Pro Oracle SQL Development

Best Practices for Writing Advanced Queries

Second Edition

Jon Heller

Apress®

Pro Oracle SQL Development: Best Practices for Writing Advanced Queries

Jon Heller
Clive, IA, USA

ISBN-13 (pbk): 978-1-4842-8866-5 ISBN-13 (electronic): 978-1-4842-8867-2
https://doi.org/10.1007/978-1-4842-8867-2

Managing Director, Apress Media LLC: Welmoed Spahr
Acquisitions Editor: Jonathan Gennick
Development Editor: Laura Berendson
Coordinating Editor: Jill Balzano

Cover Photo by Avinash Kumar on Unsplash

Distributed to the book trade worldwide by Springer Science+Business Media New York, 1 New York Plaza, Suite 4600, New York, NY 10004-1562, USA. Phone 1-800-SPRINGER, fax (201) 348-4505, e-mail orders-ny@ springer-sbm.com, or visit www.springeronline.com. Apress Media, LLC is a California LLC and the sole member (owner) is Springer Science + Business Media Finance Inc (SSBM Finance Inc). SSBM Finance Inc is a **Delaware** corporation.

For information on translations, please e-mail booktranslations@springernature.com; for reprint, paperback, or audio rights, please e-mail bookpermissions@springernature.com.

Apress titles may be purchased in bulk for academic, corporate, or promotional use. eBook versions and licenses are also available for most titles. For more information, reference our Print and eBook Bulk Sales web page at http://www.apress.com/bulk-sales.

Any source code or other supplementary material referenced by the author in this book is available to readers on GitHub (https://github.com/Apress). For more detailed information, please visit http://www.apress.com/source-code.

Printed on acid-free paper

I dedicate this book to my wonderful wife, Lisa, and to my awesome children, Elliott and Oliver.

Table of Contents

About the Author

Jon Heller is an expert SQL and PL/SQL programmer with 20 years of Oracle experience. He has worked as a database developer, analyst, and administrator. In his spare time, he is active on Stack Overflow where he is a top user in the Oracle and PL/SQL tags. He enjoys creating open source software, has a Master of Computer Science degree from North Carolina State University, and lives in Iowa with his wife and two sons.

About the Technical Reviewer

 **Michael Rosenblum** is a software architect/senior DBA at Dulcian, Inc., where he is responsible for system tuning and application architecture. He supports Dulcian developers by writing complex PL/SQL routines and researching new features. He is the coauthor of *Oracle PL/SQL for Dummies* (Wiley Press, 2006) and *Oracle PL/SQL Performance Tuning Tips and Techniques* (Oracle Press, 2014), contributing author of *Expert PL/SQL Practices* (Apress, 2011), and author of many database-related articles and conference papers. Michael is an Oracle ACE and frequent presenter at conferences (Oracle OpenWorld, ODTUG, IOUG Collaborate, RMOUG, NYOUG, etc.).

Acknowledgments

A lot of people helped make this book possible. First, I'd like to thank the technical reviewer, Michael Rosenblum, who provided many corrections and insightful comments.

Thanks to Jonathan Gennick, who reached out to me years ago about writing a book and who has provided excellent guidance and feedback since. Thanks to everyone else at Apress, especially Jill Balzano, Laura Berendson, Silembarasan Panneerselvam, and Clement Wilson. And thanks to the people who sent me useful feedback on the first edition.

So many people helped me flourish and get to a point in life where I was able to write a book: my parents, who created an environment where success seemed inevitable; my coworkers at National Instruments, Talecris, PPD, IFMC, Terra Technology, GDIT, Ventech Solutions, Businessolver, and R+L Carriers; users who helped me improve my open source programs; conference organizers who gave me a chance to present; and users on Stack Overflow who motivated me to do a ridiculous amount of work to win meaningless Internet points.

I'm grateful for the people who created and curated the wealth of knowledge that helped create this book: Jonathan McDowell for creating the JSR Launch Vehicle Database, which is used for the space data set, and the countless people who contributed to the Oracle manuals, blogs, and Wikipedia articles that helped me throughout this book.

Most importantly, I would like to thank my wife, Lisa, for always supporting me while still doing so much to help our family and our community. And thanks to my kids, Elliott and Oliver, who encouraged me and waited for me to finish so I could spend more time with them.

Introduction

This book will inspire you to write more powerful database queries, and it will set you on the path to becoming an Oracle SQL expert. This book is not a copy of the SQL Language Reference, will not quiz you about syntax trivia, and will not prepare you for an exam. But it will challenge the way you think about writing Oracle SQL. And I hope you have fun reading it.

Why Learn More About Oracle SQL?

Any database can *store* data, but Oracle is designed to help us *process* data. Many applications only treat the database as a glorified text file, and there are many opportunities to use SQL to improve our programs.

Oracle SQL is a great programming language, and it has many advantages compared with other languages and SQL implementations:

1. *Declarative*: Declarative languages let us tell the computer what we want, without having to specify how to do it. Declarative languages are different than traditional imperative languages and can be difficult at first. For example, whenever we find ourselves wanting to use a loop in SQL, that's a clue we're thinking in the wrong programming paradigm. SQL lets the compiler handle the implementation details, which leads to simpler and faster code.

2. *Popular*: Oracle is one of the most popular databases, and SQL is one of the most popular programming languages.

3. *Portable*: SQL and PL/SQL are entirely platform independent. Other than a rare bug, we never need to worry about which operating system is running our SQL.

4. *Clear and concise*: The basic syntax is simple and readable, and the relational model is built on a few simple ideas. If this description doesn't match your reality, Part III will explain how to make your code look better.

5. *Interpreted*: Statements run immediately, without a separate compilation step. Integrated development environments (IDEs) can take advantage of interpreted languages and let us instantly run programs, debug our code, and get results.

6. *Powerful*: Oracle SQL has enough features to solve almost any problem. For those rare exceptions, where we need to control precisely how our database code runs, we have well-integrated imperative options, such as PL/SQL, hints, and the MODEL clause.

7. *Fast*: Oracle SQL is powerful enough to let us bring our algorithms to our data, instead of bringing our data to our algorithms. Ignore those shallow benchmarks that compare running SELECT * FROM EMPLOYEE a thousand times. Real-world performance depends on an optimizer choosing the right data structures and algorithms and a language that enables solving more problems with set-based processing, not the speed of repeatedly running trivial commands.

Despite all those advantages, Oracle SQL is scandalously underused. There are huge opportunities to improve our systems by using SQL more often.

Target Audience

This book is for anyone who already knows Oracle SQL and is ready to take their skills to the next level. For those of you who are already skilled at Oracle SQL, this book will give you a different way to think about the language.

There are many groups of people who frequently use Oracle databases. Their reasons for using the database may differ, but they can all benefit from improving their SQL knowledge.

1. *Database developers*: If you're already frequently using an Oracle database, then you have the most to gain from this book. Even if you already know many of the advanced features, you will still benefit from the discussions about setting up the environment, SQL programming styles, and SQL performance tuning.

2. *Application/front-end/full-stack developers*: Many applications only use simple queries, like SELECT * FROM EMPLOYEE, or have a framework that automatically takes care of database access. This book won't try to convince you to put all your business logic inside the database. But it will help you find great opportunities to simplify your code and improve performance, by using new SQL programming styles and advanced features.

3. *Data analysts and testers*: Oracle SQL is the perfect language for analyzing, testing, and comparing data. Much of the advice in this book will help with those tasks.

4. *Data scientists*: You probably won't use Oracle SQL for data mining and machine learning (although Oracle does have tools for those tasks). But if your data is stored in an Oracle database, Oracle's advanced features can at least help you efficiently extract, preprocess, and format data.

5. *Database administrators*: SQL is the lifeblood of an Oracle database. If you administer Oracle, you'll need to work with SQL statements and help others improve them. And there are many times when an advanced SQL statement can help you perform administrative tasks better.

Book Structure

This book is divided into five parts. There is a progression between the sections and chapters, but they are not tightly coupled, and you should be able to skip between chapters without much difficulty.

Part I: Learn How to Learn (Chapters 1–5): The first part helps you create the foundation for advanced Oracle SQL development. However, these are not merely introductory topics. This part contains controversial opinions, and if you already have a foundation, this book may suggest that you tear it down and start over.

Part II: Write Powerful SQL with Sets and Advanced Features (Chapters 6–10): This part provides a clear mental model for thinking about queries. Then it introduces you to the advanced features, schema objects, concepts, and architectural information you need to start writing advanced SQL statements.

Part III: Write Elegant SQL with Patterns and Styles (Chapters 11–15): This part teaches you the art of building beautiful SQL statements. You can't simply take the advanced features and throw them together. Instead, you must develop a style for constructing readable queries while avoiding common anti-patterns.

Part IV: Improve SQL Performance (Chapters 16–18): This part helps you build a deeper understanding of performance with practical algorithm analysis, and it explains many tuning concepts and performance tricks.

Part V: Solve Anything with Oracle SQL (Chapters 19–21): The last chapters show you how to take your skills to the final level. This part introduces some of the most advanced SQL features and briefly discusses PL/SQL.

This book is meant to introduce new ideas, features, styles, theories, and ways of thinking. It may challenge you to think differently about your styles and processes, but it is *not* meant to frustrate you with syntax trivia. Don't try to memorize all the syntax – it's only important that you remember the concepts.

Example Schema

The examples in this book use a data set generated from the JSR Launch Vehicle Database. The data set, and the simple installation instructions, can be found at `https://github.com/apress/pro-oracle-sql-dev-2e`. If you want to run the examples, but don't have a convenient database to run them, Chapter 2 provides advice for creating a development environment.

The schema is simple, small, real, and hopefully interesting. Instead of a meaningless list of imaginary EMPLOYEES, this example schema contains data for all 70,000 orbital and suborbital launches attempted up until 2017. If you're interested in space flight, you can use the data to answer real questions.

The following are the main tables, listed roughly in order of importance and their relationships. The columns and relationships are simple and are not explained here in detail. There's no need to study a large entity-relationship (ER) diagram – just spend a few seconds to become familiar with the table names:

```
LAUNCH
        LAUNCH_PAYLOAD_ORG
        LAUNCH_AGENCY
SATELLITE
```

        SATELLITE_ORG
ORGANIZATION
        ORGANIZATION_ORG_TYPE
SITE
        SITE_ORG
PLATFORM
LAUNCH_VEHICLE
        LAUNCH_VEHICLE_MANUFACTURER
        LAUNCH_VEHICLE_FAMILY
STAGE
        STAGE_MANUFACTURER
LAUNCH_VEHICLE_STAGE
ENGINE
        ENGINE_MANUFACTURER
        ENGINE_PROPELLANT
PROPELLANT

The most important tables in the schema are LAUNCH and SATELLITE. Figure 1 shows the columns and the simple relationship between these two tables. Any nonobvious columns will be explained before they are used in examples.

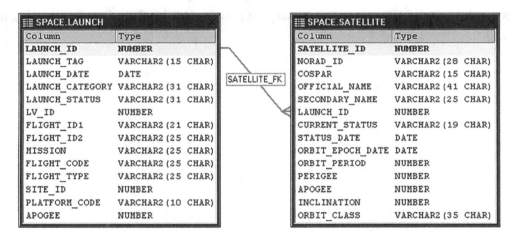

Figure 1. *Diagram of the two most important tables*

Running Examples

The examples should work with any currently supported platform, edition, and version of Oracle. This book conservatively assumes you are running on version 12.2, and it mentions whenever a feature is new to 18c, 19c, or 21c. In practice, the database version isn't as important as recruiters would make you believe, and most of the information in this book applies to any version of Oracle.

While the examples and results are usually shown as text, I strongly recommend you use a graphical IDE to run the examples and view the results. An IDE is essential for creating, reading, and debugging large, advanced SQL statements.

To avoid repeating the schema name, the examples assume you installed the space data set in your personal schema. If you install the data set on a separate schema, run a command like this in your session before you run the examples:

```
alter session set current_schema=space;
```

Just like the data set, you can find all the code examples used in this book at https://github.com/apress/pro-oracle-sql-dev-2e. You can clone that repository and create a GitHub issue if you find any mistakes.

Don't let the data set and examples scare you. This book is about SQL development processes, advanced features, programming styles, and performance concepts. Running the examples is helpful but is not necessary for reading this book and understanding the material.

PART I

Learn How to Learn

CHAPTER 1

Understand Relational Databases

Understanding the history and theory behind relational databases helps us achieve a deeper understanding of Oracle SQL. This information helps us avoid repeating old mistakes, and it gives us the confidence needed to occasionally ignore the theory and build practical solutions. This book assumes you are already familiar with relational databases and SQL, so the information provided here is not merely *introductory*; it is *foundational*.

History of Relational Databases

A brief history of relational databases helps us appreciate the importance of this technology and helps us understand Oracle Corporation's decisions. The Oracle database is a huge product that inevitably contains mistakes. Some of those mistakes are unimportant historical curiosities, but others are huge pitfalls we need to avoid.

Relational databases are built on relational algebra and the relational model, which was first popularly described by E. F. Codd in 1970.[1] The relational model is built on set theory, a mathematical way of dealing with collections of objects. The relational model is discussed in more detail in the next section.

IBM started working on relational technology and products in 1968 but did not release a commercial product for many years. Here's the first history lesson: best is the enemy of good enough. Larry Ellison, the co-founder of Oracle Corporation, heard

---

[1] Codd, E. F. (1970). "A Relational Model of Data for Large Shared Data Banks." Communications of the ACM. 13 (6): 377–387.

© Jon Heller 2023
J. Heller, *Pro Oracle SQL Development*, https://doi.org/10.1007/978-1-4842-8867-2_1

about IBM's project, implemented it, and released the first commercially available SQL database in 1979.[2] He has a huge presence in the database world and is still involved with many database decisions to this day.

Oracle Corporation has certainly used its first-mover advantage. The Oracle database has been the most popular database product for a long time. There are current trends to move away from Oracle and SQL, but we shouldn't overlook how incredibly popular they are. The database scores high on almost any database popularity metric.[3]

Oracle's age explains many of its unexpected behaviors. The following list contains the features that are most likely to confuse database developers who are new to Oracle:

1. *(+)*: Oracle originally used syntax like (+) instead of keywords like LEFT JOIN. That old-fashioned syntax is bad coding practice and is discussed in more detail in Chapters 6 and 7.

2. *Date*: An Oracle date also contains the time and probably should have been called a DATETIME. Date formatting was awkward before the introduction of ANSI date literals, as discussed in Chapter 15.

3. *Empty string*: Oracle treats an empty string as null, instead of a distinct value as most programmers expect. (However, I would argue that Oracle is not necessarily wrong here. We don't have zero-length dates or zero-length numbers; why should we have zero-length strings?)

4. *30-byte name limit*: The SQL and PL/SQL languages have an English-like syntax, but we'll quickly hit the 30-byte limit if we use regular words for names. And good variable names are crucial to make our programs more readable. Luckily this problem is fixed in version 12.2, which allows 128 bytes.

5. *SQL*Plus quirks*: SQL*Plus is a great tool for some tasks, but it's really showing its age in many ways.

---

[2] See www.ukcert.org.uk/history_of_oracle_scott_hollows_oncalldba.pdf and https://docs.oracle.com/database/121/SQLRF/intro001.htm#SQLRF50932

[3] Such as https://db-engines.com/en/ranking

In Oracle's defense, those mistakes were made before any standards existed. On the other hand, Oracle doesn't always make a good effort to comply with standards. For example, Oracle used to claim "partial" compliance for allowing long names. While 30 bytes is "part" of a bigger number, that doesn't really meet the spirit of the standard.[4]

More important than excusing Oracle's mistakes, it helps to see how Oracle Corporation responds to industry trends. Sometimes it feels like they have a "fire and motion" strategy for their technologies. They add so many features that nobody can possibly keep up with them.[5] However, adding a huge number of features may be backfiring now. The Unix philosophy of building small tools for each task seems to be taking over.

The following list shows the largest architectural and conceptual changes made to Oracle, along with the version they were introduced. These are not necessarily the most important features, but the features that tried to redefine what a database is:

- *Multiversion concurrency control (MVCC)*: 4

- *PL/SQL*: 6

- *Object-relational, Java*: 8

- *OLAP, XML (Extensible Markup Language), RAC*: 9

- *JSON, sharding, in-memory, containers (multitenant)*: 12

- *Property graph, autonomous database, documents*: 18

- *Cloud integration*: 19

- *MLE (multilingual engine)*: 21

Adding new features rarely hurts sales, but some of those new features arguably move Oracle in the wrong direction. For example, object-relational and Java in the database have significant problems. Those shortcomings are discussed in Chapters 10 and 15.

---

[4] The Oracle manual lists its compliance with different standards, although I'm not sure why they bother: https://docs.oracle.com/cd/B19306_01/server.102/b14200/ap_standard_sql004.htm

[5] Joel Spolsky discusses this strategy here: www.joelonsoftware.com/2002/01/06/fire-and-motion/

Oracle will always add a new feature to catch up with competitors, even if that feature doesn't make sense. Not everything Oracle Corporation does is the "future." Oracle is a huge product that sometimes moves in multiple, contradictory directions at the same time. We need to remember to not drink the Kool-Aid and not throw out proven technology for shiny new things.

On the other hand, it's good that Oracle supports almost everything. It's a Swiss Army knife for database solutions. We don't need a new database for each new technology trend.

The pace of technological change is accelerating, and nobody can predict the future. Given the past, it's safe to say that Oracle will add or invent new and important features. We don't always want to start using new features immediately, but we should at least take the time to read about them in the "New Features" chapter of the manual.

Relational Model and Why It Matters

The relational model has been immensely influential in computer science and programming. There are many papers, books, and classes related to the theory of relational database systems. We can be successful SQL developers without a thorough understanding of the relational model, but we should at least have an introductory understanding.

History

The relational model is the theoretical foundation for the Oracle database. It was first described by E. F. Codd's 1970 paper, "A Relational Model of Data for Large Shared Data Banks." I recommend you read that paper; it's surprisingly accessible and still relevant. Most of this section is based on that original paper, although E. F. Codd and others have expanded on the relational model in other works.

Terminology

Understanding the relational model can at least help us understand other people. There's rarely a good reason to use the theoretical words *relation*, *tuple*, and *attribute*, instead of the more common words *table*, *row*, and *column*. Even E. F. Codd's paper uses those common words in several places. But since some people insist on using the fancy words, we might as well learn them.

Table 1-1 is copied straight from Codd's original paper. There's a *relation* (table) named SUPPLY. It has three *tuples* (arrays or rows) and four *simple domains* (attributes, fields, or columns), meaning it has a *degree* of four. The *primary key* uniquely identifies each row and is the combination of SUPPLIER, PART, and PROJECT, each of which is also a *foreign key* to another relation. Foreign keys ensure that lookup values actually exist in the tables they refer to.

Table 1-1. *supply*

supplier	part	project	quantity
1	2	5	17
1	3	5	23
2	3	7	9

Simplicity

The relational model is all about simplicity. It's not more powerful than other systems, just easier to use. (So don't worry. There won't be any proofs or formulas in this section.)

Simplicity is achieved by removing *redundancy* and *nonsimple domains* through *normalization* with *primary keys*. In practice those concepts translate into two simple rules: do not store lists of values and do not repeat a column. In the preceding SUPPLY table, it would be a huge mistake to add columns like DELIVERY_DATES or SUPPLIER_ NAME, even though those columns may seem convenient at first. DELIVERY_DATES, possibly a comma-separated list of values, would be easy to read but difficult to filter or join. SUPPLIER_NAME might look good right next to the supplier number, but it would be a duplicate of the value already in the SUPPLIER table. Those duplicate columns would lead to *update anomalies*, where the columns won't agree on the values.

The rules of the relational model can be summarized as follows: make the schema smart but keep the tables dumb. It's the *relationships* between the tables that matter. Those relationships take place through constraints and joins, but those constraints and joins can't work if the data is not simple.

Sets and Tables

Thinking about the database in terms of simple relationships, or just as simple sets, is one of the keys to writing great Oracle SQL. We use the relational model to retrieve sets, join them into new sets, join those sets together, etc. Like with user interface design, two simple choices are better than one difficult choice. Forming a good mental model of database sets and tables is going to take a while, so don't feel bad if you don't get it yet. This topic is discussed a lot throughout the book.

It's easy to take tables for granted because they're so common now. We use them not just in databases but in spreadsheets, HTML, and many other places. We shouldn't avoid important data structures just because they appear too simple at first glance. When we run into a problem putting data into a table, the answer is to create more tables, not create a more complicated table.

Problems Implementing a Relational Model

Codd's paper predicted difficulties implementing the relational model. His fears have proved to be well founded.

Abstracting the storage mechanisms gives the database system a lot of responsibilities. The database must create and maintain the physical data structures and choose the algorithms to access those data structures. If the title of Niklaus Wirth's book *Algorithms + Data Structures = Programs* is true, then databases have a lot of work to do. This extra work is a problem, but Oracle does the heaving lifting for us. For example, although we need to choose which columns to index, we don't normally need to know exactly how Oracle will physically create and maintain those data structures. Index maintenance algorithms are a problem for Oracle Corporation programmers and the reason we pay them for their software.

Unfortunately, Oracle cannot automate everything. Oracle provides many storage options like indexes, caches, in-memory column stores, etc. And it provides ways to gather metadata about those relationships through things like table and column statistics. There are many complicated trade-offs between performance and storage, and we must help decide when a trade-off is worthwhile. When dealing with N columns, there are at least N! permutations[6] of how to store them.

Despite Codd's insistence on normalization in his paper, Codd also knew that redundant data was inevitable. Inconsistency of redundant data is hard to prevent because inconsistency is a state, not a specific action. E. F. Codd predicted the use of a metadata system to identify redundancies, and those redundancies could be prevented either in real time or as a batch job. As far as I know, an automated system to prevent redundancies does not exist. Perhaps some future version of Oracle will have an ASSERT functionality to fill this gap in our relational model implementation. For now, it is up to us to be aware of inconsistency problems and use a disciplined approach to mitigate them. Simply stated, if we create a wrong column, it's *our* problem.

Relational Model and Why It Doesn't Matter

There is no perfect model for the world. Abstractions are built to simplify things, but inevitably those abstractions don't fit, or they cover up an important detail that must be dealt with. Fanatically adhering to the relational model will cause problems.

Don't be fooled by books and products that offer a false choice; we don't have to choose between implementing a pure relational solution and completely abandoning the relational model. Current relational databases, and the SQL language, don't have to be perfect to be useful. We must avoid the temptation to search for pure and true solutions and embrace practical compromises.

The following sections discuss parts of the relational model that don't always work in practice. The good news is that there's always a workaround.

The NULL Problem Isn't a Problem

One of the biggest theoretical complaints about relational databases is the way they use NULL. Three-valued logic with nulls is weird and takes time to get used to. Table 1-2 is a truth table that explains how NULL works.

---

[6] "!" is the factorial operation. It can be used to calculate the number of ways to order N items. It is the product of all integers less than or equal to N. For example, 3! = 3 * 2 * 1 = 6. The numbers grow very rapidly, even faster than exponential growth. 4! = 24, 5! = 120, 6! = 720, etc. This operation will show up a few times throughout the book.

Table 1-2. *NULL Three-Valued Logic*

A	B	=	!=
1	1	True	False
1	0	False	True
1	NULL	Unknown	Unknown
NULL	NULL	Unknown	Unknown

NULLs are weird, but so is our data. There are many times when we don't know something. It might be tempting to replace NULL with a list of reasons we don't know something. But there are many times when we don't even know *why* we don't know something. And those lists of reasons can grow quickly and become ridiculous.

NULLs *could* be eliminated by creating a separate table for every nullable column. But creating such a large collection of tables quickly becomes a huge mess.

For example, some people don't have a first name or a middle name or a last name. Instead of using nullable columns to store an employee's name, we could create separate tables EMPLOYEE_FIRST_NAME, EMPLOYEE_MIDDLE_NAME, and EMPLOYEE_LAST_NAME. Each table only has two values, an EMPLOYEE_ID and a NAME. If an employee is missing a middle name, there will be no row in EMPLOYEE_MIDDLE_NAME for their EMPLOYEE_ID. Congratulations! We just created a schema without any NULLs. But now we need to join four tables just to find a person's name. And if other columns become nullable in the future, we have to make significant changes to the schema, instead of just altering a single column. Names can be complicated, and it may sometimes make sense to store them in multiple tables, but don't do it out of a fear of NULL.

It feels unnatural the way NULL = NULL returns unknown, which in most contexts translates to FALSE. And it's annoying when we write a NOT IN expression that compares against a NULL and doesn't return any results. But those problems don't mean our databases contain a ticking time bomb, like some horrible Y2K bug waiting to ruin everything. Unknown data creates challenges, but we need to be comfortable with uncertainty.

Column Order Is Important

The physical order of columns and rows does not matter in the relational model. Physical data independence is a big improvement over systems where the order did matter. Data independence is not merely a historical problem; it still happens if we mistakenly add complex, formatted data in a single value.

E. F. Codd's paper does not imply that the *logical* column order is unimportant. The examples in his paper have a meaningful order that helps the reader understand the relationships between the columns. Grouping similar columns, and listing them in the same order across different tables, makes his examples easier to read. A meaningful column order can also make our schemas easier to read.

Our systems might have a user guide, a fancy entity-relationship (ER) diagram, and other forms of documentation. But the primary interface to our schema is a simple SELECT statement. Other SQL developers view and understand our tables based on the output from SELECT * FROM SOME_TABLE, not from an out-of-date PDF file.

We shouldn't just throw new columns on the end of tables. We should take the time to shift the columns around, if it makes sense. Changing column order is a simple operation that only requires setting columns temporarily to INVISIBLE and then setting them back to VISIBLE. Those few minutes are only spent once; a bad table design will annoy us for years.

Denormalization

Ideally our relational databases are fully normalized, contain no non-atomic values, and contain no redundant values. It is reasonable to have a firm "no non-atomic values" rule and forbid anyone from ever storing comma-separated lists. However, it's not always realistic to insist on preventing redundant values. Not every system should be in third normal form.

There are times when performance requires writing the data multiple times, in order to improve read time. This may mean adding a second version of a column somewhere and synchronizing them with triggers or possibly creating a materialized view, like taking a point-in-time snapshot of pre-joined tables. This is a complex trade-off between storage, speed, and consistency.

There are many systems where this trade-off must be made, and those trade-offs do not break the relational model. E. F. Codd's paper discussed the problems with denormalization, but his paper also acknowledged that denormalization is going to happen anyway.

All Rows Are Distinct

The relational model is built on sets, and a set cannot have duplicate elements. This implies that all rows, and all query results, should be unique.

It could be helpful to have a system that enforced the uniqueness of all SQL query results. It almost never makes sense to have truly duplicate values – there should always be a unique way to identify a value. We've all been guilty of throwing an extra DISTINCT operator at a query, just in case.

But it is not practical to always enforce that rule. There are only so many ways to detect duplicate values, and each way requires either a large amount of storage, extra processing time, or both. Sorting and hashing large data sets is so painful that it's better to live with the possibility of duplicates than to always check the results.

SQL Programming Language

A relational *model* is not enough; we also need a specialized programming language to interact with the data. There have been many attempts to create such a language, and SQL is the winner.

History and Terminology

In 1970, E. F. Codd's paper discussed the need for a data language – a *relational algebra* formed by combining *relational operators* – and preferably a simple language that can deal with simple relations.

Like with the relational model, knowing the official names of these relational operations can at least help us understand what other people are talking about. *Projection* is choosing only certain columns. *Join*, of course, is combining relations together. *Restriction* or *selection* limits the tuples of a relation, by applying *predicates*. (That means results are filtered by functions that return true or false.) A *Cartesian product* (CROSS JOIN) results in a set that includes all possible combinations of elements from two sets. *Set union* (UNION ALL) combines all elements of a set, and *set difference* (MINUS) returns the difference between sets.

In the 1960s, IBM created the Structured English Query Language, SEQUEL. But don't use history to prove a point about how to properly pronounce "SQL." Just accept the fact that it's commonly pronounced "S-Q-L" with databases like PostgreSQL and MySQL. And it's commonly pronounced "SEQUEL" with databases like SQL Server and Oracle.

SQL is somewhat similar to COBOL in that they both have English-like syntaxes and were both initially designed for business users. When PL/SQL was added, it continued the trend of an English-like syntax, for example, by using BEGIN and END instead of curly brackets. Another natural language–like feature of Oracle is that lists start with 1, not 0. If we find ourselves creating a program that looks like a screen in "The Matrix", we have strayed far from the intended path.

SQL frequently appears near the top of programming language popularity lists.[7] And those sites likely still underestimate the language's real popularity, since many nonprogrammers use SQL but aren't responding to developer surveys. PL/SQL isn't a top-tier language, but it's surprisingly close.[8]

SQL Alternatives

The world is full of query languages. There's XQuery for dealing with XML, Cypher for querying graph databases, REST APIs for querying data over the Internet, and many more. But when it comes to querying relational data, SQL is by far the best choice.

For querying relational data, the SQL alternatives are only of academic or historical interest. Languages like QUEL, Rel, and Datalog may be interesting, but not practical. Technology is not always a popularity contest, but SQL is so dominant that it would be ridiculous to not use it for relational queries. Even if another language was better, it wouldn't have the huge number of programs built to use it or the huge number of people familiar with it.

---

[7] SQL was the fourth most used language on the Stack Overflow developer survey, https://insights.stackoverflow.com/survey/2021#most-popular-technologies-language-prof

[8] PL/SQL is often in the top 20 of this common programming language ranking: www.tiobe.com/tiobe-index/

Is SQL a safe bet for the future? It's foolish to predict that a better technology won't be invented, but it's reasonable to predict that a significantly better technology will not replace it in the near future.

Some languages grow old and fade away, but some languages are timeless. C and Lisp are older than SQL, but they're not going away anytime soon. Writing about technology over 30 years ago, Fred Brooks warned us to not expect any "silver bullets" for software development. That is, don't expect a single new technology to provide order-of-magnitude improvements. SQL is a high-level language that's always evolving, and it's possible the language is as good as we'll ever get for querying relational data.

Some people hold out hope that a visual programming language will someday make database queries easier. Unfortunately, that is not likely to happen, for several reasons.

Visual query builders are as old as SQL itself, starting with Query by Example (QBE) in the 1970s. The idea has been implemented many times, but it's rarely used for non-trivial queries. Programming in pictures looks cool, but it's easy to forget how great text is. Text can be easily shared, modified, and version controlled. In programming, a picture is not worth a thousand words: it's only worth 50.

> *The problem with visual programming is that you can't have more than 50 visual primitives on the screen at the same time.*
>
> —L. Peter Deutsch

The exact number of visual primitives is debatable, but the information density of visual programming languages is definitely lower than text.

When I interned at National Instruments, I was able to work at the company that created LabVIEW, which is arguably the best visual programming language. The language is fun to use and well suited to test and measurement tasks. But even the employees of that company would readily admit that visual programming is not a panacea.

As an example of visual programming, Figure 1-1 shows a simple query against the space schema that was briefly explained in the "Introduction."

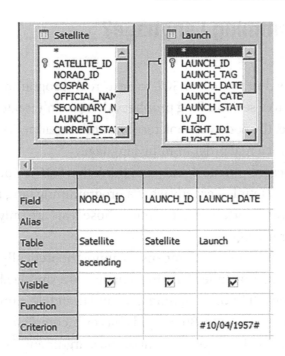

Figure 1-1. *A visual query in LibreOffice Base*

The preceding query finds all satellites that were launched on October 4, 1957. At a first glance, the image looks fine. But visual queries only look nice for simple examples. Visual query builders do not scale, and the connection lines between tables will quickly look like spaghetti. The following is the same query using Oracle SQL:

```
select
    satellite.norad_id,
    satellite.launch_id,
    launch.launch_date
from satellite
join launch
    on satellite.launch_id = launch.launch_id
where trunc(launch.launch_date) = date '1957-10-04'
order by satellite.norad_id;
```

Although text is superior to images, Chapter 2 will explain why we still need to program with an integrated development environment (IDE).

Is SQL a Programming Language?

Yes.

Some programmers don't consider SQL to be a "real" programming language, and that mistake leads to a self-fulfilling prophecy. If SQL isn't treated like a real programming language, the code will look terrible, and developers will avoid SQL, which makes them think it's not a real programming language.

There's no theoretical or practical reason to think that SQL is not a "real" programming language. Defining exactly what a programming language is, and what it can do, *is* theoretically important. But too often those tests are only applied to a strawman version of Oracle SQL.

SQL is not Turing complete, which means it cannot theoretically solve every problem that is solvable by a Turing machine. A Turing machine is a simple abstract machine that can run forever. SQL doesn't have an infinite loop and therefore cannot run forever, so technically it's not Turing complete. But nobody has ever complained that their query *didn't* take forever to run, so it's a pointless theoretical argument.

And Oracle SQL has many extensions that can make SQL act like a procedural language. With recursive common table expressions (discussed in Chapter 7) and the model clause (Chapter 19), Oracle SQL can run imperative code. Oracle SQL and PL/SQL have been slowly merging for many years, and PL/SQL is a traditional, imperative programming language.

There is no theoretical or practical limit to what we can accomplish with Oracle SQL.

Different Database Types

This book is focused on Oracle SQL. For some people, that focus is too narrow; they may use a different relational database or a non-relational database. For some people, that focus is too wide; they may only use an Oracle database in a specific context. This section gives a brief overview of the entire database landscape and drills down into specific Oracle database environments.

Alternative Database Models

There are many database products, and it would be foolish to try to quickly compare them. An Oracle software installation is larger than most operating systems. We should be skeptical of shallow comparisons between databases, since it's difficult to accurately summarize so much functionality.

But it is helpful to have at least a cursory understanding of the other *types* of databases available. Databases are difficult to precisely categorize and are often labeled with buzzwords like NoSQL, big data, NewSQL, etc. The following list contains common database selling points, but these items are not necessarily mutually exclusive architectures:

1. *Key-value*: Uses associative arrays or hashes

2. *Object*: Uses objects, as in object-oriented programming

3. *Graph*: Uses graphs, like nodes and the edges between them (this is perhaps the successor to the network model)

4. *Document*: Uses semi-structured files, like JSON or XML

5. *Hierarchical*: Uses tree-like structures, like a file system or XML document

6. *Online analytical processing (OLAP)*: Uses multidimensional data

7. *In-memory*: Stores everything in memory for high performance

8. *Embedded*: Small database that can be bundled within another program

9. *Streaming*: Reads and writes streams of data in real time

10. *Column oriented*: Stores data in columns instead of rows

11. *Distributed/sharded*: Stores data in multiple locations

12. *Blockchain*: Decentralized, cryptographically secured list of records

There are interesting technologies in the preceding list, but new technologies and products also attract a lot of myths and hype. Relational databases have been working well for decades. Given the "no silver bullet" rule, we should be skeptical of claims of huge advances in programming technologies.

I'm not saying don't investigate or use those products. But if we've already paid for Oracle, we should think carefully about moving to a different system. Oracle is much more than a relational database; Oracle is a converged database (previously called a multi-model database) and supports almost every item on the preceding list. Whenever a vendor claims that "Oracle cannot do X," they are wrong (unless they add the qualification "for less than a mountain of money").

Our databases won't grow to the size of Facebook's databases. Our programs may be mission critical, but they don't need to be as reliable as the software monitoring nuclear reactors. Software used at the extreme edges of technology may not necessarily be appropriate for the average system. A single, smart database is good enough for most business applications. Be careful not to over-engineer solutions.

There are times to consider an alternative, specialized database solution. But Oracle is almost certainly capable of handling any database workload.

Different Oracle Databases (OLTP vs. DW)

Oracle databases are traditionally divided into two categories: online transaction processing (OLTP) and data warehousing (DW). Those two environments have different goals and require different techniques.

OLTP systems manage transactions as part of a live application. Those systems generally run a large number of fast queries, have precise application logic, have a normalized schema, and require all the ACID properties. ACID stands for a*tomicity* (statements in a transaction either all succeed or all fail), *consistency* (data integrity is never lost), i*solation* (concurrent sessions don't corrupt each other), and d*urability* (data is never lost).

Data warehouses allow for querying and analysis of large amounts of data, often from multiple sources. Those systems generally run a small number of complex queries; have lots of imprecise extract–transform–load (ETL) code; have a denormalized schema; and don't need to be ACID compliant.

Oracle defaults to OLTP behavior, which is a reasonable default since it is the style that best protects our data. It's up to us to tell Oracle what data we don't care about and when we're willing to sacrifice ACID properties for better performance.

That reasonable default has led some people to mistakenly think that Oracle isn't designed for data warehousing. A quick glance at Oracle's documentation, or the following features, makes it obvious that Oracle has invested a lot of effort into data warehousing. Data warehousing is not simply bolted on to the database – it's been baked into the database for decades. There are many Oracle features geared toward data warehousing: partitioning, parallelism, direct-path writes, materialized views, large temp/undo/redo, bitmap indexes, dimensions/hierarchies/attributes, materialized zone maps, attribute clustering, etc.

There's a large cultural difference between OLTP and data warehouses. OLTP databases are run by application developers, lovingly crafted, well maintained, and fanatic about never losing data. Data warehouses are run by database programmers, have lots of ugly and repetitive code, accumulate lots of junk data, don't care about losing data (it can be reloaded), and are constantly worried about performance. When we move from one database style to another, we need to adjust our attitude accordingly.

This section only scratches the surface of the differences. There are many books dedicated to data warehousing, such as Oracle's 732-page *Data Warehousing Guide*. However, a lot of the features in that guide are just cool query techniques and can apply to any Oracle database. In practice, a lot of systems have some combination of both OLTP and data warehousing.

Key Concepts

ANSI join syntax and *inline views* are the keys to writing great SQL statements. The ANSI join syntax uses the JOIN keyword, instead of a comma-separated list of tables. Inline views are nested subqueries in the FROM clause.

That's the most important lesson in this book, but it may be a difficult lesson to learn. SQL developers who spent years using the old comma-separated list syntax will have a hard time changing. Unlearning language patterns takes time, which is why the ideas are briefly introduced here. ANSI joins and inline views are used throughout this book and are fully discussed in Chapters 6 and 7.

But before that detailed discussion is possible, it's critical that we have a firm grasp of two key SQL concepts – nulls and joins. Oracle SQL is a vast language. It has thousands of keywords and thousands of public objects, such as packages, procedures, functions, views, etc. No matter how many of those features we memorize, we will not truly understand Oracle SQL until we understand nulls and joins.

This is the only part of the book that you must completely understand. Do not continue until these ideas click in your mind.

NULL

Nulls are weird. The three-valued logic takes a while to get used to. Even defining null is tricky. When I see a null, I think "the absence of a value," even though that description isn't 100% theoretically accurate. The important thing is that you have a quick mental definition that works for you.

SQL null is different than null in other languages. Null does not default to 0 or an empty string or a specific date. Sometimes we don't really know what a null means, and sometimes we don't even know why it's there. That's OK. We shouldn't expect to understand all of our data perfectly.

Null is not equal to null. Null is also not *not equal* to null. That's counterintuitive at first, but it will make sense after a while.

For example, let's say we want to compare launch apogees. The apogee is the furthest distance from Earth and is a good way to quickly categorize rocket launches. A launch over 80 kilometers is often considered to be in "space."

First, let's find all launches without a known apogee and then find all launches with a known apogee:

```
SQL> select count(*) from launch where apogee = null;

  COUNT(*)
----------
         0

SQL> select count(*) from launch where apogee <> null;

  COUNT(*)
----------
         0
```

Neither query worked because the comparisons = NULL and <> NULL will never return any results. Comparing directly with null will always return unknown, which then gets translated to false.

The correct way to query for the presence or absence of null is with the expressions IS NULL and IS NOT NULL:

```
SQL> select count(*) from launch where apogee is null;

  COUNT(*)
----------
      5276

SQL> select count(*) from launch where apogee is not null;

  COUNT(*)
----------
     65259
```

There's one more way that null expressions frequently confuse people: never use a NOT IN expression if the subquery can return null.

For example, let's find all launches where the launch had no satellite. A lot of rocket launches don't have a payload – they're just testing the rockets themselves:

```
SQL> select count(*)
  2  from launch
  3  where launch.launch_id not in
  4  (
  5      select satellite.launch_id
  6      from satellite
  7  );

  COUNT(*)
----------
        0
```

The preceding query returns an obviously wrong number because there is a single satellite with a null LAUNCH_ID. That sounds impossible at first – how can there be a satellite that wasn't launched into orbit? Turns out there's a satellite for "unknown Oko debris." (Oko were the Soviet Union's missile defense satellites.) It's not that the satellite wasn't launched into space; we just don't know which launch it was a part of.

A total of 99.998% of all satellites have a known launch. But it only takes a single null to ruin all the results. For each LAUNCH.LAUNCH_ID, Oracle compares it to a list that includes a null, and it can't be certain whether the values match or not, so it returns no rows.

Be careful when you assume a column is always set, especially if the column does not have a NOT NULL constraint. The next section will show a better way to get the results, using a join.

JOIN

Joins are the central operation of the Oracle database. Without joins, a database is just a glorified text file. Everything done in a database should be designed around joining data. We must be completely comfortable with the most popular join types. We must be able to read and write joins without even thinking about them.

This section provides visualizations, descriptions, and sample code to help us understand and visualize joins. We don't all need to visualize joins in the same way. As long as we all have a convenient mental model of a join, that's good enough.

Join Visualizations

The basic join types are shown in Figure 1-2, using two different types of visualizations – a join diagram and a Venn diagram. Most people think about joins as Venn diagrams, but some people are more comfortable thinking about them as join diagrams.[9]

---

[9] Lukas Eder makes a good argument that using Venn diagrams here is just plain wrong and that Venn diagrams can only accurately represent relational operations such as union, intersection, and difference. He may be right, but at the end of the day, whatever works for you is fine. https://blog.jooq.org/2016/07/05/say-no-to-venn-diagrams-when-explaining-joins/

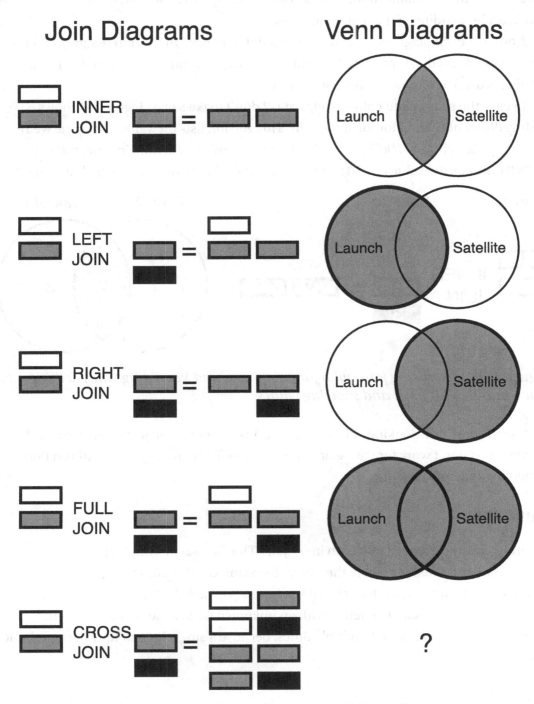

Figure 1-2. *Visualizing joins with join diagrams and Venn diagrams*

Only the basic join types are visualized in Figure 1-2. The other join types, many of which defy simple visualization, are discussed in Chapter 7. For now, it is enough to have a solid understanding of the main join types.

Note that each diagram uses shading in a different way. In the join diagrams on the left, shading is used to represent different values. In the Venn diagrams on the right, shading is used to represent overlapping values.

In case the shapes and colors of Figure 1-2 don't make sense, Figure 1-3 shows a slightly different version for the inner join. This version lists the values. Imagine we're joining by the column LAUNCH_ID, which is in both tables. And imagine that the table LAUNCH only has the values 1 and 2 and the table SATELLITE only has the values 2 and 3.

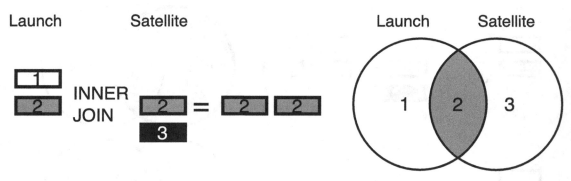

Figure 1-3. *Visualizing joins with join diagrams and Venn diagrams, drilling down into INNER JOIN and showing values*

Spend some time looking at Figures 1-2 and 1-3 until the diagrams make sense. If my diagrams don't work for you, search the Internet for "join diagram" until you find something that makes sense.

Inner Join

The most common type of join is an inner join. This first set of sample queries returns all launches and satellites where they share the same LAUNCH_ID. This does not return all launches, because many launches don't have a payload. And it does not return all satellites, because of satellite debris with an unknown launch. Some rows from the LAUNCH table will be returned multiple times, because a single launch may have multiple satellites.

There are three common ways to perform inner joins. First is using the explicit keywords INNER JOIN:

```
select *
from launch
inner join satellite
    on launch.launch_id = satellite.launch_id;
```

Inner join is the default, so the keyword INNER is not necessary:

```
select *
from launch
join satellite
    on launch.launch_id = satellite.launch_id;
```

The preceding queries use what is called the "ANSI join syntax," after the join syntax introduced by the ANSI SQL standard. Alternatively, the query can be built with what is sometimes called the "Cartesian product" approach. These types of joins existed before the SQL standard was created. Tables are listed in a comma-separated list, and the joins are done in the WHERE clause. This approach is strongly discouraged, as discussed in Chapter 7:

```
select *
from launch, satellite
where launch.launch_id = satellite.launch_id;
```

Left and Right Outer Joins

The next most common types of joins are left outer joins and right outer joins. These joins allow us to retrieve all the rows from one table along with any rows from another table that match the condition. Left and right outer joins are the same operation, only mirrored. In practice, most people only use the left outer join. The table that drives the joins is listed first and then left-joined to optional tables.

For example, here's how to retrieve all rocket launches, with their relevant satellites, if any:

```
select *
from launch
left outer join satellite
```

```
   on launch.launch_id = satellite.launch_id;
```

Since a left join is always an outer join, the keyword OUTER is not necessary:

```
select *
from launch
left join satellite
   on launch.launch_id = satellite.launch_id;
```

Alternatively, the query can be built with the Oracle (+) operator. The (+) operator means "this is the optional part of the condition." This old-fashioned syntax is strongly discouraged. But we must be familiar with it because people still use it and, in a few rare cases, Oracle requires it. This syntax will be discussed more in Chapter 7:

```
select *
from launch, satellite
where launch.launch_id = satellite.launch_id(+);
```

Changing the query from a left outer join to a right outer join is trivial. Simply change the keyword LEFT to RIGHT, or place the (+) on the other side of the condition. Changing from left to right will make the queries return all satellites, even if they do not have a matching LAUNCH_ID. This will include the "unknown debris" satellite. Right join queries are simple variations on the preceding left joins and are not shown.

(If it annoys you that the data set contains debris, you're not alone. In the worst case, this is the beginning of what's called the Kessler syndrome. If irresponsible satellite operators don't properly dispose of their satellites or if they blow them up with antisatellite missiles, the debris may cascade and increase the chance of more collisions. Eventually some orbits may become unusable.)

Full Outer Join

Full outer joins return all rows from both tables. For example, the following three queries return all launches, even those without satellites, and all satellites, even those without launches. Similar to the other join types, the outer keyword is optional and is not included in the second query. Note that the third query is invalid – the old-fashioned (+) syntax does not work here. We must use the modern ANSI join syntax to get a full outer join:

```
--Full outer join with optional "outer" keyword.
```

```
select *
from launch
full outer join satellite
   on launch.launch_id = satellite.launch_id;

--Without optional "outer" keyword.
select *
from launch
full join satellite
   on launch.launch_id = satellite.launch_id;

--This does not work. It raises the exception:
--ORA-01468: a predicate may reference only one outer-joined table
select *
from launch, satellite
where launch.launch_id(+) = satellite.launch_id(+);
```

Cross Join

Cross joins, also called Cartesian products, return every possible combination of the two tables. This join type is rare and is generally only useful as part of a complicated query where we need to generate extra rows.

Most cross joins happen by accident when we either forget to join the tables or don't understand our data and under-join the tables. There's no reason to use a cross join with our launch and satellite data, so the following cross join queries will run for a long time and return three billion pointless rows.

```
--ANSI join syntax:
select *
from launch
cross join satellite;

--Old-fashioned syntax:
select *
from launch, satellite;
```

> **Caution**   Stop and reread this section if any of this doesn't make sense. You will never reach your full potential with Oracle SQL until you are comfortable with joins.

Summary

After this brief introduction to the relational model, the history of Oracle and SQL, and a review of two key concepts, we're ready to create our development environment. While many of the details of the relational model don't matter, there are a few rules we should always remember while we're developing – avoid storing lists of values in a column and avoid duplicating data. SQL is the primary language for relational data, and everything we create in a database should be easy to use in SQL. There are many kinds of databases and even different ways of using an Oracle database; not all the features and styles we discuss will suit your environment. A firm understanding of NULL and joins is crucial before moving on to creating development processes.

CHAPTER 2

Create an Efficient Database Development Process

Most Oracle database development environments are set up like a fragile china shop. There's an intricate structure that must be maintained at all costs, and the smallest change can break things and stop everyone from working. Nobody knows exactly how the database got to be the way it is, and everybody is worried they won't know how to fix it when it breaks. Typical Oracle database development processes are woefully behind industry norms. This chapter shows a better way to work. There are simple processes that can help us create, scale, experiment, and learn without interrupting anyone else.

This chapter does not discuss the entire software development life cycle or agile vs. waterfall. Without building the right foundational processes, it's meaningless to even talk about adapting agile or some other high-level process. This chapter focuses on low-level database concepts: creating databases, creating database objects, and then managing those objects.

Shared Database vs. Private Database

There are two main approaches to Oracle database development. The most common approach is to create a shared database server for development. Multiple developers work on the same database at the same time and possibly even in the same schema. The less common approach is to create a private database for each developer. I strongly advocate private database development for most projects.

© Jon Heller 2023
J. Heller, *Pro Oracle SQL Development*, https://doi.org/10.1007/978-1-4842-8867-2_2

This chapter does not discuss the shared database approach in detail. Shared database development is the default choice for most Oracle projects, and setting up those environments is a topic for database administrators (DBAs).

There are times when shared database development may be a good choice. For example, if we have a small development team or a relatively static application or a process that has been in place for a long time, shared database development may be good enough. And there are technologies we can use to improve shared database development. But no technology can erase the sociological difference between the two models. Shared database development is ultimately controlled and limited by administrators, and private database development is ultimately controlled by developers.

Believe it or not – and I know that most of you do not – private database development works wonderfully. For SQL developers who have worked on shared systems for decades, it's hard to imagine simply getting rid of all that infrastructure and administration. A new development style is something we have to see to believe. My goal is just expose you to new ideas and convince you to keep an open mind.

It can be scary at first to rethink the way we deal with environmental differences, security, testing, sample data, licensing, performance, and deployments. Most of those concerns will be addressed later in this chapter, and you can rest assured that many successful organizations and projects have solved these issues before.

We still probably need to keep some shared servers around, for different kinds of testing. But I've worked on many projects where over 90% of the database development and testing was done on Oracle databases installed on laptops.

There are many things to consider when we make the important decision on how to set up our development process. We have to make several trade-offs. The rest of this chapter only discusses the private database development model, because I believe the trade-offs can be summarized as follows: it's better to have full control over an imperfect copy of production than to have almost no control over a perfect copy of production.

Create an Infinite Number of Databases

The first step in building an Oracle database solution is to create a system where everyone has an unlimited number of databases and unlimited privileges on those databases.

Advantages of Private Databases

Few Oracle shops use private databases, but it is not a radical idea. Java programmers don't share a compiler and don't worry that someone else is compiling a package at the same time. C programmers aren't limited to building only one executable at a time and don't worry about overwriting someone else's work. JavaScript programmers don't have to ask someone's permission to use a function that is a default part of the language. Application developers almost always have access to the near-infinite capabilities of their programming languages. Why shouldn't Oracle developers have the same power?

There are many advantages to developing on private databases instead of a single, shared server:

1. *Create, learn, and experiment*: Innovation does not ask permission; it is spontaneous, fleeting, and disruptive. On a shared server, we can't modify certain objects, or we need to ask someone's permission, or we need to warn the rest of the team. But we don't want to be embarrassed by our potentially stupid ideas. And we can't have good ideas unless we're allowed to have stupid ideas first. To thrive, developers need freedom and privacy. Even the slightest barrier to entry can prevent innovation and squash that first spark of an idea. This is especially true for new developers who don't yet have the confidence to try new things.

2. *Work in parallel*: With an unlimited number of databases, we can have an unlimited number of versions. Even for internal projects with only one customer, it's important to support multiple versions. We should never limit ourselves to only being able to develop a small number of versions at the same time.

3. *Standard configuration*: If it's not automated, it's not standardized. Shared servers with artisanal configuration will inevitably drift, due to the different people using and changing them.

4. *Data*: Free yourself from large data sets. Developing against large production data sets is used as a crutch to make up for a lack of meaningful test data. Artificially created test data is smaller, more secure, and more useful than production data. There are certainly times when we need to test against large data sets, but most of our

development is faster with smaller test data and smaller feedback loops. This topic is discussed in more detail in Chapter 3.

5. *Security*: If it's not automated, it's not secure. Manual audits and scans are a hassle. Audits are so difficult that we subconsciously make excuses for issues and spend a long time between audits. Security parameters, patches, and hardening programs must be automated to maintain security. Private instances can be thoroughly locked down, making them more secure than shared environments. For example, in the listener.ora file, set `HOST =` `LOCALHOST`, and no external users can connect to the database. If nothing is shared and there is no sensitive data, there are fewer privilege concerns. If we all have DBA access on our private databases, we have a place to test security features, such as granting roles and creating users. However, elevated access on private databases isn't an excuse to ignore security. Elevated access gives developers the responsibility to practice security early and often. This will create more initial work for developers, as they must be aware of what elevated privileges are not available in higher environments. But that extra work is a long-term investment. We cannot solely rely on administrators to harden things later.

6. *Performance*: Personal computers (PCs) often outperform development servers. Shared servers are often old and optimized for reliability and durability instead of performance. I've seen plenty of times when an insanely expensive server was much slower than a surprisingly cheap laptop. Don't blindly accept management's sunk cost fallacy reasoning that the servers must be fast because we paid a lot of money for them; compare the CPU performance with the SPEC CPU benchmarks, and roughly compare I/O with a few simple full table scans. Even if the shared server is much faster than our laptops, we obviously have to share that server with others. For performance testing in a lower environment, consistency is just as important as mirroring the production environment. It's easier to isolate tests on a private system.

7. *Licensing*: Oracle licenses are complex and expensive, but only
    for shared servers. Many of Oracle's developer tools are free,
    and virtually every product can be freely downloaded from
    `https://download.oracle.com`. Spend a few minutes to read
    the OTN License Agreement. Without paying any money, we can
    use Oracle databases for "developing, testing, prototyping, and
    demonstrating" our applications. If that license doesn't work,
    then we can buy Personal Edition for only a few hundred bucks.
    Personal Edition has almost all the same features as Enterprise
    Edition and even comes with Oracle Support. The biggest
    difference is that Personal Edition is only for one user on one
    personal computer. Personal Edition doesn't include options
    like Real Application Clusters (RAC), but we don't need RAC for
    most of our development anyway. Oracle licensing can be a real
    nightmare, and we need to be careful, but sometimes we can
    simply go to their website and buy the software we need. But we
    still need to be aware of what options we have licensed, because
    an option that is free on our laptop may still cost a lot of money in
    production.

8. *Initial setup is easier*: Setting up a large number of private
    databases is easier than setting up a small number of servers. This
    happens because creating a large number of databases forces us
    to standardize and automate. And private databases make the
    process more democratic; everyone is involved, has the same
    privileges, and can work together to incrementally improve the
    processes.

Moving from shared databases to private databases gives us a huge boost in
productivity. Distributed development even makes us happier – without artificially
scarce resources, there will be no yelling or finger-pointing when someone blocks a
resource. There's no need for a developer tragedy of the commons; everyone can have a
near-infinite supply of Oracle databases.

There are a few cases where shared databases are required for development.
Typically, the reasons are historical; once a project is headed down the shared database
or private database path, it's hard to change course. And some complex software and
resources cannot be easily redeployed. But don't use deficiencies in tools as an excuse

to do things the old-fashioned way. It's perfectly reasonable to say, "If we can't automate this tool, the tool is not worth using anymore." The information technology industry is always moving toward more automation. Infrastructure is not like an untouchable mainframe – infrastructure should be code that can be easily changed.

Create Private Databases: Local Installation

Once we decide to create private databases, how exactly is it done? There are many ways to give every developer multiple, private database instances. The trendy way to do this is with some combination of the cloud, virtual machines (VMs), and containers. But private databases do not require any fancy new technology. The simplest way to achieve our goal is to install Oracle on our personal computers (PCs). The choice isn't between accessible cloud computing and an unapproachable mainframe; the PC revolution is still alive.

The actual software installation is easy – download and install Enterprise or Personal Edition on our laptop or desktop. We should use a version of Oracle as powerful as the version used in production. That means we should probably avoid Oracle Express Edition, which has hardware restrictions, is unsupported, and is missing important features.

Installing a local instance of Oracle is simple and only requires a few steps. Administering an Oracle database can be difficult, but it's much easier when we don't have to worry about reliability and durability. Database administrators stay up at night worrying about backups and the many layers of software needed to keep shared servers running smoothly. Administration is much easier for our private development databases; we can ignore backups, and if we can't fix the database after a few minutes, we can simply reinstall it.

It might be difficult to create a private database that perfectly matches the production environment. For example, we don't want to install Real Application Clusters (RAC) or Automatic Storage Management (ASM) on our laptops. And our laptops likely won't even have the same operating system as production. Luckily, for 99.9% of Oracle development, those underlying technologies don't matter. RAC, ASM, the operating system, and many other components are invisible to users. Oracle is a highly portable system and has abstracted much of the underlying architecture. Our private databases won't be quite as stable without RAC, but the difference between 99.9% uptime and 99.99% uptime doesn't matter for development.

Even if our development must stay a shared database, there are still benefits to giving everyone a private database. It's always helpful to have a sandbox to play around in and not worry about breaking anything. A lot of testing and learning can be done on a private database, even if the database is empty.

The next section covers other options that are more advanced but require more work up front. We don't need to implement one of those technologies to be agile; a personal computer with "plain old on-premise software" is often all we need.

Create Private Databases: Other Options

There are many ways to create a database, and it's worth at least briefly mentioning the different options. In practice, you may end up with some combination of different approaches, such as the cloud, virtual machines, containers, the multitenant option, or just multiple schemas. As long as one of these more complicated solutions provides an infinite number of databases, they can all help us achieve our goal of creating an efficient development process.

Cloud platforms have risen in popularity in recent years. There are obvious advantages to farming out the low-level tasks so we can stay focused on the high-level tasks. Moving to the cloud can easily have big advantages to your organization, by freeing you from worrying about managing things like electricity, operating systems, patching, etc. But keep in mind that, as a SQL developer, the cloud will not help you much if you're still suck sharing a small number of databases.

There are many books written about cloud computing platforms, and this isn't the place to compare them. Oracle was late to the cloud, but their offerings have finally started to get interesting since their 19c autonomous database. While I can't recommend a specific cloud for your business, I do recommend Oracle's Always Free tier if you just need a small database for learning, testing, or running the examples in this book. Although Oracle's cloud isn't nearly as popular as other's, you will appreciate the enormous difference between "Always Free" and "Trial" if you've ever received a scary billing email.

Virtual machines are great for rapidly creating entire environments. For example, Oracle's Developer Day VM contains almost everything you need to start database programming immediately. Using the free VirtualBox program, you can quickly load the VM image and have an entire system with Oracle Linux, an Oracle database, Oracle SQL Developer, and more. You can easily customize the image, save it, and share it with your team to ensure that everyone is using an identical configuration. If we use virtual machines everywhere, we can rapidly clone production, use that image for development, and avoid almost all platform differences.

Having a gold image of your configuration on a virtual machine is useful especially for tasks that require rollbacks, such as tests that are part of a continuous integration and delivery (CI/CD) system. In theory, our deployment changes have a rollback section, but history tells us that our rollbacks are going to fail, and the system will gradually drift from what it should be. Constantly restarting from an image helps prevent that configuration drift.

Containers can alleviate the inevitable resource problems caused by using virtual machines. Each VM instance has an entire copy of an operating system, which will waste a lot of space and memory. Container programs like Docker will enable multiple images to share some of those operating system resources while keeping the applications isolated. The only downside to containers is that they require packaging the application binaries, and historically Oracle has not always played well with Docker. This might be because Oracle prefers you to use their own type of container solution, the multitenant option.

The *multitenant* option uses Oracle as the container engine. For each database instance, a single *container database (CDB)* holds much of the base configuration and data dictionary. The application schemas live in lightweight *pluggable databases (PDBs)*, each of which looks just like a regular old database. The (considerable) downsides are that extra configuration is required, the database must have been installed with the multitenant architecture, and you must have a multitenant license for more than three PDBs. The payoff is that once multitenant is working, creating a clone of an existing database may literally be as easy as `CREATE PLUGGABLE DATABASE orclpdb2 FROM orclpdb1`.

As a last resort, we can at least install our programs on multiple schemas and give everyone a separate schema. This approach has its own challenges, such as dealing with multiple schemas that all reference each other (synonyms may help), shared global resources like directories, etc.

I've worked at businesses with shared databases, and I've worked at businesses with private databases. It's always been a night-and-day difference. Organizations with shared databases have more missed deadlines, uglier code, and a developer class system that breeds finger-pointing and fear. Organizations with an unlimited number of databases have better products, cleaner code, and an egalitarian environment that makes people happy and helps them reach their full potential.

There are many choices for installing the database software, but that's still the easy part of creating a good development environment. The hard part is recreating custom schemas.

Rapidly Drop and Recreate Schemas

Deploying database changes is easy – if we deploy frequently. There are many fancy ways to create and run database scripts, but good old-fashioned text files and SQL*Plus are the best tools.

Why Deploy Often?

Database deployments are full of errors, uncertainty, and performance problems. Databases are more difficult to deploy than traditional applications, because databases have more persistent data. But we can't blame our deployment problems solely on databases being difficult. Deployment problems will happen to any process that is rarely used.

Practice makes perfect. If deployments are run by many people, many times a day, they will become easy and painless. But easy deployments are only possible if everyone works on private databases, as discussed in the previous section. As soon as we are done with our work, we should drop and recreate the schemas to test the build scripts. (Or, more frequently nowadays, that process is done automatically as part of a commit.) Dropping and recreating schemas, even for complicated database programs, can be done in less than a minute. Constantly recreating schemas lets us find failures immediately. Mistakes can be fixed instantly, since the code is still fresh in our minds.

Everyone on the team should be involved with creating build scripts. Deployments are a natural part of any database change, so building deployments should not be farmed out to a separate team. In some organizations the senior developers look down upon mere deployments and assign that drudge work to the junior developers. But we should take pride in our work, so we should take pride in the way it is packaged and delivered and see it through to the end. Once an efficient system is put in place, creating and testing deployment scripts will be easy anyway.

It helps to create a culture that strongly discourages breaking the build. Breaking the build is the ultimate sign of disrespect in the programming world; other people can't do their job because one person was too lazy to run a simple test. We don't need to publicly shame people, but we do need to make it clear that creating roadblocks for other people is not acceptable. This can be a hard lesson for people accustomed to shared database development. Those developers come from a world where breaking code is inevitable, and they may not understand that breaking the build is no longer acceptable. (Alternatively, we can avoid this whole situation by configuring our repository to automatically check builds before a commit.)

How to Deploy Often?

Creating and maintaining database deployment scripts is not magic. It does not even require twenty-first-century technologies. Text files and SQL*Plus are almost always good enough. But the most important ingredient is discipline.

There are many products that claim to automate database deployments. But this is one of those areas where we should ignore automated tools and build it ourselves, using the simple programs that Oracle already provides. Many automated deployment programs are either database agnostic or assume a shared server model.

There's nothing inherently wrong with being database agnostic. Clearly, many frameworks and programs benefit from working with a large number of databases. But managing and deploying schema objects requires an intimate knowledge of a database. Most deployment automation tools focus on quantity over quality. Those tools don't fully understand Oracle SQL and force us into using a simpler "standard SQL," which makes it difficult to take advantage of Oracle's unique capabilities. If we paid for Oracle, we should get to use all of its features.

Many database deployment tools assume the obsolete shared database model. Do not be fooled; there is no way to be agile if everybody shares the same development server. Slightly improving our shared database deployments is not good enough, and we should not settle for less. Technologies like cloning, data pump, export/import, flashback database, transportable tablespaces, and replication are clearly useful. But those technologies should not be at the heart of our deployment process.

This leaves us with SQL*Plus. That program is showing its age in many ways, and it is a bad choice for tasks like programming and ad hoc querying, as discussed in Chapter 5. But SQL*Plus is the lingua franca of Oracle scripts. It's not a full shell language, it's not an integrated development environment, and it's not particularly good at ad hoc querying. But SQL*Plus hits a sweet spot between those tasks. It's free, easy to configure, already installed, and platform independent. (Oracle has a new command line tool named SQLcl, but as discussed in Chapter 5, I don't recommend using it yet.)

SQL*Plus Installation Scripts

The following is a high-level outline of database installation scripts:

1. Comments: purpose, example, prerequisites, etc.

2. SQL*Plus settings and start message.

3. Check prerequisites.

4. Drop old schemas.

5. Call install script for each schema:

   a. Start message.

   b. Create user.

   c. Call one or more files per object type.

   d. End message.

6. Grant to roles.

7. Validate the schemas and print end message.

Don't try to do everything in one file. Treat the installation file like we would any program, and create lots of small, reusable parts. The top-level install script should be relatively small and should be mostly comments and calls to other scripts, such as @schema1/packages/install_package_specs.sql.

There are a lot of tricky details that will take time to get right. The scripts must grow along with our program. Creating installation scripts is not a task we can leave until the end of the project.

You don't need to read the entire *SQL*Plus User's Guide and Reference*, but you should at least scan through the commands in the table of contents. I won't try to repeat the whole user guide here, but the following paragraphs describe the important parts.

Comments

Comments at the beginning of the script are often overlooked. It's important to add details about the program and how to use it. As an example, look at many of the readme. md files on GitHub. The most successful projects almost always have meaningful documentation to help people quickly get started.

SQL*Plus Settings and Messages

There are lots of SQL*Plus settings we can use to precisely control how the commands are run and displayed. The installation script should show enough details to help us troubleshoot mistakes, but not so many details that it's difficult to find the real problem. Common settings are SET DEFINE ON|OFF (enable or disable considering ampersands to be substitution variables), SET VERIFY ON|OFF (show the substitution variable changes), SET FEEDBACK ON|OFF (show messages like "x rows created"), SET SERVEROUTPUT ON|OFF (show DBMS_OUTPUT), PROMPT TEXT (display a message), and DEFINE VARIABLE = &1 (set variables, possibly to the value of input parameters by using &NUMBER).

Two important and underused SQL*Plus settings are WHENEVER SQLERROR EXIT FAILURE and WHENEVER OSERROR EXIT FAILURE. Do not sweep installation errors under the rug. It's often safer to immediately stop the entire installation as soon as anything goes wrong instead of trying to troubleshoot a half-broken installation days later. When we make a mistake, we should at least try to make it obvious.

The preceding script outline contains lots of messages. The messages can be generated from PROMPT, DBMS_OUTPUT.PUT_LINE, or a SELECT statement. It can be difficult to tell exactly where a script fails, so those messages are important for troubleshooting. It may also help to use SET ERRORLOGGING ON to catch errors.

Check Prerequisites

We may need to limit the program to specific platforms or editions, check for sufficient tablespace, etc. Whenever the program hits an error because of a configuration problem, we should add a check for that problem in the prerequisites section. If SQL*Plus is set to exit on errors, we can stop the installation as soon as a missing prerequisite is found, with a PL/SQL statement like RAISE_APPLICATION_ERROR(-20000, 'Prerequisite X failed...').

Drop Old Schemas

It may look scary at first, but it's important to frequently drop the schemas. To be safe, we may want to put the drop commands in a separate script with a scary file name, to ensure it's never run on the wrong environment. During development, our schemas get cluttered with unnecessary junk. And sometimes we may add an object to our schema but forget to add the object to the scripts. It's better to clean up the schemas and catch missing objects as soon as possible. Dropping and recreating schemas will force us to become disciplined and build cleaner code.

Scripts for Object Types

Each schema's install script is where the real work happens. It's important to have separate install scripts for each object type. Some objects, like tables, can be grouped together in a single file. Other objects, like packages, procedures, and functions, should have a separate file for each. Those separate files allow our code editors to easily read and write to the file during development. Splitting the install script by object types also allows us to avoid most dependency issues. For example, `install_schema1_tables.sql` should run before `install_schema1_package_specs.sql`. Separating the scripts also allows them to be called in different contexts. For example, the packages, procedures, and functions will be called by both the installation and the patch scripts.

Grant to Roles

Build a script to grant to roles from the beginning of the project, even if we don't think we'll need it. Roles are one of those things we always forget, especially when we drop and recreate an object. Build a single script that always grants everything to the appropriate roles and call the script during every installation and every patch, just in case. There's a good chance that every project will eventually need a read or read–write role for important schemas.

Validate the Schemas

Always finish with a small script to validate the schemas. Even if `WHENEVER SQLERROR EXIT FAILURE` is set, there are still subtle ways for errors to go unnoticed. The validation script should at least check for invalid objects and raise an exception if anything is found. Objects may become invalid during the installation, but a call to `DBMS_UTILITY.`

COMPILE_SCHEMA usually fixes everything at the end. For systems with complex dependencies, you may need tricks such as adding a few ALTER ... COMPILE statements. The script may also check other status tables, or possibly the table SPERRORLOG, if SQL*Plus error logging was enabled.

SQL*Plus Patch Scripts

Our program may work great on our private databases, but eventually the code has to move to higher environments. It's convenient to drop and recreate our schemas, but we obviously cannot do that in production. We need scripts to upgrade the schema to include our changes.

Every developer should be involved with creating deployments and should be responsible for integrating their changes into the installation and patch scripts. Designing patch scripts requires some difficult decisions, but it's important to not take any shortcuts.

The installation scripts already take care of things like SQL*Plus settings, checking for errors, and installing code objects. If we separated the installation scripts by object type, half of the work would be already done. Installing code objects, such as packages, procedures, and functions, can be done the same way whether we're installing or patching. Our patch template can simply call those pre-built code scripts. It's easier to recompile everything, every time, instead of trying to find specific code changes.

The tricky part is handling changes to persistent objects, such as tables. Once again, it is better to do this step by hand than to buy a tool and try to automate the process. The reason for manually building change scripts is discussed in the next section. For now, there is still one more decision left – how are those table changes backported into the installation scripts? Do we constantly update the installation scripts, or do we simply run the original installation scripts and then call the patch scripts at the end?

Creating patch scripts is one of the few areas where it is beneficial to repeat ourselves and duplicate our code. Our installation scripts are not just used to recreate the system; they are also our best documentation for understanding how our databases were created. Those installation scripts are often more useful than looking at a live database, because the scripts may contain switches that install different versions of objects depending on things like the database version or edition.

Patch scripts full of ALTER commands are ugly and difficult to follow. To see how a table was built, we shouldn't have to find the original CREATE TABLE statement, then look through the patch scripts, and then put together a history of ALTER TABLE statements. We should take the extra time to make our scripts more readable for future developers; when we create the patch script, we should also add those changes to the installation script. It's annoying, and there's a chance of making a mistake when the code is duplicated, but in this case the duplication is worth the risk.

Control Schemas with Version-Controlled Text Files

Never use a database for version control. This book is about promoting *practical* solutions with Oracle SQL. Although it's fun to push Oracle to its limits and write esoteric queries to solve weird problems, there are some things that should not be done in a database. Version control should be done with manually created text files.

Single Source of Truth

Understanding why we need version-controlled text files begins with a difficult question: Where is the ideal version of our schema? There are many possible answers, such as on a production database, on our private database, in our head, on a floppy disk in a drawer somewhere, etc. This is not merely a theoretical question; every program needs a single source of truth, a single place to find and maintain the real version of the program. (Ironically, the phrase "single source of truth" may have originated with databases, for database normalization. But now the phrase applies better to version control, which shouldn't be done in a database.)

The single source of truth must be convenient and accessible by everyone. It must allow us to store, manipulate, compare, fork, and track the history of everything. While databases are good at most of those tasks, databases don't offer quite enough flexibility and don't help at all with tracking changes. This problem was solved a long time ago, and the solution is text files stored in version control software. The specific version control program doesn't matter. Whether we use Git, Subversion, or something else, any of those choices are significantly better than using a database. The ability to branch, merge, and resolve conflicts is a lot better than simply writing over someone else's work. And modern version control programs form the basis of incredibly useful platforms, such as GitHub.

Unfortunately, a lot of Oracle shops only use version control software as a glorified backup. Version control isn't just a place to store an "official copy" or to store something before it's promoted to another environment. Version control is where our programs need to *live*. If we could wave a magic wand and make all of our development databases disappear, it should only set us back a few hours. Recovery should be easy – get the latest version-controlled files and run the installation script.

Load Objects from the Repository and File System

The first step in development should be to clone a repository or pull the latest files onto your file system. When we want to modify an object, we should load that object from the *file system*, not the database. Modern IDEs, like Oracle SQL Developer, Toad, or PL/SQL Developer, make it trivial to work from the file system. In fact, working from the file system is even easier than working directly from the database objects, because we can carefully arrange the files and folders.

For example, when building the data set and examples for this book, everything is stored on my hard drive and eventually committed to the GitHub repository. Figure 2-1 shows what this looks like when I'm working in PL/SQL Developer. The menu has the same file structure as the GitHub repository, and the tabs are color-coded to quickly identify which files have not been saved to the file system and which objects have not been compiled since the last change.

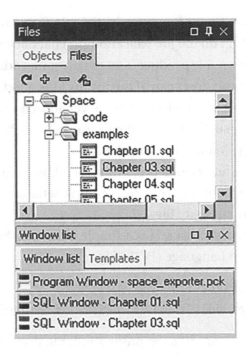

Figure 2-1. *Viewing the database objects through a version-controlled file system*

Most IDEs also have version control interfaces that let us directly work with the repository, but it's often easier to use the file system and the default version control client. If you're not comfortable with the command line interface, there are many open source programs that visually integrate version control with the file system, such as TortoiseGit and Windows File Explorer.

Create and Save Changes Manually

Whichever approach we use to interact with version-controlled files, we should manually commit and verify the files. When we push our changes or merge our branch, we might once again find version control conflicts if other people have changed the same files. Our work is integrated through the version control system, not a shared database. Relying on version control adds a step to our workflow, but the extra step is worth the cost because it enables parallel development.

There are products that attempt to look at our database and guess the changes, but we should avoid those products. Automation is great for *applying* changes. But when it comes to building the changes, they should be lovingly handcrafted. We can't trust a program to tell us how to program – that's our job.

45

Creating automatic change sets is extremely difficult. Even Oracle's solution, DBMS_METADATA_DIFF, doesn't do the job well enough. That package can create a good starting point, but it will inevitably produce a lot of ugly junk code. Those programs don't understand our style and don't care if the results look good. Those programs don't understand that objects must also look good in the version-controlled text files. And of course those programs are usually not free. For example, DBMS_METADATA_DIFF requires a license for the OEM Change Management option.

Most importantly, those automated programs don't know what we don't care about. Those programs produce a lot of junk that drowns out useful features, and they make it impossible to meaningfully compare files.

For example, the following code creates a simple table and then asks Oracle to generate the Data Definition Language (DDL) for it:

```
create table test1 as select 1 a from dual;
select dbms_metadata.get_ddl('TABLE', 'TEST1') from dual;
```

We might expect Oracle's output to be pretty similar to the original command. Instead, we get the following horrendous output:

```
CREATE TABLE "JHELLER"."TEST1"
  (    "A" NUMBER
  ) SEGMENT CREATION IMMEDIATE
 PCTFREE 10 PCTUSED 40 INITRANS 1 MAXTRANS 255
NOCOMPRESS LOGGING
 STORAGE(INITIAL 65536 NEXT 1048576 MINEXTENTS 1 MAXEXTENTS 2147483645
 PCTINCREASE 0 FREELISTS 1 FREELIST GROUPS 1
 BUFFER_POOL DEFAULT FLASH_CACHE DEFAULT CELL_FLASH_CACHE DEFAULT)
 TABLESPACE "USERS"
```

The preceding output is technically correct. But the output misses so much and adds so much that is worthless. Programs like DBMS_METADATA provide a useful starting point, but the output needs a lot of cleanup. The spacing is ugly, there are unnecessary double quotes, and there are many settings that should always be based on the default. The schema should be parameterized and controlled elsewhere in the script, with a command like ALTER SESSION SET CURRENT_SCHEMA = SCHEMA_NAME. Things like the tablespace, segment, and storage options should almost always use the default options.

When scripts look like the preceding automated output, people will not update them, especially a junior developer – they will be too scared to touch any of that mess. It's impossible to tell what part of that CREATE TABLE command is important and what isn't.

There are times when we want to edit one of those unusual options. For example, if we have a large, read-only table, we can save 10% of the storage space by specifying PCTFREE 0. But if we manually change the number ten to the number zero in the preceding script, would anyone ever notice?

Version control is an integral part of virtually all development environments, and Oracle SQL development should be no exception. Our database schemas must truly live in version-controlled text files. We should use version control software to manage differences and to create a social coding platform. We should use our IDE to work with those files, but we must handcraft any objects that are automatically generated.

Empower Everyone

Making schemas easy to install and improving collaboration with version control are part of a larger goal – empowering everyone on our team. No one should have to ask permission, fill out forms, or wait on other people to start developing and experimenting with our programs. This chapter gives specific ideas for how to democratize an Oracle schema, but there are many other ways to accomplish the same goal. Technology alone cannot break down strict social hierarchies and make our organizations and projects more accessible.

This chapter barely scratches the surface of everything needed to set up efficient development processes. This book is not about generic software development life cycle methodologies, but it is worth discussing a few sociological problems that tend to infect Oracle environments. Oracle shops can benefit from fixing the power imbalance between developers and administrators, increasing transparency, and lowering the barriers to entry.

Power Imbalance

There's often a power imbalance between database developers and database administrators. Oracle is mostly used in large businesses and government agencies, and DBAs pick up bad habits from those bureaucracies. There are often nonnegotiable requirements for Oracle database environments – the databases must always be secure, must always be available, and must never lose data. DBAs can be fired for allowing one of those requirements to slip, so there are times when a DBA must put their foot down and tell a developer they can't have what they want.

But administrators would be wise to remember that their databases are worthless if no one can use them. DBAs may protect the organization, but the people creating value for the organization are just as important.

Developers: Don't be afraid to ask the DBAs to explain their decisions. Keep in mind that DBAs understand Oracle's architecture and administrative commands, but they often don't know SQL or PL/SQL. There are different kinds of DBAs, and it's important to know which kind you're talking to. For example, an operations DBA won't understand your application or even know what database you're working on. But an applications DBA should know that information.

DBAs: Don't get mad when developers break things, especially in the lower environments. If developers don't break things, for example, if they never generate ORA-600 errors, then they're not trying hard enough. Developers have to learn through mistakes more than DBAs, so don't make things worse for them. And whenever you say "No" to a developer request, always add an explanation for why you can't do something. Try to think of a workaround, especially for privilege issues. Between roles, object privileges, system privileges, proxy users, and definer's rights procedures, there's almost always a workaround. For example, if a developer asks for the ability to kill sessions on production, you probably can't give them the ALTER SYSTEM privilege. But you can create a SYS procedure that kills sessions only for their user and then grant execute on that procedure to the developer.

Transparency

Transparency requires a willingness to make mistakes and be embarrassed. This is another area where the Oracle culture lags behind the rest of the software industry. Oracle Corporation has a history of secrecy, like hiding their bug tracker behind a paywall, forbidding benchmarks, and opposing open source. Don't follow their example. Let people look into our systems. Share our code repository, project plans, bug tracker, and other documentation with everyone. Some people will use our mistakes against us, and some people will find embarrassing bugs. But bugs are easier to fix the sooner they're found. According to Linus's Law, "given enough eyeballs, all bugs are shallow." If we shorten our feedback loops, we can fail fast and fix our mistakes as soon as possible.

Lower Barriers to Entry

We must constantly look for ways to lower the barrier to entry for our systems – not just the programs we build but for all the surrounding knowledge. Large "enterprise" companies want to harvest our data, granularly control everything, and charge money up front. That strategy might work for large corporations selling to C-level executives, but it's not a good idea for our projects. Put the documentation on a Wiki and let *anyone* modify *anything*. Use a version control system that makes forking software as easy as clicking the "fork" button. People may make annoying edits to our favorite page or use our software in the wrong way; that's simply the price we pay for encouraging participation.

Summary

It's worth spending time thinking about our development processes. Don't simply follow what everyone else does – they may not know what they're doing either. Many Oracle developers, DBAs, testers, and data analysts are only following a specific process because that's the way it's always been done. Oracle was invented in the twentieth century, but that doesn't mean we have to code like it's the twentieth century. We can find a way to make our resources appear infinite. We can make our programs trivial to install, modify, and share. And we can create a culture that fosters learning, experimentation, and teamwork. Now that our development environment is set up, we can move to the next chapter and discuss how to test what we build.

CHAPTER 3

Increase Confidence and Knowledge with Testing

Testing is more than simply demonstrating a program is correct. We must constantly challenge ourselves to make ourselves better. Likewise, we must also challenge our programs and our ideas. Testing is how we bring science into our craft and replace guesses and myths with real knowledge about how the world works. Building good tests can take a lot of time and effort, and Oracle databases present unique challenges for building reproducible test cases. Luckily, Oracle provides many tools to help us test, such as SQL, PL/SQL, the data dictionary, dynamic performance views, and much more.

Build Confidence with Automated Tests

Automated testing requires a significant investment but is almost always worth the extra effort. After we decide to use automated testing, we must decide how to handle data and how to build the automated testing framework.

Fix Bugs Faster

Programming is hard and is full of ambiguous requirements, unexpected side effects, and regressions. Fully automated testing will obviously improve the quality of our programs. The surprising thing about automated testing is that the most important benefits are subtle and only indirectly related to quality.

© Jon Heller 2023
J. Heller, *Pro Oracle SQL Development*, https://doi.org/10.1007/978-1-4842-8867-2_3

Less time fixing bugs is the first obvious, direct benefit. Testing is painful, and few of us enjoy doing it. We're always looking for excuses to avoid it, and there are plenty of cognitive biases that help us ignore testing. Manual testing is easier than automated testing – if it's only done once. We lie to ourselves and think, "We'll only need to test this part once; after the code is working, we'll never change it, so there's no chance of it breaking again." Or maybe testing is someone else's job, and we think we don't have to worry about it.

When our assumptions about our superhuman programming ability are inevitably proven wrong, there is a large price to pay. Fixing bugs is orders of magnitude easier when we do it ourselves right after creating the bugs. The context is still fresh in our minds, and there's no communication overhead. There's no need to discuss errors with testers or log bugs in a tracking system or explain problems to management several times. Building an automated test system is in our own selfish interest, even if there is a separate testing team.

Gain Confidence and Avoid Biases

Automated testing gives us confidence in our programs. Not only can automated testing help us literally sleep better at night but it also frees us to make more changes.

There are many horror stories about the unintended side effects of small programming changes. To avoid those nightmares, many programmers make only the smallest change possible. But to save time on expensive manual testing, programmers need to bundle changes together. With manual testing, every release is a compromise. Either we risk bugs by skimping on expensive testing, or our code doesn't improve over time because we avoid changes.

Automated testing completely changes how we release software. When running the full test suite is effortless, we don't have to worry as much about making changes. The cost of each release decreases, and we can release more often. Don't even think about saying the word "agile" until you have automated testing.

With automated testing we can change whatever we want, whenever we want, for any reason we want. As long as the tests pass and fully cover everything, go for it. Nothing calls that private function anymore? Remove it. Wish that variable had a better name? Rename it. There's this one package, and you just don't like the cut of its jib? Change it. Constant, small amounts of refactoring will compound over time and pay off our technical debt.

Automated testing also helps us avoid biases. Having a structured and standardized system for evaluating our programs makes lying to ourselves harder. When the deadline is looming and we're working late at night, it's awfully tempting to squint our eyes and say the results look good enough. It's always possible to lie about the results, but it's harder to ignore the poor quality of our code when we're staring at a large "FAIL" message and the entire system stops working.

Test-Driven Development

Instead of being treated as a second-class citizen in the software development life cycle, we can promote testing to a prominent role through test-driven development. In test-driven development, the automated tests are created before we start adding features or fixing bugs. The test cases can become the primary form of the requirements. When the tests pass, the requirements are met, and our job is done.

Test-driven development also helps us avoid our biases. The tests are the standards, and it's best to define our goals before we start doing something. It can be irritating to start on an exciting new project and not be able to start coding immediately. But keep in mind that we're going to get fatigued by the end of the project. If we save the testing for the end, we won't define the criteria for success until we're tired of the project and just want it to be over.

However, automated testing is not always appropriate. Sometimes we just need to experiment, and we don't know where our code will take us. Sometimes the task is a one-off or just isn't that important. Sometimes, like for large data loads, the data is too dirty and ill-defined. If we don't understand the project well enough yet, we don't want to create a fake standard. Automated testing should be a practical tool, not a fanatic ideal.

Create Useful Test Data

The biggest difference between application programming unit tests and database programming unit tests is the focus on data. Don't simply import as much data as possible. Instead, focus on creating the right amount of relevant data.

Even for a relational database designed to handle petabytes of data, less is more. It is tempting to import a huge amount of data for testing. Creating good sample data is hard, and there's often pre-generated data in other environments or maybe even live data. Do not give in to that temptation.

Using production data in development is asking for trouble. Production data may be immediately convenient, but it could turn into a disaster later. Organizations will eventually update their data security rules. It's not unusual for an organization to allow production data in lower environments one day and then forbid it the next. Getting rid of that data, or deidentifying it, can be painful.

Production data isn't that useful anyway. Production data may only represent what users have generated so far, not necessarily the limits of what users can ever generate. Don't induce requirements only from production data.

When creating sample data, every byte should mean something. One of the biggest problems with loading production data is that it's overwhelming. For test data, quality is much more important than quantity. No human being can understand a gigabyte of data, so we shouldn't load that much data into our system. Our systems are complex enough. Let's not confuse ourselves further by loading unnecessary data. It's better to take the time to create only the data necessary.

Generating data is only as difficult as the business logic. Don't bother looking for a program to help generate fake data. There is no commercial program that understands our custom systems. Once we understand the business rules and exactly what data we need to generate, there are a few simple Oracle SQL patterns that make the job easy.

The simplest way to generate fake data is with the LEVEL trick:

```
--Generate three rows.
select level a from dual connect by level <= 3;
A
-
1
2
3
```

To load specific data, SELECT from DUAL and combine statements with the UNION ALL set operator:

```
--Generate specific data.
select 1 a, 2 b from dual union all
select 0 a, 0 b from dual;
A   B
-   -
1   2
0   0
```

Create Large Test Data

While accuracy and ease of use are the most important characteristics of test data, occasionally we need to use large data sets for performance testing. Large, complex systems will ideally have at least two data sets: a small data set for automatic unit tests and a large data set for rarer performance testing. We need to ensure our programs can scale up before they are moved to production.

Combining and tweaking the tricks learned in the previous section is almost good enough for generating large amounts of test data. The LEVEL trick has memory limitations we need to work around. After about one million rows, the level trick generates an error:

```
--Raises: ORA-30009: Not enough memory for CONNECT BY operation
select count(*) from
(
    select level from dual connect by level <= 999999999
);
```

When the preceding error happens, we simply have to break the load into multiple steps. Create the table, load the initial data with LEVEL, and then insert the table into itself repeatedly to double the table size. Creating data can get tricky when there are unique or foreign keys. But normally when we're loading a large amount of data, it's for performance testing, and the data doesn't have much meaning:

```
--Generate large amounts of data.
create table test1(a number);
insert into test1 select level from dual connect by level <= 100000;
insert into test1 select * from test1;
insert into test1 select * from test1;
insert into test1 select * from test1;
...
```

For extremely large data loads, a few more tricks can help, such as creating tables with the NOLOGGING option and using INSERT /*+ APPEND */ to enable faster direct-path writes. There are risks with loading large data, and direct-path inserts are discussed in later chapters. Loading relevant data is more of a business logic challenge than a technical challenge. The preceding simple tricks are good enough to get us started.

We may want to use a hybrid approach, where we use carefully crafted data for frequent unit testing and we use a copy of production for less frequent user acceptance and performance testing. While frequently running unit tests increases our confidence in our changes, there are still a few risky changes where we want the additional peace of mind of running them in a near-production environment. For some performance tests, since query execution plans depend largely on the table and column statistics, it helps to have an environment that perfectly matches the data distribution of production. The inconvenience of using production data isn't so bad if we only need to periodically clone production to one database. But we certainly don't want to use production clones as the only source of our test data.

Remove Test Data

Part of creating test data is removing that data when we're done. Test data can pollute our environment and cause problems if we're not careful. Automated unit testing frameworks often have a `TearDown` procedure to handle cleaning up after testing is done. Cleaning up from tests is not always trivial; inserting data in one table may lead to results scattered throughout the schema.

Instead of trying to remove the test data piece by piece, it may be easier to reset the whole schema. With private database development, this is as easy as dropping and recreating the schema. On a shared database, where we don't have scripts to rebuild the environment, there are still technologies that can help us test faster. We can recreate the environment using flashback, virtual machines, multitenant, etc.

How to Build Automated Tests

If you're not already using automated unit tests, it's easy to get started. There are many different frameworks available, and even writing your own simple testing program is fine. Don't get overwhelmed by the choices – whatever program we choose, it's better than doing nothing.

JUnit is the most popular unit testing framework, although it is meant for Java. That program is a member of the xUnit family, and there are similar programs for almost every programming language. Unit testing isn't as common in Oracle as it is in Java, but there are still several choices. The most popular option is currently utPLSQL.

Installing and using utPLSQL is simple: download a free and open source program, unzip it, and run a single SQL*Plus script. The detailed steps can be found in the program repository at https://github.com/utPLSQL/utPLSQL.

This chapter only covers a small part of that program. The point is not to recreate a utPLSQL tutorial but to show you how simple it is to get started. Don't be intimidated by all the options. The program can still reshape our entire development process even if we only use 5% of the features.

utPLSQL requires us to add "annotations" to our code. Annotations configure the unit tests through formatted comments in package specifications. The test is performed by an "expectation," a statement that compares the actual value with the expected value. Tests are executed by calling a pre-built package, and the output can be viewed in multiple formats.

For example, let's say we want to test the data in the space database. To start we might want to check the number of rows in the two main tables, LAUNCH and SATELLITE. First, we create a package specification to hold the annotations. The annotations define a single test suite, named "Space," and two tests:

```
create or replace package space_test as
    -- %suite(Space)
    -- %test(Check number of rows in launch)
    procedure test_launch_count;
    -- %test(Check number of rows in satellite)
    procedure test_satellite_count;
end;
/
```

Next, we need to implement the specification and call the expectations. The following package body shows the two procedures. Each procedure counts the number of rows, saves the count into a variable, and compares that variable with the hard-coded expected number. There are 70,535 launches and 43,113 satellites. But to make the results interesting, let's expect the wrong number for the satellite count:

```
create or replace package body space_test as
    procedure test_launch_count is
        v_count number;
    begin
        select count(*) into v_count from space.launch;
```

```
      ut.expect(v_count).to_(equal(70535));
   end;

   procedure test_satellite_count is
      v_count number;
   begin
      select count(*) into v_count from space.satellite;
      ut.expect(v_count).to_(equal(9999));
   end;
end;
/
```

Here's one of several ways to run the unit tests:

```
begin
   ut3.ut.run();
end;
/
```

The following is the DBMS_OUTPUT of the run. The output contains the program name and the results of the two tests. One of the tests was successful and doesn't show anything. But one of the expectations failed, and the output explains why it failed:

```
Space
  Check number of rows in launch [.004 sec]
  Check number of rows in satellite [.005 sec] (FAILED - 1)

Failures:

  1) test_satellite_count
     Actual: 43113 (number) was expected to equal: 9999 (number)
     at "JHELLER.SPACE_TEST.TEST_SATELLITE_COUNT", line 13 ut.expect(v_
     count).to_(equal(9999));

Finished in .013 seconds
2 tests, 1 failed, 0 errored, 0 disabled, 0 warning(s)
```

That's it. A fully functioning, automated test suite in less than an hour, in only a few lines of code. Automated testing can be that simple.

There are many more features available. We can generate fancier reports, check the code coverage to ensure that all lines of code are tested, use automated testing in a continuous integration system, etc. But those features are not always necessary, so don't let them intimidate you into not using unit testing.

Now that we've started writing unit tests, where do we go from here? First, treat those test packages like regular code. Test packages can get ugly and full of repetitive boilerplate code and include complicated setups for each test. Don't be surprised if the unit test code is larger than the rest of the code. To help manage unit tests, split the code into logical packages and files and give them good names and comments.

The standard manual testing advice applies just as well to automated unit tests. Try to test every line of code and ideally every path. When there is a loop, create a test for the boundary conditions – off-by-one problems will happen at the beginning or end of the loop, not in the middle. Sometimes a test should focus on one small thing, so that when the test fails, we know exactly what to fix. Other times a test should cover lots of things, to ensure we catch as much as possible. Whatever our style, we must make failures obvious; a single failure should break the build and stop everything.

Build Knowledge with Minimal, Complete, and Verifiable Examples

Building informal test cases is difficult but important. Creating a test case that is minimal, complete, and verifiable requires time and discipline. We must ensure our test cases are easily shared with others, and we must watch out for the XY problem.

Why Spend So Much Time Building Reproducible Test Cases?

Developers need help and need to ask a lot of questions. Despite what we heard in kindergarten, there are lots of bad questions. The best way to ask a question about programming is to include a reproducible test case.

The first advantage to building a test case is that we are likely to solve the problem ourselves. Restating the problem and imagining explaining it to someone else will help us see the problem from a different perspective.

Occam's razor says that the simplest answer is usually the right one. For Oracle SQL problems, the simplest answer is one of these: we forgot to commit, we made a typo, or we're not really getting the error message we claim we got. It's frustrating and common for people to respond to our questions with one of those simple answers, so we might as well answer their concerns ahead of time. Before people will invest their time solving our complex problem, we must demonstrate that we don't have a simple problem.

A good test case is also a great way to prove something to ourselves and help us avoid biases. When we're heavily invested in making something work or making it fast, we may only see what we want to see. Building tests with reproducible, clear, and objective results makes it harder to deceive ourselves.

Reproducible test cases are also necessary for dealing with potentially adversarial situations. Many people have an incentive to not believe us, and they think, "*Our software is perfect – that failure or behavior isn't possible.*" Those responses can make us angry, but we shouldn't take it personally. Unhelpful responses are often the result of biased people who subconsciously know they can go home early if our complaints are groundless. Or perhaps their management only cares about the number of tickets opened and closed; making a ticket go away counts just as much as solving a real problem. Sometimes we need to play stupid games to get the support we paid for.

The easiest way for a support engineer to make a ticket go away is to ask for more information. If they ask for enough information, eventually we will give up and let them close the ticket. Creating a good test case will avoid many of those games.

The phrase "minimal, complete, and verifiable examples" comes from Stack Overflow and has developed over time to help people post useful questions. You can read the full description at `https://stackoverflow.com/help/mcve`. The following sections explain the different components of that phrase in an Oracle context.

Minimal

Omit needless code.

I'm tempted to only use that one sentence for the entire section. Unfortunately, simplifying isn't simple, and we need to work hard to make things look easy.

Programming is hard, and bugs can multiply quickly. The more code in the test case, the more chances there are to introduce irrelevant problems, and the more chances there are for people to focus on the wrong thing and nitpick unrelated mistakes. Large code takes more time to understand, and fewer people will be willing to look at it. If we have a purely technical issue, exclude as much business logic as possible. We must shine a focused light on the smallest possible amount of code. (But we must measure the code by the number of lines and variables, not by the number of characters; don't use single-letter variable names just to make the file size smaller and don't forget to add helpful comments.)

The same rules apply to schema objects and data. Do not create two columns when one column will do. Do not insert two rows of data when one row will do.

The tricky part is that our problem may happen in a large context. A problem might happen in a query with dozens of tables, reading billions of rows. It can take hours to remove as much code and data as possible but still reproduce the bug. Cutting a large query in half, checking if it fails, and repeating can take a long time. Eventually we will be left with a problem that fits inside a small SQL worksheet.

Minimizing code is time consuming and tedious. But the process lets us pinpoint the precise problem, is easier than arguing about the code and data, and avoids uploading massive files that nobody wants to read.

Complete

We must create a test case that is runnable and self-contained. Then we must write the code on a fresh database, to ensure that there are no unexpected dependencies missing from the test case. People won't install other products to help us with a problem, so make sure everything is in one place.

The following is an example of a complete test case. The code creates the objects, adds the data, gathers optimizer statistics, and runs the problem query:

```
--Create the table.
create table simple_table(simple_column number);

--Add sample data.
insert into simple_table select 1 from dual;

--Gather statistics if it's a performance problem.
begin
    dbms_stats.gather_table_stats(user, 'simple_table');
end;
/
```

```
--This is the query that fails or is slow.
select *
from simple_table;
```

The preceding code is the ideal, but our entire schema is the reality. We need to meet somewhere in the middle. Sometimes it helps to start with the preceding code and add real code until something breaks. Other times it helps to start with the real schema and subtract until the code works.

Along with code, we should also provide the full version number and edition. The version and edition are relevant to finding specific bugs, and they also limit what kind of troubleshooting and workarounds are available. The platform rarely matters, but it doesn't hurt to include it anyway. For example: The preceding code works on Oracle 19.3.0.0.0, Enterprise Edition, and 64-bit Windows 10.

It's also important to gather system parameters. There are literally hundreds of parameters, and it's hard to know which of them matter. We can narrow down the search by only looking for non-default parameters, with this query:

```
select name, value
from v$parameter
where isdefault = 'FALSE'
order by name;
```

But even the preceding query is not always good enough. For example, on certain processors, the default value for CPU_COUNT is wrong and can cause performance problems. And many parameters can be changed at the session level, either as part of a logon script or through a trigger. Unfortunately, there is no way to get a list of all non-default session parameters.

It's impossible to make a test case truly complete – if you wish to make a test case from scratch, you must first invent the universe. But with a little effort, we can get enough information 99% of the time. At the very least, our reproducible test case shows others that we're serious, which makes it more likely for other developers to try the sample code and investigate the problem.

Verifiable

Nobody can verify code that "doesn't work." We need objective measures for our code, such as a complete error message or detailed performance expectations.

We all hate error messages and wish they would go away. But we must resist the urge to quickly dismiss and ignore error messages. By default, an Oracle error will generate the object name, an error number, an error message, and the line numbers. If the error propagated through multiple levels, all levels of the error message will be included. By default, Oracle includes all the information we need to solve most problems. But the error message only helps if we write down the *entire* message. Developers go to great lengths to raise useful exception messages. Don't throw out their work by ignoring the messages and saying, "There was an error."

SQL*Plus is not good at interactive querying and programming. The greatest strength of SQL*Plus is its simple, universal, text-only interface to Oracle. If we can do something in SQL*Plus, anybody can copy the text, run the code, and verify the results for themselves.

Programs like Oracle SQL Developer are much nicer for most database work, but they are not as helpful for creating test cases. If we send a screenshot, other developers can't extract the code as easily. If we send just the text we used in SQL Developer, other developers may be missing information about how we ran the code – there are different window types with different behaviors. And the output and error messages are not always easy to copy in SQL Developer.

SQL*Plus looks ugly, but at least it's an ugly we can all agree on. With a few simple tricks, we can create a SQL*Plus environment that shows exactly what we ran, where we ran it, and how long it took:

```
SQL> set sqlprompt "_user'@'_connect_identifier> "
JHELLER@orcl9> set timing on
JHELLER@orcl9> select count(*) from dba_objects;
  COUNT(*)
----------
     74766
Elapsed: 00:00:00.21
JHELLER@orcl9>
```

Changing the SQL prompt makes it obvious what user ran the code and what database it was run on. People are rarely rude enough to directly ask, "Are you sure you're on the right database?" But in their head, they're thinking it, so we might as well put their mind at ease. On the other hand, sometimes the database name is sensitive, and we need to hide it. With text output, it's simple to find and replace the name, whereas screenshots often include unintended details, perhaps even from other programs.

The `SET TIMING ON` command shows the wall-clock run time of each statement. And the statements themselves are easily copied and pasted. With a tiny amount of effort, we can eliminate much of the uncertainties of a test case.

For performance tuning it is critical to include the precise timing expectations. An OLTP system processing one row might expect a result in less than a second. A data warehouse processing a billion rows might expect a result in less than a week. We must provide more information than "it's slow." It helps to explain how much time our code takes, how much time we think it should take, and why. It helps to list our performance assumptions, because sometimes our expectations are unrealistic. Perhaps the process that we think should take less than a second couldn't possibly take less than a second with our current data structures, algorithms, and hardware.

Sharing Tests

Creating reproducible test cases is beneficial for our own education, but most of the time we need to share those test cases with others. If we want to add to the world's knowledge, we need to release all the details of our tests, so that others can prove us wrong. Without a fully reproducible test case, we're not doing science.

Organizations like to keep all their test cases to themselves, but there's rarely a need to hide that information, especially in an agile environment, where the customer should be given access to view all the tests. If we're lucky, the customer will find a problem or missing assumption early in the development process.

To optimize sharing, use text as much as possible. It's easier to create a test case with an IDE, but it's worth recreating the final version in SQL*Plus to ensure everything can be copied and pasted. If we must use a screenshot, we should take the time to rearrange the windows to make them as small as possible and edit the picture to only include relevant details.

Ideally, the audience for our test case has a private Oracle database with full access to create an unlimited number of objects. If our audience does not have that environment, there are a growing number of "fiddle" websites for building and sharing code snippets. One popular database website is `https://dbfiddle.uk`. That site lets anyone create a schema, query the schema, and share the schema with others as a simple URL. Oracle has a similar site at `https://livesql.oracle.com`. Oracle's website has more features than other sites, but it requires an account to run the snippets.

Avoiding the XY Problem

Before sending the final version of the test case, we need to take a step back and try to avoid the XY problem. Programming tends to lead us down a deep garden path. We want to do X, and we think Y is the solution. When Y doesn't work, we ask a question about Y, when our real problem is with X.

A common example of the XY problem is when people ask, "How do I split a comma-separated list into different rows?" It's an important question, and there are times when it's necessary. But splitting strings implies that someone is not following the most basic rules of the relational model. The developer asking the question and the person who will someday replace them are in for a lot of trouble trying to use a broken data model. The correct answer is "don't do that." It's not the answer people want to hear, but it is the answer they need to hear.

We fall into this XY trap because programming occasionally requires focusing on minor details, and we don't see the big picture. The way out of the trap is to occasionally stop and ask ourselves "Why?" a few times.

When we find ourselves asking for help to do something weird, it's important to explain why we need to do it the weird way. We're more likely to get sympathy and help if we explain that *we're* not stupid; it's the business rule or technical limitation that is stupid. If we're lucky, someone will interrupt us and say, "Your premise is wrong – that limitation doesn't apply to version A anymore, and you can use feature B instead."

Oracle Performance Testing

Building reproducible test cases for Oracle performance problems is especially challenging. Oracle performance test cases tend to be full of heisenbugs – errors or behaviors that disappear when someone else looks at them. Since Oracle SQL is a declarative language, Oracle has a lot of leeway on how to execute things, including the ability to change its mind. Part IV covers advanced performance tuning concepts, such as using sampling and profiling to drill down into our PL/SQL programs to find the slow SQL and then using hints and monitoring to drill down into our SQL to find the slow operations. Before we get to those details, the first step in performance testing is learning how to accurately measure the overall performance of a single statement.

The wall-clock run time is the central unit of measurement for performance tests. If something runs faster, it is using less resources and is better for both the users and the system. Don't worry too much about measuring CPU, I/O, locks, mutexes, etc.

But there are important exceptions to the rule of only measuring run time. For example, we don't want to create a parallel solution that decreases run time by a few seconds but increases CPU utilization from 1% to 99%. Run time doesn't always correlate to resource consumption. Some Oracle developers find it helpful to proactively monitor resource consumption with programs such as RUNSTATS.[1]

The most frustrating part of performance tests is when the run time is not consistent. Oracle databases warm up and tune themselves over time, so it's quite common for the second or third execution of a query to be significantly faster than the first execution.

Caching is the largest factor in performance test inconsistency. When we run the query the first time, Oracle reads the table and index blocks from disk and stores the blocks in memory. The second time we run the query, the database can read the blocks with much faster memory access. Depending on our environment, we may want to test the system either "hot" or "cold." On a data warehouse, where our large tables likely won't be cached, testing a cold system is better. On an OLTP system, where popular tables should be in memory, testing a hot system is better. We can clear Oracle's memory with the command ALTER SYSTEM FLUSH BUFFER_CACHE. But that command won't clear the operating system cache, and we may not want to run it on a shared database where other users could be affected.

Intermittent system activity can also spoil our thorough test cases. This is more of a problem on a shared database, but even our laptops may suddenly start running an antivirus scan and slow down. Instead of measuring system activity, which is difficult, we can run the tests multiple times and alternate between the competing approaches. Alternating between the different options will make it more obvious if the system suddenly gets faster or slower. We may also want to throw out the minimum and the maximum run times.

Execution plans will also change over time. If we wait long enough, the system will likely automatically gather missing statistics. The Oracle optimizer is also able to learn from its mistakes and may use statistics feedback, adaptive cursor sharing, and SQL plan directives during the second or third run. (Those features are briefly discussed in Part IV.) Carefully check the Note section of the execution plan to see if there are any weird tricks being applied. To create a blank slate for testing, it is sometimes necessary to run ALTER SYSTEM FLUSH SHARED_POOL and to regather statistics. But as with flushing the buffer cache, we need to be careful running those commands if we're running on a shared database.

---

[1] There are many implementations of this idea, such as https://github.com/ oracle-developer/mystats

Oracle Detective Kit

The first of E. F. Codd's rules for relational databases is that a database must be able to manage itself entirely through a relational interface. In Oracle databases there is a wealth of information available about the database, and that information can be accessed through the database. When our tests inevitably need to look under the hood of our programs and schemas, we can use the data dictionary, dynamic performance views, Oracle packages and functions, and other Oracle tools.

Data Dictionary Views

There are roughly 1000 data dictionary views that provide metadata about virtually everything inside the Oracle database. There are four different prefixes for data dictionary views: USER_, ALL_, DBA_, and CDB_. The USER_ views provide information for the current user, the ALL_ views provide information for all users that we have access to, the DBA_ views provide information for all users, and the CDB_ views provide information for all users for all containers.

The data dictionary has great backward compatibility. This means we can write a script for version X and safely expect the script to work in version X+1. The column names almost never change, except for columns added at the end of the views. The downside to this backward compatibility is the data dictionary contains some deprecated features. The LONG columns in the dictionary are difficult to work with. There is *still* no easy way to use SQL functions against LONG values, so searching those columns takes a few extra steps.

For example, finding all columns that default to zero *should* be this easy:

```
SQL> select table_name, column_name, data_default
  2  from dba_tab_columns
  3  where to_char(data_default) = '0'
  4  order by 1,2,3;
where to_char(data_default) = '0'
      *
ERROR at line 3:
ORA-00932: inconsistent datatypes: expected CHAR got LONG
```

Unfortunately, we need to add an extra step to make the preceding query work. First, we must convert and save the data, and then we can filter the results:

```
create table convert_tab_columns as
select table_name, column_name, to_lob(data_default) data_default
from dba_tab_columns
where data_default is not null;

select table_name, column_name, to_char(data_default) data_default
from convert_tab_columns
where to_char(data_default) = '0'
   and rownum = 1
order by 1,2,3;
```

```
TABLE_NAME             COLUMN_NAME    DATA_DEFAULT
--------------------   -----------    ------------
CDB_LOCAL_ADMINAUTH$   LCOUNT         0
```

Another problem with the data dictionary is that some column names don't make sense anymore. In an ancient version of Oracle, privileges were only granted on tables, and the view name DBA_TAB_PRIVS made sense. Unfortunately, that view now contains privileges for all object types.

There are also some ancient, deprecated data dictionary views that should be avoided. Those views are available for backward compatibility, but do not contain nearly as much data as the views that replaced them. Avoid CAT, COL, COLS, TAB, and TABS. Note that Oracle does not contain an INFORMATION_SCHEMA like many other databases.

Minor problems aside, the data dictionary has a wealth of information. We don't need to memorize the 1000 views or put a poster on our office wall. But we may want to search for and bookmark the *Database Reference* for our Oracle version. The following is a list of the most important data dictionary views, some of which are self-explanatory:

1. *_ADVISOR_*: Status and results of automatic advisors, which may become increasingly important with the new autonomous database features.

2. *_AUDIT_TRAIL: The audit data depends on the configuration but typically includes useful information about logon history.

3. *_AUTOTASK: Special system jobs to gather stats, auto-tune, etc.

4. *_CONSTRAINTS: Unique, check, primary, foreign.

5. DUAL: A table with only one row – useful for when we want to create data.

6. *_ERRORS: Errors in our code causing invalid objects.

7. *_HIST_*: Views used for the automatic workload repository, for performance tuning (but requires a diagnostics pack license).

8. *_INDEXES, DBA_IND_COLUMNS.

9. *_JOBS/SCHEDULER: Scheduled jobs.

10. *_OBJECTS: All schema objects – useful for finding things.

11. *_RESUMABLE: Sessions waiting for resources.

12. *_ROLE_PRIVS/SYS_PRIVS/TAB_PRIVS: Role, system, and object privileges.

13. *_SOURCE: Source code for all code objects, except views.

14. *_SYNONYMS.

15. *_TABLES, TAB_COLUMNS.

16. *_USERS.

17. *_VIEWS: Includes the source of view (not included in *_SOURCE).

Dynamic Performance Views

Over 850 dynamic performance views contain information about the current state of an Oracle database. These views are more about Oracle than about our data, so they tend to be more cryptic, but just as useful, as the data dictionary. There are two types of dynamic performance views: V$ and GV$. The only difference is that V$ views contain data about the current instance we are connected to and GV$ contains data about all instances. If we're not connected to a Real Application Clusters database, then the two types of views will be almost identical.

Like the data dictionary, the dynamic performance views also have good backward compatibility. The full list can be found in the *Database Reference*. The following is a list of the most common views, with an explanation for the ones that are not self-explanatory:

1. V$ASM*: Automatic Storage Management data

2. V$DATABASE: Database information from the control file

3. V$INSTANCE: Current state of the database

4. V$PARAMETER: Initialization parameters

5. V$PGASTAT, V$PGA*: Program Global Area (PGA) data (session memory, like for sorting and hashing)

6. V$PROCESS: Active processes, can be tied to an operating system process

7. V$PX*: Parallel processes

8. V$SESSION: Current sessions and where they connect from

9. V$SESSMETRIC, V$SESSTAT: Session metrics and statistics, useful for measuring resource consumption and performance tuning

10. V$SGASTAT, V$SGA*: System Global Area (SGA) data (system memory, for things like caching data and execution plans)

11. V$SQL*: Data about SQL statements and their execution plans

12. V$SYSMETRIC*, V$SYSSTAT: System metrics and statistics, useful for measuring total resource consumption

13. V$VERSION: The precise version of the database in column `BANNER_FULL`

The dynamic performance view `V$PARAMETER` is especially important, and each row in that view can be critical. There are over 400 rows, and each row is thoroughly documented in the *Database Reference*. It's hard to say which parameters are most critical; even a single wrong parameter can break the database in weird ways. While administrators need to understand most of the parameters, the following parameters are most likely to be of interest to SQL developers:

1. compatible: The compatibility version of the data files may limit the available features. Once we change this parameter, there is no going back.

2. cpu_count: Should be the number of processors, but on some platforms, it's incorrectly set to the number of supported threads; this number is important for parallel processing.

3. cursor_sharing: If our application cannot use bind variables, changing from the default EXACT to FORCE can alleviate some performance issues. (Bind variables are discussed in Chapter 14.)

4. ddl_lock_timeout: Allows DDL statements to wait instead of immediately failing if the object is locked.

5. memory_target/pga_aggregate_target/sga_target: Oracle memory settings are ridiculously complicated; read the manual a few times for each of these settings before you touch them.

6. nls*: National Language Support (NLS) parameters control how data is stored, compared, sorted, and formatted – whether by binary values or according to specific language rules. Do not rely solely on the database formatting settings – they are frequently overridden by session settings.

7. optimizer_index_caching/optimizer_index_cost_adj/db_file_multiblock_read_count: Frequently abused parameters – do not set these unless you are looking for trouble.

8. parallel*: Control parallel processing; think carefully and read the parallel processing guide before changing these parameters.

9. processes, sessions: Limit the number of Oracle operating system processes and connections. These numbers frequently need to be increased.

We should not change the preceding parameters unless we think we are smarter than the engineers at Oracle. There will be plenty of times when we *are* smarter than Oracle engineers, like when we know something specific about our environment. For example, only we know how many sessions our database is intended to handle. If we have a database that must allow a thousand connections, then it's necessary to increase SESSIONS and PROCESSES, even though the change will slightly increase the memory requirements.

On the other hand, we don't know how much faster or slower our indexes are than Oracle's expected performance; changing OPTIMIZER_INDEX_COST_ADJ is almost certainly a bad idea. There are times when changing that parameter will improve a specific query's performance, by changing an execution plan from a full table scan to an index scan. But we shouldn't alter the entire system to fix a problem for just one statement. The solution should be proportional to the size of the problem, and Oracle allows us to set that parameter per session or per query. The reason I included this parameter on the preceding list is not because we need to customize it, but because we frequently need to change it back to the default after someone else mistakenly modifies it.

Relational Tools for Inspecting Databases

There are many other tools scattered throughout the database that let us investigate the database.

VSIZE is a useful function that tells us the size of a value in bytes. That may sound like a trivial feature at first, but a surprisingly large number of architectural decisions hinge on the size of data types. There is a silly but persistent myth that Oracle always allocates as much space as possible. A few calls to VSIZE will dispel that myth. VSIZE also demonstrates that small numbers may take up more space than we might expect:

```
--Byte size of values:
select
    vsize(0) zero_size,
    vsize(1) one_size,
    vsize(10) ten_size,
    vsize(date '2000-01-01') date_size,
    vsize(cast('a' as varchar2(4000))) string_size
from dual;
ZERO_SIZE   ONE_SIZE   TEN_SIZE   DATE_SIZE   STRING_SIZE
---------   --------   --------   ---------   -----------
        1          2          2           7             1
```

DUMP displays the internal contents of a value. This function can be useful when dealing with non-ASCII characters. For example, imagine a table that contains links. When we query the table, everything looks fine:

```
select * from random_links;
URL
---------------
google.com
```

Hold on a minute – let's dig deeper. That string looks like "google.com", but is the value in the database really "google.com"? Look at this output and see if you can spot the problem:

```
select dump(url,16) from random_links;
DUMP(URL,16)
-----------------------------------------------
Typ=1 Len=11: 67,6f,c3,b6,67,6c,65,2e,63,6f,6d
```

The first thing you might notice is Len=11. The length is 11 bytes, but "google.com" only has ten characters. If you look carefully at the hexadecimal values, you'll notice that the second "o" is not really "o", it's "ö". It's an "o" with a dieresis, or two dots on top.

This trick is called visual spoofing. It's intentionally hard to see, and without a function like DUMP, we may have never spotted the problem. If you're curious, the malicious string was created like this:

```
insert into random_links values('go'||unistr('\00f6')||'gle.com');
```

In theory we can recreate any object using the data dictionary. For example, all the features related to a table can be found in data dictionary views such as ALL_TABLES, ALL_TAB_COLUMNS, ALL_CONSTRAINTS, etc. In practice it is difficult to reconstruct the full DDL for objects, especially for the obscure features. The function DBMS_METADATA.GET_DDL can make our lives much easier and has many options for adjusting the formatting. For example, the following is to find the statement behind the table LAUNCH:

```
select dbms_metadata.get_ddl(
    object_type => 'TABLE',
    name        => 'LAUNCH',
    schema      => 'SPACE') ddl
```

```
from dual;
DDL
--------------------------------------------------
  CREATE TABLE "SPACE"."LAUNCH"
   (    "LAUNCH_ID" NUMBER,
        "LAUNCH_TAG" VARCHAR2(15 CHAR),
        "LAUNCH_DATE" DATE,
...
```

But if we find ourselves playing schema detective, we've already lost. As discussed in Chapter 2, the best way to find schema scripts is to look in version-controlled text files. The full output for the preceding query, while technically correct, has some formatting issues and includes a huge amount of worthless information, whereas our installation scripts are all signal and no noise. There should be no need to put up with meaningless bytes.

The SYS_CONTEXT function can retrieve data about the current session's contexts. We can create custom contexts, but the most common context is the default USERENV. It's a convenient way to find out information about the current session, without having to look through multiple tables. For example, the following is to get the name of the host machine that we used to connect to the database:

```
select sys_context('userenv', 'host') from dual;
```

For code analysis, PL/Scope can be useful for tasks that require understanding the code. PL/Scope can find specific dependencies, unused variables, etc. And the package DBMS_DEBUG can help us step through our code line by line as it executes. Those are interesting tools, but they are generally only helpful when combined with an IDE.

Non-relational Tools for Inspecting Databases

Oracle includes many non-relational tools to also help inspect the database. (Performance tuning tools are a large topic and are covered in Part IV.) A program can work with a database and maybe even run inside a database program, but not necessarily be relational. This distinction is important because non-relational tools cannot be used in as many contexts as relational tools.

For example, the DESC command in SQL*Plus is a neat way to quickly get information about a table:

```
SQL> desc space.launch
 Name                      Null?     Type
 --------------------      --------  -----------------
 LAUNCH_ID                 NOT NULL  NUMBER
 LAUNCH_TAG                          VARCHAR2(15 CHAR)
 LAUNCH_DATE                         DATE
...
```

While the DESC command is useful, we may want to avoid becoming too dependent on it, because it's only available in SQL*Plus. Even though SQL*Plus is available to almost all developers, most developers use a graphical IDE. Using a query against the data dictionary, or a call to DBMS_METADATA.GET_DDL, may take a bit more work, but it's worth it to ensure that we build purely relational solutions.

The traditional export and export data pump programs, EXP and EXPDP, can also be used to find useful data and metadata. The undocumented ORADEBUG command can output individual blocks and help us see exactly how data is stored on disk. Oracle tracing can help us understand the optimizer's decisions and see exactly what is running in the background to support our queries. And there's a whole world of tools that are generally only useful to database administrators: listener control, server control, etc.

Oracle is closed source, but if we are familiar with all these metadata tools, we can figure out exactly what is going on. It's helpful to know a wide variety of database tools, because different people have different styles and preferences for investigating database problems. For example, I typically work in PL/SQL Developer and use Ctrl+right-click to describe a table. But when I'm working with DBAs who prefer SQL*Plus, I'll show them the table metadata by using the DESC command.

Summary

When we start programming, we should be skeptical of our programs and ideas. Eventually we must become confident of our programs and knowledge, but that confidence should be the product of automated unit testing and concise test cases. Luckily, Oracle provides a wealth of views and tools to help us build that confidence. But there's only so much we can do by ourselves, and eventually we'll need help from other people. The next chapter will help us find reliable sources for Oracle knowledge.

CHAPTER 4

Find Reliable Sources

Oracle SQL programming has an epistemic problem. Epistemology is the study of knowledge, or simply asking ourselves what do we know and how do we know it. We don't need to take a philosophy class before we start programming, but we do need to carefully consider our sources. The Oracle programming culture places too much weight on unreliable epistemologies, such as tradition and scripture, and not enough weight on science and reason. If we listen to the wrong sources, we will learn the wrong lessons.

Why is finding reliable sources a problem with Oracle more than other technologies? Oracle is geared toward business users, not academics or traditional programmers. Computer science students rarely learn about Oracle and don't focus their obsessive curiosity on SQL or PL/SQL. Students, technology thought leaders, and hobby programmers tend to ignore business-oriented programming languages. Oracle is often used for boring "enterprise" software that slowly and painfully evolves and avoids experiments and refactoring. And it certainly doesn't help that Oracle is closed source and that Oracle Corporation has a history of being hostile toward open source.

A disproportionate number of people only use Oracle to help earn a paycheck and don't spend time deciphering and testing the internals of their database. Not everyone needs to be a hobby programmer, but there needs to be a minimum number of curious people to create the right cultural norms.

There's a knowledge gap, and that gap has been filled by an annoying amount of tradition, appeals to authority, clickbait, and myths. We can't reasonably test everything; the development processes and testing techniques described in Chapters 2 and 3 require a lot of time and effort, and real-life performance problems contain too many uncontrollable variables. We'll never accomplish anything if we always challenge *every* assumption. But our thought leaders should be the kind of people who are always willing to support their ideas with reproducible test cases.

We need to avoid experts who make wild claims about things they saw happen once but cannot demonstrate again. We need to be cautious of websites that make extraordinary claims about Oracle but don't provide a way to challenge those claims.

© Jon Heller 2023
J. Heller, *Pro Oracle SQL Development*, https://doi.org/10.1007/978-1-4842-8867-2_4

We learned in the previous chapters how to create scientific experiments in our databases. When we don't have time for experiments, we at least need to follow the *right* authority and the *right* traditions. This chapter provides tips for how to find good resources online and how to find good resources locally. With enough time and practice, someday you will become one of those good resources for your community.

Places to Go

Finding relevant, accurate information about Oracle is not as simple as googling it. The top results frequently have problems, especially if those results are forums or static websites. The best resources are sites like Stack Overflow, the official documentation, and My Oracle Support.

The Problems with Forums

Forums are not optimal for narrow technical questions. They focus on the person asking the question, instead of the much larger number of people who will read the answers years later. That misguided focus creates constant arguments and long meandering conversations that draw attention away from the simple solutions that we care about. Forums focus on a single point in time, but technology changes, and a good answer today may be a bad answer tomorrow. Forums that lock posts, or complain when people reply to old posts, prevent users from curating information.

Sites like Stack Overflow have mostly replaced forums. The key to Stack Overflow is that it doesn't focus on a conversation between two people. The site focuses on a question and an answer, and it ignores personalities and meta discussions. Stack Overflow is a combination of a Wiki, a blog, a forum, and an aggregation site like Reddit. Those technologies make the site difficult for new users to ask questions, but they make the questions and answers smaller, more up to date, and more readable. The real audience for a tech website is the readers, not the people asking and answering questions. We should spend our time on websites that have the best information, not necessarily the sites that are friendliest to new users.

On the other hand, few problems have a simple, objective answer. Large questions with subjective answers are a better fit for the conversational tone of forums. We can't always simply copy and paste code from Stack Overflow, and participating in question

-and-answer sites can feel unfair and dehumanizing. We should occasionally take the time to read in-depth discussions of difficult technical topics.

The Problems with Static Websites

We should be skeptical of static websites that don't allow any reader feedback. I don't expect every blogger to engage in debates and answer every question, but every technical resource should have a way to add comments. We at least need the ability to warn each other with comments such as "This feature is deprecated in version X."

Oracle is an old program, and many of the first websites about Oracle are correspondingly old. Since those websites were built first, they have the most links and are at the top of search results, regardless of their quality.

We also need to watch out for websites that post unusual information to get traffic. It's not as bad as regular clickbait; I have not yet seen an article titled "You won't believe these 8 shocking tips for indexing your database!" But some of the most popular Oracle-related websites post wild and unsubstantiated performance claims.

There are plenty of times when changing one irrelevant detail makes our program run faster. Seemingly magical performance gains happen frequently because of issues described in Chapter 3, such as caching and execution plan changes. For example, COUNT(1) is not faster than COUNT(*), but as a side effect of rewriting a query, it may initially seem faster.

When someone posts irrational performance tips, we need the ability to point out the likely root cause and to demand a fully reproducible test case. But if there's no way to challenge that information, the mistakes may never get corrected.

It's also important that technical websites include metadata such as publication date and the Oracle version. A lot of technical advice expires with each new version. For example, many PL/SQL websites still discuss cursor processing with the OPEN/FETCH/CLOSE syntax. But that feature has been almost entirely superseded by cursor FOR loops.

Do not blindly trust nonofficial sources that don't allow comments. Those sources are still useful, but we need to remain skeptical about them.

Read the Manual

The official Oracle documentation is almost always our best source of information about the Oracle database. The documentation is so thorough that it can be intimidating at times. It's frustrating that there is a learning curve to even learn about Oracle. But after we understand how to navigate the documentation and read the syntax diagrams, the official documentation will be our primary source.

The Oracle documentation library starts at this link: `https://docs.oracle.com/en/database/oracle/oracle-database/index.html`. From there, we can access all the manuals and even download the entire 679-megabyte bookshelf.

Unfortunately, by the time this book is published, that link will probably be broken. The biggest problem with the Oracle documentation is that the links frequently change.

We want to reference the latest version, but the latest version is the one most likely to change and have broken links. For temporary messages like emails, it's fine to reference the latest version. For long-term messages, like a blog or Stack Overflow post, it's best to use the most recent long-term release. As of 2022, the Oracle 19c documentation is usually the best choice. While there is documentation available for 21c, that version is an "innovation release" that is not supported for long, won't be as popular as a long-term release, and is likely to have the links change again. This book won't often link to the manual, because we can easily find the relevant book by searching for the book title and the version. For example, we can search for "Oracle SQL Language Reference 21c."

For Oracle developers, these are the most useful books, listed in order of importance:

1. *SQL Language Reference* (2,271 pages): This is the most relevant book for SQL developers. Even though it's incredibly large, it's worth reading the entire thing eventually. I almost always have a browser tab open to this manual and will use the table of contents instead of a search engine.

2. *Database Concepts* (622 pages): This book explains how the database works. While the book is written for administrators, we should reference it whenever we're curious about the inner workings of Oracle. For example, if we want to know "What exactly is REDO?" or "What do blocks look like?", this book is a good place to start.

3. *PL/SQL Language Reference* (865 pages): It's worth reading this entire book if you do PL/SQL programming. Even if you only write SQL statements, it's useful to scan through this book, since SQL and PL/SQL are gradually merging into a single language. And there's a decent chance that if you're a SQL programmer today, you will become a PL/SQL programmer in the future.

4. *PL/SQL Packages and Types Reference* (4,894 pages): Nobody
    needs to read this entire, massive book. There are many
    archaic packages nobody will ever use. But there are also a few
    unexpected gems that will help you someday. And this book can
    be a good way to learn practical applications of Oracle features
    that are implemented through a PL/SQL API. It's worth at least
    reading the description of every package.

5. *Database Reference* (2,664 pages): When we need information
    about a parameter, data dictionary view, or dynamic performance
    view, this is the place to look.

6. *SQL*Plus® User's Guide and Reference* (392 pages): Even if you're
    not doing much with SQL*Plus, you might want to at least look
    through the command reference list. There is a separate book for
    SQLcl, but the common, popular features are best described in the
    SQL*Plus documentation.

7. *Database New Features Guide* (50 pages): Scan through this guide
    to see what features you're not taking advantage of or to justify
    upgrading.

8. *SQL Tuning Guide* (878 pages): Read this entire book if you do a
    lot of performance tuning. If you only have time for one chapter,
    read "Optimizer Statistics Concepts," because optimizer statistics
    are the key to many performance issues.

9. *Data Warehousing Guide* (732 pages): This book is not just for data
    warehouses. Features like materialized views and the advanced
    querying techniques can be used in many contexts.

10. *VLDB and Partitioning Guide* (425 pages): Read this book if you
    plan to use partitioning or parallelism. This book is not just for
    "very large" databases – it can also help with medium-sized
    databases.

11. *Database Performance Tuning Guide* (396 pages): This book is for
tuning the entire database, as opposed to tuning individual SQL
statements. In practice, tuning the SQL statements will also fix
most database performance issues, so this book is less important
than the *SQL Tuning Guide*.

The preceding list of books contains 14,189 pages of dense technical documentation.
Reading it all would be ridiculous, but it's important to at least be familiar with the first
four books in the list. The answers to most of our programming questions about SQL
syntax, concepts, and functions are in the documentation.

We should also occasionally scan through the list of books. There may be a specific
book we'll need to read, depending on the technologies we're using. For example, if
we're storing and processing a lot of JSON or XML data, there are several guides just for
those data types.

The Manual Is Not Perfect

The official documentation is not perfect, but it's the most accurate and thorough
source available. The syntax diagrams are particularly helpful. The diagrams can
be intimidating at first, but once we get used to them, they are the perfect way to
understand the syntax options.

For example, the numeric literal format has a lot of options. It's hard to explain those
options with words, but luckily the *SQL Language Reference* uses the picture shown in
Figure 4-1.

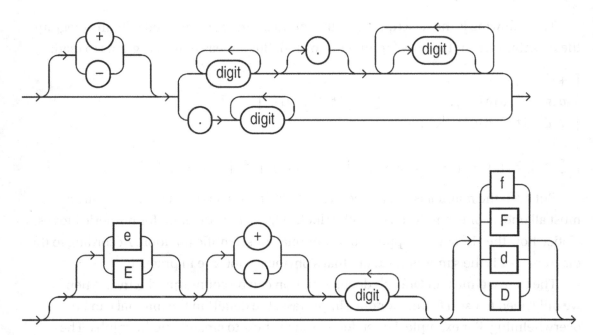

Figure 4-1. *The syntax for numeric literals. From the SQL Language Reference, copyright by Oracle Corporation*

The preceding diagram contains a surprising number of features that most developers aren't aware of. For example, the following are all valid Oracle literals:

```
select
    -.5,
    1.0e+10,
    5e-2,
    2f,
    3.5D
from dual;
```

The diagrams are a great visual representation of the SQL language syntax. In addition, underneath each image in the manual, there is a link to a text description. Those text descriptions are also useful for understanding Oracle SQL. The descriptions are similar to Backus–Naur form, which is a way to formally define a programming language. If necessary, we could even use the syntax descriptions as a starting point for recreating a full language specification. A thorough language description can help for certain programming tasks, such as building a parser.

The following is the description for the number syntax. Compared with the diagram, the description is not as easy for humans to read. But it is easier for programs to read:

```
[ + | - ]
{ digit [ digit ]... [ . ] [ digit [ digit ]... ]
| . digit [ digit ]...
}
[ [ e | E ] [ + | - ] digit [ digit ]... ] [ f | F | d | D ]
```

But even the manual is not perfect. The Oracle manual is not a holy text that we must all obey. For example, take another look at the syntax diagram for numeric literals. Notice how the "E" and "e" appear to be optional for scientific notation. According to the diagram, 1-1 is the same as 1e-1, but that's obviously not true in practice.

The thoroughness of Oracle's documentation can be counterproductive. When we only need to use a feature for one simple task, the details in the manual can be overwhelming. For example, I often forget exactly how to create scheduler jobs. The "DBMS_SCHEDULER" chapter of the *PL/SQL Packages and Types Reference* contains every possible detail about job scheduling. But I'm not going to read 131 pages of documentation every time I want to do something simple. For how-to guides that are practical instead of encyclopedic, I usually prefer Tim Hall's website oracle-base.com. As you become more familiar with Oracle, you'll build your own list of trustworthy websites, instead of randomly clicking the top search result.

My Oracle Support

My Oracle Support, previously known as Metalink, is an excellent resource that every Oracle developer should have access to. The website is `https://support.oracle.com`. The site is behind a paywall, but we shouldn't let that barrier stop us.

My Oracle Support is full of information that is not available on public search engines, especially information about patches and bugs. Accounts on that website must be associated with a valid support identifier. If we ask around the office, we can find someone who knows our organization's support identifier, and we can use that identifier to request access. Alternatively, we can buy Oracle Personal Edition for a few hundred bucks; as part of the support contract, we will get our own support identifier and the ability to create service requests.

One of the most important features of My Oracle Support is the "ORA-600/ORA-7445/ORA-700 Error Look-up Tool." On the My Oracle Support website, search for "ORA600 tool" to find that special page. On that page we can enter the first argument of a cryptic ORA-600 or ORA-7445 error, and the tool will usually take us to a relevant article. Most ORA-600 error codes cannot be found on search engines.

Documents on My Oracle Support frequently include descriptions of the problem, lists of possibly related bugs, patches, and workarounds. While those documents are usually accurate, the version numbers tend to be optimistic. Don't be surprised if the website says, "Fixed in version X," but the problem happens again in version X+1.

Creating service requests is notoriously challenging, and I have not yet found some magic trick to get good help. Following the advice in Chapter 3 about creating a minimal, verifiable, and complete example can occasionally help. But sometimes, no matter how good our test case, Oracle Support will ask us to upload tons of irrelevant information until we give up. My advice is that you don't bother creating a service request unless you absolutely need one.

People to See

The people we work with are the best resource for our Oracle SQL questions. Coworkers who originally architected the system will know the context for our questions and can help us avoid XY problems. More importantly, phone calls and face-to-face conversations are better than communicating through emails, instant messages, and posts. No matter how much we invest in digital collaboration tools, two people in a room with a white board is still the best way to communicate.

But first we need to know who to contact about database questions. Before we start bugging our coworkers, it might help to understand a few things about DBAs and developers and what they can help us with.

Not all developers can help us with SQL, even if they frequently work with a database. Application developers may use an object-relational mapping tool like Hibernate to handle database access. Business intelligence developers, data analysts, and ETL programmers may use a proprietary language or a graphical query builder. There are many ways to use Oracle, so don't be surprised if you meet people who program for Oracle databases but don't know SQL.

Database administrators are usually the top Oracle experts wherever Oracle is used. Unlike other software companies, Oracle Corporation focuses on administrators more than developers. Also, developers tend to spend a huge portion of their time on business logic, whereas administrators may spend almost all their time on purely technical problems. For technical problems, an administrator with 5 years of experience may be equivalent to a developer with 10 years of experience. Yet there are many rockstar DBAs with no SQL skills.

Many organizations only have operations DBAs, who work on problems like backup, recovery, installation, account maintenance, and resolving alerts. Those topics are complicated but may not require much SQL knowledge. All the development, architecture, data analysis, and tuning may be done by the developers.

But don't give up on asking DBAs for help just because a few of them don't know SQL. Oracle is a huge system, and there are many ways to divide database work. Many organizations may have application DBAs or DevOps engineers. Those administrators may write code and understand our applications, and they may be the SQL gurus we're looking for.

Aside from help with our queries, we have lots of other questions. The most important thing is to create direct lines of communication. Your company may have people with job titles like "requirements analyst" or "project manager." But we can't always depend on those people. We should always be willing to directly contact a client, tester, developer, administrator, vendor, or even some random person on the Internet. There may be a few times when someone will get upset that you went around them, but we can't let anyone stop us from getting the information we need. It's easier to ask forgiveness than to ask permission.

Summary

We must be willing to invest our time to find good resources, both online and in person. Now that we've discussed how to learn, the next chapter will focus on what to learn – the entire stack of technologies used to write SQL.

CHAPTER 5

Master the Entire Stack

Oracle SQL development requires more than just knowledge about Oracle SQL. While this book focuses on the Oracle SQL part, this chapter looks at the entire technology stack we use to write SQL. This is not a generic technology how-to book, so we will look at our technology stack through the eyes of a SQL developer. We need to invest in all our tools and processes, from low-level hardware to high-level project management.

Right now, you may only use Oracle SQL for a small part of your job. As your SQL skills grow and you find yourself doing more work in the database, it pays to invest more in the tools that support your SQL code. Even if you're not going to be a full-time SQL or PL/SQL developer, much of the advice in this chapter applies to any programming environment.

Not Just Faster

Our jobs are full of hierarchies, levels, abstractions, and technology stacks. For example, there are the seven layers of the OSI model for networking systems. Another example of a technology stack is the Linux, Apache, MySQL, and PHP in LAMP. Even when writing an email, we start with letters and build our way up to words, phrases, sentences, paragraphs, and finally the entire message.

SQL is a high-level programming language, but it's worth revisiting the lower levels of our technology stack. If you're reading this book, you already know how to use those technologies. But it's important that we're not merely scraping by on foundational skills.

We want to learn the fundamental technologies well enough that we don't have to think about them. When we write a SQL statement, we want to think of one and only one thing: that SQL statement. We need to master other technologies to free ourselves from them. For example, we don't need to learn everything about our operating system, but we need to know enough so that the operating system doesn't slow us down. We need to make an investment: master these technologies now, so we don't have to continually think about them for the rest of our career.

© Jon Heller 2023
J. Heller, *Pro Oracle SQL Development*, https://doi.org/10.1007/978-1-4842-8867-2_5

There are many ways to define a technology stack for SQL development. This chapter is organized according to the following list, which starts with the lowest level and ends with the highest level:

1. *Computer science and math*: The relational model was discussed in Chapter 1. Other computer science and math topics will appear throughout the book.

2. *Hardware*: Although choosing the right hardware is obviously important, this topic is too broad and is not covered by a specific section of this chapter.

3. *Basic input/output system*: The importance of touch typing is discussed in the second section of this chapter.

4. *Operating system and supporting programs*: Operating system commands and helpful programs are discussed in the third section.

5. *SQL and PL/SQL*: This entire book covers SQL, and the "Introduction" discussed why we should learn it. The fourth section discusses why we may want to master SQL and learn related technologies like PL/SQL.

6. *SQL*Plus*: The fifth section discusses the importance of using just the right amount of SQL*Plus.

7. *Integrated development environment (IDE)*: The sixth section discusses the tools we use for developing and querying Oracle.

8. *Worksheets, notebooks, snippets, scripts, and Gists*: The last section discusses how to organize our queries.

9. *Project management and architecture*: There's no specific section on these topics, but this book occasionally discusses related issues.

Typing

Typing is the most underrated skill in programming. Typing isn't exactly the most exciting part of our jobs, but we can benefit from mastering it.

The precise typing speed doesn't matter. One hundred twenty words per minute is not really twice as fast as 60 words per minute, because we don't often type at full speed. But 60 words per minute is more than twice as fast as 30 words per minute, because at that speed we're touch typing instead of looking at the keyboard. We must be able to type as fast as we can think. Then we can concentrate on what matters and not constantly lose our train of thought. If we can type properly, we won't be tempted to take shortcuts, like using one-letter variable names or avoiding comments. If we spend most of our workday on a keyboard, then we really ought to master it.

Learning how to properly type isn't difficult anyway. If we already have some typing skills, it's trivial to find typing tutorials online to help us improve. We don't need to learn the optimized Dvorak keyboard layout (although that layout may help people with repetitive strain injuries.) And we don't need to enter typing competitions. Just a few minutes a day and we can quickly fill in any gaps in a fundamental skill.

Learning relevant keyboard shortcuts also helps us work faster and spend more time thinking about things that matter. At the operating system level, we should be able to cut, copy, paste, switch between windows, open menus, switch tabs, and move between words, lines, and pages, without looking at our keyboard. And it's worth learning or configuring keyboard shortcuts for popular programs, like our IDE.

With a highly optimized environment, we can write and run simple queries in seconds instead of minutes. That time difference doesn't just make us work faster; it makes us work differently. Like the way we subconsciously avoid websites that take too long to load, we also avoid writing queries if the process is slow. Speed matters when we're in a data analysis mode, and we need dozens or hundreds of queries to thoroughly investigate an issue.

If you want to challenge yourself to learn the keyboard better, hide the mouse for a day. For most programming tasks, using the mouse only slows us down. Browsing the Web will be painful, but working without a mouse will make us better at most of our programs.

Operating Systems and Supporting Programs

Advanced SQL development requires knowledge of many other programs. We have to run our SQL on different systems and in different contexts. We need programs to help us interpret, manage, and share the results. This section lists many programs and skills we should be familiar with.

Operating Systems

When developing SQL, we may have two operating systems to deal with – the client that creates the SQL and the server that runs the SQL. Even if there's a GUI for every operating system task, it's worth understanding the command line. The command line is more powerful and faster, after the learning curve. If you're not familiar with your server or client operating systems, try to learn one new command a day. We don't necessarily need to write shell scripts, but we can at least benefit from being able to navigate the file system and move things around.

Text Editors

Text editors are important, even if we do most of our work in an IDE. SQL development involves lots of data, and much of that data starts as text. Every programmer needs to use a text editor more powerful than Notepad. There are plenty of free options for all platforms, like Notepad++, Notepad2, vi, etc. If we have corporate IT policies preventing us from installing programs, we can download an executable-only version. Most graphical text editors are easy to figure out – we just have to spend a few minutes exploring toolbars and menus. Unix editors, like vi, can be more challenging. Luckily there are online video game tutorials that teach vi, such as `https://vim-adventures.com`.

Any decent text editor supports regular expressions. Regular expressions are invaluable to data processing, and we should use them often. For example, a common SQL problem is converting lists of values into SQL data. Instead of manually modifying the data, regular expressions can make the data conversion much faster.

Imagine a large text file with comma-separated data. We want to turn the following file of data into a table of data:

```
a,1
b,2
c,3
```

Our goal is to convert the preceding text into the following SQL statement:

```
select 'a',1 from dual union all
select 'b',2 from dual union all
select 'c',3 from dual;
```

With regular expressions we can convert the data in only four small steps. Open the editor's find and replace dialog, usually with Ctrl+F. Enable regular expression mode, usually by clicking a check box. Then make four replacements:

1. Replace "^" with "`select '`".

2. Replace "," with "`','`".

3. Replace "$" with "` from dual union all`".

4. Manually remove the last "` union all`".

Regular expressions are cryptic and confusing at first. But they are powerful tools for finding and changing data. They can also be used in Oracle SQL through the `REGEXP_` functions. Chapter 7 briefly discusses those functions and the regular expression syntax.

Comparison Tools

Comparison is a core part of SQL development. If we stick to the relational model, most of our comparisons can be done with SQL joins and predicates. But inevitably we must compare semi-structured data, like text files or source code. We need a way to quickly compare large amounts of text and drill down to the precise byte differences. There are many free and open source programs to compare data, such as WinMerge. Most version control clients can also compare files.

For example, text comparison programs can help with comparing long CREATE TABLE statements. Let's use the simple example from Chapter 2, where we saw how weird the output from DBMS_METADATA.GET_DDL can be. The following commands are identical, except that the table TEST2 is created with the option PCTFREE 0. The difference is easy to spot when we're creating the tables:

```
create table test1 as select 1 a from dual;
create table test2 pctfree 0 as select 1 a from dual;
select dbms_metadata.get_ddl('TABLE', 'TEST1') from dual;
select dbms_metadata.get_ddl('TABLE', 'TEST2') from dual;
```

But when we compare the output, there's so much worthless information it's hard to find any meaningful differences. (As discussed in Chapter 2, this abundance of metadata is why we want to save the handmade SQL statements, not the system-generated ones.) The differences between the two tables become obvious in a comparison tool, and we can tell exactly which characters are different in Figure 5-1.

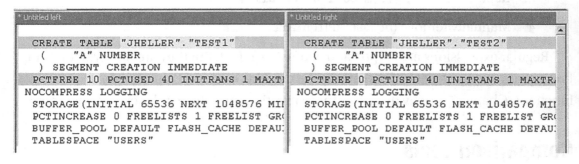

Figure 5-1. *Using WinMerge to compare* DBMS_METADATA.GET_DDL *output for two similar tables*

Reporting Tools and Excel

IDEs are great at retrieving results from SQL queries, but those initial results don't always look pretty. Spreadsheets and reporting tools can help us present the results in a better format. Reporting software and business intelligence are large topics and outside the scope of this book. But for many purposes, Microsoft Excel is good enough to enhance our results.

Most IDEs let us export data to Excel with just a few clicks. In Excel, we should learn how to do simple operations like sort, filter, remove duplicates, create a header row, create simple formulas like =SUM(A1:A100), and create simple charts. We can learn the basics of any spreadsheet program in just a few hours. The presentation of our data matters more than we think. Before sharing data with nontechnical people, we should at least put the results in Excel.

We need many more programs for our daily work, like browsers, email clients, terminal emulators, version control, etc. There's no need to discuss those programs here, since there's nothing SQL-specific about them. But the theme of this chapter applies to those programs as well: invest time to learn about our tools.

SQL and PL/SQL

If you're reading this book, you're already dedicated to learning SQL. But it's worth briefly discussing why it is beneficial to spend so much time to *master* a single language. We need to justify this investment to ourselves, our coworkers, and our employers.

Developers frequently claim that it's easy to learn a new programming language. But learning a programming language is only easy in three cases: the rare genius who can learn anything quickly, a language without much depth, or a developer who doesn't mind writing average code.

People undervalue expertise. Sometimes we forget how painful it is to master a skill. Think about all the words in this sentence – when and where did we learn them? We can't remember, but our parents and teachers can tell us stories about our years of struggle to master a language. Sometimes we don't value expertise because of the Dunning–Kruger effect; we overestimate our skills because we don't even know enough to accurately judge our knowledge.

Becoming an expert can take a long time. Ten years is a common estimate, but it's impossible to find an exact number. It takes a long time to get good enough at something to be able to do it without thinking about it. It takes a long time, and intentional practice, to know by intuition when our code isn't right. Those 10 years of experience can't be 1 year of experience repeated ten times. We need to work hard, continually improve, and put ourselves in situations where we are not the smartest person in the room.

SQL's English-like syntax makes the language easy for beginners to store, update, and retrieve data. But it's Oracle SQL's extra features that let us optimally process and manage that data. The entire Oracle database ecosystem includes not only SQL but the procedural extension PL/SQL, pseudo-scripting languages like SQL*Plus, hundreds of packages and utilities, converged database features like support for XML and JSON, and even low-code website building tools like APEX.

The extra keywords, functionality, and concepts are why we must spend more time to master Oracle SQL than a traditional programming language. The extra work, and extra knowledge, can justify our time and money spent on things like training and going to conferences.

Is it worth the time and money to become an expert? In many cases, the answer is no. Most of our projects don't significantly benefit from being great instead of merely good. Career-wise, the jack-of-all-trades developers usually do better than the specialists, especially with the industry shift toward DevOps. For me, it's a personal choice to be an expert in one language instead of being OK in two languages. I'm sick of all the mediocre software in the world. If we want to create amazing programs, we must spend the time to become experts.

SQL*Plus

SQL*Plus is a great tool but only in specific contexts. SQL*Plus is the simplest way to use the database. That simplicity is an advantage for scripting, demos, troubleshooting, and when we can't use a graphical tool. But SQL*Plus will stunt our growth as developers if we use it for development, debugging, and ad hoc querying.

When We Should Use SQL*Plus

SQL*Plus is great for scripting installations, as described in Chapter 2. And it's great for building reproducible test cases, as described in Chapter 3. The simple, text-only format leaves nothing hidden and makes the program helpful for troubleshooting. There are times when we don't have a desktop environment available, and SQL*Plus is our only choice. For some administrative tasks, we only have a terminal available. Even when we have a remote desktop, sometimes the connections are too slow to use graphical programs, and we're stuck with the command line. We're going to have to use SQL*Plus sometimes, so we might as well get used to it.

When we use SQL*Plus, we must use the real thing. Many IDEs have a built-in SQL*Plus clone that we should avoid. Those clones are always missing important features, and sometimes they're missing important bugs. The main benefit of SQL*Plus is the portability and compatibility across different platforms and versions. If something works in your SQL*Plus, but fails in mine, one of us isn't using the real thing. I've seen many deployments fail because a developer used a SQL*Plus clone that didn't have the 2,499-character-per-line limit. The code worked on their machine, but it failed on production when a real SQL*Plus was used. Those limits are annoying, but we need to be aware of limits as early in the development cycle as possible.

When We Should Not Use SQL*Plus

SQL*Plus is no longer adequate for our day-to-day development work. There are many mature IDEs that can significantly improve our productivity. Text is better than pictures for programming languages, but with a graphical IDE, we can have multiple windows of code and metadata, improved visualization of code, and quick access to hundreds of powerful options.

For writing queries, we need to be able to quickly run and view the results of different parts of a query. SQL*Plus makes it hard to run inline views or subqueries – we can't simply highlight code and press the run shortcut. And the command line formatting of SQL*Plus makes it almost impossible to meaningfully view the results of complex or ad hoc queries. If we already know the columns and only select the columns we want and set formatting options ahead of time, we can view a small set of columns fine in SQL*Plus. But that's an extremely limited way of using a database. We should be able to effortlessly view *all* the data in our tables.

It's ridiculous to believe we can remember what all the values in our databases look like and be able to select the relevant columns each time we query a table. When we use SQL*Plus for ad hoc queries, we're limiting ourselves to only the few things we remember well. We'll never improve if we limit ourselves to what we already know.

For example, during performance troubleshooting, it's common to look at the view V$SQL. We rarely know what the problem is ahead of time; we're just looking for something weird, so we need to look at everything. When we run the following query in SQL*Plus, the output is a worthless mess. I'm not even going to show the output – my conscience won't let me kill a tree to print gibberish:

```
SQL> select * from v$sql;
```

When we run the preceding query in a graphical user interface, like Oracle SQL Developer, the results are infinitely more usable. The results in Figure 5-2 are not exactly pretty, but we can scroll back and forth and more easily explore and understand the data.

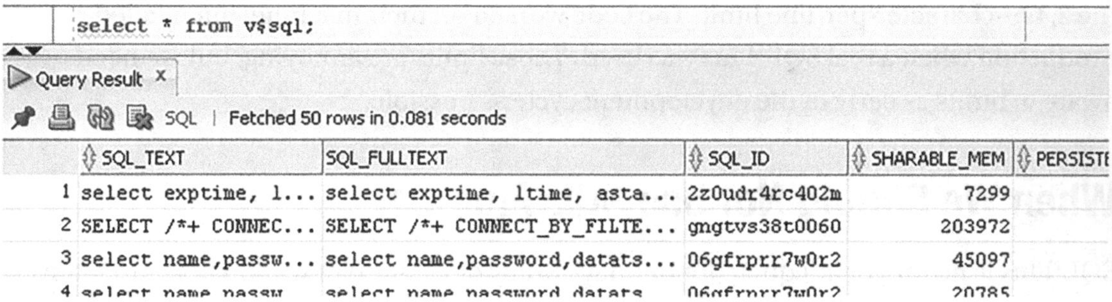

Figure 5-2. *A simple data dictionary query in Oracle SQL Developer*

We live in an information age, and we need tools that can display large amounts of information. Many database professionals never reach their full potential because they refuse to use modern tools. Those old-fashioned developers also slow down the rest of us when we have to dumb down our programs to support 72 characters per line.

Using an IDE is one of the few areas where we need to convince our coworkers to change their habits. We don't want to start pointless flame wars about Oracle SQL Developer vs. Toad. But when we see someone stuck in the twentieth century, doing everything on the command line, it's worth trying to gently convince them to upgrade their tools.

The command line program SQLcl is designed to replace SQL*Plus, but that day is probably years away. That program has some interesting new features, but it also has bugs and Java installation issues, and it is not as ubiquitously available as SQL*Plus. We should stick with SQL*Plus to make our code more accessible.

Integrated Development Environment

Our IDE is vital to writing advanced SQL queries, and we should invest a significant amount of time learning these tools. Different IDEs have a wide variety of features, and this book does not assume you are using one specific program. This chapter discusses the core features available in all the major IDEs, as well as a brief comparison between the top three Oracle SQL IDEs.

Learn an IDE

The best way to learn an IDE is to watch an expert use it. When we watch someone use their IDE, there will be moments when we're following along and then suddenly they'll leap ahead of us. When we lose track, ask the other developer to explain their magic trick. Most developers are happy to share their IDE secrets with someone else, but only if we ask. There are many personal preferences in IDEs, and developers are nervous about explaining their favorite program to others, because they want to avoid disagreements. We should signal to those experts that we're willing to learn all the tips and tricks we can, even if it does get us into the occasional argument about tabs vs. spaces.

The most important thing to know about our IDEs is that there is always a way to change anything we want. Don't like the default fonts and colors? Change them. Find it tedious to accomplish a repetitive task? Create a keyboard shortcut or a macro to automate it. Wish the tabs were ordered differently? Reorder them. Don't like the cut of its jib? Look online and find a plug-in to alter the jib. We should never have to settle for anything with our IDE.

This book is IDE agnostic and will not go into details about how to learn each IDE. But we should learn how to do at least the following things in our IDE: run the SQL at the cursor (learn the shortcut for running commands without having to highlight anything), view database objects in different schemas, open and change file system objects, create new database objects, view the DDL behind an object in the editor (usually by clicking the text), change syntax and formatting rules (such as changing tabs to spaces), change the NLS properties (such as the date format), debugging (how to quickly set breakpoints, step in, step out, etc.), run saved scripts or snippets, code navigation (such as right-clicking objects inside a package to go to different sections), refactor variable names, and much more. If any of those features are new to you, spend some time in your IDE to learn them. By learning how to run those tasks quickly, we can run more SQL statements, shorten our feedback loop, and improve our code faster.

If you've never looked through your IDE's options before, stop right now and spend 10 minutes. Open the properties or settings menu, right-click in different windows, and look through the pop-up menus. Looking through the menus is faster than reading the manual, and I guarantee you'll find at least one useful setting you'll want to change.

When Not to Use an IDE Feature

We don't want to use all the features of our IDE. Some developers use an IDE as a crutch to create code and can only program with point-and-click wizards. Just because those wizards exist doesn't mean we have to use them. For advanced developers, the IDE is like a text editor on steroids. For example, we don't want to use a "New Table" wizard in our IDE to create a table. We can still create tables with text, and our IDE will help us with things like syntax highlighting, auto complete, and much more.

IDEs often contain features that may look useful or pretty but can be dangerous. As previously discussed, we should avoid our IDE's imitation version of SQL*Plus. We should also avoid features that let a single instance of the program connect to multiple databases at the same time. One window should only be used for one connection, with the connection alias prominently displayed at the top of the window. Developers who use multiple tabs, each connected to a different database, inevitably run commands on the wrong database. We must configure our IDEs so that it is always blindingly obvious which database we are connected to.

Oracle IDE Comparison

We can't always choose our IDE. Our company may have already purchased one, or our projects may require a specific tool. If we're lucky, we'll have a say in which program we use. And if we're doing hobby programming at home, then we'll definitely need to decide for ourselves. Use Table 5-1 to help decide which program to use.

Table 5-1. *Simple Comparison Between the Most Popular Oracle IDEs*

	Oracle SQL Developer	**PL/SQL Developer**	**Toad**
Cost	Free	Cheap	Expensive
Features	Better	Good	Best
Quality	Good	Best	Better

It's impossible to say that one IDE is always better than another. The best tool depends on personal preference, where the tool will be used, the budget, etc.

Oracle SQL Developer is free and is installed by default with all Oracle clients. If Oracle SQL Developer is missing, it's trivial to install it – just download and run a file, no admin privileges required. Because of cost and ease of installation, Oracle SQL

Developer is the most common choice. There will be times when Oracle SQL Developer is the only choice, so it's worth becoming at least familiar with it. But it's the stereotypical slow Java program, and many of the features don't feel polished.

Quest's Toad has the most features and is part of a large ecosystem of tools sold by Quest. If we have a large and complex work environment, full of data analysts, testers, DBAs, and developers, then we should look at Toad. The biggest downside is the massive cost.

Allround Automations's PL/SQL Developer is my personal favorite. It's cheap, fast, and high-quality. PL/SQL Developer doesn't have as many features as the other programs, but what it does, it does better. PL/SQL Developer is not free like Oracle SQL Developer, but an unlimited site license is cheaper than a single Toad license.

Comparing IDEs is difficult and involves a lot of personal preferences. Many people will strongly disagree with my analysis. As long as we all have an IDE and know how to use it, we'll be fine.

Worksheets, Notebooks, Snippets, Scripts, and Gists

Our whirlwind tour of the Oracle SQL development stack has gone from low-level theories to high-level IDEs. Most developers would stop at this point. But there's one final, important piece that most SQL developers forget – we need to organize our SQL statements. We need to store the files in a convenient, backed-up, unforgettable location. And we need to write our ad hoc SQL statements in worksheets and notebooks, not old-fashioned scripts.

Get Organized

Most of our SQL will eventually be stored in a program. Organizing SQL inside programs is important, but internal code structure is not what we're discussing here. This section is about the ad hoc SQL statements and worksheets that we use to support our day-to-day work. As we learn more about SQL, we will build a large library of helpful statements and worksheets. Our library will come in handy thousands of times, and we may be able to carry that knowledge with us for many years.

The first step toward building a library of statements is to create a memorable location to store this information. Sadly, very few SQL developers do this critical step, and it's painful to watch them struggle to remember where they put a statement they built yesterday. The details of our filing system are not important, but we *must* use something.

For me, building a SQL library is as simple as three separate folders – one folder for worksheets (ad hoc SQL statements that I may need in the future), one folder for version-controlled repositories, and another folder for temporary files that I'll only need in the near future. In Windows 10, we can easily add folders to the "Quick access" list, and those folders will always appear in every open or save dialog. Figure 5-3 shows an example of a simple structure.

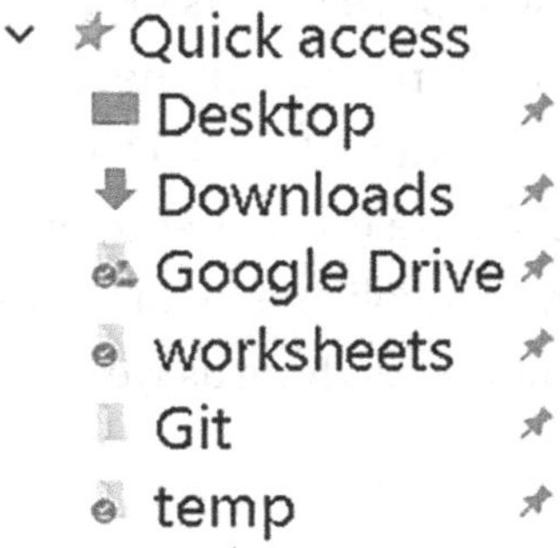

Figure 5-3. *Example of a Windows Explorer Quick access list*

Worksheets

Now that we know where to store the files, how exactly do we store our SQL statements in them? Script management is another area where Oracle's history does more harm than good. Forty years ago, it was pretty cool to be able to save a single command in a single file and then run that file. Many DBAs have a large directory of SQL*Plus scripts they frequently reference for common problems. Those scripts contain one SQL statement, perhaps with arguments passed to the file, and a small number of outputs.

But those single-purpose scripts have all the problems discussed in the "SQL*Plus" section of this chapter. It's hard to predict the relevant columns ahead of time, and it's hard to get those scripts to flow together.

The best way to store ad hoc SQL statements is in a notebook or worksheet. A worksheet is a simple concept – store multiple, related SQL statements in a single file. Put the statements in a meaningful order, add comments, load the worksheet into an IDE, run the statements one at a time, and view the results. The results from one statement may be the input into another statement later in the worksheet.

The idea of worksheets and notebooks has really taken off in data science and math programming environments. There are a growing number of programs that let us combine code, documentation, and visualizations. Figure 5-4 shows an example of an IPython Notebook. (You don't need to understand the math.)

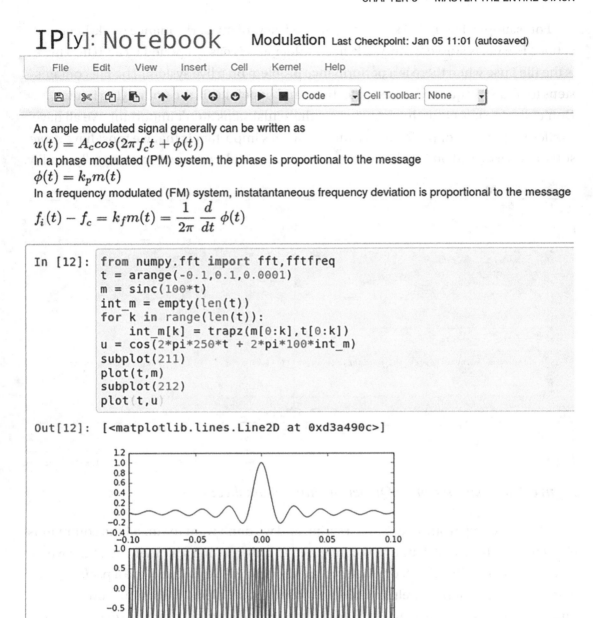

An angle modulated signal generally can be written as

$$u(t) = A_c cos(2\pi f_c t + \phi(t))$$

In a phase modulated (PM) system, the phase is proportional to the message

$$\phi(t) = k_p m(t)$$

In a frequency modulated (FM) system, instatantaneous frequency deviation is proportional to the message

$$f_i(t) - f_c = k_f m(t) = \frac{1}{2\pi} \frac{d}{dt} \phi(t)$$

```
In [12]:  from numpy.fft import fft,fftfreq
          t = arange(-0.1,0.1,0.0001)
          m = sinc(100*t)
          int_m = empty(len(t))
          for k in range(len(t)):
              int_m[k] = trapz(m[0:k],t[0:k])
          u = cos(2*pi*250*t + 2*pi*100*int_m)
          subplot(211)
          plot(t,m)
          subplot(212)
          plot(t,u)
```

```
Out[12]:  [<matplotlib.lines.Line2D at 0xd3a490c>]
```

Figure 5-4. *"IPython Notebook interface" by Shishirdasika is licensed under CC BY-SA 3.0.*

The most popular Oracle SQL IDEs don't look quite as nice as the picture in Figure 54. But most of the value of a worksheet is being able to run multiple statements in one file. It doesn't matter much if the worksheet is not perfectly formatted.

For example, Figure 5-5 shows a simplified view of my performance worksheet in action. The file is stored in my worksheets folder and is easily opened by an IDE. This is the file I use when there is a performance problem on a live system. The file contains steps to find slow queries, investigate them, and hopefully fix the underlying issue. Don't look too closely at the details, since the actual steps aren't important. We all have a different process for performance tuning. What's important is that we must have *some* sort of process. And our worksheets must be easy to find, run, and incrementally modify.

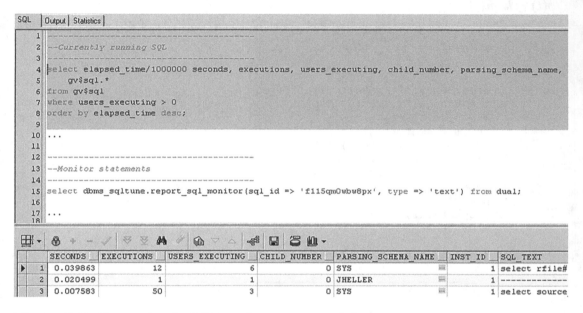

Figure 5-5. *Example of a SQL performance worksheet*

The preceding worksheet is not a script, and we don't want to run all the commands every time. (Make sure your IDE is configured to only run one statement at a time when you press F8, F9, Ctrl+Enter, or whatever the shortcut is.) Worksheets are a pseudo automated set of steps to help troubleshoot complex problems. Depending on the output of the first step, we may need to run the second step, or maybe we can skip to the third step. It's not a fully automated program; it's more like a mind map for performance problems.

Storing worksheets in a public repository like GitHub is a popular option. GitHub Gists may be a good choice, since they are geared toward storing a single file. Oracle's livesql.oracle.com has a good notebook-like interface. Unfortunately, LiveSQL only runs against a sample cloud database and cannot connect to our real databases.

Saving worksheets online is not always possible. Many companies won't let employees release code online without going through a long approval process. Releasing open source software is great, but our ad hoc worksheets aren't very reusable by other people anyway. In this case, flexibility is more important than openness. Storing worksheets locally is good enough.

Caution   Do not continue until you have created a convenient place to store your SQL worksheets.

Most IDEs allow us to save and run snippets. It's convenient to be able to right-click and instantly get a SQL statement. Snippets can be useful for tiny tasks, but they are still no replacement for powerful worksheets.

Summary

Before we dive into advanced Oracle SQL features, we need to build and learn a technology stack that will fully support us. These supporting technologies aren't always very exciting, but it's important to master the low-level stuff so we can focus on what matters. If we decide to invest more in learning SQL, then it is also worthwhile to invest in things like typing skills, operating systems and programs, SQL*Plus, IDEs, and SQL worksheets.

PART II

Write Powerful SQL with Sets and Advanced Features

CHAPTER 6

Build Sets with Inline Views and ANSI Join Syntax

We're almost ready to dive into advanced SQL features. In Part I we built a solid foundation for SQL programming, but before we start using advanced features, we need to discuss how to construct our SQL statements.

The best way to write SQL statements is to create nested sets using inline views and the ANSI join syntax. First, we need to discuss common SQL problems – spaghetti code caused by the old join syntax and too much context. Sets, chunking, and functional programming can help us create simpler queries. We will combine those three concepts and implement them with inline views. Inline views will be the small, independent building blocks for our SQL statements. The ANSI join syntax will help us take those inline views and construct large, but understandable, queries. Finally, we'll put those ideas together to build a large example and learn something from our space data set.

Spaghetti Code from Nonstandard Syntax

The old join syntax throws all the tables in a comma-separated list and joins the tables together later. That programming process leads to code that is hard to read, hard to debug, prone to accidental cross joins, and nonstandard. The old join syntax is still valid, and occasionally useful, but should be used sparingly.

As a quick refresher, the following code shows the old join syntax and the newer ANSI join syntax. (The examples use * for brevity, but most of our production queries should explicitly name the columns we need to use.)

© Jon Heller 2023
J. Heller, *Pro Oracle SQL Development*, https://doi.org/10.1007/978-1-4842-8867-2_6

```
--Old join syntax we should avoid.
select *
from launch, satellite
where launch.launch_id = satellite.launch_id(+);

--ANSI join syntax we should embrace.
select *
from launch
left join satellite
   on launch.launch_id = satellite.launch_id;
```

Hard-to-Read Old Syntax

The first problem with the old join syntax is that it separates the tables from their join conditions. The tables are thrown together in a comma-separated list and then tied together later. Separating tables from join conditions makes it harder to tell how the tables are connected. In theory, we can construct the list of tables in a meaningful order and then follow that same order when we write the join conditions. In practice, that orderly development process never happens, and we end up with a disorganized query that's hard to read.

When writing, we want to describe items in the order they are introduced. We should follow the same rule with our tables. We should list and join tables in the same order. The table order doesn't matter to the compiler – the compiler can rearrange tables however it wants. (In ancient versions of Oracle, or in extremely rare cases, the order of tables can affect performance. But those exceptional cases should not dictate the way we write our code today.) Although the compiler doesn't care about the order, *people* are the true audience. The old join syntax fails us because it promotes a bad style.

There are $N!$ ways to order any set of items. That means there is an impossibly large number of different ways to join a large list of tables. When we see a comma-separated list of tables, we have no idea what to expect for the rest of the query.

Throwing a bunch of tables onto a screen and then drawing lines between them is a poor way to think about joining tables. Our minds have a hard time processing everything at once. The old syntax misleads us into creating SQL statements like the nightmarish Figure 6-1. The Oracle programming world is full of ugly SQL statements, and they drag down the whole ecosystem. Those ugly SQL statements are why so many programmers hate Oracle SQL and why I'm spending so much time trying to convince you to change your SQL syntax.

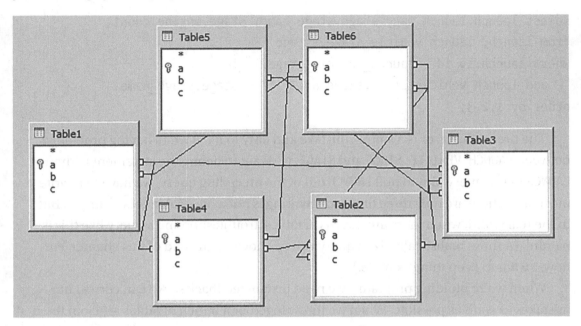

Figure 6-1. *The wrong way to think about SQL joins*

Hard-to-Debug Old Syntax

Debugging is difficult, and it's especially difficult with the old join syntax. When we debug large SQL statements, we want to test one small piece at a time. If we don't write our queries properly, there won't be an easy way to isolate and run small pieces.

This debugging problem doesn't show up in most SQL tutorials and books. Good examples omit needless code and are small. Most SQL examples only need one or two tables. When there are only two tables, the join syntax doesn't matter. Many SQL developers learn techniques and styles that work fine with small examples but do not scale to large queries.

When our queries grow to three tables or more, the problems become apparent. After you've read this book, you should be willing to create SQL statements with much more than three tables.

For example, let's say we want to find the number of engines used per rocket launch. Rockets can have multiple stages, and each stage can have a different number of engines. To find this information, we need to join LAUNCH, LAUNCH_VEHICLE_STAGE, and

STAGE. There's an intentional mistake in the following join, next to the exclamation mark. The query joins the stage *number*, when it should use the stage *name*:

```
select launch.launch_tag, stage.stage_name, stage.engine_count
from launch, launch_vehicle_stage, stage
where launch.lv_id = launch_vehicle_stage.lv_id
   and launch_vehicle_stage.stage_no /*!*/ = stage.stage_name
order by 1,2,3;
```

The preceding error is a simple mistake and easy to fix. If we're having problems between LAUNCH_VEHICLE_STAGE and STAGE, we want to debug the statement without LAUNCH in the query. But to pull LAUNCH out of the preceding query, we have to rewrite most of it. There are only three lines, so rewriting is not a big deal in this example. But in the real world, when there are dozens of tables, troubleshooting a query like this is painful. (A more realistically sized query will be shown at the end of this chapter. For now, I want to keep things simple.)

When we're building programs, we need instant feedback so we can correct our mistakes as soon as possible. When we throw together a bunch of tables and join them later, we're delaying the time until we find our mistakes. Then we may not notice the problem until there are dozens of tables and it's harder to guess where the problem is. To make debugging easier, we need to use a more modular and iterative process.

Accidental Cross Joins in Old Syntax

The old-fashioned join syntax frequently leads to unintended cross joins, also known as Cartesian products. These cross joins cause wrong results and horrible performance. Cross joins might run fine in development but fail horribly in production, when the data is larger.

Cross joins multiply the number of result rows by the number of rows in the unjoined table. A bad cross join can effectively stop the entire database from working. When Oracle generates a large number of rows, those rows must be stored on disk in a temporary tablespace. If that temporary tablespace is shared with another application, that application won't have any space left to sort or hash data. Then the application queries will either immediately raise an exception or go into a suspended state and wait for more space. When DBAs see suspended session errors, they often immediately add more space. But adding a 32-gigabyte file won't help when Oracle is trying to write an exabyte of junk data. Those extra temp files are why many databases end up with uselessly large temporary tablespaces.

The old join syntax makes unintentional cross joins much more likely to happen. When we write a large list of tables, it's easy to forget about one of them later. The query syntax is still valid, and the compiler won't complain. It's hard to catch these mistakes, especially with large queries. In the following example, if the relevant code wasn't bold, would we have noticed that the ENGINE table is not joined to anything?

```
select launch.launch_tag, stage.stage_name, stage.engine_count
from launch, launch_vehicle_stage, stage, engine
where launch.lv_id = launch_vehicle_stage.lv_id
  and launch_vehicle_stage.stage_no /*!*/ = stage.stage_name
order by 1,2,3;
```

There's no way to ban cross joins, since the syntax is sometimes necessary. And we can't catch all bad cross joins with testing, because cross joins can happen on production with ad hoc queries. Converting to the ANSI join syntax will almost completely eliminate accidental cross joins.[1]

In addition to under-joining data with accidental cross join, the old join syntax also makes it easier to over-join data. For example, if we left-join table A to table B, then we also want to left-join table B to table C. A common mistake is to use a left join between A and B and an inner join between B and C. That mistake effectively turns the outer join into an inner join. With the (+) operator, and disorganized join conditions, that mistake is easy to make in the old join syntax.

Nonstandard but Still Useful

The old join syntax was created before joins were fully standardized in SQL-92. In the early days, every database had to create its own join style. All relational databases can use the list-of-tables style for inner joins, but there are many ways to represent outer joins. In Oracle, the outer join is marked by adding the (+) operator to the side of the join that is optional.

To most advocates of the ANSI join syntax, following the standard is the biggest argument in its favor. And it's true that queries with the (+) operator will not work

---

[1] It's rare, but still possible to have an accidental cross join with ANSI joins. For example, a cross join can happen if we join a multicolumn foreign key but only use one column.

on other databases. But the lack of standardization and portability is not really that important. In practice, if we're taking advantage of useful Oracle features, our queries will not be portable anyway. Choosing the ANSI join syntax is mostly a style choice (although there are rare cases where the old syntax simply does not work, such as full outer joins).

However, there are times when the old join syntax is required. We still need to be familiar with the (+) operator and be able to translate between the two syntaxes. There are rare performance problems and syntax bugs that can be solved by switching to the old syntax. And bitmap join indexes and fast refresh materialized views require the old syntax. But those exceptions shouldn't dictate our style.

Too Much Context

The wrong SQL features create too much context and too many dependencies within our SQL statements. We want to create our SQL from small, independent blocks of code and connect those blocks as simply as possible. We should avoid features that increase the context, like correlated subqueries and common table expressions.

The Importance of Reducing Context

Context is king. We cannot understand code in isolation. We need to see the big picture and all the metadata. Code is more easily understood when we know who wrote the code, why they wrote the code, and the code before and after the block of code we're looking at. Context gives us a deeper understanding of whatever we're reading.

But programming context is different. In programming, context refers to the background state of our programs. That information can be helpful, but it's more likely to cause problems when unexpected side effects change things in the background. Code is not literature with multiple valid interpretations. Our code should be brutally plain with as little background information as possible. When programming, the context is more likely to play tricks on us than to help us.

When we have a problem with a SQL statement in a program, we want to copy that statement into our IDE and run it independently. Then we'll want to run small pieces of the query to look for the bug. But context gets in the way. The SQL statement might depend on our session's uncommitted data, bind variables based on local and global variables, objects, operating system files for external tables, etc.

Good programming practices, such as avoiding global variables, can reduce the context. It's inevitable that queries have at least some context, but we can still minimize it. We especially want to minimize the context within our queries. Intra-query dependencies must be kept to a minimum. In practice, reducing context means avoiding correlated subqueries and common table expressions.

Avoid Correlated Subqueries

Correlated subqueries are subqueries found in the SELECT and WHERE clauses that reference another part of the query. Correlated subqueries are not always evil, but they will ruin our queries if we consistently overuse use them as a replacement for joins. For example, let's rewrite the query for finding the number of engines used per launch. Instead of joining to the STAGE table directly, let's create a correlated subquery:

```
select launch.launch_tag, launch_vehicle_stage.stage_name,
   (
      select stage.engine_count
      from stage
      where stage.stage_name = launch_vehicle_stage.stage_name
   ) engine_count
from launch
join launch_vehicle_stage
   on launch.lv_id = launch_vehicle_stage.lv_id
order by 1,2;
```

The correlated subquery in the preceding example increases the complexity of the statement. At first glance, the subquery appears to isolate STAGE from the rest of the query. But the correlated subquery doesn't create an independent block of code because of the link between the two STAGE_NAME columns. Information is now passing in two directions, and we can't simply highlight and run the subquery to understand it. The new query still effectively joins the tables, but the join is performed indirectly and requires slightly more code.

This example doesn't suffer greatly from the correlated subquery, because this example is simple enough to keep in our head. But in a larger query, correlated subqueries make it impossible to understand the query in small pieces. The preceding example used a correlated subquery in the SELECT clause, but the problem is just as bad in the WHERE clause.

Avoid Common Table Expressions

Common table expressions are a useful feature, but they are frequently overused and needlessly increase the context of a query. Common table expressions are also known as the WITH clause or subquery factoring. For example, the following query returns recent deep space missions:

```
with launches as
(
    select *
    from launch
    where launch_category = 'deep space'
        and launch_date >= date '2000-01-01'
)
select *
from launches
join satellite
    on launches.launch_id = satellite.launch_id;
```

There are small advantages to using a common table expression in the preceding query. Common table expressions flow from top to bottom, which is the more traditional direction of program flow. The common table expression separates the LAUNCH predicates and makes it easier to test just those two predicates. But the common table expression doesn't truly create two separate pieces. We still cannot highlight the bottom half of the query and run it in our IDE. The entire query is still all tied together and must be understood as a single piece. The common table expression increased the amount of context.

There are many times when correlated subqueries and common table expressions are useful. Sometimes correlated subqueries just seem to make sense, and they may improve performance with features like scalar subquery caching. If referenced more than once, a common table expression can reduce the amount of code and possibly improve performance by materializing the results. But if we want to create small, modular code, we need to use different techniques.

Sets, Chunking, and Functional Programming to the Rescue

Enough about the problems with traditional SQL syntax – let's talk about the solutions. How do we write powerful SQL statements but make them readable? First, we need to think about SQL statements as nested sets, instead of the mess of linked tables we saw in Figure 6-1. Chunking can help us manage those sets. And applying functional programming ideas can help us simplify our code.

Sets

Thinking in sets helps us understand and visualize our SQL statements. Most SQL guides emphasize set-based processing to help us write faster SQL. Indeed, the performance benefits are enormous and are discussed multiple times throughout Parts III and IV of this book. But this chapter focuses on how set-based thinking can also help us write *readable* SQL.

A mathematical set is simply a collection of objects – an amorphous blob of stuff. We can describe a set as text, like A = {1, 2, 3, 4}. It's also helpful to visualize sets, like in Figure 6-2.

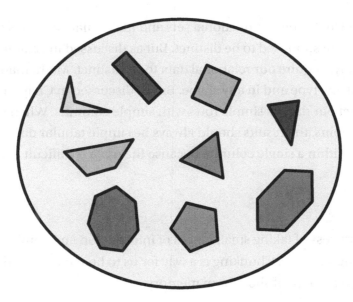

Figure 6-2. *"An example of a set" by Stephan Kulla is licensed under CC0*

Sets can contain other sets. Nesting sets is a powerful way of representing any kind of information. There are many ways to visualize sets, such as the Venn diagrams from Chapter 1 or the following diagram in Figure 6-3. The exact way of thinking about sets is unimportant. It only matters that we have a solid mental model of sets.

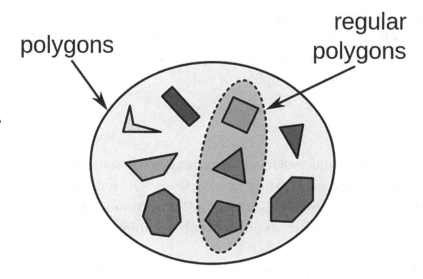

Figure 6-3. *"Set of polygons, with a highlighted subset of regular polygons. Part of a set theory series" by Stephan Kulla is licensed under CC0*

But the analogy between our relational sets and mathematical sets is not perfect. Mathematical sets are supposed to be distinct. But as discussed in Chapter 1, it's impractical to always require our relational data to be distinct. Mathematical sets can contain subsets of any type and in any shape. But as discussed in Chapter 1, we need to store and project our data as simple rows with simple columns. When we combine multiple sets with joins, the results should always be simple tabular data. We should avoid storing sets within a single column, because that data is difficult to filter and join.

Chunking

Chunking is the process of taking small pieces of information and combining them into a new and meaningful entity. Chunking is a way for us to hold complex ideas in our head despite our limited amount of short-term memory.

There's no clear consensus on how many items we can hold in short-term memory, although 7 ± 2 seems to be a popular answer.[2] We use chunking all the time, such as when we use a mnemonic device to remember the colors of the rainbow (Roy G. Biv) or when we try to remember a phone number by breaking it into small and memorable pieces. We can also use chunking to improve our SQL statements.

It's time to introduce the first and only complex example, using the space data set. Let's find out which rocket fuels are the most popular for each year and look for trends. As technology changes, are rockets moving toward using a specific kind of fuel? To answer that question with the old join syntax, here's the FROM clause:

```
from launch, launch_vehicle_stage, stage, engine, engine_propellant,
propellant
```

Those six tables, their columns, and their relationships are too much to handle at one time. Instead, we can think of the query as a set of three different sets: the launches, launch vehicle engines, and engine fuels. Each one of those sets is a small, easily understandable query. And putting the sets together is easy.

Since SQL statements have more connectivity than a typical set, we should adjust the rule of thumb from 7 ± 2 to 3 ± 1. Figure 6-4 shows a Venn diagram of the joins between those three sets. Join Venn diagrams typically show tables, but in the relational model, there's no difference between a table and a result set. Inner joins, left outer joins, and all other operations work the same way on tables and sets.

---

[2] Based on the paper "The Magical Number Seven, Plus or Minus Two" by George A. Miller.

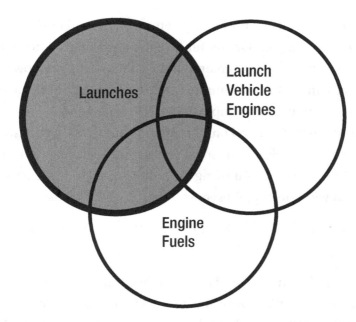

Figure 6-4. *Venn diagram of joins between three relational sets*

Nesting sets is the key to simplifying our SQL. In some programming languages, a deeply nested structure is a problem. But in SQL, a deeply nested structure lets us simplify our code. Each level of our statements will have a small number of easily understandable chunks. The interface between chunks is always the same – boring old relational data. If one chunk is causing a problem, we can drill down and look at the next level of chunks and repeat until the entire query is correct.

Functional Programming

Functional programming can reduce dependencies and context. In functional programming, deterministic mathematical functions return the same values for the same inputs and do not depend on the program state. (This kind of function is different than PL/SQL functions, which may sometimes return different results for the same inputs.) Functional programs are declarative, which means we tell the program what we want but not how to do it.

Removing program state removes unexpected side effects that cause many bugs. But it's hard to completely remove program state – our programs must change things eventually. That limitation might explain why functional programming has never really taken off. The most widely used functional programming languages are R, Lisp, and

Haskell. Those languages are popular but are rarely in a top ten list of programming languages. But the *idea* of functional programming has seeped into other languages.

SQL was not designed to be a functional programming language, but our programs can easily implement functional programming ideas. Instead of passing in parameters and returning values, SQL statements deal with relational data: relational sets are the input, and a relational set is the output. That simplicity may feel limiting at first, but that limitation frees us from worrying about context. If we use simple inputs and outputs, we can easily understand a small chunk of SQL.

SQL data should be passed through nested sets and only nested sets. By sticking to that rule, we only have to think about the data coming from one direction. That rule reduces the dependencies and the context. We want to minimize passing data through global variables, bind variables, correlated subqueries, and other side effects. At the lowest level of our SQL statements, sets come from relational tables. To pass results to the higher levels of our SQL statements, we must use inline views.

Inline Views

Inline views are the perfect way to create and assemble small chunks of SQL. Inline views help us simplify code by combining sets, chunks, and a functional programming style.

What Is an Inline View?

The terms "inline view," "subquery," and "correlated subquery" are often used interchangeably, but it's important to understand the difference between them. A subquery is any query inside a query. A correlated subquery is found in the SELECT or WHERE clause and references a column value from the outer query. An inline view is a subquery in the FROM clause:

```
--Both of these are subqueries:

--Correlated subquery:
select (select * from dual a where a.dummy = b.dummy) from dual b;

--Inline view:
select * from (select * from dual);
```

Inline views are useful because they are independent from each other. In the preceding example, we can run the subquery in the inline view all by itself. In an IDE, running separate pieces is as easy as highlighting and clicking a button. Running separate pieces is not possible with a correlated subquery, which requires understanding the entire query at once.

Each inline view is simply a set and behaves like a normal table or view. Similar to functional programming, inline views pass in one thing (sets) and always return the same result (another set) and depend on nothing else.[3]

Inline views can be infinitely nested, but we need to strike a careful balance. We don't want a query that's too deep, because each level of inline views requires more code. We don't want a query that's too shallow, because then we have to join all the tables at once. It's up to us to decide what a useable chunk is, and our definition may change over time. When we first use a data model, we may only join a few tables at once, but the number of tables will grow as we become familiar with the data. When our chunk size increases, we must remember we're writing queries for other people, not ourselves.

Inline Views Make Code Larger but Simpler

There's a paradox with inline views. Simplifying should make our code smaller, but adding inline views makes the overall code larger. For example, the shortest way to query ten tables is to join them together all at once. If we split the list into two groups, we still need to join all the tables, and now we also need to join those two groups. That splitting and joining causes more code, but it is still a good idea.

In the following pseudo-code, the first query may initially look simpler than the second query:

```
--#1: Join everything at once:
select ...
from table1,table2,table3,table4,table5,table6,table7,table8,table9,table10
where ...;

--#2: Use inline views:
select *
```

---

[3] It is technically possible for an inline view to reference external objects by using the join options LATERAL, CROSS APPLY, and OUTER APPLY. But those rare features defeat the whole purpose of inline views and should be avoided.

```
from
(
    select ...
    from table1,table2,table3,table4,table5
    where ...
),
(
    select ...
    from table6,table7,table8,table9,table10
    where ...
)
where ...;
```

The inline view version requires more characters, so how can we measurably say that the second version is simpler? First, think of the possible ways to join those ten tables. When joined all at once, there are $10! = 3,628,800$ possible ways to visualize and order those tables in the WHERE clause. In the inline view version, there are $(5! + 5!) * 2 = 480$ ways to visualize and order those tables in the WHERE clause.

The preceding math is overly precise. I'm not claiming the second version is literally 7,560 times simpler than the first version. The point is that our code complexity doesn't grow linearly. Adding one table to a ten-table join is worse than adding one table to a five-table join. The problem is related to our short-term memory, or the rule of 7 ± 2. Since we have to remember the tables and how to join them, we should cut the rule in half and use 3 ± 1.

Simple Inline Views for a Large Example

Let's look at the inline views for our first real example – finding the most popular rocket fuels per year. There are three pieces in this query: launches, launch vehicle engines, and engine fuels. First, we want to find the relevant launches:

```
(
    --Orbital and deep space launches.
    select *
    from launch
    where launch_category in ('orbital', 'deep space')
```

121

```
) launches
```

Next, we want to find the engines used for each launch vehicle. Launch vehicles, typically rockets, can have multiple stages. Each stage can use a different engine:

```
(
    --Launch Vehicle Engines
    select launch_vehicle_stage.lv_id, stage.engine_id
    from launch_vehicle_stage
    left join stage
        on launch_vehicle_stage.stage_name = stage.stage_name
) lv_engines
```

Finally, we want to find the fuels used in each engine:

```
(
    --Engine Fuels
    select engine.engine_id, propellant_name fuel
    from engine
    left join engine_propellant
        on engine.engine_id = engine_propellant.engine_id
    left join propellant
        on engine_propellant.propellant_id = propellant.propellant_id
    where oxidizer_or_fuel = 'fuel'
) engine_fuels
```

The preceding inline views are the bulk of our query, in three small, independent pieces. Arguably some of those inline views are too simple. For example, the first inline view doesn't even join a table; it only filters. But we should err on the side of caution. It's tough to gauge when an inline view is too complex. Query writers, like all writers, suffer from the curse of knowledge; we unconsciously assume other people know everything we know. Since we're just starting with this data set, we want to start small. The less we know, the smaller the chunks should be.

We can craft elegant, nested structures using sets. But putting so much work into a single SQL statement can cause issues. Chapter 12 discusses the style and performance issues caused by building large, nested queries. Now that we have the small pieces, the next section discusses how to put them together with the ANSI join syntax.

ANSI Joins

If sets and inline view chunks are the ingredients, then ANSI joins are the recipe for creating readable SQL statements. Using the JOIN keyword makes our queries a bit wordier, but readability is more important than the number of characters.

The ANSI join syntax forces us to write our SQL statements one step at a time. Our queries start with a single set, we combine that set with something else to create a new set, and we repeat the process until done. Those sets could be tables, views, inline views, materialized views, table collection expressions, partitions, remote objects, a point-in-time snapshot of a table using flashback, a CSV file represented as an external table, and who knows what else. The beauty of the relational model is that the origin of the sets doesn't matter. As long as sets return rows and columns, they can all be treated the same way.

The simplicity of the ANSI join process is the key. We can easily get confused when a dozen tables are thrown together quickly. But it's difficult to lose track of the set when we're only adding one thing at a time.

Breaking a query into multiple inline view chunks and combining them with JOIN keywords uses more characters. But readability is paramount. Everything else mentioned in the syntax debates is irrelevant. The debates about standards compliance, rare optimizer bugs, rare syntax features, tradition, Cartesian products, and character count are meaningless if we can't read our SQL statements.

Example

Let's finally put together our first complex SQL statement. The following query shows the most common rocket fuels used per year. The query starts by creating three simple inline view chunks: launches, launch vehicle engines, and engine fuels. Next, the query combines these three inline views, counts the number of uses of fuel per year, ranks the counts, and then selects the top three.

Building queries with nested inline views will look inside out at first. Unlike imperative programming, our query does not flow from top to bottom; the code starts in the middle and moves to the outside. In the following example, each inline view is numbered to help us navigate the code[4]:

```
--Top 3 fuels used per year using ANSI join syntax.
--
--#6: Select only the top N.
select launch_year, fuel, launch_count
from
(
  --#5: Rank the fuel counts.
  select launch_year, launch_count, fuel,
    row_number() over
      (partition by launch_year order by launch_count desc) rownumber
  from
  (
    --#4: Count of fuel used per year.
    select
      to_char(launches.launch_date, 'YYYY') launch_year,
      count(*) launch_count,
      engine_fuels.fuel
    from
    (
      --#1: Orbital and deep space launches.
      select *
      from launch
      where launch_category in ('orbital', 'deep space')
    ) launches
    left join
    (
      --#2: Launch Vehicle Engines
```

---

[4] Numbering isn't generally necessary with inline views. Showing code in a book is a bit more challenging than using code in an IDE. Without IDE features such as parenthesis matching, highlighting, and code folding, the numbering is helpful to keep track of how the data flows.

```
    select launch_vehicle_stage.lv_id, stage.engine_id
    from launch_vehicle_stage
    left join stage
      on launch_vehicle_stage.stage_name = stage.stage_name
  ) lv_engines
    on launches.lv_id = lv_engines.lv_id
  left join
  (
    --#3: Engine Fuels
    select engine.engine_id, propellant_name fuel
    from engine
    left join engine_propellant
      on engine.engine_id = engine_propellant.engine_id
    left join propellant
      on engine_propellant.propellant_id = propellant.propellant_id
    where oxidizer_or_fuel = 'fuel'
  ) engine_fuels
    on lv_engines.engine_id = engine_fuels.engine_id
  group by to_char(launches.launch_date, 'YYYY'), engine_fuels.fuel
  order by launch_year, launch_count desc, fuel
  )
)
where rownumber <= 3
order by launch_year, launch_count desc;
```

The preceding code and all other code samples are available on https://
github.com/apress/pro-oracle-sql-dev-2e. This book assumes you are using
Oracle 12.2 or greater. Examples and syntax that require version 18c or greater will be
individually noted.

This book doesn't often have large chunks of code, and it's OK if you're not running
the examples while reading this book. But this one time I recommend you at least
load that large query into an IDE and play around with it. Notice how we can easily

highlight different sections and debug the query. Each numbered section can be run independently, and we can easily watch the result set grow until the query is complete.

The first five rows from the query are shown as follows. Old science fiction fans may be disappointed – the most popular rocket fuels haven't changed much in the past 60 years. Other than the first few years, the top results are usually UDMH (unsymmetrical dimethylhydrazine) and different versions of kerosene. However, in the past 20 years, fuels like liquid hydrogen have started to become more popular. (This data is clearly not perfect, and some of the values should probably be grouped together. But those small errors don't mean our query is invalid.)

```
LAUNCH_YEAR   FUEL            LAUNCH_COUNT
-----------   -------------   ------------
1957          Kero T-1                   4
1957          Kero                       1
1957          Solid                      1
1958          Solid                     39
1958          JPL 136                   21
...
```

Summary

Joins are the most important operation in a database. We've got to get the joins right if we're ever going to be successful in a database. The traditional way of building queries, with the throw-all-the-tables-in-a-list style, causes many problems. Our queries will be much better if we can think in sets, break the query into chunks with inline views, and then combine the inline views with the ANSI join syntax.

CHAPTER 7

Query the Database with Advanced SELECT Features

SELECT is the most important SQL statement type. Even when we're changing data, most of the logic will go in the SELECT and WHERE clauses of the statement. Before we can insert, update, or delete a set, we must be able to choose a set.

This chapter introduces intermediate and advanced Oracle SQL SELECT features. Each topic could fill a whole chapter or maybe even a whole book. Instead of showing all the options and quizzing you on the syntax, this chapter focuses on breadth over depth and only tries to show you what is possible. The first step to advanced programming and tuning is to simply remember what features are available. When we recognize that our SQL can be improved by one of these advanced features, we can then look up the syntax in the *SQL Language Reference*.

The following topics are listed roughly in the order of importance. SELECT statements almost always have expressions and conditions in the SELECT and WHERE clauses. Most statements will join and sort data. Some statements may combine queries with set operators. Tougher problems require advanced grouping, analytic functions, regular expressions, row limiting, and pivoting and unpivoting. Rarer problems require features like alternative table references, common table expressions, and recursive queries. If we have non-relational data, we may need to process XML and JSON. Finally, we must occasionally consider National Language Support (NLS) issues.

© Jon Heller 2023
J. Heller, *Pro Oracle SQL Development*, https://doi.org/10.1007/978-1-4842-8867-2_7

Operators, Functions, Expressions, and Conditions

Oracle has a huge number of operators, functions, expressions, and conditions. We need to understand the precise definition of these four terms, to be able to identify situations where we're missing something, the precedence rules, and how to simplify our syntax.

Semantics

Operators and functions both take inputs and return a value. The difference between the two is that operators have a special syntax. For example, we can concatenate values with an operator like `'A'||'B'`, or we can concatenate values with a function call like `CONCAT('A','A')`.[1] An expression is a combination of literals, functions, and operators that returns a value. Conditions are combinations of expressions and operators that return a Boolean value. To put it simply, operators are symbols that return a value, functions are passed-in arguments and return a value, expressions combine things and return a value, and conditions combine things and return a Boolean value.

The preceding definitions for operators, functions, expressions, and conditions are confusing and may seem pedantic, but the difference between them is important. In some contexts, not all those four things can be used. For example, a `WHERE` clause can have a stand-alone condition, but cannot have a stand-alone expression. This statement with a condition is valid: `SELECT * FROM DUAL WHERE 1=1`. This statement with an expression is not valid: `SELECT * FROM DUAL WHERE 1+1`.

How to Know When We're Missing Something

We'll never memorize all the operators, functions, expressions, and conditions, no matter how many times we read the *SQL Language Reference*. We can only learn enough to develop a sense for when we're missing something and when we ought to check the manual for a way to simplify our code. Oracle provides enough operators, functions,

---

[1] You could argue that a programming language doesn't need operators, only functions. Removing operators would make a language more consistent. But realistically, we would rather write 1+1 than `PLUS(1,1)`. On the other hand, a language with too many operators can lead to cryptic syntax, like many Perl programs.

expressions, and conditions for the most common tasks. If we find ourselves doing a lot of type conversions, then we're not using the right features. These syntax-soup problems most commonly happen with date manipulations.

For example, let's say we want to find information about the first artificial Earth satellite, Sputnik. We may remember the launch took place on October 4, 1957. But nobody remembers the exact time, so we should only check the date. The following query might work but has dangerous and unnecessary type conversions:

```
select *
from launch
where to_char(to_date(launch_date), 'YYYY-Mon-DD') = '1957-Oct-04';
```

There is a simpler, safer, and faster way to accomplish the preceding query. The TRUNC function can remove the time portion of a date without any conversion. With enough practice and SQL knowledge, we will intuitively know that the preceding query can be transformed into something like the following query:

```
select *
from launch
where trunc(launch_date) = date '1957-10-04';
```

Alternatively, if there is an index on the LAUNCH_DATE column, the query might be significantly faster with a BETWEEN condition instead of a TRUNC function. There are trade-offs between simplicity and performance, and we should start with the simplest version first.

Precedence Rules

There are a few non-trivial rules for the order of precedence of operators and conditions. For operators, the most important rule is to follow the traditional math precedence rules: multiplication and division first and then addition and subtraction. For conditions, the most important precedence rule is AND comes before OR.

More important than any precedence rule is the user interface rule: don't make me think. Don't create complex expressions that require readers to perfectly understand the precedence rules. Use parentheses and spacing to make the logic simple. For example, even this simple statement can be quite confusing:

```
select * from dual where 1=1 or 1=0 and 1=2;
```

It's safer to add parentheses whenever we mix ANDs with ORs. For example, rewrite the preceding SQL to this:

```
select * from dual where 1=1 or (1=0 and 1=2);
```

Simplify

Inline views are not only for simplifying joins. When we have an extremely long expression, with many chained functions, it may make sense to split up the expression with multiple inline views. There's no universal rule that tells us how many functions we can chain. The decision to chain or split depends on the query and what makes sense to us.

For example, doing everything in one step in the following query may be too difficult to understand:

```
select a(b(c(d(e(f(g(h(some_column))))))))
from some_table;
```

Sometimes it makes sense to break expressions into multiple steps, like with the following query. Using multiple inline views can make it easier to debug the query and quickly check the values as they move between inline views. On the other hand, we don't need an inline view for every additional operator, function, expression, or condition. Whichever style we use, we don't need to worry about performance, since Oracle can easily combine expressions:

```
select a(b(c(d(result1)))) result2
from
(
    select e(f(g(h(some_column)))) result1
    from some_table
);
```

Combining conditions is deceivingly difficult. Logic that sounds reasonable in the natural language requirements does not always translate into a readable query. Some discrete math tricks can help us deal with complex queries. For example, with De Morgan's law, we can rewrite NOT(A OR B) to NOT(A) AND NOT(B), or we can rewrite NOT(A AND B) to NOT(A) OR NOT(B). Even if rewriting a statement doesn't make it clearer, the process of rewriting will help us understand the statement and requirements better.

For especially tricky expressions and conditions, it may help to build a large truth table. These truth tables aren't needed to demonstrate basic logical properties – we already know that TRUE AND TRUE = TRUE. These tables are convenient ways to show all combinations of the different inputs. When I get confused by the wording of a requirement, I'll put the different pieces into something like Table 7-1.

Table 7-1. *Example of a (Not Mathematically Precise) Multi-valued Truth Table*

Foo	Bar	Baz	...	Result
True	True	True	...	A
True	True	False	...	B
True	False	True	...	A
True	False	False	...	C
...	...	...	...	...

CASE and DECODE

CASE expressions are perfect for adding conditional logic to SQL. CASE and DECODE are the IF statements of SQL, and they both use short-circuit evaluation. CASE is usually preferred over DECODE because it is more readable, it is available in both SQL and PL/SQL, and it does not have any unexpected behavior with nulls.

The following example uses both CASE and DECODE to solve the fizz buzz programming question. Fizz buzz is a children's game and a common entry-level programming interview question: count from 1 to 100; if the number is divisible by 3, say "fizz"; if the number is divisible by 5, say "buzz"; and if the number is divisible by both 3 and 5, say "fizz buzz."

The following code shows that CASE uses more characters than DECODE, but is also more readable. CASE is more powerful because it allows any kind of condition, not just an equality condition. Both approaches use short-circuit evaluation, which means they stop processing as soon as one match is found:

```
--Fizz buzz.
select
   rownum line_number,
   case
```

```
      when mod(rownum, 15) = 0 then 'fizz buzz'
      when mod(rownum,  3) = 0 then 'fizz'
      when mod(rownum,  5) = 0 then 'buzz'
      else to_char(rownum)
    end case_result,
    decode(mod(rownum, 15), 0, 'fizz buzz',
      decode(mod(rownum, 3), 0, 'fizz',
      decode(mod(rownum, 5), 0, 'buzz', rownum)
      )
    ) decode_result
from dual
connect by level <= 100;

LINE_NUMBER  CASE_RESULT  DECODE_RESULT
-----------  -----------  -------------
          1  1            1
          2  2            2
          3  fizz         fizz
          4  4            4
          5  buzz         buzz
          6  fizz         fizz
          7  7            7
...
```

The preceding example uses the more powerful searched case expression. There is also a simple case expression – a shorter syntax for comparing against a long list of values. The following example shows another way to write the fizz buzz program by hard-coding the values. This query is clearly not the best way to write this program, but this query demonstrates there are different CASE and DECODE syntaxes that can simplify queries with many hard-coded values:

```
--Hard-coded fizz buzz.
select
    rownum line_number,
    case rownum
      when 1 then '1'
      when 2 then '2'
```

```
      when 3 then 'fizz'
      else 'etc.'
   end case_result,
   decode(rownum, 1, '1', 2, '2', 3, 'fizz', 'etc.') decode_result
from dual
connect by level <= 100;
```

DECODE is one of the few places where NULL = NULL is true. The following query returns "A" instead of "B". This behavior is one of those exceptions we just have to memorize:

```
select decode(null, null, 'A', 'B') null_decode from dual;
```

Joins

There are many ways to classify joins, and there is much overlap between those classifications. The terminology may sound confusing, and some of the options may seem esoteric. Keep in mind that joining is the most important database operation, and we should expect an advanced database to have many join options. (Measuring join features is also a quick way to evaluate alternative databases. If a database doesn't take joins seriously, it's only a program for storing data, not processing data.) This chapter only discusses the join syntax and functionality; the algorithms used to implement joins are discussed in Chapter 16:

1. Inner, left outer, right outer, full outer, cross (Cartesian product), partitioned outer, lateral, cross apply, or outer apply

2. Old syntax or ANSI join syntax

3. Equijoin or non-equijoin

4. Semi-join, anti-join, or neither

5. Self-join or not a self-join

6. Natural join or not a natural join

7. ON clause or USING clause

Some of the preceding items were already discussed and demonstrated in examples throughout the previous chapters. We don't need to further discuss inner, left, right, full, cross, or old syntax vs. ANSI join syntax. Since joins are so important, the rest of this section will discuss every remaining item on the preceding list.

Partitioned Outer Joins

Partitioned outer joins are useful for data densification. Densification happens when we are counting the number of times something happens per group and we want to show the results against a time period. We want to see the counts, per item, per time period, even if the counts are zero. Creating multiple empty rows is hard to do with a regular left join – the left join might include all the time periods, but not all time periods *per* item. A partitioned outer join is like a multi-join – it joins the time periods for each item.

Partitioned outer joins are tricky to understand without an example. For a concrete example, let's say we want to count the number of rocket launches, per launch vehicle family, per month, for 2017. If there were no launches for a month, we still want to see a row, but with a count of zero:

```
--Launches per launch vehicle family, per month of 2017.
select
    launches.lv_family_code,
    months.launch_month,
    nvl(launch_count, 0) launch_count
from
(
    --Every month in 2017.
    select '2017-'||lpad(level, 2, 0) launch_month
    from dual
    connect by level <= 12
) months
left join
(
    --2017 orbital and deep space launches.
    select
        to_char(launch_date, 'YYYY-MM') launch_month,
        lv_family_code,
```

```
        count(*) launch_count
    from launch
    join launch_vehicle
        on launch.lv_id = launch_vehicle.lv_id
    where launch_category in ('orbital', 'deep space')
        and launch_date between
            date '2017-01-01' and timestamp '2017-12-31 23:59:50'
    group by to_char(launch_date, 'YYYY-MM'), lv_family_code
) launches
    partition by (launches.lv_family_code)
    on months.launch_month = launches.launch_month
order by 1,2,3;

LV_FAMILY_CODE   LAUNCH_MONTH   LAUNCH_COUNT
--------------   ------------   ------------
Ariane5          2017-01                   0
Ariane5          2017-02                   1
Ariane5          2017-03                   0
...
Atlas5           2017-01                   1
Atlas5           2017-02                   0
Atlas5           2017-03                   1
...
```

The preceding results don't look that special at first. But those rows with zeroes would have been a real pain to generate without a partitioned outer join. There's no other easy way to repeatedly join tables based on a group.

Lateral, Cross Apply, and Outer Apply

Lateral, cross apply, and outer apply joins are evil and should be avoided. Those features were mostly added to Oracle to help migrate SQL Server queries. Those three join types allow inline views to access values outside of them, which destroys the reason for using inline views in the first place. Those three join types increase the context of our queries and prevent building small, independent sets. Lateral, cross apply, and outer apply joins are reading something they're not supposed to, like reading private variables from another class.

135

Equijoin or Non-equijoin

Equijoin vs. non-equijoin seems like a meaningless distinction at first. An equijoin is a join based on the equality operator, =. A non-equijoin uses something else, such as <> or BETWEEN. The distinction matters because there can be serious performance issues when using non-equijoins. Only equijoins can be used for hash join operations. Hash joins are discussed in more detail in Chapter 16. For now, it's only important to understand that hash joins are often the fastest join method. If there are performance problems, it may help to rewrite a non-equijoin into an equijoin, to allow a hash join. But it's not always possible to rewrite a query to use an equality predicate.

Semi-join or Anti-join

Semi-joins and anti-joins are join types where Oracle may not need to process all rows to get the results. For semi-joins, Oracle can stop joining as soon as it finds one row that matches. For anti-joins, Oracle can stop joining as soon as it finds one row that doesn't match. These join types often happen when the query uses a correlated subquery along with an IN, NOT IN, EXISTS, or NOT EXISTS.

As an example of a semi-join, let's say we want to count all the satellites that have an associated launch. A similar query was created in Chapter 1 to discuss nulls, but now we're going to slightly rewrite the query to emphasize the semi-join:

```
--Satellites with a launch.
select count(*)
from satellite
where exists
(
    select 1/0
    from launch
    where launch.launch_id = satellite.launch_id
);
```

The result is 43,112 satellites, which is just one smaller than the total number of satellites. Let's use an anti-join to find the satellite without a launch. The following query returns one row, for "Unknown Oko debris":

```
--Satellites without a launch.
select official_name
from satellite
where not exists
(
    select 1/0
    from launch
    where launch.launch_id = satellite.launch_id
);
```

You may have noticed something seemingly impossible in the preceding examples – both of the preceding queries divide by zero. EXISTS conditions don't use the results of the subquery, since the conditions only care about whether there are rows or not. The subquery must have an expression to fulfill the syntax rules, but that expression is ignored and not even executed. To emphasize the unimportance of the value, I used 1/0. As a rule, whenever I do something weird, like create a value that doesn't matter, I like to make the code look obviously weird. If the query had just used a normal value like "1" or "A", future readers might wonder what those values mean. The expression 1/0 will hopefully make it clear to others how irrelevant the value is.

Semi-joins and anti-joins are notable because they often cause performance problems. The way semi- and anti-joins are coded looks like we're asking Oracle to do work for each row, almost like we're trying to break out of the declarative programming model and tell Oracle how to do its job. Luckily, Oracle is usually smart enough to know when these queries are best rewritten to use normal joins. But sometimes we can improve performance and readability by rewriting queries to not have correlated subqueries.

Self-Joins

Self-joins are when a table is joined to itself. At a first glance there's nothing special about self-joins – they work the same way as any other join. The following example shows a simple self-join of the ORGANIZATION table, to find each organization's parent organization. When joining the table to itself, the table is listed twice in the FROM clause, and at least one of the tables must have an alias:

```
--Organizations and parent organizations.
select
    organization.org_name,
```

```
   parent_organization.org_name parent_org_name
from organization
left join organization parent_organization
   on organization.parent_org_code = parent_organization.org_code
order by organization.org_name desc;

ORG_NAME                PARENT_ORG_NAME
--------------------    --------------------
iSpace
exactEarth Ltd.         Com Dev International
de Havilland Aircraft
...
```

The results may look a little odd at first because of case-sensitive sorting. By default, Oracle sorts are case sensitive, and when sorting descending, the lowercase letters come first. You may get different results on your database, depending on NLS parameters, as described later in this chapter.

Self-joins are worth a separate category because they can be so complicated. The preceding example was simple because we only looked for one parent. But that parent might also have a parent, which also has a parent, etc. Finding all of the ancestors, or finding the root ancestor, requires a recursive query. Recursive queries are extra tricky and are dealt with in a later section.

Natural Joins and USING Considered Harmful

Natural joins should never be used. Natural joins automatically determine the join conditions based on the column names. Wherever the column names match, the tables will be joined based on equality conditions of those columns. Natural joins can be inner, left, right, or full outer. Natural joins are meant to save a trivial amount of typing, but they can lead to surprising results.

It's rare to remember all of the column names of our tables, so we might end up joining more than we expect. Or we may break existing queries when we add new columns.

The following query is an example of a natural join between the LAUNCH table and the SATELLITE table. We've joined these tables before, and both tables have a column named LAUNCH_ID that links them together. We might expect there to be 43,112 rows returned. Instead, the following query only returns 19 rows:

```
--Natural join between LAUNCH and SATELLITE.
select *
from launch
natural join satellite;
```

The two tables in the preceding query have an additional column with the same name – APOGEE. The apogee is the furthest distance from Earth, and it makes no sense to join on those two columns. Most launches do not have apogee data. And when a launch does have an apogee, it rarely matches the satellite apogee. Although a rocket might launch a satellite into orbit, most satellites have their own fuel and can maneuver into a different orbit.

We should also avoid the USING syntax, at least in our production queries. That syntax also saves us a trivial amount of typing by simply listing the columns, instead of listing the entire conditions. For example, to join LAUNCH and SATELLITE, we can save some typing like this:

```
--USING syntax:
select *
from launch
join satellite using (launch_id);
```

The USING syntax is at least safer than a natural join. We have to manually list the columns, so we won't accidentally join unexpected columns. But a few weird things happen with the USING syntax. We can no longer use the * syntax with a specific table, and we can no longer reference the joined column with the table name. Both of the following examples raise an exception:

```
--ORA-25154: column part of USING clause cannot have qualifier
select launch.*
from launch
join satellite using (launch_id);
```

```
select launch.launch_id
from launch
join satellite using (launch_id);
```

There are workarounds to the preceding problems, but the workarounds are annoying. Those workarounds can be especially annoying when we're debugging large SQL statements and want to temporarily see all the results from a specific table. Instead of just adding TABLE.*, we may have to significantly rewrite our SELECT expressions.

Joins are the most important SQL feature, and we need to thoroughly understand them. Joins are one of the few areas where we should memorize the syntax. If we want to be fluent in SQL, we need to be able to join tables effortlessly.

Sorting

The ORDER BY clause has several features and some potentially surprising behavior. We also need to consider the effects of sorting to help us decide when to sort.

Sorting Syntax

We can sort by multiple columns, expressions, or positions. Sorting can be in either ascending or descending order and can specify exactly how to handle nulls. For an example of sorting, let's find the satellites most recently launched into orbit:

```
--Most recently launched satellites.
select
    to_char(launch.launch_date, 'YYYY-MM-DD') launch_date,
    official_name
from satellite
left join launch
    on satellite.launch_id = launch.launch_id
order by launch_date desc nulls last, 2;

LAUNCH_DATE   OFFICIAL_NAME
-----------   -------------
2017-08-31    deb IRNSS-R1H
2017-08-31    deb IRNSS-R1H
2017-08-31    IRNSS-R1H

...
```

There's a lot going on in the preceding ORDER BY clause. The clause looks ambiguous – LAUNCH_DATE is both a date column and an expression that returns a text value. Which one is being used? The expression takes precedence, and in this case, we are sorting by the text value. (If we wanted to sort by the date column value, we would need to prefix the name with the table name, like LAUNCH.LAUNCH_DATE.) Luckily, the text value uses the ISO-8601 date format, so the text version sorts the same way as a date value. If the date format was "DD-Mon-YYYY", the "latest" rows would be from October 31. The NULLS LAST puts satellites without a launch date at the end of the results. (Some of the satellites are junk, and we don't know when they were launched.) Finally, the number 2 means to sort by the second column, which is helpful to break any ties.

We should always fully sort results that are displayed. SQL query results often *appear* to be sorted but are not. People may make a bad assumption based on the appearance of the first few rows and may come to the wrong conclusion. To avoid misrepresenting the data, it's best to fully sort the rows, starting from the leftmost column. On the other hand, if the results are not displayed, but are only used for internal processing, we do *not* want to sort the results. Sorting, especially for huge amounts of data, can take a huge amount of time.

Sorting Performance, Resources, and Implicit Sorting

The performance impact of sorting is complicated. There are two main topics to consider – the algorithmic complexity of sorting and when sorting requires disk access instead of memory access. Chapter 16 contains a quick crash course in algorithmic complexity. For now, let's just accept that the number of operations required to sort N rows is roughly N*LOG(N). Sort operations get slower faster than we may think. If sorting 1000 rows requires 1000*LOG(1000) = 1000*3 = 3000 operations, then sorting 2000 rows requires 2000*LOG(2000) = 2000*3.3 = 6600 operations. The input doubled, but the amount of work more than doubled.

Sorting is ideally done in the Program Global Area (PGA) memory buffer. PGA memory is split among server processes and is mostly controlled by the instance parameter PGA_AGGREGATE_TARGET. Sorting is CPU intensive and also requires space to store temporary result sets. If those temporary results can't fit in the PGA, the results get written to disk in the temporary tablespace. Disk access is orders of magnitude slower than memory access. In the worst case, adding a single row to the input can make the sorting run ridiculously slower.

On the other hand, there are times when sorting is much faster and less resource intensive than we expect. For example, Oracle may be able to transform queries to avoid redundant or unnecessary sorting, and Oracle may be able to read presorted data from an index.

These complicated performance issues cause many developers to look for alternative ways to sort, but the ORDER BY clause is the *only* way to guarantee ordered results. Looking for workarounds to return ordered results as a by-product is a fool's errand. In some versions of Oracle, in some cases, there are tricks that sort the results without actually asking to sort them. For example, older versions of Oracle automatically sorted results in GROUP BY. Years later, many programs broke when Oracle introduced new parallel features and grouping algorithms that don't implicitly sort. We must never rely on undocumented features to sort data.

If we have more than just ASCII data, we also need to consider Oracle's National Language Support. NLS settings also affect comparisons and are discussed later in this chapter. For now, the most important NLS property to remember is that Oracle sorts are case sensitive by default.

Set Operators

Set operators combine query results with UNION, UNION ALL, INTERSECT, and MINUS. The difference between joins and set operators is that set operators depend on *all* of the values in the sets, not just the values used in join conditions. Since set operators depend on all of the values, both sets must have the same number and types of columns. Like joins, we can visualize set operators through the Venn diagrams in Figure 7-1.

SQL Set Operators

select ...
union [all]
select ...

select ...
intersect
select ...

select ...
minus
select ...

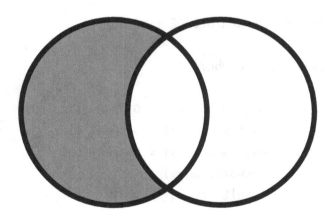

Figure 7-1. *Venn diagram of SQL set operators*

UNION and UNION ALL

The most common set operators are UNION and UNION ALL. These set operators are used when we want to combine sets of data, even if there are no relationships between the sets. UNION creates a distinct set, whereas UNION ALL allows for duplicates. Removing duplicates can have a huge performance impact, so we should use UNION ALL by default.

The most common use of UNION ALL is to generate data. In Oracle we must always select from *something*, so there is a special pseudo table named DUAL. The DUAL[2] table only has one row, so if we want to create multiple rows, we must combine statements with UNION ALL like this:

```
select '1' a from dual union all
select '2' a from dual union all
select '3' a from dual union all
...
```

INTERSECT and MINUS

INTERSECT returns rows where every value is identical between both queries. MINUS returns rows in the first query that are not in the second query. INTERSECT and MINUS are helpful for comparing data. For example, let's take the preceding fizz buzz example and compare the CASE and DECODE techniques. A query like this can help us prove that both versions return the exact same data:

```
--Compare CASE and DECODE fizz buzz.
select
    rownum line_number,
    case
        when mod(rownum, 15) = 0 then 'fizz buzz'
        when mod(rownum,  3) = 0 then 'fizz'
        when mod(rownum,  5) = 0 then 'buzz'
        else to_char(rownum)
    end case_result
```

---

[2] In old versions of Oracle, the DUAL table was a real table. Since DUAL was a real table, it was possible to change it, which led to strange bugs. In current versions, DUAL is a special memory structure that can't be changed and performs better than a regular table.

```
from dual connect by level <= 100
minus
select
    rownum line_number,
    decode(mod(rownum, 15), 0, 'fizz buzz',
        decode(mod(rownum, 3), 0, 'fizz',
        decode(mod(rownum, 5), 0, 'buzz', rownum)
        )
    ) decode_result
from dual connect by level <= 100;
```

Since the two subqueries in the preceding example are equal, the full query returns no rows. If we replace the MINUS with an INTERSECT, we could demonstrate the subqueries are identical by counting that all 100 rows are returned.

Set Operator Complications

Set operator comparisons are not always trivial. With the preceding example, we cannot simply say, "The minus query returns 0 rows; therefore, the sets are equal" or "The intersect returns 100 rows; therefore, the sets are equal."

What if the first subquery in the preceding example had LEVEL <= 99 instead of LEVEL <= 100? The full query would still return 0 rows, but the sets aren't completely equal. Or what if the first subquery had LEVEL <= 101 and we used INTERSECT? The full query would return 100 rows, even though the sets are not equal. We need to carefully count the rows of each subquery before comparing with MINUS or INTERSECT, and we also need to watch out for duplicates.

Similar to the rules of DECODE, set operators treat two nulls as identical values. Set operators are another place where Oracle breaks its own rules. But at least this time the broken rule makes sense. In practice, when comparing sets, we always want nulls to match. For example, the following query returns just one row, which is what we want:

```
select null from dual
union
select null from dual;
```

Set operators cannot work on unusual data types, such as CLOB, LONG, XMLType, user-defined types, etc. Those types will generate an error message like "ORA-00932: inconsistent datatypes: expected - got CLOB." Large objects could theoretically contain gigabytes of data, which cannot be easily compared or ordered. The same limitations on large data types also apply to joining and sorting.

Oracle 21c introduced new set operator features. INTERSECT and MINUS now have an ALL option, so you can perform those operations without getting unique results. To match the SQL standard, the keyword EXCEPT was added, but it works exactly the same way as MINUS.

Advanced Grouping

Oracle SQL has many options to help us group our data and aggregate results. This book assumes you are familiar with basic grouping concepts, so let's start with a simple example and then add on to it. Let's count the number of orbital and deep space launches per launch vehicle family and launch vehicle name:

```
--Count of launches per family and name.
select lv_family_code, lv_name, count(*)
from launch
join launch_vehicle
   on launch.lv_id = launch_vehicle.lv_id
where launch.launch_category in ('orbital', 'deep space')
group by lv_family_code, lv_name
order by 1,2,3;

LV_FAMILY_CODE   LV_NAME     COUNT(*)
--------------   ---------   --------
ASLV             ASLV               4
ASLV             SLV-3              4
Angara           Angara A5          1
...
```

The results are ordered and start with the Augmented Satellite Launch Vehicle (ASLV, an Indian rocket from the 1980s) and Angara (a new Russian rocket). This simple type of grouping is enough for most queries. Occasionally we may need to limit the results with the HAVING clause. For example, if we only want to see the launch counts for the most popular rockets, we could add this line of code between the WHERE and the ORDER BY clauses: HAVING COUNT(*) >= 10. Note that the HAVING conditions cannot reference the aliases in the SELECT clause, so we may need to duplicate our logic.

ROLLUP, GROUP*, CUBE

More complicated reports require multiple levels of groupings. Let's expand on the previous example. In addition to counting launches per family and name, we also want the counts only per family, as well as a grand total. The ROLLUP syntax lets us perform multiple groupings in the same query. ROLLUP starts at the most detailed level, the rightmost column in the list, and keeps adding subtotals for each column to the left:

```
--Launch count per family and name, per family, and grand total.
select
    lv_family_code,
    lv_name,
    count(*),
    grouping(lv_family_code) is_family_grp,
    grouping(lv_name) is_name_grp
from launch
join launch_vehicle
    on launch.lv_id = launch_vehicle.lv_id
where launch_category in ('orbital', 'deep space')
group by rollup(lv_family_code, lv_name)
order by 1,2,3;
```

LV_FAMILY_CODE	LV_NAME	COUNT(*)	IS_FAMILY_GRP	IS_NAME_GRP
ASLV	ASLV	4	0	0
ASLV	SLV-3	4	0	0
ASLV		8	0	1
Angara	Angara A5	1	0	0
...				
		5667	1	1

The preceding results show multiple levels of grouping, including the grand total at the bottom. The nulls indicate which columns are aggregated in each row. For example, the third row has a null for LV_NAME, because that row shows totals for all values of the ASLV family.

It's not always easy to tell which rows are subtotals. Oracle provides multiple ways to distinguish the row's grouping level. The group level of each row can be precisely determined with the function GROUP_ID, GROUPING, or GROUPING_ID. GROUPING is the easiest to use – that function returns a 1 or 0 to indicate whether or not the row is a group of a specific set of columns. That function is used in the preceding results to generate the columns IS_FAMILY_GRP and IS_NAME_GRP. Columns that tell us the grouping level can be used for things like filtering out unwanted rows or changing the display to emphasize grand totals. GROUP_ID and GROUPING_ID are more powerful but are also more difficult to use. These two functions return an encoded number to distinguish between row types.

In addition to ROLLUP, Oracle also provides CUBE and GROUPING SETS to define even more types of groupings. CUBE groups all combinations of columns, and GROUPING SETS lets us specify multiple sets to group together. These grouping functions can quickly get crazy, so I'm not going to show any more huge examples. If we find ourselves creating multiple summary queries and concatenating them with UNION ALL, we should look for an advanced grouping function to simplify our code.

After the data is grouped, the values inside each group need to be combined with the proper aggregate functions. Most aggregation is satisfied by combinations of MIN, MAX, AVG, SUM, and COUNT. There are many more aggregate functions for different types of statistical operations. And all of the aggregate functions can use expressions, such as a CASE expression, making them even more powerful.

Every column returned by an aggregate query must either be in the **GROUP BY** clause, have an aggregate function, or be a literal. That rule occasionally leads to queries with logically redundant grouping. For example, let's say we want to add the launch vehicle classification, LAUNCH_VEHICLE.LV_CLASS, to the preceding query. That column will always return the same value for each group, but Oracle doesn't know that. We need to either add the column to the GROUP BY clause or add a meaningless aggregate function like MAX in front of the column. Since Oracle 21c, if we want to avoid the overhead of extra grouping and make the code clearer, we can use the expression ANY_VALUE(LV_CLASS). But we must fully understand our data, or that expression could return unexpected values.

LISTAGG

LISTAGG aggregates strings, and that function was shamefully absent from Oracle for decades. In the past, every Oracle developer had to create their own custom solution for string aggregation. There is a lot of old code and old forum posts that discuss different strategies for aggregating strings: CONNECT BY, MODEL, Oracle data cartridge, COLLECT, undocumented functions like WM_CONCAT, etc. None of that code is needed anymore. If we need to generate a comma-separated list of strings, we should always use LISTAGG.

For example, this query displays the name of all rockets in the Ariane rocket family and lists the names in alphabetical order:

```
select
   lv_family_code,
   listagg(lv_name, ',') within group (order by lv_name) lv_names
from launch_vehicle
where lower(lv_family_code) like 'ariane%'
group by lv_family_code
order by lv_family_code;

LV_FAMILY_CODE  LV_NAMES
--------------  --------
Ariane          Ariane 1,Ariane 2,Ariane 3,Ariane 40,...
Ariane5         Ariane 5ECA,Ariane 5ES,Ariane 5ES/ATV,...
```

Creating lists of strings is a common task, and there can be many tricky requirements. If the string could be larger than the 4,000-byte limit, we might need to add the ON OVERFLOW TRUNCATE option. (If we really need to aggregate more than 4,000 bytes, we can look online for advanced solutions using XMLAGG or ODCI.) If we want to return unique values and we are on version 19c or higher, we can add the DISTINCT keyword. But if we have more complicated requirements or are stuck on an older version of the database, we can always use multiple inline views to preprocess the data before aggregation.

Advanced Aggregate Functions

The COLLECT function is useful when we need to aggregate "anything." The COLLECT function works together with the CAST function to take a bunch of values and convert those values into a single nested table. That nested table can then be passed to a custom PL/SQL function for further processing. COLLECT gives us complete control over aggregation. COLLECT and custom PL/SQL functions are briefly discussed in Chapter 21.

Aggregate functions also have a FIRST and a LAST mode. Those modes are useful when we want to find the minimum or maximum value, but we want to define the minimum or maximum based on a different column. For example, let's compare launch apogees – the furthest distance from Earth. For each launch vehicle family, let's find the first launch apogee. We pass the column APOGEE to the MIN function, but we want to calculate the minimum based on LAUNCH_DATE:

```
--For each family find the first, min, and max apogee.
select
    lv_family_code,
    min(launch.apogee) keep
        (dense_rank first order by launch_date) first_apogee,
    min(launch.apogee) min_apogee,
    max(launch.apogee) max_apogee
from launch
join launch_vehicle
    on launch.lv_id = launch_vehicle.lv_id
where launch.apogee is not null
group by lv_family_code
order by lv_family_code;
```

LV_FAMILY_CODE	FIRST_APOGEE	MIN_APOGEE	MAX_APOGEE
10KS2500	10	10	10
48N6	40	40	40
A-350	10	0	300
...			

The results show us that the first apogee is usually the same as the minimum. That result makes sense – when testing a launch vehicle, it's best to start with small launches. But for the anti-ballistic missile A-350, the first launch went further than the minimum launch. That difference is because some of the later launches failed and had an apogee of 0.

Analytic Functions

Analytic functions, also known as window functions, can significantly improve the power of our SQL statements. So far, we have seen operators, functions, expressions, and conditions operate on two levels – for every row or for all the rows in a group. Analytic functions let us combine those two levels. With analytic functions we can calculate a value per row, but that value is based on a window of data. Calculations like running totals and moving averages are best done with analytic functions. Analytic function syntax can be quite complicated, and we need to occasionally use the syntax diagrams in the manual, but the most common usage looks like ANALYTIC_FUNCTION(ARGUMENTS) OVER (PARTITION_CLAUSE ORDER_BY_CLAUSE WINDOWING_CLAUSE).

Analytic Function Syntax

There are many analytic functions to choose from, including almost all of the aggregate functions previously discussed. AVG, COUNT, LISTAGG, MIN, MAX, and SUM can operate as either aggregate or analytic functions. The most popular analytic functions are DENSE_ RANK, RANK, LAG, LEAD, and ROW_NUMBER. Those functions are shown in examples later in this section.

The arguments to analytic functions can be any valid expression and can involve columns, operators, etc. CASE expressions are a common argument for aggregate and analytic functions. For example, we can create a conditional sum with an expression like SUM(CASE WHEN X = 'Y' THEN 1 ELSE 0 END). But some analytic functions, such as ROW_NUMBER, don't take any arguments and have empty parentheses after the function name.

The partition clause defines the group, or window, for the analytic function. The partition clause is a list of columns or expressions, similar to the list of columns or expressions we might use in a group by clause. If we want to use *all* the rows, for example, to show a grand total per row, simply leave the partition clause empty.

The order by clause defines the order the rows are processed. For example, in a running total the values must be totaled in a specific order. That clause is also a list of comma-separated columns or expressions. Similar to the partition clause, we can sometimes leave the order by clause blank to mean the order doesn't matter.

The windowing clause is less common. That clause lets us specify a more precise group of rows, also called a window. After the partition by clause specifies a group, the window clause can narrow it down. For example, a common window clause is ROWS BETWEEN UNBOUNDED PRECEDING AND CURRENT ROW. This clause is tricky and isn't fully explained here. If you're ever writing a query and wish you could specify X rows before or after, look up the full syntax in the manual.

Analytic Function Examples

The following example demonstrates the RANK analytic function, along with the order by clause and the partition by clause. Let's find the most popular launch vehicle families. But it's not fair to compare small sounding rockets with enormous orbital rockets, so we want to determine the most popular overall and the most popular per launch category. To find the most popular overall, don't partition by anything. To find the most popular per category, partition by the category. And in both cases, we want to order the results descending – the largest number of launches is ranked first:

```
--Most popular launch vehicle families.
select
    launch_category category
    ,lv_family_code family
    ,count
    ,rank() over (order by count desc) rank_total
    ,rank() over (partition by launch_category
        order by count desc) rank_per_category
from
(
    --Launch counts per category and family.
    select launch_category, lv_family_code, count(*) count
    from launch
    join launch_vehicle
        on launch.lv_id = launch_vehicle.lv_id
```

```
    group by launch_category, lv_family_code
    order by count(*) desc
)
order by count desc, launch_category desc;
```

```
CATEGORY            FAMILY      COUNT RANK_TOTAL RANK_PER_CAT
----------------    ----------- ----- ---------- ------------
suborbital rocket   Rocketsonde 21369          1            1
suborbital rocket   M-100        7749          2            2
suborbital rocket   Nike         2948          3            3
suborbital rocket   Loki         2495          4            4
orbital             R-7          1789          5            1
suborbital rocket   Arcas        1716          6            5

...
```

Pay close attention to the numbers in the preceding results. Analytic queries are tricky, and even something as simple as counting and ranking is complicated because the data seems to be moving in so many directions. The vast majority of popular launch vehicles are sounding rockets in the "suborbital rocket" category. Sounding rockets are relatively small and usually carry a small payload of scientific experiments. Look carefully at the total rank and the rank per category. Notice how the numbers mostly go in order, until the R-7 rocket. The R-7 rocket might be fifth overall, but it is first for orbital launches. Launching tiny experiments is different than launching satellites and people, so that rocket may deserve first place, depending on how we count.

RANK, DENSE_RANK, and ROW_NUMBER are similar functions. We're getting close to syntax trivia here, but these functions are so common it's worth knowing the exact differences between them. RANK uses what is called "Olympic ranking"; if two rows tie for first place, the next row is third place. DENSE_RANK does the opposite; if two rows tie for first place, the next row is second place. ROW_NUMBER never allows ties; if we don't fully specify the order by clause, the function will randomly pick a winner. ROW_NUMBER is useful when we must limit the number of rows returned, but we don't particularly care about the rank. For example, a screen may only be able to display 20 rows regardless of ties.

The functions LAG and LEAD are useful for seeing the previous and next values. The following example uses LAG to find the days between deep space launches of a family of rockets. The query also includes a running total of launches per rocket family:

```
--Deep space launches with analytic functions per family.
select
    to_char(launch_date, 'YYYY-MM-DD') launch_date,
    flight_id2 spacecraft,
    lv_family_code family,
    trunc(launch_date) - lag(trunc(launch_date)) over
        (partition by lv_family_code
        order by launch_date) days_between,
    count(*) over
        (partition by lv_family_code
        order by launch_date) running_total
from launch
join launch_vehicle
    on launch.lv_id = launch_vehicle.lv_id
where launch_category = 'deep space'
order by launch.launch_date;
```

LAUNCH_DATE	SPACECRAFT	FAMILY	DAYS_BETWEEN	RUNNING_TOTAL
1959-01-02	Luna-1	R-7		1
1959-03-03	Pioneer 4	Jupiter		1
1959-09-12	Luna-2	R-7	253	2

...

In the preceding example, the analytic clause OVER (PARTITION BY LV_FAMILY_CODE ORDER BY LAUNCH_DATE) was specified twice. The duplication wasn't a big deal with this query, but real-life queries may have a more complicated analytic clause that may repeat many times. Since version 21c, we can avoid repeating ourselves by replacing each analytic clause with a simpler OVER MY_WINDOW and then defining that window after the WHERE clause like this: WINDOW MY_WINDOW AS (PARTITION BY LV_FAMILY_CODE ORDER BY LAUNCH_DATE).

Analytic functions can solve many advanced problems, and there's not enough space to list them all here. One interesting example is finding consecutive or non-consecutive patterns, sometimes called islands and gaps, using a technique named tabibitosan. The core of the technique is simple – convert each row to a number and then subtract the ROW_NUMBER from that number to generate a group ID. Fully demonstrating that technique would take several pages. If you're interested, there's an example in the repository that shows ranges of consecutive launches per launch family.

This section only touched on some of the uses of analytic functions. As always, I recommend you look at the manual if you need to learn more about this topic. We should use analytic functions whenever we're trying to calculate something where one row depends on other rows. However, even analytic functions are not powerful enough to help us with recursive relationships – when a row depends on a row, which depends on a row, etc. For those more difficult cases, see the later section in this chapter about recursive queries, or see the "MODEL" section in Chapter 19.

Regular Expressions

Regular expressions are powerful pattern-matching text strings that can be used to filter, validate, and change text data. Oracle SQL provides several ways to apply regular expressions to our queries.

All programmers should be familiar with regular expressions. For readers who are new to regular expressions, the beginning of this section provides a brief introduction. For readers who are experienced with regular expressions, this section ends with important warnings about overusing regular expressions.

Regular Expression Syntax

Oracle SQL allows regular expressions through the condition REGEXP_LIKE and the functions REGEXP_COUNT, REGEXP_INSTR, REGEXP_REPLACE, and REGEXP_SUBSTR. These features are similar to the features without the REGEXP_ prefix. For example, just like the normal REPLACE, REGEXP_REPLACE allows us to specify the position and the occurrence of the text to replace. The main difference between the two feature sets is that the REGEXP_ features expand the pattern searching from "_" and "%" to more powerful regular expressions.

The following list explains the most common regular expression options:

. – Matches any one character.

* – Matches zero or more occurrences.

+ – Matches one or more occurrences.

? – Matches zero or one occurrence.

| – An "or" operator.

^ – Matches the beginning of a string.

$ – Matches the end of a string.

[] – Creates a list of values to match. Can use hyphens to make a range, such as "a-z" or "0-9". Can use carats to mean "do not match this."

() – Creates a group of matched values.

\ – Do not interpret the next letter as a command, for example, if we want to match a period instead of using a period to mean "anything." If used with a number, it becomes a reference to a group.

Oracle also includes many Perl regular expression extensions, to match digits (\d), non-digits (\D), word characters (\w), non-word characters (\W), whitespaces (\s), non-whitespaces (\S), and many more.

Regular Expression Examples

Let's try to order the launch vehicles by their name and their version. But the names are confusing – sometimes they contain numbers, and other times they contain Roman numerals. To properly sort the names, we need to convert Roman numerals. That process is a lot of work for a sort order, so we'll only include with the first few steps. First, let's look at the popular Canadian sounding rocket Black Brant and find names that look like Roman numerals:

```
--Launch vehicle names with Roman numerals.
select lv_name
from launch_vehicle
```

```
where regexp_like(lv_name, '\W[IVX]+')
    and lv_name like 'Black Brant%'
order by lv_name;

LV_NAME
---------------
Black Brant I
Black Brant II
Black Brant IIB
Black Brant III

...
```

The key ingredient in the preceding query is the cryptic regular expression '\W[IVX]+'. That expression finds any rows where the vehicle name contains a nonword character followed by one or more of either "I," "V," or "X."

The next step is to convert the Roman numerals to numbers. To simplify things, we're going to cheat and just hard-code a few Roman numeral conversions. The important part of the following query is the way REGEXP_REPLACE is used to break the name into different pieces. After the name is broken apart, we can modify the Roman numeral portion and then put the pieces back together:

```
--Convert Roman numerals and re-assemble pieces into a name.
select
    part_1||part_2||
        --This hard-coding is clearly not the best way to do it.
        case part_3
        when 'I' then '01'
        when 'II' then '02'
        when 'III' then '03'
    end||
    part_4 new_lv_name
from
(
    --Launch vehicles with Roman numerals, broken into parts.
    select
        regexp_replace(lv_name, '(.*)(\W)([IVX]+)(.*)', '\1') part_1,
        regexp_replace(lv_name, '(.*)(\W)([IVX]+)(.*)', '\2') part_2,
```

```
    regexp_replace(lv_name, '(.*)(\W)([IVX]+)(.*)', '\3') part_3,
    regexp_replace(lv_name, '(.*)(\W)([IVX]+)(.*)', '\4') part_4
  from launch_vehicle
  where regexp_like(lv_name, '\W[IVX]+')
    and lv_name like 'Black Brant%'
  order by lv_name
);

NEW_LV_NAME
---------------
Black Brant 01
Black Brant 02
Black Brant 02B
Black Brant 03

...
```

The regular expression in the preceding WHERE clause is still simple and just finds the pattern. But the regular expression in the REGEXP_REPLACE has to find four different patterns – anything at the beginning, a non-word character, the Roman numeral, and anything at the end. The parentheses create four groups, and the backslash and number reference those groups. Each REGEXP_REPLACE replaces the entire string with just one of the four parts.

Regular expressions can solve many problems, and there are several patterns worth learning. The most popular example is how to use regular expressions to split a delimited string into different parts. To split by a delimiter, we first use the CONNECT BY row trick to generate extra rows. For each row, we match a group of characters that contain anything *other* than the delimiter, with an expression like '[^,]'. Finally, in the REGEXP_SUBSTR function, we choose the LEVEL occurrence of the match. The following query is small but uses a lot of features:

```
--Split a comma-separated string into its elements.
select regexp_substr(csv, '[^,]', 1, level) element
from
(
    select 'a,b,c' csv
    from dual
)
connect by level <= regexp_count(csv, ',') + 1;
```

```
ELEMENT
-------
a
b
c
```

Regular Expression Limitations

The cryptic syntax of regular expressions may make us feel like coding superheroes, but it's very easy to make a mess. When using regular expressions, we must take extra care to make our code readable. We must resist the urge to create one uber-expression, and instead we must break our code into small pieces.

The examples in this chapter are good examples of what *not* to do. The examples demonstrate the concepts of regular expressions, but we're not close to our goal of actually finding and replacing Roman numerals. If we look at all the different launch names, we'll notice that there are a huge number of exceptions to our simplistic rule. Converting these Roman numerals is one of those "90–10" tasks; we easily built a solution for 90% of the problem, but solving the remaining 10% will take 90% of our time.

These 90–10 tasks happen a lot when parsing text, and we have to know our limitations. Even for the seemingly simple task of splitting strings, there are many cases that might break our simple regular expressions – such as empty lists. The real solution to splitting strings is to not store delimited strings in the database in the first place.

Even tasks as seemingly simple as finding numbers can be unexpectedly difficult. Recreating the numeric literal syntax diagram discussed in Chapter 4 requires a surprisingly nasty regular expression. The Internet is full of half-baked answers that forget things like an initial negative sign. And forget about validating email addresses – the official regular expression to validate email addresses is over 6,000 characters long.

Finally, there are many tasks that are literally impossible to solve with one regular expression. Figure 7-2 shows a hierarchy of formal languages. Even though regular expressions are powerful tools, the regular languages they define are at the bottom of the hierarchy. Many languages, such as HTML, XML, and almost all programming languages, are context-free or higher. Regular expressions alone cannot fully parse HTML, XML, and programming languages. Regular expressions can easily find many patterns in complex languages, but finding simple patterns can give us a false sense of confidence. We must be careful not to try to use a regular expression for a task that requires a full language parser. We don't want to invest time in a regular expression that is 99% accurate but will never be 100% accurate.

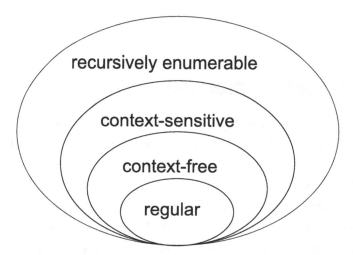

Figure 7-2. *"A graphical representation of the sets of languages included in the Chomsky hierarchy" by J. Finkelstein is licensed under CC BY-SA 3.0.*

Row Limiting

Sometimes we only want to retrieve a subset of the results from our SQL statements. When applications only display N rows at a time, our queries should only return N rows. Oracle's row limiting clause lets us specify exactly what subset of rows to return. Although the row limiting clause was introduced in 12c, there's still a lot of code that uses the old ROWNUM technique, so we need to understand it. And sometimes we need to limit rows with analytic functions, using ROW_NUMBER.

Row Limiting Clause

The row limiting clause lets us easily specify how many results to return from a query. We can choose either a number of rows or a percentage of rows. The number can be exact or can also return ties for the Nth number. We can also specify an offset, which can help with pagination. However, the row limiting clause cannot instantly retrieve rows from the middle of a result set and may lead to performance problems. For faster pagination it might be better to keep a cursor open and iterate through the results.

The rows returned by the row limiting clause will respect the order by clause, if there is one. Without the order by clause, the syntax will return the first N rows it finds. (Those rows will be neither deterministic nor truly random. Remember – we can never assume anything about the order of results unless we specify the order by clause.)

For example, let's find the first three satellites, based on their launch date:

```
--First 3 satellites.
select
   to_char(launch_date, 'YYYY-MM-DD') launch_date,
   official_name
from satellite
join launch
   on satellite.launch_id = launch.launch_id
order by launch_date, official_name
fetch first 3 rows only;
```

```
LAUNCH_DATE   OFFICIAL_NAME
-----------   -------------
1957-10-04    1-y ISZ
1957-10-04    8K71A M1-10
1957-11-03    2-y ISZ
```

The official names are cryptic, but you know those satellites. If you're old enough, you may have literally seen those satellites in the sky. The first two rows are Sputnik 1 and its rocket, and the third row is Sputnik 2.

ROWNUM

In 11g and lower, the syntax for row limiting was a bit trickier. Even if we're only using version 12c and above, we should still be familiar with the old techniques, because we will inevitably inherit old code.

The traditional way to get the top N rows is with the ROWNUM pseudo-column and an inline view. ROWNUM returns a number that represents the order the row was returned from the query, starting with 1. There's a common mistake that everyone makes with ROWNUM; the ROWNUM pseudo-column cannot be filtered in the same subquery as the ORDER

BY. ROWNUM is generated *before* the order by clause. If we filter by ROWNUM in the same
subquery as the order by clause, the query will return a few random rows and then order
those random rows. The following query is the only correct way to use ROWNUM filtering:

```
--First 3 satellites.
select launch_date, official_name, rownum
from
(
    select
        to_char(launch_date, 'YYYY-MM-DD') launch_date,
        official_name
    from satellite
    join launch
        on satellite.launch_id = launch.launch_id
    order by launch_date, official_name
)
where rownum <= 3;


LAUNCH_DATE   OFFICIAL_NAME   ROWNUM
-----------   -------------   ------
1957-10-04    1-y ISZ              1
1957-10-04    8K71A M1-10         2
1957-11-03    2-y ISZ             3
```

Analytic Function Row Limiting

More complex row limiting requires the ROW_NUMBER analytic function. The partition by
clause in ROW_NUMBER allows us to get the top N rows for multiple groups. The following
example returns the first two satellites of each year:

```
--First 2 satellites of each year.
select launch_date, official_name
from
(
    select
        to_char(launch_date, 'YYYY-MM-DD') launch_date,
        official_name,
```

```
    row_number() over
    (
        partition by trunc(launch_date, 'year')
        order by launch_date
    ) first_n_per_year
  from satellite
  join launch
      on satellite.launch_id = launch.launch_id
  order by launch_date, official_name
)
where first_n_per_year <= 2
order by launch_date, official_name;

LAUNCH_DATE   OFFICIAL_NAME
-----------   -------------
1957-10-04    1-y ISZ
1957-10-04    8K71A M1-10
1958-02-01    Explorer 1
1958-03-17    Vanguard I
...
```

There's rarely a significant performance difference between FETCH, ROWNUM, and analytic functions, so we should use whichever approach feels more natural. If we do encounter performance problems, keep in mind that FETCH is internally implemented as an analytic function, so we shouldn't bother rewriting between those two styles. Although the ROWNUM technique is older, in this case older may be better, since Oracle has some optimizations that only work with ROWNUM.[3]

Pivoting and Unpivoting

Pivoting moves data from rows to columns, and unpivoting moves the columns back to rows. These features are useful when we want to summarize data for a report or want to load summarized report data into a table. There's a simple aggregation and UNION ALL

---

[3] See https://jonathanlewis.wordpress.com/2020/07/15/fetch-first-vs-rownum/ for more details.

trick to pivot and unpivot data. Oracle also provides a PIVOT and an UNPIVOT syntax that can help simplify code. We should know both the old and new techniques, since they are both still useful.

Pivoting combines rows of data into a single row with more columns. Our relational tables are often skinny, with just a few columns that list a type, a value, and a status. But our reports are often wide, with one type per row and a column with the values for each status. Figure 7-3 is a visual representation of the way pivoting and unpivoting change the shapes of the results.

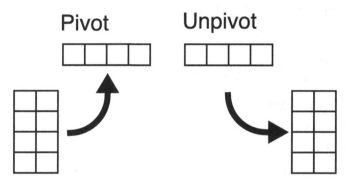

Figure 7-3. *Visual representation of pivot and unpivot*

Old Pivot Syntax

Let's start with a simple grouping example – the counts of launch statuses per year. The query returns skinny rows, with a different status for each row:

```
--Launch success and failure per year.
select
    to_char(launch_date, 'YYYY') launch_year,
    launch_status,
    count(*) status_count
from launch
where launch_category in ('orbital', 'deep space')
group by to_char(launch_date, 'YYYY'), launch_status
order by launch_year, launch_status desc;
```

```
LAUNCH_YEAR   LAUNCH_STATUS   STATUS_COUNT
-----------   -------------   ------------
1957               success               2
1957               failure               1
1958               success               8
...
```

The preceding results are in a good format for further processing. But if we want to display the results, we can fit more information in a single row. The following query pivots the results, using the old-fashioned aggregation technique:

```
--Pivoted launch successes and failures per year.
select
    to_char(launch_date, 'YYYY') launch_year,
    sum(case when launch_status = 'success' then 1 else 0 end) success,
    sum(case when launch_status = 'failure' then 1 else 0 end) failure
from launch
where launch_category in ('orbital', 'deep space')
group by to_char(launch_date, 'YYYY')
order by launch_year;
```

```
LAUNCH_YEAR   SUCCESS   FAILURE
-----------   -------   -------
1957                2         1
1958                8        20
1959               13        10
...
```

The preceding results show more information per row because the status value was pivoted into multiple columns. The pivoted columns make it much easier to compare data across years. If we look at all the data, we discover that 1958 was by far the worst year for launches, both in the number of failures and the percentage of failures. The large number of failures was not just because rocket technology was new. There was a push to cut corners and launch as soon as possible. That push was fueled by the cold war and the Sputnik crisis.

New Pivot Syntax

The following query returns the same results as the preceding query but uses the new PIVOT syntax. The pivot clause is given the aggregate function, the list of columns to pivot, and the values to include:

```
--Pivoted launch success and failure per year.
select *
from
(
    --Orbital and deep space launches.
    select to_char(launch_date, 'YYYY') launch_year, launch_status
    from launch
    where launch_category in ('orbital', 'deep space')
) launches
pivot
(
    count(*)
    for launch_status in
    (
        'success' as success,
        'failure' as failure
    )
)
order by launch_year;
```

For this small example, the new syntax is more complex and larger than the old-fashioned syntax. I always find the PIVOT syntax a bit weird, and I have to look it up every time I use it. The syntax doesn't help until we have a large number of columns to pivot. Even then, there is still a lot of manual typing – we still need to list each status, create an alias, and possibly deal with nulls. In most cases we might as well stick with the old SUM(CASE syntax.

UNPIVOT

Unpivoting turns multiple columns into multiple rows. As an example of why we might want to unpivot, let's look at the LAUNCH columns FLIGHT_ID1 and FLIGHT_ID2. Any time we have multiple columns with the same names, but a number at the end, we should be suspicious. Should those columns be stored in a separate table, to allow an unlimited number of flight identifiers? What happens if a rocket launch has a third flight identifier? Instead of having to add new columns, it might make sense to create a separate table to store flight identifiers. (In this case, the flight identifiers don't add much value, and it's not worth the trouble, but let's pretend for the sake of the example.) First, let's look at the initial, wide data:

```
--Multiple FLIGHT_ID columns per launch.
select launch_id, flight_id1, flight_id2
from launch
where launch_category in ('orbital', 'deep space')
order by launch_id;
```

```
LAUNCH_ID   FLIGHT_ID1   FLIGHT_ID2
---------   ----------   ----------
4305        M1-PS        PS-1
4306        M1-2PS       PS-2
4476        TV-3         Vanguard TV3
...
```

The old-fashioned way to convert the columns into skinny rows uses a UNION ALL for each column, shown as follows:

```
--Unpivot data using UNION ALL.
select launch_id, 1 flight_id, flight_id1 flight_name
from launch
where launch_category in ('orbital', 'deep space')
    and flight_id1 is not null
union all
select launch_id, 2 flight_id, flight_id2 flight_name
from launch
```

```
where launch_category in ('orbital', 'deep space')
    and flight_id2 is not null
order by launch_id, flight_id;

LAUNCH_ID   FLIGHT_ID   FLIGHT_NAME
---------   ---------   -----------
     4305           1   M1-PS
     4305           2   PS-1
     4306           1   M1-2PS
     4306           2   PS-2
     4476           1   TV-3
     4476           2   Vanguard TV3
...
```

The following query uses the UNPIVOT syntax to return the same results:

```
--Unpivot data with UNPIVOT syntax.
select *
from
(
    select launch_id, flight_id1, flight_id2
    from launch
    where launch_category in ('orbital', 'deep space')
) launches
unpivot
(
    flight_name for
    flight_id in (flight_id1 as 1, flight_id2 as 2)
)
order by launch_id;
```

The preceding UNPIVOT query is much smaller than the original version and even runs faster, whereas the PIVOT syntax is hardly any better than the original version and usually isn't any faster. The poor syntax and performance of PIVOT are unfortunate, because in practice we're much more likely to pivot data than to unpivot data.

One of the most common Oracle SQL questions is: How can we dynamically pivot data, where we don't have to specify all the columns to display? The simple answer is there is no dynamic pivot option. A more thorough answer is Oracle does allow dynamic pivoting, but only if we ask for the output to be in XML, which is then harder to consume. An even more thorough answer is we *can* dynamically pivot if we create advanced dynamic SQL solutions, such as Method4 discussed in Chapter 20.

But the real, unsatisfying answer to the question about how to dynamically pivot is we don't want to dynamically pivot our queries. Overly generic and dynamic solutions are a huge pain for little gain. At some point we have to know our columns, or we can't do any meaningful work with our data.

Table References

There are many sources of relational data in Oracle. We can select from tables, views, materialized views, inline views, table functions, synonyms, remote objects, clusters, and others. Selecting from a table sounds like the easy, boring option. But Oracle SQL provides a surprising number of different ways to get data from a table. Table data can be selected point in time with a flashback query, as a sample, or as specific partitions.

Flashback

A flashback query lets us query data the way it used to look. Flashback can be a literal job saver when we have logical table corruption. Having a time machine for our tables can help us quickly back out incorrect changes. Imagine if someone had deleted rows from the LAUNCH table 9 minutes ago. We can look back in time and find the table as of 10 minutes ago with this query:

```
--LAUNCH table as it looked 10 minutes ago.
select *
from launch as of timestamp systimestamp - interval '10' minute;
```

Whenever someone makes a bad change, try to find the change with a flashback query. But don't wait – the clock is ticking. Flashback queries use Oracle undo data, and that data ages out. There may be a magic fix to our production data issue, but that fix is going to expire. It's difficult to predict how long the undo data will be available, since the retention period depends on instance parameters and system activity.

Flashback has a VERSIONS BETWEEN syntax and multiple pseudo-columns that can help us find exactly what change was made and when. We can combine flashback with set operators like MINUS to find missing data.

In addition to querying data, flashback can also be used to restore tables and entire databases. Those features share the name "flashback" but work with different storage mechanisms – the recycle bin and flashback logs. Speak to your DBA if you need to do frequent time traveling.

Sample

Querying a small sample of data can help with testing, especially with large tables. The sample clause lets us specify an estimated percentage of table data to retrieve. By default, the sampling is random and will return a slightly different result most times. If we want a deterministic sample, we can specify a seed number. The following queries return approximately 1% of the rows from the LAUNCH table:

```
--Sample query that returns a different number each time.
select count(*) from launch sample (1);

--Sample query that returns the same number each time.
select count(*) from launch sample (1) seed (1234);
```

The sample clause does not return results that are statistically random. And if the sample size is small enough, there is a chance the query will return zero rows. If we need to be precise with our randomness, we need to avoid SAMPLE and use ORDER BY DBMS_RANDOM.VALUE instead. Unfortunately, the DBMS_RANDOM approach is ridiculously slow.

Partition Extension Clause

The partition extension clause lets us choose data from a specific set of partitions or subpartitions. (Partitioning is briefly described in Chapter 9.) The partitions can be referenced either by partition name or by the partition key value. For example, the following queries read from a partitioned table. (Since we don't all have a license for partitioning, the example uses an existing system table instead of creating our own partitioned table.)

```
--Reference partition name.
select *
from sys.wrh$_sqlstat partition (wrh$_sqlstat_mxdb_mxsn);
```

```
--Reference partition key values.
select *
from sys.wrh$_sqlstat partition for (1,1);
```

Normally the partition extension clause is not necessary, since partitioning is meant to be invisible to the end user. We should be able to query a table, ask for a value, and let Oracle automatically determine the partitions. In practice, Oracle partition pruning can't always figure out the partitions at compile time. For example, if we're doing operations that lock partitions, like direct-path writes, Oracle may have to lock the entire table, unless we use the partition extension clause.

Common Table Expressions

Common table expressions allow us to replace repetitive SQL logic with a single subquery, function, or procedure. Common table expressions are defined at the top of the SQL statement and can be referenced many times below. In Oracle, this feature is also called subquery factoring and the grammatically awkward "WITH clause." Common table expressions can help us simplify our queries, improve performance, solve tricky recursive problems, and follow one of the cardinal rules of programming: don't repeat yourself. But we also need to be careful to not overuse this feature.

Example

Let's combine several advanced features to answer a frequently asked question: What changed? By combining flashback queries (to get old data), set operators (to find differences and combine results), and common table expressions (to avoid repeating ourselves), we can find the precise changes made to a table.

Before we create the large query, let's run some code to set up a test. Run the following statements to make two pseudorandom changes to the table ENGINE_ PROPELLANT. This code removes one row and switches one value from "fuel" to "oxidizer" or vice versa:

```
--Delete and update a row from a not-so-important table.
delete from engine_propellant where rownum <= 1;

update engine_propellant
set oxidizer_or_fuel =
```

```
case when oxidizer_or_fuel = 'fuel' then 'oxidizer' else 'fuel' end
where rownum <= 1;
```

For the next 5 minutes, the following query will show all the changes made by the preceding statements. This query is a bit complicated for an example, but this pattern of finding differences through set operators and common table expressions is worth learning. I build a query similar to the following at least once a month:

```
--Changes made to ENGINE_PROPELLANT in past 5 minutes.
with old as
(
    --Table as of 5 minutes ago.
    select *
    from engine_propellant
    as of timestamp systimestamp - interval '5' minute
),
new as
(
    --Table right now.
    select *
    from engine_propellant
)
--Both row differences put together.
select *
from
(
    --Rows in old table that aren't in new.
    select 'old' old_or_new, old.* from old
    minus
    select 'old' old_or_new, new.* from new
)
union all
(
    --Rows in new table that aren't in old.
    select 'new' old_or_new, new.* from new
    minus
```

```
    select 'new' old_or_new, old.* from old
)
order by 2, 3, 1 desc;

OLD_OR_NEW  ENGINE_ID  PROPELLANT_ID  OXIDIZER_OR_FUEL
----------  ---------  -------------  ----------------
old                 2            100  fuel
new                 2            100  oxidizer
old                62              1  fuel

--Don't forget to rollback the changes:
rollback;
```

The results show the row that was changed – it has a value for both "old" and "new," and the OXIDIZER_OR_FUEL column changed. The results also show the row that was deleted – the last row that is listed in "old" but not in "new." The common table expressions are like macros for our SQL statement, and they help us avoid having to repeat the "as of 5 minutes ago" logic. We could have used a view instead, but then we would have had to create and maintain separate objects just for one query.

PL/SQL Common Table Expressions

Functions and procedures in the WITH clause allow us to add imperative code to our queries. This feature can help minimize the objects in our schema, and it can help if our database user does not have the privileges to create objects.

Let's use a PL/SQL declaration to solve another common business problem: finding numeric values in text fields. As discussed in Chapter 4, determining if a string is a number is more complicated than most programmers appreciate. Using a regular expression is a bad idea because we'll forget to check for things like negative signs, decimals, etc. The following code looks for numeric values in FLIGHT_ID1:

```
--Launches with a numeric FLIGHT_ID1.
with function is_number(p_string in varchar2) return varchar2 is
    v_number number;
begin
    v_number := to_number(p_string);
    return 'Y';
```

```
exception
   when value_error then return 'N';
end;
select
   to_char(launch_date, 'YYYY-MM-DD') launch_date,
   flight_id1
from launch
where flight_id1 is not null
   and is_number(flight_id1) = 'Y'
order by 1,2;
/

LAUNCH_DATE   FLIGHT_ID1
-----------   ----------
1942-06-13    2
1942-08-16    3
1942-10-03    4
...
```

(There's actually a simpler way to write the preceding query, by using a type-safe conversion mode available in many built-in functions: TO_NUMBER(FLIGHT_ID1 DEFAULT NULL ON CONVERSION ERROR) IS NOT NULL. In a real query, a useful PL/SQL declaration would be more complicated.)

The PL/SQL WITH syntax is a bit strange, and many IDEs have problems parsing it. Even SQL*Plus treats the preceding statement a bit differently than normal SELECT statements, which is why there's a slash at the end of the preceding code.

Performance and Overuse

Common table expressions can help improve performance in some cases. If the common table expression is referenced two or more times, Oracle may materialize the results by storing them in a temporary table. Materializing can reduce the number of times the tables are read. Oracle automatically decides whether it's worth transforming intermediate results into a temporary table, but we can force the decision with the hint /*+MATERIALIZE*/. Also, the PL/SQL WITH clause is tightly integrated with SQL and can run faster than regular functions and procedures.

But many SQL developers overuse common table expressions. The performance benefits of materializing results only directly help if the common table expression is called more than once. (However, materializing results forces Oracle to perform operations in a certain order, which may limit the ways the query can be transformed. It's possible that rewriting a query to use common table expressions will indirectly improve performance, but we shouldn't blindly rewrite queries and hope to get lucky.) And while it's nice to avoid the overhead of calling PL/SQL functions, we don't want to repeat ourselves and copy and paste business logic from a package into individual SQL statements. And if we need to reduce the overhead of PL/SQL functions, we can use PRAGMA UDF to get the same performance improvement. Also, if we're worrying too much about PL/SQL function overhead, it probably means we're not using enough SQL.

As discussed in Chapter 6, the top-down data flow of common table expressions is a bad thing. Common table expressions that are only used once increase the context of our SQL statements and make our statements harder to debug and understand.

Common table expressions are a great feature that can save a lot of code and improve performance, if used correctly. Additionally, common table expressions can refer to themselves. Recursive common table expressions are a powerful feature and are described in the next section.

Recursive Queries

When data references itself an unknown number of times, we must use recursive or hierarchical queries. If data only references itself a single time, for example, if we want to find the parent record, we can write that query with a self-join. Or if our row only needs to access the one row before it, we can write that query with the analytic function LAG. But when we want the parent's parent or the previous row's previous row or we want to generate something that looks like a tree, we need Oracle's recursive query syntax.

Oracle provides two ways to process hierarchical data: the original CONNECT BY syntax and the newer recursive common table expression syntax (also known as recursive subquery factoring). Newer syntax is usually the best option, but in this case the newer syntax is not always better. Both syntaxes have their advantages. The CONNECT BY syntax is the original syntax, is less wordy, and is more convenient for handling traditional hierarchical data. The recursive common table expression syntax is based on a standard, wordier than CONNECT BY, not as convenient for processing traditional hierarchical data, but more powerful and better suited to advanced queries. Each syntax seems to be a better fit for certain problems. If one style gives us trouble, with either the syntax or performance, we should try the other style.

CONNECT BY Syntax

In the original syntax, we start with a set and then use CONNECT BY conditions to define how the set joins to itself. Conditions in the CONNECT BY clause can use the special PRIOR operator, which lets us reference the value from the previous row of the set. Optional START WITH conditions let us pick the initial rows. Picking the initial rows is important because it prevent duplicates. If we're building trees of results from a flat table, we only want to start building trees from the root. If we build trees starting from the root, *and* starting from every other level, we'll end up with many subtrees.

The CONNECT BY syntax also provides useful pseudo-columns such as LEVEL. LEVEL is a number that tells us what level of the tree each row is on. CONNECT_BY_ROOT returns the value from the root row. SYS_CONNECT_BY_PATH walks the tree and creates a string aggregation of all the values. The ORDER SIBLINGS BY clause preserves the tree structure of the results.

For example, let's look at the ORGANIZATION table. That table is used frequently in the data set; there are organizations for the launch, satellite, stage, engine, and more. Each organization has a parent organization, which can have a parent organization, etc. If we wanted to count launches or satellites per organization, it might help to count by the top-level organization. First, we need to generate a hierarchy of organizations with this query:

```
--Organization hierarchy with CONNECT BY.
select
    lpad(' ', 2*(level-1)) || org_code org_code,
    parent_org_code parent,
    org_name
from organization
connect by prior org_code = parent_org_code
start with parent_org_code is null
order siblings by organization.org_code;
```

```
ORG_CODE    PARENT   ORG_NAME
---------   ------   --------
...
USAF                 United States Air Force
  ...
  HAFB      USAF     Holloman Air Force Base
    ...
    HADC    HAFB     Holloman Air Development Center
      HAM   HADC     Holloman Aeromedical Lab, Holloman ...
  ...
```

The preceding partial results show one of the many trees. Unsurprisingly, there are many organizations under the United States Air Force (USAF). The results are formatted like a tree, with the LPAD trick that multiplies the spaces by the LEVEL. The query starts with the root organizations at the top – the ones where PARENT_ORG_CODE IS NULL. The SIBLINGS in the order by clause ensures that the tree order is preserved. The CONNECT BY condition is the most difficult part of the query and requires some thought. Imagine we started with the USAF row and are trying to find the second row. To decide if each row is in the tree, we need to compare the current PARENT_ORG_CODE to the PRIOR ORG_CODE.

Don't feel bad if these recursive queries don't make sense yet. Recursive queries are notoriously complicated; it might take a few times before the recursion feels natural.

Recursive Common Table Expressions

Let's recreate the previous results with a recursive common table expression. In this syntax we define a table in the WITH clause, but this time we also need to predefine the column names. Inside the common table expression, there are two subqueries. The first subquery primes the pump by generating the initial rows. The second subquery generates parent or child rows by joining a table to the common table expression itself. Finally, the common table expression is queried to get the results:

```
--Organization hierarchy from recursive CTE.
with orgs(org_code, org_name, parent_org_code, n, hierarchy) as
(
    --Start with parent rows:
    select org_code, org_name, parent_org_code, 1, org_code
    from organization
```

```
    where parent_org_code is null
    union all
    --Add child rows by joining to parent rows:
    select
        organization.org_code,
        organization.org_name,
        organization.parent_org_code,
        n+1,
        hierarchy || '-' || organization.org_code
    from orgs parent_orgs
    join organization
        on parent_orgs.org_code = organization.parent_org_code
)
select
    lpad(' ', 2*(n-1)) || org_code org_code,
    parent_org_code parent,
    org_name
from orgs
order by hierarchy;
```

The preceding query returns the same results as the CONNECT BY version but uses more code to do the same thing. There's no convenient LEVEL or SIBLINGS syntax, so we have to create those ourselves. To recreate LEVEL, the "n" column starts with 1 and adds 1 after each join. And to order by siblings, we need to create a string to represent the whole tree and then order by that tree. The "hierarchy" column represents a tree by starting with the org code and appending a new org code at each level.

For simple examples, the CONNECT BY syntax is best. For complex examples, where we need more fine-grained control over how the statement recurses, the common table expression syntax is best.

No matter which syntax we use, recursive queries can get painfully difficult. Making sense of recursive queries requires creating an intricate mental model of a tree. When creating recursive queries, we must be careful to keep our inline views small and to thoroughly document everything.

XML

Oracle is a converged database that supports much more than just relational data. This book is about SQL development and focuses on relational data, but there are many times when the relational model needs to merge with semi-structured data stored as XML. There are whole manuals written about the subject, such as the *XML DB Developer's Guide.* This section only shows the basics, but keep in mind that Oracle is designed to handle vastly more complicated scenarios.

XMLType

Extensible Markup Language documents can be created, stored, and processed in Oracle. XML is semi-structured, not unstructured. We never want to allow invalid XML, so we don't want to just throw XML into a string field. XML data should be stored as an XMLType, which will automatically validate the structure. Converting text into an XMLType is trivial; just pass the text into the default constructor like this:

```
--Convert text to XML.
select xmltype('<a></a>') from dual;
```

The output of the preceding statement depends on our IDE. Not every program understands XMLType. Programs may display the result as a generic message or as a text string or perhaps in an XML editor. The text itself may look different. The results could be "<a></a>", "<a/>", or some other equivalent. Just like relational data has display properties that don't matter (such as row order), XML also has display properties that don't matter (such as tag style and insignificant whitespace).

Converting from an XMLType back to text is a little trickier. When using object types like XMLType, there must be an alias, a column name, and parentheses for function calls (even if there are no parameters). In the following code, ideally we would only need to use the expression XML_COLUMN.GETCLOBVAL. But the real code is a bit more complicated:

```
--Convert to XMLType and convert back to CLOB.
select table_reference.xml_column.getClobVal()
from
(
    select xmltype('<a></a>') xml_column
    from dual
) table_reference;
```

Just as we never want even a single byte of corrupt relational data, we never want a single corrupt XML. Always store XML as XMLType to prevent invalid data. Corruption in even one of our XML files may prevent us from processing *any* of our files. The following code shows an example of what happens when we try to load bad XML into XMLType:

```
select xmltype('<a></a') from dual;

ERROR:
ORA-31011: XML parsing failed
ORA-19202: Error occurred in XML processing
LPX-00007: unexpected end-of-file encountered
ORA-06512: at "SYS.XMLTYPE", line 310
ORA-06512: at line 1
```

Storing XML in XMLType columns also gives us more storage options. Oracle can store the XML internally in different, optimized formats. And we can also create XML indexes on properly typed XML data.

DBMS_XMLGEN and Creating XML

There are many ways to create XML, and the simplest technique is the function DMBS_XMLGEN.GETXML. That function accepts any SQL statement and returns the results as a single XML file. The results are a CLOB, but it's easy to convert that CLOB into an XMLType if necessary. Chapter 20 shows a few advanced tricks we can do with DBMS_XMLGEN. For our current example, let's convert some of our launch data into an XML file:

```
--Create XML file for launch data.
select dbms_xmlgen.getxml('
    select launch_id, launch_date, launch_category
    from launch
    where launch_tag = ''1957 ALP''
    ')
from dual;

<?xml version="1.0"?>
<ROWSET>
 <ROW>
```

```
  <LAUNCH_ID>4305</LAUNCH_ID>
  <LAUNCH_DATE>04-OCT-57</LAUNCH_DATE>
  <LAUNCH_CATEGORY>orbital</LAUNCH_CATEGORY>
 </ROW>
</ROWSET>
```

Oracle automatically adds an XML prologue (the version information at the top), creates a "ROWSET" element for all the results, creates a "ROW" element for each row, and creates one element for each column value. There may be issues with the type conversions. For example, the preceding LAUNCH_DATE format is terrible because my session was set to use a two-digit year format. It would be better to do the conversion ourselves in the SQL statement, like with an expression such as TO_CHAR(LAUNCH_DATE, 'YYYY-MM-DD') LAUNCH_DATE.

Oracle SQL has many other ways to create more precise XML statements. We can control the element names, attributes, and other features, using SQL functions such as XMLELEMENT, XMLATTRIBUTES, XMLAGG, and XMLFOREST. XML data can be modified with SQL functions like INSERTXML*, UPDATEXML, and DELETEXML.

Oracle also has multiple ways to read and process XML data. There are SQL functions like XMLQUERY and EXTRACTVALUE, PL/SQL packages like DBMS_XML*, and interfaces for other programming languages. Oracle's XML features change frequently, so we should reference the most recent versions of the manuals to ensure we're using the latest features and avoiding deprecated features.

XMLTABLE

The function XMLTABLE is the most convenient and powerful way to access XML stored in the database. XMLTABLE accepts at least three parameters: an XQuery string to find the relevant elements, the column that contains the XML, and a path for each column we want to project.

Mapping SQL and XML has a few quirks. SQL keywords are case insensitive, whereas XML is case sensitive. Many minor XML mistakes won't throw errors but will instead return null or no rows. But when everything is done correctly, we can quickly turn an XML file into relational data in a single statement.

For our example, we must first create XML data, which is easy in Oracle SQL. The following code converts the entire LAUNCH table into LAUNCH_XML:

```
--Create a single XML file for launch data.
create table launch_xml as
select xmltype(dbms_xmlgen.getxml('select * from launch')) xml
from dual;
```

The following is an XMLTABLE query that reads from LAUNCH_XML. This query counts the number of launches per launch category:

```
--Count launches per category using LAUNCH_XML table.
select launch_category, count(*)
from launch_xml
cross join xmltable(
    '/ROWSET/ROW'
    passing launch_xml.xml
    columns
        launch_id number path 'LAUNCH_ID',
        launch_category varchar2(31) path 'LAUNCH_CATEGORY'
)
group by launch_category
order by count(*) desc;

LAUNCH_CATEGORY     COUNT(*)
------------------  --------
suborbital rocket      48880
military missile       12641
orbital                 5483
...
```

The preceding results are normal relational data that can be read from like any other table or inline view. The results show why many of our sample queries filter by the launch category. Most of the launches in the space data set are for weather experiments and military tests. But the most interesting launches are the ones that go into space and try to stay there.

XML Programming Languages

Oracle XML features include several powerful languages. The XMLISVALID function can validate an XMLType against an XML schema. The XMLTRANSFORM function can apply XSLT (eXtensible Stylesheet Language Transformations) to XML. Those transformations can be used to convert XML into HTML, PDF, or other formats. The XQuery processing in XMLTABLE allows FLWOR expressions (for, let, where, order by, return). For example, we can use XQuery to create a simple row generator:

```
--XQuery FLWOR row generator.
select *
from xmltable
(
    'for $i in xs:integer($i) to xs:integer($j) return $i'
    passing 1 as "i", 3 as "j"
    columns val number path '.'
);

VAL
---
   1
   2
   3
```

I'm going to stop listing XML features before this chapter looks like alphabet soup. There's a huge range of SQL functionality that can help us generate, read, and process XML data. There are tools that can handle XML better than Oracle, but using the database's built-in functionality can reduce our program's dependencies and can improve performance by reducing the overhead of transferring large XML data.

JSON

Similar to XML, the converged Oracle database can generate, read, and process JSON data. Oracle's JSON support has grown significantly in recent years. If we're working with a lot of JSON data, we need to pay close attention to the precise version of our database and use the newest features listed in the *SQL Language Reference* and the *JSON Developer's Guide*.

JSON stands for JavaScript Object Notation. JSON is a file format built on top of two simple ideas: a collection of objects, each with a name and value, and arrays. For example, this is a valid JSON document that contains one string named "string" and an ordered array of two numbers named "array": {"string":"a", "array":[1,2]}.

Store JSON in the Database

The preceding example JSON file can be generated with the JSON_OBJECT function:

```
--Simple JSON example.
select json_object('string' value 'a', 'array' value json_array(1,2))
from dual;
```

Until 21c introduced the JSON data type, storing JSON data was slightly more complicated than storing XML. In older versions, JSON was stored in a string data type such as VARCHAR2 or CLOB. Columns were marked as being JSON files with a constraint, such as CONSTRAINT SOME_TABLE_CK CHECK (SOME_COLUMN IS JSON). For the next examples in this chapter, let's create a simple table to hold launches:

```
--Create a table to hold JSON launch data.
create table launch_json
(
    launch_id number,
    --19c and below - Use VARCHAR2 or CLOB datatype, and a constraint:
    json clob,
    constraint launch_json_ck check (json is json),
    --21c and above - Use JSON datatype:
    --json json,
    constraint launch_json_pk primary key(launch_id)
);
```

Like with storing XML, it is critical that we use the correct data types and constraints to enforce data integrity. A single invalid JSON file can break many queries. And using the correct data types and constraints allows us to build indexes on JSON files.

Create JSON Data

There is not a JSON equivalent of DBMS_XMLGEN.GETXML, but we can create JSON files with a combination of functions like JSON_OBJECT (to convert values into an object), JSON_ARRAY (to convert a list into an array of values), and JSON_ARRAYAGG (to combine a bunch of JSON objects into one object).

Before 19c, the syntax for building JSON was inconvenient and required explicitly listing each value. The following statement converts LAUNCH into LAUNCH_JSON, but for brevity the statement only includes a few columns:

```
--Populate LAUNCH_JSON with some of the LAUNCH data.
insert into launch_json
select
   launch_id,
   json_object
   (
      'launch_date' value to_char(launch_date, 'YYYY-MM-DD'),
      'flight_ids' value json_array(flight_id1, flight_id2)
   ) json
from launch
where launch_category in ('orbital', 'deep space');
commit;
```

The preceding JSON table is a bit different than the XML table created in the previous section. While the XML table stored everything in a single XML file, LAUNCH_JSON has one JSON string per row. We could have reversed it and stored one XML file per line and put everything in a single JSON string. Both techniques are valid, and which one we use depends on the data and how the data is accessed.

Since 19c, the improved JSON_OBJECT syntax greatly simplifies converting a row into a JSON file by allowing a wildcard or a simple list of columns. For example, the following query transforms each SATELLITE row into a JSON file:

```
--Convert each SATELLITE row into a JSON file.
select json_object(*) satellite_json
from satellite
order by satellite_id;
```

```
SATELLITE_JSON
----------------------------------------------------------------
{"SATELLITE_ID":1,"NORAD_ID":"000001","COSPAR":"57 Alpha 1",...}
{"SATELLITE_ID":2,"NORAD_ID":"000002","COSPAR":"57 Alpha 2",...}
{"SATELLITE_ID":3,"NORAD_ID":"000003","COSPAR":"57 Beta 1",...}
```

Since 19c, converting an entire table into a single JSON file is also easier. The following example creates a JSON file for satellite data by combining JSON_OBJECT and JSON_ARRAYAGG. JSON functions often return data as a VARCHAR2, so we may need to specify RETURNING CLOB to ensure the data will not exceed the byte limit. This example only includes the first three rows – not because Oracle SQL can't handle more rows, but because your IDE may not be able to handle displaying such a large document:

```
--Convert multiple SATELLITE rows into a single JSON file.
select json_arrayagg(json_object(*) returning clob) satellite_json
from satellite
where satellite_id <= 3;
```

```
SATELLITE_JSON
----------------------------------------------------------------
[{"SATELLITE_ID":1,"NORAD_ID":"000001","COSPAR":"57 Alpha 1",...}]
```

Query JSON

The JSON data we inserted into LAUNCH_JSON can be viewed as simple strings with the following query:

```
--View JSON data in LAUNCH_JSON.
select to_char(json) launch_data
from launch_json
order by launch_id;
```

```
LAUNCH_DATA
----------------------------------------------------------------
{"launch_date":"1957-10-04","flight_ids":["M1-PS","PS-1"]}
{"launch_date":"1957-11-03","flight_ids":["M1-2PS","PS-2"]}
{"launch_date":"1957-12-06","flight_ids":["TV-3","Vanguard TV3"]}
...
```

On 21c, the preceding query will return the error "ORA-00932: inconsistent datatypes: expected NUMBER got JSON," because the TO_CHAR function does not accept a JSON data type. Instead, we need to use the JSON_SERIALIZE function. Although JSON_ SERIALIZE has more functionality than TO_CHAR, the error demonstrates that the JSON data type is not a drop-in replacement for storing JSON as a VARCHAR2 or a CLOB.

The preceding query shows us how JSON works, but the results aren't useful in SQL. The great part about JSON in SQL is that the columns are easily accessible with a few syntax extensions. Like with XML, to access the data, we must use a table alias. Then we add a dot, followed by the object name. For arrays, we can use square brackets and numbers, starting with 0:

```
--Simple JSON query on table LAUNCH_JSON.
select
    launch_id,
    substr(launch_json.json.launch_date, 1, 10) launch_date,
    launch_json.json.flight_ids[0] flight_id1,
    launch_json.json.flight_ids[1] flight_id2,
    launch_json.json.flight_ids[2] flight_id3
from launch_json launch_json
order by launch_date;


LAUNCH_ID   LAUNCH_DATE   FLIGHT_ID1   FLIGHT_ID2     FLIGHT_ID3
---------   -----------   ----------   ------------   ----------
4305        1957-10-04    M1-PS        PS-1
4306        1957-11-03    M1-2PS       PS-2
4476        1957-12-06    TV-3         Vanguard TV3
...
```

The preceding query generates relational data from JSON. Like with XML, there are a few quirks when mapping to SQL. For example, the preceding query references a third FLIGHT_ID, even though we cannot possibly have a third flight ID. That mistake demonstrates one of the pitfalls of semi-structured data – our queries can be wrong but will not generate a compilation error.

This section only covers the simplest ways to handle JSON. Oracle provides many other functions to process JSON, including JSON_DATAGUIDE and DBMS_JSON (a sort of data dictionary for JSON), JSON_MERGEPATCH and JSON_TRANSFORM (update a JSON

document), JSON_QUERY (retrieve fragments of a document), JSON_SCALAR and JSON_
VALUE (retrieve a value as a JSON scalar or a SQL scalar), and JSON_TABLE (creating a
relational view of JSON, similar to XMLTABLE).

For those of us stuck with versions of Oracle lower than 12.1, the most popular
choice for working with JSON is the open source project PL/JSON. Even for the newer
versions of Oracle, if we need advanced JSON functionality, it might be worth looking
into that program, although PL/JSON is more resource intensive than the native features.

We don't want to overuse XML and JSON. Theoretically we could store our entire
database in a single XML or JSON value, but then why are we using a database? The
extra dynamic abilities of semi-structured data are tempting, but there must be a model
somewhere. To query files, they must have some type of dependable structure, or else
the files are useless. Even though Oracle can make XML and JSON look like a table, the
mapping isn't perfect. Querying XML and JSON is not nearly as convenient as querying
relational data. Despite all the features built into Oracle, the best way to load XML and
JSON into the database is probably to convert the files to rows and columns.

National Language Support

Internationalization and localization are complicated. Oracle's National Language
Support architecture lets us store, process, and display information for any language
and locale. Even if we're only storing simple English text, we still need to be aware of
character sets, length semantics, NLS comparing and sorting, and display formats. These
topics apply to all programmers, no matter how much we try to wish them away.

Character Sets

Oracle has great character set support but also has horrible character set defaults.
If possible, our databases should always use UTF8, instead of old character sets like
US7ASCII, WE8ISO8859P1, WE8MSWIN1252, etc. Oracle has officially recommended
UTF8 for a long time but inexplicably didn't default to UTF8 until version 12.2.

A lot has been written about character set differences, but the trade-off boils down to
this: UTF8 supports every character but may be slightly larger. Unless we have specific,
objective reasons to not use UTF8, it would be foolish to pick something else. I've seen
many problems caused by using old character sets, and I've seen many weird bugs

caused by databases that were later converted to UTF8. We need to choose the correct character set from the start of our project. The examples in this section won't work correctly if our database does not use UTF8.

There are Unicode data types NVARCHAR2, NCLOB, NCHAR, and N' ' text literals. These types exist in case we are using an old character set but need to support a few columns of Unicode data. These data types use UTF16 or UCS2 – these are slightly different from, but compatible with, UTF8. Ideally, we should never need to use the "N" data types.

When dealing with character set issues, the Oracle functions DUMP and UNISTR come in handy. DUMP displays the internal representation of data, as discussed in Chapter 3. UNISTR lets us create Unicode characters even if our database client doesn't support Unicode. Most IDEs support UTF8, but don't forget that our installation scripts might be run by a misconfigured SQL*Plus client.

If we're worried our source code files may get corrupted, the safest way to store non-ASCII data is with the UNISTR function. For example, the column LAUNCH.ORG_UTF8_NAME contains many non-ASCII characters. Loading the UTF8 data would be safer if the strings were defined like this:

```
--Store unicode characters in a text file of any encoding.
select unistr('A\00e9ro-Club de France') org_utf8_name
from dual;

ORG_UTF8_NAME
-------------------
Aéro-Club de France
```

Notice the "é" in the preceding output. In practice, the UNISTR syntax is too cumbersome to use frequently. The function is only helpful when we have text that is almost entirely ASCII with just a few exceptions.

Length Semantics

How we count the length of strings has important consequences. Oracle defaults to byte length semantics, where string size is measured by the number of bytes. Sometimes we need to change to character length semantics, where string size is counted by the number of characters. When we use varying-width character sets, like UTF8, we need to remember that X bytes does not always equal X characters.

The following code demonstrates the importance of character length semantics. If we create a table with a column of the type VARCHAR2(1), that column can only store 1 byte of data. When we try to insert one multi-byte character, the example raises the exception "ORA-12899: value too large for column "SCHEMA". "BYTE_SEMANTICS_TEST". "A" (actual: 2, maximum: 1)". That error happens because the character being inserted is the non-ASCII "é" that doesn't fit in 1 byte in UTF8. (But if we're using an extended-ASCII character set, the following code might work because the character may fit in 1 byte.)

```
--Byte length semantics causes an error.
create table byte_semantics_test(a varchar2(1));
insert into byte_semantics_test values('é');
```

If we add the keyword CHAR after the number in the data type definition, Oracle uses character length semantics instead. Now the column will fit one character, regardless of how many bytes that character uses:

```
--Character length semantics works correctly.
create table character_semantics_test(a varchar2(1 char));
insert into character_semantics_test values('é');
```

Even if we think our database only contains ASCII characters, chances are good our database will eventually contain word processing markup characters. For example, the Microsoft smart quote might look like a regular quote but may use 2 bytes instead of 1.

NLS Comparing and Sorting

Text comparisons and sorting are done by binary values by default. Binary sorting means that two strings are only considered equal if they have the same internal representation. And characters are ordered based on their numeric values in the character set. Binary sorting is why uppercase characters show up before lowercase characters; "A" is number 65 in ASCII, and "a" is number 97 in ASCII. (The first 127 ASCII characters work the same way in UTF8.)

The parameters NLS_COMP and NLS_SORT enable us to change the comparison and sorting behavior to be more linguistically meaningful. We can compare and sort values regardless of case or accents or according to the rules of a specific language. (But beware of huge performance penalties for using non-binary sorting and comparisons. Indexes built on binary comparisons cannot be used for linguistic comparisons and vice versa.)

For example, let's find the French aviation club founded by Jules Verne in 1898. The "Aéro-Club de France" is in the space data set because that organization was involved with launching Sputnik 41. Let's find the organization without having to type the accented character:

```
--Use accent-independent linguistic comparison and sorting.
alter session set nls_comp=linguistic;
alter session set nls_sort=binary_ai;

select org_utf8_name
from organization
where org_utf8_name like 'Aero-Club de France%';

ORG_UTF8_NAME
-------------
Aéro-Club de France
```

The NLS_COMP and NLS_SORT parameters can be set per system, session, schema, table, column, or statement. As with all parameters, we only want to set them at the smallest possible level. For example, don't change the NLS settings for the entire system if you only need them for a specific statement.

NLS capabilities are also available through the NLS_* functions. When we don't want to change parameters, we can call an NLS function precisely when needed. For example, most of the space data set works fine with binary sorting and comparisons. But if we're using the internationalized names for sorting, by default the order may not make sense. We might expect "Aéro-Club de France" to show up next to other organizations with names like "Aero." But by default, that string shows up somewhere else:

```
--Regular sort.
--(Reset session sort to the default.)
alter session set nls_sort=binary;

select org_utf8_name
from organization
order by org_utf8_name;
```

```
ORG_UTF8_NAME
-------------
...
Aeritalia Sistemi Spaziali (Torino)
AeroAstro, Inc
...
```

The NLSSORT function with BINARY_AI sorting displays "Aéro-Club de France" in the right place:

```
--Accent independent sort.
select org_utf8_name
from organization
order by nlssort(org_utf8_name, 'nls_sort=binary_ai');
```

```
ORG_UTF8_NAME
-------------
...
Aeritalia Sistemi Spaziali (Torino)
Aéro-Club de France
AeroAstro, Inc
...
```

Display Formats

NLS functionality is also important for displaying data. There are a dozen parameters that control the format of dates, timestamps, money, error messages, and numbers. The most popular and abused parameter is NLS_DATE_FORMAT. Like with almost all parameters, there is a hierarchy of ways that NLS_DATE_FORMAT can be applied. That parameter can be set per database, per session, or per function call. We should never assume a specific value of NLS_DATE_FORMAT at the database level. Many tools and programs automatically change the session settings and override the database settings.

NLS_DATE_FORMAT and similar parameters are only for ad hoc display formatting. Never rely on an implicit date format for processing. The following code, looking for the first satellite launch on October 4, 1957, is dangerous. Depending on our IDE's settings, the code may fail with the error "ORA-01858: a non-numeric character was found where a numeric was expected":

```
--Dangerous NLS_DATE_FORMAT assumption.
select *
from launch
where trunc(launch_date) = '04-Oct-1957';
```

The following code uses an explicit date format conversion with the TO_CHAR function. It is much safer than the previous code. But even this version has problems; "Oct" is not always the correct abbreviation for "October." But using an explicit date format in our programs is still much safer than an implicit date format. Chapter 15 explains how to make this code completely safe with date literals:

```
--Somewhat safe date format conversion.
select *
from launch
where to_char(launch_date, 'DD-Mon-YYYY') = '04-Oct-1957';
```

Summary

This chapter briefly introduced many advanced SELECT features. Each topic could easily fill an entire chapter, and some of them could fill an entire book. Don't expect to remember the syntax details. It's more important we remember the features and patterns and when to use them. SQL is easy to learn but hard to master.

This is the longest and most code-intensive chapter. Selecting data is the most important part of database operations. But ultimately, we need to create and change data. The next chapter discusses advanced features for modifying our data.

CHAPTER 8

Modify Data with Advanced DML

Now that we learned how to write advanced SQL statements to retrieve data, it is time to learn how to write advanced SQL statements to change data. Oracle Data Manipulation Language (DML) lets us insert, update, and delete data.[1]

Oracle provides four main statements for changing data: INSERT, UPDATE, DELETE, and MERGE. Each of these statements has advanced options specific to that command. There are also advanced features relevant to all DML statements: updatable views, hints, error logging, and the returning clause. Some additional commands are not technically DML statements but are used to help us change data: TRUNCATE, COMMIT, ROLLBACK, SAVEPOINT, ALTER SYSTEM, ALTER SESSION, and others. Using and modifying data not stored in Oracle is challenging, and Oracle has many different options for file input and output. Finally, although PL/SQL is mostly outside the scope of this book, there are PL/SQL packages we need to use to manage our data.

This chapter, like all chapters, assumes you are already familiar with basic SQL concepts. Each section is going to jump right into an advanced feature. To save space, the examples directly modify tables in the data set. Remember to roll back the changes when you're done with each example.

---

[1] Arguably, a SELECT statement is also a DML statement, especially a SELECT FOR UPDATE that locks rows. SELECT doesn't permanently change tables, but it does manipulate data. In practice, developers treat SELECT different than other statements, so when this book says "DML," it does not include a SELECT statement.

© Jon Heller 2023
J. Heller, *Pro Oracle SQL Development*, https://doi.org/10.1007/978-1-4842-8867-2_8

INSERT

The INSERT ALL syntax was intended to add data to multiple tables in one statement. The feature supports conditional logic, where we read from a large source table and use WHEN-THEN-ELSE logic to decide which rows go to which destination table. But in practice the syntax is most commonly used to generate data and insert multiple rows into the same table.

For example, let's say we want to load new fuels into the PROPELLANT table. There are several ways to generate data, and previous chapters already demonstrated the UNION ALL trick. The following code demonstrates the INSERT ALL trick:

```
--Generate new PROPELLANT rows.
insert all
into propellant values (-1, 'antimatter')
into propellant values (-2, 'dilithium crystals')
select * from dual;
```

Note how the preceding INSERT ALL does not use sequences but instead hard-codes the primary keys. Hard-coding is necessary, because INSERT ALL only increments the sequence once per statement, not once per row.

There's a debatable style choice with the INSERT ALL statement – the preceding code doesn't list all the column names. Normally, an INSERT should explicitly list the column names, to make it clear what values are being set. And listing the column names ensures the values go in the right place, even in the unlikely situation where the column order changes. On the other hand, we don't want to repeat ourselves and list the column names multiple times.

The INSERT ALL trick is neat, but the UNION ALL trick is better for generating data. The INSERT ALL statement is slower to parse than UNION ALL, especially for large statements with hundreds of rows.

If our applications are generating lots of data, an INSERT ALL is much better than multiple INSERT statements. But an INSERT ALL is not as good as using the application's batching API. Don't get carried away with INSERT ALL. It's a neat trick, but it's not meant for generating enormous amounts of data.

UPDATE

There are not a lot of exciting features specific to UPDATE statements. Most of the advanced features and side effects of UPDATE also apply to other DML commands and will be discussed in later sections. But there are a few UPDATE topics worth discussing.

UPDATE always performs the same amount of work regardless of whether the values change. Updating a column to itself is just as expensive as updating the column to a new value. For example, the following statement doesn't change anything, but the statement still generates REDO, UNDO, and row locks. (REDO and UNDO are discussed in Chapter 10.)

```
--Updating a value to itself still uses a lot of resources.
update launch set launch_date = launch_date;
```

Avoid UPDATE statements that reference the same table twice. We can rewrite those UPDATE statements to make them faster and simpler. For example, let's pretend there is a mistake in our data set and fix the mistake with an UPDATE statement. (Remember to always roll back the changes in this chapter.) Launches and satellites have many names and identifiers, and there's a lot of overlap between them. For example, one of the Pioneer missions has a LAUNCH.FLIGHT_ID2 set to "Pioneer 5," but the SATELLITE. OFFICIAL_NAME is set to "Pioneer V." Just for the sake of this example, let's pretend the data is wrong and we need to fix the satellite data for deep space missions. Our first instinct might be to write the following UPDATE statement:

```
--Update SATELLITE.OFFICIAL_NAME to LAUNCH.FLIGHT_ID2.
update satellite
set satellite.official_name =
(
    select launch.flight_id2
    from launch
    where launch.launch_id = satellite.launch_id
)
where satellite.launch_id in
(
    select launch.launch_id
    from launch
    where launch.launch_category = 'deep space'
);
```

The preceding UPDATE statement has issues. The first part of the SQL statement includes a correlated subquery, which increases the context and makes the SQL harder to debug. The second subquery reads from the LAUNCH table again, but in a different way.

There are two ways to rewrite the preceding UPDATE statement. We can change the UPDATE to use an updatable view, or we can change the UPDATE into a MERGE statement. The MERGE statement is the better choice, and both options are discussed in later sections.

DELETE

Similar to UPDATE, DELETE statements also don't have many unique advanced features. But DELETE statements have issues with relationships, locking, and space. We need to be careful when deleting, and not just because of the obvious problem of losing the wrong data.

When we delete from a table, we need to think about that table and all of its relationships. If there's a parent–child relationship, we can't simply delete from the parent table. Trying to delete a parent row that is referenced by a child row will usually raise an exception like this:

```
SQL> delete from launch;
delete from launch
       *
ERROR at line 1:
ORA-02292: integrity constraint (SPACE.LAUNCH_AGENCY_LAUNCH_FK) violated -
child record found
```

There are four ways to delete parent–child data: deleting in a specific order, deferrable constraints, cascading deletes, and triggers.

Deleting parent–child data in a specific order is usually the simplest and best way. It's normally easy to know which table comes first. If we're lucky, the constraint name in the error message gives us a good clue where to look. In the preceding example, the constraint is LAUNCH_AGENCY_LAUNCH_FK, which refers to the LAUNCH_AGENCY table. Prior to Oracle version 12.2, when Oracle names were limited to 30 bytes, we couldn't always give our constraints obvious names, since there wasn't always enough space to list both tables. If we're stuck with cryptic names, we can look up the constraint in DBA_CONSTRAINTS.

Finding the correct deletion order for a deeply nested table structure can be annoying. But that annoyance is a speed bump that may prevent bad deletions. If we have a giant tree of tables, do we really want to make it easy for someone to delete from all of the tables at once? If so, the safest solution is to find the correct order and put the DELETE statements in a stored procedure. To generate the code for that stored procedure, we can write a recursive query using the data dictionary view ALL_CONSTRAINTS. Using a stored procedure has the advantage of ensuring everyone deletes data in the same order, thus preventing deadlocks.

Deferrable constraints let us temporarily violate the rules of our relational database. With deferred constraints we can delete data in any order, as long as everything is correct before the next COMMIT. But we shouldn't blindly use deferred constraints all the time, since deferred constraints can cause performance issues. Deferred constraints use regular indexes, never unique indexes. Deferred constraints cause a temporary relaxing of metadata rules. Those relaxed metadata rules can no longer be used by the Oracle optimizer to pick better execution plans.

Cascading deletes let the system automatically delete child rows when the parent row is changed. As previously discussed, we may not always want to make it easy to delete large amounts of data. Personally, I always try to avoid dangerous side effects, especially when deleting data. A fear of side effects is also why we should try to avoid using triggers to solve our DELETE problems.

When our DELETE statements are successful on parent tables, we need to be careful to avoid locking problems. Every time a parent row is deleted, Oracle checks child tables for references to that value. If the foreign key columns in the child table do not have indexes, those lookups will be slow – so slow that Oracle will lock the entire child table instead of just locking the deleted rows. That escalated locking is why we want to create indexes on all foreign key columns. On the other hand, there are many relationships where we will never realistically delete parent rows, and those indexes aren't needed. And the lock escalation isn't quite as bad as it might sound at first. Table locks are bad, but a foreign key table lock only lasts for the duration of the statement, not the duration of the transaction.

When we delete data, that data isn't scrubbed from the file system. DELETE statements generate a lot of REDO and UNDO, but the actual data files don't initially change much. The deleted rows in the data files are just marked as being available for new rows and will get gradually overwritten with new data.

Keeping the space from deleted rows is usually a good thing. When we delete data from a table, there's a good chance new data will be inserted later. We don't want to release the space if we're just going to request more space again. On the other hand, there are times when we delete data and we're never going to put more data back in the table. In those cases, we want to reset the high-water mark and reclaim our space with a TRUNCATE statement. TRUNCATE is not technically DML, but it will be described in more detail in a later section.

Removing rows can be so expensive that we may want to architect our systems to avoid using DELETE for large data purges. Databases frequently contain tables with large amounts of historical data that are no longer needed after a certain amount of time. If we have licensed the partitioning option, we can partition those tables based on a date column that represents the age of each row and then periodically truncate or drop old partitions. Creating a maintenance job to clean up old partitions is more complex than a simple delete, but the job will consume few resources and will run instantly.

MERGE

The MERGE command lets us update or insert rows, depending on whether the rows already exist. Other databases name this command UPSERT, and occasionally Oracle will also use that name. For example, the command is named "UPSERT" in V$SQLCOMMAND. In addition to letting us combine inserts and updates, the MERGE command is also a simpler and faster way to perform complex updates.

The MERGE syntax may look confusing at first. But a few extra keywords are better than writing multiple INSERT and UPDATE statements and checking for the existence of a value. For example, the following code modifies the PLATFORM table with space elevator data. The MERGE statement adds the row if it doesn't exist or updates the row if it does exist.

A space elevator would let us travel to space by climbing a large cable. One end of the cable would be attached to Earth, and the other end would be attached to a counterweight in space. Space elevators are common in science fiction books, but space elevators aren't entirely science fiction as Japan has launched tiny, experimental space elevators:

```
--Merge space elevator into PLATFORM.
merge into platform
using
```

```
(
   --New row:
   select
      'ELEVATOR1' platform_code,
      'Shizuoka Space Elevator' platform_name
   from dual
) elevator
on (platform.platform_code = elevator.platform_code)
when not matched then
   insert(platform_code, platform_name)
   values(elevator.platform_code, elevator.platform_name)
when matched then update set
   platform_name = elevator.platform_name;
```

One minor syntax annoyance in the preceding code is the parentheses around the ON condition. Joins don't normally require parentheses, but the MERGE statement does require parentheses here.

If we ran the preceding code in SQL*Plus, we would see a feedback message like "1 row merged." Unfortunately, there is no way of telling whether that row was updated or inserted, which can complicate logging or making decisions based on the behavior of a MERGE.

The preceding MERGE statement has both an update and an insert section, but we don't always need to include both. Let's use MERGE to rewrite the UPDATE statement from the previous section. The following statement does the same thing – updates SATELLITE. OFFICIAL_NAME to LAUNCHES.FLIGHT_ID2, for deep space launches:

```
--Update SATELLITE.OFFICIAL_NAME to LAUNCH.FLIGHT_ID2.
merge into satellite
using
(
   select launch_id, flight_id2
   from launch
   where launch_category = 'deep space'
) launches
   on (satellite.launch_id = launches.launch_id)
when matched then update set
```

```
satellite.official_name = launches.flight_id2;
```

The preceding rewrite using MERGE is simpler and faster than the previous UPDATE statement. The new statement only references the LAUNCH table once. And the LAUNCH table is used in an inline view, making it easier to debug the input rows. Additionally, MERGE statements support more join methods than UPDATES. For example, a MERGE statement can use a hash join, but an UPDATE statement cannot.

MERGE isn't just for upserts. We should consider using MERGE for any complex UPDATE statement that either references the same table multiple times or changes a large number of rows.

Updatable Views

Updatable views let us insert, update, and delete rows from a query, instead of working directly on a table. The updatable view can be stored in a view object, or it can be a subquery. The updatable view can contain joins with multiple tables, but only one table can be modified at a time. There are several other important restrictions on updatable views.

For example, let's create yet another version of our SQL statement to set SATELLITE. OFFICIAL_NAME to LAUNCH.FLIGHT_ID2:

```
--Update SATELLITE.OFFICIAL_NAME to LAUNCH.FLIGHT_ID2.
update
(
    select satellite.official_name, launch.flight_id2
    from satellite
    join launch
        on satellite.launch_id = launch.launch_id
    where launch_category = 'deep space'
)
set official_name = flight_id2;
```

Of the three versions of this change, the preceding updatable view version is the smallest. Despite the feature working well in this example, updatable views should usually be avoided.

One of the main problems with updatable views is the large number of restrictions on the queries they can contain. The query or view must not contain DISTINCT, GROUP BY, certain expressions, etc. Queries using those features may raise the exception "ORA01732: data manipulation operation not legal on this view." Luckily, we don't have to examine or experiment with each view to find out what we can modify. The data dictionary view DBA_ UPDATABLE_COLUMNS tells us what operations are possible for each view column.

The updatable view query must unambiguously return each row of the modified table no more than one time. The query must be "key-preserved," which means Oracle must be able to use a primary key or unique constraint to ensure that each row is only modified once. Otherwise, the query will raise the exception "ORA-01779: cannot modify a column which maps to a non key-preserved table."

The UPDATE statement checks for possible ambiguities at compile time and raises exceptions if the statement could theoretically be ambiguous. Updatable views can fail at compile time even when they *would* work at run time.

The MERGE statement checks for possible ambiguities at run time and raises the exception "ORA-30926: unable to get a stable set of rows in the source tables." The MERGE statement is more powerful but also lets a few statements run that *shouldn't* work.

Demonstrating key-preserved tables is tricky and would require a lot of pages.[2] It's best to avoid updatable views completely. But if we're stuck on a system that only gives us views, and no direct access to tables, updatable views are our only option. If we must use a view, but the view can't meet all the key-preserved requirements, we can use INSTEAD OF triggers.

DML Hints

Hints are instructions that tell Oracle how to process a SQL statement. Hints are mostly used for performance and will be more thoroughly discussed in Chapter 18. This section only focuses on hints for DML statements. DML hints can affect more than just the execution plan of statements.

The first difficulty with hints is to understand that they're not really "hints." Hints are not merely recommendations that the database can randomly choose to ignore. Hints *will* be followed, if possible. When our hint is not followed, something has gone wrong, but it can be difficult to figure out why the hint didn't work.

---

[2] If you're interested in seeing an example of the problems key-preserved tries to avoid, look at my answer to this question: https://stackoverflow.com/questions/17092560/

Hints are formatted as comments with a plus sign. Hints can be single-line comments like `--+ APPEND` or multiline comments like `/*+ APPEND */`. Hints must be placed directly after the first keyword in the statement. For example, `INSERT /*+ APPEND */` is correct, but `INSERT INTO /*+ APPEND */` is incorrect. Incorrect hints silently fail instead of raising errors.

Hints are frequently abused. Some SQL developers will litter their statements with hints, trying to force the perfect execution plan and outsmart the optimizer. Hints used for DML are generally considered "good" hints because they are telling the optimizer something it can't figure out for itself. However, some of these "good" hints can affect recoverability and can be quite dangerous if they are misused. The most important DML hints are `IGNORE_ROW_ON_DUPKEY_INDEX`, `APPEND`, and `PARALLEL`.

The hint `IGNORE_ROW_ON_DUPKEY_INDEX` is useful when we're inserting data and want to ignore duplicates. This hint is a semantic hint – the hint changes the logical behavior of the SQL statement. For example, if we try to load duplicate data into a table, the statement will generate an error like this:

```
SQL> insert into propellant values(-1, 'Ammonia');
insert into propellant values(-1, 'Ammonia')
*
ERROR at line 1:
ORA-00001: unique constraint (SPACE.PROPELLANT_UQ) violated
```

The typical workaround to the preceding error is to check for the existence of a row before inserting it. But checking for rows requires extra code and extra run time. Instead, we can add the hint `IGNORE_ROW_ON_DUPKEY_INDEX`, and then the statement will simply ignore the duplicate rows:

```
SQL> insert /*+ignore_row_on_dupkey_index(propellant,propellant_uq)*/
  2  into propellant values(-1, 'Ammonia');
0 rows created.
```

The `APPEND` hint enables a direct-path `INSERT`. Direct-path inserts are an important topic and are discussed in Chapter 10 and elsewhere in this book. Here's the short version: direct-path `INSERT`s are good because they write directly to data files and are faster; direct-path `INSERT`s are bad because they exclusively lock objects and are not recoverable. That trade-off is what makes DML hints special – this is a decision the optimizer cannot make by itself. There's no painless hint for /*+ FAST=TRUE */. We must think carefully before we use potentially dangerous DML hints. We should only use the APPEND hint if we're OK with extra locking and potentially losing data.

The PARALLEL hint is tricky and has performance implications that are discussed in Chapter 18. The PARALLEL hint also has consequences for DML. The query part of a statement can run in parallel without us worrying too much about the consequences. But running the INSERT, UPDATE, or DELETE part of the statement in parallel uses direct-path mode, and we're back to the previously discussed trade-offs.

If we want both direct-path writes and parallel DML, then we should use both the APPEND and PARALLEL hints, like this: /*+ APPEND PARALLEL(... */. Parallel DML implicitly requests direct-path mode, but we should still list both hints separately. If the statement gets downgraded to serial, perhaps because all the parallel sessions are being used, then the PARALLEL hint alone will not enable direct-path mode. Downgraded statements are bad enough; we don't also want to lose direct-path mode. (On the other hand, there are times when we only want to parallelize the SELECT part of a statement, not the DML part.)

Parallel DML is disabled by default. That default may feel annoying in a large data warehouse, but that annoyance protects us from two important things: the lack of recoverability from direct-path mode and the expensive overhead of parallelism for small statements. Parallel processing sometimes happens automatically, but we never want direct-path mode to happen automatically. To request parallel DML, we must either use the hint /*+ ENABLE_PARALLEL_DML */ or run this statement in our session before any DML:

```
alter session enable parallel dml;
```

Error Logging

DML error logging lets us ignore errors and continue processing. The errors, along with the data causing those errors, are saved in an error logging table. Error logging is useful when we don't want a few bad values to stop the entire process.

For example, let's try to load new rows into the LAUNCH table, but use a value that is too large. By default, our query generates an error and stops processing:

```
SQL> --Insert into LAUNCH and generate error.
```

```
SQL> insert into launch(launch_id, launch_tag)
  2  values (-1, 'A value too large for this column');
values (-1, 'A value too large for this column')
            *
ERROR at line 2:
ORA-12899: value too large for column "SPACE"."LAUNCH"."LAUNCH_TAG"
(actual:33, maximum: 15)
```

Before we can use error logging, we must generate an error logging table. Oracle provides a PL/SQL package to create a table with the right format:

```
--Create error logging table.
begin
    dbms_errlog.create_error_log(dml_table_name => 'LAUNCH');
end;
/
```

The default error log name is the table name prefixed with "ERR$_", so the preceding statement creates a table named ERR$_LAUNCH. The error logging clause works with INSERT, UPDATE, DELETE, and MERGE. To use the error logging table, we must add the error logging clause to our statements. We want to include at least two different sections of the error logging clause – which table to use and the reject limit.

The default reject limit is 0, which means the statement will log the error but immediately stop processing. A more common value is UNLIMITED. The following example shows the same bad INSERT statement as before, but this time the statement completes and logs the error:

```
SQL> --Insert into LAUNCH and log errors.
SQL> insert into launch(launch_id, launch_tag)
  2  values (-1, 'A value too large for this column')
  3  log errors into err$_launch
  4  reject limit unlimited;
0 rows created.
```

The preceding INSERT didn't raise an error, but the SQL*Plus feedback message shows "0 rows created." That statement created a row in the ERR$_LAUNCH table, and that row will still be there even if the session is rolled back.

The ERR$_LAUNCH table contains several ORA_ERR_* columns with metadata, as well as all the LAUNCH table columns for the failed row. There is a lot of data in that error logging table, and the following query only returns the most useful columns:

```
--Error logging table.
select ora_err_number$, ora_err_mesg$, launch_tag
from err$_launch;
```

ORA_ERR_NUMBER$	ORA_ERR_MESG$	LAUNCH_TAG
12899	"ORA-12899: value too large..."	A value...

The preceding results are perfect for debugging because they also show the values we tried to use. Default SQL exceptions don't include the actual values that caused the errors.

Error logging is a useful feature when we have a job that absolutely must finish, regardless of errors. On the other hand, we don't want to overuse error logging to sweep all our bugs under the rug. Most problems are best handled the moment they happen, not later.

Returning

The returning clause lets us save columns from rows changed by DML statements. We don't always know the values that we changed or created, such as when we use a sequence. We may want to save those values for later processing.

The returning clause works best in a PL/SQL context, and PL/SQL is out of the scope of this book. But a little PL/SQL is necessary when discussing advanced SQL. The following anonymous block inserts a row into the LAUNCH table, returns the new LAUNCH_ID, and then displays the new value:

```
--Insert a new row and display the new ID for the row.
declare
    v_launch_id number;
begin
    insert into launch(launch_id, launch_category)
    values(-1234, 'deep space')
    returning launch_id into v_launch_id;
```

```
    dbms_output.put_line('New Launch ID: '||v_launch_id);
    rollback;
end;
/
```

The DBMS output from the preceding statement should be "New Launch ID: -1234." A more realistic example would use something like SEQUENCE_NAME.NEXTVAL instead of a hard-coded number.

The returning clause works with INSERT, UPDATE, and DELETE, but does not work with MERGE. The returning clause can return multiple columns into multiple variables and can also return multiple sets of values into collection variables. The collection variable example is only shown in the repository, since the example requires complex PL/SQL.

TRUNCATE

The TRUNCATE command is the fastest way to remove all the rows from a table. The command is officially Data Definition Language (DDL), instead of Data Manipulation Language (DML). In practice, TRUNCATE is used more like DML than DDL. TRUNCATE has many advantages compared with deleting all the rows from a table, but TRUNCATE also has significant disadvantages. Understanding the trade-offs requires understanding Oracle architecture, which is described in more detail in Chapter 10.

Deleting all the rows from a table is an expensive operation. When deleting a row, Oracle must first store the information in the REDO log (a write-ahead log, in case the database crashes and needs to be recovered) and then in the UNDO tablespace (in case the command is rolled back and all the changes need to be undone), and then the actual rows are changed. Deleting rows is much slower than inserting rows, whereas the TRUNCATE command runs almost instantly. Instead of changing individual rows, truncating the table simply removes the segment, which is the entire storage area for the table. A TRUNCATE command can finish in less than a second, regardless of the table size.

Another advantage of truncating instead of deleting is that truncating the table also releases the storage immediately. That space can then be used for other objects. A DELETE removes the rows, but the space used by those rows will only be available for the same table.

The main problem with TRUNCATE is that it automatically commits, even if the command fails, and there's no undoing it. A TRUNCATE cannot be rolled back, and we cannot use a flashback command on the table to view old data. TRUNCATE also requires an exclusive lock on a table, so we can't TRUNCATE a table if anyone else is modifying it (although if we're trying to TRUNCATE a table that someone else is modifying, something has gone horribly wrong).

The following test cases demonstrate a few properties of TRUNCATE. The test cases are also good examples of how to investigate Oracle's storage properties. These are the kind of tests all SQL developers must learn to create. These test cases help us prove how Oracle works, instead of merely guessing.

First, we need to create a table, load it, and measure it:

```
--Create a table and insert rows.
create table truncate_test(a varchar2(4000));

insert into truncate_test
select lpad('A', 4000, 'A') from dual
connect by level <= 10000;

--Segment size and object IDs.
select megabytes, object_id, data_object_id
from
(
    select bytes/1024/1024 megabytes
    from dba_segments
    where segment_name = 'TRUNCATE_TEST'
) segments
cross join
(
    select object_id, data_object_id
    from dba_objects
    where object_name = 'TRUNCATE_TEST'
) objects;


MEGABYTES  OBJECT_ID  DATA_OBJECT_ID
---------  ---------  --------------
       80     196832          196832
```

The results show the table uses 80 megabytes of space and has the same OBJECT_ID and DATA_OBJECT_ID. The size may be different on your system, because Oracle's segment space allocation and compression defaults vary depending on your settings and version. Your values for OBJECT_ID and DATA_OBJECT_ID will be different than mine, but notice that your two values are identical.

Let's TRUNCATE the table and check the segments and objects again. Notice that the following TRUNCATE command is commented out. You'll have to either remove the comment or highlight and run the command. This example is intentionally inconvenient – the TRUNCATE command is dangerous, and we want to ensure that nobody runs it by accident. Inevitably, someone will load our worksheets or notebooks and run all the commands like it's a script. This example table isn't important, but we want to get into the habit of commenting out potentially dangerous commands:

```
--Truncate the table.
--truncate table truncate_test;

--(Re-run the above segments and objects query)
MEGABYTES   OBJECT_ID  DATA_OBJECT_ID
---------   ---------  --------------
   0.0625      196832          196833
```

The preceding results show the segment space has decreased to almost zero. The OBJECT_ID stayed the same, but the DATA_OBJECT_ID has slightly changed. The new DATA_OBJECT_ID is Oracle's ways of saying the table may look the same, but the data has completely changed in an unusual way. The sudden change to our segment can affect other operations and cause strange errors if we're using the table while it's being truncated.

You may have heard the Oracle mantra "readers don't block writers, and writers don't block readers." That phrase refers to the consistency model of the Oracle database. If we start reading from a table, someone else can change the table at the same time. None of the users get blocked, and both users get a consistent view of the table as of the time their statements began.

Those rules about readers and writers don't apply to TRUNCATE. TRUNCATE doesn't write to the table; TRUNCATE destroys and recreates the table. If someone else was reading from a table while the table was truncated, their read operation may fail. When the client asks Oracle for the next N rows, Oracle won't be able to find any rows. The rows obviously aren't in the table, but the rows won't even be in the UNDO tablespace either, so Oracle doesn't know where the data went. The DATA_OBJECT_ID has changed, the client is trying to read from an old table, and the SELECT statement will generate the error "ORA-08103: object no longer exists." That error message is a bad omen, implying someone is destroying our tables at the wrong time.

COMMIT, ROLLBACK, and SAVEPOINT

COMMIT, ROLLBACK, and SAVEPOINT are transaction control commands and are important for controlling our DML statements. This book assumes you are familiar with the basics of COMMIT (making the changes permanent), ROLLBACK (undoing the changes), and SAVEPOINT (creating places we can later roll back to). For advanced SQL development, we need to know more about transactions, what causes transaction control statements, what happens when transaction control statements are executed, and when to use transaction control statements.

Transactions are logical, atomic pieces of work. It's up to us to decide what a transaction should be. When a user clicks a button, what changes should either completely happen or not happen at all? Many developers get transactions backward – they try to find out what the database can support and then size their transactions accordingly. Instead, we should find our maximum transaction and then size our database accordingly. If our transactions run into resource problems and don't have any obvious bugs or missing optimizations, we should resize or reconfigure our database.

Oracle transactions start automatically. We don't need to worry about starting transactions, but we do need to worry about ending transactions. Most transactions should be ended explicitly with either a COMMIT or a ROLLBACK. Transactions are automatically committed if we run any DDL statement. Since DDL statements issue a COMMIT before they execute, the transaction will be committed even if a DDL statement fails. Unlike some other databases, Oracle DDL statements cannot be part of a transaction and cannot be rolled back.

Exiting a session also automatically ends a transaction. A normal exit typically issues a COMMIT, and an abnormal exit typically issues a ROLLBACK. But that behavior may be configurable. We should check our IDE and clients before we make assumptions about how our transactions will end. Or better yet, we should always specify exactly how our transactions end, by running either COMMIT or ROLLBACK.

When a COMMIT is executed, not much happens right away. A simple database change requires a lot of work to meet the ACID properties – atomic, consistent, isolated, and durable. Oracle is designed to do as little of that work as possible before the COMMIT.

211

The COMMIT command almost always executes immediately, but that speedy execution doesn't mean COMMIT is free. A lot of work happens asynchronously. Creating lots of tiny transactions creates more overhead and makes it harder for Oracle to optimize the background work. We should avoid splitting large changes into multiple statements and transactions.

When a ROLLBACK is executed, a lot of work may be required. Unless the operation was an insert or direct-path write, the time to run the ROLLBACK command will be about as long as the time to run the statement. ROLLBACK automatically runs when a statement fails or the session is killed. When a statement fails, only that statement is rolled back. When a session is killed, the entire transaction is rolled back.

We need to understand ROLLBACK performance to help us decide when to kill a long-running statement. When a statement has been running for too long, sometimes the statement is so close to finishing that we might as well let it continue. Other times, that statement will not finish soon enough, and we must kill the session, let the transaction ROLLBACK, and run the original statements in a different way. The decision hinges on how long the statement will take to complete vs. how long the ROLLBACK will take.

Estimating statement run time is difficult or impossible, as described in Chapter 16. Luckily, we can easily estimate the ROLLBACK time – it should take about as long as the original DML. Rolling back large SQL statements is a bit scary, and it helps to track the progress. The simplest way to measure ROLLBACK progress is with V$TRANSACTION.USED_UREC. The column USED_UREC is the number of used UNDO records. That value depends on the number of table rows changed and the number of indexes. For example, let's make a small change and measure the activity:

```
--Insert temporary data to measure transactions.
insert into launch(launch_id, launch_tag) values (-999, 'test');
select used_urec from v$transaction;

USED_UREC
---------
        3
```

The single INSERT statement generated three UNDO records. The number is a bit tricky to understand. The number represents one row change and two index changes. The table LAUNCH has five indexes, but only two of the indexes are used, because nulls are not stored in indexes. Now let's ROLLBACK the change and watch the numbers decrease:

```
--Now get rid of the data.
rollback;
select used_urec from v$transaction;

USED_UREC
---------
```

After the ROLLBACK, the transaction entry is gone, and the row disappears. For long-running statements, we should wait a minute, rerun the query against V$TRANSACTION, and find the difference. That difference gives us UNDO rows per minute, which we can use to estimate when the ROLLBACK will complete. This whole ROLLBACK estimate process may not be important in an OLTP environment, where all changes are small. In a data warehouse environment, where we have to explain to management why a critical job must wait another day, this estimate can prevent a lot of panic.

We all understand that our changes can't be seen by other sessions until we run a COMMIT. But forgetting a COMMIT is still a common bug that happens to the best of us. Whenever we're building a test case or reporting a bug, we must make it obvious that the code was committed. Someone will eventually ask the question, so we might as well answer it ahead of time.

COMMIT has a few options with risky trade-offs. The option NOWAIT means that the change doesn't have to be fully written to disk before the COMMIT returns. The option BATCH will group several COMMIT commands together and write them all at once. Both options improve performance, but at the cost of durability. A normal COMMIT doesn't return control until everything necessary for recovery is written to permanent storage. If we ask for different COMMIT options, we could potentially lose our data. Since COMMIT is so fast anyway, if we're looking at those two options, we should step back and ask ourselves why we're committing so frequently.

ALTER SYSTEM

The ALTER SYSTEM command is not a DML command, but there are times when it's necessary for SQL development. As described in Chapter 2, we should do most of our work in an environment where we have full control over everything. Even when we have full control, we don't want to run ALTER SYSTEM commands frequently. But there are a few specific commands that SQL developers may find handy. And there are easy ways to grant access to those commands without granting elevated privileges.

For performance testing it may help to clear database memory structures. Sometimes we want to force Oracle to generate a new execution plan, using this command: `ALTER SYSTEM FLUSH SHARED_POOL`. Sometimes we want to clear the cache, to test the system running cold, using this command: `ALTER SYSTEM FLUSH BUFFER_CACHE`. Sometimes we need to kill runaway sessions, using a command like this: `ALTER SYSTEM KILL SESSION '...' IMMEDIATE`.

The commands in the previous paragraph require the powerful privilege `ALTER SYSTEM`. Even if we have that privilege in our primary development environments, it's likely we don't have that privilege in higher environments. But we can always use PL/SQL to grant a highly targeted privilege. We can create a definer's rights procedure that allows only the specific commands we need. There is no system privilege specific to `ALTER SYSTEM FLUSH SHARED_POOL`, but the following statements will allow a user or role to run *only* that specific command:

```
--Let users run a few specific ALTER SYSTEM commands.
create procedure sys.flush_shared_pool is
begin
    execute immediate 'alter system flush shared_pool';
end;
/
grant execute on sys.flush_shared_pool to DEVELOPER_USERNAME;
```

There are a few things about the preceding code that may concern a database administrator. The Oracle manual says to not store objects in system schemas and to be careful about flushing the shared pool. But those concerns shouldn't prevent us from creating this procedure. We don't want to store *data* in the system schema (because the SYSTEM tablespace is special and not meant for large amounts of data), and we don't want to store *all* our code in SYS, because of security concerns. But there are times when we *have* to create objects in SYS anyway, like password verification functions. Creating a precisely targeted procedure in SYS can help us limit our privileges and automate common tasks. And in practice, flushing the caches rarely has a huge impact.

The important lesson here is that even `ALTER SYSTEM` commands should be available for everyone. We just have to be careful, depending on which environment we're in and which specific commands we're granting.

Organizations with shared development databases that can't give SQL developers the ability to run `ALTER SYSTEM` commands end up with a parameter mess. Parameters only get changed when absolutely necessary, but over the years those custom values outlive their usefulness. Eventually nobody knows why we set all those cryptic values, and nobody is empowered to test changing the parameters. We have to be careful about changing parameters, but it's important to have everyone invested in our database configuration.

ALTER SESSION

The `ALTER SESSION` command is also not a DML statement, but it supports our DML statements.

As discussed in Chapter 3, there are hundreds of instance parameters listed in `V$PARAMETER` and explained in the *Database Reference*. Most of those parameters can also be set at the session level. When possible, we should set parameters at the session level instead of the instance level. If there's unusual behavior in our application that requires a configuration change, that change should only apply to *our* application. We don't want to modify other programs that also happen to be running on the same database.

For example, let's say someone set the parameter `OPTIMIZER_INDEX_COST_ADJ`. The parameter was changed years ago, nobody knows why, but everyone is scared to touch the parameter now. Using a non-default value for that parameter is almost certainly a bad idea, but once the parameter is set, how do we prove it's not necessary? We can start by changing the parameter just for one session at a time and slowly testing the change with other users:

```
--Change OPTIMIZER_INDEX_COST_ADJ at the session level.
alter session set optimizer_index_cost_adj = 100;
```

If we only want to change a parameter for one user, we can put an `ALTER SESSION` statement in a logon trigger. Eventually, we can change the system parameters back to their default values and use the optimizer the way it was designed.

Other common session parameters are National Language Support parameters. But NLS parameters are overused, even at the session level. Setting parameters like `NLS_DATE_FORMAT` at the session level is like using a global variable. Our code shouldn't do that much format conversion in the first place, although for some tasks it's unavoidable.

Setting `CURRENT_SCHEMA` is helpful when we are constantly querying another schema and don't want to repeatedly type the schema name. Setting `ENABLE|DISABLE PARALLEL`

DML | DDL | QUERY helps set parallelism. Setting RESUMABLE can make our session either wait or immediately fail if the database runs out of space. Sometimes we want to wait for the DBA to add space, and sometimes we want to throw an error immediately. Several PLSQL_* parameters can help us control program compilation.

The following are four quick examples of the previously mentioned ALTER SESSION commands:

```
--Use the SPACE schema by default.
alter session set current_schema=space;
--Allow parallel DML.
alter session enable parallel dml;
--Wait for adding space.
alter session enable resumable;
--Enable debugging in newly compiled programs.
alter session set plsql_optimize_level = 1;
```

Input and Output

As much as we might like to do all our work inside one database, there are times when we need to move data between systems. For transferring data, there are many powerful extract–transform–load (ETL) tools, like Informatica, and extract–load–transform (ELT) tools, like Oracle Data Integrator. Before we build complex workflows with those programs, we should consider the pros and cons of using Oracle's built-in tools to transfer data between databases, file systems, and object stores.

Oracle's built-in utilities are the simplest, fastest, and most robust programs for copying data between two Oracle databases. It is foolish to use a third-party program built for generic data when both source and destination are an Oracle database. Exporting tables to simple INSERT statements or CSV files is much harder than most people realize. Unless we're willing to spend a huge amount of time dealing with issues like character sets, large and rare data types, batching, and referential integrity, we should stick to Oracle's binary data transfer tools:

1. *Import/export data pump* (impdp, expdp, DBMS_DATAPUMP): The only transfer process that supports all data types and features. Data pump is fast, has both command line programs and a PL/SQL API, and can be used for creating and reading external tables.

The only downside is that data pump only works on the server, so we need operating system access.[3] But since version 21c, these utilities can also directly access Oracle Cloud Infrastructure (OCI) object stores; copying files to and from OCI is generally easier than directly loading files onto a server.

2. *Original import/export* (imp, exp): An older, less capable version of data pump that runs directly on the client. Only use those deprecated programs when we need to access an ancient version of Oracle or don't have server access.

3. *Database links*: Great for small and fast querying. Links don't support all data types and are slow for moving large amounts of data (although database link limitations do not apply when links are used with programs like DBMS_DATAPUMP or pluggable database cloning).

4. *SQL*Plus COPY*: Deprecated program that is only useful for small, simple transfers, where the source and destination can't directly communicate.

5. *Transportable tablespaces*: The fastest way to transfer data, but it copies an entire tablespace and has restrictions.

When we're transferring data between Oracle and a non-Oracle system, that data will often be transferred through text files. Even though Oracle has many ways to read and generate text files, dealing with text files is still a challenge. Text file input and output in Oracle is not as convenient as it is in most databases, which means we need to be aware of many alternatives. The best solution depends on the context. The following list shows different ways of moving text in and out of Oracle:

1. *UTL_FILE*: This package gives us complete control over how every byte is read and written. The downside is that we have to code the file format ourselves and the file must be on the server. Conforming to even a simple file format like CSV is harder than

---

[3] We may be able to access server files without direct access to the server, using Oracle directories and the open source program Oracle Copy (OCP): https://github.com/maxsatula/ocp

most developers appreciate. When possible, we should look for pre-built packages on top of UTL_FILE.[4]

2. *SQL*Loader*: Fast tool that comes with Oracle by default, can work on the client or the server, and has many configuration options for things like delimiters and fixed width formats. The configuration files and syntax are complicated. SQL*Loader is only useful for reading files.

3. *External tables*: A table whose data comes from a flat file, a data pump file, or cloud object storage (configured via DBMS_CLOUD). External tables are the fastest way to access files, but are read-only and require server access. Since 18c, inline external tables allow queries to read from external files without creating objects. Querying a file can be as simple as SELECT * FROM EXTERNAL ((VALUE1 VARCHAR2(100)) DEFAULT DIRECTORY DATA_PUMP_DIR LOCATION ('test.csv')).

4. *DBMS_XSLPROCESSOR*: Convenient functions READ2CLOB and CLOB2FILE for CLOB I/O. Since 19c, these functions are better used from the package DBMS_LOB.

5. *SQL*Plus scripts*: Reading from SQL*Plus scripts to load data is convenient, if we're able to get files in that format. Writing from SQL*Plus scripts can be deceivingly difficult, even for simple file formats like CSV. Be careful of SQL*Plus export scripts that poorly implement CSV instead of using a command like SET MARKUP CSV ON.

6. *Oracle SQL Developer, SQL CL, or other third-party tools*: Most IDEs have options for exporting table data to different formats, such as CSV or INSERT statements. These tools also have options for either importing data from files or helping configure SQL*Loader.

---

[4] The popular DATA_DUMP.SQL is useful for quickly outputting data to a CSV file. There are many versions of this utility, including one I have worked on: https://github.com/jonheller1/ data_dump

Useful PL/SQL Packages

Advanced SQL development inevitably requires PL/SQL. PL/SQL is Oracle's procedural extension for SQL, is available wherever Oracle SQL is available, and integrates seamlessly and optimally with SQL. If we're building a program that primarily runs SQL statements, then PL/SQL should be our first choice to glue those statements together. While PL/SQL has many important uses, this section only discusses the most popular PL/SQL packages that help us write better SQL.

First, we need to discuss how to run PL/SQL packages, without going into a full PL/SQL tutorial. Most packages contain functions that we can simply call from a SQL statement. For other PL/SQL functionality, we can either create procedural objects or use anonymous blocks. Procedural objects are things like packages, procedures, functions, types, etc. But we may not have the privileges to create and run PL/SQL objects, and we may not want to deal with managing more schema objects. Anonymous blocks are perfect for ad hoc tasks.

Anonymous blocks are groups of statements that are run together. The block isn't stored anywhere, doesn't require an extra compilation step, and doesn't require extra privileges. Blocks contain an optional DECLARE section to create variables, a body with BEGIN and one or more statements, and an END. We can nest blocks; create functions, procedures, and other objects inside the blocks; etc. We could build our entire program in one anonymous block, but that would be a bad idea.

Let's start with the simplest anonymous block. Not all the syntax is optional; there has to be at least one statement, so this is the smallest PL/SQL block we can write:

```
--The most boring anonymous block.
begin
    null;
end;
/
```

Let's make a more useful anonymous block by outputting data:

```
--Anonymous block that does something.
declare
    v_number number := 1;
begin
    dbms_output.put_line('Output: ' || to_char(v_number + 1));
```

```
end;
/
Output: 2
```

If you don't see the preceding results, you may need to configure your IDE to display DBMS output. Some IDEs, like PL/SQL Developer, automatically detect and display DBMS output. Some IDEs, like Oracle SQL Developer, require us to manually enable DBMS output before we run the example. In SQL*Plus, we would run this command to enable the output: SET SERVEROUTPUT ON.

SQL*Plus has an EXEC command to run PL/SQL statements. The EXEC command takes the input statement and wraps it inside a BEGIN and an END. We should almost always use a regular PL/SQL block instead of the EXEC command. A PL/SQL block works in every IDE, but EXEC only works in some IDEs. As described in Chapter 5, we should avoid doing PL/SQL development in SQL*Plus. (But there are always exceptions.)

```
SQL> set serveroutput on
SQL> exec dbms_output.put_line('test');
test

PL/SQL procedure successfully completed.
```

We've already seen DBMS_OUTPUT a few times in this book. The package has multiple functions for sending strings to the output buffer. That output may be displayed on the screen, captured by DBMS_OUTPUT.GET_LINES, displayed as the output for our scheduler jobs, etc.

DBMS_RANDOM generates pseudorandom text and numbers. This package is useful for generating or selecting random test data:

```
--Not-so-randomly generate a number, since the seed is static.
begin
    dbms_random.seed(1234);
    dbms_output.put_line(dbms_random.value);
end;
/
.4278990469059150424734967392105241463 9
```

DBMS_STATS is a vital package for performance tuning. Optimizer statistics are essential for good performance, and there are an enormous number of options for gathering statistics. Luckily, 99% of the time, the default settings are perfect, and the package is easy to use. (You may need to adjust the first parameter in the following examples, depending on the schema used to install the data set.)

```
--Gather stats for a table.
begin
   dbms_stats.gather_table_stats('SPACE', 'LAUNCH');
end;
/
--Gather stats for a schema.
begin
   dbms_stats.gather_schema_stats('SPACE');
end;
/
```

DBMS_SCHEDULER lets us create and manage jobs. DBMS_SCHEDULER is another vital package and has many powerful and complex scheduling features. We can create a set of jobs to manage complicated systems, build our own parallelism, or just kick off something and have the code run in the background. The following code creates and runs the simplest possible job and then checks the job's status:

```
--Create and run a job that does nothing.
begin
   dbms_scheduler.create_job(
      job_name   => 'test_job',
      job_type   => 'plsql_block',
      job_action => 'begin null; end;',
      enabled    => true
   );
end;
/

--Job details.
--(The first two rows may be empty because one-time jobs
-- automatically drop themselves when they finish.)
```

```
select * from dba_scheduler_jobs where job_name = 'TEST_JOB';
select * from dba_scheduler_running_jobs where job_name = 'TEST_JOB';
select * from dba_scheduler_job_run_details where job_name = 'TEST_JOB';
```

DBMS_METADATA and DBMS_METADATA_DIFF were briefly described in Chapter 2 but are worth repeating. Those packages have lots of options for retrieving, formatting, and comparing code. Hopefully we have all our code in version control and don't need to rely on those packages too often.

Summary

This chapter shows there's much more to changing data than a simple INSERT, UPDATE, or DELETE. These three commands have interesting options and pitfalls, and there's also the powerful MERGE statement. DML statements can use updatable views, but we should avoid that feature. Hints can significantly change our DML behavior, but we must use them with caution. DML can log errors and return data from affected rows. There are many other commands that are not DML but can help us change our data: TRUNCATE to quickly remove table data, COMMIT and ROLLBACK to end transactions, and ALTER SYSTEM and ALTER SESSION to control the environment. Oracle has many ways to get data into and out of the system, and it's worth learning each tool's pros and cons. Finally, this chapter introduced useful PL/SQL packages and how to use them in anonymous blocks.

We've seen how to read and write data with advanced SQL. The next chapter discusses how to create the objects to hold that data.

CHAPTER 9

Improve the Database with Advanced Schema Objects

So far, this book has used pre-built objects, but now it's time to start making our own. This book assumes you are familiar with basic Data Definition Language commands like `CREATE TABLE`. This chapter describes advanced features of Oracle schema objects and the advanced DDL commands to create and maintain them.

This chapter does not create an exhaustive list of features and expect you to memorize the syntax. Instead, the goal is to introduce a wide variety of interesting features. Exposure to these new features and commands will give you ideas for your current and future projects. When the time comes to implement these new features, look them up in the *SQL Language Reference* for more details.

There's a chance that running the commands in this chapter will break things in our schemas. But none of these commands will break things in *other* schemas. If we followed the advice in Part I about setting up efficient database development processes, breaking things in our own schema shouldn't be an issue. In fact, if we're not breaking things, we're not trying hard enough.

ALTER

The `ALTER` commands let us change our database to match our ever-changing requirements. This section does not discuss specific `ALTER` commands, such as the precise syntax to add columns to tables or to recompile objects. And this section does not include the `ALTER SESSION` and `ALTER SYSTEM` commands, which are for "session

© Jon Heller 2023
J. Heller, *Pro Oracle SQL Development*, https://doi.org/10.1007/978-1-4842-8867-2_9

control" and "system control." Instead, this section only discusses two ALTER anti-patterns: using ALTER to modify code and not using ALTER to modify persistent objects.

Oracle has 51 different ALTER commands. Developers who are scared of rebuilding schemas from scratch may read too much into the power of those ALTER commands. Many developers have asked a variant of this question: How can we use ALTER to add a new function to a package?

The shallow answer to the preceding question is that we cannot ALTER procedural code objects.[1] The ALTER PACKAGE command is only for recompiling; the command does not give us the ability to add one function at a time.

The deeper answer to the preceding question is that something is wrong with our development process if we're even asking such a question in the first place. Creating objects is hard, but eternally maintaining and deploying a set of changes is even harder. As described in Chapter 2, we should build an installation script for all procedural objects, like packages, functions, and procedures. We should run that same script for every deployment.

Recompiling everything, every time, may not work well in some environments, but it works great in Oracle. Having only one way to create code objects keeps our scripts simple and organized. And if we're working with version-controlled files, when we add a function to the package, we save the function inside the whole package anyway. It would be more work to create a separate ALTER PACKAGE ... ADD FUNCTION command, if such a thing were even possible.

On the other hand, our development process suffers when we're scared of altering *persistent* objects, such as tables. The ALTER TABLE command lets us change almost anything about a table. We do have to be more careful about altering tables than simply changing data; since DDL auto-commits, it is possible to lose data if something goes horribly wrong. But if we have a fully automated development and testing process, we shouldn't fear DDL.

Fear of altering tables is the primary cause of the entity–attribute–value (EAV) pattern. EAV is when our tables have only a few simple columns, such as NAME and VALUE. EAV is discussed as an anti-pattern in Chapter 15, but it is not inherently evil. The real problem occurs when organizations are so scared of altering tables that they will store everything in an EAV, making their systems painful to use.

---

[1] There are ALTER commands that affect object-relational code. But those exceptions demonstrate why we should avoid object-relational technology. It's a nightmare when altering code permanently breaks our data.

My simple rule is this: always recreate code from scratch and always try to alter persistent objects.

Tables

Tables are the central objects in a relational database, so it's not surprising that Oracle has many different types of tables, table properties, ways of altering and dropping tables, and column types and properties. Some important table features, such as constraints and partitioning, are discussed in a later section.

Table Types

All tables look the same in a SQL statement. But under the covers, Oracle can implement tables in many different ways: heap, global temporary, private temporary, sharded, object-relational, external, index-organized, immutable, and blockchain.

Heap tables are the default table type. The word "heap" means the table is an unorganized pile of stuff. The following CREATE TABLE and data dictionary queries show how even the simplest table contains a huge number of options. The results are too large to show here, so you'll have to run the following queries to explore the results:

```
--Create a simple table and see its metadata.
create table simple_table2(a number, b varchar2(100), c date);

select dbms_metadata.get_ddl(
   object_type => 'TABLE',
   name        => 'SIMPLE_TABLE2',
   schema      => sys_context('userenv', 'current_schema')
) from dual;

select *
from all_tables
where table_name = 'SIMPLE_TABLE2'
   and owner = sys_context('userenv', 'current_schema');

select *
from all_tab_columns
where table_name = 'SIMPLE_TABLE2'
   and owner = sys_context('userenv', 'current_schema');
```

Global temporary tables store temporary values that only the current session can see. The data can be preserved either until the next commit, with the option ON COMMIT DELETE ROWS, or until the end of the session, with the option ON COMMIT PRESERVE ROWS. The following example creates a global temporary table and shows how the value disappears after a commit:

```
--Global temporary table that holds data until next commit.
create global temporary table temp_table(a number)
on commit delete rows;

--Insert data and it shows up ONLY in your session.
insert into temp_table values(1);

select count(*) from temp_table;

COUNT(*)
--------
       1

--But once you commit, the data is gone.
commit;

select count(*) from temp_table;

COUNT(*)
--------
       0
```

Global temporary tables tend to be misused in several ways. First, Oracle's global temporary tables are *global*; the *definition* is viewable by other sessions, but the *data* is not. The table definition is permanent, and the table doesn't need to be constantly dropped and recreated. Second, Oracle's global temporary tables are not memory structures. Writing to global temporary tables writes to disk, just like a heap table. Global temporary tables are useful for holding temporary results of programs, but global temporary tables are not meant for frequent ad hoc creation. Unlike SQL Server, Oracle's global temporary tables are not primarily intended to boost performance. They may improve performance in some cases, but we should not blindly add global temporary tables and expect an improvement.

The biggest problem with global temporary tables is when they are used as a poor replacement for inline views. Complex queries are best built with multiple inline views, which simplify the program and let Oracle decide when to read and write data. Global temporary tables are only useful when the results will be read multiple times in different queries or when doing everything in one query is infeasible. Chapter 12 discusses how to create large SQL statements, and in practice there are few queries that need to be broken up with global temporary tables.

Private temporary tables were introduced in 18c. They are similar to global temporary tables, except they are stored in memory in the PGA, and both the definition and the data are private to the session. Similar to global temporary tables, private temporary tables are not a panacea for improving SQL. The following example creates a private temporary table, which can then be used like any other table, but only in the same session. Note that private temporary tables must have a specific prefix, which is ORA$PTT by default:

```
--Create a private temporary table.
create private temporary table ora$ptt_private_table(a number)
on commit drop definition;
```

The worst part about private temporary tables is the confusion over the name. Prior to 18c there was only one kind of temporary table. References to "temporary tables" are almost certainly referring to "global temporary tables."

Sharded tables are tables where the rows are distributed among multiple shared-nothing databases. The administration and use of this feature is too complex for an example in this book. In my experience, a single database is the best way to solve most of our problems. When we try to replicate and shard, we often end up creating more problems than we're solving. The technologies needed to build Facebook or Google do not necessarily apply to our simpler, internal applications.

Object-relational tables let us create tables based on user-defined types. Storing complex objects in a column doesn't extend the relational model – it breaks the relational model. The disadvantages of breaking the relational model, such as ruining SQL, almost certainly outweigh the advantages, such as simplifying a few specific use cases. There are exceptions, such as JSON and XML, but those exceptions were carefully designed. Object-relational anti-patterns will be discussed in more detail in Chapter 15.

External tables are tables whose data comes from flat files or data pump files managed by the operating system. To create an external table, we specify the Oracle directory (which maps to an operating system directory), a file name, and a list of columns similar to a SQL*Loader format. Then we can read from a text file just like a regular table.

External tables are the fastest way to load flat files into Oracle tables, and they are also convenient for reading archived data without fully restoring all the data. In practice, our text files are never as clean as relational data, so I recommend keeping the external tables as generic as possible. Instead of doing conversion and processing through SQL*Loader column definitions, create external tables with VARCHAR2(4000) columns. Then we can do the conversion and processing in a separate PL/SQL step. Keeping the external tables simple allows us to at least query the raw data if there are problems. Exception handling in PL/SQL is more useful than exception handling with external table definitions.

External tables also let us run an executable preprocessor before loading data. That preprocessor is intended for things like unzipping a file before loading it. But there are several creative uses for shell scripts that generate table data. For example, we can create a preprocessor script with a simple DIR command to list all the files in a directory.[2]

Index-organized tables (IOTs) are stored inside an index. Normally, an index is an optional data structure, used for performance and constraint enforcement. An index-organized table combines the table data with the primary key index. If one index is always used to access the table data anyway, we might as well put more table data inside that index, instead of requiring a separate table lookup. Index-organized tables can also reduce the amount of space, since the indexed data is not duplicated. The following code is a simple example of creating an index-organized table:

```
--Create index-organized table.
create table iot_table
(
    a number,
    b number,
    constraint iot_table_pk primary key(a)
)
organization index;
```

---

[2] Adrian Billington's excellent website describes how to use a preprocessor to generate a list of files in a directory: www.oracle-developer.net/display.php?id=513

Immutable and **blockchain** tables, available since 19c, allow us to limit or verify the operations on our tables. Immutable tables allow only reads and inserts (with some exceptions), which can help us ensure our tables haven't been modified. Blockchain tables also prevent updates and deletes, but they use cryptographic hashes to further ensure our data hasn't been tampered with. The following example shows an immutable table in action:

```
--Create immutable table.
SQL> create immutable table immutable_test(a number)
  2   no drop until 16 days idle
  3   no delete until 16 days after insert;

Table created.

SQL> insert into immutable_test values(1);

1 row created.

SQL> update immutable_test set a = -1;
update immutable_test set a = -1;
                      *
ERROR at line 1:
ORA-05715: operation not allowed on the blockchain or immutable table
```

We should be cautious before using immutable or blockchain tables. Aside from the inconvenience of not allowing updates and deletes, performance penalties, technical restrictions, and the bugs that affect those new table types, there's a good chance of those data structures being misused. Blockchains are notoriously overused because they are oversold as a technical solution to a sociological problem. The cost of development and administration can skyrocket if we insist on not trusting any of our developers and DBAs.

Table Properties

After we define the table type, we can control even more behavior through the many available table properties. The most important properties are logging, compression, parallel, deferred segment creation, physical attributes, and flashback archiving. The tablespace setting is important but is covered later in the chapter when users are discussed; ideally tables only need one tablespace that is inherited from the user.

The **logging** clause lets us set the table to either LOGGING or NOLOGGING. This feature is easy to enable, but the effect of the logging clause is complicated and depends on many factors. The logging clause helps Oracle decide when to use direct-path writes. Direct-path writes are faster, but they are not recoverable since they don't generate redo. (Redo data is described in Chapter 10.) We must tell Oracle when it is acceptable to make that trade-off. By default, Oracle tries hard to never lose data.

The difficulty with the logging clause is that there are so many ways to tell Oracle whether or not it is OK to lose data. We can tell Oracle at the database level (is the database in ARCHIVELOG mode or NOARCHIVELOG mode), at the object level (is the table set to LOGGING or NOLOGGING), and at the statement level (did the statement ask for APPEND or NOAPPEND). When Oracle gets conflicting directions, Oracle chooses the option that does not risk losing data. Table 9-1 shows what happens when we mix logging settings.[3]

Table 9-1. *When Will Oracle Generate Redo*

Table Mode	Insert Mode	Log Mode	Result
LOGGING	APPEND	ARCHIVELOG	Redo generated
NOLOGGING	APPEND	ARCHIVELOG	No redo
LOGGING	NOAPPEND	ARCHIVELOG	Redo generated
NOLOGGING	NOAPPEND	ARCHIVELOG	Redo generated
LOGGING	APPEND	NOARCHIVELOG	No redo
NOLOGGING	APPEND	NOARCHIVELOG	No redo
LOGGING	NOAPPEND	NOARCHIVELOG	Redo generated
NOLOGGING	NOAPPEND	NOARCHIVELOG	Redo generated

Even the preceding table is not an exhaustive list of when redo will be generated. There are other things that can prevent direct-path inserts and cause redo generation, such as tablespace settings, foreign keys, triggers, etc.

---

[3] This table is based on an old Ask Tom thread: https://asktom.oracle.com/pls/asktom/f?p=100:11:0:::::P11_QUESTION_ID:5280714813869.

Basic table compression can save a huge amount of space and improve performance. Oracle has many compression options, but only basic table compression is free. Luckily, the free option is usually good enough. Basic table compression is easy to implement and has virtually no downsides. The problem with basic table compression is that it's hard to effectively use.

A table can be compressed but have uncompressed data in it. Only direct-path writes, or reorganizing the table, will compress table data (unless we buy the advanced compression option, which can compress data all the time). To know when to use compression, we need to understand how compression works. It also helps to understand how data is stored in Oracle, in blocks, as described in Chapter 10.

Oracle compression uses a simple pattern substitution. Each block of data, 8 kilobytes by default, has a symbol table with common values. When those common values are found in the data, the symbol is used instead of repeating the data. The following text shows a logical representation of how basic table compression works:

```
--Launch data as uncompressed comma-separated-values.
LAUNCH_ID,LAUNCH_CATEGORY,LAUNCH_STATUS
4305,orbital,success
4306,orbital,success
4476,orbital,failure
...
--Launch data with simple pattern substitution compression.
LAUNCH_ID,LAUNCH_CATEGORY,LAUNCH_STATUS
LAUNCH_CATEGORY:£=orbital
LAUNCH_STATUS:€=success,¢=failure
4305,£,€
4306,£,€
4476,£,¢
...
```

The preceding compression example is not the literal data format. A real block is much more complex and uses short numbers instead of long names for metadata. But the preceding text is enough to understand when compression may help. The column values must be identical for compression to save space. The column values must also repeat within the same column, not across columns. And the repeated values must appear within the same block, which means within about 8 kilobytes of each other. Only each block is compressed, not the entire table. Block compression means the overall compression ratio may significantly improve if we order the data in the table before we compress it.

The space saved by compression completely depends on our data. I've seen many tables not shrink at all, and I've seen tables shrink up to 33% of their original size. The following code shows how to create tables with basic table compression enabled and how to compress tables if we can't use direct-path inserts:

```
--Create a compressed table.
create table compressed_table(a number) compress;

--Compression will only happen for direct-path inserts.
--Periodically MOVE table if we can't use direct-path inserts.
alter table compressed_table move compress;
```

The **parallel** clause lets us set a degree of parallelism for tables and other objects. Parallelism is a powerful mechanism to significantly improve performance, but parallelism may come at the expense of other processes. Parallelism is best defined at the query level, unless we are absolutely sure that a table should always run in parallel.

The parallel clause can be set to NOPARALLEL (the default), PARALLEL X (where X is an integer indicating the degree of parallelism), or simply PARALLEL (which uses the system-determined degree of parallelism – the number of CPUs multiplied by the parameter PARALLEL_THREADS_PER_CPU). The following code shows an example of creating a table with a default degree of parallelism:

```
--Create table with parallelism enabled by default.
create table parallel_table(a number) parallel;
```

Deferred segment creation lets us create a table without allocating any space. In older versions of Oracle, whenever we created a table or partition, Oracle would automatically allocate a segment to hold the data. Those empty segments typically use a few megabytes of space, although if we use manual segment space management, we can define our own sizes. In extreme cases, like if we pre-build thousands of tables or create a table with thousands of partitions, those empty segments can waste a considerable amount of space. With deferred segment creation, that space is not added until it is needed.

Deferred segment creation is enabled by default and doesn't have any performance implications – so why are we even talking about it? A few weird things can happen when deferred segment creation is used. We can create a table and see that table immediately in DBA_TABLES, but we won't see the segment in data dictionary views like DBA_SEGMENTS. Missing segments can be a problem for programs and scripts that assume the segments always exist. Deferred segment creation is why the deprecated EXP program may miss some of our tables.

Deferred segment creation can be disabled when we create a table. Or we can force Oracle to allocate space, regardless of the data in the table. The following code shows both options:

```
--Create a table without deferred segment creation.
create table deferred_segment_table(a number)
segment creation immediate;

--Force Oracle to create a segment.
alter table deferred_segment_table allocate extent;
```

The **physical attributes clause** lets us control about a dozen different parameters related to table storage. These parameters include PCTFREE, PCTUSED, INITRANS, and the parameters in the STORAGE clause. Don't touch those parameters unless we know something that Oracle doesn't. Many of those parameters aren't even used anymore. And if the parameters are used, the defaults are almost always good enough.

The only physical attribute we should set is PCTFREE, which controls how much space Oracle leaves empty for changes. We want Oracle to pack our data as densely as possible to save space. On the other hand, if the data is packed too densely, adding a single byte requires moving a lot of data around. Oracle's default value is 10%. If we know that our table will never be updated, we can save 10% of the space by changing PCTFREE to 0. If our table is updated frequently and we see performance issues from row migration and row chaining (discussed in Chapter 10), increasing PCTFREE might help.

Flashback archiving and **row archival** let Oracle tables archive data. Flashback archiving is tricky to set up and maintain, but it lets us perform flashback queries on a table indefinitely. Row archival is simpler to enable and use, but it only allows us to archive or unarchive rows. When row archival is enabled for a table, each row has a hidden column. That hidden column makes data disappear from queries unless we specifically ask for archived data.

ALTER and DROP Table

In addition to creating the right types of tables with the right properties, we also need to know how to alter those properties and drop tables. The ALTER TABLE syntax is massive, and we can change just about anything in our tables. ALTER TABLE statements are non-transactional and can require a lot of downtime. Online table redefinition allows us to change tables without significant downtime, but that's a complicated topic not covered in this book.

Dropping tables is simple but obviously dangerous. Statements like DROP TABLE TABLE_NAME will put the table in the recycle bin. The recycle bin is enabled by default, but we should check the RECYCLBIN parameter in V$PARAMETER before we assume it's enabled.

Until the table is purged from the recycle bin, the table still uses the same amount of disk space. We can skip the recycle bin and reclaim that space immediately by adding the keyword PURGE to the end of the command. Every time we drop a table, we need to stop and ask ourselves – do we need the space back, and are we 100% sure we will never need the table again?

The DROP TABLE command also has a CASCADE CONSTRAINTS option. That option drops any referential constraints that refer to the soon-to-be-dropped table. To be safe, we should avoid the CASCADE CONSTRAINTS option. It's hard enough to be 100% confident that we can drop a specific table. It's another thing to be 100% confident about a table *and* all other tables in the database that might refer to it. It's safer to manually disable constraints, use a regular drop command, and generate exceptions if we forgot to disable a relationship.

Column Types and Properties

Just like tables, columns come in many types and have many properties. We don't need to review the basic types, like VARCHAR2 and NUMBER. But the advanced types have different storage options, and columns can be defined with several important properties.

XML data can be stored in tables in three different ways. When using the XMLType, we can choose binary, structured (object-relational), or unstructured (CLOB). Binary XML storage is the default and is good for document-centric storage where we don't know the exact structure of each file ahead of time. Structured (object-relational) storage is good for data-centric storage, where we know the precise XML schema and we want to optimize and index the data. Unstructured (CLOB) storage is obsolete, but that option is good for storing our XML data byte for byte in the original format. We should use the default storage options unless we have a significant XML workload that may benefit from the complicated performance trade-offs between the three options and if we are willing to read the *XML DB Developer's Guide.*

JSON data also has multiple storage options, and these options also have complicated performance trade-offs. Until 21c, JSON data was stored as either VARCHAR2 or CLOB, depending on the maximum file size, and it was important to add an IS JSON constraint. Since 21c, we should probably use the native JSON data type.

Large objects (LOBs) also have different storage options. The main difference is between the old BasicFiles and the new SecureFiles. SecureFiles is backward compatible, performs better than BasicFiles, and offers unique features, such as compression, deduplication, and encryption. (But those extra features require additional licenses.) LOBs can have other storage properties, such as a tablespace different than the table. As always, we should use the default settings unless we have a special case. When we upgrade, we should consider changing from old defaults to new defaults. For example, SecureFiles has been the default since 12.1, so if we inherited an old database, we may want to convert our LOBs from BasicFiles to SecureFiles.

Column definitions have several advanced features. Columns can have a *default value,* which is useful for tasks like storing auditing data, such as the current user and data. *Virtual columns* do not store any data but instead return an expression. Virtual columns can help us avoid denormalization – we can store data both in its natural format and in a display format, without worrying about synchronization problems. Column definitions can have *inline constraints,* with a syntax that is simpler than out-of-line constraints. But it's generally better to create out-of-line constraints because inline constraints have system-generated names that will be different on every database. That name difference can cause schema comparison headaches. *Invisible columns* can be used but won't show up in a SELECT *. The following code demonstrates all of these unusual column properties:

```
--Default, virtual, inline check, and invisible.
create table weird_columns
(
   a number default 1,
   b number as (a+1),
   c number check (c >= 0),
   d number invisible
);
```

```
insert into weird_columns(c,d) values (3,4);

select * from weird_columns;

A  B  C
-  -  -
1  2  3
```

Column defaults are especially helpful for setting primary key values. In old versions of Oracle, we needed to either manually call a sequence with each INSERT, create a trigger that calls a sequence, or use a function like SYS_GUID as a default. Modern versions allow identity columns and using a sequence as the default. Both identity columns and sequence defaults are simpler and faster than previous solutions. Creating an identity column automatically creates a sequence and connects that sequence to the table and column. Unfortunately, with identity columns we lose some important details, such as the sequence name. I prefer to manually create a sequence and then set the column default to SEQUENCE_NAME.NEXTVAL. Creating the sequence manually is an extra manual step, but it avoids system-generated sequence names that will never match between environments. The following are examples of using an identity column and sequence default:

```
--Identity column and sequence default.
create sequence test_sequence;

create table identity_table
(
    a number generated as identity,
    b number default test_sequence.nextval,
    c number
);

insert into identity_table(c) values(1);

select * from identity_table;

A  B  C
-  -  -
1  1  1
```

Constraints

Constraints restrict values to enforce relationships and data rules in our relational databases. I assume you are familiar with the basic constraint types: primary key (columns that are non-null and unique), unique (columns with no duplicates), foreign key (columns that share values with a parent table), and check (a condition that must always be true). But there are other types of constraints and advanced ways of using constraints.

Constraint Performance Impact

Constraints are necessary for data integrity, but they can significantly harm performance. Direct-path writes are not possible on a child table with a foreign key. (But at least foreign keys don't stop direct-path writes on the parent table, and the limitation does not apply to reference partitioned tables.) To enable direct-path writes, constraints can be disabled and re-enabled, but that process can be slow. Every constraint requires time to validate, and primary key and unique constraints must spend time maintaining indexes. (But most constraint enforcement time either is trivial, like for check constraints, or has workarounds, such as the way direct-path writes will perform index maintenance in bulk instead of row by row.)

Constraints can also significantly *improve* performance. For example, NOT NULL check constraints can enable the optimizer to use an index. The following statements perform a distinct count on two indexed columns, SATELLITE.SATELLITE_ID and SATELLITE.LAUNCH_ID. The query on SATELLITE.SATELLITE_ID can use an index – the column is NOT NULL, and therefore the index contains all values. The query on SATELLITE.LAUNCH_ID cannot use an index – the column is nullable, and therefore the index may not contain all the values. If possible, setting columns to NOT NULL can enable new index access paths. (But in our data set, that NOT NULL constraint is not possible – there is one satellite without a known launch.)

```
--This statement on a NOT NULL column can use an index.
select count(distinct satellite_id) from satellite;
--This statement on a nullable column cannot use an index.
select count(distinct launch_id) from satellite;
```

Performance issues shouldn't prevent us from using constraints. Data integrity is more important than performance. And the performance benefits of constraints may outweigh the performance costs. And when we encounter performance problems caused by constraints, there is always a workaround.

Altering Constraints

Constraints can be added, dropped, enabled, and disabled. To preserve our configuration, it's better to enable and disable constraints than to drop and re-add them. Constraints belong to tables, and most constraint commands happen through ALTER TABLE. To demonstrate some constraint properties, let's make an empty copy of the ORGANIZATION table. The following code creates an initially empty table, adds a unique constraint, disables the constraint, and loads the data:

```
--Create separate table for organization data.
create table organization_temp nologging as
select * from organization
where 1=2;

--Create a unique constraint.
alter table organization_temp
add constraint organization_temp_uq
unique(org_name, org_start_date, org_location);

--Disable the constraint.
alter table organization_temp
disable constraint organization_temp_uq;

--Load data.
insert into organization_temp
select * from organization;
```

Constraint Exceptions

The preceding code runs, but it contains a mistake. Our unique constraint is not unique enough. There are a few organizations that share the same name, start date, and location. The constraint is disabled, and as soon as we try to enable the constraint, we'll get an error.

Constraint errors don't tell us the data that caused the error. That lack of details isn't a problem with our small tables, since we can easily find the duplicates. But with complicated constraints, or huge amounts of data, those errors can be difficult to track down. We can use the *exceptions clause* to find the values that caused constraint errors, similar to the way DML error logging can find the values that caused DML errors.

Setting up constraint exceptions is more complicated than setting up DML error logging. There's no convenient DBMS_ERRLOG package to create exception tables. Instead, we need to call a script stored in the server installation directory. If our ORACLE_HOME environment variable is set correctly, we can run the script like this:

```
SQL> @?\rdbms\admin\utlexpt1
Table created.
```

Make sure you run the preceding script as the owner of the data set or set the CURRENT_USER before running the script. If the preceding code doesn't work, then we can find the small script online and recreate the table manually. Once we have the table, we can use the following syntax to save any exceptions:

```
--Try to enable a constraint that isn't valid.
alter table organization_temp
enable constraint organization_temp_uq
exceptions into exceptions;
```

The preceding code still throws the error: "ORA-02299: cannot validate (SPACE. ORGANIZATION_TEMP_UQ) – duplicate keys found." But now it's easy to find the culprits, with the following SQL:

```
--Rows that blocked the constraint.
select *
from organization_temp
where rowid in (select row_id from exceptions);
```

NOVALIDATE and Parallel Constraints

There are a few duplicates in our sample schema, but that's understandable for 80-year-old data. We can't always fix bad data, but we can at least prevent more bad data from happening. The NOVALIDATE option lets the constraint ignore existing exceptions and prevent future exceptions.

The NOVALIDATE option is a bit tricky to use with unique constraints because unique constraints must also work with indexes. To create a not-so-unique unique constraint, we must first create a non-unique index. The following code creates a non-unique index, enables the constraint, ignores existing bad data, and uses a specific index to maintain the constraint:

```
--Create a non-unique index for the constraint.
create index organization_temp_idx1
on organization_temp(org_name, org_start_date, org_location)
compress 2;
```

```
--Enable NOVALIDATE the constraint, with a non-unique index.
alter table organization_temp
enable novalidate constraint organization_temp_uq
using index organization_temp_idx1;
```

The USING clause and disabling and validating constraints are also helpful for performance. Data warehouses often improve the performance of loading data by removing constraints and indexes. But those constraints and indexes need to be re-added when the data load is complete. The USING clause lets us create our index however we want, perhaps with performance-enhancing options such as compression, parallelism, and NOLOGGING. To re-enable constraints in parallel, we must first create them with DISABLE and then VALIDATE them as a separate step.

Demonstrating parallel constraint re-enabling is difficult and requires a lot of setup work. To conserve space, the prep work for creating a large version of the ORGANIZATION table is only shown in the repository. Let's assume that we have created a large table and loaded data, and now we want to re-add the constraints in parallel. The following four steps show how to re-enable constraints in parallel:

```
--Set the table to run in parallel.
alter table organization_parallel parallel;
```

```
--Create constraint but have it initially disabled.
alter table organization_parallel
add constraint organization_parallel_fk foreign key (parent_org_code)
references organization_parallel(org_code) disable;
```

```
--Validate constraint, which runs in parallel.
alter table organization_parallel
modify constraint organization_parallel_fk validate;

--Change the table back to NOPARALLEL when done.
alter table organization_parallel noparallel;
```

Running constraints in parallel may seem like an unusual case, but these steps are important and also demonstrate a larger principle. Because of Amdahl's law (discussed in Chapter 16), if we're going to parallelize a process, we need to parallelize *all* of the steps. There are many data warehouse processes that parallelize and optimize the obvious data loading steps, only to spend the majority of time recreating indexes and rebuilding constraints serially. Oracle has all these weird constraint features for a reason. Don't bother trying to memorize the constraint syntax – just remember that there is always a workaround to constraint performance problems.

Other Constraints

Views can be created using a `WITH READ ONLY` constraint, preventing them from being changed as part of an updatable view. Views also have the `WITH CHECK OPTION` constraint, which allows updatable views to only modify specific values. View constraints don't prevent bad data; they only prevent bad data from being created through views. As discussed in Chapter 8, updatable views are difficult and should be used with caution.

Oracle constraints are limited to enforcing rules within a single table or between two tables for referential integrity constraints. We should use constraints instead of triggers when possible, but constraints can't compare multiple tables. Hopefully, a future version of Oracle will include an `ASSERT` command that lets us define complex business rules in a single statement. For now, there is a workaround discussed later in the "Materialized Views" section.

This book focuses on practical solutions, yet this section used a lot of weird code to demonstrate obscure features. And other unusual constraint features were discussed in previous chapters, such as cascading deletes and deferrable constraints. Constraints are one of the few areas worth discussing in depth. Constraints are critical, and we need to keep our data as clean as possible. Once again, don't worry if you can't remember all the syntax. The important point to remember is that there's always a way to enforce the data rules we need. And there's always a way to enforce those rules efficiently.

Indexes

Indexes are data structures that mirror table data but are organized in a way to improve performance. Oracle has a ridiculous number of index options, and they are only briefly discussed in this section. Before we discuss the options, it's important to have a good understanding of what indexes are and how indexes work. We need a good theoretical understanding of indexes to know how to use them and when they won't work. Many databases are littered with useless indexes because a developer thought an index would magically solve a performance problem. And many databases suffer because their indexes are missing that one, small feature that would make the indexes useful.

Index Concepts

To understand indexes, we must first think about searching for data. Let's start with a simple children's guessing game, where we have to find a number between 1 and 8. The simplest way to search for the number is to start with 1, then guess 2, then guess 3, etc. On average, using that linear search algorithm, it will take four guesses to find the number.

Luckily, we all know a better way to play the guessing game – guess a number in the middle, ask if the number is lower or higher, and repeat. This binary search algorithm eliminates as many numbers as possible each time and narrows down the results quickly. We can visualize this binary search strategy with Figure 9-1. The diagram is shaped like a tree, and at each branch of the tree, we must make a simple decision: go left if our guess is too high and go right if our guess is too low.

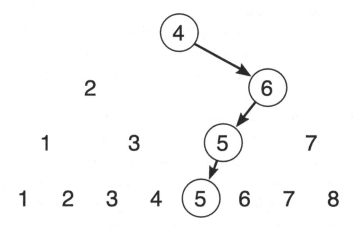

Figure 9-1. *A binary search to find the number 5*

Using the binary search algorithm, on average we can find the number in three guesses. So far, our binary search algorithm is only slightly better than our linear search algorithm: three guesses instead of four. The difference in the algorithms becomes more noticeable when we increase the size. If we double the number range to 16, the average number of linear search guesses also doubles, to eight. But the average number of binary search guesses only increases from three to four.

Let's scale up the example to our data set. Let's say we want to find a launch, with the following query:

```
select * from launch where launch_id = :n;
```

The data is stored in a heap table, in no particular order. If we search through the table of 70,535 launches with a linear search, it will require an average of 35,268 comparisons. A binary search could find the row in at most 17 comparisons, since 2^17 = 131,072, which is greater than 70,535. The principles of a children's guessing game scale up nicely to help us quickly find real data.

It is helpful to use a more mathematical explanation for what's going on with our searching. When we count in binary, the powers-of-two exponentiation grows quickly. We probably understand binary growth intuitively; for example, we know that 32 bits allows for about four billion numbers: 2^32 = 4,294,967,296. Binary searching works in reverse, and logarithms are the opposite of exponents. Therefore, we can say that a binary search of N rows requires approximately LOG2(N) comparisons. Compare that with a linear search on N rows, which requires approximately N/2 comparisons. Those mathematical expressions will be useful for understanding indexes in just a minute.

An index is a data structure that is similar to the binary tree displayed in Figure 9-1. Of course, the actual index structure is more complicated than our example. Oracle's default index uses a B-tree index; there's a root branch block at the top, branch blocks in the middle, and leaf blocks at the bottom. Each block contains hundreds of values instead of just one. The leaf blocks don't just contain the column value; they also contain a ROWID that references the table row, as well as pointers to the next and last leaf blocks in order. (The pointers are why Figure 9-1 seems to have an extra row at the bottom – there is a lookup from the leaf block to a table block.) In practice, it's extremely rare to have an index more than four levels deep. (We can count the height of an index using DBA_INDEXES.BLEVEL+1.) Also, real indexes have empty space for new values and may be unbalanced.

We can learn a lot about indexes by combining the tree data structure in Figure 9-1 with our simple algorithm for traversing the tree. The most important lesson is why index access is not always faster than a full table scan. For finding a single value, the number of comparisons is LOG2(N) for an index vs. N/2 for a full table scan. For finding one value, the index is clearly the winner.

But what if we're looking for a value that exists in almost every row? Searching an index for every row means we need to walk the tree N times. Now the number of comparisons is N*LOG2(N) for the index vs. N for the full table scan. For finding all values, the full table scan is clearly the winner.

Index access comparisons get even more complicated when we consider block access time. Storage systems can read a large amount of data more efficiently than they can read multiple small amounts of data. In the time it takes the system to read two index blocks, one at a time, the system may be able to read 64 blocks from a full table scan. A dumb multi-block read may be better than a smart single-block read.

The clustering factor may also work against indexes. For example, let's say we only need to scan 1% of an index. One percent sounds like a small number of searches, but that number is not the whole story. After we read the index blocks, we also need to access the table blocks. If the rows we need are randomly distributed, we may still need to read 100% of the table, one block at a time. DBA_INDEXES.CLUSTERING_FACTOR is a measure of how much the data is disordered. A good, low clustering factor means the values in one index block all refer to the same table block. A bad, high clustering factor means the rows in an index block are scattered all over the place.

Indexes are perfect for accessing a small amount of data from a table. Indexes may be a bad choice for accessing a large amount of data from a table. It's hard to know where the tipping point is and when an index isn't worth it anymore. We need to consider how an index works, multi-block reads, and the clustering factor.

Index Features

Indexes are an indispensable part of database performance. It's a great feeling when a statement as simple as CREATE INDEX SOME_INDEX ON SOME_TABLE(SOME_COLUMN) makes our queries run a million times faster. But performance tuning is not always that easy. Simple indexes aren't always enough, so we need to be aware of the many different ways to use, create, and alter indexes.

First, we need to understand how Oracle can use an index. The tree traversal we saw in Figure 9-1 is the most common algorithm, but there are several others:

1. *Index unique and index range scan*: The traditional way to read an index, by traversing the tree from top to bottom. Ideal when we only need a small percentage of rows from a table.

2. *Index fast full*: Reads the entire index with multi-block reads. Ideal when we need a large percentage of rows and all of the columns we need are in the index. The index can be used as a skinny version of the table.

3. *Index full*: Reads the entire index, in order. Slower than an index fast full, because single-block reads are used instead of multi-block reads. The advantage is that the data is returned in order, which can avoid sorting.

4. *Index skip scan*: Uses a multicolumn index even though the leading index columns aren't referenced. This access method is slow, especially if the leading columns have a high cardinality, but it's better than nothing.

5. *Index joins*: Reads data from multiple indexes and joins the indexes instead of the tables.

Bitmap indexes are useful for low-cardinality data – columns with a small number of distinct values. A bitmap is a list of ones and zeroes that map whether each row has a specific value. For example, in our data set, LAUNCH.LAUNCH_CATEGORY is a good candidate for a bitmap index. The following code creates a bitmap index, along with a simple visualization of what that bitmap index might look like:

```
--Create bitmap index on low-cardinality columns.
create bitmap index launch_category_idx
on launch(launch_category);

military missile  : 111000000...
atmospheric rocket: 000111000...
suborbital rocket : 000000111...
...
```

Each bitmap stores 70,535 ones or zeroes, where each bit corresponds to a row. This format is why bitmap indexes only work well for low-cardinality columns. Although 70,535 bits is not a lot of data, that size must be repeated for each unique value. On the other hand, Oracle can compress the bitmap indexes, so the actual storage may be much smaller. LAUNCH.LAUNCH_CATEGORY only has ten distinct values, so even in the worst case of using 70,535 bits for each value, not a lot of space is used.

The bitmap format makes it easy to perform comparison operations. If we also created a bitmap index on LAUNCH.LAUNCH_STATUS, we could quickly run queries that filtered on both the category and the status. Oracle could combine the two bitmaps with a BITMAP AND operation. Comparing lists of ones and zeroes is something any computer can do efficiently.

Bitmap indexes have concurrency issues and should not be used on tables that are frequently changed. While we may think of the bitmap format as a list of ones and zeroes, Oracle's bitmap compression may significantly shrink that format. Oracle may compress a range of values and store the equivalent of a note that says, "Rows 1 to 10,000 are all 0." If we update the table and change a value in the middle of that range, Oracle has to recompress the bitmap index. That recompression means changing a single value may lock many of rows. Frequently updating a table with bitmap indexes will lead to long waits and deadlock errors.

Index compression can save a lot of space and improve performance. Index compression is similar to basic table compression – they both use a simple pattern substitution. But index compression is better than table compression in several ways. Index compression works regardless of the types of table changes and does not require direct-path inserts. And index compression has virtually no CPU overhead. Indexes are stored with the leading columns first, so compression only works if the leading columns are repetitive.

Oracle indexes can include **multiple columns**. If we know certain columns will always be queried together, it may make sense to put them in the same index. Or we can have a separate index for each column. Or we can have both – one multicolumn index and many individual indexes. But we don't want to go crazy creating indexes. Each index uses space and requires extra time to maintain when the table is changed.

Function-based indexes are built on expressions. Function-based indexes are useful when we query a column by a modified version of the value. For example, when looking for launches, most of the time we only care about the date, not the time. If we add a normal index on the LAUNCH.LAUNCH_DATE, we could use a BETWEEN query to get an index range scan. But we would also have to define two dates and specify the seconds, which is annoying. It's easier to query the table using the TRUNC function and only compare dates. But the TRUNC function does not work with a normal index. The following code creates and uses a function-based index on the launch date:

```
--Create function based index.
create index launch_date_idx
on launch(trunc(launch_date));

select *
from launch
where trunc(launch_date) = date '1957-10-04';
```

Rebuilding Indexes

Indexes can be turned on or off, similar to constraints. But instead of ENABLE and DISABLE, indexes are USABLE or UNUSABLE. Making indexes unusable is as simple as ALTER INDEX LAUNCH_DATE_IDX UNUSABLE, and making indexes usable is as simple as ALTER INDEX LAUNCH_DATE_IDX REBUILD. In addition to enabling and disabling indexes, we can keep an index enabled but make it invisible. An invisible index is still maintained but is ignored by the optimizer. We can change the visibility of indexes to test the performance impact of index changes.

Unless we're rebuilding the entire schema, modifying an index is simpler than dropping and recreating an index. Our indexes may have lots of properties set, and we don't want to lose those properties during an index rebuild.

Indexes have many of the same configuration options as tables. Indexes can be set to parallel, but like with tables, we should avoid setting a default degree of parallelism. Indexes can have separate tablespaces, but like with tables, we should avoid creating many tablespaces. (And please ignore the myth that indexes and tables need separate tablespaces, unless you are an expert in your storage system and are prepared to thoroughly test performance.) Indexes can also be set to NOLOGGING, but unlike tables the repercussions of using NOLOGGING are not as bad; if an index is unrecoverable, we can simply recreate the index from the table data. Similar to tables, indexes can also be partitioned, which is described in a later section.

Oracle index rebuilding is a contentious topic. There are clearly times when we must rebuild an index, like if the index was made unusable during a maintenance operation or if we want to change index properties. But we should not rebuild indexes frequently for performance reasons or as part of a periodic "maintenance" procedure. Other than a few rare exceptions, Oracle indexes are self-balancing and don't need to be rebuilt.

When we do need to rebuild indexes, there are several options to make the process faster and nondisruptive. The ONLINE option will let the index still be used in queries while a new version of the index is built. We can combine the ONLINE option with other options to rebuild the index quickly and then change the properties back to their original values:

```
--Rebuild online, quickly, and then reset properties.
alter index launch_date_idx rebuild online nologging parallel;
alter index launch_date_idx logging noparallel;
```

Partitioning

Partitioning divides tables and indexes into smaller pieces to improve performance and manageability. Partitioned tables look like regular tables to our SQL statements. Behind the scenes, Oracle can adjust our statements to only access the relevant partitions, instead of reading the entire table. Partitioning is fully described in the 425-page *VLDB and Partitioning Guide*. This section gives a brief overview of partitioning and is more focused on understanding why partitioning works than listing the hundreds of partitioning features.

Partitioning Concepts

Although partitioning is described in the "Very Large Database" manual, partitioning can help databases of any size. Partitioning is about the *percentage* of the data we're accessing, not just the *size* of the data. Partitioning and indexing solve two different kinds of performance problems; indexes work best for retrieving a small percentage of rows, and partitions work best for retrieving a large percentage of rows.

Let's use an example to understand the fundamental mechanism of partitioning. Most of the examples in this book filter the LAUNCH table by the column LAUNCH_ CATEGORY. We rarely want to query across all launches, since there's a huge difference between sounding rockets that perform weather experiments and orbital launches that put a satellite into orbit.

Our goal is to optimize this SQL statement: SELECT * FROM LAUNCH WHERE LAUNCH_ CATEGORY = 'orbital'. That SQL statement retrieves a relatively large percentage of rows. As discussed in the last section, there are several reasons indexes cannot help us retrieve a large percentage of rows. We want the efficiency of multi-block reads from a full table scan, but we don't want to read the entire table. To understand partitioning, let's first achieve our goal the hard way by using an old technique called "partitioned views." We can get multi-block read efficiency and exclude most of the rows by creating multiple tables and putting them together in a view.

First, we create a table for each launch category. There are only ten launch categories, so creating the tables doesn't take too long. (Only the first part of this large example is listed here. See the repository for the full example code.)

```
--Create a table for each LAUNCH_CATEGORY.
create table launch_orbital as
select * from launch where launch_category = 'orbital';

create table launch_military_missile as
select * from launch where launch_category = 'military missile';
...
```

Next, create a view named LAUNCH_ALL that stitches together those tiny tables:

```
--Create a view that combines per-category tables together.
create or replace view launch_all as
select * from launch_orbital
where launch_category = 'orbital'
union all
select * from launch_military_missile
where launch_category = 'military missile'
...
```

When we query from the preceding view, the results are the same as querying directly against the original LAUNCH table, but the view query provides optimal performance. Oracle can read the view definition, can understand that only one of the ten tables can satisfy the predicate LAUNCH_CATEGORY = 'orbital', and will only read from that table. At first this solution looks like the best of all worlds; we query the view like it's a huge table, but the view acts like a small table:

```
--These return the same results but LAUNCH_ALL is faster.
select * from launch where launch_category = 'orbital';
select * from launch_all where launch_category = 'orbital';
```

We just built a bargain-basement partitioning scheme. Our specific example worked fine, but the solution is horribly broken. We can't update LAUNCH_ALL, since we'll run into problems with updatable views. Creating the tables and views was a chore and required repeating the predicates. If we wanted to create indexes, we'd have to create an index for each table.

Real partitioning automates the previous steps and creates a table that works optimally and flawlessly. Oracle creates a segment for each partition, which behaves just like a table. Oracle perfectly understands the mapping between those segments and the table, and all table operations work automatically on the partitioned table.

The following code shows how to create a real partitioned LAUNCH table. (Alternatively, we could have used ALTER TABLE to add partitioning to an existing table.) There's some new syntax, but this code is much simpler than explicitly creating extra tables, views, and indexes:

```
--Create and query a partitioned launch table.
create table launch_partition
partition by list(launch_category)
(
    partition p_sub values('suborbital rocket'),
    partition p_mil values('military missile'),
    partition p_orb values('orbital'),
    partition p_atm values('atmospheric rocket'),
    partition p_pln values('suborbital spaceplane'),
    partition p_tst values('test rocket'),
    partition p_dep values('deep space'),
    partition p_bal values('ballistic missile test'),
    partition p_snd values('sounding rocket'),
    partition p_lun values('lunar return')
) as
```

```
select * from launch;
```

```
select *
from launch_partition
where launch_category = 'orbital';
```

Why didn't we simply create the preceding partitioned table and skip the poorly built version with multiple tables and views? It's important to understand that partitioning is not magic. Too many SQL developers always partition large tables and assume partitioning will help performance. Partitioning is just an automatic system to break large tables into small tables. If we can't think of a way that querying multiple smaller tables could improve our SQL statements, then partitioning won't help.

In addition to improving the performance of our SQL statements, partitioning can also make our data more manageable. For example, it's easy to create a data retention system with a scheduler job that reads partition metadata from the data dictionary and truncates or drops old partitions. And since 19c, we can create a hybrid partitioned table where some of the partitions are based on external files or other external data sources.

Partitioning Features

Partitioning has a huge number of features. Oracle provides many ways to divide tables into partitions, use partitions, and index partitions.

The most important partitioning decision we have to make is how to divide our table into partitions. We need to determine the "chunks" of data that our SQL statements will most often reference. The following list includes the most common partition options:

1. *List*: Each partition maps to a list of values and can include a
    DEFAULT value to cover everything else. Useful for low-cardinality
    discrete values, such as a status or category column.

2. *Range*: Each partition contains a range of values. Each partition
    is defined as values less than a specific literal, or the MAXVALUE
    to cover everything else. Useful for continuous values, such as
    numeric and date values.

3. *Hash*: Each partition contains a random row, based on the hash of a value. Useful for data that we want to split into groups but we don't care about the precise grouping. Typically, only useful if multiple tables are partitioned the same way and we plan to use partition-wise joins.[4] The partition number should be a power of 2, or the partition sizes will be skewed.

4. *Interval*: Same as range partitioning, except the ranges do not need to be fully specified. Only an initial value and an interval must be defined, and Oracle will automatically create the necessary partitions. Useful for continuous values that will grow.

5. *Reference*: Uses list, range, hash, or interval partitioning, but lets the child table automatically follow the partitioning scheme of the parent table. The partitioned columns are not repeated, so this is useful for saving space in parent–child tables.

6. *Composite*: Combinations of list, range, hash, and interval, into partitions and subpartitions.

After we choose the partition type, we must choose the number of partitions. The number of partitions involves trade-offs and depends on how we are going to access the table. A large number of small partitions let us more quickly access only the data we need. But the larger the number, the larger the overhead and the more difficult it is to manage. Oracle does a good job of managing things like metadata and statistics for partitions; but if we end up with a million partitions, the data dictionary is going to grind to a halt. We might want to err on the side of fewer partitions. For example, even if our queries retrieve data one day at a time, weekly interval partitioning might be good enough.

Partitions, like tables, have many properties. Partitions inherit their properties from their table, but it may make sense to customize properties for different partitions. With partitioning, we can implement tiered storage within a single table. For example, for a

---

[4] Partition-wise joins work one partition at a time. Joining per partition instead of per table can significantly decrease the memory requirements and improve performance. But partition-wise joins only happen if the tables are partitioned the exact same way and the join uses the partition column. Most hash-partitioned tables are a mistake because programmers incorrectly think partition-wise joins happen with every join.

table range partitioned by a date, new partitions can be stored in tablespaces that use fast storage, while older partitions can be compressed and stored in tablespaces that use slower, cheaper storage.

Parallelism is the most misunderstood partitioning feature. Parallelism and partitioning tend to go together, since both of them help with large data. But we do not need to use one to take advantage of the other. On the surface, parallelism and partitioning sound similar – they both break large tables into smaller pieces. But parallel SQL works just as well on non-partitioned tables as on partitioned tables. Parallelism doesn't have to use the partition chunks; parallelism can just as easily divide up the table by itself into pieces called granules.

Partition exchange is used in data warehouses to help load data. We can take our time loading data into a temporary staging table. When we're done with the load and we've verified the data, we can swap that whole staging table with the production partition. The exchange operation is only a metadata change and runs much faster than inserting the data.

There are multiple syntax options for performing partition maintenance. The following code shows an example of deleting from a partitioned table using the partition extension clause and truncating the same partition using an ALTER TABLE command:

```
--Partition administration examples.
delete from launch_partition partition (p_orb);
alter table launch_partition truncate partition p_orb;
```

Partitioned tables can have indexes. Mixing partitioning and indexing gives us the best of both worlds – we can use the partitions to efficiently retrieve a large percentage of data, and we can use the indexes to efficiently retrieve a small percentage of data.

Indexes on partitioned tables can be either global or local. While the table data for a partitioned table is physically separated into multiple partitions, the index data does not need to follow the same pattern. A global index is a single, large tree that covers all the partitions. A local index contains multiple, smaller trees where each tree covers a single partition. A global index works best for searching for a small number of values that are spread across multiple partitions. A local index works best for retrieving a small number of values that are all within the same partition.

Views

Views are stored SQL statements. We can reference views instead of repeating the same SQL statements multiple times. Views only store the logic, not the data. Materialized views include actual data and are discussed later in this chapter. There aren't many advanced features for views, and previous chapters and sections have already discussed updatable views and view constraints. But there are important issues with creating and expanding views.

Creating Views

Creating views is simple. Two of the view creation options are OR REPLACE and FORCE. There's not much mystery to how those options work; OR REPLACE means the view will overwrite an existing view, and FORCE means that the view will be created even if something in the view doesn't exist. The following code demonstrates these two options:

```
--View with "OR REPLACE" and "FORCE".
create or replace force view bad_view as
select * from does_not_exist;

--The view exists but is broken and throws this error:
--ORA-04063: view "SPACE.BAD_VIEW" has errors
select * from bad_view;
```

The interesting thing about these two options is that they are *not* properties of the view – they are simply instructions for how to create a view. When we look at view source code through DBMS_METADATA.GET_DDL or by clicking a button in our IDE, the programs do not necessarily return the options we used to initially create the view. The programs only return the options they think we might want to use next time.

This difference between our original DDL and the DDL returned by metadata tools is another example of why we should store our code in version-controlled text files, instead of relying on the database to recreate our objects. Maybe we don't want to replace the view if the view already exists – perhaps the view creation was part of a non-repeatable process. Maybe we don't want to force the creation of the view – perhaps we want our script to fail as soon as an error is detected. The data dictionary cannot perfectly recreate our processes and has to make guesses. We should aim for 100% reproducibility in our build scripts, so we have to watch out for these tiny differences.

Expanding Views

In theory, views are a wonderful tool for improving our code. "Don't repeat yourself" is perhaps the most important programming rule, and views can help us follow that rule. In practice, views often become a mess. Too many SQL developers don't follow common programming advice, like using meaningful names, indenting, adding comments, etc. We must treat SQL, and especially views, as miniature programs.

One of the most annoying problems with views is when they become deeply nested. Nesting *inline* views is great, because each step is simple and we can easily see and debug the entire statement. Nesting regular views is often different, especially when the views are large and poorly built.

Oracle provides tools like DBMS_UTILITY.EXPAND_SQL_TEXT to help us expand our views and view all of the code at once. The following code demonstrates creating a nested view and expanding the view to show all the code at once:

```
--Create nested views and expand them.
create or replace view view1 as select 1 a, 2 b from dual;
create or replace view view2 as select a from view1;

declare
   v_output clob;
begin
   dbms_utility.expand_sql_text('select * from view2', v_output);
   dbms_output.put_line(v_output);
end;
/
```

Unfortunately, the output from the preceding anonymous block looks horrible. The following results are technically correct but almost unreadable:

```
SELECT "A1"."A" "A" FROM  (SELECT "A2"."A" "A" FROM  (SELECT 1 "A",2 "B"
FROM "SYS"."DUAL" "A3") "A2") "A1"
```

The preceding mess is why some organizations have guidelines to not nest views more than one level deep. Another potential issue with nesting views is performance. Oracle has many ways to rewrite and transform our SQL. When we reference a huge view, but only use a small part of it, Oracle may be able to avoid running the unnecessary parts – but not always. It's difficult to tell exactly when Oracle can throw out the unnecessary parts of views. If we're constantly using large views, only for one small piece, we're going to run into performance problems.

Don't let the preceding problems prevent you from using views. With the right features, styles, and discipline, we can build impressive systems with views. For example, if we combine views and INSTEAD OF triggers, we can create an abstraction layer that can be simpler than our tables and isolated from data model changes.

Users

Oracle users serve two purposes – they are a schema[5] that contains objects, and they are an account that can log on to the database. Many SQL developers are given an account by a more privileged user and never consider user management. But to create an efficient database development process, we need to be comfortable with creating, altering, and dropping user accounts. The advice in this section is for developers creating application accounts, not for DBAs creating user accounts.

Creating users can be simple – all we need is a username and a password. But we should put more thought into user management, or we will regret it later. Every organization struggles with passwords, and Oracle has multiple mechanisms to ease our password pains. Instead of sharing application passwords with developers, we can grant proxy access that lets a user connect to another account with their personal password. For example, ALTER USER APP_USER GRANT CONNECT THROUGH YOUR_USER would let you log in to the application account with the username YOUR_USER[APP_USER] and your personal password. The odd syntax is a small price to pay for not having to share and change application passwords. And since 18c, we can use LDAP authentication for our Oracle user. Or if nobody ever needs to log in as the application user, since 18c, we can create the application account with the option NO AUTHENTICATION and not have to worry about password management at all.

Our application user passwords need to be long and complicated. There are many password verification functions out there, so we might as well generate a password that will satisfy them all. Always combine multiple lowercase and uppercase characters,

---

[5] To make things even more confusing, Oracle has an unrelated CREATE SCHEMA command. That command does not create a user; instead, it is for creating multiple objects in one statement. This rarely used command is useful for creating tables with circular dependencies.

numbers, and a few special characters. And use the full 30 bytes. Oracle's password hashing algorithms are often insecure, and having a longer password will at least make the hashes harder to crack.

Applications should also have a non-default profile. Profiles are used to limit user connections, require periodic password changes, etc. Even if we don't care about the security implications and just want infinite connections and unlimited password lifetimes, we still need to worry about the profiles. Most databases use a default profile that limits the concurrent sessions and expires the password. If we don't choose the right profile, our application may break when the activity increases or when the password expires. Since 21c, profiles allow us to create a gradual password rollover time. If our environment has a large number of applications and connections, being able to temporarily use the old and new passwords at the same time can greatly simplify password changes.

Ideally, the only time we ever need to worry about tablespaces is when we create a user. Applications should have their own tablespace or at least not share the default USERS tablespace with other accounts. The USERS tablespace tends to fill up from ad hoc SQL statements, and we don't want a full USERS tablespace to break our application. In addition to setting a default tablespace, application schemas also need quota for that tablespace, usually through `QUOTA UNLIMITED ON TABLESPACE_NAME`.

The following command is an example of how we may want to create an application or application user account:

```
--Create an application user account.
create user application_user
identified by "ridiculouslyLongPW52733042#$%^"
--Schema account option:
--  account lock
--18c schema account option:
--  no authentication
profile application_profile
default tablespace my_application_tablespace
quota unlimited on my_application_tablespace;
```

We're getting close to database administration, which is not the topic of this book. But SQL developers should be involved with creating, altering, and dropping application accounts.

We should be careful, but not scared, of dropping accounts – at least in our sandbox environments. Other than production, we don't often perform maintenance on application accounts, which means those non-production accounts get full of junk and should be frequently dropped and recreated. The process was described in Chapter 2 and begins with the following command. Even though this is a nonworking sample command, I have intentionally commented it out. Dangerous commands need an extra level of protection. Commenting isn't the only way to protect us from dangerous commands; we might put an extra prompt in our scripts, give the script a dangerous-sounding name, etc.:

```
--Drop user and all its objects and privileges.
--drop user application_user cascade;
```

Sequences

Sequences generate unique numbers, typically for surrogate primary keys. Sequences are another object that's simple to create but has a few unexpected behaviors.

A common request for sequences is to generate a sequence without gaps. Gapless sequences are not possible, so don't bother trying. Sequences are built for scalability, whereas creating a gapless sequence of numbers would require serializing transactions. If the user Alice increments a sequence as part of a transaction and then Bob increments the same sequence for another transaction, what happens if Alice executes a rollback? There are two ways to handle that situation: either Alice's sequence number is given up and creates a gap, or Bob's transaction cannot start until Alice is done. Oracle has chosen the first option, enabling sequences to scale for large multiuser environments. If we really need a gapless sequence (and chances are good we don't – we just think removing gaps would look nicer), we'll need to create our own custom serialization process that ensures only one user gets a number at a time.

We should avoid dropping and recreating sequences, other than in our initial build scripts. For basic sequence maintenance, we should use ALTER SEQUENCE commands when possible. Recreating sequences is not trivial, mostly because sequences may be granted to roles and users.

The most common sequence maintenance is resetting the sequence to a new value. Applications or ad hoc SQL statements may forget to use the sequence to insert a value, which means the sequence may eventually generate the same value and cause unique constraint violations. The simplest way to reset a sequence, since version 12.1, is this command:

```
--Create and alter a sequence.
create sequence some_sequence;
alter sequence some_sequence restart start with 1;
```

Resetting sequences in 11g is more painful: change the sequence interval to a large value, call the sequence, and then change the interval back to 1. Or perhaps we can simply call SOME_SEQUENCE.NEXTVAL repeatedly.

Calling the sequence many times is much slower than altering the sequence but has the advantage of avoiding any DDL commands. This approach can be useful in a production environment when we might need to fill out lots of paperwork to run a "change," but simply selecting from a sequence does not count as a change.

Sequences don't have to start with 1 and increment by 1; sequences have several other options. Sequences can START WITH any number, and they can INCREMENT BY any number, even a negative number to make the sequence decrease. Sequences can CYCLE back to the MINVALUE after the MAXVALUE is reached.

The sequence default values are usually good enough. The most common option that SQL developers change is the CACHE value, which determines how many sequences are pre-generated and stored in memory until they are used. The default value of 20 is usually fine. Similar to bulk collect, prefetch, and other batch size options, there is little benefit to setting large values. Batch sizes are discussed in more detail in Chapter 16.

For extreme concurrent insert performance, we may need to use the scalable sequence feature introduced in 18c. Sequences typically increment linearly and are typically used for primary key generation. Since indexes are stored in order, new values will tend to be written to the same block on disk. Accessing the same blocks is sometimes a good thing, because it means the data will be cached in memory. But frequently writing to the same block causes contention, especially in a clustered environment where multiple processes across multiple servers need to coordinate changes. We need a sequence to create a unique value, but sometimes we don't want all the new values to be stored in the same block.

The traditional solution to primary key index contention is to create the index with the keyword REVERSE to store the values in reverse order. While index values like 123 and 124 will likely be stored together, reversed values like 321 and 421 will likely be stored separately. Reverse key indexes solve contention problems, but writing every value to an almost random location causes other performance issues. In practice, reverse key indexes rarely solve a performance problem.

Scalable sequences solve the contention problem a better way, by prefixing the instance and session id to the sequence number. Each session will tend to write index values to the same blocks, minimizing the number of blocks that are accessed. And since a session cannot have contention with itself, and each session has a significantly different value, there is no inter-session contention either. The only downside is the ridiculously large sequence value, which isn't really much of a problem, but the values look suspicious at first:

```
--Create a scalable sequence and show the first value.
create sequence scalable_sequence_test scale;

select to_char(scalable_sequence_test.nextval) nextval from dual;

NEXTVAL
-------
10282800000000000000000000001
```

Synonyms

Synonyms are useful for creating aliases for schema objects. A layer of synonyms can hide ugly environmental differences that we don't want users or developers to worry about.

For example, the data set in this book can be installed on any schema. The data set installation instructions include steps for creating a user named SPACE. Imagine we're building an application on top of our data set, but the name SPACE is already taken on one database. The schema name will be different across environments. Our application could hide that difference with a synonym:

```
--Create synonym example.
create synonym launch for space.launch;
```

Another use for synonyms is to minimize downtime during large data loads. We can have two tables, or two materialized views, with a synonym pointing to one of them. When new data arrives, we load the data into the unused table. When the loading is complete, we CREATE OR REPLACE SYNONYM to switch the synonym to point to the new data. That approach is not as robust as online table redefinition, but it's simpler.

Similar to views, we should minimize our layers of indirection and avoid creating synonyms that refer to synonyms. We should also avoid creating PUBLIC synonyms. Public synonyms don't grant access to all users, but public synonyms do pollute the namespace.

Materialized Views

A materialized view stores the results of a query. Materialized views are mainly intended to improve the performance of data warehouses but can also enforce multi-table constraints. This section only briefly discusses materialized view topics; for more detailed information, there are several hundred pages about materialized views in the *Data Warehousing Guide*.

Materialized views share all the properties of tables, along with a query and directions for how to rebuild the materialized view. Materialized views can have indexes and can be built off of other materialized views. Refreshing materialized views can be done on demand, as part of a schedule, or automatically after a relevant statement or commit. The refresh can either be COMPLETE, where the entire table is rebuilt, or FAST, where only the necessary parts of the table are rebuilt. The package DBMS_MVIEW can help with refreshing a set of materialized views. The DBMS_MVIEW.REFRESH procedure has many options for refreshing, such as degree of parallelism, atomic (refresh all materialized views in one transaction), out of place (build a separate table and then swap out the old data), etc.

Materialized views are complex and should only be used after we have exhausted all other query tuning options. Materialized views can solve difficult performance problems, but at the cost of extra complexity, extra space, and extra time spent refreshing.

Materialized Views for Multi-table Constraints

Outside of a data warehouse, materialized views can be useful for enforcing multi-table constraints. For example, let's try to enforce a rule across the SATELLITE and LAUNCH tables. Both tables have an important date column; launches have LAUNCH_DATE, and satellites have ORBIT_EPOCH_DATE. Those dates are related but not always the same. Satellite orbits will change over time, such as when orbits decay due to atmospheric drag. The column ORBIT_EPOCH_DATE is the date when the orbital information was last obtained.

ORBIT_EPOCH_DATE is often later than the launch date, since the orbit changes after the launch. But it doesn't make sense for the orbit epoch date to be *before* the launch date. If Oracle had assertions, perhaps this statement could keep our data correct:

```
--LAUNCH.LAUNCH_DATE must be before SATELLITE.EPOCH_DATE.
--(Use "-1" because there are small deviations in times.)
create assertion launch_before_epoch_date as check
(
    select *
    from satellite
    join launch
        on satellite.launch_id = launch.launch_id
    where launch.launch_date - 1 < orbit_epoch_date
);
```

Unfortunately, the preceding feature does not exist yet. Most SQL developers would recreate that rule using triggers, which requires procedural code that is difficult to make both correct and fast. We can solve the problem declaratively using materialized views.

First, we must create materialized view logs on the relevant tables. Every time the table is changed, that change is also automatically written to the materialized view log. With that change information, our materialized view can quickly determine which rows to examine, so Oracle only has to compare changed rows, not the entire table:

```
--Create materialized view logs on base tables.
create materialized view log on satellite with rowid;
create materialized view log on launch with rowid;
```

Next, we create a FAST ON COMMIT materialized view that will list the rows we *don't* want to see. The following code flips the date comparison and has a few other odd changes. The view includes the ROWID from both tables and uses the old-fashioned join syntax instead of the ANSI join syntax. Fast refresh materialized views have many strange restrictions and can be difficult to create:

```
--Materialized view for the condition we don't want to happen.
create materialized view satellite_bad_epoch_mv
refresh fast on commit as
select satellite.orbit_epoch_date, launch.launch_date,
    satellite.rowid satellite_rowid,
```

```
    launch.rowid launch_rowid
from satellite, launch
where satellite.launch_id = launch.launch_id
    and orbit_epoch_date < launch.launch_date - 1;
```

(If you are using tables from another schema, you will need to grant `CREATE TABLE` directly to that schema, or else the preceding statement will fail with "ORA-01031: insufficient privileges." Even though *your* user may have the ability to create a table, when you create a materialized view, the *materialized view owner* needs to create another table in the background.)

The preceding materialized view contains all the bad rows. Because of the materialized view logs, the materialized view won't have to re-read the entire LAUNCH and SATELLITE tables to validate changes.

The last piece of the puzzle is to add a constraint. This materialized view shouldn't have any rows, so we create a constraint that will fail if anything exists. But since there are a few preexisting bad rows, we will create the constraint with the NOVALIDATE option to ignore those rows:

```
--Add constraint that prevents new rows.
alter table satellite_bad_epoch_mv add constraint
    satellite_bad_epoch_mv_no_row check (launch_rowid is null)
    enable novalidate;
```

Finally, let's try to make a bad update. Let's set an orbit epoch date to a value much earlier than the launch date. The following UPDATE will run, but the COMMIT statement initiates a series of events that end with the error "ORA-02290: check constraint (SPACE.SATELLITE_BAD_EPOCH_MV_NO_ROW) violated." The COMMIT causes the materialized view to try to refresh. The materialized view reads the changed rows from the materialized view log and then tries to build the results for our query that should not return any rows. When the query does return rows, the materialized view violates the constraint, causing an error:

```
--Set a bad value.
update satellite
set orbit_epoch_date = orbit_epoch_date - 100
where norad_id = '000001';

commit;
```

Materialized view assertions are useful for enforcing complex data rules, but there are several disadvantages. Each imitation assertion requires several new objects. The logic behind the materialized view is backward – we have to write a query for what we don't want. That query must adhere to several odd and poorly documented syntax rules. And DML on the base tables will have a performance penalty, because all changes also need to be written to the materialized view logs. This was a lot of painful code to create a simple constraint, but the effort is worth it to maintain the integrity of our data.

Database Links

Database links are the easiest way to access data on another database. With a few extra keywords, and a few tricks, we can build large, powerful inter-database systems.

Creating a database link is simple and only requires basic connection information. If we don't have access to multiple databases, we can still test database links by creating a database link that refers to itself. After we create a database link, remote objects are as easy to access as adding the "@" symbol. Oracle automatically figures out the privileges, data types, etc.:

```
--Create a database link to the same database, for testing.
create database link myself
connect to my_user_name
identified by "my_password"
using '(description=(address=(protocol=tcp)(host=localhost)
(port=1521))(connect_data=(server=dedicated)(sid=orcl)))';

select * from dual@myself;

DUMMY
-----
X
```

(The preceding commands will not work if we have the CURRENT_SCHEMA set to a different schema, since database links can only be directly created in our own schema. And, of course, we'll need to enter the correct details for our connection string.)

Database links have some odd behaviors, but there is almost always a workaround to our problems. Database links are not great for importing or exporting huge amounts of data. If we want to move gigabytes of data, we should look into tools like data pump. The "@" syntax also does not natively support DDL statements. The workaround for running DDL is to call `DBMS_UTILITY.EXEC_DDL_STATEMENT` over a database link. And database links always generate a transaction, even if the statement doesn't include DML.

Too many organizations have rules prohibiting database links for security reasons. There's nothing wrong with database links, although there are certainly problems with `PUBLIC` database links. We need to be very careful granting anything to public. But we shouldn't let a non-default option stop us from using the most convenient solution. Organizations that outright ban all database links would be wise to heed AviD's Rule of Usability: security at the expense of usability comes at the expense of security. If we block the easy, secure way, people will find an easy, insecure way. The worst security violations I've ever seen happened because an organization didn't allow database links.

With the right code and workarounds, database links can be used to help us query and control a large environment from a single database.

PL/SQL Objects

There are many interesting PL/SQL objects, but unfortunately those objects are out of the scope of this book. If you continue to learn more about Oracle SQL, you will inevitably start to use PL/SQL, so I will quickly list the objects here. You can start using PL/SQL with anonymous blocks and PL/SQL common table expressions. Eventually you'll want to start creating these PL/SQL schema objects:

1. *Function*: Runs PL/SQL statements and returns a value. Used for small lookups or data transformations.

2. *Procedure*: Runs PL/SQL statements but does not return a value. Used for small changes.

3. *Package specification and body*: Encapsulates functions, procedures, and variables. Used for creating programs.

4. *Trigger*: PL/SQL statements that are fired when an event happens, such as table changes or system events. Used for side effects of changes, such as adding a primary key to a new row.

5. *Type specification and type body*: Encapsulates functions, procedures, and variables. Similar to packages but meant to be used to hold data. Used for custom collections in PL/SQL programs or for object-relational tables.

PL/SQL is both overused and underused. The language is *overused* by programmers who come from a more traditional programming background and want to program procedurally. A PL/SQL program should not be used when a SQL statement can do the same thing. The language is *underused* by programmers who think databases should only store data, not process data. While I won't say Oracle is the best database, I'm comfortable saying Oracle PL/SQL is the best database procedural language. Just a little bit of PL/SQL can open up a lot of opportunities. The PL/SQL language is powerful enough to solve almost any problem.

Other Schema Objects

This section briefly lists other, less important schema objects. Even this section is not a complete list; there are still many more schema object types, although those objects are likely not relevant to SQL development:

1. *Cluster*: Physically stores multiple tables together. For example, the LAUNCH and SATELLITE tables are frequently joined together. It might help performance if the tables were pre-joined and stored in a cluster. Clusters sound good in theory but are not used in practice.

2. *Comment*: Documents tables, columns, and views. Can be useful since many IDEs read the comments and display them when we query the data.

3. *Materialized zone map*: Stores information about the min and max values within a "zone." Similar to partition pruning, a zone map can be used to quickly eliminate large chunks of data from full table scans. Unlike partitioning, zone maps are only metadata and do not require redesigning tables.

4. *OLAP objects*: Oracle has a full online analytical processing option. OLAP technology has faded recently, and Oracle has started to create more of the OLAP functionality as regular database objects. This includes analytic views, attribute dimensions, dimensions, and hierarchies.

Global Objects

Global objects are not owned by a specific Oracle user. Global objects are easy to forget because they are not directly owned by our applications. Our applications may depend on these objects, but these objects will often not show up when we export schemas or metadata. We need to remember these exceptions, or our applications may only get partially installed:

1. *Context*: Custom namespace that contains global data for each session. Can be set by a custom package and can be referenced by the SYS_CONTEXT function. For example, the default USERENV has many helpful values, such as SYS_CONTEXT('USERENV', 'HOST').

2. *Directory*: Mapping between a name and a file system directory. Oracle packages like UTL_FILE don't directly reference file system directories, only the Oracle directory object. This level of indirection is useful because the file system directories frequently change across environments and platforms.

3. *Profile*: Sets limits for users. Oracle recommends using the Resource Manager instead, since it's more powerful. But in practice the Resource Manager is overly complicated, and we rely on profiles.

4. *Restore point*: A name associated with a timestamp or System Change Number (SCN). Useful for flashback operations.

5. *Role*: A set of object and system privileges that can be granted to other users and roles. It's much simpler to grant a privilege once to the right role instead of granting a privilege to multiple users.

GRANT and REVOKE

The GRANT and REVOKE commands control database access. There are three things that must be controlled: object privileges (access to tables, views, etc.), system privileges (CREATE SESSION to log on, powerful privileges like SELECT ANY TABLE, etc.), and role privileges (custom application roles, powerful preexisting roles like DBA, etc.).

Privileges can only be granted on existing objects. That restriction sounds reasonable, but it means that there is no way to give the user Alice eternal access to all objects owned by the user Bob. We can simplify grant script by using the ALL PRIVILEGES option, but we still need to run the GRANT for every relevant object in Bob's schema. And if a new object is created in Bob's schema, Alice will not have access until we run another GRANT statement.

Another difficult privilege scenario is when grants get transitive: when X is granted to Y and Y is granted to Z. Creating chains of grants is difficult. When we grant an object to a user, that user cannot grant the object to someone else, unless they have the WITH ADMIN option. When we grant an object to a user, that user cannot create a view on top of that object and then grant that view to others, unless they have the WITH GRANT option.

Tracking privileges is not trivial. There are three kinds of privileges and three sets of data dictionary views, such as DBA_TAB_PRIVS, DBA_SYS_PRIVS, and DBA_ROLE_PRIVS. Since roles can be granted to roles, if we want to thoroughly list all the role privileges, we need a recursive query. If we want to truly know which roles we have access to, we must use a query like this:

```
--Roles granted directly or indirectly to the current user.
select *
from dba_role_privs
connect by prior granted_role = grantee
start with grantee = user
order by 1,2,3;
```

The queries get more complicated when looking for object and system privileges. We must take the preceding query and use it as part of another query. The following example finds all the system privileges granted to the current user:

```
--System privileges granted directly or indirectly to current user.
select *
from dba_sys_privs
where grantee = user
   or grantee in
   (
      select granted_role
      from dba_role_privs
      connect by prior granted_role = grantee
      start with grantee = user
   )
order by 1,2,3;
```

Finding object privileges requires a query very similar to the preceding query, but replace DBA_SYS_PRIVS with DBA_TAB_PRIVS. That view name is misleading – that view contains privileges for all objects, not just for tables.

Summary

Our whirlwind tour of advanced features is complete. We know how to build sets, how to read and write data, and how to create schema and global objects. We don't need to memorize the SQL syntax, but we do need to remember what our different options are. When we start combining advanced features and try to get the best performance out of Oracle, we need to look behind the curtain and see how Oracle works. The next chapter completes our discussion of advanced features by introducing Oracle's architecture.

CHAPTER 10

Optimize the Database with Oracle Architecture

SQL and the relational model are logical constructs built on top of our slow, physical machines. Even E. F. Codd's original paper warned that implementing the relational model would run into physical limitations. The more advanced features we use and the more stress we put on the database, the more likely it is for Oracle's abstractions to fail. Oracle has put a lot of effort into making our SQL code atomic, consistent, isolated, and durable. But no system can hide all of its implementation details, and we need to understand Oracle internals in order to make things work efficiently.

This chapter is focused on practical architectural information that we need to know for SQL development. Database administrators will need to learn much more about Oracle's architecture and should read all 622 pages of the *Database Concepts* manual. Developers can get by with just skimming that manual or with the information in this chapter.

Storage Structures

SQL developers need to be aware of how data is stored. Even if we're not responsible for administering our databases and storage, Oracle's storage architecture affects the performance and locking of our SQL statements. And we may need to understand how space is allocated, so we know how much space to request and how to not waste that space.

The storage structures, ordered from smallest to largest, are column values, row pieces, blocks, extents, segments, data files, tablespaces, and ASM or file systems. All of the items in that list are logical storage structures that only exist inside the database, except for data files that are physical storage structures that exist on the operating system. Oracle has other physical storage structures, such as control files and parameter

© Jon Heller 2023
J. Heller, *Pro Oracle SQL Development*, https://doi.org/10.1007/978-1-4842-8867-2_10

files, but those structures are more important to DBAs than developers. Our list of storage structures is not a perfect hierarchy, but it's good enough to be helpful. The list is shown in Figure 10-1.

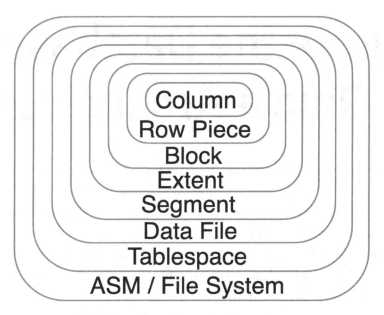

Figure 10-1. *Storage structure hierarchy*

Column Values

We've already encountered column values many times in this book. And we've seen how we can use the DUMP function to view the internal representation of data. The simplest data types, NUMBER, VARCHAR2, and DATE, are easy to understand and need no further explanation. These data types should make up the vast majority of our columns.

The storage of large objects (LOBs), such as BLOB, CLOB, and BFILE, can get quite complicated. BFILEs are pointers to binary files stored on the file system and are managed by the operating system. BLOBs and CLOBs can be stored inline, where a value less than 4000 bytes can be stored along with other data. BLOBs and CLOBs larger than 4000 bytes must be stored out of line, separate from the rest of the table data.

Each BLOB and each CLOB column has a separate segment to store large out-of-line data. In some cases, the vast majority of table data is stored in a LOB segment instead of the table segment. LOB segments can make calculating storage sizes tricky. For tables with large LOBs, we cannot simply look for the table name in DBA_SEGMENTS – we also have to find the LOB segment using DBA_LOBS. LOBs also have many storage properties, such as tablespace, compression, encryption, deduplication, logging, retention, etc. If we're storing a huge amount of data in LOBs, we need to think carefully about the settings for each LOB column.

Out-of-line LOBs still store a small amount of data in the table segment. Each LOB value has a locator that points to the LOB. An index is automatically created for each LOB to help quickly look up LOB data. Those LOB indexes are given system names like SYS_IL0000268678C00010$$, and we should not directly modify those indexes.

Non-atomic types, such as XMLType and object types, are more complicated. But even these complicated types are still stored in regular columns and rows behind the scenes. Data dictionary tables like DBA_NESTED_TABLES and DBA_TAB_COLS[1] show that the fancy types are stored the same way as the regular types. No matter what we do, our data is stored as columns and rows, so we shouldn't expect magical performance improvements by using advanced types.

Row Pieces

As we would expect from a relational database, all values are stored in columns, and the columns are stored in rows. These rows may be broken into multiple row pieces and scattered across multiple blocks (which are discussed next). Everything in Oracle must fit inside a block, which is usually 8 kilobytes. That size limitation means that large rows must be broken into multiple pieces, called row chaining. If we update a row and the row suddenly grows too large for the block, the entire row may migrate to another block. In rare cases, row chaining and row migration can lead to performance problems. Chaining and migrating rows require creating extra pointers to the row pieces or new location, which can lead to extra reads.

Every row can be identified by a ROWID pseudo-column, which is like a physical address for each row. The ROWID is the fastest way to look up a row – even faster than a primary key. But the ROWID can change, for example, if we compress or rebuild a table. We should not permanently store a ROWID value and expect the value to work later.

The way column data is stored within a row can have important implications for our table design. For each row, Oracle stores the number of columns. For each column, Oracle stores a byte size and then the data. (There is other row metadata, but that's not important here.)

---

[1] DBA_TAB_COLS shows the system-generated columns, whereas the data dictionary view DBA_TAB_COLUMNS only shows the user-generated columns.

For example, let's imagine three rows in the LAUNCH table, where LAUNCH_ID is the only column with a value. That table has 14 columns, so almost all of the values in those three rows are NULL. Let's also imagine that we chose to put the LAUNCH_ID as the *last* column. Each row starts with the number of columns, 14. Then there are 13 zeroes, for the null columns that have 0 bytes. Then there is a 1, the size of the last column, which only takes 1 byte. Finally, there are the LAUNCH_ID values themselves, which are simple integers. The first three rows may look like this:

```
14|000000000000011
14|000000000000012
14|000000000000013
```

Oracle uses a simple trick to save space with trailing NULLs. If we have the LAUNCH_ID at the *beginning* of the table, and every other value is NULL, the number of columns will be set to only 1. For the first column, the size is set to 1 byte, and then the data is included. For the rest of the columns, nothing is needed. Oracle infers that if only 1 out of the 14 columns is included, the rest must be NULL:

```
1|11
1|12
1|13
```

That trailing-NULL trick can save a significant amount of space for wide, sparse tables. But the trick only saves space if the nullable columns are put at the end of the table. We don't normally need to know this kind of information. But if we're going to build something extreme, like a table with a thousand columns, working with Oracle's physical architecture can make a big difference.

Blocks and Row-Level Locking

All columns and rows must fit inside blocks. A block is the atomic unit of Oracle read operations. Although we may only care about a single row, data is always read at least one block at a time. The default size of blocks is 8 kilobytes, so even if we only want 1 byte of data, Oracle will always read at least 8 kilobytes. (The operating system and storage device may read and write larger chunks as well.) Blocks can impact the performance and behavior of our database in several ways.

Basic table compression is done per block. Each block contains metadata about common values, and the block can save space by not repeating those common values. If the same value is repeated, but not within 8 kilobytes of the previous value, the value won't be compressed. But if the table is ordered by a column, repetitive values show up next to each other, and the compression ratio improves. We can make our compressed tables significantly smaller if our INSERT statement also has an ORDER BY.

The block size is configurable, but we shouldn't change it. There are many myths surrounding block sizes. I've never seen a reproducible test case demonstrating performance improvements from block size changes. But I have seen plenty of systems with a confusing mix of block sizes and incorrectly set parameters. Changing the block size won't help with large reads anyway; Oracle will adjust the DB_FILE_MULTIBLOCK_READ_COUNT parameter to never exceed the operating system maximum. Unless you're willing to spend a huge amount of time researching and testing, don't use a custom block size.

The PCTFREE parameter controls how much free space is left in new blocks and defaults to 10%. It's important to have a little bit of free space, to prevent row migration. If the blocks were completely full, adding a single byte would require moving the entire row. If the table is read-only, and rows will never move, then changing PCTFREE to 0 can save space.

Retrieving data in blocks explains why indexes don't perform as well as we would like. Our SQL statements may only select 1% of all rows, but if we're unlucky, that 1% is spread across 100% of the table blocks. Oracle may have to read a large percentage of the table to read a small percentage of the rows. This problem is represented by the clustering factor. Similar to compression, we can improve things by inserting data into the table in a specific order. But if we have multiple indexes, we may only be able to improve the clustering factor for a small number of them.

Oracle's row-level locking is implemented inside blocks. Whenever a transaction changes a row, that row is locked until the transaction is committed or rolled back. Only one transaction can modify the same row at the same time. Locks are not stored in a separate table – locking information is stored with the data blocks. Each block has an Interested Transaction List (ITL) that records which transaction is modifying which row, as well as a pointer to the relevant undo data.

This row-level locking architecture means there's no easy way to find out which rows are locked. Since lock information is stored inside each table, Oracle would have to read the entire table to know which row is locked and who locked it. And Oracle only stores the transaction that locked a row, not the specific statements. When we encounter a locking problem, we should ask *who* is blocking our statement, not *what* is blocking our statement. The following query is a simple way to find out who is blocking sessions:

```
--Who is blocking a session.
select final_blocking_session, gv$session.*
from gv$session
where final_blocking_session is not null
order by gv$session.final_blocking_session;
```

Once we have found the blocking session, it's simple to figure out who owns that session, what they are doing, and how they locked the row. There are lots of complex locking scenarios, hidden parameters, lock modes, and other details. But most of the time, when our row is locked, it means somebody else was updating the row and forgot to commit their transaction.

Extents

An extent is a collection of blocks that belong to the same segment. Oracle may modify data one block at a time, but Oracle allocates new space one extent at a time. There are two algorithms for deciding how many blocks to allocate per extent; we can let Oracle decide with AUTO, or we choose a static size ourselves with UNIFORM.

We should use the default, AUTO, and not worry about this setting unless we have an extreme case. For example, if we have thousands of tiny objects or partitions, we might want to save space by creating a small uniform size (although if we have that many objects, we have other problems and may need to rethink our design). There's not much to worry about for extents, as long as we don't mess with extent settings when we create tables and tablespaces.

Segments

A segment is a collection of extents. A segment is the entire storage structure for one logical object, although the definition of "object" can be a bit tricky. These objects are most commonly tables and indexes but can also include clusters, materialized views, LOBs, partitions and subpartitions, etc. Segments are usually the best storage structure for answering questions about object size, but the calculations can be tricky, especially when dropped objects are involved.

It's important to understand that a segment only applies to one logical object at a time. Space allocated to one table segment cannot be used by another table. For example, if we fill up a segment with a large table and then delete all the rows in that table, the space in that segment cannot be used by anything else. Unused space is why the TRUNCATE command is so important. Every segment has a high-water mark, to mark the largest amount of space used by that segment. The high-water mark is easy to increase but needs a DDL command to shrink. The empty space in a segment is not truly free space until we reset the high-water mark with a command like TRUNCATE.

It is impossible to perfectly measure the size of our data. The difficulty of that task seems absurd at first. Data is just 0s and 1s. Shouldn't it be trivial to count them? The problem is that there are so many ways to define "data." It's easy to include the table data by using DBA_SEGMENTS.BYTES. But since LOBs aren't stored in the table, we should at least use DBA_LOBS to find related LOB segments. If we also want to count indexes, we should use DBA_INDEXES to find related index segments. But the default answers will include empty space in the blocks and the segments and will measure the compressed size. With all these variables, whatever number we come up with will never match the size of a text file of our data. It's usually best to admit the answers won't be perfect and just use the sum of all relevant segment sizes.

When we want to measure or remove space, we also need to consider the recycle bin. Dropped objects disappear from our applications, but if the PURGE option wasn't used, those objects may not disappear entirely. Instead, the segments related to the objects may have been prefixed with BIN$ to mark them as being in the recycle bin. Oracle automatically removes the oldest objects from the recycle bin based on "space pressure." Space pressure occurs when the system is running out of space. But it's not clear what the criteria are; the old version of the manual was ambiguous, and the new version of the manual doesn't discuss space pressure at all. To be safe, we should purge objects when possible. Data objects can be dropped permanently with the PURGE option, or we can use a command such as PURGE USER_RECYCLEBIN or PURGE DBA_RECYCLEBIN.

Other non-permanent segment types include redo, undo, and temporary tablespaces. Those segment types are discussed elsewhere in this chapter.

Data Files

Data files are the physical storage structure for all data and are exactly what they sound like – files on the operating system. Data files are not truly parents of segments, so the hierarchical model used in this chapter is not perfect. A large table segment can span multiple data files. But in practice, data files tend to be much larger than segments.

Unfortunately, adding data files is something that SQL developers need to be aware of. Adding data files is a database administration task, but it is frequently done wrong and causes problems. The following is a simple example of adding a data file:

```
--Add data file.
alter tablespace my_tablespace add datafile 'C:\APP\...\FILE_X.DBF'
size 100m
autoextend on
next 100m
maxsize unlimited;
```

The first line of the preceding example is pure database administration. Finding the tablespace name, the directory (or the ASM disk group), and the file name depends on our system configuration. It's the last four lines that are important to developers and worth a brief discussion. There is no performance advantage to creating initially large data files, so starting with a small SIZE 100M can save space, especially in large environments with many data files. We almost always want to increase the size of the data files as our data grows, so AUTOEXTEND ON is an easy choice. We want our data files to grow at a reasonable pace, and NEXT 100M is a good size. If we set the next clause to 1, that will cause horrible performance problems since the system will have to extend the data file for every 8 KB of data. On the other hand, we don't want to set the next clause too high and waste space. And we might as well use as much space as possible, so setting MAXSIZE UNLIMITED is also a good default.

Another important decision is how many data files to add. As developers, we are responsible for providing an initial estimate of the data size. But we also need to recognize that our estimate will be wrong. If possible, we should try to set up rules for how to grow the data files. A good rule is to always double the number of data files. If we follow the preceding settings, adding extra data files is almost free. Doubling the number of data files doesn't hurt anything, and it provides lots of breathing room.

This data file discussion may feel irrelevant to the job of a SQL developer. But it's worth thinking about space growth ahead of time. Running out of space is the most common reason for Oracle outages. Nothing is more frustrating than having terabytes of space allocated, yet watching an application fail because one data file wasn't set to grow or watching the application repeatedly fail because a DBA adds one data file at a time, instead of doubling the number of data files.

There are other ways to ensure we don't run out of space. For example, we can use a single bigfile data file instead of multiple smallfiles. Once again, as SQL developers we may not particularly care about those details. Whatever approach our DBAs choose, we need to ensure that there is a system in place to not frequently run out of space.

Data files also have a high-water mark, and we may need to occasionally defragment our data files. Defragging above the high-water mark is easy, but it can be painful to defrag below the high-water mark. If we clean up a lot of objects, but are still wasting space on large data files, we need to talk to our DBAs. But don't be surprised if our DBAs tell us we can't easily reclaim the space.

Tablespaces

Tablespaces are logical collections of segments and have one or more data files. Tablespaces are used to group together storage, typically for an application or specific type of data.

Every object with permanent data can be assigned to a different tablespace. But we don't want to have to worry about the tablespace for every table. The simplest way to manage storage is to create one tablespace per user and let every object in that schema use the default tablespace. Managing the database is easier with fewer tablespaces. The more tablespaces we have, the more likely one of our tablespaces will run out of space and break things. On the other hand, we don't want to use only *one* tablespace; a runaway application could fill up the tablespace and break the entire database.

Many utilities and features can work per tablespace, such as data pump import and export, backup, and transportable tablespaces. Transportable tablespaces let us copy and paste data files between servers, to quickly move data. If we have a set of large tables that we want to frequently copy, it may help to isolate those tables in a tablespace.

Oracle comes with the default tablespaces SYSTEM, SYSAUX, USERS, UNDOTBS1, and TEMP. The SYSTEM and SYSAUX tablespaces are for system-generated objects, and we should avoid storing anything in these tablespaces. When a tablespace is full, the application that writes to that tablespace is going to break; if SYSTEM or SYSAUX is full, the entire database breaks. The USERS tablespace is helpful for ad hoc users but shouldn't be shared with applications. We don't want a user's ad hoc table to consume all the space and break our application. UNDOTBS1 unsurprisingly holds undo data, as described earlier in this chapter. The TEMP tablespace will be discussed later in this chapter.

Automatic Storage Management

Automatic Storage Management (ASM) is an Oracle tool to manage file systems inside a database, instead of using the operating system. SQL and administrative commands can reference a single disk group name instead of using operating system directories and files. Oracle can take care of things like striping, mirroring, file locations, etc. ASM can help with performance and reliability and can enable technologies like Real Application Clusters (RAC). ASM mostly affects administrators, but it may also impact SQL development in minor ways.

ASM has a huge footprint – it requires another database installation and instance. If we're setting up a personal sandbox, creating a separate ASM database is not worth the trouble.

Although ASM is a separate database, we rarely need to directly connect to it. Our regular databases automatically connect to the ASM instance. If we want to write queries to find the space available, instead of looking at data files and the operating system, we need to look at data dictionary views such as V$ASM_DISKGROUP.

We have to be careful to avoid duplicates when querying the ASM data dictionary. Each database returns the ASM information for *all* the databases connected to that ASM instance. If we want to query and aggregate data from all of our ASM instances, we need to only query from one database per ASM instance. Depending on how ASM is set up, those queries can be tricky. But usually there is one ASM database per host or one ASM database per cluster.

Wasted Space

There are many layers of storage structures, and each layer has wasted space. Some layers have extra space for updates or growth; other layers may maintain space unless they are resized. In addition, administrators have to pre-allocate extra space for future growth and emergencies. Most organizations try to keep their space usage below a certain threshold, such as 80%. And a lot of space may be used for supplementary data structures such as indexes and materialized views. And we need space for the database binaries, operating system files, trace files, data pump files, flat files, redo, archive logs, undo, temporary tablespaces, etc.

One way to avoid wasting so much space is to change from a simple storage threshold rule to a storage forecast. Instead of adding space when ASM is 80% full, we should only add space when an algorithm predicts we will run out in the near future. As SQL developers, it's tempting to ignore space problems and let the administrators handle them. But SQL developers are well suited to create programs that track space and predict future growth. (But this entire discussion may not apply to cloud environments where getting extra space is simple.)

Before we calculate our environment's ratio of allocated space to actual data, we should prepare to be disappointed. At my current job, we have a 5-to-1 ratio; it takes 5 terabytes of SAN space to store 1 terabyte of data. That high ratio seems ridiculous at first. But when we examine each storage layer individually, the extra space seems unavoidable. Wasting a huge amount of space is just something we have to live with.

These eternal space problems mean we need to have an honest conversation with our DBAs about storage management. We need to talk about the overhead and make sure we're not *both* multiplying the storage requirements by a fudge factor. We need to be prepared to be disappointed and understand that storing X bytes of data requires much more than X bytes of storage.

Redo

Oracle is designed to never lose our data, and redo is a central part of that design. Redo is a description of the changes being made to the database. When we run a DML statement, Oracle doesn't synchronously modify the data files; writing directly to data files would cause contention and performance issues. Instead, Oracle uses a process that is faster but is more complex and uses more resources. Most modern databases do something similar, but with a different name, such as write-ahead logging or transaction logging.

Redo in Theory

When data is changed, Oracle quickly writes the redo data into a redo log buffer, a memory structure. Before a commit can finish, that redo log buffer must be flushed to disk, into the online redo logs. The online redo logs are multiplexed files – losing one copy will not lose our data. Once the data is safely written to multiple locations, Oracle can finish the changes asynchronously. Background processes will copy the temporary online redo log into a permanent archive log. Background processes will also read the change data and eventually update the permanent data files.

The redo process feels like a lot of extra steps at first. But redo allows Oracle to batch the changes and write them together, instead of updating data files one tiny change at a time. And redo lets much of the work happen asynchronously while allowing Oracle to maintain durability. If we pull the plug on the database server, nothing will get lost. When the database restarts, Oracle can read from both the permanent data files and the redo log files to reconstruct the state of the database.

Redo in Practice

The redo architecture affects our SQL performance in several ways. DML is more expensive than we might anticipate. When we make a change to a table, that change must be written multiple times. Let's recreate the LAUNCH table, change the new copy, and measure the amount of redo data generated. The following query uses the view V$MYSTAT to measure redo generation:

```
--Cumulative redo generated by this session, in megabytes.
select to_char(round(value/1024/1024, 1), '999,990.0') mb
from v$mystat
join v$statname
    on v$mystat.statistic# = v$statname.statistic#
where v$statname.name = 'redo size';
```

To measure redo, we must re-run the preceding query after each statement. But to save space, the following examples do not reprint the statement each time. The following code shows different commands and how much redo is generated by each one. The redo sizes printed in the comments may not precisely match the values generated on your database because of version differences, configuration differences, and rounding:

```
--Create an empty table.  +0.0 megabytes.
create table launch_redo as
select * from launch where 1=0;

--Insert data.  +7.0 megabytes.
insert into launch_redo select * from launch;
commit;

--Delete data.  +24.6 megabytes.
delete from launch_redo;

--Rollback the delete.  +21.5 megabytes.
rollback;
```

According to DBA_SEGMENTS, the LAUNCH table only uses 7 megabytes of space. Notice how the preceding DELETE statement generates almost three times as much redo data than the actual size of the data. Even the rollback is expensive.

If we want to avoid generating redo, we need to use different SQL commands. The following code shows that a direct-path INSERT and a TRUNCATE statement both generate very little redo. Unfortunately, there is no way to stop redo from being generated by DELETE and UPDATE statements:

```
--Direct-path insert.  +0.0 megabytes.
alter table launch_redo nologging;
insert /*+ append */ into launch_redo select * from launch;
commit;

--Truncate new table.  +0.0 megabytes.
--truncate table launch_redo;
```

Notice how we're measuring redo in bytes, not rows. When we're thinking about SQL logic, the number of rows is more important. When we're thinking about the physical performance and impact of our SQL, the number of bytes and blocks is more important.

Redo generation can happen in unexpected places. DDL commands like TRUNCATE don't generate redo for the data, but they do generate a tiny amount of redo for changes to the data dictionary. There's a small chance you will see "+0.1" instead of "+0.0" for some of the DDL examples. Also, redo is also generated by global temporary tables, unless the parameter TEMP_UNDO_ENABLED is set to TRUE.

The problem with redo generation can be even worse than simply waiting for all those bytes to get written to disk. If our system is in ARCHIVELOG mode, then those online redo logs get saved again as archive logs. Those archive logs may consume a lot of space before they are backed up and deleted. Developers don't usually care about backups, but if we're changing a massive amount of data, we may want to check with a DBA first.

Redo is useful for more than just recovery. LogMiner can use redo data to read the changes and find the source of logical corruption. Data Guard uses redo data for maintaining logical and physical standby databases. GoldenGate uses redo for replication and synchronization with other databases.

Undo and Multiversion Read Consistency

Undo data is used for rollback, flashback, and multiversion read consistency. Undo is similar to redo – both represent changed data, and both can cause performance problems. But undo causes different kinds of problems and at different times.

Undo for Rollback

Redo represents the new data, and undo represents the old data. There are many times when our SQL statements need to reference the old data. Even when we issue a DELETE command, Oracle cannot simply remove all the data. The most obvious problem is – what happens if we roll back the statement or transaction? When Oracle is halfway through deleting a table, Oracle must be able to put everything back to the way it was.

Before data is changed, an old version of the data is saved in the undo tablespace. While redo is stored on the file system, undo is stored inside the database. But to make matters worse, undo also generates redo. The undo–redo combination may be necessary if the database crashes during a rollback.

All this transaction logging data sounds ridiculous at first. Aside from the change itself, Oracle saves multiple copies of the new data and multiple copies of the old data. All those extra copies are why direct-path writes can be so important. Our processes don't always have enough time and resources to make so many extra copies.

At least undo tends to be less expensive than redo. We can measure undo similar to the way we measured redo. The following query on V$MYSTAT is almost exactly the same as before – simply change "redo size" to "undo change vector size":

```
--Cumulative undo generated by this session, in megabytes.
select to_char(round(value/1024/1024, 1), '999,990.0') mb
from v$mystat
join v$statname
    on v$mystat.statistic# = v$statname.statistic#
where v$statname.name = 'undo change vector size';
```

Similar to calculating redo, we can use the output from the preceding query as a baseline for measuring undo generation. Then we can determine the undo generated by any statement by re-running the preceding query. If we re-run the previous test cases, but this time measure undo, we'll find that the undo generated is less than the redo generated:

```
--Create an empty table.  +0.0 megabytes.
create table launch_undo as
select * from launch where 1=0;

--Insert data.  +0.3 megabytes.
insert into launch_undo select * from launch;
commit;

--Delete data.  +13.9 megabytes.
delete from launch_undo;

--Rollback the delete.  +0.0 megabytes.
rollback;

--Direct-path insert.  +0.0 megabytes.
alter table launch_undo nologging;
insert /*+ append */ into launch_undo select * from launch;
commit;

--Truncate new table.  +0.1 megabytes.
--truncate table launch_undo;
```

Like with redo, creating the preceding empty table generates almost no undo data. Inserting data is where the undo looks better than redo; neither conventional nor direct-path INSERT statements generate significant undo data. Deleting does create a lot of undo data, about twice as much data as the size of the table, but that undo is still less than the redo size. Rollback *uses* the undo data but doesn't generate any undo data.

285

Another good thing about undo is that it ages out. There's no such thing as undo archive logs that need to be saved or backed up. The undo tablespace will eventually clean itself out, based on the size of the tablespace, the parameter UNDO_RETENTION, and system activity. But we may still need to allocate a lot of space for the undo tablespace, depending on how big and slow our transactions are. If we get errors about not being able to find undo segments, either from DML or flashback, we may need to either increase the undo tablespace size or increase UNDO_RETENTION. If our undo problem is related to LOBs, which store their undo data differently, we may need to change individual column retention settings.

Undo for Multiversion Consistency

Aside from the obvious use of undo for rollbacks, undo is also used to maintain multiversion consistency. Undo is Oracle's mechanism to achieve the consistency and isolation in ACID (as opposed to databases that use the simpler mechanism of locking entire objects, which causes horrible concurrency problems).

Oracle uses a System Change Number (SCN) to identify the version of each row. The SCN increases with every commit and can be queried through the pseudo-column ORA_ROWSCN, as shown in the following example:

```
--System Change Number (SCN) example.
select norad_id, ora_rowscn
from satellite
order by norad_id
fetch first 3 rows only;

NORAD_ID   ORA_ROWSCN
--------   ----------
000001       39300415
000002       39300415
000003       39300415
```

If we made a change to those rows, and committed the change, the ORA_ROWSCN would increase. If we rewrote the query using flashback, for example, if we added the expression AS OF TIMESTAMP SYSTIMESTAMP - INTERVAL '1' MINUTE after the table name, we would see the old values and the old SCN. When we query a table, we may be reading from other data structures; some table data may be in the table, and some table data may be in the undo tablespace.

We need to be careful about using the SCN for our own purposes, such as optimistic locking. Despite the name, ORA_ROWSCN does not necessarily return the SCN for each row. By default, Oracle records one SCN per block, and updating one row may change the ORA_ROWSCN for other rows. If we want to track an SCN for each row, we can create the table with ROWDEPENDENCIES enabled, which uses an extra 6 bytes in each row to store the SCN.

But even with ROWDEPENDENCIES enabled, the ORA_ROWSCN pseudo-column is not 100% accurate and can appear to randomly change. Oracle's internal use of the SCN is accurate, but the external presentation of the SCN is imprecise. Before we use ORA_ROWSCN to implement a locking mechanism, we should carefully read all the caveats described in the *SQL Language Reference*.

Undo and SCN enable multiversion consistency because every row effectively has a timestamp. While we were running the preceding query against the SATELLITE table, imagine if another user changed the table and committed their transaction. Even if the table is changed in the middle of our query, the query results will not include those changes. Every query returns a *consistent* set of data – the data that existed as of the time the query began. Imagine if another user changed the SATELLITE table *before* we started our query, but the transaction is not committed. Our query results are *isolated* from that session, and we don't see uncommitted data from other transactions.

Every time Oracle reads from a table, it must compare each row's SCN with the SCN at the beginning of the query. If the row SCN is higher than the query SCN, that means someone else recently changed the data, and Oracle must look in the undo tablespace for an old copy of the data.

Oracle queries are always consistent and isolated. Although redo can be disabled, there is no way to disable undo to get a "dirty read" in Oracle. Reading undo data is so fast we rarely notice it happening anyway. And since the undo data is not stored with the table data, we don't have to worry about our tables running out of space or about periodically cleaning up that undo information.[2] But there is a price to pay for Oracle's undo architecture.

Long-running SQL statements may fail with the error "ORA-01555: snapshot too old." That error means the table has changed since we started reading it and the old versions of the table data could not be found in the undo tablespace. We can avoid those errors either by making the query run faster, increasing the timeout for undo data with the

---

[2] In PostgreSQL, the changes are stored within the tables. That approach has advantages, but it requires periodically vacuuming tables to reclaim space.

UNDO_RETENTION parameter, or increasing the space available to the undo tablespace. The UNDO_RETENTION parameter is not a guarantee; Oracle will only keep undo data for that long *if* there is space available.

While redo and archive logs need to be sized for to the *largest* possible DML, undo needs to be sized for the *longest* possible SELECT.

Temporary Tablespace

A temporary tablespace is used for storing intermediate results for sorting, hashing, and large object processing. We need to allocate enough space to support our SQL statements, but we don't want to over-allocate space that will never be used.

Oracle first tries to process everything in memory, but the amount of memory allowed for sorting and hashing depends on the parameter PGA_AGGREGATE_TARGET, with a hard limit set by the parameter PGA_AGGREGATE_LIMIT. The memory for intermediate results is shared among many sessions, and when operations cannot fit in memory, they are written to disk through the temporary tablespace.

The amount of space required to sort or hash data is roughly equal to the size of that data. If we have to process large amounts of data in a single query, as is common in a data warehouse, there's no way all that data will fit in memory. The minimum size of our temporary tablespace should be equal to the size of the largest objects that will be hashed or sorted at the same time.

It can be difficult to predict how much data needs to be hashed or sorted at the same time. We might have to find a good value through trial and error. Trial and error is a painful way to configure a system, but Oracle provides features that can help us with this task.

First, we can look at the data dictionary to check current and historical values. We can look at DBA_SEGMENTS.BYTES for large objects that will be sorted and hashed. We can check the column DBA_HIST_ACTIVE_SESS_HISTORY.TEMP_SPACE_ALLOCATED for the temporary tablespace used in previous SQL statements. And we can check the view V$TEMPSEG_USAGE for current usage.

When we start running our large workloads, we can enable resumable sessions. A resumable session will become suspended when it runs out of space, instead of immediately throwing an error. When the session is suspended, we can quickly add space, and then the session will automatically continue processing. Resumable sessions are enabled with the parameter RESUMABLE_TIMEOUT. We can monitor for suspended sessions with the data dictionary view DBA_RESUMABLE. Database administrators can set up alerts, with a program like Oracle Enterprise Manager, to get an email or text when a session is suspended.

If all the temporary tablespace is full, nothing can be hashed or sorted, which effectively breaks the database. To avoid that problem, we could create multiple temporary tablespaces and assign them to different users or applications. With multiple temporary tablespaces, a single runaway query won't take down everything on the database. On the other hand, the more we divide the temporary tablespace, the more storage we will have sitting idle.

There are many times when we do *not* want to add more space, even if the system has run out of temporary tablespace. If we create an unintentional cross join, the SQL statement may need a virtually infinite amount of space. If we blindly increase the temporary tablespace whenever we get space alerts, we may end up wasting a lot of space to support a statement that will never finish anyway. In practice, many of our temporary tablespaces are oversized and waste a lot of space. If we're running out of space and getting desperate, we may want to look at shrinking our temporary tablespaces.

Once again, this book about SQL development is discussing database administration. We don't need to be experts in space administration, but we need to be able to help administrators plan ahead, to keep our applications working. And we need to know how to respond to emergencies – administrators will not always know if a query is intentionally large or just a mistake.

Memory

Oracle's memory architecture is complex and difficult to configure. Although DBAs are primarily responsible for memory configuration, developers need at least a basic understanding of Oracle's memory architecture, so we can become familiar with the memory trade-offs and choose the correct strategies for our systems.

One of the first memory-related decisions is the server architecture. Oracle defaults to a dedicated server architecture, where each connection has a separate process or thread with its own memory. Oracle also offers a shared server architecture, where a single operating system process or thread handles multiple connections. There's a trade-off between the reduced process and thread overhead of dedicated server mode and the reduced memory of the shared server mode. As always, we should stick with the default settings unless we have a good reason to change. For example, if our application has thousands of active connections or constantly reconnects because it doesn't use an application pool, we should consider changing to shared server mode. (Alternatively, there is a feature called Database Resident Connection Pooling that allows Oracle to create an internal connection pool.)

Oracle memory is divided into two main categories: System Global Area (SGA) and Program Global Area (PGA). Oracle will only use the memory we configure it to use. I've seen plenty of servers with hundreds of gigabytes of memory, yet the installed databases were only configured to use a few gigabytes. Even if system configuration is not our job, we may want to occasionally check parameters like SGA_TARGET and PGA_AGGREGATE_TARGET and ensure we are sufficiently using our resources. If we want a quick estimate about whether adding memory will help, we should look at the views V$PGA_TARGET_ADVICE and V$SGA_TARGET_ADVICE.

The SGA contains memory components that are shared between connections. The largest part of the SGA is the buffer cache, which caches table and index blocks.

The PGA contains memory components that are private to each session. The PGA mostly contains space for sorting, hashing, and session variables.

For an OLTP system, with many small queries that constantly read from the same tables and indexes, the SGA is most important because those small objects may all fit in memory. For a data warehouse system, with large queries that sort huge amounts of data that won't fit in memory anyway, the PGA is most important.

Getting the memory settings correct is tricky, but we shouldn't worry *too* much about memory. We've all heard that memory access is 100,000 times faster than hard drive access, but that ratio is not always applicable. First of all, that large number is for random access, but disk drives are much more competitive for sequential throughput. Also, we can't do *everything* in memory anyway. Data must be frequently written to disk, or we lose durability. And with Oracle's asynchronous I/O, much of that writing can be batched and run in the background. We should not blindly add memory when we run into performance problems.

Caches

Oracle has many ways to use high-speed memory structures to cache data and results. Before we buy a separate, expensive caching solution, we should make sure we're taking advantage of the Oracle features we're already paying for. The previous section described the high-level memory system. This section describes more granular caching options. The following is a list of the different types of caches in Oracle:

1. *Buffer cache (SGA)*: The largest and most important cache. It stores blocks of tables, indexes, and other objects. The buffer cache does not store the actual results of queries, which are frequently different and become invalidated. By storing blocks, the SGA caches data that can be used many times by many different queries. Data is aged out based on a least recently used algorithm. We can calculate the effectiveness of our cache with the buffer cache hit ratio, which tells us what percentage of blocks are read from memory instead of disk. (But do not obsess over this ratio, because there are some operations that can never be done in memory.)

```
--Buffer cache hit ratio.
select 1 - (physical_reads / (consistent_gets + db_block_
gets)) ratio
from (select name, value from v$sysstat)
pivot
(
    sum(value)
    for (name) in
    (
        'physical reads cache' physical_reads,
        'consistent gets from cache' consistent_gets,
        'db block gets from cache' db_block_gets
        )
);

RATIO
-----------------
0.982515222127574
```

2. *Shared pool (SGA)*: Multiple caches that contain parsed SQL queries, stored procedures, data dictionary, etc. This cache is important, but unlike the buffer cache, we rarely need to adjust it. The most common task for the shared pool is to flush it with the command ALTER SYSTEM FLUSH SHARED_POOL, to force Oracle to regenerate execution plans.

3. *Session memory (PGA)*: Contains session and program data, such as package variables. With package variables, especially collections, we can build our own caches if necessary.

4. *Client result cache*: Caches statement results instead of only the data blocks. A cached statement is much faster than processing cached blocks. On the other hand, caching statements only helps if the exact same statement is executed multiple times and if none of the underlying objects have been modified. This feature requires configuring the server, client, and statement or table.

5. *In-memory option (SGA)*: An extra-cost option to cache data in a special columnar format. This option can significantly improve performance of some types of analytic queries, but it requires extra memory and configuration. Since 19c, this option is free for the first 16 GB.

6. *SQL result cache (SGA)*: Caches the results of a specific SQL query. This cache must be manually enabled with a `/*+ RESULT_CACHE */` hint.

7. *PL/SQL function result cache (SGA)*: Caches the results of a function. This cache also must be manually enabled, by adding the keyword `RESULT_CACHE` to function definitions.

8. *Scalar subquery caching (PGA)*: Scalar subqueries may be automatically cached, dramatically improving query performance. For example, `SELECT (SELECT COUNT(*) FROM LARGE_TABLE) FROM ANOTHER_LARGE_TABLE` is a poorly written query, but it may run much faster than we'd expect.

Whenever we find Oracle repeating the same, slow task, we should look for a cache to reduce the run time.

Multitenant

Oracle's multitenant architecture lets us have multiple pluggable databases inside a single container database. Multitenant is another database administration subject that at first appears to be irrelevant to developers. But understanding this architecture can help us take advantage of powerful features or at least avoid common pitfalls.

The multitenant architecture can efficiently handle many database instances on a single machine. With the traditional architecture on a shared database server, each database instance requires a large amount of administration time and hardware resources, which is why DBAs are hesitant to create many instances for developers. The multitenant option changes that equation by making it easy to perform tasks such as creating, dropping, cloning, or relocating a database. Multitenant may give us an opportunity to use shared servers but still provision multiple instances per developer.

Unfortunately, unless we buy the multitenant option, we are limited to three pluggable databases per container. That's enough databases to play around with new features, but not enough to radically alter our development process. Licensing may be the main reason most organizations do not yet even install the multitenant architecture. But since the multitenant architecture is mandatory starting with 21c, we will eventually need to learn it.

For developers, the biggest problems with multitenant systems happen at the very beginning, when we try to connect to the database. Developers should almost always connect to a pluggable database (PDB), not a container database (CDB). Unfortunately, it's easy to mistakenly connect to a CDB, since most Oracle documentation is written for DBAs who *do* need to connect to a CDB. And if we're using the multitenant architecture, the default database name "ORCL" now refers to the CDB instead of a PDB.

Developers should have connection strings that connect directly to the PDB. We do not want to connect to the CDB and then run a command like ALTER SESSION SET CONTAINER = ORCLPDB. Constantly juggling two databases, when we only care about one of them, causes confusion and errors.

If we accidentally run a user creation script on the CDB instead of a PDB, we may get the error "ORA-65096: invalid common user or role name in oracle." That error message is potentially misleading because Oracle does allow us to create common users – a user that exists on all PDBs. But that is a rare feature, and it has some weird requirements like prefixing the username with C##. Many developers foolishly avoid that error by setting the undocumented parameter _ORACLE_SCRIPT. That workaround allows the script to run, but it creates the user the wrong way and will cause weird problems later. The real solution is to install the application in a PDB instead of the CDB.

If we're installing a personal database or if we're installing a shared database without buying the multitenant option, we may want to choose the traditional architecture over the multitenant architecture.

Database Types

There are many different types of Oracle databases. The vast majority of features discussed in this book apply to any type of Oracle database. And this book is not an administration guide that explains how to install and manage Oracle. But SQL developers occasionally need to be aware of their underlying database type. The following are different ways to categorize Oracle databases and how they impact SQL developers. These items aren't simply different features. These are large architectural changes that may affect the way we use our databases:

1. *Edition*: A choice between Enterprise Edition, Standard Edition 2, Express Edition, and Personal Edition. The features, and price, are wildly different between the editions. Virtually every source of Oracle information assumes you are using Enterprise Edition, so if you're using a different edition, you should investigate what features you're missing. (Some cloud platforms, like Amazon RDS, add so many restrictions that they practically create their own custom edition.)

2. *Version*: For SQL development, we only care about the first two numbers. For example, developers don't need to worry much about the feature differences between 12.2.0.1 and 12.2.0.2 (although DBAs have to worry about such differences, since the latter version is a terminal release and is supported much longer). But developers do need to worry about the feature differences between versions like 12.1 and 12.2. And developers certainly need to worry about the first number, and they need to know the difference between long-term releases and innovation releases. For example, 19c is a long-term release, which means it will be

thoroughly tested and supported. If you're not on version 19c yet, it's a safe bet that you will be some day. On the other hand, 21c is an innovation release, which means it is only supported for a short amount of time. Innovation releases are good for testing bleeding-edge features, but the chance of your organization using an innovation release in production is very small.

3. *Platform*: Oracle has excellent cross-platform support. It is extremely rare to have to worry about the operating system when writing SQL.

4. *Real Application Clusters (RAC)*: RAC is a shared-everything solution, where every node contains the same information. The shared-everything architecture makes it easier for developers, because we don't care which node we connect to. But we still need to know if we are using a RAC system. At the very least, RAC affects the way we connect to the database. For example, we may want to use a service name for load balancing and high availability, but we want to directly connect to a specific node when debugging. (Debugging creates a background session, and debugging won't work unless both sessions connect to the same node.) We also need to know if we're on RAC so we can appropriately query the data dictionary. For example, we need to use GV$ instead of V$ on RAC. RAC also significantly affects parallelism, and we may need to adjust our parallel strategies accordingly.

5. *Autonomous*: Oracle is increasingly adding automated processes to their cloud and on-premise software. Most of the features are meant for DBAs: automated scaling, backup, patching, and temporary and undo tablespace shrink. But there are also automated processes that can affect developers: automated indexing, SQL plan management, materialized views, and zone maps. Some of the autonomous database settings, such as the parameter OPTIMIZER_IGNORE_HINTS being set TRUE by default, can cause unexpected performance problems.

6. *Engineered systems*: By controlling the entire hardware and software stack, Oracle's engineered systems are able to offer unique features and optimizations. For example, Exadata machines have execution plan operations not available on other systems.

7. *Packs and options*: Although Oracle does not physically block us from using all database features, there are advanced features that require buying an extra license. We should ask around and see if our databases are licensed to use common management packs and options such as advanced compression, data masking, database in-memory, diagnostics, multitenant, partitioning, and tuning.

8. *ASM*: ASM is useful for management but doesn't affect our code much. As previously described in this chapter, there are only a few SQL command differences that depend on our ASM choice.

9. *Sharding*: Oracle sharding breaks away from the shared-everything architecture of RAC. Now our systems can store different data on different databases. Unlike with RAC, sharding may have a huge impact on our SQL code.

Not all of the items in the preceding list must match between all of our environments. It doesn't matter if our sandbox database matches production for the platform, RAC, autonomous, or ASM. The vast majority of our database code will stay the same regardless of those four items. The minor differences between the choices for those four items can be abstracted relatively easily. And many of the differences simply don't matter. For example, we may want 99.999% uptime for our production databases, but it doesn't matter if our personal sandbox uptime is much worse.

But it is important to use the same edition, version, and sharding options. These three choices may fundamentally alter our code. For example, some organizations use Enterprise Edition in production and Express Edition for development. Mixing those editions is a huge mistake. SQL developers will never be able to take full advantage of Enterprise Edition features if those features are not easily available for testing.

When it's time to choose our options for new systems, we don't want to over-engineer it, and we don't want to let Oracle Corporation upsell us. Oracle's core database technology is great, but a lot of their extra options are only good on the surface. When we choose technology stacks, we must remember that the money we spend on extra licenses may compete with our salaries. I've been in situations where the original architects always selected the high-priced options and inevitably our business or customers got sick of the exorbitant costs and decided to migrate away from all Oracle products. Don't set yourself up for a similar failure.

Summary

This chapter contains advice about times when SQL developers need to step up and perform administrative work, even if that work is not in our job descriptions. There is always overlap between developers and administrators, especially with the DevOps movement. Instead of thinking of ourselves as just a developer, we need to care about the end results, regardless of whose job it is.

Understanding Oracle's architecture can help us improve our programs, work better with other teams, and future-proof our code. Hopefully we can use our knowledge of Oracle's architecture to identify and prevent bottlenecks before they happen.

PART III

Write Elegant SQL with Patterns and Styles

CHAPTER 11

Stop Coding and Start Writing

Part I explained the importance of SQL and built a solid foundation for SQL development. Part II discussed sets and advanced features needed to build powerful SQL statements. We now have the motivation, efficient processes, and advanced knowledge, but that is not enough. Part III discusses the styles and patterns needed to write elegant SQL.

Why should we care about writing elegant SQL? It's true there are many times when our code quality doesn't matter. Despite what we were promised about the reusability of software, in practice most of our code is only used once and then forgotten. For most development, great is the enemy of good enough.

But the world is full of mediocre software. Developers should strive to occasionally rise above our boring day-to-day code and write something amazing.

This book discusses "writing" SQL, not merely "programming" SQL or "coding" SQL. The word "write" is important because it helps us focus on the true audience of our code. Our audience is not the end users; the end users are the audience of our programs and don't care about the source code. Our audience is not the compiler; the compiler must verify and build our code, but the compiler doesn't care if our code makes sense. Our true audience is other developers.

The scarcest resource in the software life cycle is the attention of developers. Our programming mantra should be "don't make me think." That statement is the title of a popular book about website usability. While we can't make our source code as simple as a website, we still want to maximize the usability of our code for other developers.

We must spend extra time up front to make our code easier for developers later. Making our code readable encourages other people to use our code and will even help our future selves. Instead of programming cryptic statements, we should write easy-to-follow stories. But making something look easy is hard.

301

© Jon Heller 2023
J. Heller, *Pro Oracle SQL Development*, https://doi.org/10.1007/978-1-4842-8867-2_11

Part III is a style guide and the most opinionated part of the book. I hope you strongly disagree with some of my suggestions. Disagreement means you are paying attention and you care about your code quality. If we disagree, we can still learn, as long as we can justify our beliefs. Having any carefully considered style guide is better than having none. Oracle SQL has a lot of historical baggage, but we shouldn't rely on the excuse "that's the way we've always done it." If we don't know both sides of an argument, then we don't know either side.

The Hypocrisy of Examples

This book promotes one set of styles yet occasionally deviates from them. It's difficult to not be hypocritical when writing about programming styles, because writing and programming are not exactly the same thing. It's great to have a preferred coding style, but we also need to be flexible and adapt to our context. We should cultivate an idealistic style, but we should also have a pragmatic willingness to occasionally abandon our ideals.

Writing *about* programming is a bit different than writing actual programs. For example, tabs work great in an IDE but not in a book. Writing everything in uppercase looks silly, but uppercase creates a helpful contrast when embedding code in a paragraph. A long line of code may look fine in an IDE, but the code won't look good in a blog post. It's often helpful to include the table name in front of the column name, but extra table names can take up too much space on a forum post. We must be willing to occasionally ignore our own rules.

The problem with most SQL programming styles is that they only look good for small examples. But we don't need help writing code that is less than one line long. We need help writing SQL statements that span more than a page. The large query in Chapter 6, which shows the top rocket fuels used per year, is an example of when we need to start applying helpful styles. The styles advocated in this book are meant to help with large SQL statements, not trivial examples.

It's good to program with a sense of idealism and beauty, but we should try to keep the dogmatism out of it. After a while we should all evolve a sense of when code "just looks right." Eventually we'll know that when our code looks right, it will run right. But sometimes we need to ignore our feelings and stop insisting one style is always best. For example, if we're modifying existing code, we should imitate the existing style. It's better to be successful than to be right.

Comments

We will never program in a natural language. Human languages are too complicated and ambiguous to be accurately parsed and executed. Even laudable attempts to fuse programming and natural languages, such as Donald Knuth's literate programming, have failed. Our programs are inevitably cryptic and complex. If we want to lower the barrier of entry to our programs and enable more people to participate, we shouldn't make people think any more than necessary. We must use comments to make our programs readable.

Comment Styles

It's debatable exactly where to place comments and how much to use them. I recommend using enough comments so that someone can read our programs using only the comments. For PL/SQL, we should add comments at the top-level objects, at the definition of any function or procedure, in front of any large collection of statements, and whenever we're doing something unusual. For SQL, we should add a comment at the top of every statement, the top of every inline view, and whenever we're doing something unusual. We don't want to restate everything in the comments, but we want to create signposts to help others quickly navigate our code.

Some people say, "If it was hard to write, it should be hard to read." I prefer the aphorism "If you can't explain it to a six-year-old, you don't understand it yourself." We shouldn't literally write for a six-year-old, but we do need to spend extra effort to distill the truths of our program and present those simple truths to readers who have not seen our code before.

It's difficult to know exactly who our audience is when we add comments. Are we targeting specific coworkers who already know our business logic, developers familiar with the programming language, our future selves, or someone else? There's no easy answer, so we should spend at least a small amount of time writing and revising our comments. On the first pass, we may want to overshare to avoid the curse of knowledge – the cognitive bias where we assume everyone knows what we know. On the second pass, we can revise our comments to keep them clear and simple.

Ideally, we can use our comments as our documentation. Developers rarely want to read large, out-of-date PDF files. Text files, simple HTML, and markdown files are sufficient for documenting noncommercial programs. The advantage of those simple formats is they can be automatically generated. There are several open source programs, such as pldoc and plsql-md-doc, that can turn specially formatted comments into documentation. Or it may be good enough to have a Readme.md file that merely directs the reader to look at package specifications for details.

It's difficult to say exactly what the content of our comments should be – it's too subjective. But one mistake we should avoid is we should not use comments to record a history of all changes. Version control comments belong in the version control system. Seeing a list of names, dates, and changes at the top of a file is a red flag. That metadata makes us wonder if the program was built with a version control system, which is the same as wondering if the program was built competently.

Comment Mechanics

There are two kinds of comments in SQL and PL/SQL. Single-line comments start with --. Multiline comments start with /* and end with */. SQL*Plus also allows single-line comments that start with either REM or REMARK. But we should ignore features exclusive to SQL*Plus when there are alternatives that work with all SQL clients. There is also the COMMENT object that we can attach to tables and columns. Those COMMENT objects can be useful, especially when IDEs automatically read the comments and display them in the result grid.

Comments are also used as hints, if the comments start with either --+ or /*+. Optimizer hints are always suspicious, so when we create a hint, we should also include a text comment. Hints are read left to right and do not throw syntax errors, so if we include our text *after* the real comment, everything will work fine:

```
--Hint and comment example.
select /*+ cardinality(launch, 9999999) - I know this is a bad idea but...
```

Some people say that comments are an apology. Even if that statement is true, when we're programming, we have a lot to apologize for. For example, the hint in the preceding code is generally considered a "bad" hint. We're lying to the optimizer, telling the optimizer to pretend the table is much larger than its true size. There are better approaches to tuning SQL statements, but we may have constraints preventing us from using the best approach. In case those constraints change in the future, it helps to explain why we're doing something bad now. It's better to have a developer find bugs or faulty assumptions through our comments than to have someone else discover the problem in production.

There are a few limitations on Oracle comments we need to watch out for. Comments cannot occur after a statement terminator. For example, the following code does not work correctly in SQL*Plus or other contexts:

```
SQL> --Don't use a comment after a line terminator.
SQL> select * from dual; --This doesn't work.
  2
```

Multiline comments should contain a space after the opening /*, or there may be problems on some SQL*Plus clients. The following SQL*Plus session looks confusing, because SQL*Plus gets easily confused. SQL*Plus doesn't have a full parser, and it may incorrectly interpret a multiline comment without a space as a forward slash requesting another execution of the SELECT statement. We can avoid the following problem by using /* a */ instead of /*a*/. (The following problem does not happen on the latest version of SQL*Plus. But the rule about adding a space after the first slash-asterisk is still in the manual.)

```
SQL> --Example of bad comment.
SQL> select 1 from dual;

         1
------
----
         1

SQL> /*a*/

         1
------DO
UBLEHYPHEN--
         1
```

Multiline comments are useful for when we're debugging or testing and want to quickly remove a lot of code. But for permanent code, it helps to stick with single-line comments, since multiline comments cannot be embedded inside each other. Once we start using multiline comments in permanent code, we cannot quickly comment out large blocks of code.

Comment ASCII Art

We can make the most out of our text-only comments with ASCII art. We don't want our comments to look like goofy forum signatures, but there are times when we can benefit by using something fancier than plain text. If there are critical variables we don't want developers to mindlessly modify, an extra-large "STOP" or "DANGER" can help. We don't have to hand-draw our own ASCII text; there are many ASCII text generators online.

To explain complex processes, it helps to create small flowcharts. There are also several ASCII diagram tools readily available online.

We should focus the vast majority of our effort on writing plain text. But we must recognize that programmers are going to skim through the program and not heed our dire warnings. We can catch their eye with ASCII art like the following comment:

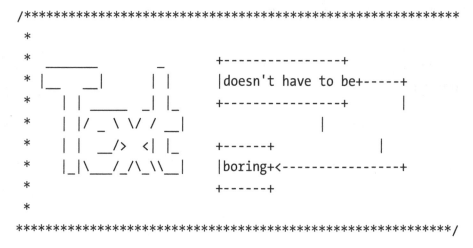

```
/******************************************************
 *
 *   _____          _       +----------------+
 *  |_     _|        | |      |doesn't have to be+-----+
 *    | |  ____   _| |_     +----------------+        |
 *    | |/ _ \ \/ / _ |                   |           |
 *    | | _/> <| |_     +------+                 |
 *    |_|\___/_/\_\\__|  |boring+<----------------+
 *                       +------+
 *
 ******************************************************/
```

SQL is a real programming language and deserves useful comments. Always remember that the audience for our code is not the computer – the audience is other humans.

Choose Good Names

It's important to choose good names for our databases, schemas, schema objects, functions, procedures, variables, aliases, inline views, and all other programming objects. Choosing good names isn't just about creating aesthetically pleasing code. We need to create logical, memorable chunks, to help make the most of people's short-term memory. When we're writing source code, we're at a significant disadvantage compared with normal writing. Choosing names is one of the few things we have control over, so we should spend extra effort picking the right names.

Name Styles

As we gain experience, we build our own personal set of styles and naming rules. The specific rules don't matter that much, as long as we are trying to achieve consistency, simplicity, and flexibility. One common rule is to use nouns for things like packages and tables and to use verbs for procedures and functions. Another example is to use singular nouns for table names, instead of plural. Avoid single-letter variable names like "A" and "B." On the other hand, "i" and "j" are common names for loop variables. Avoid abbreviations, unless the abbreviations are standard in our domain. Avoid names that are listed in V$RESERVED_WORDS; those names may not work in all contexts, may not work in future versions, and may confuse syntax highlighters and other programming tools. Whatever we do, we should spend more than the bare-minimum amount of time to give everything a proper name.

On the other hand, we don't want to discuss every name in a team meeting, create a spreadsheet of approved table names, or have a formal process to verify all new column names. Those three examples are not straw men – I've literally had to endure each of those scenarios. Aside from being a bureaucratic nightmare, creating too much process leads to *worse* table and column names. In a previous job, we didn't always have time to go through the process for approving new column names, so we would settle on the least-worst existing name. We should strive for good names, but we must be pragmatic about it.

It can help to include values in our names. For example, if we use an analytic function to find the first occurrence of something per year, we can name the column FIRST_WHEN_1. When we want to limit the results to the first occurrence, the predicate becomes obvious: FIRST_WHEN_1 = 1. We can do the same thing with small lists of values, to make it clear what values can be included in the expression. Our names can become tiny contracts that guarantee we're using the values correctly.

Avoid Quoted Identifiers

We should avoid case-sensitive names with double quotes. Oracle identifiers normally only allow alphanumeric characters, underscores, dollar signs, and pound signs. It might feel liberating to get around those limitations using quoted identifiers, but it is a pain to reference those quoted identifiers in SQL. Case-sensitive names break many of our data dictionary queries and DDL generation programs. Some database objects, like database links, don't even support case-sensitive names. And our SQL looks ugly when every name is surrounded by double quotes.

In theory, quoted identifiers can save us a step. When we're writing SQL for a specific purpose, such as a single report, we can use quoted identifiers to give columns the precise name we want to see on the report.

In practice, those queries we use "just once," for a single report, will eventually be used for something else. Case-sensitive column names are like a virus that will infect all our code. We should avoid case-sensitive names, such as in the following SQL statement:

```
--Avoid case sensitive column names.
select *
from
(
    select 1 "Good luck using this name!"
    from dual
)
where "Good luck using this name!" = 1;
```

Name Length and Changes

Although all modern versions of Oracle allow names to use 128 characters, we need to be aware that previous versions were limited to 30 characters. If our programs were written for an older version, there's a good chance there are columns or variables set to VARCHAR2(30) that should be upgraded to VARCHAR2(128).

Programs change over time, and it's important that we refactor our code and keep the names up to date. Most IDEs have a simple refactor option, where we can right-click variable names and change them in many places at once. If we set up a fully automated build and test process, as described in Chapters 2 and 3, we shouldn't be scared of changing names. Changing schema object names is simple, as shown in the following code:

```
--Change table and column names.
create table bad_table_name(bad_column_name number);

alter table bad_table_name
rename column bad_column_name to good_column_name;

rename bad_table_name to good_table_name;
```

If you're still not convinced of the importance of good names, a few humbling code reviews can be convincing. The best cure for the curse of knowledge is to watch someone else look at our code and wonder out loud, "What does this mean?"

Whitespace

Whitespace is one of the limited number of tools available to help us write better code. Without as many formatting options as writing a document or email, we must rely on whitespace to separate items and shift the reader's gaze to what's important.

Consider the way we use whitespace when writing. Whether we're writing in a programming language or in a natural language, there is a hierarchy of elements. For example, this book starts with characters, which aggregate into words, sentences, paragraphs, pages, chapters, parts, and finally the entire book. Each one of these elements has an increasingly large amount of whitespace to separate them. We all intuitively know that rule and follow it. But it's worth explicitly stating that rule, because we sometimes forget to apply it to our programs.

In PL/SQL, the hierarchy is character, word, statement, and nested block. In SQL, the hierarchy is character, word, expression or condition, clause, and nested query. Most programmers and code formatters make a mistake at the top of the SQL hierarchy. Every query, including every correlated subquery and inline view, is important and deserves extra space. As discussed in Chapter 6, inline views are the key to writing good SQL. Inline views deserve lots of space, like in the following code:

```
--Give inline views lots of space.
select * from
(
    --Good comment here.
    select * from dual
) good_name;

--Don't cram everything together.
select * from (select * from dual);
```

The parentheses in the preceding example are like a BEGIN and END in PL/
SQL. Parentheses deserve their own line when they are used to separate inline views.
And, of course, everything inside the parentheses must be indented an additional level.
The indenting is critical to understanding the nested structure of our code. Giving lots of
space to inline views also makes them easier to highlight and run, which we will do often
for debugging.

Even if our inline views are small, they are still a high-level SQL concept and deserve
extra whitespace. Unless the inline views are trivial, we should clearly separate them
from other parts of the query. Both queries in the preceding example might look fine, at
first. But this tiny example is misleading, because the second, more compressed format
does not scale well. For comparison, we would almost never put a procedure all on one
line, like in the following example:

```
--Typical way to format a procedure.
create or replace procedure proc1 is
begin
    null;
end;
/

--Weird way to format a procedure.
create or replace procedure proc1 is begin null; end;
/
```

Whitespace is not just important within a query; whitespace is also important
between queries, like in our SQL worksheets. The examples in this book and in the
GitHub repository follow this whitespace advice. Each chapter has its own file; each
heading is separated by three blank lines and a comment; each group of commands in

an example is separated by two blank lines; each command is separated by one blank line. Worksheets are an important part of SQL development, and we must all develop a style to help us quickly navigate worksheets.

The exact number of lines and spaces doesn't matter. What's important is that we have a consistent and easy-to-use system and that we use increasingly larger amounts of whitespace for larger units of work. Even though our IDE provides a navigation pane, we still need to make our worksheets, programs, and queries readable.

Make Bugs Obvious

We can't make bug-free programs. But we can write our programs in a way to make bugs easier to find and fix. Code is inevitably cryptic, but we should try to make it as transparent as possible. Our goal is to make our code as clear and simple as the truth, even if the truth is embarrassing. This section includes generic programming advice and how to apply that advice in a SQL or PL/SQL context.

Fail Fast

Failing fast is the most important technology concept in recent history. It is laughable that we ever believed we could build something right on the first try. We need to tolerate and even encourage failures, to more rapidly create something that works.

The most important parts of failing fast are software engineering ideas like automated testing, agile, building a minimum viable product, transparency, etc. Some of these ideas are discussed in earlier chapters, but most of those large topics are not in the scope of this book. The idea of failing fast, and being honest about our mistakes and limitations, can percolate down to many of our small day-to-day programming decisions. The next sections discuss specific ways to fail fast in SQL and PL/SQL.

Avoid Pokémon Exception Handling

Low-level failures in SQL or PL/SQL are exceptions. Exception handling is more of a PL/SQL topic than a SQL topic. Unfortunately, we need to discuss exception handling because it is frequently done wrong. When our exception handling is broken, we don't even know what SQL statement to debug. Most SQL developers, including myself, will waste weeks of their lives trying to find the *real* line number and error message.

311

The best way to handle exceptions in Oracle is to do nothing. By default, many useful things happen when an exception occurs. The exception stops the current block, propagates up through all the calling blocks, and crashes the entire program. The final exception generates all the error codes and messages, along with all the relevant line numbers and object names.

The default exception handling behavior provides enough information to troubleshoot almost all of our problems. Our unnatural fear of failure leads to bad practices that make failures harder to find and harder to diagnose.

For example, many PL/SQL programs catch and log all exceptions instead of crashing the program. It's great if our programs can catch and handle an exception. It's great if our programs can continue after an error. But we shouldn't create an unrealistic expectation that *all* programs can work through *all* exceptions.

Most SQL developers know that we should not catch and ignore all errors, like in the following code:

```
--Example of bad exception handling that ignores all errors.
begin
    --Do something here...
    null;
exception
    when others then null;
end;
/
```

But many SQL programmers don't realize that the following code is almost as bad. The following code logs the error and continues processing:

```
--Example of potentially bad exception handling.
begin
    --Do something here...
    null;
exception
    when others then
        log_error;
end;
/
```

The preceding code should have at least re-raised the error. Or the code should not have caught OTHERS in the first place.

In practice, error logs are rarely checked. When something bad happens to our program, sometimes we need to admit defeat and crash the program. Crashing is better than sweeping errors under the rug. It's better to find the error immediately, when the problem is fresh in our minds, than to investigate it later.

Custom logging functions almost always fail to log the entire call stack and all the line numbers. If we build an error logging function, we must always use both DBMS_ UTILITY.FORMAT_ERROR_STACK and DBMS_UTILITY.FORMAT_ERROR_BACKTRACE. If we need more precise control over the error stack or call stack data, we can use the package UTL_CALL_STACK.

Printing only the last error, and only the last line number, may not show the underlying problem. Sadly, most custom error logging only shows the location of the exception handler, not the original error. If we build a custom error logging function, the function must include at least as much information as when we do nothing at all. A logging utility that only stores SQLERRM is a huge mistake.

Unless our programs are specifically handling an error or logging extra information that only exists in one program scope, we only need to catch exceptions at the program entry points. We shouldn't add an exception handler to every procedure or every PL/SQL block. We should take advantage of exception propagation.

Exceptions are not like Pokémon – we don't want to catch them all.

Use Bad Names and Weird Values

We often write bad code even though we know it's bad. We know we shouldn't hard-code that value or call that dangerous function or depend on that unproven assumption. But we write bad code anyway because we don't have the time to make our programs perfect. When we have to compromise quality, we instinctively want to hide what we're doing. We need to fight that instinct and do the exact opposite: make our bad decisions obvious to anyone reading our code.

If we don't know what we're doing, we should say so in the comments. If we're falsely confident, programmers who know better than us might hesitate to change our code. By making our ignorance clear, we're inviting others to help us.

If we think our column or function is dangerous, put that uncertainty in the name. We don't want to drag other programmers down with our mistakes.

If we have to hard-code a non-real value, use a weird value that will stick out. For example, with dates, choose an unrealistic date that obviously has no meaning. The following example is painfully close to real code I've used several times:

```
--This works but I don't know why!
select date '9999-12-31' dangerous_last_date
from dual;
```

New programmers might feel nervous about admitting mistakes, but admitting mistakes is much better than the alternative. Experts don't fear bad programmers – experts fear bad programmers who don't know they're bad programmers. We're all bad programmers in some contexts, so we all understand time constraints and being confused by a program. Let's be honest with each other.

Use Fragile SQL

There is a difference between writing robust programs that can handle unexpected problems and writing careless programs that suppress errors and encourage bad input. We have been trained to avoid errors and exceptions in our SQL statements at all costs. As discussed in a previous section, the simplest away to avoid that trap is to avoid code like EXCEPTION WHEN OTHERS THEN NULL. In addition, there are several helpful SQL constructs that shouldn't be used to suppress useful errors.

Correlated subqueries that return more than one row generate the error "ORA-01427: single-row subquery returns more than one row." We may be conditioned to always use IN instead of = to avoid that error. But if our data is only supposed to return one row, we want to know when that assumption is wrong. For example, the DUAL table should only contain one row. If that table contains multiple rows, we want to see an error immediately. For example, in the following code, the IN operator is not protecting us; instead, it's ignoring potentially serious problems:

```
-- "=" is better than "in" if there should only be one value.
select * from dual where 'X' in (select dummy from dual);
select * from dual where 'X' = (select dummy from dual);
```

Queries in PL/SQL code that return no rows generate the error "ORA-01403: no data found." Queries that return more than one row generate the error "ORA-01422: exact fetch returns more than requested number of rows." We can avoid those errors by using an aggregation that always returns one, and only one, row. But like with the preceding subquery problem, we don't always want to hide our errors. If the DUAL table contains no rows, then we want to generate a no data found exception, not hide it. The following PL/SQL block shows that sometimes the simplest, most fragile code is best. If someone messes with the DUAL table, which was possible in older versions, there's no point in trying to protect ourselves from the problem. Our system is going to break, so we might as well find out in the most straightforward way possible:

```
--Don't hide NO_DATA_FOUND errors.
declare
    v_dummy varchar2(1);
begin
    --This generates "ORA-01403: no data found".
    select dummy into v_dummy from dual where 1=0;
    --We might be tempted to avoid errors with aggregation.
    select max(dummy) into v_dummy from dual where 1=0;
    --But we want an error if this code fails.
    select dummy into v_dummy from dual;
end;
/
```

Outer joins are clearly necessary for our SQL statements. But we should not use an outer join by default to avoid returning empty sets. If our program depends on both tables having data, then we don't want to hide it. The error generated by an empty set may be more useful than returning a set with missing values.

When our SQL queries make a mistake, errors are better than wrong results. Exceptions are obvious and can be traced. Subtle, wrong results can linger for a long time and cause unexpected problems that are hard to trace back to the source.

The Path to Writing Good SQL

Writing good code, or writing anything well, takes a lot of work. While I certainly hope this book helps you become a good SQL writer, this book is not enough. Parts I and II gave you the processes and knowledge needed to write powerful SQL, and this chapter introduces SQL writing styles and tips. Ultimately, the only way to be good at writing something is to frequently practice. Just doing our daily work isn't enough to master a skill. To become good at writing SQL, we must *deliberately* practice it.

We need to find ways to get slightly out of our comfort zone and exercise our SQL writing skills. There are many ways to practice with SQL. We can answer questions on Stack Overflow, help people on forums, email useful tricks to our coworkers, present at a team meeting, attend local user groups or peer reviews, etc.

Contributing to work and open source projects is important, but those contributions won't significantly improve our SQL *writing* skills. The trick is to find something with a short feedback loop, so we can quickly learn what we're doing wrong. We want to be comfortable enough with the medium to participate, but not entirely comfortable with our posts. The best way to learn something is to teach it to others, even though teaching can be intimidating.

Summary

Creating elegant SQL statements requires more than rote knowledge of SQL syntax. We need to think about our true audience – other human beings. Writing *good* SQL requires efficient processes and technical knowledge. Writing *great* SQL requires extra effort to tell a story in a limited format. This chapter introduced many tips and styles for telling our stories in SQL. We should use comments to explain ourselves, use carefully selected names, use whitespace to emphasize important code, and make our code honest to make our bugs obvious.

It's fine if you disagree with many of my specific suggestions; there are many opinions, and there's no one-size-fits-all style guide. We just need to ensure that our programming style is not driven by a simple desire to make our code compile. Our programming style must be driven by a desire to be understood by others.

CHAPTER 12

Write Large SQL Statements

We must write large SQL statements to take full advantage of the power of Oracle SQL. Large procedures are an anti-pattern in procedural programming languages; we need to understand why SQL is different. Large SQL statements create several risks and opportunities; we must be aware of the consequences of parsing, optimizer transformations, resource consumption, context switches, and parallelism. Finally, we need to learn how to read and debug large SQL statements.

Imperative Programming Size Limits Do Not Apply

Not all of the rules we learned from imperative programming apply to declarative SQL. One of the first things we learned from traditional programming is to keep each statement, procedure, and function as small as possible.

Keeping each line and procedure small is great advice and should be followed for our PL/SQL code. It's best to build a procedure that only does one small thing. Keeping procedures small minimizes unexpected side effects, makes code easier to understand, simplifies debugging, etc. Likewise, each line of code should also be small, although there's no precise, objective definition for what is too big.

A SQL statement is arguably a single line of code. Consider the large example built in Chapter 6 that shows the top rocket fuels used per year. That single line of code is over 1,500 characters long. In a procedural context, that much code in one statement would be a monstrosity. But in Oracle, that single statement is the best way to get the information. A procedural version of that example would require more code, more context, and more supporting objects.

© Jon Heller 2023
J. Heller, *Pro Oracle SQL Development*, https://doi.org/10.1007/978-1-4842-8867-2_12

The rules about procedure length apply to SQL, but not to the entire SQL *statement*. In Oracle SQL, the declarative equivalent of a procedure is an inline view. It doesn't matter if our SQL statements are a hundred lines long, but it does matter if our inline views are a hundred lines long.

One Large SQL Statement vs. Multiple Small SQL Statements

To demonstrate the advantages of one large SQL statement over multiple small statements, ideally, we would reuse the large example from Chapter 6. Unfortunately, that example would take up too much space, so we'll reuse a smaller example from Chapter 7. The following is a SQL statement to find the first three satellites, based on their launch date:

```
--SQL version of first 3 satellites.
select
    to_char(launch_date, 'YYYY-MM-DD') launch_date,
    official_name
from satellite
join launch
    on satellite.launch_id = launch.launch_id
order by launch_date, official_name
fetch first 3 rows only;

LAUNCH_DATE  OFFICIAL_NAME
-----------  -------------
1957-10-04   1-y ISZ
1957-10-04   8K71A M1-10
1957-11-03   2-y ISZ
```

That SQL statement is recreated in the following in an imperative language, using PL/SQL:

```
--Imperative version of first 3 satellites.
declare
    v_count number := 0;
begin
    for launches in
```

```
  (
    select *
    from launch
    order by launch_date
  ) loop
    for satellites in
    (
      select *
      from satellite
      where satellite.launch_id = launches.launch_id
      order by official_name
    ) loop
      v_count := v_count + 1;
      if v_count <= 3 then
          dbms_output.put_line(
              to_char(launches.launch_date, 'YYYY-MM-DD') ||
              '   ' || satellites.official_name);
      elsif v_count > 3 then
          return;
      end if;
    end loop;
  end loop;
end;
/
```

The most obvious difference between the preceding two examples is the SQL version is much smaller. This comparison is not criticizing PL/SQL. PL/SQL is a great language, and PL/SQL almost perfectly integrates with SQL. *Any* imperative solution is going to be much larger than the equivalent declarative SQL statement.

The imperative version of the code requires us to do much more work. We need to define a variable and increment our own counter. We need to create our own loops and iterate the results. We need to tie the two SQL statements together, using a value from a higher scope. We need to think about which table is iterated first, LAUNCH or SATELLITE – the order is important because we're only getting the top three. Debugging the PL/SQL code requires stepping through the code and viewing variables one value at a time, instead of viewing entire sets of data at once.

As with any small example, we need to ask ourselves if the lessons we learn from this example will apply to large, realistic SQL. In this case, the answer is a resounding yes. If we think the preceding PL/SQL block is bad, it would be even worse for the large Chapter 6 example. Gluing SQL statements together in PL/SQL isn't rocket science, but it's much more complicated than passing data through joins or inline views. There are multiple ways to split large queries into procedural pieces, but each way either requires more code or more helper objects, like temporary tables.

However, the readability advantages of SQL disappear if we do not use inline views and ANSI joins. If we throw all the tables together, with no discipline, the result will be more confusing than the imperative alternative.

For many SQL developers, the preceding PL/SQL version already looks bad. It's not too hard to spot a simple join done in PL/SQL. But the more advanced our SQL knowledge and experience, the more frequently we'll be able to identify procedural code that can be replaced with declarative code. Every experienced SQL developer can tell you stories about times they replaced a hundred lines of procedural code with a dozen lines of SQL. And this lesson certainly does not only apply to PL/SQL. PL/SQL is the ideal language for running SQL statements. In other procedural languages, the equivalent of a SQL statement is even more complicated than the preceding example.

Performance Risks of Large SQL Statements

Large Oracle SQL statements are a great way to simplify our code and increase performance, but they also introduce performance risks. When we start using advanced features, we're going to run into problems, but we should solve those problems instead of giving up. We need to keep an eye out for problems with parsing, optimizer transformations, and resource consumption.

Large SQL Parsing Problems

The first problem with writing or generating large SQL statements is parse time. Every SQL statement is a program that goes through many parsing steps – checking syntax, checking privileges, optimizing, etc. Oracle effectively compiles a new program for each statement, and compiling is traditionally slow. Luckily, Oracle's SQL parsing is much faster than traditional compilation. But there are still some edge cases with SQL parsing.

There is no theoretical limit to the size of a SQL statement. The Oracle database server can easily handle megabytes of data in a SQL statement, although our clients and programs may complain. The physical size of a query is not a problem, except in extreme cases when we're using SQL to store lots of data.

SQL is a convenient format for storing data. We can store data by selecting constants from DUAL and combining rows with UNION ALL. Compared with a CSV or JSON file, a SQL statement is a bit larger and maybe a bit slower. But SQL has the huge advantage of not needing any import tools or conversions, and the SQL can easily be plugged into many contexts.

Problems start to happen when the number of rows concatenated by UNION ALL or INSERT ALL approaches several hundred. Old versions of Oracle had a bug where concatenating 499 rows worked fine but concatenating 500 would take hours. The parse time is much better in modern versions, but we should still avoid concatenating more than 100 rows in a single statement. Part IV describes how combining 100 rows at a time is good enough. Large SQL is useful, but ginormous SQL causes slow parse times.

Storing too many megabytes of data in a PL/SQL object can cause compilation errors like "Error: PLS-00123: program too large (Diana nodes)." Those errors can be avoided by using multiple objects. But at some point, when our imported data becomes large enough, we need to look at other formats.

Common table expressions also have parse problems when they are nested more than a few dozen levels deep. But that is an extremely unlikely scenario. I don't want you to learn the wrong lesson here. Batching operations is a great idea; we just need to be a little cautious when using extreme sizes.

Large SQL Increases Optimizer Risks

A common SQL performance problem is having two queries that run fast independently but run slowly when combined. Our initial experience might lead us to believe that combining large inline views causes performance problems. Our first impression is wrong, and we need to understand why these problems happen, how to fix the root causes, and how to work around the problems.

The Oracle optimizer is discussed in more detail in Part IV. For now, all we need to know is that Oracle does not have to execute our queries in the order we write them. When we write SQL, we're not asking Oracle to "run these commands"; we're asking Oracle to "get data where these conditions are true." The optimizer can transform our code into a different but logically equivalent version. The SQL statement actually run by Oracle may look significantly different than the one we wrote. We need to provide helpful information to the optimizer through accurate statistics, and we need to tune the optimizer's SQL, not our SQL.

For example, when we join two inline views, Oracle does not necessarily execute each inline view separately and then join them together. Oracle can rewrite the inline views into a single query, move conditions from one inline view into the other, etc.

Those transformations are the reason putting inline views together may lead to better or worse performance. Combining queries gives Oracle more opportunities to optimize and improve performance. But combining queries also creates more opportunities to make a mistake and decrease performance.

For example, the following code is almost certainly not executed in the order it appears. The predicate at the end of the SQL statement will be pushed into the inline view. Pushing that predicate allows Oracle to use an index, which can quickly look up the single row that matches the LAUNCH_ID. There's no need for Oracle to read the whole table first and *then* filter the results. These transformations are an important feature that Oracle frequently uses to significantly improve performance:

```
--An inline view that should be transformed.
select *
from
(
    select *
    from launch
)
where launch_id = 1;
```

Optimizer transformations can go horribly wrong and cause performance problems. Instead of simply turning off transformations, it's best to understand *why* Oracle made a bad transformation. Finding the root cause of a bad transformation is difficult, but the root cause will reveal problems that affect other code. Part IV discusses transformations and performance tuning in more detail.

In practice, we can't get to the bottom of every performance issue. We may not have time to look at execution plans, optimizer settings, statistics, etc. Or we may have a monstrous execution plan, with hundreds of operations, and we don't even know where to begin. In rare cases, a SQL statement is simply too complex for the optimizer to correctly estimate. Luckily, there's a simple code trick to disable transformations and force the optimizer to view one SQL statement as two separate statements.

When we know that two queries run fast independently, but slowly when run together, we can disable all transformations between them. The best way to disable transformations, and force Oracle to execute things in a specific order, is to use ROWNUM. The following example has a ROWNUM in the inline view, which prevents the LAUNCH_ID predicate from being pushed inside:

```
--An inline view that cannot be transformed.
select *
from
(
    select *
    from launch
    --Prevent query transformations.
    where rownum >= 1
)
where launch_id = 1;
```

ROWNUM is a pseudo-column that is meant to be generated at the end of query execution, to add a simple incrementing number to each row. Since ROWNUM is meant to be used for the display order, Oracle will never transform an inline view that uses ROWNUM. This simple trick ensures our inline views will run as if they were executed separately.

This ROWNUM trick is stupid, but it's the least-worst option to a difficult problem. No other fix works reliably. There are combinations of hints that can do the same thing, but those hints are difficult to get right, and it's easy to lose hints when queries are changed. I don't like using cryptic code that doesn't solve the root problem and looks logically redundant. But in practice this is an important trick worth remembering. As our SQL writing skills improve, we're less likely to make mistakes that cause performance problems. As our database version increases, optimizer bugs get fixed, and new features solve more performance problems. On the other hand, those new skills and features will help us write larger queries, and we'll still need to use this ROWNUM trick to handle exceptional cases. This trick is also used to fix type conversion bugs, as described in Chapter 15.

Large SQL Resource Consumption Problems

Batch processing with one large SQL statement is faster and more efficient than using multiple small SQL statements. While a large SQL statement uses less *cumulative* resources, that statement consumes more resources at a specific point in time. This consumption can cause issues with CPU, I/O, locks, redo, temporary tablespaces, and, most importantly, undo.

Most changes need to be written to the undo tablespace. The larger the DML statement, the larger the amount of undo needed at one time. Multiple small changes will generate more undo overall, but that undo can be flushed in between commits. In addition, a longer-running query also needs to access more undo data. If a query has been running for an hour, the query may need to access undo data from an hour ago.

It's better to size our systems to support large DML, but allocating enough resources is not always feasible. There are times when we need to break statements into pieces, but that should not be our default behavior.

Performance Benefits of Large SQL Statements

Large SQL statements are more risky than small SQL statements when it comes to performance. But no risk, no reward. There are enormous potential performance benefits of using large SQL statements. Each of the risks and problems discussed in the previous section must be measured against the improvements and opportunities discussed in this section. If we follow the style suggestions in this chapter, we can increase performance through improved clarity, optimizer opportunities, reduced I/O, fewer context switches, and improved parallelism.

Large SQL Improves Clarity

The key to SQL tuning is to understand the meaning of a SQL statement. Understanding the SQL lets us rewrite the statement more efficiently and apply advanced features. We should always start from understanding the query; don't jump right to execution plans, indexing, cryptic hints, etc. "Understand your business logic" is boring advice, but that doesn't make it wrong.

Large SQL statements, when built with the proper features and styles, will be easier to understand than the equivalent imperative programs. Writing good code invites others to participate, creating a virtuous circle. Improving performance is a wonderful side effect of writing clean code.

Large SQL Increases Optimizer Opportunities

The more code and information we give to Oracle, the more opportunities the optimizer has to do something clever. The optimizer builds SQL execution plans and only works on one SQL statement at a time. Building large SQL statements gives the optimizer more to work with.

As previously discussed, the optimizer can push predicates into inline views and potentially filter out rows before those rows are joined to something else. Instead of pushing predicates down, Oracle can also pull joins up and can execute joins that weren't explicitly asked for. That transformation is called view merging.

For example, consider the following pseudo-query. The pseudo-code has two inline views and then joins the views together:

```
--Pseudo-query using inline views.
select *
from
(
    ... a join b ...
) view1
join
(
    ... c join d ...
) view2
    on view1.something = view2.something;
```

The optimizer can merge these views into a statement like this:

```
--Pseudo-query caused by view merging.
select *
from a
join b ...
join c ...
join d ...
```

Oracle doesn't have to join tables in the same order they are displayed. Oracle can take advantage of transitive joins; if A joins to B and B joins to C, then Oracle can join A to C instead. Perhaps tables A and B are large and unfiltered – joining them together takes forever. And maybe table C is small and is filtered to only return one row – joining with that table is fast. We can save a lot of work by rearranging joins through view merging, reordering the joins, and many other optimizer transformations.

Large SQL Reduces Input/Output

Large SQL statements can help us dramatically decrease the amount of I/O generated. Processes with intermediate steps have to save temporary data, often in a global temporary table. Those temporary tables require writing data to disk and then later reading the data from disk, whereas a single SQL statement may be able to keep everything in memory and not need to write anything to disk.

When a SQL statement can't process everything in memory, Oracle can automatically use temporary tablespaces. For example, when sorting or hashing data, Oracle needs about as much space as the data being sorted or hashed. But there's an important difference between using temporary tables and temporary tablespaces. Writing to tables, even global temporary tables, also generates redo and undo. Writing to temporary tablespaces because of sorting and hashing does not generate any redo or undo.

Large SQL Reduces Context Switches

Every change from a procedural language to SQL incurs extra overhead. With a large SQL statement, we only pay that price once. If we use a procedural language to repetitively call a SQL statement, we pay a price for each SQL call. Likewise, if our SQL statement calls a custom PL/SQL function, we pay a price for each function call.

There can be a huge amount of overhead for calling multiple SQL statements, especially if that call involves a network round trip. Sending and receiving messages and parsing the SQL may take longer than actually executing the SQL. Replacing row-by-row solutions with set-based solutions can improve performance by orders of magnitude.

The overhead generated by calling PL/SQL from SQL is not huge, but it can quickly add up. Even though SQL and PL/SQL are closely integrated, we still want to avoid too many context switches between them. When we create user-defined functions in PL/SQL, every call to those functions takes a small amount of time to change between languages. And since the optimizer cannot accurately estimate the time to run procedural code, there is a chance the execution plan will call the function an unnecessarily large number of times.

There are many tricks demonstrated in the preceding and following chapters that can help reduce PL/SQL overhead: PL/SQL optimization levels, the compiler instruction PRAGMA UDF, using ROWNUM to ensure that functions are called less often, function caching, SQL macros, creating custom statistics to provide cost estimates for the function, etc. Those tricks are important and often necessary, but they should always be the backup plan for when we can't write everything in a single SQL statement.

Large SQL Improves Parallelism

Large SQL statements are the most efficient way to use parallelism. If we have enough resources, we can improve program performance by orders of magnitude with parallel processing. In traditional programming, building parallel solutions can be ridiculously difficult. With SQL, parallel programming can be as easy as adding the hint /*+ PARALLEL */. We don't have to tell Oracle how to build concurrent programs; Oracle will do all the hard work for us.

Oracle can also take advantage of parallelism through single instruction multiple data (SIMD) processing. Modern CPUs don't just have many cores and many threads. Each thread can process multiple values at the same time. Oracle can use SIMD for in-memory operations on most modern processors. On a few processors, Oracle has SQL-in-silicon features that can execute parts of SQL in hardware. It's not clear exactly how those features work, but chances are the more data we process at once, the more likely Oracle can use processor parallelism.

With parallel processing, bigger is always better. One statement processing a ginormous amount of data is better than multiple statements processing large amounts of data. A single statement only has to pay for process startup and shutdown once and only has to worry about one set of partition granule skewing.

Every time Oracle uses parallel processing, it must create a lot of processes, allocate memory, and then eventually deallocate those resources. Oracle divides the data into partition granules and feeds the granules to the parallel processes. If the granule sizes are skewed and if each parallel process is only given a small number of granules, that skew can significantly impact performance. If one parallel server has more work than the others, then all the processes have to wait on one thread. Even a small amount of serial overhead can erase much of the benefits of parallelism and is discussed further in Chapter 16.

For example, let's count the number of rows in a large, partitioned table. Many programmers hesitate to read the entire table at once and prefer to process the table one partition at a time. Figure 12-1 is the SQL Monitor Active Report, which shows the activity generated by reading each partition in parallel. (See the GitHub repository for the code to generate a similar example on your system.) Don't worry about the details of the image; just look at the shape.

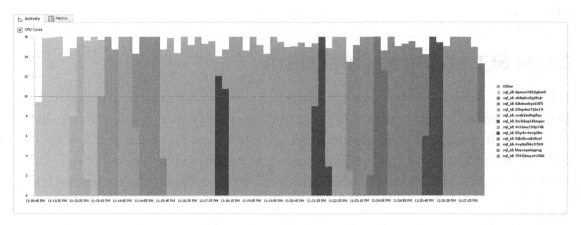

Figure 12-1. *Processing a large table in parallel, one partition at a time*

Notice the jagged edges at the top of the preceding image. Each SQL statement in the process asked for a degree of parallelism of 16. Yet there are many times when the number of active SQL sessions is less than 16. The code ran for 10 minutes, and if the report could zoom in further, we would see many peaks and valleys.

Contrast Figure 12-1 with Figure 12-2, which shows the SQL Monitor Active Report for counting the entire table with one statement. This image is more boring, but in this case boring is good. Oracle is doing one thing and doing it well – the average number of active sessions is almost always 16. There's almost no time wasted scaling up and down the processes. The process runs faster when we give Oracle the entire job in one statement and let Oracle decide how to divide the work.

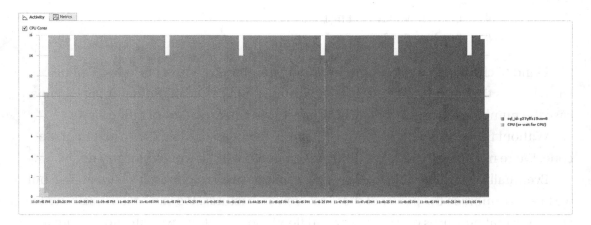

Figure 12-2. *Processing a large table in parallel in one statement*

Reading and Debugging Large SQL Statements

The size and structure of SQL statements can be challenging initially. But with a good style, an IDE, and practice, we can quickly dissect any code into readable chunks.

Inside Out

It takes time and effort to get used to the way Oracle SQL executes starting from the deepest inline view. This inside-out flow is different than the traditional top-to-bottom flow every programmer is used to.

For example, let's take another look at the code behind the large example in Chapter 6. But this time we're going to focus on the *shape* of the query, not the code. That query found the top three rocket fuels used per year. The query was broken into six steps and used inline views, joins, conditions, grouping, ordering, and analytic functions. If we strip away the code and look only at the comments, these comments tell the story of the query:

```
--Top 3 fuels used per year.
--
--#6: Select only the top N.
   --#5: Rank the fuel counts.
      --#4: Count of fuel used per year.
         --#1: Orbital and deep space launches.
```

```
--#2: Launch Vehicle Engines
--#3: Engine Fuels
```

I kind of cheated in the example, by adding numbered comments to each inline view. Unless the code is particularly complicated, I don't typically add numbers. In this case the numbers are useful for teaching how to visualize the flow of inline views.

Without those numbers, indenting is the key to understanding the structure of the code. We're not using Python, we don't *have* to indent, but it would be crazy not to.

Eventually we will be able to easily read those nested structures. It's hard at first, but we need to embrace the power of these recursive structures. We can't realistically write SQL code that only uses one subquery and flows top to bottom; we will end up with a mess of spaghetti code if we join all the tables at once. Nor can we use common table expressions to enforce a top-down structure. Common table expressions are useful to prevent repetition, but otherwise they make our statements more complicated by increasing the context and making debugging harder.

We need to learn this inside-out structure anyway, in order to understand execution plans. For example, Figure 12-3 is the execution plan for the Chapter 6 example code. Just like with inline views, we start with the most indented level and then read top to bottom within that level. Then we move out a level and repeat.

```
-------------------------------------------------------------------------
| Id | Operation                  | Name                     |
-------------------------------------------------------------------------
|  0 | SELECT STATEMENT           |                          |
|  1 |  VIEW                      |                          |
|  2 |   WINDOW SORT PUSHED RANK  |                          |
|  3 |    VIEW                    |                          |
|  4 |     SORT ORDER BY          |                          |
|  5 |      HASH GROUP BY         |                          |
|  6 |       HASH JOIN RIGHT OUTER|                          |
|  7 |        VIEW                |                          |
|  8 |         HASH JOIN RIGHT OUTER |                       |
|  9 |          TABLE ACCESS FULL | PROPELLANT               |
| 10 |          INDEX FAST FULL SCAN | ENGINE_PROPELLANT_PK |
| 11 |        HASH JOIN RIGHT OUTER |                        |
| 12 |         VIEW               |                          |
| 13 |          HASH JOIN RIGHT OUTER|                        |
| 14 |           TABLE ACCESS FULL | STAGE                   |
| 15 |           INDEX FAST FULL SCAN| LAUNCH_VEHICLE_STAGE_PK |
| 16 |         TABLE ACCESS FULL  | LAUNCH                   |
-------------------------------------------------------------------------
```

Figure 12-3. *Execution plan example*

You don't need to understand all the operations in the preceding execution plan; just look at the shape of the execution plan and note how it's similar to the shape of the comment outline at the beginning of this section. When we read nested inline views, we're trying to understand the SQL statement similar to the way the optimizer does.

Navigating Inline Views

With nested views, proper indenting, and putting parentheses on lines by themselves (sometimes called the Allman style), it's easy to navigate the code and highlight only the inline views we want to run. Without changing any code, we can quickly debug most of a large SQL statement.

Figure 12-4 shows how we could highlight and run the first three inline views. Don't even try to read the code; the text is too small and doesn't matter anyway. Just focus on the *shape* of the highlighted selections. Also, notice how we can see the result set after each execution, at the bottom of the IDE window.

Figure 12-4. *Debugging the example from Chapter 6 by running the first three inline views*

This debugging is easier and more powerful than traditional imperative debugging. We don't need to compile the code for debug, we don't need another interface to step through the code, and we can inspect entire *sets* of data at each level, not merely a few scalar values. It would be trivial to find any problem with the first three inline views.

After we've run the innermost inline views, we can start combining the inline views and generating higher-level result sets. Figure 12-5 shows how we're now selecting *groups* of inline views and moving up the hierarchy. Once again, don't try to read the code; just look at the shape of the highlighted sections. At each additional level, we can see our data get combined and transformed. With any modern IDE, it's trivial to see huge amounts of data at one time, making debugging much simpler.

Figure 12-5. *Debugging the example from Chapter 6 by running the last three inline views*

Figures 12-4 and 12-5 simply run a pre-built query. We can easily modify and rerun any level of the query and see how that change affects the results. For example, we might want to run the query with a finer granularity, to only focus on one problem row. To narrow our debugging scope, we might add a condition like LAUNCH_ID = 1 to the first inline view.

Since each highlighted block is independent, we can replace inline views with any relational source. We can tweak the inline view code to add more or less rows, completely rewrite the query, or replace it with a view. We could even procedurally generate the source data with a PL/SQL table function that returns a collection. (That advanced technique is described in Chapter 21.)

We can easily view columns that are not projected by changing one of the inline views to start with a SELECT *. Using a SELECT * at the top level of a query is a bad idea – we don't want to return more data than we need. But using a SELECT * in one of the nested inline views can make debugging easier.

Summary

The best advice for a new programmer is the less you know, the less you should do. Start small instead of trying to build everything at once and ending up with a bewildering number of errors. This advice is a tiny version of failing fast. Nested inline views help us start small. The most colossal query starts with a simple SELECT * FROM SOME_TABLE.

Unfortunately, with SQL, too many developers start small and end small. But you now have the ability, environment, knowledge, and style to start writing progressively larger SQL statements. Start programming out of your comfort zone. Try building things in SQL that might seem too complicated or maybe even a bad idea.

You will certainly run into problems when trying to build large SQL statements. Large SQL statements create performance risks and require a new way of reading and debugging. But if you don't give up, you will certainly solve most of those problems and create SQL statements that are faster and easier to use.

CHAPTER 13

Write Beautiful SQL Statements

The most important thing about programming styles is to have one. This subjective and opinionated chapter shows how traditional SQL styles can prevent us from realizing Oracle SQL's true potential.

Beauty is in the eye of the beholder, but we should base our sense of beauty on sound principles. Too many developers spend all their time heads-down coding and don't stop to ask important meta-questions. We should occasionally look at our code and ask ourselves, "*Why* does this code look good?"

Let's start with a concrete example. The following query counts the orbital and deep space launches per launch agency. There may be more than one organization responsible for a launch, so we need to use the bridge table LAUNCH_AGENCY to join LAUNCH and ORGANIZATION. This first query is my preferred style and is the same style used throughout this book:

```
--My preferred SQL programming style.
--Organizations with the most orbital and deep space launches.
select organization.org_name, count(*) launch_count
from launch
join launch_agency
    on launch.launch_id = launch_agency.launch_id
join organization
    on launch_agency.agency_org_code = organization.org_code
where launch.launch_category in ('deep space', 'orbital')
group by organization.org_name
order by launch_count desc, org_name;
```

© Jon Heller 2023
J. Heller, *Pro Oracle SQL Development*, https://doi.org/10.1007/978-1-4842-8867-2_13

```
ORG_NAME                                        LAUNCH_COUNT
----------------------------------------------- ------------
Strategic Rocket Forces                                 1543
Upravleniye Nachalnika Kosmicheskikh Sredstv             905
National Aeronautics and Space Administration            470
...
```

The following query returns the same results as the preceding query but is written in a more traditional SQL programming style:

```
--Traditional SQL programming style.
--Organizations with the most orbital and deep space launches.
SELECT o.org_name, COUNT(*) launch_count
  FROM launch l, launch_agency la, organization o
 WHERE l.launch_id = la.launch_id
   AND la.agency_org_code = o.org_code
   AND l.launch_category IN ('deep space', 'orbital')
 GROUP BY o.org_name
 ORDER BY launch_count DESC, o.org_name;
```

The rest of this chapter compares and contrasts the styles used in the preceding two examples. Regardless of our opinions about the styles, there is one style choice that we can all agree on: use SQL as much as possible. If we rewrote the preceding queries using imperative, row-by-row logic, the code would be slower and more complex.

We're not just trying to make our SQL look visually pleasing. The true purpose of a programming style is to reduce the complexity and improve the readability of our code. After we internalize the goals of simplicity and readability, our opinions of what constitutes beautiful SQL should reflect an objective goal of better code.

How to Measure Code Complexity

Our programming styles should reduce the complexity of our programs, which then improves readability. But how do we measure code complexity? Programming is hard enough, and trying to formally classify and measure our programs is even harder.

We don't have a perfect way to measure code, but that doesn't mean we can't reason about our code. On one end of the spectrum of code metrics, we have complicated metrics like cyclomatic complexity, which counts the number of paths in a program.

Those advanced metrics are meant for imperative programming languages and don't help with SQL. On the other end of the spectrum, we have simple metrics like comparing the number of characters of a program.

In practice, most SQL developers compare program complexity by counting the number of characters – which is a mistake. Characters are the atomic unit of code to the *compiler*, but we're only interested in the atomic unit of code to a *human*. If we're worried about human comprehension, the number of *words* is much more meaningful than the number of characters.

It's worth briefly discussing the importance of words, even though we all intuitively understand this idea. We think in words – it's easier to remember a word than a collection of random characters. We read in words – we don't sound out the characters, except for unfamiliar words. We type in words – touch typists memorize whole words and don't think about individual characters. A good programming style should minimize the number of words and ignore the number of characters.

Focusing only on the word count leads naturally to the next two rules – avoid unnecessary aliases and avoid abbreviations.

Avoid Unnecessary Aliases

We should not create an alias without a good reason. Aliases are sometimes required, but most aliases are optional. There is a trade-off when aliasing columns, expressions, inline views, or table references; aliases let us create more meaningful names, but aliases also create more variables.

There are clearly many times when it helps to rename things. We certainly want to use aliases for expressions. We could reference the expression with double quotes, but quoted identifiers are painful to use. When we return two different columns that share the same name, we obviously want to change at least one of the names to something different. When we self-join a table, we need to give at least one instance of the table a different name. For example, we may use the same name but with a suffix like _PARENT or _CHILD. XML, JSON, and object-relational types may require an alias to access the values inside the object. And inline views deserve a good alias, especially when inline views are joined together like tables.

But we must not create aliases simply to save a few characters. The advantages of single-letter aliases are trivial, and it doesn't matter if we save a few bytes or a few seconds of typing. The disadvantages far outweigh the advantages. Adding unnecessary aliases adds more variables and consumes the most precious resource – the short-term memory of a developer. As described in the previous section, it's the number of *words* in our SQL statements that matters, not the number of characters.

For example, we should never use the trivial alias in the following example:

```
--Without alias.
select launch.launch_date from launch;
```

```
--With alias.
select l.launch_date from launch l;
```

If we were really creating a program with the space data set, we would be intimately familiar with the LAUNCH table. After the hundredth time, typing the word LAUNCH becomes automatic and is just as fast as typing the letter L. In the preceding simple example, the alias isn't that bad. But that alias is only tolerable because the example is trivial. Imagine if there were many other tables in a SQL statement, spaced dozens of lines apart; our short-term memory would be full of useless, one-letter variables, and we would have to spend a nonzero amount of thought to remember what the alias L stands for.

Unnecessary aliasing reduces the number of characters but increases the number of words and variables. We quickly grow accustomed to our most common table and column names. We should take advantage of that familiarity and reuse the same names when possible. Never create a new variable without a good reason.

Prefixes and Suffixes

Naming things is hard, and even referring to things by their proper name can be hard. Should we add prefixes and suffixes to our object and variable names? And when we reference objects, should we prefix the schema or table name? There are no strict rules in this section, only a discussion of the relevant trade-offs and advice to be flexible.

SQL Object and Column Names

When we create SQL objects and columns, we should avoid adding simple data type information to the name. For example, avoid adding TBL_ in front of table names or _NUM at the end of column names. Adding simple type information to names is called Hungarian notation and is generally considered a bad idea in most programming languages.[1]

The object types and column data types are easy to look up, and we don't need constant reminders. SQL is a high-level language with English-like syntax; a lot of meaning can be embedded into a simple SQL statement, and adding a few trivial prefixes and suffixes can distract from the real meaning of our queries. Compared with the number of variables in procedural languages, we will have much fewer SQL object and column names to remember, so it's worth the time to make the names easily readable.

When it comes to SQL object and column names, the type information is a very tiny part of the story anyway. Our persistent data cannot be adequately explained by a simple prefix or suffix. To get the full story, we need to look at the relationships, check constraints, table and column comments, and data itself. Over time, we'll become familiar with the names and know what they really mean.

On the other hand, I occasionally break my own rule and add _VW to the end of views. There are many times when a view and a table are almost identical, but those two objects can't share the same name.

There's another, more interesting exception to the rule to avoid adding type information to variable names. The original idea behind Hungarian notation was to add *useful* type information to a variable, which would make mistakes in our code more obvious. Prefixing each column name with the table name can help make our joins and expressions easier to understand. If the preceding example used this style, where every column in LAUNCH was prefixed by LAUNCH_ and every column in LAUNCH_AGENCY was prefixed by LAUNCH_AGENCY_, the join between those two tables would be ON LAUNCH_ID = LAUNCH_AGENCY_LAUNCH_ID.

Using consistent, unique prefixes makes it blindingly obvious where the columns from each join and expression come from. The downside to this approach is that the names get ridiculous pretty fast. In this case I would break another of my rules and allow abbreviations; if we are forced to consistently use a unique abbreviation for each table,

---

[1] See www.joelonsoftware.com/2005/05/11/making-wrong-code-look-wrong/ for the story behind Hungarian notation.

those abbreviations will quickly have real meaning to the developers. Personally, I don't think this naming system would be helpful for a schema as simple as the space data set. But I've seen the system work well in a schema with hundreds of tables. There are no objective answers here – only trade-offs.

PL/SQL Variable Names

Prefixes and suffixes tend to be more useful in PL/SQL than SQL. PL/SQL variables don't have as much history as SQL names, and they usually only apply to a small block of code. Within those small blocks of code, the variables will only serve a small purpose and won't have as much context as a table or column name. Prefixes and suffixes can create miniature contracts, to make it obvious how the variables should be used. For large PL/SQL systems, it's not uncommon to have a naming standard to help differentiate between things like constant and nonconstant variables, global and local variables, input or output parameters, etc.

Prefixes and suffixes are especially useful in PL/SQL when we have a variable that contains the same information as a column. It's tempting to give that PL/SQL variable the exact same name as the column, but duplicate names lead to ambiguity.

For example, if a PL/SQL function had a parameter named LAUNCH_ID, a SQL statement inside that function might contain an ambiguous expression, such as WHERE LAUNCH.LAUNCH_ID = LAUNCH_ID. Is the second LAUNCH_ID the value from the table or the value from the parameter? To avoid those situations, I prefix parameters with P_, for "parameter," and I prefix local variables with V_, for "variable." With a naming scheme like that, ambiguous expressions would be changed to a nonambiguous expression like WHERE LAUNCH.LAUNCH_ID = P_LAUNCH_ID.

Referencing Tables and Columns

We have several choices for how to reference tables and columns. Should we add the schema name in front of the table? Should we add the table name or alias in front of the column? The following example shows some of the different options for a simple query. The correct style depends on the context:

```
--Four ways to run the same query.
select launch_date from launch;
select launch.launch_date from launch;
```

```
select launch.launch_date from space.launch;
select space.launch.launch_date from space.launch;
```

The examples in this book do not reference the schema name. The space data set is installed in the schema SPACE by default, but there's not much value in adding that schema name to every query. There's little chance of confusion when the examples reference SATELLITE instead of SPACE.SATELLITE.

There's a trade-off between reliability and readability. It's *possible* that we already have a table in our schema named SATELLITE, and we could confuse that table with SPACE.SATELLITE. Or a table with the same name could be added in the future. But that small risk doesn't seem worth the cost of adding hundreds of additional words to our examples.

If we're constantly querying tables from another schema, we can create synonyms to hide the schema name. Or we can change our default schema with this command:

```
--Default to the SPACE schema.
alter session set current_schema=space;
```

The examples in this book only put the table name in front of the column name when the table name is not obvious. It's good to know where the columns come from, but many times the source table is unmistakable.

For example, after using the space data set for a non-trivial amount of time, it is obvious that LAUNCH_DATE comes from the LAUNCH table. But "obviousness" is subjective. Prefixing *every* column with the table name is more consistent and may help us when we're unfamiliar with the code, but all that prefixing clutters the SQL. Prefixing *none* of the columns will make the code smaller and may look better to someone intimately familiar with the data model, but it could be confusing to other developers. We need to find the right balance and adjust our style depending on the context.

Avoid Abbreviations

We should avoid uncommon abbreviations and use the unabridged form of words instead. Abbreviations use less characters but generate the same number of words. Code complexity is better measured by the number of words than the number of characters, and not all words are equal.

Uncommon abbreviations are harder to type and harder to read than full words. The definition of "uncommon" is subjective and depends on the context. If every programmer on our project instantly recognizes an abbreviation, then we should use it. But we shouldn't invent new abbreviations in every SQL statement.

As a quick example, imagine if our data set used abbreviations for everything:

```
--Abbreviated.  (This code does not work.)
select * from lnch;
```

```
--Not abbreviated.
select * from launch;
```

The first of the preceding two statements is smaller but is less readable. The abbreviation LNCH only requires a tiny amount of thought – but why make readers think any more than they have to? Reading the full word requires no thought and lets the readers focus all their attention on more important things.

There are certainly times when abbreviations are useful or necessary. But the hacker tendency to remove vowels from all variable names is not helpful. Writing without vowels technically means we're not even using an alphabet anymore; writing systems that only use consonants are called abjads. Abjads work fine in some languages but not in English or SQL. If we insist on abbreviating everything, we're fighting against thousands of years of language evolution.

Use Tabs for Left Alignment

Tabs vs. spaces is an old technology holy war, but it's worth re-evaluating the arguments through the lens of an advanced SQL developer. For building large SQL statements, using left-aligned tabs instead of right-aligned spaces helps us program faster and focus on the important parts of our SQL statements.

In most programming languages, the tabs vs. spaces argument is pointless – IDEs can auto-indent and effortlessly convert between the two. Unfortunately, that kind of auto-formatting is not always available to SQL developers. As described in the next section, automatic SQL formatting is not always a good idea. And SQL is often used in administrative tasks, where we frequently don't have access to IDEs. And when we're using dynamic SQL, where the code is stored as a string, we're stuck manually styling our code anyway.

We need to be able to write SQL relatively quickly, without the aid of a fancy IDE or auto-formatter. We should be able to make good-looking code without spending a lot of time adding individual spaces. There are times when our SQL needs to be extra beautiful, and then it's worth spending the time getting every space exactly right. But for most of our code, best is the enemy of good enough.

Programming is not a race, but using tabs when creating SQL will help us code faster and think more clearly about our code. With tabs we can quickly get the code good enough – indented and left-aligned – vs. trying to make the code look perfect with right-aligned spaces.

Small examples are deceiving when discussing whitespace and alignment. When we have a trivial SQL statement, like the following code, right-aligning the keywords looks just as nice as left-aligning. The right alignment can even produce a nice river of whitespace after the keywords:

```
--Left-aligned.
select *
from dual
where 1 = 1;

--Right-aligned with spaces.
SELECT *
  FROM dual
 WHERE 1 = 1;
```

But the preceding right-aligned style is not scalable. When we compare a more realistic SQL statement, like the large example from Chapter 6, the right alignment of the traditional SQL style quickly breaks down. The traditional right-aligned style works fine when there is only one level to our query. But as soon as we start nesting inline views, we need the alignment to quickly tell us what level we're looking at. With left-aligned tabs, we can more easily navigate inline views.

For large queries we don't need visual help to identify keywords like SELECT and FROM. We need visual help to identify the inline views. Figure 13-1 shows the example code from Chapter 6 and compares left-aligned tabs with the traditional right-aligned spaces. Don't try to read the code – just quickly scan the image to get a feeling for the shape of the query. To emphasize the shape of the queries, Figure 13-1 only shows the first word of each line.

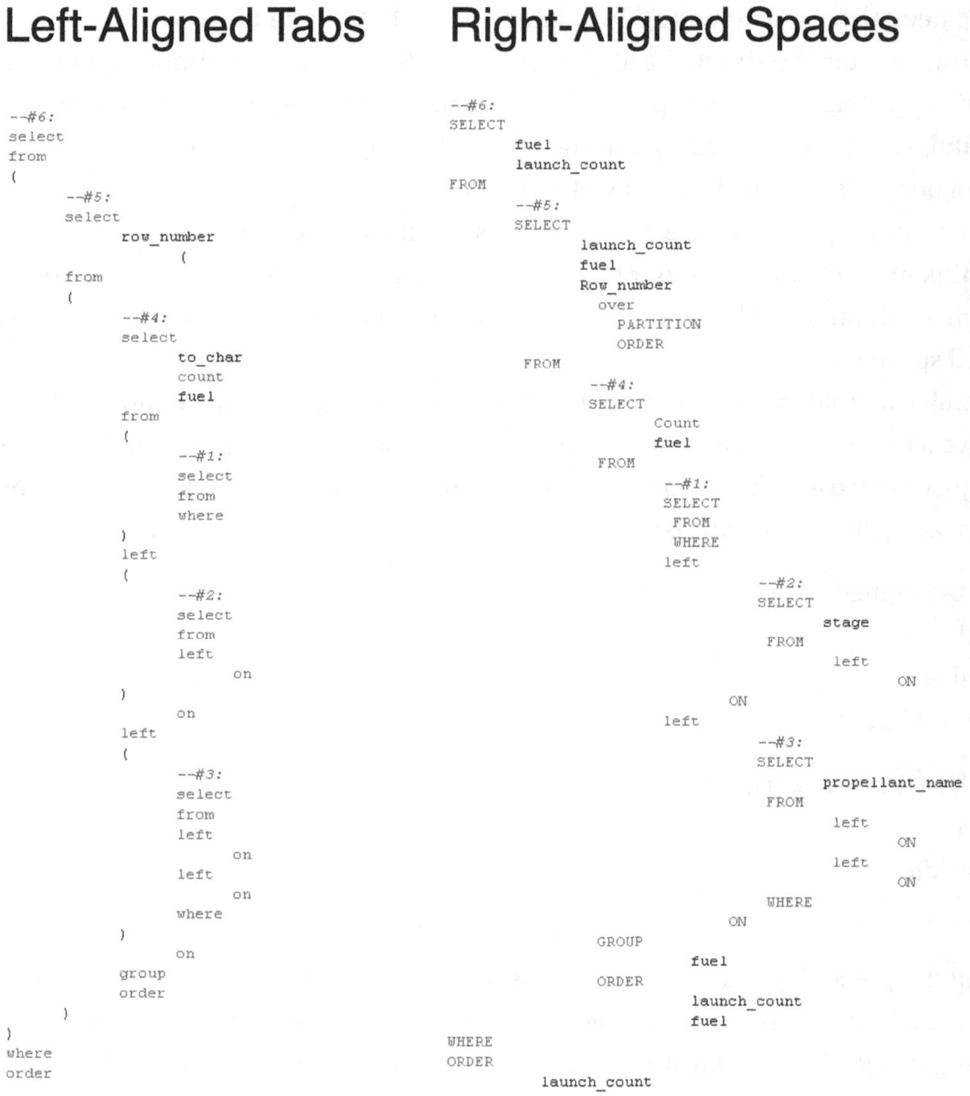

Left-Aligned Tabs   Right-Aligned Spaces

Figure 13-1. *Left-aligned tabs vs. right-aligned spaces*

In the preceding image, the left-aligned tabs version has a simpler and more accurate shape than the right-aligned spaces version. The left-aligned tabs version uses an entire line for each inline view parenthesis and equally indents those parentheses. That style is called the "Allman style," and it makes the inline views easier to read, write, and debug.

In addition, if we look closely at the right-aligned spaces style, we can see that the indenting is wrong. Inline views #1, #2, and #3 should all be indented at the same level. But the right-aligned spaces version incorrectly makes #1 look like the parent of #2 and

#3. Every popular SQL code formatter makes the same huge mistake. Indenting is meant to convey the parent–child relationships in our code. Simply being the first line of code does not make it a parent to the next line of code.

The left-aligned tabs style also makes it much easier to copy and paste inline views. Highlighting and copying inline views is easy because they don't share a line with unrelated code. Pasting and formatting the inline view is easy because all we have to do is highlight and press either Tab or Shift+Tab, to indent or unindent. Compare that with adding inline views using traditional right-aligned spaces; we have to either change many individual spaces or reformat the entire statement. Our coding style should enable us to copy snippets of code in a few seconds.

The main drawback with tabs is that the exact size is undefined. When we're writing an email, a post, or a book, to be safe we might want to convert the tabs to spaces when we're done.

We want a style that helps us focus on what's important in realistic SQL statements, not a style that adheres to what people traditionally used. Left-aligning with tabs helps us read and write inline views more easily.

Avoid Code Formatters

We should not become dependent on automatic code formatters, beautifiers, or pretty printers. While I appreciate the soulless efficiency of automation, we still need to maintain the ability to artisanally craft code. Automatic code formatters work well for most programming languages, but none of them consistently work well for Oracle SQL.

Code formatters have a hard time with Oracle SQL because the language is so complicated. Whereas most programming languages add features in libraries, SQL tends to add features as new syntax. That huge syntax makes automatically formatting code difficult.

A code formatter that works 99% of the time is not good enough. SQL code formatters are most likely to fail when our SQL statements become large and use advanced features – which is exactly when the code formatting is most important.

We don't always have an IDE available. If we're doing administration work on a server or helping a coworker, we may not have our favorite IDE. And when we're creating SQL in a string, for dynamic SQL, no code formatter will help us. Code formatters either won't recognize the string as SQL, or the string will be invalid SQL until run time, when we have all the variables. Even our generated dynamic SQL should look good, as discussed in Chapter 14.

SQL code formatters also focus on small, simple code. As demonstrated in the previous section, SQL code formatters focus on the obvious keywords, instead of properly spacing and aligning the important inline views.

There are times when we care about precise spacing, but only *we* can decide on how to set that spacing. Large SQL statements frequently have to repeat long lists of columns. We may have many columns we don't care about, along with one important column we want to highlight. Putting that important column or expression on a line by itself can help emphasize what's important to the reader.

For example, we may have to project 26 columns, but only one column is modified in an expression. We don't want to waste 26 blank lines for each column. But we also don't want to squish all the columns on one line and miss the important part. The following code uses a separate line for the important expression but crams everything else together in a simple list. If we want to use space to emphasize important things, we have to set the space manually:

```
--Use space to highlight what's important.
select
    a,b,c,d,e,f,g,h,i,j,k,l,m,
    n+1 n,
    o,p,q,r,s,t,u,v,w,x,y,z
from some_table;
```

We should disable IDE options that automatically format code on compilation. Even if we have coding standards, someone may have a good reason for breaking the standard. Luckily, some IDEs let us disable automatic code formatting for specific code blocks.

SQL developers are going to be stuck in many situations where we need to hand-build our code. We must be able to write code quickly, without relying on a specific code formatter.

Lowercase

SQL should be written mostly in lowercase, like all modern programming languages. Lowercase code looks better and is easier to read.

Uppercase keywords are associated with older programming languages, such as assembly, Fortran, and COBOL. SQL is an old language, which has some advantages, but there are negative connotations with our code looking ancient. Decades ago, there were good technical reasons to use uppercase, but those reasons no longer apply.

The cultural convention today is to use lowercase for programming. And lowercase, or mixed case, is obviously the typical choice for normal writing. (There is a consensus that it is easier to read lowercase writing than uppercase writing. But it's debatable why lowercase is easier to read, and I'm not sure if the research applies to monospaced fonts used in programming languages.)

But there are certainly still times when uppercase is helpful. When embedding small SQL statements inside other languages, it helps to use uppercase to contrast the SQL with the other language. Uppercase is also useful when writing emails or posts. And uppercase can be useful for helping parts of our PL/SQL programs stick out, like for global constants.

Most of our time looking at code is in an IDE, where the syntax highlighting is more important than using case for identifying keywords. There aren't huge advantages to using lowercase, but if it looks better, is more readable, and is easier to type, we might as well abandon uppercase.

Summary

This concludes the most controversial opinions in this book, and I will now get off my soapbox. Style tips and tricks have been included in many different parts of this book and are quickly summarized in "Appendix A: SQL Style Guide Cheat Sheet."

Writing SQL, and especially writing large SQL, can benefit from nontraditional programming styles. We can reduce the complexity of our code by avoiding unnecessary aliases and uncommon abbreviations. Our programming style should help our code emphasize what's important, which is usually the relationship between inline views. Using left-aligned tabs can help us read and write nested inline views. Automatic code formatters will eventually let us down, so we might as well get used to manually styling our code. Using lowercase can help our code look modern and be more readable.

I hope you are willing to reconsider at least some of the traditional "best practices" used for writing SQL. No matter which style we prefer, it's helpful to understand the reasons we prefer that style. In practice, we can't always write code the way we want, and we have to be willing to compromise. But it's helpful to have an idealistic style and to strive to write beautiful SQL statements.

CHAPTER 14

Use SQL More Often with Basic Dynamic SQL

Dynamic SQL is a powerful tool that helps us get the most out of Oracle SQL. With dynamic SQL we can build our code at run time. Writing code in code is challenging but offers many opportunities.

First, we need to understand when we must use dynamic SQL, when we want to use dynamic SQL, and when we do not want to use dynamic SQL. The basic features of dynamic SQL are simple, but we have to be careful to preserve performance and security. Generating source code is tricky, and we need to use specific programming styles to make dynamic code manageable. When we're comfortable with dynamic SQL, we can apply it to several complex scenarios and significantly improve the clarity and performance of our programs.

This chapter only briefly introduces dynamic SQL. More advanced and more powerful dynamic SQL solutions are described in Chapters 20 and 21.

When to Use Dynamic SQL

Dynamic SQL is commonly used in four different contexts: to run DDL commands, when the objects or properties or structure is not known until run time, to simplify privileges, and to build rule engines. It's also important to not use dynamic SQL when there are better alternatives.

Run DDL

The most common use of dynamic SQL is to run DDL commands, because PL/SQL does not natively support static DDL. The following example shows how DDL must be executed as a string and not hard-coded into PL/SQL:

J. Heller, *Pro Oracle SQL Development*, https://doi.org/10.1007/978-1-4842-8867-2_14

```
--Working PL/SQL block that compresses table with dynamic SQL.
begin
    execute immediate 'alter table launch move compress online';
end;
/

--Broken PL/SQL block that compresses table using static SQL.
--This block raises a PL/SQL compilation error.
begin
    alter table launch move compress online;
end;
/
```

Initially, it feels wrong that PL/SQL doesn't natively support static DDL, especially since PL/SQL and SQL are so tightly integrated. In practice, that limitation isn't a big deal, since executing dynamic SQL only requires a few extra keywords. We probably wouldn't want to use static DDL in our PL/SQL anyway, since most DDL commands are destructive and require recompiling dependent PL/SQL code. If a procedure directly references an object and then alters that object, the procedure will have to recompile itself. Oracle is fine with constantly parsing SQL statements, but recompiling procedural code while that code is running is a bad idea.

There are several dynamic SQL traps we must avoid. Although we must always use dynamic SQL for DDL, we should rarely use dynamic SQL for DML. We don't want to use dynamic code when static code works just fine. Also, just because we can manage objects at run time does not mean we *should* manage objects at run time. In other databases it might be common to frequently drop and recreate tables to hold intermediate values, but that is not a best practice in Oracle. In Oracle, we should hold intermediate values either in inline views, PL/SQL collections, or global temporary tables that are only created once.

Unknown Until Run Time

The second most common use of dynamic SQL is when we don't know the objects, properties, or structure of the SQL statement until run time. Dynamic SQL works with any string, so there's no limit to how much we can change the statement. We can swap table names, add conditions, change columns, or completely rebuild the entire statement.

For example, let's create a function to count the number of rows in any table. The table name is passed into the function and then concatenated into the SQL statement string. The query is executed, the result is stored in a variable, and then the variable is returned:

```
--Use dynamic SQL to count the number of rows in a table.
create or replace function get_count(p_table_name varchar2)
return number authid current_user is
   v_count number;
begin
   execute immediate
   'select count(*) from '||
      dbms_assert.sql_object_name(p_table_name)
   into v_count;
   return v_count;
end;
/

select get_count('LAUNCH') row_count from dual;


ROW_COUNT
---------
    70535
```

Notice how the preceding code calls the function DBMS_ASSERT.SQL_OBJECT_NAME. This function ensures that the parameter is a simple string that matches an object name. If we try to call the function with a dangerous string like GET_COUNT('LAUNCH; DROP TABLE STUDENTS;'), the DBMS_ASSERT package raises the exception "ORA-44002: invalid object name." The DBMS_ASSERT package contains several functions that can help us avoid SQL injection. We must always be careful to not let unauthorized users run arbitrary code.

Another popular use for dynamic SQL is when we don't know the structure of the WHERE clause until run time. That scenario can happen when we're building SQL statements based on values entered on forms. A static query using every element from a form may get littered with compound conditions like COLUMN1 = P_VALUE1 OR P_VALUE1 IS NULL. The resulting query would be huge and more likely to have performance issues. That final query might be simpler and faster if it's dynamically generated to only include relevant conditions.

Even when we know the dependent objects at compile time, we may still want to avoid creating static dependencies. For example, database links create complicated dependencies, and changing underlying objects on one database can lead to errors like "ORA-04062: timestamp of function "OWNER.OBJECT" has been changed" in another database. Running code dynamically can help avoid weird compilation issues with remote databases.

Simplify Privileges

One of the lesser-known advantages of dynamic SQL is simplifying privileges. When compiling PL/SQL objects, the owner of the PL/SQL object must have direct access to all of the statically referenced objects, at compile time. Unfortunately, that access cannot be granted through a role. The privileges must be granted directly to the owner of the PL/SQL object.

For example, imagine if we changed the preceding function and hard-coded a static reference to DBA_TABLES. Even if our user has the DBA role, the function will fail to compile with the error "ORA-00942: table or view does not exist." That error occurs because the access was only granted through a *role* and not directly to the *user*.

Our first instinct might be to solve the problem by granting direct access to the DBA_TABLES view. A direct grant would work, but we might regret it later when our privileges are a mess and auditors are asking why we have so many individual grants.

A better workaround is to use dynamic SQL, which is the way the preceding function already works. The clause AUTHID CURRENT_USER tells Oracle that when the function runs, the function can use the roles of the user invoking the function. As long as we have a role that grants us access to the DBA views, we can call the function like this:

```
--Use dynamic SQL to access DBA views.
select get_count('DBA_TABLES') row_count from dual;

ROW_COUNT
---------
     2302
```

This discussion is veering off into complicated PL/SQL topics like definer's rights vs. invoker's rights. The important part to remember is that even though dynamic SQL may require a few more keywords, dynamic SQL can simplify our privilege requirements. In most organizations it's easier to add a few lines of code than to get elevated privileges.

Rule Engines

Dynamic SQL can be used to build powerful rule engines. Rule engines can be helpful for tasks like scoring claims based on a large set of criteria. Many medical and insurance systems have hundreds of rules, many of which contain simple and repetitive logic, such as `IF A AND B THEN 0`, `IF B OR C THEN 1`, etc.

SQL is a high-level language, with an English-like syntax. If we carefully set up the columns and expressions, our SQL statements can look surprisingly close to our requirements. Instead of hard-coding each rule as a query, we can store the rules in a table and then dynamically generate the SQL statements to implement the rules. Ideally, the rules in that table can be validated or created by a business analyst, without any programming knowledge.

In practice, rule engines are difficult to get right. It's not always easy to store dynamic code in a relational database. Source code, like any language, is inherently hierarchical. Oracle is certainly capable of storing and manipulating hierarchical data, but SQL is not the ideal language for solving difficult hierarchical problems. And while databases are certainly capable of containing simple text strings, versioning our code is still best done with version control software.

Whether or not we want to build a rule engine is a difficult decision. If we do decide to build a rule engine in Oracle, then we should definitely use dynamic SQL as the cornerstone of our engine. Building a rule engine can quickly devolve into the quagmire of creating a custom programming language, so we want to stay as close to SQL and PL/SQL as possible.

When Not to Use Dynamic SQL

Dynamic SQL is intended for when we don't know the *structure* of the query until run time. Dynamic SQL should not be used simply because we don't know the *values* until run time. If only the values are changing at run time, then bind variables are a better solution.

It's a common misconception that dynamic SQL is inevitably slower, less secure, or messier than regular SQL. It's true that dynamic programming presents challenges, but it also provides amazing opportunities. An unhealthy fear of dynamic SQL can lead to huge anti-patterns and cause us to miss great opportunities to use SQL to solve problems. Later in this chapter, we'll see how to tame dynamic SQL with the right programming style.

Basic Features

There are many dynamic SQL options, but most of our programs only need a few basic features. We have to decide which version of dynamic SQL to use and understand the syntax and how to pass information in and out of the SQL statement.

Oracle has two different kinds of dynamic SQL. In ancient versions of Oracle, dynamic SQL could only be executed through the complex PL/SQL package DBMS_ SQL. Modern versions of Oracle allow native dynamic SQL, which uses the simpler EXECUTE IMMEDIATE and OPEN/FOR syntax. Native dynamic SQL is almost always the best choice. Native dynamic SQL is faster and much simpler to use than DBMS_SQL. There are some rare challenges that require DBMS_SQL, which are discussed in Chapter 20.

As we've seen in the previous examples, EXECUTE IMMEDIATE is easy to use – simply pass the statement as a string. But we must remember to remove the terminator. For dynamic SQL, the statement should not end with a semicolon. For dynamic PL/SQL, the PL/SQL block should not end with a forward slash.

Just like static SQL, the results of a dynamic SQL statement can be assigned to variables using INTO. The following code shows a simple native dynamic SQL example:

```
--Simple INTO example.
declare
    v_dummy varchar2(1);
begin
    execute immediate 'select dummy from dual'
    into v_dummy;

    dbms_output.put_line('Dummy: '||v_dummy);
end;
/

Dummy: X
```

The INTO clause can also include a comma-separated list of variables, if there are multiple columns returned. If the SQL statement is not a SELECT statement, simply leave out the INTO clause. Multiple rows of data can be captured with either a BULK COLLECT and collection variables or a dynamic SQL cursor. But those advanced PL/SQL features are not discussed here. The important point to remember is that there's always a way to run any statement dynamically.

Bind Variables for Performance and Security

Even though dynamic SQL executes concatenated strings, we should still take advantage of bind variables. Bind variables can significantly improve the performance and security of our dynamic SQL.

Bind variables are placeholders for real values in SQL statements. Bind variables let Oracle reuse the same SQL statement for different values, saving a lot of compile time.

Although bind variables and dynamic SQL seem like opposites, they can still be used together. For example, the following code uses string concatenation to choose the table name, but it uses a bind variable to choose the value:

```
--Count either LAUNCH or SATELLITE rows for a LAUNCH_ID.
declare
  --(Pretend these are parameters):
  p_launch_or_satellite varchar2(100) := 'LAUNCH';
  p_launch_id number := 4305;
  v_count number;
begin
  execute immediate
  '
    select count(*)
    from '||
      dbms_assert.sql_object_name(p_launch_or_satellite)||'
    where launch_id = :launch_id
  '
  into v_count
  using p_launch_id;

  dbms_output.put_line('Row count: '||v_count);
end;
/

Row count: 1
```

In the preceding code, using the bind variable significantly reduces the number of SQL statements that need to be parsed. There may be multiple parsed statements to handle the dynamic table name, but there won't be a new statement for every LAUNCH_ID. Bind variables don't have to eliminate parsing; they only have to reduce parsing.

Bind variables work slightly differently for SQL and PL/SQL. In dynamic SQL, bind variables are set once per occurrence, regardless of the bind variable name. In dynamic PL/SQL, bind variables are set once per unique bind variable name. In the following example, both the SQL and PL/SQL code reference the bind variable A twice. The dynamic SQL code requires two input values, while the dynamic PL/SQL requires only one input value:

```
--SQL requires variables for each bind variable.
--PL/SQL requires variables for each unique bind variable.
declare
    v_count number;
begin
    execute immediate
    'select count(*) from dual where 1=:A and 1=:A'
    into v_count using 1,1;

    execute immediate
    '
        declare
            v_test1 number; v_test2 number;
        begin
            v_test1 := :A;   v_test2 := :A;
        end;
    ' using 1;
end;
/
```

More important than performance, bind variables can save us from huge security problems. If we allow untrusted users to enter arbitrary values, those users can change the meaning of our SQL statements. For example, imagine a program with a partial line of code like this: EXECUTE IMMEDIATE 'SELECT * FROM LAUNCH WHERE LAUNCH_ID = '||V_VALUE. We expect the variable to be a number, but what happens if the variable is a string like this: '1 or 1=1'? We can use DBMS_ASSERT to check values, but even that package is not as safe as bind variables.

Breaking out of a concatenated string value is called SQL injection, which is one of the worst security holes. We must *never* allow untrusted user input to run in dynamic SQL. There are many sneaky ways to escape out of a variable. Even numbers and dates are not safe, because it may be possible to alter the session and use weird strings for numeric and date formats.

Dynamic SQL is an awesome, powerful feature. But every time we use it, we must consider the performance and security implications. And just because we use dynamic SQL doesn't mean we shouldn't also use bind variables.

How to Simplify String Concatenation

Dynamic SQL can get ugly. It's hard enough to build code with code. On top of that, we have to deal with strings inside strings. To get the most out of dynamic SQL, we need to be able to write decent-looking code. There are three simple tricks we can combine to make our dynamic SQL infinitely more readable: multiline strings, the alternative quoting mechanism, and templates.

Multiline Strings

Oracle supports multiline strings, and they are trivial to use. There are still programming languages that don't support multiline strings, and many developers are stuck in the bad habit of concatenating every line.

The previous code example used this multiline string:

```
'
    declare
        v_test1 number; v_test2 number;
    begin
        v_test1 := :A;  v_test2 := :A;
    end;
'
```

Without multiline strings, we would be left with this mess:

```
'declare'                             ||chr(10)||
'    v_test1 number; v_test2 number;'||chr(10)||
'begin'                               ||chr(10)||
'    v_test1 := :A;  v_test2 := :A;' ||chr(10)||
'end;'
```

There is almost never a reason to avoid multiline strings, even though there are potential ambiguities with line endings. Does the code use ASCII character 10 (new line), 13 (line feed), or a combination of the two? In practice, the line ending doesn't matter. The readability of our code is more important than irrelevant ambiguities, so we should use multiline strings as much as possible.

Alternative Quoting Mechanism

Embedding single quotation marks in strings is painful if we only use escape characters. The alternative quoting mechanism can help us write much cleaner code.

The most common way to embed single quotation marks is to escape them, by using two single quotation marks next to each other. Escaping can lead to visually confusing code, as seen in the following:

```
--Single quotation mark examples.
select
    'A'     no_quote,
    'A''B'  quote_in_middle,
    '''A'   quote_at_beginning,
    ''''    only_a_quote
from dual;


NO_QUOTE   QUOTE_IN_MIDDLE   QUOTE_AT_BEGINNING   ONLY_A_QUOTE
--------   ---------------   ------------------   ------------
A          A'B               'A                   '
```

The preceding code is only the beginning of concatenation hell. When we plug SQL statements into strings or nest SQL inside PL/SQL inside strings, our code quickly becomes repulsive. My personal, shameful record is 12 consecutive quotation marks.

The alternative quoting mechanism helps us avoid concatenation problems. We can define our own delimiters and not have to worry about escape characters. With this improved syntax, we can more easily copy and paste SQL statements into code.

To use the alternative quoting mechanism, begin the string with the letter Q, then a single quote, and then the opening delimiter. If the opening delimiter is one of [, (, <, or {, then the closing delimiter is the matching],), >, or }. For other delimiters, the opening and closing characters are the same.

The following example uses the alternative quoting mechanism and returns the same results as the escape character version. This example demonstrates how the syntax works, but at first this feature looks like a huge step in the wrong direction:

```
--Alternative quoting mechanism examples.
select
    q'[A]'    no_quote,
    q'<A'B>'  quote_in_middle,
    q'('A)'   quote_at_beginning,
    q'!'!'    only_a_quote
from dual;
```

This is another case where we can learn the wrong lesson from trivial examples. If there is only one single quotation mark, then escaping is much simpler. But when we're copying and pasting code as strings, the alternative quoting mechanism makes a world of difference. The following example is a more realistic comparison of escaping vs. the alternative quoting mechanism:

```
--Escape character.
begin
    execute immediate
    '
        select ''A'' a from dual
    ';
end;
/

--Custom delimiter.
begin
    execute immediate
    q'[
        select 'A' a from dual
    ]';
end;
/
```

With the alternative quoting mechanism, it is trivial to copy and paste entire blocks of code. If we want to debug the code in an IDE, we can simply highlight and run the innermost block. When we use escaping, we have to manually change the SQL before we can test the SQL independently.

This section may sound like syntactic sugar, but the alternative quoting mechanism is more like syntactic steroids. Without the ability to write clear code, we would avoid dynamic SQL, which means we would also avoid SQL.

Templating

String concatenation is still ugly, even with multiline strings and the alternative quoting mechanism. We can improve our code readability by replacing concatenation with a simple templating system. There are template libraries, but in practice all we need is simple variable names and the REPLACE function.

For example, imagine we are constructing a dynamic SQL statement with unknown columns, tables, and conditions. The typical approach may end up looking something like this:

```
'select '''||v_column_1||''', '||v_column_2||'
 from '||v_table||'
 where status = ''OPEN''
    '||v_optional_condition_1
```

Dynamic SQL will never look quite as good as static SQL, but the preceding code is almost unreadable. And that code is still only a trivial example. Imagine concatenating an advanced SQL statement.

Instead of concatenating results, the following code replaces variables with the real values:

```
replace(replace(replace(replace(
q'[
    select '$V_COLUMN_1', $V_COLUMN_2
    from $V_TABLE
    where status = 'OPEN'
       $V_OPTIONAL_CONDITION_1
]',
'$V_COLUMN_1'              , v_column_1),
```

```
'$V_COLUMN_2'              , v_column_2),
'$V_TABLE'                 , v_table),
'$V_OPTIONAL_CONDITION_1', v_optional_condition_1)
```

The overall code is larger because we need to add four REPLACE functions. But the SQL statement is much more readable. The variable replacing is unimportant boilerplate code – the SQL statement is what's important. Making our PL/SQL uglier to make our SQL prettier is a good trade-off. This templating approach is also vital if we want to store templates in a repository and use them to create a rule engine.

Dynamic SQL looks much better when we combine multiline strings, the alternative quoting mechanism, and a simple template system. Dynamic code can quickly grow out of control, so we need to spend a little extra time to keep our code clean. That effort will be well worth it if we get to use SQL more often. Dynamic SQL is not perfect, but it's better than the alternatives.

Code Generation, Not Generic Code

Dynamic SQL is typically used for generating code or temporary objects at run time. But we can also use dynamic SQL to create permanent code. Instead of building one complex object to handle multiple scenarios, we can dynamically build multiple simple objects instead.

Dynamic code generation is considered evil in most programming languages. For example, the EVAL function in JavaScript is frequently abused. Most programming languages use features like reflection, generics, or polymorphism to create dynamic programs. But the best practices are different in Oracle.

The reason for the difference in programming styles is that Oracle is more structured than other environments, and Oracle is better prepared for frequent compiling. Oracle is a relational database and has taken to heart the idea of making everything available through relational interfaces. The data dictionary and dynamic performance views offer a wealth of information that lets us easily reason about our environment, objects, and code. Compiling is slow in other languages, but Oracle is able to quickly parse a large number of statements.

Many of the advanced features in other programming languages don't work well in Oracle. Common alternatives to dynamic SQL are object-relational features and the ANYDATA type. Those alternative technologies are useful in some limited contexts, but they are not nearly as powerful as SQL.

361

For example, let's say we need to create auditing triggers for our tables. Whenever a value is changed, we want to store the old value in a history table, along with metadata. The code is going to look relatively simple and repetitive; there will be lots of triggers, and the triggers will insert data only if the new values are different than the old values.

Instead of copying and pasting code, we might be tempted to build triggers and a smart procedure that can handle "any" data change. But we'll quickly find that converting "anything," and using generic data types, is painful in SQL and PL/SQL.

Instead of building one smart procedure, it's better to generate lots of dumb triggers. With the data dictionary, we can easily figure out the column names and types and can automatically generate the boilerplate code.

If we use a code generator approach, we need to spend extra effort to make both the code generator and the generated code look good. The compiler doesn't care if triggers look nice, but eventually other programmers will see the code. We should also add a warning comment, such as "Do not modify; this code was automatically generated by <package name>."

There are many systems where we have to choose between a smart generic solution and an automatically generated simple solution. In Oracle, if we know how to tame dynamic SQL, generated code is usually the best solution.

Summary

Dynamic SQL is a great feature and can be used for running DDL, simplifying privileges, building code that is only known at run time, and constructing large rule engines. The basic features are simple, but to get the most out of dynamic SQL, we need a programming style that incorporates multiline strings, the alternative quoting mechanism, and templates. If our code looks good, it will run good. We need to consider performance and security and use bind variables when possible. There are many cases where generating dumb code is better than writing smart generic code. With dynamic SQL we can leverage Oracle's greatest strength – SQL.

CHAPTER 15

Avoid Anti-patterns

So far, this book has focused on what we *should* do. But it is also helpful to discuss what we should *not* do. This chapter lists common anti-patterns – programming concepts and styles that we should avoid.

Anti-patterns are not merely trivial compiler errors that we can immediately fix. Anti-patterns are subtle mistakes that might save us time today but will cost us more time tomorrow. We need to proactively avoid certain shortcuts, so we don't accumulate too much technical debt.

All the items in this chapter are real mistakes I've seen happen many times in my career, and most of them I've fallen for myself. These are not simply beginner mistakes that experts can skip over; these are choices that appear alluring even to expert programmers who have not yet seen the far-reaching consequences of these choices.

The anti-patterns are ordered roughly by how disastrous they can be for our projects. Listed first are architectural blunders that can very nearly doom a project. At the end of the list are relatively minor mistakes that may only doom a single query. This chapter only focuses on Oracle SQL anti-patterns. There are obviously many generic programming and business anti-patterns that we don't want to learn the hard way.

Avoid the Second System Syndrome and Rewriting from Scratch

Before we grab our pitchforks and torches and start trashing everyone else's code, we need to hear a few words of caution. If we're too negative and pessimistic about existing code and we only focus on the problems, our negativity can lead to other problems. Focusing only on software mistakes can lead to the second system syndrome and foolishly rewriting from scratch.

© Jon Heller 2023
J. Heller, *Pro Oracle SQL Development*, https://doi.org/10.1007/978-1-4842-8867-2_15

The second system syndrome is our tendency to go overboard with expectations for the second version of a system. We say to ourselves, "The first version worked fine, but it was too simple and full of architectural mistakes. When we create the second system, we can realize our utopian vision and add all these awesome new features we didn't get around to the first time."

Agile development can fix some of the problems related to the second system syndrome. Hopefully we won't spend too much time architecting features only later to discover that those features aren't important. It's easy to look at old code and see problems with it, because it's easier to write code than it is to read code. It's easy to be negative in software development, and we need to fight our biases. We need to ask ourselves if maybe the old system was limited for a reason. Maybe the old development team painfully discovered that those hundreds of new features are worthless. Or maybe the original team already tried and failed to implement features that don't make sense.

Overly pessimistic thinking can lead us to foolishly rewrite from scratch.[1] That old, large code isn't necessarily ugly and full of junk. That old code might be battle-hardened and full of fixes that handle rare, unexpected problems. Chances are good we're not smarter than the people who wrote the original code. We'll make plenty of mistakes when we write our own version.

The anti-patterns listed in this chapter are problems that can plague our code. But none of these anti-patterns are programming death sentences, making our code completely unusable. We can refactor our way out of many problems without throwing everything out. And a lot of problems we can live with.

We're biased to think everyone else's code is trash and our code is great. It's fun to poke holes in other people's code and talk about how bad it is. Anti-patterns can definitely teach us a lot about programming and help us avoid mistakes. But we should keep a positive attitude, especially when sharing our opinions with someone else. Instead of saying, "Your code sucks because of X," we should say, "Our code could be better because of Y."

---

[1] Joel Spolsky has written about the problems with rewriting code from scratch: `www.joelonsoftware.com/2000/04/06/things-you-should-never-do-part-i/`

Avoid the Stringly Typed Entity–Attribute–Value Model

Entity–attribute–value (EAV) models allow extreme flexibility for storing data in relational tables, but we must not use the wrong data types. EAV is a contentious topic in database design, with several pros and cons. Although it is reasonable to relax some of our database norms when using an EAV, we must never abandon type safety.

EAV Pros and Cons

EAV is a table structure where each value is stored in a separate row, instead of using multiple columns to store multiple values per row. EAV tends to be preferred by architects and application programmers, while database administrators and database developers tend to avoid EAV.

Simply using an EAV is not an anti-pattern. There are several ways to build an EAV model, and the following table is a simple and safe way (although a real EAV table should include constraints, comments, etc.):

```
--Simple and safe EAV.
create table good_eav
(
    id              number primary key,
    name            varchar2(4000),
    string_value    varchar2(4000),
    number_value    number,
    date_value      date
);

insert into good_eav(id, name, string_value)
values (1, 'Name', 'Eliver');
insert into good_eav(id, name, number_value)
values (2, 'High Score', 11);
insert into good_eav(id, name, date_value)
values (3, 'Date of Birth', date '2011-04-28');
```

With the preceding table, we don't have to add columns to add new types of data. We can add any kind of value at any time, using only an INSERT statement. The EAV table is skinnier and denser than a regular table that holds the same data.

Table 15-1 summarizes the different trade-offs of using an EAV model vs. using multiple columns.

Table 15-1. *Comparison of EAV and Non-EAV Tables*

	EAV	**Non-EAV**
Flexibility	Allows any value without DDL	Requires DDL for new columns
Performance	Difficult to index, opaque to optimizer	Easy to index, transparent to optimizer
Appearance	Looks nicer in an ER diagram	Looks nicer in an IDE
Type safety	No constraints, requires dangerous conversions	Allows constraints, no dangerous conversions
Size	Smaller for sparse tables	Smaller for dense tables
Querying	Difficult – requires more tables, conditions, and conversions	Simple – just reference the column

Depending on the context, different items in the preceding list will carry more or less weight. For example, if the table is only going to hold a dozen rows, then the performance difference doesn't matter.

As long as we're honestly considering and weighing the pros and cons, there's nothing wrong with choosing an EAV model. The anti-pattern occurs when EAV models are implemented incorrectly.

Never Use the Wrong Type

This anti-pattern happens when an EAV table uses only a *single* column to store all values. One of the few absolute rules of *relational* databases is that we must never store data as the wrong type. The only exception is using staging tables to temporarily hold data before it is cleaned up and moved to the real tables. Even if we have unstructured data like XML or JSON, we can still store it as an XMLType or with the IS JSON check constraint. We must never create an EAV table like this:

```
--Never create a table like this:
create table bad_eav
(
    id      number primary key,
    name    varchar2(4000),
    value   varchar2(4000)
);
```

```
insert into bad_eav values (1, 'Name'        , 'Eliver');
insert into bad_eav values (2, 'High Score'  , 11);
insert into bad_eav values (3, 'Date of Birth', '2011-04-28');
```

Storing all values as a VARCHAR2(4000) is one of the worst mistakes we can make in a database. Since the database can no longer ensure type safety, we have to implement our own logic to ensure that numbers and dates are properly formatted. (As discussed in Chapter 7, verifying number and date formats is not a trivial task, especially when we consider internationalization and localization.) Every time we use an incorrectly typed value, we need to remember to use the right conversion functions. The numeric and date values will use more space than their native values. The optimizer will be completely unable to reason about the values and will have a hard time building good execution plans.

Systems that store all their values as strings are jokingly referred to as "stringly typed" (a pun based on the phrase "strongly typed"). This problem can occur in many places; columns, parameters, variables, and expressions can be incorrectly processed as strings. This problem is tricky because the implicit conversion will work *most* of the time. It's easy to miss these problems during testing and have bugs suddenly appear in production.

Subtle Conversion Bugs in Oracle SQL

Stringly typed data is especially bad in Oracle SQL because it creates subtle, nondeterministic bugs. For example, look at the following code. I normally dislike quizzing readers, but in this case, I want you to try to spot the bug:

```
--Simple query against stringly-typed EAV that will likely fail.
select *
from bad_eav
where name = 'Date of Birth'
    and value = date '2011-04-28';
```

The preceding query will likely fail with the error message "ORA-01861: literal does not match format string." Per the implicit data type conversion rules in the *SQL Language Reference*, Oracle will try to convert the string column VALUE into a date to match the date literal. (Don't bother trying to memorize the implicit data type conversion rules – the best solution is to never use implicit data type conversion in the first place.) But that conversion of VALUE from a string into a date only works if our server or client date format is set to something similar to the format we used when we populated the table.

A common, but terrible, solution to the preceding error is to change the date format on the client or the server. Running ALTER SESSION SET NLS_DATE_FORMAT = 'YYYY-MM-DD' will enable Oracle to correctly convert some of the strings into dates. But now we are forever fighting battles with client settings. We cannot reasonably expect every tool and every user to always set the date format parameter a specific way.

Another common, but terrible, solution is to use a simple, explicit conversion of the VALUE column into a date:

```
--Insidiously wrong way to query a bad EAV table.
select *
from bad_eav
where name = 'Date of Birth'
    and to_date(value, 'YYYY-MM-DD') = date '2011-04-28';
```

The obvious problem with the preceding query is that the "Date of Birth" values in the table must always be formatted correctly. A single incorrectly formatted date string can ruin many queries. Since this is a generic column, it's hard to prevent bad values with a constraint. And since this column may serve many purposes, there may be many other pieces of code that write to it that we need to validate.

If we have perfectly formatted data in the EAV table, the preceding query will *probably* work. But the query is still not *guaranteed* to work because Oracle may execute the last two predicates out of order. The TO_DATE function can only successfully work for "Date of Birth"; it is going to fail if it runs against "Name" or "High Score." Even if the data in the table is perfect, depending on the order of execution, the query will fail.

The best way to write this query is using the new 12.2 conversion error syntax. The syntax in the following query is a bit more complicated, but it is the safest way to query the table. Unfortunately, even this new syntax does not work in a few specific cases,[2] but at least when the syntax fails, it will fail consistently:

```
--New type-safe way to query a stringly-typed EAV.
select *
from bad_eav
where name = 'Date of Birth'
    and to_date(value default null on conversion error, 'YYYY-MM-DD') = date
    '2011-04-28';
```

If we're stuck using a version before 12.2, the solution gets even trickier. Without the improved conversion syntax, we must force a specific query execution order, which is difficult. Merely reordering the query does not work, and hints are difficult to set up correctly. One of the only safe ways to query the bad EAV table is to use the ROWNUM trick discussed in Chapter 12:

```
--Old type-safe way to query a stringly-typed EAV.
select *
from
(
    select *
    from bad_eav
    where name = 'Date of Birth'
        and rownum >= 1
)
where to_date(value, 'YYYY-MM-DD') = date '2011-04-28';
```

What did we gain by replacing the three columns STRING_VALUE, NUMBER_VALUE, and DATE_VALUE with the single column VALUE? Nothing. In practice, we rarely have data so generic that we can't even be bothered to learn its type. Even if we're only going to display data on a screen, we still need to know the type so we can properly justify and format the displayed values. If we have unstructured documents, we can create another EAV column named XML_VALUE and make the column an XMLType.

---

[2] See this Stack Overflow answer for an explanation of the weird times when DEFAULT NULL ON CONVERSION ERROR does not work: https://stackoverflow.com/a/66037721/409172

Incorrectly typed data is a horrible situation that we should never be in. Using the wrong data types may doom us and all future SQL developers to writing weird queries and dealing with tricky random bugs. We must use the right data type every time, so we don't have to worry about these problems.

I've seen the negative long-term effects of stringly typed data several times. Some systems randomly generated type errors that nobody could reliably reproduce, and everyone just learned to live with it. On other systems we had to add protective layers to any query that touched the EAV. On the other hand, some systems can get away with it; perhaps their data is only accessed in one specific way, or they just got lucky. But we shouldn't design our systems to require luck, so spend the extra minute to create a few extra columns.

Avoid Soft Coding

All developers understand the importance of avoiding hard-coding. We're always looking for ways to create abstractions that hide our code from implementation details. We want to be able to change our program's behavior without changing a lot of code and without recompiling. In SQL, we can improve the safety and performance of our queries by using bind variables instead of hard-coding literals. But any best practice can be taken too far; an unhealthy aversion to changing code can lead to the soft coding anti-pattern.

We all want to make our programs smart and flexible. As we discussed in Chapter 14, our code can be *too* smart. It's better to automatically generate simple code with dynamic SQL than to create a super-complex block of code with esoteric PL/SQL. As we saw in the previous section, our tables can be *too* flexible. The most flexible database schema is a single EAV table, but that would be a nightmare to query. Building the mother of all EAV tables would eliminate the need to ever run a DDL command, but that solution would create a database in a database.

We don't want to build an infinitely generic, infinitely configurable program. Any sufficiently advanced configuration is indistinguishable from a programming language. If we try too hard to avoid programming, we're only going to invent a new programming language...poorly. This anti-pattern is sometimes called the inner-platform effect.

Things like variable lookups, table-driven configuration, and parameterizing programs are great ideas. But we must not take those ideas to extremes. We don't want to reinvent SQL and PL/SQL with configuration files or tables.

I wish I could tell you that this section is merely theoretical. But unfortunately, I have wasted much of my life trying to tame different soft-coded rule engines. And I have spent a lot of time unintentionally recreating PL/SQL…poorly.

There are times when we need to build configurable engines. But we must have an excellent reason for doing so, we must carefully limit the scope, and we should build them with dynamic SQL instead of obscure PL/SQL features.

Avoid Object-Relational Tables

Oracle is a converged database that supports multiple programming paradigms. We have to be careful when mixing paradigms because not all combinations are useful. Storing data in a relational model and accessing that data with procedural code work fine. And mixing procedural code with object-oriented programming works fine. But storing object-oriented data in relational tables is a bad idea.

Object types are useful for processing and passing data into PL/SQL. Ideally, we want to do all our processing in SQL, but that's not always realistic. To help integrate SQL with PL/SQL, we can create an object type to hold a record of data. If we want to store or process multiple records at once, we can create a nested table type of that object type. The following code shows a simple example of creating object types:

```
--Object type to hold a record of satellite data.
create or replace type satellite_type is object
(
    satellite_id number,
    norad_id     varchar2(28)
    ---Add more columns here.
);

--Nested table to hold multiple records.
create or replace type satellite_nt is table of satellite_type;
```

Our problems begin when we use SATELLITE_TYPE or SATELLITE_NT for storing data in tables. Saving object types in tables is marketed as a simple extension of the relational model. But storing object types is more like a betrayal of the relational model. Object types can be almost infinitely complex, which means our columns no longer have atomic values.

As soon as we start creating object-relational tables, the complexity of our data model increases significantly. We can no longer rely on the huge number of tools that support the traditional data types. And we can no longer rely on an army of existing developers who know SQL.

To follow the spirit of the relational model, we should keep our columns and tables dumb and make our schemas smart. With object-relational tables, a single column can be confusing. Trivial things like inserting data or joining tables become ridiculously complex. If we can't easily join our data, there's no point in using a relational database.

There are other practical concerns with object-relational technology. If we mix code and data too tightly, it becomes painful to change either one of them. You don't want to learn object-relational programming the hard way; if we change the wrong *code*, we can permanently destroy our *data*. Object databases were a fad in the 1990s, and Oracle rode that wave, but the technology hasn't been significantly upgraded for a long time.

Object types are fine for PL/SQL collections, but we should keep them out of our tables.

Avoid Java in the Database

The primary languages of Oracle databases are SQL and PL/SQL. Despite what the official sources claim, Java in the database is a distant third place and should be avoided when possible.

This section is not a rant about the Java programming language. Java is a popular, powerful language and is frequently used with databases. Regardless of how great Java is, there are several reasons to avoid putting Java stored procedures *inside* an Oracle database.

Java Is Not Always Available

The biggest problem with using Java inside Oracle is that Java is not always available. Oracle owns Java and has been advertising Java in the database for decades, but in practice we cannot dependably rely on Java being installed.

Java is not available for the Express Edition. I'm not a fan of Express Edition, but a lot of people use it, so this lack of support is a showstopper for many products.

Java is an optional component in all other database editions. Java is installed by default, but the component is frequently deselected or removed by DBAs. The Java component is often removed because it can cause problems during patching and upgrades. And unfortunately, the Java components are not trivial to reinstall and may require planning and downtime. And recent versions of Oracle have made this even worse – Java patching isn't even included in normal database patching anymore. Some cloud service providers, such as Amazon RDS, didn't allow the Java option until recently and still place limitations on how it's used.

Java Does Not Fit Perfectly

It may seem unfair to fault a product for not integrating perfectly. But when SQL and PL/SQL integrate so seamlessly, it's hard not to get annoyed when dealing with Java stored procedures.

The types don't perfectly match. There's nothing wrong with Java types, but whenever we pass data back and forth, we have to worry about string sizes, character sets, precision, etc.

Java object names are case sensitive and long, which is especially annoying in versions before 12.2 that only supported names up to 30 bytes long. The object names may look different in the data dictionary, and many DBA scripts fail to properly handle Java objects. This problem can be fixed by translating the names with DBMS_JAVA. LONGNAME, but constantly translating names is a pain.

SQL and PL/SQL Are Almost Always Better Choices

Java has more powerful language features than PL/SQL, but those features are irrelevant to the type of processing that happens inside a database. A good Oracle database program will do almost all of the heavy lifting in SQL. Procedural languages are mostly used to glue together SQL statements. PL/SQL's improved integration with SQL more than makes up for PL/SQL being a less powerful language than Java.

It's a shame that Oracle and Java don't get along better. It would be great to be able to reliably take advantage of existing Java libraries. Perhaps the new multilingual engine (MLE) will work better someday, but that experimental feature currently only supports JavaScript in the 21c innovation release. For the foreseeable future, unless we need functionality that only Java can provide, are absolutely sure that all our databases have the Java component installed, and are willing to put up with integration issues, we should avoid Java in the database.

Avoid TO_DATE

TO_DATE is a code smell. A code smell isn't always a bug, but it's a sign that there may be a deeper problem or anti-pattern lurking in our system. There are certainly times when we need to use TO_DATE, but an excessive number of TO_DATE calls imply our system is using the wrong types.

Oracle date creation and processing are surprisingly confusing. Based on the thousands of questions I've seen on Stack Overflow, date processing is one of the largest sources of bugs for SQL developers. This chapter isn't the place for an entire date tutorial, but luckily, we don't need one. As long as we avoid using the function TO_DATE, we are on the right path to processing and creating dates.

Avoid String-to-Date Conversion

Unless we are loading data from an external source, we should never have to convert strings to dates. Data processing is simpler and faster when values are processed in their native type. Oracle has many functions for handling dates, and we almost never need to convert back and forth between dates and strings.

One of the most common date processing mistakes is to use TO_DATE to remove the time. For example, the pseudo-column SYSDATE includes the current date and time. To remove the time, and only get the date, a common mistake is to write code like this:

```
--(Incorrectly) remove the time from a date.
select to_date(sysdate) the_date from dual;

THE_DATE
---------
30-NOV-18
```

The preceding code is dangerous and may not always work, because it depends on implicit data conversion. TO_DATE expects a string input, not a DATE. So SYSDATE is converted to a string and then back into a DATE. The conversion only indirectly removes the time because most clients and servers have an NLS_DATE_FORMAT that excludes the time.

The system parameter NLS_DATE_FORMAT is frequently overridden by a session-level parameter. That parameter is intended to be used for how dates are *displayed*, not for how dates are *processed*. If our server-side code depends on an Oracle client setting, we're in trouble.

We can't control a client's NLS_DATE_FORMAT setting. What if the user wants to view the time in the output? If a user runs the following command or their IDE runs a command like this by default, the preceding code will no longer work:

```
--Change default date format display.
alter session set nls_date_format = 'DD-MON-RR HH24:MI:SS';
```

We do not need to use string processing to remove the time from a date. Oracle has a built-in function for this operation – TRUNC. The following code reliably removes the time portion of a date, regardless of client settings:

```
--(Correctly) remove the time from a date.
select trunc(sysdate) the_date from dual;
```

This section only includes one example of bad date processing, but there are many other common bugs. If we ever find ourselves converting dates to strings and then back to dates, we're probably doing something wrong. There is likely an Oracle function that can do the work more quickly, safely, and easily, in the same data type.

If we're having date problems, we might want to read the "Datetime Functions" section in the *SQL Language Reference*. There are 28 built-in functions that can handle most of our date processing needs.

Use DATE, TIMESTAMP, and INTERVAL Literals

Datetime creation is best done with DATE and TIMESTAMP literals. The TO_DATE function is not a good way to create dates. It's difficult to change our date format habits, but there are so many advantages to using date literals that it's worth the effort to change.

The following code compares date creation using literals vs. using the TO_DATE function:

```
--DATE literal versus TO_DATE.
select
    date '2000-01-01' date_literal,
    to_date('01-JAN-00', 'DD-MON-RR') date_from_string
from dual;
```

The date literal always uses the ISO-8601 date format: YYYY-MM-DD. Date literals never have any ambiguity about days vs. months, the century, the calendar, or the language. They also have the advantage of being easily sorted when we view them as strings. (We don't normally want to convert our dates to strings, but the format is also useful outside of database programming, such as when we need to save a date in a file name.)

In practice, TO_DATE almost always has ambiguity, even if we use an explicit format. Those of us old enough to remember the Y2K bug already know that a two-digit year is just begging for trouble. But there's a lot more wrong with the way TO_DATE was used in the preceding code.

For example, "JAN" is not a valid month abbreviation in every language. And not every locale uses the same calendar. If you're reading this book, the chances are good that you program in English and use the Gregorian calendar. And many Oracle programs don't need to worry about localization and internationalization. But why limit our programs? Are we sure nobody will ever run our queries and programs with a non-English client setting?

Date literals also occasionally help the optimizer build better execution plans. Date literals are completely unambiguous, and the optimizer can be sure that two different users will always execute the same statement in the same NLS context. An ambiguous TO_DATE means that the optimizer may need to parse the same text differently, depending on client settings. It's a rare problem, but why risk it?

The preceding discussion also applies equally to TIMESTAMP literals vs. TO_TIMESTAMP. In fact, TIMESTAMP literals have even more advantages because of standardized time zone formatting. If we want precise dates and timestamps, we should avoid TO_DATE and TO_TIMESTAMP and use date and timestamp literals instead.

We should also use INTERVAL literals for date arithmetic and storing date ranges. Default date math is done in days – the current date plus one is equal to tomorrow. In old versions of Oracle, more advanced date math required converting days to other units, which is error prone. Modern versions of Oracle simplify the date arithmetic and let us specify a literal value for a YEAR, MONTH, DAY, HOUR, MINUTE, or SECOND. For example, the following code compares using date math against an INTERVAL literal:

```
--Date arithmetic using math or INTERVAL.
select
    sysdate - 1/(24*60*60)          one_second_ago,
    sysdate - interval '1' second one_second_ago
from dual;
```

Avoid CURSOR

CURSOR is also a code smell. Like TO_DATE, there are certainly times when we need to use CURSOR, but we should be skeptical of code that frequently uses that keyword.

There's nothing wrong with cursor *processing*; the problems happen when we write code with the CURSOR keyword. Similar to TO_DATE, it's perfectly fine to use CURSOR when we're passing information from a database to an external application.

The main problem with the CURSOR keyword is that it's used for explicit cursor processing, instead of the simpler and faster cursor FOR loop processing. This anti-pattern is another PL/SQL topic in a SQL book. But it's worth briefly discussing cursor processing because it so frequently affects how we write SQL. We want a PL/SQL style that makes it easy to use SQL statements.

For example, let's say we want to print all the launch dates in order. The following PL/SQL block uses explicit cursor processing, with the CURSOR, OPEN, FETCH, and CLOSE commands. This syntax is outdated and should almost never be used:

```
--Explicit cursor processing: complex and slow.
declare
    cursor launches is
        select * from launch order by launch_date;
    v_launch launch%rowtype;
begin
    open launches;
    loop
        fetch launches into v_launch;
        exit when launches%notfound;
        dbms_output.put_line(v_launch.launch_date);
    end loop;
    close launches;
end;
/
```

Compare the preceding code with the following much simpler cursor FOR loop processing:

```
--Cursor FOR loop processing: simple and fast.
begin
```

```
    for launches in
    (
        select * from launch order by launch_date
    ) loop
        dbms_output.put_line(launches.launch_date);
    end loop;
end;
/
```

The second code example is much simpler, and it even runs faster. The explicit cursor processing example only retrieves one row at a time and spends a lot of time context switching between SQL and PL/SQL. The cursor FOR loop example automatically grabs 100 rows at a time and almost completely eliminates context switching.

Almost all of the things the CURSOR keyword are used for are unnecessary, or they can be replaced by a simpler cursor FOR loop or a larger SQL statement.

Explicit cursor processing allows us to manually bulk collect and limit the results. But the simpler cursor FOR loop automatically collects 100 rows at a time. As Chapter 16 discusses, collecting 100 rows at a time is almost always good enough.

Explicit cursor processing is often used with FORALL statements. But instead, we can almost always do both the reading and the writing with a single SQL statement.

Multiple cursors are often defined at the beginning of a procedure and then run in a loop inside each other. Instead, we should combine the two SELECT statements and run a single SQL statement.

Cursors are sometimes used for pipelined functions, an advanced PL/SQL feature. But even pipelined functions are often just a poor way of writing a large SQL statement.

There are certainly good uses for the CURSOR keyword, such as dynamic ref cursors, and I'm not advocating that we ban CURSOR from our code. But every time we see CURSOR, we should ask ourselves if we're missing an opportunity to replace slow, complex, procedural code with faster, simpler, declarative SQL.

Avoid Custom SQL Parsing

Sometimes when we're confronted with a difficult SQL language problem, we think, "I know. I'll parse the SQL." Now we have two problems.

There are times when it would be helpful to parse an Oracle SQL or PL/SQL statement. We may want to find problems in our code, convert between syntaxes, find references to specific objects, etc. Unfortunately, parsing SQL is so hard that many language problems can rarely be solved in practice. When we run into a complex SQL problem and think we need a parser, we've probably hit a dead end. Unless our code only uses a small, well-defined subset of the SQL language, we should find another solution.

The SQL language syntax is orders of magnitude more complex than most other programming languages. This complexity doesn't mean that SQL is more powerful than Java or C. The complexity is because SQL adds many features through syntax, instead of through libraries or packages. That extra syntax helps our code look nice, but the extra syntax makes Oracle SQL ridiculously hard to parse.

Most programming languages only have a few dozen keywords, but Oracle has over 2500 keywords, and many of the keywords are unreserved. For example, BEGIN is used to mark the beginning of PL/SQL blocks. But BEGIN can also be used as a column alias. We can't simply search for keywords to parse our code. Some keywords also serve multiple purposes, such as "$", which has four different meanings. And in Oracle, multiple languages can work together. Fully parsing SQL also requires parsing PL/SQL, hints, and Java. There is also a lot of legacy syntax that's still supported but not even listed in the current version of the manual. Even breaking SQL into lexical units, like numbers and whitespace, is difficult.

There are lots of difficult programming problems. Why is parsing worthy of a special mention? The problem with parsing is that there is not a linear relationship between accuracy and difficulty. There are many parsing problems that can be solved with 90% accuracy in a few hours. But 99% accuracy may take days, and 100% accuracy may take months. As discussed in Chapter 7, a regular expression is theoretically incapable of parsing a language like SQL. Even if we use powerful parsing tools, like ANTLR or YACC, the problem is still almost impossible to get right.

For example, consider a common and deceivingly simple language problem – determining if a SQL statement is a SELECT. If we create a website that accepts code, like https://dbfiddle.uk, we need to classify each statement to know how to run it. I've seen many solutions to this problem, but very few of them can correctly classify all of the following SELECT statements:

```
--Valid SELECT statements.
SeLeCt * from dual;
```

```
/*asdf*/   select * from dual;
((((select * from dual))));
with test1 as (select * from dual) select * from test1;
```

If we try to parse SQL, we can very easily program ourselves into a corner and waste a huge amount of time. Unless we can identify a special case, like if we can ensure our parsed code always has a specific format, we should avoid creating SQL parsers.

Avoid Automating Everything

Automation is great, but not every automated process or technology is worth using. For every painful, manual task, there is a long line of vendors willing to sell us software, whether that software makes sense or not. We need to remember that many information technology projects fail, and we need to avoid the sunk-cost fallacy. Sometimes we need to avoid small features that sound useful, but don't work in practice.

The following list includes examples of automation features that don't quite work in Oracle:

1. *Automatic memory management:* This feature was never officially recommended, and in 12.2 it is effectively disabled. This feature failure doesn't make sense to me – it seems like it shouldn't be that hard to dynamically size PGA and SGA.

2. *Recycle bin space pressure:* Dropped tables are supposed to be automatically cleaned up when the system needs the space. But the algorithms to reclaim the space are poorly documented, and in practice tables don't always purge themselves when we need space. For now, every time we drop a table, we still have to worry about adding the PURGE clause.

3. *Tuning advisors:* The optimizer works great, Oracle's performance monitoring tools work great, but the programs that suggest performance changes are rarely helpful. The advisors might work fine for simple problems, like adding an obvious index. But in my experience, the advisors are rarely helpful for complex problems. But as Oracle invests in their autonomous database, many of those automated performance processes ought to improve with each version. It's worth re-evaluating the advisors when we upgrade.

4. *Version control:* As discussed in Chapter 2, we cannot fully automate version control. We can't just willy-nilly change whatever we want in a development database and expect tools to magically copy it into production for us. Programming is still best done using version-controlled text files and manually checking the conflicts.

Remember that standardization is a prerequisite for automation. If we have a perfectly standard environment, some of the preceding items might work fine. If we have a completely-out-of-control environment, we may have a hard time even automating tasks like patching.

Some things are just best done the old-fashioned way. But some things change over time. Hopefully most of the items in the preceding list will work perfectly in future versions of Oracle or in an autonomous Oracle database cloud environment.

Avoid Cargo Cult Syntax

Too much copy-and-paste programming can lead to cargo cult programming. Cargo cult programming is when we ritualistically include things in our code, even though we have no reason to believe those things will bring about the desired result, for example, changing COUNT(*) to COUNT(1), changing <> to !=, the (incorrect) NOLOGGING hint, or any minor syntax change that is supposed to improve performance for no discernable reason.

We're all guilty of copying and pasting code we don't understand. This book even occasionally advocates the use of weird syntax, such as using ROWNUM to control optimizer transformations. But we need to occasionally question what we're copying and pasting. If these miraculous syntax changes are real, we should be able to measure them. If we can't build a reproducible test case to demonstrate something, then we shouldn't promote it.

Avoid Undocumented Features

Our code should not rely on undocumented or unsupported functionality. Oracle has interesting features just sitting around, gathering dust, but we must resist the urge to use something that we may regret later. Those undocumented features may be part of an optional component that will go away, or they may be an experimental feature that doesn't work as expected.

The most famous example of an undocumented feature is the WM_CONCAT function. WM_CONCAT was a string concatenation function, used internally as part of Workspace Manager. Before Oracle 11.2, there was no standard string concatenation function, and developers had to create their own. Many developers noticed that WM_CONCAT already existed and started using that function. Unfortunately, WM_CONCAT was dropped in version 12.1, breaking many queries and programs during upgrades.

Many features are unofficially available in versions before they are documented. Maybe those features were experimental and too buggy or weren't thoroughly tested yet. Either way, it is foolish to use undocumented features. There are arguably some exceptions to that rule; if we find a useful feature, and if we can easily test that the feature works, and if it's only going to be used in temporary ad hoc scripts, then it might be fine to use that undocumented feature.

We should also avoid undocumented parameters – the parameters that start with an underscore. Theoretically, we're only supposed to set undocumented parameters if an Oracle support engineer tells us to. But in practice, we can read the My Oracle Support notes and usually figure out when an undocumented parameter is necessary. And it's not like an Oracle support engineer is going to stop helping us as soon as they discover any hidden parameters. In practice, all databases have a few hidden parameters set.

Avoid Deprecated Features

We should avoid deprecated features. When Oracle discourages the use of certain features, we should heed their warning and switch to newer and better options. We should periodically check the "Database Upgrade Guide" for chapters full of newly deprecated and desupported features. Oracle usually keeps deprecated features around for a long time, but those features won't be improved. The old versions will likely be buggier, less convenient, and slower than the new versions.

For example, we can still use the old EXP and IMP utilities, but they're not nearly as good as the new EXPDP and IMPDP utilities. Or we could still use many XML functions that were deprecated a long time ago, but they may run significantly slower than new XML functions.

Do not confuse deprecated with desupported. Deprecated features still work fine and *might* be desupported in the next version. We should be cautious when using deprecated features, because we don't want to tie our code to something that is going to break in the future. But we should also be skeptical of deprecation, because sometimes Oracle deprecates the cheap features to encourage us to buy the expensive features.

Avoid Simplistic Explanations for Generic Errors

Oracle has generic error messages that represent a large number of more specific errors. Using search engines to look up generic error messages doesn't help, because each answer only covers one of the many possible root causes. We need to drill down to find the precise error message and all the relevant arguments and settings. There are several classes of these generic error messages: dead processes, deadlocks, and the top of the error stack.

Dead Processes

Oracle bugs can cause server processes to die. Processes can die so abruptly that they can't even generate and return the full error message to the client. Oracle reports a *generic* error message to the client and only stores the detailed error information in the alert log or trace files.

When we see one of the following error messages, there's no point in googling only the error message itself:

1. ORA-00600: internal error code

2. ORA-07445: exception encountered

3. ORA-03113: end-of-file on communication channel

4. No more data to read from socket

Finding the real error can be a complex process: open the alert log file on the database server (use V$DIAG_INFO if you don't know the file location), find the relevant occurrence of the error based on the error codes and the timestamps in the alert log, find the first argument of the error, go to the My Oracle Support website at https://support. oracle.com, search for the "ORA-600/ORA-7445/ORA-700 Error Look-up Tool," enter the first argument, and search through the relevant documents to find the possible causes. (If that tool does not find any relevant bugs, we need to either create a service request or find some way to work around the problem.) Occasionally these errors can be found on search engines if we search for both the error number and the first argument. But if we search for just the first error number, without the argument, we'll waste a lot of time.

Deadlocks

When we see the error message "ORA-00060: deadlock detected while waiting for resource," the first thing we need to do is find the relevant trace file. The alert log will contain an entry for deadlock errors and will point to a trace file that contains all the information necessary for debugging.

A deadlock is an application problem. Deadlocks are not Oracle bugs, and they are not just a "really bad lock." Deadlocks are resource consumption problems that can only be fixed by rolling back one of the two relevant sessions.

Deadlocks happen when two different sessions try to lock the same rows but in a different order. The length and number of locks don't matter; it's all about the *order* of the locking.

For example, the following code creates a deadlock that will roll back one of the statements. The tricky thing about creating deadlocks is we need to alternate between two sessions and precisely control the order the rows are changed:

```
--Deadlock example.  One session will fail with ORA-00060.
--Session #1:
update launch set site_id = site_id where launch_id = 1;

--Session #2:
update launch set site_id = site_id where launch_id = 2;
update launch set site_id = site_id where launch_id = 1;

--Session #1:
update launch set site_id = site_id where launch_id = 2;
```

The preceding simple example only updates one row at a time. In the real world, the problems are more complex. When we update multiple rows, we can't easily control the order the rows are locked. Different statements can lock rows in a different order. Even the same statement can lock rows in a different order, if the execution plan changes. For example, a full table scan may lock rows in a different order than index access. Deadlocks can occur on indirectly locked objects, such as bitmap indexes that aren't supposed to be created on transactional tables.

Diagnosing real-life deadlocks can be tricky. Don't even try to solve deadlocks until you understand the theory of deadlocks and have the specific details from the trace file. The trace file tells us exactly what objects and statements are involved in the deadlock, so we don't need to guess what caused the problem.

Top of the Error Stack

The error on the top of the error stack is not always important. Buried errors happen with error messages like "ORA-12801: error signaled in parallel query server PXYZ." That initial error message only tells us that a parallel query server died, but it doesn't tell us *why* the parallel query server died. Like with deadlocks, these errors are not Oracle bugs. If we look in the full error stack or check the alert log, we will find a much more useful error message hidden inside.

We must always read the entire error message stack, especially for custom exceptions. In a custom exception handler, the last line number may only point to the last RAISE command, not the original line that caused the error. As discussed in Chapter 11, there is a tendency among PL/SQL developers to capture and hide every error message, instead of letting exceptions naturally propagate. We may need to dig around for the error message.

For example, the following code uses a BAD_EAV query with a few modifications: the query is run in parallel and inside a PL/SQL block. (This exact problem may be difficult to reproduce, because there are several reasons our systems may not run queries in parallel.) The exception handler may look helpful because it's catching and printing the error code. But this exception handler is doing more harm than good:

```
--Incorrectly catch and print error code:
declare
    v_count number;
begin
    select /*+ parallel(8) */ count(*)
    into v_count
    from bad_eav
    where value = date '2011-04-28';
exception when others then
    dbms_output.put_line('Error: '||sqlcode);
```

```
end;
/
```

```
Error: -12801
```

The preceding PL/SQL block only printed the last error code. The error code -12801 tells us that a parallel query server died, but it does not tell us the underlying cause. If we comment out the exception handler and rerun the block, it will raise a more meaningful exception, like this:

```
ORA-12801: error signaled in parallel query server P001
ORA-01861: literal does not match format string
```

Avoid Unnecessarily Small Parameters

There are many complicated trade-offs when setting Oracle parameters. For example, every administrator has a story about cranking the memory settings for one database but not seeing any performance improvement. Those administrators also have stories about databases crashing because there wasn't enough available memory. DBAs tend to think about most parameters in terms of conservative compromises, and they are hesitant to set parameters to a value that seems unreasonably high.

But there are parameters where a conservative approach is harmful. Parameters that prevent users from logging on are a hard limit, and hitting those limits can be as bad as a database crash. For many of these parameters, setting the limit high doesn't cost anything, unless the resources are actually used.

For the parameters SESSIONS, PROCESSES, MAX_PARALLEL_SESSIONS, and the profile limit SESSIONS_PER_USER, it is best to use a trust-but-verify approach. We should set these parameters high, even higher than we think we need, and then periodically monitor resource consumption. A moderately high value in those parameters is better than running out of sessions late at night and breaking an application. For example, I've seen literally dozens of errors on databases when PROCESSES was set too low, and I've only ever seen one problem caused by setting it too high.

An administrator is likely responsible for setting and maintaining these parameters. But as developers it is in our own best interest to have good values for parameters and avoid creating an artificial scarcity that can effectively break our programs.

Avoid Conflating Planning with Premature Optimization

Developers worry too much about Donald's Knuth's quote "premature optimization is the root of all evil." There's a lot of context behind that quote, and it is a mistake to use that quote as an excuse to ignore performance until the end of a project. We certainly want to avoid obsessing over the performance of every query and every line of PL/SQL code before they are proven to be a problem. But as we gain experience with database development, we can accurately predict bottlenecks. Every large project should spend time thinking about data growth and opportunities for denormalization.

Planning for data growth is more than simply estimating the amount of space needed in the future. Forecasting performance is complicated, and we cannot simply assume that performance will grow linearly with the data. As described in the next chapter, there are many situations where performance grows very slowly, like with index access, but there are also times when performance grows exponentially, like with locks or bad table joins. Not every problem can be fixed by adding an index, so we would be wise to periodically test our system with a realistic amount of data and user activity.

Practical database developers shouldn't be *too* scared of denormalized data. Even the creators of the relational model and normalization rules recognized that sometimes we need to repeat data. And sometimes we need to quickly cram bad data into a simple table and clean it up later. Repetitive data may save us from joining a large number of tables in a complex data model. Removing triggers, relational integrity, and durability requirements can enable direct path writes that are an order of magnitude faster than conventional writes. When we have an enormous amount of data, we need to plan for performance.

Anti-patterns Discussed in Other Chapters

There are plenty of anti-patterns discussed in other chapters, and some of those worst practices are worth mentioning twice. We should avoid storing lists of values in columns, using the old-fashioned join syntax, writing SQL that depends on the order of execution, trying to handle all exceptions instead of using propagation, case-sensitive object names that require quoted identifiers, using advanced PL/SQL features instead of SQL, making everything publicly accessible, and overengineering systems when a single instance database works fine.

Summary

Remember that there are exceptions to every rule. Other than "storing data as the wrong data type," the anti-patterns discussed in this chapter are not always evil. We don't want to go around telling everybody that their code sucks, but we need to be on the lookout for bad coding practices that should be avoided.

PART IV

Improve SQL Performance

CHAPTER 16

Understand SQL Performance with Algorithm Analysis

Solving Oracle SQL performance issues is the pinnacle of SQL development. Performance tuning requires a combination of all the skills previously discussed in this book. We need to understand the development process (to know why problems happened and weren't caught sooner), advanced features (to find alternative ways to implement code), and programming styles (in order to understand the code and rewrite it into something better).

Programming is one of the few fields with order-of-magnitude difference in skill level between professionals. We've all had to deal with coworkers who are only one-tenth as productive as us, and we've all been humbled by developers whose code is ten times better than ours. With performance tuning these numbers get even higher, and the rewards are greater. It's exhilarating when we make a small tweak and something runs a million times faster.

But "a million times faster" is only the beginning of this story. All SQL tuning guides discuss run *times*, but none of them consider the run-time *complexity*. Database performance tuning requires more than an encyclopedic knowledge of obscure features and arcane settings. Performance tuning calls for a different mindset.

Algorithm analysis is the most underused approach to understanding Oracle performance problems. This chapter tells the story of Oracle performance through the lens of simple algorithm analysis. The sections are not listed in a traditional order, such as ordered by performance concepts and tuning tools. Instead, the sections are ordered by time complexity, from fastest to slowest.

© Jon Heller 2023
J. Heller, *Pro Oracle SQL Development*, https://doi.org/10.1007/978-1-4842-8867-2_16

Admittedly, algorithm analysis is not the most useful performance tuning technique. But algorithm analysis should not be relegated to the halls of academia – it should be a part of everyone's SQL tuning toolkit. We may solve more problems with techniques like sampling and cardinality estimates, but we'll never truly understand performance without understanding the algorithms.

Algorithm analysis can help us with both proactive and reactive tuning. For proactive tuning, we need to be aware of the advantages available if we create different data structures. For reactive tuning, we need to be able to measure the algorithms chosen by the optimizer and ensure Oracle made the right choices.

The two chapters after this one provide a more traditional approach to performance tuning; those chapters describe the different concepts and solutions used in Oracle SQL tuning. This chapter explains why the stakes are so high for the decisions Oracle must make. This material should be useful to SQL developers of any skill level.

Algorithm Analysis Introduction

With a few simple mathematical functions, we can gain a deeper understanding of the decisions and trade-offs involved in execution plan creation. Performance results are often given as simple numbers or ratios, such as "X runs in 5 seconds, and Y runs in 10 seconds." The wall-clock time is important, but it's more powerful to understand and explain our results with mathematical functions.

Algorithm analysis, also known as asymptotic analysis, finds a function that defines the boundary of the performance of something. This technique can apply to memory, storage, and other resources, but for our purposes we only need to consider the number of steps in an algorithm. The number of steps is correlated with run time and is an oversimplification of the overall resource utilization of a database system. This chapter ignores measuring different kinds of resource utilization and considers all database "work" to be equal.

A full explanation of algorithm analysis would require many precisely defined mathematical terms. Don't worry – we don't need a college course in computer science to use this approach. A simplified version of algorithm analysis is easily applied to many Oracle operations.

Let's start with a simple, naïve way to search a database table. If we want to find a single value in a table, the simplest search technique would be to check every row. Let's say the table has N rows. If we're lucky, we'll find the value after reading only 1 row. If we're unlucky, we have to read N rows. On average, we will have to read N/2 rows. As the number of table rows grows, the average number of reads grows linearly.

Our naïve algorithm for searching a table has a best-case, an average-case, and a worst-case run time. If we plot the input size and the number of reads, we'll see that the worst-case performance is *bounded* by the function N. In practice, we only care about the upper bound. Worst-case run time can be labeled with the traditional Big O notation as O(N). Although real-world solutions are full of constants and exceptions, we can ignore all those details and still meaningfully compare algorithms.

Figure 16-1 visualizes the worst case as a solid line, an asymptote that the real values can never exceed. Our not-so-smart search algorithm uses the dashed line, and it takes more or less steps[1] depending on exactly where the value is placed in the table. Our real-world results look like the messy dashed line, but to understand performance, we can use the simpler solid line.

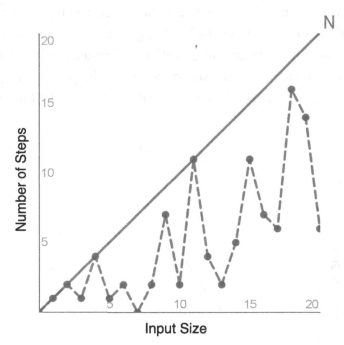

Figure 16-1. *Number of steps vs. input size for linear search algorithm, including an asymptote*

---

[1] This book uses the word "steps" to refer to the work performed by algorithms. Traditionally, that value is called "operations." But Oracle execution plans already prominently use the word "operation," so it would be confusing if I used the standard name here. This chapter isn't a mathematical proof, so it doesn't matter if our terminology is nonstandard.

The functions by themselves are meaningless; it's the comparison between the functions that matters. We want Oracle to choose the functions that have the lowest number of steps on the Y axis, even as the data increases along the X axis.

If Oracle only had to compare straight lines that begin at the graph's origin, then the task would be trivial. The task becomes difficult when each algorithm's performance is represented by a different curve and the curves intersect at different points along the X axis. Stated as an abstract math problem, to know which curve has the lowest Y value, Oracle must determine the X value. Stated as a practical database problem, to know which algorithm is fastest, Oracle must accurately estimate the number of rows. Bad execution plans occur when Oracle doesn't have the right information to accurately estimate which operation is cheaper.

Figure 16-2 shows the most important functions discussed in this chapter. 0(1), 0(∞), and Amdahl's law didn't fit together on the graph, but they are also discussed later. Luckily, the most important Oracle operations fall into a small number of categories. We don't need to look at the source code or write proofs, since most database operations are easy to classify. Spend a few moments looking at the lines and curves in Figure 16-2.

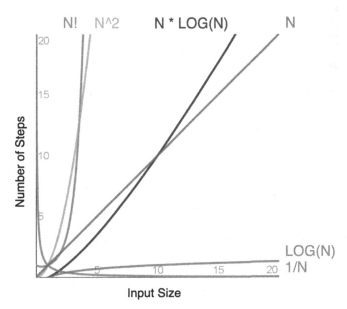

Figure 16-2. *Functions that represent important Oracle operations*

The next sections discuss each function, where we find them, and why they matter. Comparing the preceding shapes helps explain many Oracle performance problems.

O(1/N): Batching to Reduce Overhead

The harmonic progression 1/N perfectly describes the overhead of many Oracle operations. This function describes sequence caching, bulk collect limit, prefetch, arraysize, the number of subqueries in a UNION ALL, PL/SQL packages with bulk options like DBMS_OUTPUT and DBMS_SCHEDULER, and many other operations with a configurable batch size. Choosing the right batch size is vital to performance. For example, performance may be disastrous if there is a SQL-to-PL/SQL context switch for every row or if we have to wait for a network round trip for every row.

To reduce wasteful row-by-row overhead, we must combine the overhead for multiple rows. But how many rows do we combine? This is a difficult question with many trade-offs. Not combining *anything* is ridiculously slow, but combining *everything* will cause memory or parsing problems. Batching is one of the keys to good performance, so we need to think clearly about how much to batch.

Just pick 100 and stop worrying about it. We can be confident in choosing a value like 100 by understanding the following charts in Figure 16-3. The first thing to notice is that the theoretical results almost perfectly match the real-world results.

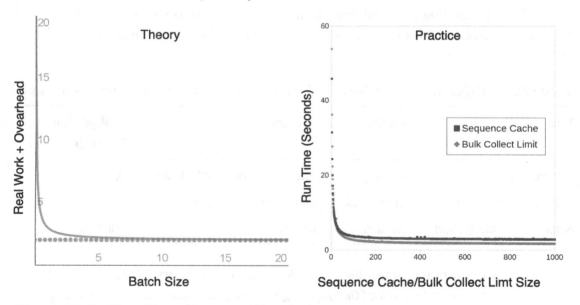

Figure 16-3. *The effect of increased batch size on run time*

For the theoretical chart on the left, the total run time is the dotted line of the "real work" plus the solid line of the overhead. Increasing the batch size rapidly reduces the overhead, but there is only so much overhead to reduce. No matter how much we increase the batch size, the total amount of work will never get to zero. Our processes are never purely overhead – there should always be a significant amount of real work to do.

The lines in the preceding graphs start near infinity and quickly plateau. As we increase the batch size, the overhead rapidly disappears. A batch size of 2 removes 50% of the overhead, a batch size of 10 removes 90%, and a batch size 100 removes 99%. A setting of 100 is already 99% optimized. The difference between a batch size of 100 and a batch size of one billion cannot theoretically be more than 1%.

The scripts I used to produce the real-world results can be found in the GitHub repository. There's not enough space to list all the code here, but the code is worth briefly discussing. The scripts created two scenarios with a ridiculous amount of overhead: inserting rows where every value is a sequence and bulk collecting a small amount of data and doing nothing with the results. The test cases are almost completely full of useless overhead. If any test case was going to show a *meaningful* improvement by increasing batch size from 100 to 1000, this was it.

Table 16-1 describes three batching scenarios in detail. These rows are three completely unrelated tasks that can be perfectly explained with the same time complexity.

Table 16-1. *Different Tasks Where Performance Depends on Reducing Overhead*

Task	Real Work	Overhead	Configurable Parameter
Bulk collect	Selecting data	SQL-and-PL/SQL context switch	LIMIT
INSERT using sequence	Inserting data	Generating sequence numbers	CACHE SIZE
Application fetching rows	Selecting data	Network lag	Fetch size

There are many practical results we can derive from this theory. The default bulk collect size of 100 used by cursor FOR loops is good enough; there's almost never any significant benefit to using a ridiculously high custom limit. The default sequence caching size of 20 is good enough; in extreme cases it might be worth increasing the cache size slightly,[2] but not by a huge amount. Application prefetch is different for each application; we should aim for something close to 100. These rules apply to any overhead-reducing optimization.

If we have an extreme case or drill way down into the results, we can always find a miniscule difference with a larger batch size. But if we find ourselves in a situation where setting a huge batch size significantly helps, then we've already lost; we need to bring our algorithms to our data, not our data to our algorithms.

In practice, bringing algorithms to our data means we should put at least some of our logic in SQL, instead of loading billions of rows into a procedural language for a trivial amount of processing. If we foolishly load all the rows from a table into PL/SQL just to count them with V_COUNT := V_COUNT+1, then increasing the batch size will help. But the better solution would be to use SELECT COUNT(*) in a SQL statement. If we load a billion rows into PL/SQL and perform real work with those rows, the few seconds we save from a larger batch size will be irrelevant. There are always exceptions, like if we have to access lots of data over a database link with horrendous network lag, but we should not let those exceptions dictate our standards.

There are trade-offs between space and run time, but with a harmonic progression time complexity, we will quickly trade space for *no* run time. Developers waste a lot of effort debating and tweaking large numbers on the right side of the preceding graphs, but almost all the bang for our buck happens quickly on the left side of the graph. When we have a 1/N time complexity, the point of diminishing returns is reached very quickly. We should spend our time looking for opportunities to batch commands and reduce overhead, not worrying about the precise batch size.

O(1): Hashing and Other Operations

Constant-time access is ideal but often unrealistic. The operations that can work in constant time are mostly trivial, such as using a predicate like ROWNUM = 1. The constant-time function is simple, just a horizontal line, and is not worth showing on a graph. The most important Oracle operation that can run in constant time is hashing. Hashing is a core database operation and is worth discussing in detail.

---

[2] Since 21c, Oracle may dynamically adjust sequence caching based on the sequence workload. Perhaps in the near future, we won't have to worry about sequence caching at all.

How Hashing Works

Hashing assigns a set of items into a set of hash buckets. Hash functions can assign items into a huge number of cryptographically random buckets, such as SELECT STANDARD_HASH('some_string', 'SHA256') FROM DUAL. Or hash functions can assign values into a small number of predefined buckets, such as SELECT ORA_HASH('some_string', 4) FROM DUAL. Hash functions can be designed with many different properties, and their design has important implications for how they are used. Figure 16-4 includes simple ways of describing hash functions.

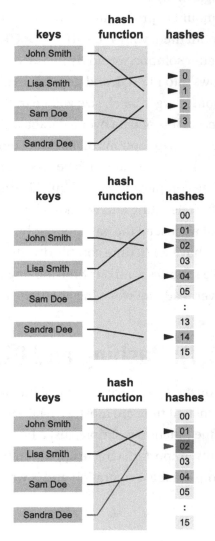

Minimal perfect hash

Every value maps to one unique hash, and there are no empty hash buckets

Perfect hash

Every value maps to one unique hash, but there are empty hash buckets

Typical Hash

Multiple values may map to the same hash, and there are empty hash buckets

Figure 16-4. *Description of different hash functions. Images were created by Jorge Stolfi and are in the public domain*

There is a huge range of performance that depends on exactly how the hash works. With perfect hashing, access requires only a single read, and the operation is $O(1)$. With a broken hashing algorithm, where every value is mapped to the same hash, we just end up with a regular heap table stuck inside a hash bucket. In that worst case, we have to read the entire table to find a single value, which is $O(N)$.

When hashing, we need to be aware of space–time trade-offs. In practice we cannot achieve a minimal, perfect hash. Oracle's hash partitioning is minimal (there are no empty buckets), but far from perfect (there are many collisions); hash partitions don't provide instant access for one row, but they don't waste much space. Hash clusters can be perfect (no collisions) but are far from minimal (many empty buckets); hash clusters provide instant access for one row, but they waste a lot of space. Hash joins are somewhere in the middle. Those three types of hashing serve different purposes and are described in detail in the next sections.

Hash Partitioning

Hash partitioning splits a table of N rows into P partitions, based on the ORA_HASH of one or more columns. Hash partitioning will certainly not be a perfect hash, since each hash bucket is a segment meant to fit many rows. The number of hash partitions should be minimal, since we don't want to waste disk space by having extra segments.

The time to insert a row into a hash-partitioned table is still $O(1)$ – the ORA_HASH function can quickly determine which partition the row goes in. But the time to retrieve a row will be $O(N/P)$, or the number of rows divided by the number of partitions. That can be an important improvement for large data warehouse operations that read a large number of rows. But for reading a single row, that improvement is not nearly as good as what we can achieve with an $O(LOG(N))$ B-tree index access. (The time complexity of B-tree indexes is described in a later section.) Don't try to replace indexes with partitions – they solve different problems.

We could theoretically build a hash-partitioned table with an amazing $O(1)$ read access by using a ridiculously large number of hashes. While that hash might be "perfect" in the sense that every row maps to a single segment, a ridiculous number of segments would waste a huge amount of space and would also cause problems with the data dictionary.

When building hash-partitioned tables, we must use the right columns for the partition key. If we use columns with a low cardinality or don't set the number of partitions to a power of two, the data will not be evenly distributed among the partitions. If all of the rows are stored in the same bucket (the same hash partition), then partitioning won't help us at all.

Hash partitioning is frequently overused in practice. To avoid abusing that feature, we need to understand the hashing trade-offs and choose a good partition key.

Hash Clusters

Hash clusters are designed to return a small number of rows, unlike hash partitions that are designed to return a large number of rows. An undocumented hash function tells Oracle exactly where to store and find each row – there's no need to walk an index tree and follow multiple pointers. In theory, hash clusters are even better than B-tree indexes for retrieving a small number of rows. In practice, hash clusters are rarely used.

The first problem with hash clusters is that we cannot add one to an existing table; we have to organize the table from the beginning to use a hash cluster. To get $O(1)$ read time on hash clusters, we need to create a near-perfect hash. But we have to worry about that space–time trade-off. There is no practical way to get perfect hashes without also creating a huge number of unused hash buckets. We can have a hash cluster with good performance or a hash cluster that uses a minimal amount of space; we can't have both.

When we create a hash cluster, we can specify the number of buckets with the HASHKEYS clause. In my experience, getting $O(1)$ read time requires so many hash buckets that the table size will triple.

Unfortunately, even after all that effort to get $O(1)$ access time, hash clusters still end up being slower than indexes. I can't explain why hash clusters are slower; this is a place where our theory breaks down in real-world applications.

Oracle measures the number of reads performed by a SQL statement using a statistic called "consistent gets." It's possible to create test cases where hash lookups require only one consistent get, while index lookups on the same table require four consistent gets.[3] But the index is still faster. For these operations, the $O(LOG(N))$ of an index is less than the $O(1)$ of a hash cluster.

---

[3] See this Stack Overflow answer, where I try and fail to create a useful constant-time index using hash clusters: https://stackoverflow.com/questions/32071259/constant-time-index-for-string-column-on-oracle-database

When comparing small numbers, such as 1 vs. 4, the constants become more important than the Big O analysis. Hash clusters are rarely used, and Oracle surely invests more time optimizing indexes than clusters. Perhaps those optimizations compensate for the small difference between the run-time complexities.

Algorithm analysis helps us drill down to the problem, but in this case the real performance difference is hidden by constants in closed source software. Perhaps this is an opportunity for a custom index type. Other databases have hash indexes that don't require reorganizing the entire table. Maybe someday Oracle will add that feature and make hash access work better. For now, we should ignore hash clusters.

Hash Joins

Hashing is a great way to join two tables when there's a large percentage of rows that match between them. A hash join starts by creating a temporary hash table based on the join column values from the first table. Next, Oracle uses the join column values from the second table and probes the hash table to see if there is a match.

The precise performance of hash joins is discussed later, but the main point to understand is that the first step of creating a temporary hash table requires a significant amount of time and space. That extra work can be a good investment because each probe in the second step can theoretically run in $O(1)$ time. But like with hash partitioning and hash clusters, the hash table is certainly not minimal and perfect. There will be some wasted space, and the probe run time ends up being something worse than $O(1)$. However, unlike hash clusters, the probe run time is significantly better than the $O(LOG(N))$ we would get from a single index lookup. Determining when that up-front investment of building a hash table is worth the cost is one of the most important decisions the optimizer makes.

It's important for us to understand that hash joins can only be used for equality conditions. The way input values are mapped to fixed-length hash values preserves some equality properties, but hashing does not preserve any other relationships between the inputs. For example, A may be smaller than B, but that relationship is not necessarily true of their hash values.

Hash joins are so useful that it is often worth going out of our way to enable them. We can enable hash joins by rewriting simple non-equality conditions into weird equality conditions. For example, `COLUMN1 = COLUMN2 OR (COLUMN1 IS NULL AND COLUMN2 IS NULL)` is a logical way of telling Oracle, "Either these columns are equal or both of them are NULL." We may be able to significantly improve the performance of joining two large tables by rewriting the condition to NVL(COLUMN1, 'fake value') = NVL(COLUMN2, 'fake value'). Writing cryptic expressions is not ideal and may cause problems from bad cardinality estimates, but it's often worth the trouble if it enables faster join operations.

Other

Constant-time operations show up frequently in Oracle, like in any system. For example, inserting a row into a table, creating objects, and altering objects often take the same amount of time regardless of the input size.

On the other hand, all those operations also have nonconstant time versions. Inserting a row into a table takes a non-trivial amount of time if there are indexes that need to be maintained. Creating objects like indexes can take a huge amount of time to sort the data. Even altering tables may or may not take constant time, depending on the ALTER command. Adding a constraint usually requires validation against the data, which depends on the number of rows; but adding a default value can be done purely in metadata and can finish almost instantly.

We can't categorize operations based purely on their command type. To estimate the run time of any command, we always need to think about the algorithms, data structures, and size of the data.

O(LOG(N)): Index Access

O(LOG(N)) is the worst-case run time for index access. Index reads are another core database operation. Indexes were described in detail in Chapter 9, but a brief summary of this important concept is included in the following paragraph.

When we search a binary tree, each step can eliminate half the rows of the index. Doubling the number of rows grows exponentially; conversely, halving the number of rows shrinks logarithmically. Index access on a simple binary tree is O(LOG2(N)). Oracle B-tree indexes store much more than one value per branch, so they have a worst-case access time of O(LOG(N)). Figure 16-5 shows an example of a binary tree search.

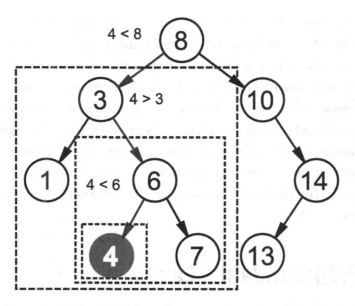

Figure 16-5. *Binary search algorithm. Image was created by Chris Martin and is in the public domain*

We know how indexes work, and we know that indexes are great for performance, but comparing the algorithms helps us understand precisely how awesome indexes can be. Figure 16-6 compares the fast O(LOG(N)) of an index read with the slow O(N) of a full table scan. This visualization is a powerful way of thinking about index performance.

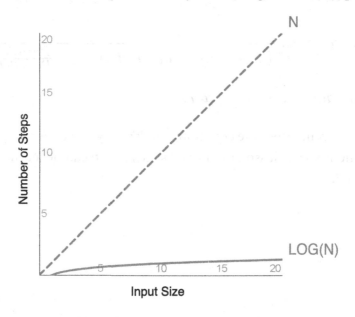

Figure 16-6. *Compare O(LOG(N)) index read vs. O(N) full table scan*

Most performance tests only compare results at a single point along a range of input sizes. Thinking about the lines and curves in the preceding visualizations helps us understand how our system's performance will change as the data grows. The amount of work required to read one row from an index rarely increases, no matter how large the table grows. In practice, our B-tree indexes will rarely even grow to a height of five levels, which means any indexed value is just a few reads away. Contrast that gradual run-time growth with the steeper growth of a full table scan, where every new row adds new work.

So far, we've mostly discussed small operations – one hash lookup, one index lookup, or one full table scan. The performance comparisons will soon become trickier as we start iterating the operations.

1/((1-P)+P/N): Amdahl's Law

For optimal parallel processing in a data warehouse, we have to worry about *all* operations. It is not enough to only focus on the biggest tasks. If our database has N cores and we want to run large jobs N times faster, we need to parallelize *everything*.

Amdahl's law is the mathematical version of the preceding paragraph. Amdahl's law is not a worst-case run-time complexity, but the function is important for understanding performance and is worth discussing here. The law can be expressed as the following equation in Figure 16-7.

$$TotalSpeedup = \frac{1}{(1 - ParallelPortion) + \frac{ParallelPortion}{ParallelSpeedup}}$$

Figure 16-7. *Amdahl's law as an equation*

We don't need to remember the equation, and it's only listed for completeness. But we do need to remember the lesson of Amdahl's law, which can be learned from the graph in Figure 16-8.

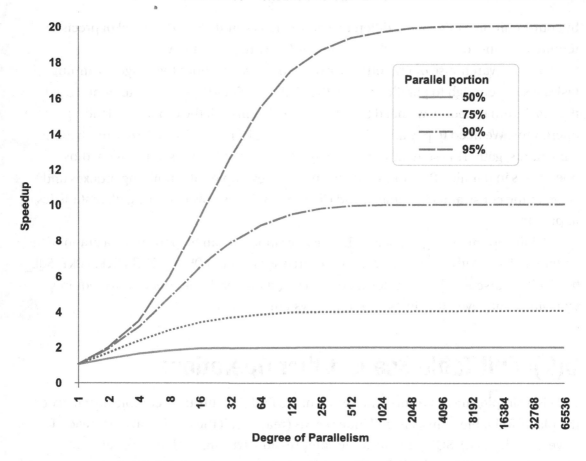

Figure 16-8. *Amdahl's law as a graph. Based on "Amdahl's Law" by Daniels220, licensed under CC BY-SA*

Notice that the preceding graph uses a logarithmic X axis and the numbers on the Y axis are comparatively small. The implications of this graph are depressing; even the tiniest amount of serialization will dash our dreams of running N times faster.

For example, let's say we've got a large data load and we've parallelized 95% of the process. Our machine has 128 cores, and (miraculously) the parallel portion runs 128 times faster. Yet the overall process is only 17.4 times faster. If we foolishly throw hardware at the problem and increase the cores from 128 to 256, the process will only run 18.6 times faster. These are disappointing diminishing returns.

Our time would be much better spent increasing the parallel portion from 95% to 96%, which would increase the performance from 17.4 times faster to 21 times faster. These surprising performance gains are why we need to spend so much effort finding exactly where our processes spend their time. We all like to tune with our gut feelings, but our intuition can't tell the difference between 95% and 96%. That level of precision requires advanced tools and a deep analysis of the process activity.

For data warehouse operations, we cannot only worry about the longest-running tasks. It's not enough to parallelize only the `INSERT` or `CREATE TABLE` statement. To get the maximum speedup, we need to put a lot of effort into all the other data loading operations. We need to pay attention to operations like rebuilding indexes, re-enabling constraints, gathering statistics, etc. Luckily, Oracle provides ways to run all of those operations in parallel. Previous chapters included examples of rebuilding indexes and re-enabling constraints in parallel, and Chapter 18 shows how to easily gather statistics in parallel.

To fully optimize large data warehouse operations, it can help to create a graph of the system activity, with tools like Oracle Enterprise Manager or `DBMS_SQLTUNE.REPORT_SQL_MONITOR`. As discussed in Chapter 12, optimizing data warehouse operations requires worrying about even the tiniest amount of system inactivity.

O(N): Full Table Scans, Other Operations

`O(N)` is a simple, linear performance growth. We find this run-time complexity all over the place: full table scans, fast full index scans (reading all the index leaves instead of traversing the tree), SQL parsing, basic compression, writing or changing data, etc. There's not much to see here, but things get interesting in the next section when we start comparing more functions.

Most Oracle operations fall into the `O(N)` category. In practice, we spend most of our tuning time hoping for linear improvements. For example, direct-path writes can improve performance by reducing the amount of REDO and UNDO data. That's only a linear improvement, but it's a significant one.

O(N*LOG(N)): Full Table Scan vs. Index Access, Sorting, Joining, Global vs. Local Index, Gathering Statistics

`O(N*LOG(N))` is the worst-case run time for realistic sorting algorithms. This run-time complexity shows up in many unexpected places, like constraint validation. Previous sections discussed data structures and algorithms that mostly focused on finding a single value, and now it's time to start iterating those algorithms to find multiple values. For finding a single value, an O(LOG(N)) index access is obviously faster than an O(N) full table scan, but what happens when we're looking up more than a single row?

Figure 16-9 compares the functions discussed in this section: N^2, variations of N*LOG(N), and N.

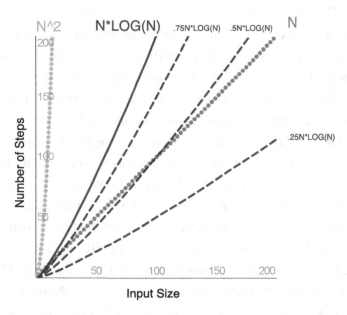

Figure 16-9. *Comparing N^2, N*LOG(N), and N*

The preceding lines and curves can be used to understand full table scans vs. index access, sorting, joining, global vs. local indexes, gathering statistics, and many other operations.

Full Table Scan vs. Index Access

Indexes are awesome for looking up a single row in a table – it's hard to beat O(LOG(N)) read time. But other than primary key or unique key indexes, most index access will retrieve more than one row. To retrieve multiple rows, Oracle must repeat LOG(N) multiple times.

If an index scan is used to look up every row in the table, Oracle has to walk the tree N times, which leads to a N*LOG(N) run time. That run time is clearly much worse than just reading the entire table one row at a time. The performance difference is obvious if you look at Figure 16-9 and compare the slower, solid line of N*LOG(N) against the faster, dotted line of N. There are many times when a full table scan is faster than index access.

The performance difference is more complicated when Oracle reads a percentage of rows other than 1% or 100%. Notice the dashed lines in Figure 16-9; they represent repeating the LOG(N) access for 25%, 50%, or 75% of the rows in the table. As the size of the table grows, each curve will eventually overtake the linear line for N. We cannot simply say that one algorithm is faster than another. The fastest algorithm depends on the size of the table and the percentage of rows accessed. An index might be a good idea today for reading 25% of a table, but a bad idea tomorrow if the table has grown.

There are other factors that can significantly change the balance. Oracle can use multi-block reads for full table scans, as opposed to single-block reads for index access. Using multi-block reads, Oracle can read several blocks from a table in the same time it takes to read one block from an index. And if the index clustering factor is high (if the index is not ordered by the value being searched for), an index lookup on a small number of rows may end up reading all of the blocks of the table anyway.

The theory tells us the *shape* of the lines, but only practice can tell us the actual values. I can't give you an exact number for your system, table, and workload. But there *is* a number – a point where a full table scan becomes cheaper than an index. Finding that number is not trivial, and it should not surprise us that Oracle doesn't always make the right decision.

When Oracle fails to make the right choice, we shouldn't throw out the entire decision-making process by using an index hint. Instead, we should look for ways to provide more accurate information, to help Oracle make better choices. Helping Oracle is usually done by gathering optimizer statistics.

Sorting

O(N*LOG(N)) is the worst-case run time for popular sorting. We always hope our processes will scale linearly, but that is often not the case. In practice, we have to deal with algorithms that get slower faster than we anticipate. Sorting is a central part of any database and affects ORDER BY, analytic functions, joining, grouping, finding distinct values, set operations, etc. We need to learn how to deal with these slow algorithms and avoid them when possible.

For planning, we need to be aware of how performance will change over time. If sorting one million rows takes 1 second today, we cannot assume that sorting two million rows will take 2 seconds tomorrow.

We also need to be aware of how the space requirements for sorting will change with the input size. Luckily, the amount of space required grows linearly. If the number of rows doubles, the amount of PGA memory or temporary tablespace required to sort will also double.

There are times when the sorting is already done for us. A B-tree index has already been sorted – the work was done during the original INSERT or UPDATE. Adding a row to a table is $O(1)$ – the process only requires adding a row to the end of a dumb heap. Adding a row to an index is $O(LOG(N))$ – the process needs to walk the tree to find where to add or update the value.

Oracle can use an index full scan to read from the index, in order, without having to do any sorting. The work has already been done; Oracle just needs to read the index from left to right or right to left.

Oracle can also use a min/max read to quickly find the minimum or maximum value. The minimum or maximum value in a B-tree will be either all the way on the left or all the way on the right. Once again, the data is already sorted, so finding the top or bottom result is a trivial $O(LOG(N))$ operation.

Oddly, there's a missing feature where Oracle can't find *both* the min and max using a simple min/max read.[4] But the following code shows a simple workaround to this problem: break the problem into two separate queries, and then combine the results. Writing an extra subquery is annoying, but it's a small price to pay for a huge improvement in run-time complexity – $O(2*LOG(N))$ is much better than $O(N)$. When we understand the algorithms and data structures used by Oracle, we know what to expect and when to look for a faster workaround:

```
--Create a table and query for min and max values.
create table min_max(a number primary key);

--Full table scan or index fast full scan - O(N).
select min(a), max(a) from min_max;
```

---

[4] See my Stack Overflow answer here for more details: https://stackoverflow.com/q/43131204/409172

```
--Two min/max index accesses - O(2*LOG(N)).
select
    (select min(a) from min_max) min,
    (select max(a) from min_max) max
from dual;
```

The set operations INTERSECT, MINUS/EXCEPT, and UNION require sorting. We should use UNION ALL when possible because it is the only set operation that does not need to sort the results.

Sorting and joining seem to go together, but in practice they are a bad combination. The next section discusses why we don't want to use sorting for joins.

Joining

Hopefully you remember the Venn diagrams and join diagrams from Chapter 1, which explained how joins logically work. Unfortunately, understanding how joins physically work is more complicated. Figure 16-10 visualizes the main join algorithms and their run-time complexity. The diagram visualizes joins as the process of matching rows between two unordered lists. Each join algorithm is also described in a separate paragraph after the diagram. You may need to flip back and forth a few times to understand the algorithms.

Join Algorithms and Time Complexity

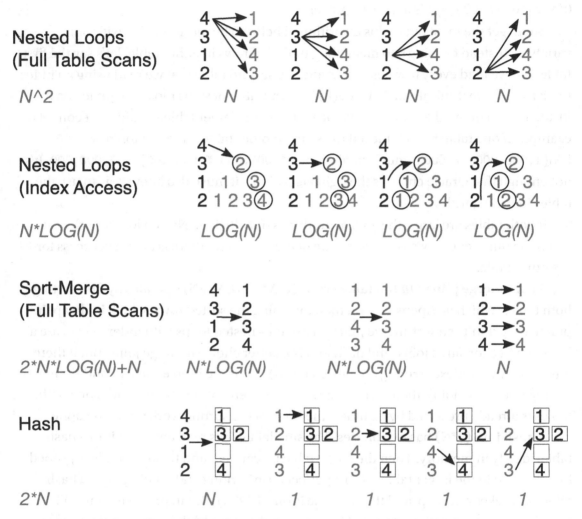

Figure 16-10. Visualization of join algorithms and time complexity

A **nested loop with full table scans (N^2)** is conceptually simple. Start with the first table and compare each row in that table with every row in the second table. We can think of this algorithm as two nested FOR loops. Each of the loops runs N time, so the run-time complexity is a horribly slow O(N^2). Recall from Figure 16-9 that the line for N^2 looks almost completely vertical. This join algorithm should only be used when the tables are trivially small, the optimizer statistics are bad, or important indexes are missing.

411

A **nested loop with index access (N*LOG(N))** is often a faster choice for joins. Instead of searching an entire table for each row, we can search an index. Reducing O(N^2) to O(N*LOG(N)) is a huge improvement.

But to get the most out of this algorithm, it helps to be more specific with our variables. Instead of using N to mean the number of rows in either table, let's say the first table that we read every row has A rows and the second table that we read using an index has B rows. If we think about O(A*LOG(B)), the number of steps mostly depends on A instead of B. The smaller table should be first, and the larger table should be second. For example, if one table has a hundred rows and another table has a million rows, 100 * LOG(1,000,000) = 600 is much smaller than 1,000,000 * LOG(100) = 2,000,000. It's not enough that Oracle chooses the right algorithm – it must also know how to use the tables in the algorithm.

If both tables are large, this join algorithm is not efficient. Nested loops work best when the number of rows is small for one of the tables and there is an index access for the other table.

A **sort-merge join with full table scans (2*N*LOG(N)+N)** operates by first sorting both tables, which is expensive, and then matching the sorted rows, which is cheap. In practice we don't see sort-merge joins very often – nested loops with index access are a better choice for small joins, and hash join is a better choice for large joins. But if there are no relevant indexes (ruling out nested loops) and there is no equality condition (ruling out a hash join), then sort-merge is the best remaining option. And if one of the tables is already presorted by an index, then half of the sorting work is already done.

A **hash join (2*N)** has two phases. The smaller table is read and built into a hash table, ideally in memory. Then the larger table is scanned, and the hash table is probed for each row in the larger table. With a perfect hash, writing and reading from a hash table only takes one step, and the run time is only O(2*N). But in practice there will be collisions, and multiple rows will be stored in the same hash bucket, so the time to perform hash joins does not grow linearly; hash joins are somewhere between O(2*N) and O(N*LOG(N)).[5]

Hash joins have a great run-time complexity, but that doesn't mean we always want to use them. Hash joins read all of the rows of both tables, even if we are only going to match a few rows. Hash joins require a lot of memory or temporary tablespace – roughly equal to the size of the smaller input table. A slow algorithm in memory might be better

---

[5] See my answer here for tests comparing sort-merge with hash: https://stackoverflow.com/a/8548454/409172. When available, hash joins are always faster.

than a fast algorithm on disk. And hash joins are not always available, because they only work with equality conditions.

There are many variations of the preceding join algorithms. Cross joins, also known as Cartesian products, are similar to nested loops with full table scans. Parallelism and partitioning can always complicate the algorithms. Hash joins can use bloom filters to eliminate values without fully comparing all of them. Joining is the most important operation in the database, and there's not enough space here to describe all of the features for joining tables.

Join performance is all about Oracle correctly estimating the size of tables. The table size determines which algorithms are used and how the tables are used in the algorithms. For example, hashing and sorting are bad ideas if one of the tables returns no rows – there's no need for all that prep work when the intermediate data structures won't be used. And a nested loop is a horrible idea for two huge tables that have a lot of matching rows. Bad execution plans happen when Oracle thinks a small table is large or a large table is small. How that mistake happens, and how to fix it, is discussed in Chapters 17 and 18.

Global vs. Local Index

The advantages and disadvantages of partitioning are different for tables and indexes. Partitioning a table is often a good choice, since there are many potential performance improvements and few costs. Indexes can be either global, one index for the whole table, or local, one index per partition. Compared with table partitioning, index partitioning benefits are smaller, and the costs are greater.

Reading from a single table partition, instead of a full table scan, significantly decreases the run-time complexity from $O(N)$ to $O(N/P)$, where P is the number of partitions. But reading from a local index, instead of a global index, only changes the run-time complexity from $O(LOG(N))$ to $O(LOG(N/P))$. That index access improvement is barely noticeable.

The cost of reading an entire partitioned table, without partition pruning, is still a normal $O(N)$. But reading from a local index without partition pruning is much more expensive than a global index read. Reading from one large index is $O(LOG(N))$. Reading from many small indexes is $O(P*LOG(N/P))$, a significant increase. Walking one big tree is much faster than walking many small trees. We need to think carefully when we partition, and we should not expect table and index partitioning to work the same way.

Gathering Optimizer Statistics

Gathering optimizer statistics is an essential task for achieving good SQL performance. Statistics are used to estimate cardinality, the number of rows returned by an operation. Cardinality is synonymous with "input size," the X axis on most of the graphs in this chapter. Cardinality is vital information for making execution plan decisions, such as knowing when to use a nested loop or a hash join.

To get good execution plans, we need to gather statistics periodically and after any significant data changes. But gathering statistics itself can be slow. Understanding the different algorithms and data structures for gathering statistics can help us avoid performance problems.

Finding the cardinality isn't just about counting the number of rows in each table. Oracle also needs to measure the distinctness of columns and specific column values. For example, an equality condition on a primary key column will never return more than one row, so it is a good candidate for index access. But an equality condition on a repetitive status column is more complicated; some statuses may be rare and benefit from index access; other statuses may be common and work best with a full table scan. Optimizer statistics gathering needs to generate information that can be used to estimate the cardinality for many complicated scenarios.

Counting distinct items is similar to sorting, which is a slow operation. To make things even worse, Oracle needs statistics for all the columns in a table, which may require multiple passes. A naïve algorithm to count distinct values would first sort those values; it's easy to measure distinctness if the values are in order. But that naïve approach would take $O(N*LOG(N))$ time. A better algorithm would use hashing, and that's exactly what recent versions of Oracle can do with the HASH GROUP BY and HASH UNIQUE operations. As with joining, the time to hash is somewhere between $O(N)$ and $O(N*LOG(N))$.

Luckily, when gathering optimizer statistics, we can trade accuracy for time. The default Oracle statistics gathering algorithm performs an *approximate* count with a single pass of the table. The single-pass algorithm runs in $O(N)$ time and generates numbers that are accurate but not perfect.

Developers rightfully worry about imperfect values. A single wrong bit can break everything. But in this case an approximate value is good enough. The optimizer doesn't need to know the *exact* value. Oracle only needs to know if the algorithm needs to be optimized for "large" or "small" queries.

The following example shows how close the approximation is, using the function APPROX_COUNT_DISTINCT, which uses the same algorithm as statistics gathering:

```
--Compare APPROX_COUNT_DISTINCT with a regular COUNT.
select
    approx_count_distinct(launch_date) approx_distinct,
    count(distinct launch_date)         exact_distinct
from launch;

APPROX_DISTINCT  EXACT_DISTINCT
---------------  ---------------
         61745           60401
```

The fast approximation algorithm[6] only works if we read the entire table. If we try to sample a small part of the table, the approximation algorithm no longer applies, and Oracle has to use a different approach. We may think we're clever setting a small estimate percentage, such as DBMS_STATS.GATHER_TABLE_STATS(..., ESTIMATE_PERCENT => 50). But in this case, a slow algorithm reading 50% of the table is slower and less accurate than the fast algorithm reading 100% of the table. We should rarely, if ever, change the ESTIMATE_PERCENT parameter.

These distinct counting tricks can also apply to partition statistics, using a feature called incremental statistics. Normally, partitioned tables require reading the table data twice to gather statistics: one pass for each partition and another pass for the entire table. The double read may seem excessive at first, but consider that we cannot simply add distinct counts together.

But incremental statistics uses an approximation algorithm that does enable adding distinct counts. Incremental statistics creates small data structures called synopses, which contain information about the distinctness within a partition. After gathering statistics for each partition, the global statistics can be inferred by merging those small synopses. This algorithm improves statistics gathering from $O(2*N)$ to $O(N)$. That decrease may not sound impressive, but remember that partitioned tables are often huge. Saving an extra full table scan on our largest tables can be a big deal.

This algorithm analysis is starting to get recursively ridiculous. We're discussing algorithms that help Oracle determine which algorithms to use. And the problem goes deeper – in rare cases, statistics gathering is slow because the optimizer chooses a bad

---

[6] Oracle uses an algorithm called HyperLogLog for distinct count approximations.

plan for the statistics gathering query. For those rare cases, we may need to prime the pump; we can use DBMS_STATS.SET_TABLE_STATS to create initial, fake statistics, to help us gather the real statistics.

Many organizations consider statistics gathering a boring maintenance task that is best handled by the DBAs. But that metadata is at the heart of Oracle performance, and it should be understood by anyone who is responsible for our database program's performance.

O(N^2): Cross Joins, Nested Loops, Other Operations

O(N^2) algorithms are getting into the ridiculously slow territory. Unless we have special conditions, such as an input size close to 0, we should avoid these run times at all costs. This run-time complexity happens from cross joins, nested FOR loops, nested loop joins with full table scans, and some other operations. As a quick reminder of their poor performance, Figure 16-11 shows N! and N^2.

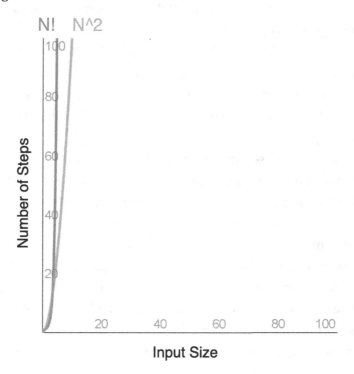

Figure 16-11. *Compare N! with N^2*

Cross joins are not always bad. Sometimes it is necessary to mindlessly combine every row in one table with every row in another table. And cross joins can be fast if the number of rows is close to zero. But cross joins that happen because of incorrectly joined tables, or because of poor cardinality estimates, are horrible for performance. Accidental cross joins are so bad that they can effectively bring down an entire database; Oracle may need an unlimited amount of temporary tablespace to build the result set, depriving other processes of space for sorting or hashing.

FOR loops inside FOR loops are the most common way to generate $O(N^2)$ run times in procedural code. If we add *another* FOR loop, the run-time complexity becomes $O(N^3)$, then $O(N^4)$, etc. Nested FOR loops can easily happen in PL/SQL, and they are all too common when using explicit cursors. Avoiding that horrible performance is an important reason we should always try to replace nested cursors with a single SQL statement.

Most developers write procedural code as nested FOR loops because loops are the easiest way to think about joins. But Oracle cannot change the algorithms used by imperative programs – Oracle is stuck doing exactly what we ask for. The advantage of switching to declarative code is that we don't have to worry about these algorithms as much. When we use SQL, we let Oracle decide which join algorithms to use.

It is possible that after switching to declarative SQL the optimizer will still choose an $O(N^2)$ algorithm. As we saw in Figure 16-10 earlier in the chapter, a nested loop join with two full table scans is a terrible way to join tables. But that worst case should only happen if we have missing statistics, missing indexes, or weird join conditions.

$O(N^2)$ shows up in other unexpected places. In extreme cases, SQL parse time grows exponentially. For example, the parse time becomes ridiculously bad if we combine thousands of subqueries with UNION ALL. (The code measuring parse time is too large to include here, but it can be found in the repository.) Writing large SQL statements is a good thing, but writing Brobdingnagian SQL statements is not.

The MODEL clause brings procedural logic to SQL statements. MODEL is a neat trick and is explained briefly in Chapter 19. That clause gives us the ability to turn our data into a spreadsheet and apply FOR loops to our rows and columns. But just like with PL/SQL, we can easily find ourselves in $O(N^2)$ performance territory.

A high run-time complexity isn't always avoidable or necessarily bad. But we should think carefully when we see cross joins or nested operations.

O(N!): Join Order

O(N!) is as bad as Oracle's algorithms get, but luckily, it's also rare. As discussed in Chapter 6, tables have to be joined in a specific order, and there are many ways to order a set of tables. The problem of ordering tables must be solved by the optimizer when building execution plans and in our minds when trying to understand queries.

The optimizer is capable of handling a huge number of tables without serious problems. But there are always unexpected problems when we push the system to the limits. For example, if we nest over a dozen common table expressions, the parse time appears to grow like O(N!). (See the GitHub repository for a code demonstration.) In practice, this problem will only happen because of a rare bug or because we're doing something we shouldn't.

Our minds can only hold a small, ordered list in short-term memory. If we build our SQL statements with giant comma-separated lists, we'll never be able to understand them. Building small inline views and combining them with the ANSI join syntax will vastly simplify our SQL. There's no precise equation for SQL complexity, but we can think of the complexity comparison like this: $(1/2N)! + (1/2N)! \ll N!$

For performance we want to batch things together, to reduce overhead. But to make our code readable, we want to split everything up into manageable pieces. That is precisely what SQL excels at; we can logically divide our queries into inline views to make them understandable, and then the optimizer can efficiently put the code back together.

O(∞): The Optimizer

The Oracle optimizer builds SQL execution plans. Building optimal execution plans is impossible, so we could say this task is O(∞). That run-time complexity sounds wrong at first; Oracle obviously builds at least *some* optimal execution plans. But it's helpful to think of the optimizer as doing an impossible task.

Building the best execution plan means the optimizer must compare algorithms and data structures and determine which one runs fastest. But it is literally impossible to determine if a generic program will even *finish*, much less how long it will run. Determining if a program will finish is called the halting problem. Before computers were even invented, Alan Turing proved that it is impossible for computers to solve the halting problem. Luckily, this is a problem that's theoretically impossible to solve in all cases, but it is practically feasible to solve in almost all cases.

To add another wrinkle to the problem, Oracle has to generate the execution plan incredibly fast. A better name for the optimizer would be the satisficer. Satisficing is solving an optimization problem while also taking into account the time necessary to solve the problem.

It's important we understand how difficult the optimizer's job is. We shouldn't be surprised when Oracle occasionally generates a bad execution plan. The optimizer isn't as bad as we think – it's merely trying to solve an unsolvable problem. When the optimizer is having trouble, we shouldn't abandon it; we should try to work with it.

When a bad execution plan is generated, our first instinct shouldn't be, "How can I work around this bad plan?" Our first instinct should be, "How can I provide better information so Oracle can make better decisions?" That information is almost always in the form of optimizer statistics, which are described in Chapters 17 and 18.

We need to resist the urge to quickly use hints and change system parameters. Think of the optimizer as a complex forecasting system. We should never change a system parameter such as OPTIMIZER_INDEX_COST_ADJ just because it helps with one query. That would be like adding 10 degrees to every weather forecast because the meteorologist was once wrong by 10 degrees.

Summary

Many performance problems fall into a small number of run-time complexities. Knowing which functions represent our problems can help us understand why Oracle is behaving a certain way and how to find a solution. Practical algorithm analysis is simply matching our problems with predefined classes of problems. We may not use this approach often, but without it we'll never be able to truly understand database performance.

Most of our performance problems are related to implementation details and those pesky constants we've been conveniently ignoring. The next chapter looks at a more traditional list of Oracle performance concepts.

CHAPTER 17

Understand SQL Tuning Theories

Algorithm analysis is a useful guide for understanding the foundations of Oracle performance. Now we must turn to the more traditional techniques and theories of database performance. First, we need to discuss performance issues from the end user's perspective. Then we will discuss several popular approaches to performance tuning. But all roads eventually lead to SQL tuning. For effective SQL tuning, we need to understand the importance of execution plans, the operations available to execution plans, cardinality, optimizer statistics, transformations, and dynamic optimization features.

Managing User Expectations

Before we jump into technical topics, we need to address the human aspect of performance tuning. We're usually not tuning for ourselves; we're tuning systems for clients or end users. We need to carefully think about the end user's perspective when we investigate problems, explain resources, present our ideas, and implement the changes.

First, we need to get a clear, objective definition of the performance problem. The end users may not have much experience troubleshooting, so it's up to us to help guide the conversation. Instead of simply asking, "What's wrong?" we should ask for specific details. We need to know if the problem is consistent or intermittent, when does it happen, how long does it take to run, has it always been this slow, how long should it take to run, are we sure the problem is in the database and not an application, etc. We must remember the curse of knowledge, and we must try extra hard to convey tuning information in simple language. An extra minute spent in the discovery phase can save us hours of needlessly tuning the wrong thing.

© Jon Heller 2023
J. Heller, *Pro Oracle SQL Development*, https://doi.org/10.1007/978-1-4842-8867-2_17

When we find and understand the problem, we have to consider the available resources that may provide context for poor performance. Many performance problems are bugs that can be fixed, but many other performance problems are caused by resource limitations. We need to understand our database and server resources and honestly discuss them with end users. I've soothed many angry users by explaining, "Our old servers are slower than your laptop, so this is as fast as we can process the data" or "You're reading X gigabytes of data. Our hard drives can only read Y megabytes per second. This job is always going to take at least Z seconds." Users are more willing to wait if they think the wait is reasonable.

Depending on the scope of the change, we may need to present a cost/benefit analysis to the end user or client for approval. The cost may be money to buy hardware, or the cost may be our time. Honesty, humility, and testing are important at this step; it's not uncommon to throw hardware at a problem and not fix anything, or for deadlines to slip. It's better to under-promise and over-deliver.

When we implement the change, we must be sure to carefully measure performance before and after. The end users will want to know precisely what they got for their investment.

Like with most development tasks, most of our performance tuning time will be spent discussing and coordinating the work instead of the work itself. But this book is focused on SQL development, so let's jump into the technical work of finding and fixing performance problems.

Performance Tuning State of Mind

This chapter is going to disappoint you. I know what you want, but it's not possible to build a single, comprehensive performance tuning checklist. Whenever we encounter a performance problem, we wish we could scan through a checklist or flip through the chapters of a book or refer to a standard operating procedure. There are plenty of lists in this book, but performance tuning is too complex to be described in simple step-by-step instructions.

Performance tuning is hard, and we need to approach it differently than other problems. We can't treat performance tuning like debugging. We need a wide variety of approaches to guard ourselves against wasting our time with motivated troubleshooting.

Performance Tuning Is Not Debugging

We have to treat performance problems different than code problems. It's tempting to apply the same problem-solving process to both tuning and debugging; find a problem, drill down to the root cause, and then fix or work around the underlying problem. We need to use a *depth-first* approach for debugging and a *breadth-first* approach for performance tuning. Developers and administrators who try a depth-first approach for performance tuning will waste a lot of time.

For debugging, we only need to find the first problem and then drill down. The program must work 100% correctly, and even a single incorrect byte is worth investigating. Even if we don't fix the right problem, we still accomplish something useful.

For performance tuning, we need to find the first *significant* problem and then drill down. The word "significant" is subjective and can mean a problem that slows down a web page, consumes so many resources that it slows down the entire system, drives up server costs, etc. But even though we can't all completely agree on what a significant performance problem even is, we can still adopt a mindset that will usually lead us to us solve important problems. Perhaps it is more useful to think of what a significant performance problem is not; a problem is not significant merely because we don't like it or it's something we know how to fix. There are always countless candidates for performance problems. The problem could be something in the application, database, operating system, network, hardware, SAN, etc. It's easy to get distracted by red herrings. If we don't quickly eliminate spurious correlations, we're going to waste a lot of time.

The art of performance tuning is to use multiple approaches to quickly gather and filter a lot of data. We must ignore the 90% that runs fine, ignore the 9% that is slow but necessarily slow, and find the 1% that is slow and fixable. If we use a simple checklist, with overly simplistic rules like "avoid full table scans," we'll spend too much time fixing the wrong problems.

Motivated Troubleshooting

We must constantly be on guard for biases that will make us waste days fixing irrelevant problems. We all have the urge to take the easy path and focus on fixing the problems we are familiar with. Following familiar paths is a good strategy for bug fixing – any cleanup is a good thing. Having a utopian view of the code is beneficial.

But performance tuning must stay firmly grounded in reality. The ugly truth is that nobody will ever fully understand all the wait events or all the execution plan operations. We only have time to fix the slow ones.

For personal education it's helpful to investigate anything that doesn't look right. But when there's a critical performance problem, we must focus on only the most important part.

Different Approaches

There are many ways to investigate our programs for performance problems. The following list includes the common approaches to performance tuning. Each approach works better in different contexts, and we must be willing to quickly change approaches if one isn't working. As we gain experience, we develop our own tuning style and develop a feeling for when something is wrong. Also, technologies change over time, so we must be willing to change our approach:

1. *Application/operating system/hardware*: We don't always have to solve the most direct problem. Improving one layer in our system may be enough to make the problem go away in another. For example, if we can't fix the execution plan of a statement, we could make up for a slow operation by increasing the hardware I/O performance. Or we could shift the problem to a different layer by moving application logic into a query or vice versa. But we can't always compensate for bad performance in one layer with a fix in another, and these solutions can be wasteful and expensive. Non-SQL approaches are not discussed in this chapter.

2. *Cardinality*: Examining the number of rows returned by each operation of a SQL statement is a useful way of gauging the accuracy of execution plans. This approach is discussed in a later section.

3. *Tracing/profiling/sampling*: Virtually every activity performed in Oracle is instrumented. Oracle can capture almost every detail of almost every SQL statement with tracing. Oracle can capture the time spent on every line of PL/SQL code with profiling. In practice, tracing has been mostly replaced by Oracle's sampling

frameworks, such as AWR (Automatic Workload Repository), ASH (Active Session History), and SQL monitoring. Tracing provides a ginormous amount of data but inconveniently. Sampling provides a huge amount of data and makes the data easily accessible. Profiling and sampling are discussed in the next chapter.

4. *Algorithm analysis*: Comparing the run-time complexity of different choices helps us understand the trade-offs and decisions made by Oracle. This approach was discussed in the previous chapter.

5. *Phone a friend*: Sometimes we need to admit defeat and seek help from others. This approach can be as simple as asking a search engine or our coworkers. Or we can create a service request and ask Oracle to tune for us. (But in my experience, Oracle Support is not helpful for performance tuning, unless we are certain we have hit a bug. Most support engineers don't seem interested in tuning and will inundate us with requests for off-topic trace files until we go away.) Or we can rely on Oracle's automated advisors to recommend and implement performance fixes. (But in my experience, Oracle's advisors are rarely helpful. Hopefully, the advisors will improve in future versions.) This approach is not discussed further in this chapter.

6. *Avoid the problem*: The fastest way to run something is to not run it at all. When we understand our code, and the code's context, we often discover a simpler implementation. This approach depends on using a good development process, understanding Oracle's advanced features, and using proper SQL programming styles to make the code's meaning more intelligible. The topics discussed in Parts I, II, and III of this book can fix the majority of our performance problems. Performance tuning cannot be studied in isolation. If you skipped to Part IV of this book, you missed the most important tuning tips. Advice like "use inline views and ANSI SQL join syntax" is indirectly related to performance, but more important than anything discussed in this chapter.

We all have different preferences, and one approach isn't necessarily better than another. We can often use expertise in one technique to compensate for a lack of knowledge in another. For example, this book uses my preferred technique of focusing on individual SQL statements instead of looking at overall resource utilization; if we take care of the queries, the databases will take care of themselves. Admittedly, that approach does not always work, so it's worth reading different sources and learning different tuning styles.

Why Not Database Tuning?

Database tuning, performance planning, system architecture, and configuration are important topics, with many books written about them. You might wonder why this book focuses on SQL tuning instead of database tuning. It's not just because this book is about SQL; it's because SQL is the central component of the database. Tuning SQL will also alleviate stress on the database, operating system, hardware, network, SAN, etc.

The converse is less likely to be true; it's easier for SQL improvements to make up for bad hardware than it is for hardware improvements to make up for bad SQL. Hardware improvements tend to be linear, while SQL improvements are frequently exponential or better. Oracle provides so many SQL tuning opportunities that we can almost always find a way to make the SQL run faster.

Plenty of systems can limp by with ancient hardware if the SQL runs well. But if our execution plans are full of bad Cartesian products, then there is no hope. Unless we have access to a quantum computer, there is no way to buy ourselves out of a terrible algorithm.

Declarative Programming (Why Execution Plans Are Important)

In traditional imperative programming, we tell the compiler exactly how to operate, and we are responsible for creating efficient algorithms and data structures to enable good performance. In declarative programming, we tell the compiler what we want, and the compiler tries to find the optimal algorithms and data structures.

Declarative Quirks

SQL is our declarative language in Oracle. We ask Oracle to modify or retrieve data, and Oracle has to decide how to join the tables, apply the filters, etc. There are many interesting consequences of this declarative environment.

For example, Oracle SQL provides consistency and tries to make many things happen at the exact same moment. The following SQL statement has two references to SYSDATE, and both of them will always return the same value:

```
--In declarative SQL, these SYSDATEs generate the same value.
select sysdate date1, sysdate date2 from dual;
```

When we write SYSDATE in SQL statements, we're asking Oracle to find the current date. When we write SYSDATE in PL/SQL, we're asking Oracle to assign the current date to a variable. This PL/SQL snippet has a small chance of passing two different values: SOME_PROC(SYSDATE, SYSDATE). Weird things can happen when we switch between the declarative and imperative worlds.

Oracle may run parts of our code more or less often than we anticipate. A function in the SELECT list may be called more than once per row – there may be an extra execution to set up result caching. A function or trigger that is part of a DML statement may be called more than once – Oracle may restart part of a statement to ensure consistency. And many times, Oracle can decide something is unnecessary and not run it at all, like the expression in the following EXISTS clause:

```
--The expression is ignored and no divide-by-zero error is raised.
select * from dual where exists (select 1/0 from dual);
```

In Chapter 15 we saw the dangers of assuming an Oracle SQL statement will run in the same order we wrote it. If our data types are wrong, like in a bad EAV data model, and the predicates are run out of order, we can get run-time errors. But the main reason this declarative-vs.-imperative discussion matters is to understand Oracle's execution plans.

Execution Plans

Execution plans are the key to SQL tuning. An execution plan shows the precise order of operations used to execute a SQL statement, along with useful information that tells us how Oracle made its decisions. These operations and details tell us the algorithms and data structures used to run our queries. The Oracle optimizer generates execution plans based on the SQL statement, the objects related to the SQL statement, statistical information about our database environment, and much more.

Execution plans are often confused with query plans or explain plans. The important difference is that an execution plan is the actual plan that was used by Oracle, while the explain plans are just the predicted plans that might be used by Oracle. The word "actual" is used a lot in the next two chapters because that's the term Oracle uses to describe real numbers vs. estimates. For example, we'll see later that "A-rows," or "actual rows," may be a wildly different number than "E-rows," or "estimated rows." It is crucial that we are always aware of whether we're looking at actual plans and numbers or estimated plans and numbers, or we will waste an inordinate amount of time tuning things that aren't worth tuning.

SQL tuning is all about finding, understanding, and fixing execution plans. The many ways to find and fix plans are discussed in more detail in Chapter 18. To summarize, the best way to find and understand plans is as plain text and with the actual numbers instead of just estimates. And the best way to fix execution plans is indirectly, by providing more information so the Oracle optimizer can make better decisions.

For example, the simplest way to generate an estimated explain plan is to start with the EXPLAIN PLAN command like this:

```
--Generate explain plan.
explain plan for
select * from launch where launch_id = 1;
```

The following command and results show the explain plan[1] for the preceding statement:

```
--Display explain plan.
select *
from table(dbms_xplan.display(format => 'basic +rows +cost'));

Plan hash value: 4075417019
```

---

[1] I used uncommon FORMAT options and removed extraneous spaces so the execution plan lines will fit the width of the page. These results are another example of formatting that is necessary when publishing our results, but not something we should typically do.

```
--------------------------------------------------------------
|Id|Operation                     |Name      |Rows |Cost (%CPU)|
--------------------------------------------------------------
| 0|SELECT STATEMENT              |          |    1|    2   (0)|
| 1| TABLE ACCESS BY INDEX ROWID|LAUNCH    |    1|    2   (0)|
| 2|  INDEX UNIQUE SCAN           |LAUNCH_PK|    1|    1   (0)|
--------------------------------------------------------------
```

You don't have to understand everything in the preceding output yet. For now, it's enough to understand how important execution plans are to understanding Oracle performance.

Operations (What Execution Plan Decisions Are Available)

Execution plans are the key to SQL tuning, and operations are the key to understanding execution plans. Many developers fail at SQL tuning because they focus on the wrong thing. It's not good enough to know how long SQL statements run or how long SQL statements wait on a specific event. It's more helpful to measure things per *operation* than per *statement*. You could argue that this chapter's title is wrong – this chapter is more about "operation tuning" than "SQL tuning."

Operation Details

Each line in an execution plan has one operation, which maps to one algorithm. The Name column in the execution plan tells us the data structure used by that algorithm.

The precise algorithm depends on a combination of an operation name and an operation option. As of 19c, there are 149 operations and 259 operation options. Usually, a single operation only has a few valid options. For example, HASH JOIN is an operation, and OUTER is an operation option. For convenience these names are combined into HASH JOIN OUTER in most execution plan formats.

The operations are indented to convey parent–child relationships. This indentation is tricky and takes a while to get used to, but it is vital information. Indentation tells us which algorithms are executed first and how the rows are passed between operations. Changing even a single space in the operation line can radically alter the meaning of an execution plan.

Execution Plans and Recursive SQL

Most operations consume rows, do something with those rows, and then produce new rows. For example, a hash join consumes rows from two different child sources, combines them, and then produces a joined set of data for a parent operation. That intermediate result set might then be joined with something else.

The nested structure of an execution plan mirrors the way we should build SQL statements with small, nested, inline views. Just like building logical SQL statements, understanding an execution plan is about understanding small sets of operations, combining them into a new set, and repeating.

But execution plans aren't always that simple. There may be a significant amount of work not shown in the execution plan. Sometimes we have to tune a *recursive* SQL statement – a SQL statement that is automatically generated to support our SQL statement. Recursive SQL (not to be confused with recursive queries that use `CONNECT BY`) can be generated in many ways: custom PL/SQL functions with embedded SQL, triggers with SQL, metadata queries needed to parse the query or build the execution plan, remote objects handled by a remote database, etc. (But a view is not a recursive SQL statement. The query in a view will be added to our SQL statement as if we copied and pasted the text.)

If we're using advanced tuning tools like `DBMS_SQLTUNE.REPORT_SQL_MONITOR`, we can tell there's slow recursive SQL if the "Activity (%)" values do not add up to 100%. Finding the slow recursive queries can be done by looking at views like `V$SQL` and is explained in the next chapter. Luckily, those recursive queries tend to stick out and are easy to catch when we know what to look for.

Why Operations Matter

To understand execution plans, we need to know what operations and operation options are available. As discussed in the previous chapter, different algorithms are optimal in different contexts. We need to know what the algorithms are and when they should be used.

This section lists the most common operations and operation options and when they should be used. There are many guidelines, but we don't always have precise instructions. For example, hash joins work well for a large amount of data, and nested loops work well for a small amount of data. But the precise definition of "large" and "small" depends on many factors.

The science of SQL tuning is getting precise measurements and finding which operations are using the most time and which operations would work better. But we don't always have time for science; the art of SQL tuning is much faster. Eventually you will be able to look at an execution plan and just know that an operation doesn't belong. You've already been introduced to many of the operations listed in this chapter and been given advice for when they are useful. But there's a lot of information, and it will take a while to build an intuition for bad execution plans.

The operation names and options in this chapter were generated based on my experience, and the most popular combinations in the 350 databases I have access to. But this list is not comprehensive, and you will likely see different operations depending on what features you use.

The following SQL statements can help you see what operations are used and available on your systems:

```
--Recently used combinations of operations and options.
select operation, options, count(*)
from v$sql_plan
group by operation, options
order by operation, options;

--All available Operation names and options.  (Run as SYS.)
select * from sys.x$xplton;
select * from sys.x$xpltoo;
```

First Operations

The first operation in an execution plan is just a copy of the command name and doesn't have much meaning. But the first operation is a useful placeholder for information that sums up the entire plan. For example, the cost for the first operation is the total cost for the entire statement.[2]

---

[2] There are exceptions where the first operation costs less than the sum of the whole query. This seems to happen when an operation may stop a child operation after N rows. For example, this happens with FILTER, COUNT STOPKEY, and subqueries in the SELECT column list. See my answer here for more information on these unusual cases: https://stackoverflow.com/a/25394748/409172

These are the most common top-level operations, which need no further explanation: CREATE INDEX STATEMENT, CREATE TABLE STATEMENT, INSERT STATEMENT, DELETE STATEMENT, MERGE STATEMENT, MULTI-TABLE INSERT, SELECT STATEMENT, and UPDATE STATEMENT.

From the preceding list, only the INSERT operations are interesting. INSERT statements have a child operation that indicates whether the INSERT used direct-path writes or conventional writes. LOAD TABLE CONVENTIONAL indicates that a normal INSERT was used, which will be recoverable but slow. LOAD AS SELECT indicates that a direct-path write was used, which is non-recoverable but fast.

Joining

There are many join operations:

1. HASH JOIN: Builds a hash table of the smaller row source and then probes that hash table for each row of the larger row source. Best operation for joins that return a large percentage of rows. Requires an equality condition.

2. MERGE JOIN: Sorts both row sources and then joins them. Best operation for joins that return a large percentage of results but do not use an equality condition.

3. NESTED LOOPS: For each row in one row source, search for a match in the other row source. Best operation for joins that return a small percentage of results. One or both of the input row sources should come from an index access.

4. JOIN FILTER: A bloom filter that can be used to quickly eliminate rows before joining. Only allowed as a child operation of a hash join. (There's not much we can do to control this operation.)

The options are especially important, and they can significantly change the behavior of join operations. Remember that not all options are valid for all operations:

1. ANTI: Anti-joins return rows where a value in one row source does not exist in another row source. Used with NOT IN and NOT EXISTS conditions. This operation stops as soon as a match is found, so it is faster than a normal full table scan.

2. SEMI: Semi-joins return rows where a value in one row source matches at least one value from another row source. Used with IN and EXISTS conditions. This operation stops as soon as a match is found, so it is faster than a normal full table scan.

3. BUFFERED: Intermediate results that are written to temporary tablespace. Rows can flow between many levels of an execution plan at the same time, but these synchronization points require retrieving all rows before moving to the next operation.

4. OUTER/FULL OUTER/RIGHT OUTER: Performs an outer join instead of an inner join. An outer join isn't directly slower than an inner join. But we should not use outer joins by default, since outer joins provide less optimization opportunities than inner joins.

5. CARTESIAN: Combines every row from one source with every row from another source. Also known as cross joins, this option is only valid for MERGE JOIN. This option is a red flag in execution plans. Unless we have an extremely small number of rows, this option may lead to horrible performance.

Table Access

Tables are the most important data structure in Oracle. The most important table access operations are as follows:

1. TABLE ACCESS: Self-explanatory.

2. MAT_VIEW ACCESS: Materialized views store the results of a query as a table. The underlying data structure is identical to a table; it just has a different name.

3. FAST DUAL: DUAL is a special table used for generating data. Reading from DUAL in modern versions of Oracle never requires reading from disk.

4. FIXED TABLE: Similar to reading from DUAL, Oracle's dynamic performance views are populated by memory structures. Reading from V$ views does not require disk access.

5. EXTERNAL TABLE ACCESS: Reads from operating system files to create a table on the fly.

The following are the options for table access operations:

1. FULL: Full table scans are the fastest way to read a large percentage of data from a table, as they can take advantage of multi-block reads.

2. BY [LOCAL|GLOBAL] INDEX ROWID [BATCHED]: Quickly accesses a row's physical location, based on a ROWID stored in an index. Indexes may store data used for filtering, but not necessarily all the data needed from the table row. Each index entry contains a ROWID that can be used to quickly access the table data. The LOCAL and GLOBAL keywords are relevant for partitioned tables. The BATCHED option is a newer feature where Oracle will try to batch the ROWIDs so it won't have to access the same table block more than once.

3. BY USER ROWID: Quickly accesses a row's physical location, based on a ROWID stored in a table or a literal. This operation is perhaps the fastest way to access data, so storing and retrieving data by ROWID can be helpful. On the other hand, rows can move locations when data changes, so be careful when storing a ROWID.

4. SAMPLE: Returns a random sample of data from a table.

5. CLUSTER: Clustered tables can store two tables pre-joined together. (In practice this option is rarely used anymore, other than a few dictionary tables.)

Index Access

The most common index operations are as follows:

1. INDEX: B-tree indexes are a vital data structure for performance. Indexes are generally used for quickly retrieving a small percentage of data from a table.

2. BITMAP INDEX/AND/OR/MINUS/CONVERSION: Bitmaps are ideal for low-cardinality columns, like statuses. Multiple AND and OR operations can be quickly performed by combining bitmap indexes. B-tree indexes can be converted into bitmaps for quick comparisons.

3. DOMAIN INDEX: Custom index types. These operations are rare unless we're using advanced options like Oracle Text.

4. FIXED TABLE (FIXED INDEX): Dynamic performance views can also have indexes that only reside in memory.

Most of these index options only apply to B-tree indexes:

1. RANGE SCAN: The most common type of index access. This option efficiently traverses the B-tree and can quickly return a small percentage of rows.

2. UNIQUE SCAN: Similar to range scan but stops after it finds one row.

3. FAST FULL SCAN: Reads the index like a skinny version of the table and can use fast multi-block reads. Good option if we need to retrieve a large percentage of rows and all of the relevant columns are in the same index.

4. FULL SCAN: Reads data from the index in order. Reading data in a specific order requires slower single-block reads but provides presorted results.

5. SCAN (MIN/MAX): Similar to a range scan, but only needs to traverse the first or last path of a B-tree to get the minimum or maximum value. (This option has a child operation named FIRST ROW.)

6. SKIP SCAN: Occurs when the leading column of a multicolumn index cannot be used. This option is inefficient and is a sign that we may want to create another index.

Grouping and Sorting

Grouping and finding distinct values can be done with either the HASH or SORT operation. Those operations can have an option of either GROUP BY or UNIQUE. Hashing is usually faster than sorting, but in rare cases we may need to force the optimizer's decision with a hint like /*+ NO_USE_HASH_AGGREGATION */.

The SORT operation can also be used for options like ORDER BY, CREATE INDEX, JOIN (to order the results before a MERGE JOIN), and AGGREGATE (which is used when there's an aggregate function without any grouping).

Other than the AGGREGATE option, which doesn't actually sort the data, we should try to avoid these slow SORT operations. However, sorting can be fast if it includes the option STOPKEY. STOPKEY means the processing stops after the first N rows, perhaps because of a ROWNUM or FETCH.

Similar to sorting and hashing, there is also a WINDOW operation, which is used for analytic functions. Analytic functions are powerful and fast and are usually a better option than writing self-joins. But watch out for nested WINDOW operations. If multiple analytic functions use different PARTITION BY or ORDER BY clauses, there will be a WINDOW SORT operation for each one. All that sorting can get expensive.

Set Operators

There are four set operators we can use to combine queries: INTERSECT, MINUS, UNION, and UNION ALL. (21c added EXCEPT as a synonym for MINUS and added an ALL option for MINUS and INTERSECT.) We might expect each command to have a separate operation, but those four commands only map to three execution plan operations: INTERSECTION, MINUS, and UNION-ALL. The UNION operator is converted to a UNION ALL operation, plus a SORT UNIQUE child operation. That extra sorting operation is why we should always use a UNION ALL if we know the values are already distinct.

Oracle may convert queries to use set operations. Instead of only using one type of access on the whole table, sometimes it is better to access a table multiple times with different techniques and combine the results. With table expansion, Oracle can query different partitions in different ways. With OR expansions, Oracle can query different conditions in different ways – usually with different indexes. For both types of transformations, the new plan may look twice as large as the original, and the two halves will be put together with a CONCATENATION or UNION ALL operation.

Optimizer Statistics

Optimizer statistics are so vital to performance that Oracle has several operations dedicated to gathering them:

1. STATISTICS COLLECTOR: Gathers optimizer statistics in the middle of an execution plan, for adaptive query plans. An adaptive query plan can dynamically change itself if the actual cardinalities are different than the expected cardinalities. For example, an adaptive query plan may default to use nested loops for what it thinks is a join involving a small number of rows, but it will switch to a hash join if the number of rows is unexpectedly large.

2. APPROXIMATE NDV: Gathers an approximate distinct count in a single pass, without sorting or hashing.

3. OPTIMIZER STATISTICS GATHERING: Gathers optimizer statistics while the table is being created. If gathering statistics only requires a single pass and we're loading a large amount of data, we might as well gather the stats at the same time.

Gathering optimizer statistics can be slow, so we want to be aware of the preceding operations. If statistics are already gathered, we don't need to duplicate the effort later. Or if the table doesn't need statistics, we can suppress those operations with hints.

Parallel

Parallelism is a great opportunity to significantly improve the performance of slow SQL statements. Optimizing parallelism is tricky and requires careful attention to the syntax and execution plan. The following are the main parallel operations:

1. PX BLOCK: Reads blocks of data in parallel.

2. PX SEND: Sends the blocks up the execution plan to the next step. The option determines how the blocks are sent, which is an important decision. For small results, a BROADCAST option may work well – it sends all rows to all parallel servers. For large results, a HASH option may work well – it divides the rows among the parallel servers. There are several other options not discussed here.

3. PX RECEIVE: Receives rows from a PX SEND.

4. PX COORDINATOR: The final parallel operation that coordinates and controls the child parallel operations.

The following example demonstrates how picky the syntax can be and how even subtle execution plan differences can be significant. First, let's look at a statement where every step is run in parallel:

```
--Fully parallel SQL statement.
alter session enable parallel dml;

explain plan for
insert into engine
select /*+ parallel(8) */ * from engine;

select * from table(dbms_xplan.display);
```

Id	Operation	...	IN-OUT	PQ Distrib
0	INSERT STATEMENT	...		
1	PX COORDINATOR	...		
2	PX SEND QC (RANDOM)	...	P->S	QC (RAND)
3	INDEX MAINTENANCE	...	PCWP	
4	PX RECEIVE	...	PCWP	
5	PX SEND RANGE	...	P->P	RANGE
6	LOAD AS SELECT (HYBRID TSM/HWMB)	...	PCWP	
7	OPTIMIZER STATISTICS GATHERING	...	PCWP	
8	PX BLOCK ITERATOR	...	PCWC	
9	TABLE ACCESS FULL	...	PCWP	

```
Note
-----

  - Degree of Parallelism is 8 because of hint
```

The following code has a small change. Instead of using the hint PARALLEL(8), the code uses the hint PARALLEL(ENGINE, 8). Spend a minute to compare the execution plans between the previous example and the following example:

```
--Partially parallel SQL statement.
alter session enable parallel dml;

explain plan for
insert into engine
select /*+ parallel(engine, 8) */ * from engine;

select * from table(dbms_xplan.display);
```

```
------------------------------- ... -------------------
|Id|Operation                  | ... |IN-OUT|PQ Distrib|
------------------------------- ... -------------------
| 0|INSERT STATEMENT           | ... |      |          |
| 1| LOAD TABLE CONVENTIONAL|   ... |      |          |
| 2|  PX COORDINATOR          | ... |      |          |
| 3|   PX SEND QC (RANDOM)    | ... | P->S |QC (RAND) |
| 4|    PX BLOCK ITERATOR     | ... | PCWC |          |
| 5|     TABLE ACCESS FULL    | ... | PCWP |          |
------------------------------- ... -------------------
```

Note

- Degree of Parallelism is 8 because of table property
- PDML disabled because object is not decorated with parallel clause
- Direct Load disabled because no append hint given and not executing in parallel

The plan differences are caused by the hint type. Parallelism has statement-level and object-level hints. We almost always want to use statement-level hints. If we're going to run one operation in parallel, we might as well run all operations in parallel. (However, there are some important exceptions. For example, we wouldn't want to run tiny, correlated subqueries in parallel.) The hint PARALLEL(8) tells Oracle to run everything in parallel. The hint PARALLEL(ENGINE, 8) tells Oracle to only parallelize the *read* from the ENGINE table.

In the first example, when we use a statement-level hint, both the INSERT and the SELECT operations are run in parallel. We can tell because there's a "PX" operation above the (poorly named) LOAD AS SELECT operation. And the LOAD AS SELECT operation also means the first example is using a fast direct-path load, whereas the second example uses a slow LOAD TABLE CONVENTIONAL.

Notice that parallel plans contain a column named "IN-OUT." Ideally, we want to use parallel servers for both the producers and the consumers of the rows. The value P->S means that the parallel results are compressed into a single server and the next steps are run serially. We want to see P->S as late as possible, which means we want to see it near the top of the execution plan. In the second, slow example, the P->S happens in the middle.

These examples demonstrate the difficulty of properly hinting statements and how carefully we need to read the execution plans. We should use hints when we're telling Oracle something that it can't figure out for itself; the statement-level parallel hint tells Oracle that this query is important enough to us that we're willing to use multiple threads to speed it up. We should not use hints to tell Oracle exactly how to do its job; the object-level parallel hint tells Oracle exactly which table to parallelize. But that simple rule for deciding how to use hints doesn't always work. The degree of parallelism, the 8 in the hint, is arguably a mistake. If the number was excluded, Oracle would automatically determine the degree of parallelism. In my experience, those automatic degrees of parallelism are not stable enough, and I prefer to hard-code a number like 8 to represent a "medium amount of resources." Clearly, that number may not work for you. Finding the right number, or relying on the automated number, is something we have to find through trial and error.

Partition

The partition operation names are self-explanatory and match the partition types. For example, it's obvious what PARTITION HASH, PARTITION LIST, PARTITION RANGE, and PARTITION REFERENCE are for.

The relevant options aren't too complicated, but they are important and worth briefly discussing:

1. ALL: Retrieves all partitions from a table. This option means that partitioning isn't helping at all. We may need to check our conditions and ensure that we're filtering by the partitioned columns.

2. SINGLE: Retrieves data from only a single partition, which means partition pruning is probably working optimally.

3. ITERATOR: Retrieves data from a range of partitions, which means partition pruning is working, but not necessarily optimally.

Similar to parallel operations, partitioning is complex and has a few special columns in execution plans. The columns "Pstart" and "Pstop" list the partition numbers being used. Those numbers tell us how well the table is being pruned to a smaller size. Sometimes the value will be KEY, which means the partition number depends on a variable or a lookup from another table.

Partition operations can also be stacked if the table is subpartitioned. Both operations are named PARTITION, but the child operation is really for the subpartitions. The following example demonstrates what a simple partition execution plan looks like. (The example uses an unusual system table because that table is already subpartitioned and simply reading the table does not require a partitioning option license.)

```
--Partition execution plan example.
explain plan for select * from sys.wri$_optstat_synopsis$;

select * from table(dbms_xplan.display);
```

```
----------------------------------  ...  -----------------
| Id  | Operation                 | ...  | Pstart| Pstop |
----------------------------------  ...  -----------------
|   0 | SELECT STATEMENT          | ...  |       |       |
|   1 |  PARTITION LIST SINGLE    | ...  |     1 |     1 |
|   2 |   PARTITION HASH ALL      | ...  |     1 |    32 |
|   3 |    TABLE ACCESS FULL      | ...  |     1 |    32 |
----------------------------------  ...  -----------------
```

In the preceding output, we can see two PARTITION operations, one for partitioning and one for subpartitioning. On my system the table has one partition and 32 subpartitions. All partitions are read since the query does not filter the table, so the Pstart and PStop values match the number of partitions and subpartitions.

Filter

FILTER is an important and misunderstood operation. Unfortunately, the word "filter" has two different meanings in execution plans. Most frequently a "filter" is a condition applied to limit the results and is listed in the "Predicate Information" section of an

execution plan. But a FILTER operation is quite different. A FILTER operation also applies
a condition, but the result of that condition dynamically changes the execution plan.

A good example of a FILTER operation happens when a query is based on a form
with many inputs. If a user enters a value for an input, the query should only return rows
that match that value. If a user leaves a value empty for an input, the query should return
all rows. Matching one value is a good candidate for an index, and matching all values is
a good candidate for a full table scan. With the FILTER operation, the execution plan can
have both paths and choose the right one at run time.

Notice how the following execution plan is really two separate plans put together.
The fastest plan will be chosen at run time:

```
--Filter example.
explain plan for
select *
from launch
where launch_id = nvl(:p_launch_id, launch_id);

select * from table(dbms_xplan.display(format => 'basic'));
```

```
-------------------------------------------------------------
| Id | Operation                    | Name            |
-------------------------------------------------------------
|  0 | SELECT STATEMENT             |                 |
|  1 |  VIEW                        | VW_ORE_D33A4850 |
|  2 |   UNION-ALL                  |                 |
|  3 |    FILTER                    |                 |
|  4 |     TABLE ACCESS BY INDEX ROWID| LAUNCH        |
|  5 |      INDEX UNIQUE SCAN       | LAUNCH_PK       |
|  6 |    FILTER                    |                 |
|  7 |     TABLE ACCESS FULL        | LAUNCH          |
-------------------------------------------------------------
```

The preceding trick does not happen with all semantically equivalent versions of the
query. For example, the FILTER operation disappears if we replace WHERE LAUNCH_ID
= NVL(:P_LAUNCH_ID, LAUNCH_ID) with WHERE LAUNCH_ID = :P_LAUNCH_ID OR :P_
LAUNCH_ID IS NULL. Searching for one or all values is a scenario where we need to use
cryptic code to ensure the best execution.

Other

Many operations are straightforward and don't tell us any actionable information. For example, the SEQUENCE operation is self-explanatory. But that doesn't mean we can ignore those operations; if a SEQUENCE operation is slow, then we should examine the sequence settings, like the cache size.

Some operations are repeated multiple times, making it difficult to monitor the progress of SQL statements. For example, a NESTED LOOPS join may call child operations a large number of times. Repetition can also happen with operations like CONNECT BY and RECURSIVE WITH PUMP. The progress estimates provided by V$SESSION_LONGOPS are meaningless if we don't know how many times an operation will repeat.

REMOTE operations also deserve special attention. Joining data on the same database is hard enough; pulling information across database links is powerful but potentially slow.

Operations may help explain how our query was transformed into a different query before execution. The VIEW operation is just a logical grouping of operations and may be an inline view or a schema object view. The operation VIEW PUSHED PREDICATE is telling us that one of the predicates in the main query was pushed into one of the subqueries. Predicate pushing is usually a good thing, but we want to know when our query is being rewritten in case we need to stop that transformation.

A single operation can represent a call to another programming language, which could represent an almost infinite amount of work. XMLTABLE EVALUATION, XPATH EVALUATION, JSONTABLE EVALUATION, and MODEL represent languages embedded in SQL. The most common non-SQL operation is COLLECTION ITERATOR, which represents rows being generated by a PL/SQL table function. We should be skeptical of execution plans that involve non-SQL languages. The optimizer does a great job of estimating times and building execution plans for declarative code. But the optimizer is almost completely blind to how procedural code will work, and it has to make wild guesses.

TEMP TABLE TRANSFORMATION occurs when a common table expression is turned into a temporary table. If the common table expression is called more than once, it may be cheaper for Oracle to store the results in a temporary table than to rerun the query.

Cardinality and Optimizer Statistics (Building Execution Plans I)

Cardinality and optimizer statistics are the keys to understanding how Oracle decides which operations to use in an execution plan. Cardinality refers to the number of items, like the number of rows or the number of distinct values. Optimizer statistics are what Oracle uses to estimate the cardinality.

The tough part of building execution plans is deciding when one set of algorithms and data structures outperform another. As Chapter 16 visually demonstrated, the fastest algorithm often depended on the "input size" of the X axis. In Oracle, that input size is the cardinality. The only way to know which operations are the fastest is to accurately estimate the cardinality.

This section tries to convince you to focus on the cardinality of execution plans and the importance of good optimizer statistics. The next chapter discusses how to gather those statistics to fix bad cardinality estimates.

Cardinality Is Important

The word *cardinality* has two slightly different meanings in Oracle. Cardinality means the number of rows returned. Cardinality can also mean the number of *distinct* rows returned. A high-cardinality column like a primary key has many distinct values, and a low-cardinality column like a status code has few distinct values.

The following are two simple examples showing the cardinality of two drastically different plans. First, let's find all the launches that took place at the White Sands Missile Range, an important military testing area in New Mexico. (For brevity, the examples use a hard-coded SITE_ID.) White Sands is a popular launch site with 6590 launches. As we can see from the "Rows" column in the following explain plan, the optimizer estimates that White Sands has 6924 launches. (The estimated cardinality may be different on your machine.) The estimate is not perfect, but it's good enough for Oracle to understand that this query returns a large percentage of rows from the LAUNCH table. Therefore, Oracle builds an execution plan with a full table scan:

```
--Full table scan example.
explain plan for select * from launch where site_id = 1895;

select * from table(dbms_xplan.display(format => 'basic +rows'));
```

```
---------------------------------------
|Id|Operation            |Name  |Rows |
---------------------------------------
| 0|SELECT STATEMENT |      | 6924|
| 1| TABLE ACCESS FULL|LAUNCH| 6924|
---------------------------------------
```

Let's change the query to count the launches from a remote pad on Johnston Island. This site was used for Operation Fishbowl, which can be summarized as "let's blow up a thermonuclear weapon in space and see what happens." Unsurprisingly, the military only used that launch site once. Oracle estimates the condition will return 14 rows, which is a small enough percentage to warrant an index range scan:

```
--Index range scan example.
explain plan for select * from launch where site_id = 780;

select * from table(dbms_xplan.display(format => 'basic +rows'));
```

```
-----------------------------------------------------------
|Id|Operation                           |Name       |Rows |
-----------------------------------------------------------
| 0|SELECT STATEMENT                    |           |   14|
| 1| TABLE ACCESS BY INDEX ROWID BATCHED|LAUNCH     |   14|
| 2|  INDEX RANGE SCAN                   |LAUNCH_IDX2|   14|
-----------------------------------------------------------
```

Without any intervention, Oracle correctly knows when to use a full table scan and when to use an index range scan. Most of the time, everything works out fine, but we can't take this magic for granted. We need to understand exactly what's going on so we can fix things when the system breaks. As you can imagine, real execution plans can get much more complicated than this.

Oracle needs to understand the cardinality (distinctness) of the columns and expressions to estimate the final cardinality of each operation (the number of rows returned). Estimating a single equality condition is tricky enough, but our SQL statements also have ranges, compound expressions, etc.

Luckily, when we focus on cardinality, there are a bunch of things we don't need to worry about. We don't need to worry about the time it takes to execute functions or expressions. If we were doing scientific programming, we might look for small loops and try to find tiny performance differences between functions like SUBSTR vs. REGEXP_ SUBSTR. In database programming, the time to process data in the CPU is almost always irrelevant compared with the time it takes to read the data. We need to worry about the algorithms used to read and process our data, not the speed of small function calls. (However, there are exceptions; if we call a custom PL/SQL function a billion times, then we need to worry about context switching and the performance of the function.)

Comparing estimated cardinalities with actual cardinalities is the best way to know if a plan is good. (The simple techniques for finding the actual cardinalities are discussed in the next chapter.) If all the relevant objects are available, such as indexes, and the estimates are accurate, there's a good chance the plan is optimal. Part of SQL tuning is finding out when and why the cardinality estimate is wrong. Another part of SQL tuning is thinking about better operations and how to make them available. Creating better paths for the optimizer requires understanding the available operations and understanding all the Oracle features and data structures that enable them. For example, if our query has a slow nested loop operation, we may need to rewrite a condition into an equality condition to enable a hash join operation.

Cardinality Differences

It's important to understand when cardinality differences matter. In the preceding examples, both estimates were wrong but were still good enough.

It can be useful to think of cardinality estimates as only returning two possible values: big or small. To check if Oracle chose the right value, the *percent* difference is more important than the *absolute* difference. In the first example, the cardinality estimate was wrong by an absolute difference of 334 rows (6924 estimate – 6590 actual). But 334 out of 6590 isn't so bad. In the second example, the cardinality estimate was wrong by an absolute difference of 13 rows (14 estimate – 1 actual).

The second example was off by an order of magnitude, but the optimizer still made a good decision. We need to adjust our expectations for the optimizer estimates. There's no precise definition of how "wrong" the result can be before it matters. But as a rule of thumb, don't worry about the estimates until they're off by more than an order of magnitude.

Think about the graphs in Chapter 16, which compared different algorithm run-time complexities like O(N) vs. O(M*LOG(N)). There is a large difference between the graphs at the extremes, but there's also a large area in the middle where the performance is about the same. Database algorithms are not highly sensitive – a small difference in cardinality won't generally cause huge problems.

But don't think this large range of acceptable values means cardinality estimates are easy. Cardinality mistakes are multiplicative, not additive. If one estimate is off by 10x and another estimate is also off by 10x, they can combine to off by 100x. Luckily, to fix this problem, we may only need to fix one of the bad estimates. Oracle can make good decisions as long as the estimates are in the right ballpark.

Cost Doesn't Matter

The optimizer is officially called the cost-based optimizer. Oracle generates an internal number, a cost, for each operation. I removed the cost from most of the execution plans displayed in this book because the cost is usually worthless for tuning.

The cost is certainly helpful internally to Oracle. And we can use the cost to quickly compare the resource consumption an execution plan will use. But the cost is just an *estimate*. And the cost doesn't always meaningfully add up in execution plans. It's pointless for us to look at an execution plan's cost and arbitrarily say, "Oh, that number is too much."

It's more meaningful to measure SQL statements by the time they take to run. The time estimate column is more useful than the cost, even though the time estimate is often wildly inaccurate. The next chapter shows how to measure *actual* time, instead of merely estimating time. With the actual time, we can tell which statements and operations are truly the most expensive, and we won't have to guess.

Optimizer Statistics

Optimizer statistics are the key to generating good cardinality estimates. In theory, due to the halting problem, it is impossible to always accurately predict run times. In practice, with the right statistics, the optimizer can almost always generate useful predictions. The following list includes all the different types of optimizer statistics, roughly ordered by importance:

1. *Table*: Number of rows and the size of the table in bytes and blocks. Cardinality is still the most important metric, but the size of the table in bytes is useful for estimating the time to read the data, especially in a data warehouse.

2. *Column*: Number of distinct values, nulls, high and low values, and column usage information. Column usage is important because the optimizer won't gather histograms on a column that's never meaningfully used in a query.

3. *Histogram*: Detailed information about the most popular values of each column. Histograms were helpful in our previous LAUNCH example because most SITE_IDs only have a few rows, but a few SITE_IDs have many rows.

4. *Index*: Number of B-tree levels, rows, distinct values, and clustering factor (which can be used to tell us how efficient an index is).

5. *Partition*: Table, column, histogram, and index statistics are also generated for each partition.

6. *Extended statistics*: Selectivity of expressions or combinations of columns.

7. *Temporary tables*: Similar to regular tables, but stats can be generated for global temporary, private, or materialized common table expressions. Global temporary table statistics can be per session or global. Getting these statistics right can be tough since the data changes so frequently.

8. *System*: I/O and CPU performance. This information can help produce more meaningful time estimates. And knowing the difference between single-block read time and multi-block read time can help more accurately estimate differences between index range scans and full table scans. Useful information in theory, but rarely used in practice.

9. *SQL plan directive*: Automatically record statistics about cardinality mistakes for expressions and joins and adjust estimates the next time. Disabled by default.

10. *SQL profile*: Contains information to modify estimates for a specific SQL statement. SQL profiles contain hints that can improve estimates or force plan changes.

11. *User defined*: Procedural code can have custom statistics information using ASSOCIATE STATISTICS or Oracle data cartridge interface.

12. *Inline view*: Through hints like CARDINALITY, we can create fake estimates for inline views.

As we should expect, almost all of the preceding information can be found in the data dictionary. Optimizer statistics are usually stored along with the main metadata tables, such as DBA_TABLES, DBA_TAB_COLUMNS, DBA_INDEXES, etc.

Optimizer Statistics Example

Understanding exactly where the cardinality estimates come from can be difficult. We rarely need to know the precise details about how an execution plan was generated. But in case we ever need those details, and to help demystify the optimizer, this section includes a simple example of generating and reading an optimizer trace (10053).

Previously, we examined the execution plan of this query: SELECT * FROM LAUNCH WHERE SITE_ID = 1895. The optimizer estimated the query would return 6924 rows. But where did the number 6924 come from? We can trace the execution plan generation and discover exactly how that estimate was derived.

The following commands generate an optimizer trace file and then find the location of that file. Finding trace files may be tricky, because trace files are constantly generated, and we need to access the server file system:

```
--Generate an optimizer trace file:
alter session set events='10053 trace name context forever, level 1';
select /* force hard parse */ * from launch where site_id = 1895;
alter session set events '10053 trace name context off';

--Find the latest .trc file in this directory:
select value from v$diag_info where name = 'Diag Trace';
```

The trace file is huge, may take a minute to generate, and is full of cryptic numbers and abbreviations. In that large file, we are only interested in the section with information about the SITE_ID column. The numbers in the trace may be different on your machine, but the math should work out the same way. The following is the relevant section of the trace file from my database:

...

```
  Column (#12): SITE_ID(NUMBER)
    AvgLen: 4 NDV: 1579 Nulls: 0 Density: 0.000195 Min: 0.000000 Max:
2.000000
    Histogram: Hybrid  #Bkts: 254  UncompBkts: 5552  EndPtVals:
254  ActualVal: yes
  Estimated selectivity: 0.098163 , endpoint value predicate, col: #12
  Table: LAUNCH  Alias: LAUNCH
    Card: Original: 70535.000000  Rounded: 6924  Computed: 6923.914805Non
Adjusted: 6923.914805
```

...

To create the final estimate of 6924, Oracle must determine how selective the predicate SITE_ID = 1895 is, and it must then multiply that selectivity by the estimated number of rows in the table. Selectivity is a number between 0 and 1 that represents the probability of a predicate returning a row from a table. Selectivity calculations can sometimes be simple. For example, if an equality predicate on a column usually returns five rows from a table with ten rows, the selectivity is 0.5. But in our more realistic example, instead of using simple averages, Oracle uses histograms to calculate the selectivity of popular values. Histograms are generated when optimizer statistics are gathered. While normal column statistics include information about the average selectivity of the whole column, histograms calculate the selectivity for both ranges of values and for popular values.

The following data dictionary query shows that SPACE.LAUNCH.SITE_ID has a hybrid histogram. The histogram was built on a 5552-row sample – the same number we saw in the trace file:

```
--Column statistics for SPACE.LAUNCH.SITE_ID.
select histogram, sample_size
from dba_tab_columns
where owner = 'SPACE'
   and table_name = 'LAUNCH'
   and column_name = 'SITE_ID';

Histogram   SAMPLE_SIZE
---------   -----------
HYBRID             5552
```

Histograms can have up to 254 buckets. Each bucket includes information about a range of values, as well as an endpoint count for the most popular values. SITE_ID 1895 is a popular value and is the endpoint with a count of 545:

```
--Histogram bucket for 1895.
select endpoint_repeat_count
from dba_histograms
where owner = 'SPACE'
   and table_name = 'LAUNCH'
   and column_name = 'SITE_ID'
   and endpoint_value = 1895;

ENDPOINT_REPEAT_COUNT
---------------------
                  545
```

Unfortunately, the number 545 is not in the trace file. We just have to know to look it up in the data dictionary. When we combine the trace file numbers with the data dictionary numbers, we can finally see how Oracle came up with the estimate of 6924 rows:

```
Selectivity = Number of Sampled Values / Number of Sampled Rows
0.098163 = 545 / 5552
Estimated Cardinality = Total Rows * Selectivity
6924 = 70535 * 0.098163
```

Playing optimizer detective is painful; if you got lost in the preceding trace files and queries, there's no need to go back and study them further. The point of this exercise is to show that generating estimates requires many optimizer statistics. If we need to, we can use tracing and the data dictionary to completely debug how estimates are generated. In the next chapter, we'll learn how to change those values to get better execution plans.

Transformations and Dynamic Optimizations (Building Execution Plans II)

When building execution plans, Oracle is not limited to precisely the query we wrote and is not limited to only the information available at one point in time. Oracle can rewrite our queries with transformations. And Oracle can make our SQL run progressively faster with dynamic optimizations.

Transformations

Oracle does not have to run the pieces of a SQL statement in the exact order they are written. Oracle can transform the query into many different, but logically equivalent, versions, to build the optimal execution plan.

For the most part, these transformations are cool magic tricks that happen behind the scenes. But it's important to know what Oracle is capable of; if we thought SQL statements really were executed exactly as is, then we would be rightfully worried about using multiple inline views in large SQL statements. And we need to know when Oracle is making a bad transformation so we can prevent it. And we need to know when Oracle is not performing a transformation so we can compensate for it with weird or repetitive code.

Transformations only occur within a single SQL statement. However, there are features where one SQL statement may indirectly affect another: SQL plan directives, statistics gathering, and block caching can cause one query to indirectly change the run time of another query.

The most common transformations don't have a specific name. Oracle frequently changes the order of items in a SQL statement. Predicates and joins are trivially reordered. The join syntax is converted from ANSI syntax to the traditional syntax and sometimes the other way around. DISTINCT operations can occasionally be moved sooner or later in an execution plan. But there are also many important transformations with specific names.

Predicate pushing is when predicates in the outer query are pushed into the inner query. This important transformation can explain why performance significantly changes when two queries are put together. The following code is a trivial example of predicate pushing:

```
--Trivial example of predicate pushing.
select * from (select * from launch) where launch_id = 1;
```

Oracle does not retrieve all the rows from the LAUNCH table in the inline view and *then* filter the rows with the predicate. Instead, Oracle rewrites the SQL statement and directly applies the predicate to the table. By transforming the statement, Oracle can then use an index unique scan to quickly retrieve a small number of rows.

View merging allows the optimizer to move tables in and out of inline views. Oracle may not need to join two large tables together if their results are going to be joined to a smaller table later. For example, in the following code, Oracle does not need to directly join the relatively large tables SATELLITE and LAUNCH. Instead, Oracle can first join the smaller tables SITE and LAUNCH. That first join generates a tiny number of rows, and then those small, intermediate results can be efficiently joined to the larger SATELLITE table:

```
--Simple view merging example.
select *
from
(
    select *
    from satellite
    join launch using (launch_id)
) launch_satellites
join site
    on launch_satellites.site_id = site.site_id
where site.site_id = 200;
```

Subquery unnesting happens when Oracle rewrites a correlated subquery as a join. If the main query returns a small number of rows, and the subquery is fast, it makes sense to run the subquery for each row. But if the main query returns a large number of rows, or the subquery is slow, it makes sense to use a regular join operation. In the following example, there are many rows in LAUNCH and SATELLITE, and Oracle will almost certainly convert the query into a regular join:

```
--Simple unnesting example.  (Launches with a satelite.)
select *
from launch
where launch_id in (select launch_id from satellite);
```

OR expansion can happen to SQL statements with multiple OR conditions. The statement can be broken into multiple pieces and then stitched together with UNION ALL.

There are many other available transformations. If we want to see the final version of our SQL statement, we can look in a 10053 trace, like the trace file that was generated a few pages earlier. If we open that trace file and search for "final query after transformations," we will find the final version of our query. Unfortunately, the transformed versions of our queries are painful to read. Luckily, we don't really care about the final version of our code; we only care about the way it runs. The execution plan tells us how the transformed SQL statement is executed, which is what really matters.

Transformations are an interesting topic, but we don't need to fully understand transformations to use them. Being aware of transformations helps because sometimes we need to make our own transformations. Sometimes rewriting a query to use a different but equivalent syntax will bring unexpected performance boosts. If predicate pushing doesn't occur, then we may need to repeat predicates. If subquery unnesting doesn't occur, then we may need to manually convert subqueries into joins.

Adaptive Cursor Sharing and Adaptive Statistics

Execution plans can change at run time depending on bind variables, previous runs, and information gathered from other queries. We got a taste of Oracle's dynamic execution plan abilities with the FILTER operation. Recent versions of Oracle have introduced many new dynamic optimizations.

Adaptive cursor sharing lets a SQL statement have multiple execution plans depending on bind variables. Consider the previous example query: SELECT * FROM LAUNCH WHERE SITE_ID = 1895. That query is not entirely realistic; in practice, we would almost certainly use a bind variable instead of hard-coding a literal.

Without access to literals, estimating cardinalities could become significantly harder. If we replaced 1895 with :SITE_ID, how would Oracle know if the predicate is selective and best served with an index or if the predicate is not selective and best served with a full table scan?

The solution is that Oracle can *peek* at the bind variable value to create the first execution plan. If the relevant column data is skewed and has a histogram, the optimizer makes a note to check the bind variable next time. During the next run, if the bind variable value skews in a different way, Oracle creates a different execution plan.

Adaptive statistics can change plans by gathering statistics during run time. These features are mostly disabled with the parameter OPTIMIZER_ADAPTIVE_STATISTICS defaulting to false. In a data warehouse environment, where it's worth spending extra time building execution plans, it might be worth enabling these features.

Dynamic statistics, also known as dynamic sampling, can make up for missing or inadequate optimizer statistics. Before a SQL statement is run, if statistics are missing, dynamic sampling gathers statistics based on a small number of blocks.

Dynamic sampling is important and can be tricky to tune through the parameter OPTIMIZER_DYNAMIC_SAMPLING. But we almost certainly want this feature enabled, so we can at least gather dynamic statistics when a table is completely missing statistics. Because of dynamic sampling, missing statistics are better than bad statistics. Oracle can compensate for missing statistics, but bad statistics will be believed. Dynamic sampling in the Note section of an execution plan is often a sign that we forgot to gather stats. This phrase in an execution plan is a big red flag: "dynamic statistics used: dynamic sampling (level=2)."

Automatic reoptimization, known in 11g as cardinality feedback, can help improve subsequent executions of the same statement. For statements that are missing statistics or are sufficiently complex, Oracle records the actual cardinality for different operations. If the actual and estimated cardinalities are sufficiently different, the optimizer may build a different execution plan the second time.

SQL plan directives store statistical information about predicates. This information can be shared among many queries. The optimizer is able to make good cardinality estimates for simple equality and range predicates, but we shouldn't expect the optimizer to be able to predict complex expressions the first time they run. With SQL plan directives, the optimizer can learn from its mistakes.

Adaptive Query Plans

Adaptive query plans let SQL statements have multiple execution plans. Queries can choose the best plan at run time, based on live cardinality numbers. When Oracle adds a STATISTICS COLLECTOR operation before a join, that operation records the actual cardinality and chooses the best plan accordingly. This feature is incredibly powerful but also makes execution plans harder to read.

Let's create an example of adaptive query plans using a simple join between LAUNCH and SATELLITE. The following two queries join the tables, but only for a specific launch year. There were many launches in 1970, but none in 2050, since the data set only goes to the year 2017. We want the first query, on a popular year, to use a hash join to deal with the large number of results. And the second query, on an unpopular year, should use a nested loop join to deal with the small number of results. But the way the predicates are written makes it hard for Oracle to accurately estimate the cardinality:

```
--Launches in a popular and unpopular year.
select * from launch join satellite using (launch_id)
where to_char(launch.launch_date, 'YYYY') = '1970';

select * from launch join satellite using (launch_id)
where to_char(launch.launch_date, 'YYYY') = '2050';
```

There are several ways we could provide more information to the optimizer. We could rewrite the predicate into a simpler date range, create an expression statistic, create a function-based index on the expression, etc. In older versions of Oracle, we would need to consider those approaches if the query was causing problems. But in modern versions, Oracle can fix the execution plan on the fly.

For this more complex example, the EXPLAIN PLAN command isn't good enough. We don't want to look at an explain plan that shows what Oracle thinks it will run – we need to view an execution plan that shows what Oracle actually ran.

For more complex SQL tuning, we typically need to start by finding the SQL_ID of the statement. Once we have the SQL_ID, we can plug it into many different programs.

But the SQL_ID is not always trivial to find. There may be many false positives, especially since queries on V$SQL will return the query on V$SQL. Programs that return their own source code are called quines. Writing quines is an interesting challenge in most programming languages. In Oracle SQL, creating quines is annoyingly easy to do, and we need to adjust our queries to avoid them.

The following SQL statement can be used to find the actual execution plan, for either 1970 or 2050. (To save space I commented out one of the relevant predicates, instead of displaying the query twice.)

```
--Find actual execution plan of either 1970 or 2050 query.
select * from table(dbms_xplan.display_cursor(
   sql_id =>
   (
      select distinct sql_id from v$sql
      where sql_fulltext like '%= ''1970''%'
      --where sql_fulltext like '%= ''2050''%'
```

```
        and sql_fulltext not like '%quine%'
    ),
    format => 'adaptive')
);
```

Notice that the preceding query gets the actual plan, not just the estimated plan, by using DBMS_XPLAN.DISPLAY_CURSOR instead of DBMS_XPLAN.DISPLAY. That new function requires the SQL_ID, which is found with the subquery against V$SQL. To avoid quines, the subquery needs the predicate SQL_FULLTEXT NOT LIKE '%QUINE% '. Finally, to get the adaptive query plan details, we must use the argument FORMAT => 'ADAPTIVE'. With these advanced, dynamic features, finding the execution plans can be tricky.

If we get the error "ORA-01427: single-row subquery returns more than one row," that means we have multiple queries that match the text. If that error happens, we'll need to add additional predicates. Or we could SELECT * FROM V$SQL in a separate step to find the SQL_ID.

The following is the execution plan for the 1970 query. Adaptive plans include all possible operations and use a hyphen to mark the inactive operations. Notice how the following plan has a NESTED LOOPS operation. But those operations are inactive, and instead a HASH JOIN is used, which is more appropriate for joins that involve a large number of rows:

```
--------------------------------------------...-
|  Id | Operation                    |...|
--------------------------------------------...-
|    0 | SELECT STATEMENT            |...|
|  *  1 |  HASH JOIN                 |...|
|-   2 |   NESTED LOOPS              |...|
|-   3 |    NESTED LOOPS            |...|
|-   4 |     STATISTICS COLLECTOR   |...|
|  *  5 |      TABLE ACCESS FULL     |...|
|- *  6 |      INDEX RANGE SCAN      |...|
|-   7 |     TABLE ACCESS BY INDEX ROWID|...|
|    8 |    TABLE ACCESS FULL        |...|
--------------------------------------------...-
...
Note
```

```
-----
    - this is an adaptive plan (rows marked '-' are inactive)
```

If we change the DBMS_XPLAN query to look for 2050 instead of 1970, we get the following execution plan. Now the operations are reversed – NESTED LOOPS is active, and HASH JOIN is deactivated. There are no rows yet for the year 2050, so a NESTED LOOPS operation is ideal:

```
---------------------------------------------...-
|  Id  | Operation                        |...|
---------------------------------------------...-
|    0 | SELECT STATEMENT                 |...|
|- *  1 |  HASH JOIN                       |...|
|    2 |   NESTED LOOPS                   |...|
|    3 |    NESTED LOOPS                  |...|
|-   4 |     STATISTICS COLLECTOR         |...|
|  *  5 |      TABLE ACCESS FULL           |...|
|  *  6 |      INDEX RANGE SCAN            |...|
|    7 |     TABLE ACCESS BY INDEX ROWID|...|
|-   8 |   TABLE ACCESS FULL              |...|
---------------------------------------------...-

...
Note
-----
    - this is an adaptive plan (rows marked '-' are inactive)
```

We need to understand dynamic optimizations because we need to know when we're not looking at the real execution plan. And if we don't see dynamic execution plans, we're potentially missing out on great optimizations. A lack of dynamic execution plans implies there are incorrectly set parameters, perhaps for OPTIMIZER_FEATURES_ENABLE, COMPATIBLE, or CURSOR_SHARING.

These dynamic options are silently running in the background and improving a huge number of statements without any intervention. But sometimes, providing additional and more accurate information can lead to a *worse* execution plan. These performance degradations are often the only time when developers and administrators directly see these optimizations happening.

Unfortunately, it is all too common for developers and administrators to disable features for everyone just because they encountered one minor problem with a feature. We must resist the urge to change something at the *system* level when we could fix the same problem at the *query* level. Dynamic optimizations don't have to be perfect to be useful. Do not disable dynamic optimizations unless you are sure they are causing more than one problem.

Summary

This chapter is only a brief summary of many complicated topics. Even the 878-page *SQL Tuning Guide* and the 396-page *Database Performance Tuning Guide* do not cover everything we need to know. My goal is merely to introduce you to multiple ways of thinking about SQL performance concepts. Execution plans, operations, cardinality, transformations, and dynamic optimizations build a great foundation for becoming a SQL tuning expert.

Inevitably, we will abuse many of the concepts in this chapter and either solve the wrong problem or try to solve the right problem the wrong way. We're going to make epic mistakes and waste a lot of time. We need to appreciate the complexity of performance tuning and have the humility to admit when we're mistaken. For every SQL tuning problem, there is an answer that is clear, simple, and wrong.

We must embrace multiple ways of thinking about performance tuning and adapt a breadth-first approach to problem solving. As developers, we dream of having that one perfect idea for a new program, instead of having ten good ideas for mediocre programs. We need to reverse that attitude for performance tuning and learn how to quickly try the ten good ideas.

CHAPTER 18

Improve SQL Performance

It's time to use our theories and start building practical SQL tuning solutions. This chapter starts with high-level applications and then drills down through databases and SQL statements, until we get to operations.

Before we start looking for opportunities to improve performance, we all need to agree to do something: stop guessing. We should *never* have to guess what program is slow, what database is slow, what statement is slow, or what operation is slow. No matter what part of our technology stack we are investigating, there are multiple tools that can easily and precisely tell us what is slow. If we ever find ourselves guessing what is slow, we're making a mistake.

Performance tuning must be guided by numbers, not guesses. Without objective measures we will become afflicted with Compulsive Tuning Disorder. We must focus on the part of the system that is slow, and we must strenuously resist the temptation to tune things that won't help. It's great to refactor and to challenge ourselves to learn more. But when we're confronted by an urgent performance problem, we need to focus on the numbers instead of only fixing things that feel slow or are easy to fix.

We earn the right to guess after years of skepticism, measuring, and testing. It takes a while to build a good intuition that we can use for quick breadth-first searches of performance fixes. But experts still need the humility to know that their guesses could be wrong.

Application Tuning: Logging and Profiling

Most performance problems start with a slow application. Application tuning is a huge topic and is outside the scope of this book. Even PL/SQL applications are not the main topic of this book, but they are worth briefly discussing. We at least need to know enough about PL/SQL to help us find our slow SQL statements.

© Jon Heller 2023
J. Heller, *Pro Oracle SQL Development*, https://doi.org/10.1007/978-1-4842-8867-2_18

Logging

It's important to instrument our PL/SQL programs. There are many free and powerful logging utilities, but don't let their complexity deter you from logging. Even creating our own simple logging is still much better than doing nothing.

This instrumentation doesn't need to be fancy. Logging can be as simple as writing messages and timestamps to a table whenever important processes start or stop. Or we could use DBMS_APPLICATION_INFO to help Oracle track data in the database or use UTL_FILE to write data to a file system. Be careful using DBMS_OUTPUT; it's useful for small debugging, but it can be slow and cause overflow errors on larger systems.

For example, we could use DBMS_APPLICATION_INFO to track the resource consumption of the examples in this chapter. We could run the following PL/SQL block at the beginning of each section, to set the session's module name and action name:

```
--Set the session's MODULE and ACTION.
begin
    dbms_application_info.set_module
    (
        module_name => 'Chapter 18',
        action_name => 'Logging'
    );
end;
/
```

At the end of the chapter, we could compare the different sections by querying the ACTION and MODULE columns in views and tables like V$ACTIVE_SESSION_HISTORY and DBA_HIST_ACTIVE_SESS_HISTORY. (Those two objects are discussed more thoroughly later in this chapter.) The following is an example of how to compare activity:

```
--Which sections in this chapter used the most resources.
select action, count(*) session_count
from v$active_session_history
where module = 'Chapter 18'
group by action
order by session_count desc;
```

Many database programs automatically set that session metadata. And Oracle's default logging already captures other metadata such as the username and the machine name. In most cases we can find performance problems without that extra session information, but we should think about adding extra logging information *before* we run into problems.

This logging information is helpful for finding historical trends. Oracle has a wealth of performance information, but the default information is not organized for our applications and is not stored for long. Instrumenting our code doesn't take much effort and should be a part of every project.

Profiling: DBMS_PROFILER

Oracle does not track the time for every execution of every line of code. That much instrumentation would quickly consume all available storage. But if we set up DBMS_ PROFILER, we can temporarily gather the total amount of time and number of calls to every line in our PL/SQL program. Profiling provides better data than logging but cannot entirely replace logging; profiling has significant overhead and should not be enabled by default.

If we're using an IDE like PL/SQL Developer or Toad, profiling is as simple as clicking a few buttons before starting the PL/SQL program. Other IDEs require a bit more setup; we have to run PROFTAB.SQL from the installation directory RDBMS/ADMIN, call DBMS_PROFILER functions to start and stop profiling, and then query the tables PLSQL_ PROFILER_DATA, PLSQL_PROFILER_RUNS, and PLSQL_PROFILER_UNITS. It is annoying that Oracle doesn't fully automate that setup process, but if we are tuning PL/SQL programs, then the setup is absolutely worth the effort.

To demonstrate profiling, let's create a simple and slow procedure:

```
--Create a test procedure that runs many COUNT operations.
create or replace procedure test_procedure is
   v_count number;
begin
   for i in 1 .. 10000 loop
      select count(*) into v_count from launch order by 1;
   end loop;
```

```
   for i in 1 .. 10000 loop
      select count(*) into v_count from engine order by 1;
   end loop;
end;
/
```

Now we need to enable profiling and run the procedure. With the right IDE, enabling means clicking a button to enable profiling and then running this PL/SQL block:

```
--Run the procedure for profiling.  (Takes about 15 seconds.)
begin
   test_procedure;
end;
/
```

Every IDE or query has a different display. Figure 18-1 shows the profiler report in PL/SQL Developer. The results are sorted by descending run time, so the most important lines are at the top. There's even a spark bar chart to quickly show us which lines use the most time.

Unit	Line	Total time ▲	Occurrence	Text
TEST_PROCEDURE	5	16,502	10000	select count(*) into v_count from launch
TEST_PROCEDURE	9	726	10000	select count(*) into v_count from engine
TEST_PROCEDURE	4	1	10001	for i in 1 .. 10000 loop
TEST_PROCEDURE	8	1	10001	for i in 1 .. 10000 loop
ANONYMOUS BLOCK	1	0	2	
TEST_PROCEDURE	11	0	1	end;
ANONYMOUS BLOCK	2	0	2	
TEST_PROCEDURE	1	0	1	procedure test_procedure is
ANONYMOUS BLOCK	3	0	1	

Figure 18-1. *DBMS_PROFILER report*

The preceding profiler report tells us exactly which part of the procedure to focus on. There's no need to guess about what part of the program we think is slow. The run time of line 5 is much greater than all the other lines put together. This report makes it clear that we would be crazy to spend time optimizing anything other than line 5.

Profiling: DBMS_HPROF

Tools like the hierarchical profiler and tracing can provide more data than DBMS_ PROFILER. I tend to avoid these advanced tools because they are harder to use and access. I'd rather have easily accessible good data than poorly accessible great data. But as long as we are using tools that tell us the actual run time, instead of just guessing, we're well ahead of the curve. The hierarchical profiler is gradually becoming more powerful and easier to use, and it may completely replace DBMS_PROFILER someday.

The main problem with the hierarchical profiler is that it requires elevated privileges and server access to set up and use. The setup scripts change with every version, and the following instructions and code will probably only work on 18c and later:

First, we must grant access to the package:

```
--Grant access to DBMS_HPROF.  Must be run as SYS.
grant execute on sys.dbms_hprof to &your_user;
```

The following code creates a table to hold the profiler report, enables the profiler, and runs and analyzes TEST_PROCEDURE:

```
--Create table to hold the results.
create table hprof_report(the_date date, report clob);

--Generate report.
declare
    v_report clob;
    v_trace_id number;
begin
    --Create profiler tables, start profiling.
    dbms_hprof.create_tables(force_it => true);
    v_trace_id := dbms_hprof.start_profiling;
    --Run the code to profile.
    test_procedure;
    --Stop profiling, create and store the report.
    dbms_hprof.stop_profiling;
    dbms_hprof.analyze(v_trace_id , v_report);
    insert into hprof_report values(sysdate, v_report);
```

```
   commit;
end;
/

--View the report.
select * from hprof_report;
```

The report contains a lot of great information but is much too wide to fit on this page. Figure 18-2 contains only a portion of one of the many tables of data in the HTML report. If we read the entire report, it would verify what we already learned from DBMS_ PROFILER – only one line in the procedure is worth tuning. The part of the report not shown also provides the relevant SQL_ID, which is needed if we want to tune the slow SQL statement.

Function Elapsed Time (microsecs) Data sorted

```
15824265 microsecs (elapsed time) & 20003 function calls
```

Subtree	Ind%	Function	Ind%	Descendants	Ind%	Calls	Ind%	Function Name
15824207	100%	37978	0.2%	15786229	99.8%	1	0.0%	SPACE.TEST_PROCEDURE.1
15301083	96.7%	15301083	96.7%		0	0.0%	10000	50.0%	SPACE.TEST_PROCEDURE.
485146	3.1%	485146	3.1%		0	0.0%	10000	50.0%	SPACE.TEST_PROCEDURE.
58	0.0%	58	0.0%		0	0.0%	1	0.0%	SYS.DBMS_HPROF. static
0	0.0%	0	0.0%		0	0.0%	1	0.0%	SYS.DBMS_HPROF.STOP_P]

Figure 18-2. *Partial hierarchical profiler report*

Application Tuning Through Batching

Batching commands is the simplest way to improve the performance of database-centric applications. Putting commands together is usually an easy change that doesn't touch any of the business logic. Batching commands helps in two ways – it reduces overhead, and it provides more opportunities for the optimizer.

There can be a significant amount of overhead for database calls. The most obvious overhead is network round-trip time. And there are many hardware and software optimizations available when multiple commands and data are processed together: improved cache and memory access, SIMD, fewer context switches, less parsing, etc.

As discussed in Chapter 16, we can quickly see huge returns from the 1/N harmonic progression of reduced overhead. We can keep our application changes simple because we don't need to aggregate everything to get huge performance improvements. Combining commands in groups of 100 is 99% optimized.

Batching commands gives the optimizer more opportunities to do something clever. Writing one large SQL statement, instead of multiple small SQL statements, lets Oracle apply a larger number of transformations and operations. On the other hand, batching also gives the optimizer more opportunities to make a mistake, but no risk, no reward. When those mistakes happen, instead of giving up on batching, we can apply our SQL tuning skills.

The biggest opportunities to batch commands are installation scripts, OLTP applications, and data warehouses.

Installation and Patch Scripts

Improving the performance of installation and patch scripts is more important than many developers realize. There are only a few *direct* benefits from tuning those scripts, since they are not seen by end users and they are rarely run on production systems. But the *indirect* benefits are huge, since faster installation and patching enable developers to more quickly experiment and test.

The difference between an installation script that takes 1 minute and an installation script that takes 10 minutes is much more than 9 minutes. When reinstalling only takes a minute, we have no excuse not to test whatever crazy idea pops into our heads. But this advice only applies to developers who are using a private database development model.

For example, the following code shows a typical installation script. The script uses nine commands to create and populate a table. Most automatic script generation programs create code that looks like this:

```
--Typical slow and wordy install script.
create table install_test1(a number);

alter table install_test1 modify a not null;

alter table install_test1
   add constraint install_test1_pk primary key(a);

insert into install_test1(a) values(1);
commit;
```

```
insert into install_test1(a) values(2);
commit;
insert into install_test1(a) values(3);
commit;
```

We can shrink that entire script into a single command:

```
--Faster and more compact install script.
create table install_test2
(
   a not null,
   constraint install_test2_pk primary key(a)
) as
select 1 a from dual union all
select 2 a from dual union all
select 3 a from dual;
```

The constraints are built inline along with the table, and the initial values are created with a CTAS (create table as SELECT). Simple changes like the preceding batching can easily make installation scripts run an order of magnitude faster.

By default, SQL*Plus reads one command and sends the command to the server, the server parses and executes the command, the server replies with a feedback message, and SQL*Plus displays the feedback message. Actually executing the commands usually isn't the slowest part of SQL*Plus scripts. Avoiding the overhead of sending commands and receiving statuses can be a huge performance boost.

There are many other tricks we can use to simplify installation scripts. For example, instead of using a huge number of UNION ALL commands, here are some tricks with hierarchical queries and predefined collections:

```
--Alternate ways to generate numbers and other values.
select level a from dual connect by level <= 3;
select column_value a from table(sys.odcinumberlist(1,2,3));
select column_value a from table(sys.odcivarchar2list('A','B','C'));
```

We could take batching a step further and use the CREATE SCHEMA syntax, which allows us to create multiple objects in a single command. In practice, that command goes a bit too far – debugging errors becomes difficult when our entire script is just a single command. And remember that we only need to batch *most* of our commands to get huge performance benefits.

Anonymous blocks can also help us improve the performance of automatically generated scripts. Many database utilities don't understand the importance of batching, and instead they create long lists of separate commands. It may be impractical to rewrite automatically generated scripts to use tricks like UNION ALL. But we can still realize most of the performance benefits by turning the list of commands into an anonymous block. Simply add BEGIN at the front of the script and END; at the end.

Anonymous blocks are sent to the database as a single PL/SQL command. The server still needs to spend extra time parsing and executing multiple commands. But at least the network traffic and SQL*Plus overhead are eliminated.

OLTP Applications

OLTP applications are by nature one-at-a-time systems. But there are still plenty of opportunities to batch commands, both by working with the applications and by working with SQL.

There used to be a battle between application developers and database developers – who would get to implement the "business logic"? The application developers won, and we database developers need to accept defeat. There's no point trying to talk application developers out of using object-relational mapping tools like Hibernate (although it might be worth considering SQL-centric frameworks like jOOQ). Instead, we need to work with the existing tools and be willing to provide advanced SQL when possible.

ORM tools may not always generate ideal SQL statements, but that doesn't mean we don't have any control over the SQL generation. Before we worry about row-by-row processing, we need to ensure the application is not making even bigger mistakes; applications should not frequently reconnect to the database, and applications should only use one command per logical change. Applications should certainly not make changes one *column* at a time. We do not want our application to INSERT an empty row and then run separate commands to UPDATE each column one at a time.

Few systems are purely OLTP; there are usually some batch processes somewhere. Those processes are good candidates for advanced SQL or at least taking advantage of the applications' batch processing features. Options like JDBC batch execution can create huge performance improvements.

We don't have to choose purely object-relational mapping or purely SQL. ORM frameworks can still run native queries and call custom PL/SQL functions. At the very least we can create views for the application. We shouldn't limit ourselves purely to database-agnostic features – otherwise, why did we pay for Oracle?

Data Warehouses

For data warehouses it's especially important to use one large SQL statement instead of multiple small SQL statements. But we have to be mindful of possible resource consumption problems.

A single, large SQL statement is faster and consumes less *cumulative* resources than multiple, small statements. However, a single, large SQL statement may consume more resources at a specific *point in time*. Statements hold on to undo and temporary tablespace until they complete. Ideally, we should size our undo and temporary tablespace to accommodate our large queries. If that's not possible, we're forced to use multiple, small statements.

For example, the fastest way to delete many rows from a table is usually with a single DELETE statement. But large DELETE statements are notorious resource hogs, and a large enough statement could potentially fail because there's not enough undo tablespace available. One easy option for breaking up large DELETEs is to repeat the statement multiple times, but with a condition like ROWNUM <= 1000000. Removing only one million rows at a time may significantly reduce the maximum undo tablespace required. But repeating DELETE statements will be much slower, because Oracle has to re-read the whole segment each time. It can be difficult to find the right number of rows that perfectly balances improved performance with reduced point-in-time resource consumption.

The fastest alternative to a large DELETE statement is a DROP or TRUNCATE command. Obviously, we can't always remove all the contents of a table. But if the table is partitioned, we may be able to drop only a single partition. For example, if we have to delete from large tables to remove old rows, we could set up the table as interval partitioned by date and simply drop the oldest partitions.

Another fast alternative to large DELETEs is to recreate the entire table, minus the rows we want to delete. If we create the table with the NOLOGGING option and insert data with the APPEND hint, we can avoid generating costly redo and undo data. The problem with that alternative process is that it's not trivial to recreate tables. Table recreation scripts often forget to handle all the dependencies, like comments and grants.

Tuning large DML gets even trickier when our process requires multiple INSERT, UPDATE, and DELETE statements. We may need to perform large changes quickly but still enable consistent access to the old version of the table. It's hard to get high performance, flexibility, lower resource usage, and consistency all at the same time. But Oracle technologies like materialized views and partition exchanging can help. Or we could simply use a synonym that points to the original table, work on a new table, and then switch the synonym when we're done.

Batching can also be implemented with DBMS_PARALLEL_EXECUTE, parallel pipelined functions, and DBMS_SCHEDULER. Those advanced options are useful, but don't get carried away with them. For example, parallel pipelined functions are a great option for parallelizing procedural code. But that advanced feature still isn't going to perform as fast as a single, parallel SQL statement.

We don't always need to sacrifice performance, availability, or consistency. In a data warehouse, the only thing we need to sacrifice is the extra time to build advanced solutions.

Database Tuning

Database tuning is a large topic, and condensing the 396-page *Database Performance Tuning Guide* into a few pages doesn't do the topic justice. This book focuses on SQL tuning, and database tuning is usually a task for a DBA instead of a developer. But we can't completely ignore database turning; there is considerable overlap between the two topics because database performance is mostly the sum of SQL performance. For developers, the most important database tuning topics are measuring performance, Automatic Workload Repository,[1] Active Session History, Automatic Database Diagnostic Monitor (ADDM), and advisors.

Measure Database Performance

Time model statistics are a good way to measure database performance. The simple wall-clock run time of an application is not always a fair way of measuring performance. It is better to measure the "DB time," the amount of time the database spends processing a request.

---

[1] This chapter assumes you have licensed the Diagnostics and Tuning Packs and are using Enterprise Edition. The Diagnostics Pack covers AWR and ASH, and the Tuning Pack covers DBMS_SQLTUNE and advisors. If your edition or license doesn't allow access to the tools discussed in this chapter, the concepts still apply, but you will need to look for free alternatives. For example, Statspack can be used in place of AWR, and Simulated ASH can be used in place of ASH.

If an application takes a minute, but the "DB time" is only 1 second, the problem is not with Oracle. One of the toughest parts of performance tuning is convincing people when the database is *not* the problem. We can use the "DB time" metric to prove our case. That metric is displayed in many places, like in AWR reports, V$SQL, etc. "DB time" can be broken down into subcategories, which we can see in views like V$SYS_TIME_ MODEL or V$SESS_TIME_MODEL.

Wait events help us classify the bottlenecks that affect our database and SQL statements. Our programs need to consume scarce resources and often must wait for them to become available. By counting the wait events and categorizing them into wait classes, we can diagnose some system and statement problems.

There are 14 wait classes, and their names are self-explanatory: Administrative, Application, Cluster, Commit, Concurrency, Configuration, CPU, Idle, Network, Other, Queueing, Scheduler, System I/O, and User I/O. (The wait class "CPU" is not a real wait class. For some strange reason, Oracle does not give a name to the most popular wait event.)

Wait classes like User I/O and CPU are generally considered "good" waits; it's inevitable that our processes will use at least some I/O and CPU resources. But a large number of waits in other wait classes are often a sign of trouble.

We can look at a summary of the wait events by wait class and quickly identify problems. Programs like Oracle Enterprise Manager use the wait events to create activity graphs, like in Figure 18-3. By looking at the following graph, we can quickly tell there was a lot of Concurrency (the red area on the left), followed by a lot of CPU (the green area on the right). Based on this chart, we would be wise to initially ignore the CPU section (which likely represents real work) and focus on the Concurrency section (which may represent a large amount of work held up by something like an uncommitted transaction).

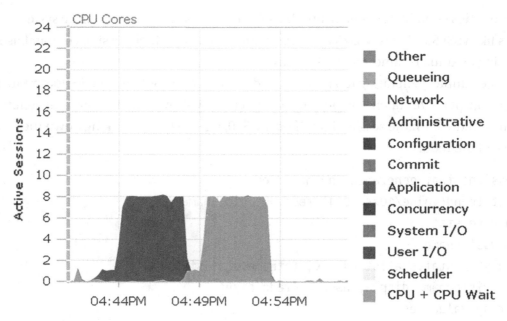

Figure 18-3. *Example of a (modified) top activity report from Oracle Enterprise Manager*

The EVENT column is stored in many tables and views, such as V$SESSION and V$ACTIVE_SESSION_HISTORY. The EVENT column is useful, but we have to remember that NULL really means "CPU." The following is an example of viewing wait events and wait classes for recent session activity:

```
--Recent wait events.
select
    nvl(event, 'CPU') event,
    nvl(wait_class, 'CPU') wait_class,
    v$active_session_history.*
from v$active_session_history
order by sample_time desc;
```

There are literally thousands of wait events, and most of them are documented in the "Oracle Wait Events" chapter of the *Database Reference*. As we look at reports on wait events, we will learn which waits are expected and which ones imply trouble. We must always focus on the most popular waits. There will always be some weird waits with a small number of occurrences. We don't want to waste our time investigating waits that rarely happen.

Statistics contain *cumulative* numbers for active sessions and the entire system. Views like V$SESSTAT and V$SYSSTAT are useful for finding which sessions or databases are using an unusual amount of resources.

For example, generating too much redo data can be a problem. Oracle doesn't track redo usage per SQL statement, but the following query shows the sessions that generated the most redo. With the session identifier, the SID, we can begin tracking down the source of the redo:

```
--Sessions that generated the most redo.
select round(value/1024/1024) redo_mb, sid, name
from v$sesstat
join v$statname
    on v$sesstat.statistic# = v$statname.statistic#
where v$statname.display_name = 'redo size'
order by value desc;
```

```
REDO_MB    SID    NAME
-------    ---    ---------
360        268    redo size
2          383    redo size
1          386    redo size
...
```

Metrics contain *ratios* of statistics per time. The most popular metric is the previously discussed "buffer cache hit ratio," which tells us what percentage of our data is read from memory instead of disk.

While statistics give us grand totals, it's more useful to know the ratios at different points in time. For example, if a database system has generated 1 petabyte of I/O that doesn't necessarily tell us much, the importance of that number depends on how long the instance has been running. But if we look at the metric "I/O megabytes per second," like in the following query, the numbers are a more meaningful measurement of system performance:

```
--Current I/O usage in megabytes per second.
select begin_time, end_time, round(value) mb_per_second
from gv$sysmetric
where metric_name = 'I/O Megabytes per Second';
```

```
BEGIN_TIME            END_TIME               MB_PER_SECOND
-------------------   -------------------    -------------
2022-08-14 20:45:13   2022-08-14 20:46:13              263
```

Sampling is the most useful way to measure performance in Oracle. We may *think* we want to know every detail about every SQL execution, but in reality, that much information would be overwhelming. In practice, it's good enough to take a picture of what is happening every second and then do our tuning based on those samples. Sampling is used in Automatic Workload Repository and Active Session History, which are described in the next sections.

We can solve 99.9% of our performance problem with sampling. Capturing all of the activity of a database, like with tracing, is almost never necessary in modern versions of Oracle. We don't have to build our own sampling system or make any decisions about how often to sample or what to sample. Oracle's sampling systems are always running, for every user and every statement, and the data is easily accessible through views. We couldn't disable Oracle's sampling even if we wanted to, whereas tracing must be manually enabled, can use significant resources, and requires external, non-relational tools to understand. Once again, easily accessible good data is better than poorly accessible perfect data.

Automatic Workload Repository (AWR)

Automatic Workload Repository and Active Session History are perhaps the most powerful database tuning features. These programs are always gathering important information; we only have to query a table or call a package to generate a report. (But beware of licensing issues. Even though Oracle makes everything available by default, that does not mean we are licensed to use it.)

To demonstrate how these tools work, let's do something stupidly slow and see if Oracle can tell us how to fix our code. First, let's run the following PL/SQL block. This block queries the table SATELLITE a large number of times, using a non-indexed column. This code doesn't do anything yet – it's only generating activity to show up on our reports later:

```
--Repeatedly count a large table using a non-indexed column.
--Takes about 10 minutes to run.
declare
    v_count number;
```

```
begin
   dbms_workload_repository.create_snapshot;
   for i in 1 .. 200000 loop
      select count(*)
      into v_count
      from satellite
      where orbit_class = 'Polar';
   end loop;
   dbms_workload_repository.create_snapshot;
end;
/
```

Automatic Workload Repository collects a huge amount of information and divides that information into snapshots. By default, a snapshot contains 1 hour of data, and that data is retained for 8 days. AWR can be configured to take more or less snapshots and retain the data for more or less time, but those changes can require more space. The snapshots let us generate reports for ranges of time, create baselines of performance, and compare time periods. There are many ways to customize AWR collection. For example, the preceding PL/SQL block called the function DBMS_WORKLOAD_REPOSITORY. CREATE_SNAPSHOT so we don't have to wait an hour for our slow query to show up on reports.

Although most DBAs still use operating system files and scripts for generating AWR reports, the easiest way to generate AWR reports is with SQL. First, we need to find the relevant snapshot range, like this:

```
--Find snapshots, for generating AWR reports.
select dbid, snap_id, begin_interval_time, end_interval_time
from dba_hist_snapshot
order by begin_interval_time desc;
```

If we pick the DBID and the latest two SNAP_ID values from the preceding query, we can plug them into the following function to generate an AWR report:

```
--Generate AWR report.
select *
from table(dbms_workload_repository.awr_report_html(
   l_dbid     => 985569476,
```

```
    l_inst_num => 1,
    l_bid      => 6709,
    l_eid      => 6710
));
```

The preceding table function returns many rows, each of which is a line in an HTML report. If we copy all of the lines, paste them into a text file, save the file as an .html file, and open the file with a browser, we'll find a wealth of information. We can also query AWR data directly using the many DBA_HIST_* views.

AWR reports can be huge and overwhelming, so I'm not even going to bother including screenshots. Open the AWR report generated earlier, and scroll down to the "Main Report," which contains a menu of the different sections. If we click "SQL Statistics" and then click "SQL ordered by Elapsed Time," we should see our SQL statement that counted the rows from the SATELLITE table. An HTML table shows how many times the statement ran, how long it took, etc.

Active Session History (ASH)

An active session is a database session that is waiting for a resource such as CPU, memory, disk I/O, a locked row, etc. Practical database performance tuning only cares about these active, waiting sessions. If a session is intentionally sleeping or waiting for a client command, then the performance problem is not inside our database. Every second, Oracle creates one row for every session that is actively waiting on something. This data is called the Active Session History (ASH).

ASH is related to AWR, but there are crucial differences. ASH data is sampled every 1 second, whereas AWR data is sampled every 10 seconds. ASH data only lasts about 1 day, whereas AWR data lasts 8 days by default. Both ASH and AWR can be viewed through reports, but it's more common to only access ASH through queries. ASH data is mainly queried through V$ACTIVE_SESSION_HISTORY, while AWR data is mainly queried through DBA_HIST_ACTIVE_SESS_HISTORY.

The 112 columns in V$ACTIVE_SESSION_HISTORY tell us a lot about what recently happened in our database. If you haven't used that view before, you should spend a minute browsing through the rows and columns. That dynamic performance view is stored entirely in memory structures, and it is always fast to query, whereas the AWR tables may contain a huge amount of historical data that can slow down our queries. Since performance tuning is best done in a breadth-first manner, the query performance advantage of ASH over AWR is important.

One of the best ways to understand ASH is to calculate the number of active sessions by counting the number of rows per `SAMPLE_TIME`. This number of active sessions is a great way to measure database activity. A database that averages only a few samples per timestamp isn't very busy. A database with a hundred samples per timestamp may be too busy.

The relational interface to sampling data is a great tuning opportunity. Canned reports are nice and can fill many needs, but eventually we'll grow our own style of performance tuning and build our own queries and reports. For example, I feel like AWR reports don't have enough details per SQL statement and that sharing and comparing HTML is difficult. In just a single query, I was able to combine AWR and ASH into a text-only chart, showing data just the way I liked it.[2]

Too many developers ignore ASH data because "it's only a sample." But sampling is all we need. If a problem occurs for less than a second and is never caught in a sample, then it's not a problem worth worrying about.

Automatic Database Diagnostic Monitor (ADDM)

Automatic Database Diagnostic Monitor analyzes AWR data and helps find database performance problems. After ADDM finds a problem, ADDM often suggests using one of the automatic advisors to find a specific fix. These processes can be set up to automatically find and fix performance problems.

In practice ADDM and the advisors are not helpful. They are only good at finding simple problems that we can find and fix ourselves. But automated tuning systems should improve in future versions of the database or in a future autonomous database environment.

There are many ways to use ADDM. The following example creates an ADDM report for the same snapshot we looked at before:

```
--Generate ADDM task.
Declare
    v_task_name varchar2(100) := 'Test Task';
```

---

[2] See https://github.com/jonheller1/SQL_Activity_Chart for this open source query.

```
begin
    dbms_addm.analyze_db
    (
        task_name       => v_task_name,
        begin_snapshot  => 6709,
        end_snapshot    => 6710
    );
end;
/
```

We can view the report with another call to DBMS_ADDM. The report may generate a huge number of recommendations, but somewhere in the report, there should be a mention of our query against the SATELLITE table. (But I can't guarantee there will be any recommendations on your system. The long-running PL/SQL block was set to run for about 10 minutes because that's usually long enough to trigger a recommendation, but the recommendation thresholds are not documented.)

```
--View ADDM report.
select dbms_addm.get_report(task_name => 'Test Task') from dual;

...
    Recommendation 1: SQL Tuning
    Estimated benefit is .39 active sessions, 96.77% of total activity.
    -------------------------------------------------------------------
    Action
        Run SQL Tuning Advisor on the SELECT statement with SQL_ID
        "5115f2tc6809t".
        Related Object
            SQL statement with SQL_ID 5115f2tc6809t.
            SELECT COUNT(*) FROM SATELLITE WHERE ORBIT_CLASS = 'Polar'
    Rationale
...
```

ADDM still hasn't actually *tuned* anything yet, but the preceding report has produced helpful information. Pay attention to the report rationales and do not just blindly implement every recommendation. Notice that the preceding output includes the number of active sessions. That number tells us how much database activity we might save by improving this query. If the active sessions benefit is too low, then it's not worth investigating further.

The preceding ADDM output also includes the SQL statement, along with the SQL_ID. The recommended action is to run that SQL statement through the SQL Tuning Advisor, and we'll need the SQL_ID to do that.

Advisors

Oracle has many ways to offer us advice. There is the SQL Tuning Advisor, SQL Access Advisor, Optimizer Statistics Advisor, and views V$SGA_TARGET_ADVICE and V$PGA_TARGET_ADVICE. The SQL Tuning Advisor can examine SQL statement executions and provide ideas for how to make them run faster.

For example, we can use the SQL_ID we previously found in our AWR and ADDM reports. First, we have to create a tuning task, execute that tuning task, and save the task name for later:

```
--Create and execute SQL Tuning Advisor task
declare
    v_task varchar2(64);
begin
    v_task := dbms_sqltune.create_tuning_task(
        sql_id => '5115f2tc6809t');
    dbms_sqltune.execute_tuning_task(task_name => v_task);
    dbms_output.put_line('Task name: '||v_task);
end;
/

Task name: TASK_18972
```

We can view the report by taking the preceding task name and plugging it into the following SQL statement:

```
--View tuning task report.
select dbms_sqltune.report_tuning_task('TASK_18972') from dual;

...
1- Index Finding (see explain plans section below)
```

```
-----------------------------------------------------------------------------
  The execution plan of this statement can be improved by creating
one or more
  indices.
  Recommendation (estimated benefit: 96.64%)
-----------------------------------------------------------------------------
  - Consider running the Access Advisor to improve the physical
schema design
    or creating the recommended index.
    create index SPACE.IDX$$_4A1C0001 on SPACE.SATELLITE("ORBIT_CLASS");
  Rationale
  ---------

...
```

The advice in the preceding report looks correct; creating an index on the ORBIT_ CLASS column would almost certainly help with the query that we just ran thousands of times. The full report also includes metadata, rationales behind the recommendations, and before-and-after execution plans if the recommendation is accepted. The SQL Tuning Advisor can recommend other kinds of changes, such as a SQL profile that can help nudge the execution plan in the right direction. SQL profiles will be discussed later.

Automatic Indexing

Oracle is constantly creating automated processes to simplify development and administration. Automatic indexing was introduced in 19c as one of the key new features in Oracle's autonomous database offerings. Optimizing indexes requires a significant amount of skill and effort, and tools like the Access Advisor and the SQL Tuning Advisor have already been offering index help. This section shows how automatic indexing can put all the automation pieces together to remove most index tasks from developers.

Even if we don't plan to use automatic indexing, we should learn about this feature because it represents the future of Oracle technology. On the other hand, at present, the technology has some significant issues and is probably not ready for use in most production systems. This powerful feature can significantly impact performance, so before using it in production, we should read all the documentation and test it thoroughly.

The first step in implementing automatic indexing is to check the current configuration by querying the data dictionary view DBA_AUTO_INDEX_CONFIG. The parameter AUTO_INDEX_MODE can be set to OFF, REPORT ONLY, or IMPLEMENT. We can begin using this feature by calling the DBMS_AUTO_INDEX package to modify the configuration. (This feature is currently only available on Exadata and autonomous databases, so the first command may fail with the error "ORA-40216: feature not supported.") By enabling report mode, Oracle will create the indexes but will set them to invisible, so they are not used:

```
--Enable REPORT ONLY (invisible indexes).
begin
    dbms_auto_index.configure('AUTO_INDEX_MODE','REPORT ONLY');
end;
/
```

Next, we need to set which schemas we want to automatically index. The following PL/SQL block adds one schema at a time. If you change the schema name, the code will not drop other schemas; it will only add the new schema name to the list:

```
--Allow automatic indexes for the SPACE schema.
begin
    dbms_auto_index.configure('AUTO_INDEX_SCHEMA', 'SPACE', true);
end;
/
```

To test the feature, let's create a large table and then run a query on that table that could obviously benefit from an index:

```
--Create large table, gather stats, run query that needs an index.
create table satellite2 as select * from satellite;

begin
    for i in 1 .. 100 loop
        insert into satellite2 select * from satellite;
    end loop;
end;
/
```

```
begin
  dbms_stats.gather_table_stats(null, 'satellite2');
end;
/

select * from satellite2 where satellite_id = 1;
```

Finally, we have to wait about 30 minutes for the auto-task to run. We should see a new index appear in the activity report generated with this command:

```
--Generate report for the last index created.
select dbms_auto_index.report_last_activity from dual;
```

The report can get quite large and may contain sections that include report dates, summary of indexes created and dropped, details about indexes created and dropped, and verification details that include before-and-after execution plans and statistics. For example, the following is a small section of the report for the slow SQL statement we ran:

```
...
INDEX DETAILS
-------------------------------------------------------------------------------
1. The following indexes were created:
-------------------------------------------------------------------------------
-------------------------------------------------------------------------------
| Owner | Table     | Index              | Key          | Type   | Properties |
-------------------------------------------------------------------------------
| SPACE | SATELLITE2 | SYS_AI_adscrw50ccvut | SATELLITE_ID | B-TREE | NONE      |
-------------------------------------------------------------------------------
...
```

There's a lot more of information available in other places. Instead of generating reports for the last activity, we can use the same package to generate reports for different date ranges. There are several DBA_AUTO_INDEX_* views that tell us what SQL statements were executed, how the indexes and related execution plans were verified, and summary data. We can also track automated indexes in the data dictionary columns DBA_INDEXES. AUTO and DBA_INDEXES.VISIBILITY. If we're not happy with our automated indexes, we can drop them with the package DBMS_AUTO_INDEX.

While the preceding example is seemingly straightforward, there are many unexpected complications that can happen with automatic indexing. First, the preceding example is not reliably reproducible, and I'm not sure why. Perhaps sometimes the query is caught by some sampling algorithm, and other times it isn't. On the other hand, the statement from the previous section, `SELECT COUNT(*) FROM SATELLITE WHERE ORBIT_CLASS = 'Polar'`, was run for 10 minutes, can obviously benefit from an index, and is even flagged by the SQL Tuning Advisor as needing an index, yet the automatic indexer never recommends an index for it. It's difficult to tell what criteria are used, but they obviously aren't sufficient to solve all our missing indexes.

Also, the `REPORT ONLY` mode name is misleading, as it actually creates indexes instead of just reporting on what the task would do if enabled. Setting the indexes to invisible seems like a poor compromise, as invisible indexes can still have real consequences. In my experience, the problem with creating too many indexes isn't that the indexes will be used incorrectly by the optimizer. The main problem with creating too many indexes is that they consume too much space and require extra work when modifying data. Invisible indexes won't be used by our queries, but they still require extra storage space and extra work for index maintenance.

This feature probably isn't ready for production use yet. There are several gotchas in the implementation, the API is a bit rough, the reports aren't always useful or consistent, the feature is only available in a small number of environments, etc.

The whole implementation feels rushed – and considering the way Oracle handled its recent versions, it probably was. But we should still pay attention to automatic indexing and see how it improves in future versions. Autonomous processes like creating indexes, materialized views, zone maps, and more will eventually change the way we work. In the future, the average developer may not need to worry about indexes at all (except for some necessary indexes like for foreign keys). Automatic indexing may take care of 75% of our performance needs, and only a single developer or administrator can handle all the exceptions. I wouldn't create an index in production if I thought it only had a 75% chance of working. But perhaps the lesson here is that we must lower our expectations of automated systems and accept that systems don't need to work 99% of the time to be useful.

Other Tools

Performance tuning requires many tools other than just those listed previously, especially since there's not always a clear difference between a database problem and an operating system problem. For database administrators it's especially important to have knowledge of the server operating system and commands that can diagnose common operating system problems.

But we should be skeptical of buying expensive, closed source programs to help us tune databases. We shouldn't spend money on extra tuning programs unless we can try them first or have a recommendation from a developer we trust. Most performance tuning programs are just expensive, shiny wrappers around the tools that Oracle provides for free.

Investing time and money in a small, proprietary tuning program is risky. Even if the program is helpful now, chances are low that we'll be able to use it in the future. Oracle shops tend to buy only a small number of expensive products. If you are an Oracle developer and change jobs to develop Oracle somewhere else, SQL and PL/SQL are the only skills that you are guaranteed to bring with you.

We should even be cautious of using Oracle Enterprise Manager. OEM is a powerful, useful program, and it has many pages to walk us through performance issues. Unfortunately, OEM is not nearly as reliable as the Oracle database itself. If we grow dependent on OEM, we will eventually have problems when OEM is unavailable or has its own performance problems. We should use the SQL and PL/SQL interfaces for database tuning whenever they are available.

SQL Tuning: Find Slow SQL

The first and most underappreciated step of SQL tuning is finding slow SQL statements. This task is harder than it sounds, especially since our databases run an enormous number of SQL statements. We need to create an organized system for performance troubleshooting, precisely define what "slow" means, and be able to find SQL that is slow right now or was slow in the past.

Get Organized

Every Oracle developer must have an organized collection of worksheets for troubleshooting Oracle performance problems. There are many options for how to organize those files – a directory on our desktop, a GitHub repository, etc. But the files must be somewhere we can easily remember and quickly find – convenience is more important than perfection.

When we run into a problem, we should be able to pull up our trusty worksheet in just a few seconds. As an example, I included my own worksheet in the book's GitHub repository, in the file "Performance.sql". I don't expect you to use my file; we all have different preferences and tuning styles. But you should have something comparable, and it should be easily accessible and allow you to incrementally improve your troubleshooting process. These files will grow into mind maps for how we think about Oracle problems, so there's no one-size-fits-all solution.

Slow Is Based on DB Time

This chapter focuses on things that are slow, but who defines what slow means? To the end users, only the wall-clock run time matters, but focusing only on the run time can cause problems. We are really looking for things that are wasteful – things that use more resources than necessary. We need a metric that is more meaningful than wall-clock run time but something simpler than a complete description of the system's resource utilization.

We don't want to improve the speed of one query at the expense of other processes. For example, replacing a 10-second index access with a 9-second parallel full table scan would improve the run time, but it would be a ridiculous waste of resources. And we don't want to improve the speed if it doesn't matter; if a procedure calls DBMS_LOCK. SLEEP, that procedure is intentionally slow, doesn't use any significant resources, and doesn't need tuning.

Luckily the "DB time" statistic accurately reflects the resource utilization of the database, SQL statements, and operations. The DB time is simply the time spent doing meaningful work in the database. The primary metrics in this chapter, ELAPSED_TIME, number of active sessions, and "% Activity," are all strongly correlated with the DB time. For example, if a parallel query is busy for 10 seconds and uses two parallel servers, the ELAPSED_TIME will be 20 seconds. If a procedure runs for a minute because of DBMS_ LOCK.SLEEP(60), the ELAPSED_TIME will be 0 seconds.

Find Currently Running Slow SQL

Everything we need to know about our SQL can be found inside the database, using SQL. Other than a good IDE, we don't want to rely on expensive, closed source programs to find slow SQL statements.

The dynamic performance view V$SQL is the key to finding currently running SQL statements. When I see a live performance problem, this is the first query I run:

```
--All SQL statements that are currently running.
select
    elapsed_time/1000000 seconds,
    executions,
    users_executing,
    parsing_schema_name,
    sql_fulltext,
    sql_id,
    v$sql.*
from v$sql
where users_executing > 0
order by elapsed_time desc;
```

The preceding query tells us exactly what statements are running on the database right now. Interpreting the columns and expressions is tricky, so the most important columns are briefly described as follows:

1. SECONDS/ELAPSED_TIME: Cumulative database time spent on all executions of the statement.[3] There are always multiple statements running; we need this column so we can focus on the slow ones.

2. EXECUTIONS: Number of times the statement was executed. Tuning a statement that runs once per hour is different than tuning a statement that runs a thousand times per hour.

---

[3] All values in V$SQL are cumulative, but only since the SQL statement has been in the shared pool. It's hard to predict how long statements will be in the shared pool. In practice, the slow statements we care about will stay around for a long time.

3. USERS_EXECUTING: Number of sessions that are running the SQL statement right now. For parallel queries, this number includes each parallel session.

4. PARSING_SCHEMA_NAME: Schema or user that is running the SQL.

5. SQL_FULLTEXT: The exact text of the SQL.

6. SQL_ID: A unique identifier based on a hash of the SQL text. This ID is used in almost all tuning tools and is one of the first things we need to find when tuning. Since SQL_ID is a hash, it is sensitive to space and capitalization. We need to be careful to precisely copy our SQL statements to get the same SQL_ID.

7. V$SQL.*: Every one of these 104 columns is potentially important. The large number of columns is one of the reasons we can't realistically tune using the command line. When there is a performance problem, we have to explore lots of data.

Don't expect to uncover all the mysteries of V$SQL. We may never understand all of the columns, values, or why there are so many seemingly duplicate rows. But don't let the complexity deter you; V$SQL is incredibly useful even if we don't fully comprehend it.

Oracle's definition of what is "running" may not match ours. A SQL statement will show up in V$SQL with one or more USERS_EXECUTING if the cursor is still open. Showing up in V$SQL doesn't mean that Oracle is necessarily doing anything with that statement. It's quite common for programs to run a query, retrieve the first N rows, and then let the query sit there for a while. Oracle doesn't track time spent by the application downloading or processing the rows. A row may appear to be active in V$SQL for a long time but have a tiny ELAPSED_TIME. From a database perspective, we only care about queries with a large ELAPSED_TIME.

Find Historically Slow SQL

Finding SQL that was slow in the past can be more challenging than finding SQL that is slow right now. We need to be able to quickly search through many sources – VSQL, VACTIVE_SESSION_HISTORY, DBA_HIST_ACTIVE_SESS_HISTORY, and DBA_HIST_SQLTEXT. And we need to look for combinations of SQL text, time, username, and many other columns. A good IDE and advanced SQL skills will come in handy.

We also need to remember that data will eventually age out of each of those sources. As a rough estimate, V$SQL will last an hour (or less if the shared pool is manually flushed), V$ACTIVE_SESSION_HISTORY will last a day, and DBA_HIST_* will last 8 days.

SQL Tuning: Find Plans

After we find the slow SQL statement, we're tempted to jump right into finding the plan. But don't overlook the importance of understanding the SQL. The best performance tuning is rewriting SQL into something simpler, finding a way to batch multiple runs of the query, or using an advanced feature. If there's no way to change the SQL to avoid the problem, then we need to dive into the plan. But first, remember that explain plans are the estimated plans and execution plans are the actual plans. It's easy to confuse the two terms, and even the documentation and Oracle programs get them mixed up occasionally.

Graphical Plans Considered Harmful

Do not use your IDE's graphical interface for viewing execution and explain plans. While those graphical reports may look pretty and may be easily generated at the press of a button, graphical plans are always wrong or misleading.

Let's start with a simple example that merely joins SATELLITE and LAUNCH:

```
--All satellites and their launch.
select *
from satellite
left join launch
   on satellite.launch_id = launch.launch_id;
```

In Oracle SQL Developer, we can generate an explain plan by simply pressing F10. Figure 18-4 shows the explain plan generated by SQL Developer.

OPERATION	OBJECT_NAME	OPTIONS	CARDINALITY	COST
⊟─ ● SELECT STATEMENT			43113	784
⊟─ ✕ HASH JOIN		OUTER	43113	784
⊟─ ♂ Access Predicates				
⌐··· SATELLITE.LAUNCH_ID=LAUNCH.LAUNCH_ID(+)				
⊟─ ✕ NESTED LOOPS		OUTER	43113	784
⊟─ ● STATISTICS COLLECTOR				
⌐··· ⊞ TABLE ACCESS	SPACE.SATELLITE	FULL	43113	106
⊟─ ⊞ TABLE ACCESS	SPACE.LAUNCH	BY INDEX ROWID	1	120
⊟─ ◁ INDEX	SPACE.LAUNCH_PK	UNIQUE SCAN		
⊟─ ♂ Access Predicates				
⌐··· SATELLITE.LAUNCH_ID=LAUNCH.LAUNCH_ID(+)				
⌐··· ⊞ TABLE ACCESS	SPACE.LAUNCH	FULL	70535	120
⊟─ Other XML				
⌐···· USE_HASH(@"SEL$2BFA4EE4" "LAUNCH"@"SEL$1")				
⌐···· LEADING(@"SEL$2BFA4EE4" "SATELLITE"@"SEL$1" "LAUNCH"@"SEL$1")				
⌐···· FULL(@"SEL$2BFA4EE4" "LAUNCH"@"SEL$1")				
⌐···· FULL(@"SEL$2BFA4EE4" "SATELLITE"@"SEL$1")				
⌐···· OUTLINE(@"SEL$1")				
⌐···· OUTLINE(@"SEL$2")				
⌐···· ANSI_REARCH(@"SEL$1")				
⌐···· OUTLINE(@"SEL$8812AA4E")				
⌐···· ANSI_REARCH(@"SEL$2")				
⌐···· OUTLINE(@"SEL$948754D7")				

Figure 18-4. *Oracle SQL Developer explain plan display*

There are several things wrong with the preceding output. This query generates an adaptive plan; sometimes the plan will use a hash join, and sometimes the plan will use a nested loop join. Yet the preceding explain plan doesn't make it clear which operations are active and which operations are inactive. Also, the "Other XML" section is confusing – that section contains advanced information that is rarely needed. At the same time, that XML section is incomplete and does not include all of the hints used by the explain plan.

I'm not trying to pick on SQL Developer – it's a great program for database development. Every SQL IDE I've ever used has suffered from similar problems with visualizing plans. For execution and query plans, we should strive for 100% accuracy. When we're working on performance tuning, even the slightest mistake can obscure the problem.

Text Is Best

The EXPLAIN PLAN command and the DBMS_XPLAN package are the best way to display explain plans. For example, the following code generates the explain plan for the simple join between SATELLITE and LAUNCH:

```
--All satellites and their launch.
explain plan for
select *
from satellite
left join launch
   on satellite.launch_id = launch.launch_id;

select * from table(dbms_xplan.display);
```

Figure 18-5 shows the output. (This is another case where I am not following my own advice due to limitations of the medium. Normally, it would be better to copy and paste the raw text of an explain plan, but the 89 characters probably would not fit the width of a printed page.)

```
Plan hash value: 2829467527

---------------------------------------------------------------------------------------
| Id  | Operation            | Name      | Rows  | Bytes |TempSpc| Cost (%CPU)| Time     |
---------------------------------------------------------------------------------------
|   0 | SELECT STATEMENT     |           | 43113 | 7831K |       |    784  (1)| 00:00:01 |
|*  1 |  HASH JOIN OUTER     |           | 43113 | 7831K | 4680K |    784  (1)| 00:00:01 |
|   2 |   TABLE ACCESS FULL  | SATELLITE | 43113 | 4168K |       |    106  (1)| 00:00:01 |
|   3 |   TABLE ACCESS FULL  | LAUNCH    | 70535 | 5992K |       |    120  (2)| 00:00:01 |
---------------------------------------------------------------------------------------

Predicate Information (identified by operation id):
---------------------------------------------------

   1 - access("SATELLITE"."LAUNCH_ID"="LAUNCH"."LAUNCH_ID"(+))

Note
-----
   - this is an adaptive plan
```

Figure 18-5. *Simple explain plan output from DBMS_XPLAN*

The preceding explain plan display is more accurate than graphical visualizations. The output only includes the active hash join, not the inactive nested loop join. The "Note" section warns us that we're looking at an adaptive plan and that there is more information under the surface. As discussed in Chapter 17, if we want to view the inactive operations, we can use this SQL statement:

```
--View all inactive rows of an adaptive plan.
select * from table(dbms_xplan.display(format => '+adaptive'));
```

EXPLAIN PLAN and DBMS_XPLAN have many benefits over graphical representations of explain plans:

1. *Simple, standard format*: DBMS_XPLAN works in any environment and produces output that every Oracle professional is familiar with. Anyone with access to Oracle can reproduce the issue, and anyone can discuss the issue with the same standard names. We cannot assume other developers have access to our favorite IDE.

2. *Easy-to-process output*: The output is easy to save, share, and search. We can store the output in a table, copy the text into Notepad, etc. It's also much easier to compare the output using a diff program, such as WinMerge. Large queries may produce hundreds of lines in the explain plan, and using a diff utility can make tuning much easier. For programming, text is better than pictures.

3. *Includes important sections*: For some bizarre reason, IDEs never display the "Note" section. That section includes essential information. Without the "Note" section, we have to guess if there's something weird going on.

4. *More accurate*: As we saw earlier, IDEs generate slightly wrong results. Another common problem is that some IDEs use a separate session to generate graphical explain plans. Session settings like ALTER SESSION ENABLE PARALLEL DML are not always applied in graphical explain plans.

5. *More Powerful*: DBMS_XPLAN can be scripted and has powerful features described in the next sections.

For a quick check, it's easier to hit F10, F5, CTRL+E, or whatever the shortcut is in our IDE. For serious plan analysis that will be shared with others, always use EXPLAIN PLAN and DBMS_XPLAN. The basic commands are worth memorizing. It's hard to remember all the details, but we can always look up EXPLAIN PLAN in the *SQL Language Reference* and look up DBMS_XPLAN in the *PL/SQL Packages and Types Reference*.

DBMS_XPLAN Functions

The function DBMS_XPLAN.DISPLAY only works for explain plans that were gathered through the EXPLAIN PLAN command. Those explain plans are still estimates, although in practice the estimates are accurate unless there are bind variables or adaptive plans.

The function DBMS_XPLAN.DISPLAY_CURSOR displays the *actual* execution plan of a SQL statement that already ran. In order to identify the SQL statement, this function must be passed a SQL_ID parameter. DISPLAY_CURSOR is especially useful because it displays actual numbers, not just estimates. The importance of actual numbers will be discussed later in this chapter. Explain plans are convenient, especially for quick demonstrations, but if you need to be absolutely certain about the plan, you may want to stick to only using execution plans.

The function DBMS_XPLAN.DISPLAY_AWR can display all of the different execution plans used by a SQL statement. The history goes back as far as the AWR retention period, which defaults to 8 days. This feature is useful for diagnosing problems where a query used to run fast but is now running slow.

DBMS_XPLAN FORMAT Parameter

The most important parameter for the DISPLAY* functions is FORMAT. The FORMAT parameter accepts a space-separated list of options. The most common of these options are BASIC (only display the ID, operation, and name), TYPICAL (display the default columns), and ADAPTIVE (display inactive operations).

In addition to those options, FORMAT also accepts keywords that act as modifiers to execution plans. For example, we may want to display the BASIC format but also include ROWS. On the other hand, we can display the TYPICAL format with everything except the ROWS. The following SQL statements show some combinations of the options:

```
--FORMAT options.
select * from table(dbms_xplan.display(format => 'basic +rows'));
select * from table(dbms_xplan.display(format => 'typical -rows'));
```

There are several other formatting options listed in the manual, as well as several useful hidden options. Either ADVANCED or +OUTLINE will generate output that includes an "Outline Data" section. That new section displays a set of hints that fully describe the plan:

```
--Display Outline Data.
select * from table(dbms_xplan.display(format => 'advanced'));
```

The output is full of cryptic, undocumented hints. The following results only show the "Outline Data" section of the execution plan. Don't spend too much time studying the output; we don't need to understand all of these hints:

```
...
Outline Data
-------------

  /*+
      BEGIN_OUTLINE_DATA
      USE_HASH(@"SEL$2BFA4EE4" "LAUNCH"@"SEL$1")
      LEADING(@"SEL$2BFA4EE4" "SATELLITE"@"SEL$1" "LAUNCH"@"SEL$1")
      FULL(@"SEL$2BFA4EE4" "LAUNCH"@"SEL$1")
      FULL(@"SEL$2BFA4EE4" "SATELLITE"@"SEL$1")
      OUTLINE(@"SEL$1")
      OUTLINE(@"SEL$2")
      ANSI_REARCH(@"SEL$1")
      OUTLINE(@"SEL$8812AA4E")
      ANSI_REARCH(@"SEL$2")
      OUTLINE(@"SEL$948754D7")
      MERGE(@"SEL$8812AA4E" >"SEL$948754D7")
      OUTLINE_LEAF(@"SEL$2BFA4EE4")
```

```
    ALL_ROWS
    DB_VERSION('12.2.0.1')
    OPTIMIZER_FEATURES_ENABLE('12.2.0.1')
    IGNORE_OPTIM_EMBEDDED_HINTS
    END_OUTLINE_DATA
  */
...
```

These hints can be invaluable for solving advanced tuning problems. If a query runs differently on two systems, the "Outline Data" may help explain the difference. And if we're desperate to force the plan to work the same on both systems, we can paste that block of hints into a query. The ADVANCED option also creates an extra section for "Query Block Name/Object Alias," which is helpful for referencing specific objects in custom hints.

Using the outline is a blunt way of tuning and doesn't solve the root cause. But we don't always have time to find the underlying cause of execution plan differences, and we just need to fix things right away.

"Note" Section

Before we go any further with execution plan analysis, we should check the "Note" section. The following are the most common and troublesome notes:

1. *Dynamic statistics used: dynamic sampling (level=2)*: Level 2 implies object statistics are missing.

2. *This is an adaptive plan*: There are multiple versions of the plan, and we're only looking at one right now.

3. *Statistics/cardinality feedback used for this statement*: This plan has corrected itself. The original plan was different.

4. *SQL profile/plan baseline/patch "X" used for this statement*: This plan was influenced or forced to behave a certain way.

5. *Direct load disabled because X*: Direct-path writes can be prevented by parent referential integrity constraints, triggers, and other limitations.

6. *PDML disabled in current session*: Parallel DML is not working, usually because we forgot to run `ALTER SESSION ENABLE PARALLEL DML`.

7. *Degree of parallelism is X because of Y*: The requested DOP and the reason that DOP was used. The DOP is vital information for large queries and will be discussed in more detail later.

Similar to "Note," the "Predicate Information" section can also be important. Our predicates may be secretly converted to a form that doesn't allow index access. For example, if we see the function `NLSSORT` in the predicates, but we didn't explicitly use that function in our query, that means a session or database parameter is forcing a linguistic sort.

Other Ways to Get Execution Plans

Execution plans can be quickly generated in SQL*Plus using the `AUTOTRACE` feature. The command `SET AUTOTRACE ON` will automatically display the results, actual execution plan, and actual statistics from the execution. If we want to ignore the results of the query, we can use the command `SET AUTOTRACE TRACEONLY`.

Execution plan information is also available in the data dictionary in the view `V$SQL_PLAN`. Building execution plans from the views is difficult, but those views can be useful for looking for specific execution plan features. For example, we can use `V$SQL_PLAN` to find out which indexes are used by which statements.

SQL Tuning: Find Actual Times and Cardinalities for Operations

Many developers make a huge mistake by not drilling down further than the execution plan. A SQL statement is a collection of algorithms and data structures – each statement is effectively a whole program. It's meaningless to say, "This program is slow"; we need to know which *part* of the program is slow. We need to drill down and focus on actual operation statistics.

Operations are the atomic unit of SQL tuning.[4] Measuring the actual execution time of operations tells us which algorithms and data structures are the slowest. Measuring the actual cardinalities tells us why Oracle picked the operation. If we have to guess which operations are slowest, we will waste a lot of time. Always use actual numbers when possible.

GATHER_PLAN_STATISTICS

Let's create a slow SQL statement to practice tuning. We'll start with an imaginary ETL process that creates a copy of the LAUNCH table. But the process makes a huge mistake; the process gathers statistics *before* the data is loaded into the table, not *after* the data is loaded. Oracle can easily handle *missing* statistics but has a harder time dealing with *bad* statistics:

```
--Create LAUNCH2 table and gather stats at the wrong time.
create table launch2 as select * from launch where 1=2;

begin
    dbms_stats.gather_table_stats
    (
        ownname => sys_context('userenv', 'current_schema'),
        tabname => 'launch2'
    );
end;
/

insert into launch2 select * from launch;
commit;
```

Before we continue, we need to more thoroughly set ourselves up for failure. This example is more complicated than previous examples because we have to avoid the many mechanisms that automatically fix performance problems. If we only make one

---

[4] Like with real atoms, operations can be divided into smaller pieces. We could trace operations to C functions, operating system calls, machine instructions, etc. In practice, the operation is as deep as we want to go.

simple mistake, Oracle will find a way to compensate for it. Newer versions, especially with the autonomous features, are hard to trick. Depending on your version, edition, and configuration, you may need to temporarily disable more than just the result cache:

```
--Temporarily disable features that may ruin the example.
alter session set result_cache_mode = manual;
```

With bad statistics, the LAUNCH2 table is more likely to cause performance problems. Let's say we find a slow statement and want to tune it. To get the actual execution plan numbers, instead of just guesses, we must run the slow query with the hint GATHER_ PLAN_STATISTICS, like this:

```
--Distinct dates a satellite was launched.
select /*+ gather_plan_statistics */ count(distinct launch_date)
from launch2 join satellite using (launch_id);
```

The next step is to find the SQL_ID with a query like this:

```
--Find the SQL_ID.
select * from gv$sql where sql_fulltext like '%select%launch2%';
```

We must take the preceding SQL_ID and use it in the following call to DBMS_XPLAN. DISPLAY_CURSOR. To view the extra data generated by the GATHER_PLAN_STATISTICS hint, we need to use the value IOSTATS LAST in the FORMAT parameter:

```
--First execution has NESTED LOOPS, bad cardinalities, bad performance.
select * from table(dbms_xplan.display_cursor(
    sql_id => '82nk6712jkfg2',
    format => 'iostats last'));
```

That was a lot of work simply to find an execution plan, but the extra effort is about to pay off. The output is displayed in Figure 18-6. Notice the execution plan includes the new columns "A-Rows" and "A-Time" – the actual values.

```
SQL_ID  82nk6712jkfg2, child number 0
-------------------------------------
--Distinct dates a satellite was launched. select /*+
gather_plan_statistics */ count(distinct launch_date) from launch2 join
satellite using (launch_id)

Plan hash value: 416301548
```

```
--------------------------------------------------------------------------------------------
| Id  | Operation            | Name          | Starts | E-Rows | A-Rows |   A-Time   | Buffers |
--------------------------------------------------------------------------------------------
|   0 | SELECT STATEMENT     |               |      1 |        |      1 |00:00:00.16 |   48092 |
|   1 |  SORT AGGREGATE      |               |      1 |      1 |      1 |00:00:00.16 |   48092 |
|   2 |   VIEW               | VW_DAG_0      |      1 |      1 |   5294 |00:00:00.16 |   48092 |
|   3 |    HASH GROUP BY     |               |      1 |      1 |   5294 |00:00:00.16 |   48092 |
|   4 |     NESTED LOOPS SEMI|               |      1 |      1 |   5295 |00:00:00.28 |   48092 |
|   5 |      TABLE ACCESS FULL| LAUNCH2      |      1 |      1 |  70535 |00:00:00.03 |     896 |
|*  6 |      INDEX RANGE SCAN | SATELLITE_IDX1| 70535 |  43113 |   5295 |00:00:00.11 |   47196 |
--------------------------------------------------------------------------------------------
```

```
Predicate Information (identified by operation id):
---------------------------------------------------

   6 - access("LAUNCH2"."LAUNCH_ID"="SATELLITE"."LAUNCH_ID")
```

Figure 18-6. *Slow execution plan with actual numbers*

The next tuning step is to find precisely *what* is slow, by finding the operation with the largest "A-time." In the preceding output, we can see that the slowest operation is the NESTED LOOPS SEMI that took 0.28 seconds. If we want to improve performance, we must focus on that operation.

This execution plan is small, and there's only one thing to tune. For larger SQL statements, with larger execution plans, the actual time is the only way to find the real problem.

Next, we want to know *why* the join operation is slow. Comparing the actual number of rows with the estimated number of rows is the best way to understand the optimizer's mistakes. The cardinality estimate doesn't need to be perfect, but it needs to be in the ballpark for the optimizer to make a good decision.

When comparing cardinalities, we're not looking for the biggest mistake – we're looking for the *first meaningful* mistake. Cardinality estimation errors propagate through the execution plan, so many of the errors are merely a consequence of the root error. Execution plans are run inside out, so we want to start with the most indented line. Lines 5 and 6 are the most indented.

Line 6 estimated 43113 rows, but the actual number of rows is 5295. That estimate is good enough. Less than a 10x difference usually doesn't matter.

Line 5 estimated 1 row, but the actual number of rows is 70535. A difference that huge is worth our attention. Line 5 is a full table scan of the LAUNCH2 table. There is no asterisk on line 5, implying there are no predicates applied to that operation. Without a predicate, it's weird for the estimate to be so wrong – unless the statistics are bad. The solution is easy – regather statistics and run again:

```
--Re-gather stats and re-run the query.
begin
    dbms_stats.gather_table_stats
    (
        ownname => sys_context('userenv', 'current_schema'),
        tabname => 'launch2',
        no_invalidate => false
    );
end;
/

--Distinct dates a satellite was launched.
select /*+ gather_plan_statistics */ count(distinct launch_date)
from launch2 join satellite using (launch_id);

--Second execution has HASH JOIN, good cardinalities, good performance.
select * from table(dbms_xplan.display_cursor(
    sql_id          => '82nk6712jkfg2',
    cursor_child_no => null, --Improved plan may be a child cursor.
    format          => 'iostats last'));
```

The preceding code generates the execution plan displayed in Figure 18-7. The join changed from a NESTED LOOPS to a HASH JOIN, which is more appropriate for joining a large percentage of data. The actual cardinalities almost perfectly match the estimated cardinalities, which strongly implies that Oracle created the best possible plan for the given statement and objects. The actual times also decreased.

```
SQL_ID  82nk6712jkfg2, child number 0
-------------------------------------
--Distinct dates a satellite was launched. select /*+
gather_plan_statistics */ count(distinct launch_date) from launch2 join
satellite using (launch_id)

Plan hash value: 1657356609

-----------------------------------------------------------------------------------------------------
| Id  | Operation              | Name          | Starts | E-Rows | A-Rows |   A-Time   | Buffers | Reads |
-----------------------------------------------------------------------------------------------------
|   0 | SELECT STATEMENT       |               |     1  |        |      1 |00:00:00.02 |    983  |   13  |
|   1 |  SORT AGGREGATE        |               |     1  |      1 |      1 |00:00:00.02 |    983  |   13  |
|   2 |   VIEW                 | VW_DAG_0      |     1  |   5295 |   5294 |00:00:00.02 |    983  |   13  |
|   3 |    HASH GROUP BY       |               |     1  |   5295 |   5294 |00:00:00.02 |    983  |   13  |
|*  4 |     HASH JOIN RIGHT SEMI|              |     1  |   5295 |   5295 |00:00:00.01 |    983  |   13  |
|   5 |      INDEX FAST FULL SCAN| SATELLITE_IDX1|   1  |  43113 |  43112 |00:00:00.01 |    104  |   13  |
|   6 |      TABLE ACCESS FULL | LAUNCH2       |     1  |  70535 |  70535 |00:00:00.01 |    879  |    0  |
-----------------------------------------------------------------------------------------------------

Predicate Information (identified by operation id):
---------------------------------------------------

   4 - access("LAUNCH2"."LAUNCH_ID"="SATELLITE"."LAUNCH_ID")
```

Figure 18-7. *Fast execution plan with actual numbers*

All the signs indicate that Oracle produced a perfect execution plan. We have to be careful comparing small numbers like 0.28 seconds to 0.02 seconds. Such a small difference could be explained by caching or system activity. To be completely certain of our results, we could run the preceding tests multiple times, possibly in a PL/SQL loop.

This test case may feel too artificial; there is a lot of setup just to demonstrate a bad cardinality estimate. That's because Oracle has become incredibly good at fixing and preventing performance problems. On modern versions of Oracle, real-world performance problems are likely caused by a combination of several weird factors. SQL tuning is less common than it used to be, but when we need to do it, it's more complicated.

Real-Time SQL Monitor Reports (Text)

Real-time SQL monitor reports are the best way to tune long-running SQL statements. These reports provide the actual number of rows, the actual amount of time, the wait events, and other important information. These reports also don't require rerunning the statement, which isn't always feasible for DML or long-running queries.

The SQL monitoring framework is yet another way to measure SQL performance. AWR stores high-level metrics for days, ASH stores samples for hours, and SQL monitoring stores granular details for minutes. SQL monitoring reports need to be generated either while the statements are running or shortly after they finish.[5] Similar to AWR and ASH, we can also access SQL monitoring data in the data dictionary, through views like V$SQL_PLAN_MONITOR and V$SQL_MONITOR.

SQL monitoring only works on statements that take longer than 5 seconds or have the MONITOR hint. Our previous example didn't run long enough to produce SQL monitoring data. Instead, let's run a really stupid SQL statement in a separate session:

```
--Ridiculously bad cross join.  (Run in a separate session.)
select count(*) from launch,launch;
```

While the preceding statement is running, we want to find the SQL_ID and call DBMS_SQLTUNE to generate the report:

```
--Find the SQL_ID, while the previous statement is running.
select *
from gv$sql where sql_fulltext like '%launch,launch%'
    and users_executing > 0;
```

```
--Generate report.
select dbms_sqltune.report_sql_monitor('7v2qjmgrj995d') from dual;
```

The function REPORT_SQL_MONITOR can produce reports in multiple formats, and the default text format is shown in Figure 18-8. There's a lot of important information, so you may want to spend a minute looking at the output.

---

[5] If SQL monitoring data ages out, we can still partially recreate the format of the reports using AWR and ASH data. I've built an open source program for historical SQL monitoring: https://github.com/jonheller1/hist_sql_mon

```
SQL Monitoring Report

SQL Text
------------------------------
select count(*) from launch,launch

Global Information
------------------------------
  Status              :  EXECUTING
  Instance ID         :  1
  Session             :  JHELLER (399:62162)
  SQL ID              :  7v2qjmgrj995d
  SQL Execution ID    :  16777216
  Execution Started   :  12/25/2018 13:35:01
  First Refresh Time  :  12/25/2018 13:35:07
  Last Refresh Time   :  12/25/2018 13:36:03
  Duration            :  62s
  Module/Action       :  PL/SQL Developer/SQL Window - Chapter 18.sql
  Service             :  SYS$USERS
  Program             :  plsqldev.exe

Global Stats
=========================================
| Elapsed | Cpu     | Other    | Buffer |
| Time(s) | Time(s) | Waits(s) | Gets   |
=========================================
|      62 |      62 |     0.17 |    220 |
=========================================


SQL Plan Monitoring Details (Plan Hash Value=2880158423)
=============================================================================================================================
|Id |        Operation          | Name     | Rows  |Cost| Time    |Start |Execs| Rows   |Mem|Activity|Activity Detail|
|   |                           |          |(Estim)|    |Active(s)|Active|     |(Actual)|   |  (%)   |  (# samples)  |
=============================================================================================================================
|->0|SELECT STATEMENT           |          |       |    |     57| +6|    1|      0| .|        |               |
|->1| SORT AGGREGATE            |          |     1|    |     57| +6|    1|      0| .|    4.84|Cpu (3)        |
|->2|  MERGE JOIN CARTESIAN     |          |    5G| 3M|     57| +6|    1|     2G| .|        |               |
|->3|   INDEX FAST FULL SCAN    |LAUNCH_PK | 70535| 41|     57| +6|    1|  28604| .|        |               |
|->4|   BUFFER SORT             |          | 70535| 3M|     62|+1|28604|     2G|2MB| 95.16|Cpu (59)       |
|  5|    INDEX FAST FULL SCAN   |LAUNCH_PK | 70535| 40|      1| +6|    1|  70535| .|        |               |
=============================================================================================================================
```

Figure 18-8. *Real-time SQL monitor report with text format*

The preceding output contains a lot of metadata about the SQL statement, and the output adjusts depending on the type of query. For example, if there were bind variables, the report would have displayed the bind values. The metadata is helpful because these reports are worth saving and comparing days later. Without the metadata, we might forget when the report was run and who ran it.

The most important part of the report is the table of operations. The format is similar to DISPLAY_CURSOR and contains the actual values. We can use "Rows (Actual)" to get the real cardinality and "Activity (%)" to find the slowest operations.

The column "Activity Detail (# samples)" provides a count of each wait event for each operation. The number in parentheses represents the number of seconds the query was waiting for that kind of resource. In the preceding example, all the waits are for "Cpu." In more realistic examples, there will be many kinds of waits. Like with operations, we should only worry about waits that have a substantial number. There will often be a strange-sounding wait event, but if the wait only happened one time, then it's not worth worrying about. The most common waits should be for CPU and I/O, such as "Cpu," "db file sequential read," and "db file scattered read." We can look up unusual events in the "Oracle Wait Events" appendix of the *Database Reference* manual.

The monitor report may also contain a "Progress" column that gives a percentage completion for the operation. That number can be useful for predicting the completion of a statement, but we must be careful to interpret the progress correctly. Many operations will iterate, so an operation may be "99%" complete many times. The column "Execs" tells us how many times an operation has executed.

Unfortunately, the SQL monitor reports do not include "Note" or "Predicate Information." Sometimes we may need to generate the execution plan with both DBMS_SQLTUNE and DBMS_XPLAN and combine the two results to get all the relevant information.

Real-Time SQL Monitor Reports (Active)

In addition to the default text format, SQL monitor reports can also be generated as XML, HTML, or active. The active report is not just a prettier interactive HTML format; it also contains extra information that is useful for advanced tuning.

Active reports contain helpful information for tuning parallel SQL, such as how many parallel servers were allocated and used throughout the life of a query. Active reports are also helpful for tuning PL/SQL processes, since the report contains detailed information about all the dependent SQL statements. Active reports aren't as popular as they should be, probably because the HTML file used to depend on Adobe Flash and many developers gave up on trying to run them.

Generating an active report starts with a SQL statement like this:

```
--Generate Active report.
select dbms_sqltune.report_sql_monitor('242q2tafkqamm',
    type => 'active')
from dual;
```

The CLOB results from the preceding statement must be saved as an HTML file and opened with a browser with Internet connectivity. An example of one of the pages of the active report is displayed in Figure 18-9. The report is crammed full of interactive information, so the screenshot doesn't do it justice.

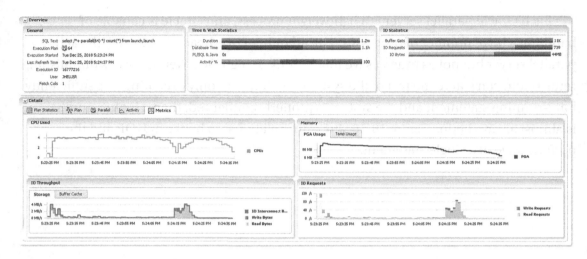

Figure 18-9. *Real-time SQL monitor report with active format*

Although active reports are one of the most powerful SQL tuning tools, there are a few reasons text is still a good default. The text format is still much easier to generate, share, and compare. But when we need more advanced tuning features or just a prettier picture to show to management, the active report is a good option.

Degree of Parallelism

If our SQL can't work smarter, we can make it work harder with parallelism. Finding the requested and allocated degree of parallelism is vital in data warehouse operations. There are many myths surrounding parallelism, so we need to carefully measure our results and use actual numbers instead of guesses.

We must remember Amdahl's law and the importance of parallelizing *every* possible operation. If the execution plan has one PX operation, then it should have many PX operations. We can achieve full parallelism by using statement-level hints instead of object-level hints.

The only time we don't want to use parallelism is with correlated subqueries. We do not want to parallelize an operation that runs a large number of times – the overhead of parallelism would be greater than the benefit. The best way to avoid that problem is to rewrite subqueries into inline views.

Choosing the optimal DOP is difficult. A higher DOP is better for the individual statement but may be unfair for other processes.

Each Oracle parallel server is a lightweight process, and Oracle is capable of handling a huge number of processes. The amount of overhead increases with each parallel server but not as much as we might think. A high DOP definitely has diminishing returns and can starve the rest of the system. But if we are only executing one sufficiently long-running statement and the system is properly configured, then a higher number is almost always better. Figure 18-10 shows the relationship between DOP and the performance of a single statement.

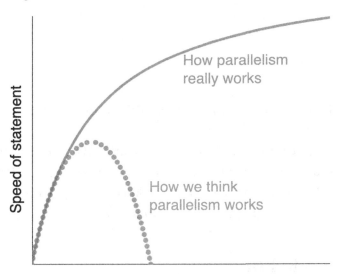

Figure 18-10. *How we think parallelism works vs. how it really works*

The default DOP is based on the parameter `CPU_COUNT` multiplied by the parameter `PARALLEL_THREADS_PER_CPU`. For this reason, it's important that the `CPU_COUNT` is set to the physical number of processors and not some marketing definition of a "logical processor."

Unfortunately, there are many times when the default DOP is not used. There are over 40 factors[6] that affect the degree of parallelism: hints, session settings, object settings, interoperation parallelism (which doubles the number of parallel servers for things like sorting and grouping), etc. Developers and administrators often worry too much about runaway parallelism. Before we decrease a critical parameter, such

---

[6] See my answer here for a long list of things that affect the DOP: `https://stackoverflow.com/a/21132027/409172`

as PARALLEL_MAX_SERVERS, we should understand exactly why statements are getting their DOP. We should also measure the performance at large DOPs instead of simply assuming a large DOP is bad.

We should always look at the execution plans for information about the DOP. But keep in mind that the execution plan only knows the *requested* number of parallel servers. The real-time SQL monitor report, and V$PX_PROCESS, can tell us the *actual* number of parallel servers. Even when our SQL statement is allocated the correct number of parallel servers, we still need to check that the SQL statement is meaningfully *using* those servers. Active reports include a chart that shows us how many parallel processes are truly used for each operation. We need to make sure our statements request, allocate, and use the proper number of parallel servers at all times.

Parallel execution is complicated. If we're working on a data warehouse, we should carefully read the entire 87-page "Using Parallel Execution" chapter in the *VLDB and Partitioning Guide*.

What to Look for in Execution Plans

Here is a quick checklist for how to investigate execution plans. These summaries are a good starting point even though they oversimplify the real-world problems we will encounter:

1. *Note, predicate*: Something weird in these sections may be responsible for everything else in the execution plan.

2. *Slow operations*: Only invest time tuning operations that are either slow or cause a slow operation.

3. *Bad cardinality*: Find the first operation that has a significantly wrong cardinality estimate.

4. *Wrong join operations*: Avoid nested loop index access for joining a large percentage of rows. Avoid full table scan hash joins for joining a small percentage of rows.

5. *Wrong access operations*: Avoid index range scans for returning a large percentage of rows. Avoid full table scans for returning a small percentage of rows.

6. *Weird waits*: A significant amount of time spent on unusual waits should be investigated. Most of the waits should be for CPU or I/O. Other waits might be a sign of a configuration problem.

7. *Large number of executions*: Are the operations fast but repeated a large number of times? This can happen with a subquery that needs to be unnested, perhaps by rewriting the SQL to use a join.

8. *Bad join order*: For hash joins, the smallest row source should be listed first. The row source listed first is the one used to create the hash table, which ideally fits in memory.

9. *Direct-path or conventional writes*: Ensure that either LOAD AS SELECT or LOAD TABLE CONVENTIONAL is used as expected.

10. *Partitioning*: Ensure that partition pruning is being used as expected.

11. *Numbers that don't add up*: If the "Activity (%)" column doesn't add up to 100%, then the remaining time is being spent by a recursive query. Check for slow data dictionary queries or for slow functions used in the query. It doesn't matter if the numbers in the other columns, like "Cost", add up.

12. *Temporary tablespace*: An unusually large amount of temporary tablespace is slow, may cause resource problems, and is a bad sign of other issues. Oracle may be joining the tables in the wrong order, merging views incorrectly, or performing DISTINCT operations at the wrong time.

13. *Parallelism*: Check the requested, allocated, and used DOP.

SQL tuning is difficult, and we must always arm ourselves with actual times and cardinalities, not just guesses.

SQL Tuning: Changing Execution Plans

After we finally understand the problem with our SQL query, there is a long list of techniques for fixing the execution plan. Each technique could fill an entire chapter, but there's only room here for brief summaries and one small example.

Changing Execution Plans

There are many ways to change the execution plans of SQL statements. The following list is ordered by which solutions are the cleanest. This subjective ranking is based on a combination of proportionality, obviousness, and simplicity.

Fixes should be proportional to the problem; rewriting a query only affects one query, whereas changing a system parameter affects many queries. Fixes should be obvious; rewriting a query makes the changes obvious, whereas using DBMS_ADVANCED_REWRITE will fool most developers. Fixes should be easy; adding a hint directly to the query is easier than adding a hint through a SQL profile.

In the real world, we have many constraints placed on our tuning. Frequently we have to fix the execution plan without directly changing the query. Sometimes we have to skip the easy steps and go to advanced steps that secretly swap out a bad execution plan for a good one.

1. *Change how the query is called*: Ensure the application is not creating a new connection for each query. Use bind variables instead of creating a large number of hard-coded queries. Use batching instead of reading and writing one row at a time.

2. *Rewrite the query*: Apply advanced features and programming styles. If our query is too large to tune in one piece, we can split it into non-transformable pieces with the ROWNUM trick.

3. *Gather statistics*: Described in more detail at the end of the chapter.

4. *Create or alter objects*: Consider adding indexes, constraints, materialized views, compression, partitions, parallelism, etc.

5. *Add hints to the query*: See the next section for details about hints.

6. *SQL profiles*: Add hints to a query without directly changing the SQL text. This feature is also described later in the chapter.

7. *SQL plan baselines*: Replace one plan with another plan. This feature is a large, complex system that can be used to control and evolve execution plan acceptance. This feature is useful for preserving performance during large system changes but is too cumbersome for most SQL tuning.

8. *Stored outlines*: An earlier, simpler, and deprecated version of SQL plan baselines.

9. DBMS_STATS.SET_X_STATS: Manually modifying table, column, and index stats can significantly change plans by making objects artificially look more or less expensive.

10. *Session control*: Change parameters at the session level. For example, if an upgrade from 12c to 19c causes problems for one process, and we don't have time to fix each query individually, we can run this command at the beginning of the session: `ALTER SESSION SET OPTIMIZER_FEATURES_ENABLE='12.2.0.1'`.

11. *System control*: Change parameters for the entire system. For example, on a data warehouse, we may want to spend more parsing time to generate good execution plans; we can enable SQL plan directives by running `ALTER SYSTEM SET OPTIMIZER_ADAPTIVE_STATISTICS=TRUE`. Or if we see lots of odd wait events, we may need to reconfigure the system. Try not to lie to Oracle, and do not change a system parameter to only fix a single instance of a problem.

12. DBMS_ADVANCED_REWRITE: Change a query into another query. This package is a neat trick but is kind of evil because we can secretly change the meaning of a query.

13. *Virtual private database*: Change a query into another query by adding predicates. This feature is not intended for performance, but we can abuse it to change execution plans.

14. *SQL translation framework*: Change a query into another query before it even gets parsed.

15. *SQL Patch* (DBMS_SQLDIAG.CREATE_SQL_PATCH): A semi-documented way to add hints to queries.

Hints

Hints are directives the optimizer must follow if possible. The name "hint" is misleading. Despite what many people believe, the optimizer does not randomly ignore hints. It only seems that way because the hint syntax is complicated. There are many reasons a hint can be invalid and cannot be followed.

There are hundreds of hints, and many of them are documented in the "Comments" chapter of the *SQL Language Reference*. There's a hint for every execution plan feature. We can generate a full list of hints for an execution plan by passing the parameter FORMAT=>'+OUTLINE' to DBMS_XPLAN. Most hints are cryptic and difficult to use. Luckily, we normally only need to add a small number of hints.

It's useful to think of there being two different categories of hints: good hints that provide useful information to the optimizer and bad hints that tell the optimizer how to do its job.

Good hints tell the optimizer something it couldn't know, like a trade-off that we're willing to accept. For example, only a developer could choose the APPEND hint, because only a developer knows if we're willing to gain performance at the risk of unrecoverable data.

Bad hints circumvent the normal optimizer logic and require developers to play the role of the optimizer. We don't always have time to fix the root cause, and sometimes we need to quickly tell the optimizer how to do its job. Overusing bad hints can make our SQL difficult to understand and may cause us to miss useful features in future versions. But sometimes a small number of bad hints is necessary for quickly solving a critical problem.

The following is a list of popular, good hints:

1. APPEND/APPEND_VALUES: Use direct-path writes; improves speed but data is initially unrecoverable.

2. DRIVING_SITE: Execute a query on a remote site; when using tables over database links, we may want to execute the join on a remote database instead of passing the rows and then joining them.

3. DYNAMIC_SAMPLING: Read blocks from the row sources to provide additional optimizer information.

4. ENABLE_PARALLEL_DML: Enable parallel DML for just one query, instead of running `ALTER SESSION ENABLE PARALLEL DML`.

5. FIRST_ROWS: Optimize the query to quickly return the first rows, instead of optimizing to quickly return the entire set.

6. PARALLEL: Use multiple threads to take advantage of more CPU and I/O resources. Try to use statement-level hints instead of object-level hints.

7. QB_NAME: Create a name for a query block; useful for referencing the query block in other hints.

The following is a list of popular, bad hints:

1. FULL: Use a full table scan.

2. INDEX*: Use a specific index or type of index access.

3. LEADING/ORDERED: Join tables in a specific order.

4. MERGE: Merge views and rewrite the two queries into one.

5. OPTIMIZER_FEATURES_ENABLE: Use an older version of the optimizer to disable newer features that cause problems.

6. OPT_PARAM: Change specific parameter values for a query; for example, if a DBA foolishly changed `OPTIMIZER_INDEX_COST_ADJ` on the system, we can at least fix it for the query.

7. PQ*: How to process parallel data.

8. UNNEST: Convert a subquery into a join.

9. USE_HASH/USE_MERGE/USE_NL: Force a hash join, a sort-merge join, or a nested loop join.

There are many more hints than what is in the preceding list. And almost every hint has a `NO_*` version that has the opposite effect. There are even undocumented hints that are helpful enough to consider using. `CARDINALITY` and `OPT_ESTIMATE` can hard-code or adjust the row estimate for an inline view or operation, and they can be especially useful for objects the optimizer cannot easily estimate, like PL/SQL table functions. Those hints are used internally by SQL profiles created by the automatic SQL Tuning Advisor. The `MATERIALIZE` hint forces Oracle to store the results of a common table expression in a temporary table, instead of rerunning the subquery. Oracle automatically decides whether to materialize a common table expression or not, but sometimes Oracle makes the wrong choice. Those undocumented hints can be useful when nothing else works.

Using hints correctly takes practice and patience. Oracle does not throw an error if the hint syntax is invalid or impossible to use. Instead, Oracle will simply ignore that hint and all the hints that come after it. In 19c we can use FORMAT=>'+HINT_REPORT' in the DBMS_XPLAN package to help understand what hints were used. The next section shows a quick example of using a hint when creating a SQL profile.

SQL Profile Example

This section demonstrates a worst-case SQL tuning example; we need to apply hints to fix an execution plan, but we do not have access to change the query. SQL plan baselines, outlines, and the SQL Tuning Advisor can preserve, evolve, and fix some problems, but it's hard to get those tools to do exactly what we want. By manually creating SQL profiles, we can precisely inject the hints we need.

For example, imagine we have an application that mistakenly decides to run all queries with parallelism enabled. The excessive parallel queries are trashing performance and need to be disabled immediately. We can't easily change the application, but we need to change the execution plans right now. The following is an example of the bad query and execution plan:

```
--Query that shouldn't run in parallel.
explain plan for select /*+parallel(2)*/ * from satellite;

select * from table(dbms_xplan.display(format => 'basic +note'));

Plan hash value: 3822448874

---------------------------------------------
| Id  | Operation            | Name         |
---------------------------------------------
|   0 | SELECT STATEMENT     |              |
|   1 |  PX COORDINATOR      |              |
|   2 |   PX SEND QC (RANDOM)| :TQ10000     |
|   3 |    PX BLOCK ITERATOR |              |
|   4 |     TABLE ACCESS FULL| SATELLITE    |
---------------------------------------------
```

Note

- Degree of Parallelism is 2 because of hint

The following code creates a SQL profile that inserts a NO_PARALLEL hint into the query. SQL profiles are normally created by the SQL Tuning Advisor. Unfortunately, the SQL Tuning Advisor doesn't always know exactly what we want to do. It's helpful to create the profiles ourselves, precisely the way we want:

```
--Create SQL Profile to stop parallelism in one query.
begin
    dbms_sqltune.import_sql_profile
    (
        sql_text      => 'select /*+parallel(2)*/ * from satellite',
        name          => 'STOP_PARALLELISM',
        force_match   => true,
        profile       => sqlprof_attr('no_parallel')
    );
end;
/
```

After running the preceding PL/SQL block, if we rerun the same EXPLAIN PLAN and DBMS_XPLAN commands, we'll see the new execution plan as follows:

```
Plan hash value: 2552139662

-----------------------------------------
| Id  | Operation            | Name      |
-----------------------------------------
|   0 | SELECT STATEMENT     |           |
|   1 |   TABLE ACCESS FULL  | SATELLITE |
-----------------------------------------

Note
-----

    - Degree of Parallelism is 1 because of hint
    - SQL profile "STOP_PARALLELISM" used for this statement
```

The new profile appears in the "Note" section, and the execution plan does not use parallelism anymore. This technique can be applied to use any combination of hints. SQL profiles are great but are not the ideal way to solve performance problems. We have to remember to deploy the profile to all databases. And if the query changes at all, even an extra space, the profile will no longer match the query.

SQL Tuning: Gathering Optimizer Statistics

Optimizer statistics should be manually gathered after any process that changes a large percentage of data. Optimizer statistics should be automatically gathered by the default auto-task for incremental data changes.

Take a minute to reread the previous paragraph; the majority of performance problems are caused by not following that simple advice. Too many developers ignore gathering statistics – perhaps because they think "gathering stats is a DBA's job." Too many DBAs mess up automatic statistics gathering, perhaps because they encountered a bug 10 years ago and think they can still create a better job than Oracle.

Manual Statistics

Without good statistics the optimizer cannot function properly. If a table is going to be involved in queries after that table is loaded or changed, we must immediately gather statistics. Large table changes should be followed by a call to DBMS_STATS.GATHER_TABLE_STATS.

There's no perfect definition for what constitutes a "large" table change. For the optimizer, the percentage is more important than the absolute number. Adding 100 rows to a table with only 1 row is more significant than adding a billion rows to a table that already has a billion rows. For global temporary tables, almost any change could be considered large, since the tables are empty to begin with.

The package DBMS_STATS should be used to gather statistics – do not use the semi-deprecated ANALYZE command. The most important functions in DBMS_STATS are GATHER_TABLE_STATS and GATHER_SCHEMA_STATS. Those functions have a large number of parameters, and it's worth becoming familiar with most of them. The following list includes the required and most important parameters:

1. ownname/tabname: The schema owner and table name.

2. estimate_percent: The amount of data to sample. We almost always want to leave this parameter alone. The default gathers 100% but uses a fast, approximate-number-of-distinct-values algorithm. For extra-large tables that don't need precise statistics, it may be helpful to use a tiny value like 0.01.

3. degree: The degree of parallelism. This parameter can significantly improve the performance of gathering statistics on large objects. Some parts of statistics gathering, such as histograms, are not improved by parallelism. For extreme statistics gathering performance, we may need to look into concurrency instead.

4. Cascade: Are statistics also gathered on related indexes? Defaults to TRUE.[7]

5. no_invalidate: By default, the statistics will not necessarily be applied to all existing execution plans. Invalidating many plans could cause performance problems, so the invalidations are done gradually over time. The default is TRUE, but in practice most dependent execution plans are immediately invalidated. However, if we want to be sure that our statistics immediately take effect, we may want to set this parameter to FALSE.

6. method_opt: Determines which histograms to gather. By default, histograms are created for columns with skewed data, and only if those columns have also been used in a relevant condition in a query.

---

[7] The default is supposed to automatically decide whether or not to gather index statistics. But in practice the default is effectively TRUE. See this question for details: https://dba.stackexchange.com/q/12226/3336

There are several times when statistics are gathered as a side effect of other operations, and we don't need to repeat the gathering. Statistics can be automatically gathered when loading table data, so if our execution plans have the operation OPTIMIZER STATISTICS GATHERING, then we probably do not need to regather statistics manually. Creating or rebuilding indexes automatically gathers index statistics, so we may be able to save a lot of time with the parameter CASCADE=>FALSE.

Automatic Statistics

By default, Oracle creates scheduler jobs to automatically gather statistics. These scheduler jobs are created by AutoTasks, which can be monitored from the data dictionary view DBA_AUTOTASK_*. By default, the AutoTask runs every night and gathers statistics on all tables that were changed by more than 10%.

There are many times when performance problems magically disappear because of automatic statistics collection. On the other hand, there are also rare times when performance problems magically appear – sometimes gathering better statistics leads to a worse execution plan. Even when performance problems disappear, it is useful to understand why. We can track the statistics collection history through columns like DBA_TABLES.LAST_ANALYZED and the data dictionary view DBA_OPTSTAT_OPERATIONS.

The statistics job should be working preventively and gathering statistics before problems happen. But we cannot rely on that job to solve all of our problems. We still need to manually gather statistics. Performance cannot always wait for the nightly stats job.

If we encounter problems with the default AutoTask, we can set preferences to help the job work better. For example, if a large table is taking too long, we can set the table preference to gather statistics in parallel:

```
--Gather optimizer statistics in parallel.
begin
    dbms_stats.set_table_prefs(user, 'TEST1', 'DEGREE', 8);
end;
/
```

We can set preferences for all of the GATHER_TABLE_STATS parameters. There are other available preferences, such as INCREMENTAL (a special algorithm for partitioned tables) and STALE_PERCENTAGE (the percentage of rows that must be modified to trigger gathering, which defaults to 10%). If we're having problems automatically gathering statistics, we should first work with the preferences before we create our own manual job.

Finally, if our table change patterns are just too weird for automatic statistics gathering, we can use DBMS_STATS.LOCK_TABLE_STATS to stop statistics gathering for individual tables. When the time is right, we can manually gather statistics by using the FORCE => TRUE option.

Other Statistics

There are many weird types of statistics, to match our weird data. The ASSOCIATE STATISTICS command lets us associate custom selectivity and costs with schema objects like functions. DBMS_STATS contains self-explanatory functions that let us GATHER_FIXED_OBJECTS_STATS and GATHER_DICTIONARY_STATS, which can improve the performance of data dictionary queries. We can even create fake statistics using DBMS_STATS.SET_* functions.

Dynamic sampling is automatically used when statistics are missing or for parallel statements that run long enough to justify spending more time gathering statistics. The optimizer has a hard enough time figuring out declarative cardinalities; it doesn't even try to estimate the cardinality of table functions or object types. For procedural code, the optimizer always guesses 8168 rows. We can use dynamic sampling to generate better estimates, as shown in the following code:

```
--Dynamic sampling to estimate object types.
explain plan for
select /*+dynamic_sampling(2) */ column_value
from table(sys.odcinumberlist(1,2,3));

select * from table(dbms_xplan.display(format => 'basic +rows +note'));

Plan hash value: 1748000095
----------------------------------------------------------------
| Id | Operation                            | Name | Rows |
----------------------------------------------------------------
|  0 | SELECT STATEMENT                     |      |    3 |
|  1 |   COLLECTION ITERATOR CONSTRUCTOR FETCH|    |    3 |
----------------------------------------------------------------
```

Note

```
- dynamic statistics used: dynamic sampling (level=2)
```

The preceding results show a perfect cardinality estimate due to dynamic sampling. When dynamic sampling doesn't work, either because it's too slow or because the estimate is bad, we may need to hard-code an estimate with the undocumented CARDINALITY hint.

Extended statistics let the optimizer capture information about expressions or relationships between columns. For example, in the table ENGINE_PROPELLANT there is a strong correlation between the columns PROPELLANT_ID and OXIDIZER_OR_ FUEL. Propellants are almost always used exclusively as either an oxidizer or a fuel.

If we query the table with two conditions, PROPELLANT_ID = 1 and OXIDIZER_OR_ FUEL = 'fuel', the optimizer incorrectly thinks that both conditions reduce the number of rows. That faulty assumption will incorrectly shrink the cardinality estimates. We can tell the optimizer about this relationship and get more accurate cardinality estimates, by using the following code to create extended statistics:

```
--Extended statistics on ENGINE_PROPELLANT.
select dbms_stats.create_extended_stats(
    ownname => sys_context('userenv', 'current_schema'),
    tabname => 'ENGINE_PROPELLANT',
    extension => '(PROPELLANT_ID,OXIDIZER_OR_FUEL)')
from dual;
```

Summary

Investigating performance problems and fixing them with cryptic hints is fun. But the most important performance tips are not found in SQL tuning guides. Performance is about having a good development and testing process that allows quick experiments, knowledge of advanced features and objects, and a style that makes SQL easier to understand and debug.

When we tune SQL statements, we must remember to use actual numbers to find the slow statements, slow operations, and bad cardinalities. We need a breadth-first approach and the ability to use multiple tools to find the most relevant information quickly. Combining our knowledge of algorithmic complexity, cardinality, operations, transformations, and dynamic optimizations, we should have an idea of what a better execution plan could look like. There are many ways to fix execution plans, and we should strive to use the cleanest approach. Ideally, we can improve the optimizer statistics and solve the root causes of our problems.

PART V

Solve Anything with Oracle SQL

CHAPTER 19

Solve Challenging Problems with Arcane SQL Features

It's time to discuss the most advanced Oracle features, the features that solve problems most developers think are impossible to solve in a database.

We need to be cautious before using these obscure technologies. Just because we *can* use a feature does not mean we *should* use it. Half of the features in this chapter I've only used for code golf to solve a ridiculous challenge. The other half I've used in real-world systems, where a rare SQL feature saved the day. Before we briefly describe Oracle's most arcane features, we need to honestly evaluate the costs and benefits of building so much logic in our databases.

Oracle vs. the Unix Philosophy

One of the age-old questions in software engineering is: Do we build one large system or multiple small systems that work together? The more we use these esoteric Oracle features, the more we're choosing a monolithic solution over of a modular solution.

We want to avoid overusing a single tool and falling victim to the golden hammer anti-pattern; when all we have is a hammer, everything looks like a nail. The technology industry is constantly moving from large proprietary systems on expensive servers to small open source programs on commodity hardware. The Unix philosophy emphasizes using many small tools and chaining them together.

On the other hand, we don't want solutions with too many pieces. A common example of this problem is system administration scripts that combine shell scripts, cron, SQL, SQL*Plus, and many operating system commands. All of those pieces are

© Jon Heller 2023
J. Heller, *Pro Oracle SQL Development*, https://doi.org/10.1007/978-1-4842-8867-2_19

fine individually. But when combined, those technologies require a lot of different skills, and there will likely be problems integrating them. Many times, it's simpler to replace a combination of technologies with a single, scheduled PL/SQL procedure. We need to consider both approaches.

I'm not trying to convince you to use Oracle for everything. Oracle is not the best tool for spreadsheet processing, pattern matching, polymorphism, web application front ends, search engines, polyglot programming, geographic information systems, or data mining. But I would like to convince you that there are times when you should consider using Oracle for all of those tasks. If we've already built an Oracle solution, there's a huge advantage to being able to leverage our existing infrastructure, knowledge, and relational interfaces.

MODEL

The MODEL clause enables procedural logic inside a SQL statement. MODEL lets us process data like a multidimensional array or a spreadsheet. We can partition our data, define dimensions and measures, and apply rules and FOR loops.

The price we pay for these cool features is a complex syntax. Every time I use MODEL, I have to reread parts of the *"SQL for Modeling"* chapter of the *Data Warehousing Guide*.

This feature is best demonstrated with an unrealistic example. Let's build a cellular automaton in SQL. A cellular automaton is a grid of cells where each cell has a state of on or off. After an initial state, all cells are recreated depending on a set of simple rules. The new state is based on the state of a cell's neighbors. You've seen cellular automata before if you've ever played Conway's Game of Life. The interesting thing about cellular automata is how complex behavior emerges from incredibly simple rules.

To keep things as simple as possible, we'll use an elementary cellular automaton, which is represented as a one-dimensional array. The cells in the array change each generation based on the state of the cell to the left, itself, and the cell to the right.

Figure 19-1 shows the cellular automata we're going to build in SQL.

Rule 18   Rule 110

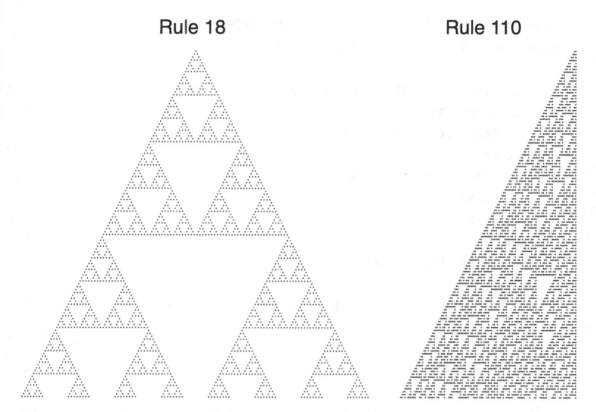

Figure 19-1. *Elementary cellular automata created by the MODEL clause*

Creating the cellular automata in Figure 19-1 is a four-step process. The first step is to create a two-dimensional array of data. The second step is where the MODEL magic happens and where we step through the two-dimensional array and populate values based on the state and the rules. The third step is a simple aggregation to turn each array into a string. Finally, we need to copy and paste the results into a text editor and zoom out to see the results:

```
--Cellular automata with MODEL.  On is "#", off is " ".
--#3: Aggregate states to make a picture.
select listagg(state, '') within group (order by cell) line
from
(
```

```
--#2: Apply cellular automata rules with MODEL.
select generation, cell, state from
(
    --#1: Initial, mostly empty array.
    select generation, cell,
        --Seed first generation with "#" in the center.
        case
            when generation=0 and cell=120 then '#'
            else ' '
        end state
    from
    (select level-1 generation from dual connect by level <= 120)
    cross join
    (select level-1 cell from dual connect by level <= 240)
)
model
dimension by (generation, cell)
measures (state)
rules
(
    --Comment out rules to set them to ' ' (off).
    --Interesting patterns: 18 (00010010) 110 (01101110)
    state[generation >= 1, any] =
        case
            state[cv()-1, cv()-1] || --left
            state[cv()-1, cv()  ] || --middle
            state[cv()-1, cv()+1]    --right
        --when '###' then '#'
        when '## ' then '#'
        when '# #' then '#'
        --when '#  ' then '#'
        when ' ##' then '#'
        when ' # ' then '#'
        when '  #' then '#'
```

```
        --when '   ' then '#'
        else ''
        end
  )
)
group by generation
order by generation;
```

The first step, creating an empty array, is simple enough. That step creates a table of data with a unique GENERATION and CELL coordinate for each value. The first step can be accomplished by using the CONNECT BY LEVEL trick twice and then cross joining the results. You may want to highlight and run the first inline view to understand how this complex query begins.

The second step is the important one, where the MODEL clause is used. We create a two-dimensional array with DIMENSION BY (GENERATION, CELL). Then we define a measure, the state that will be calculated, with MEASURES (STATE). In the RULES clause, we read and write the states.

We want to change the state for all cells, except for generation 0, which has the initial state: STATE[GENERATION >= 1, ANY] =. The left-hand side of the rule uses square brackets for array access, contains conditions to limit the dimensions, and uses the ANY keyword. The right-hand side references the array three times – for the left parent, the middle parent, and the right parent. For example, to reference the state of the left parent is STATE[CV()-1, CV()-1]. The CV() function gets the current value, and then we subtract one to get the parent generation and to get the cell to the left. The state uses a hash character for ON and a space for OFF, and the eight rules are commented out to enable a specific set of rules.

Cellular automata look cool but are not often practical. More practical examples of the MODEL clause would duplicate spreadsheet logic, such as solving inventory calculations or creating loan amortization schedules. I've only used the MODEL clause a few times for real-world queries, for solving graph problems like transitive closures. Oracle SQL is definitely not the best language for querying a graph. However, since my data was already in a database, using MODEL was much easier than adding another tool to the system.

If we ever think "this programming problem can't possibly be solved in pure SQL," we should try the MODEL clause.

Row Pattern Matching

Row pattern matching is a powerful way to find patterns in our data. The REGEXP functions enable searching for regular expressions within a single value. Analytic functions can be used to find simple row patterns, like consecutive or non-consecutive values. The MATCH_RECOGNIZE clause lets us use regular expressions to find complex patterns between rows.

For example, we can use row pattern matching to help us find patterns in the number of launches per year. While analytic functions can find years that decrease or increase, analytic functions are not good enough for finding more specific patterns. The following code uses row pattern matching to find where the number of launches decreased for two or more years:

```
--Years where launches decreased two years in a row or more.
select *
from
(
   --Count of launches per year.
   select
      to_char(launch_date, 'YYYY') the_year,
      count(*) launch_count
   from launch
   group by to_char(launch_date, 'YYYY')
   order by the_year
)
match_recognize
(
   order by the_year
   measures
      first(down.the_year) as decline_start,
      last(down.the_year) as decline_end
   one row per match
   after match skip to last down
   --Declined for two or more years.
   pattern (down down+)
   define
```

```
      down as down.launch_count < prev(down.launch_count)
)
order by decline_start;

DECLINE_START   DECLINE_END
-------------   -----------
...
         1977          1978
         1980          1986
         1988          1996
...
```

The MATCH_RECOGNIZE syntax is verbose, so I'll let most of the preceding code speak for itself. The most interesting part of the query is where we define the regular expression: PATTERN (DOWN DOWN+). Once we've got the initial query built, it's easy to play around with different patterns. We could easily find series of years where the number of launches increased, where the number of launches seesawed back and forth, etc.

Any Types

If we don't know what our data looks like ahead of time, we need the ability to process "anything." Oracle provides three object types that can help us pass and process completely generic data. ANYDATA contains a single value of any type, ANYTYPE contains type information about the data, and ANYDATASET contains a collection of any types of data.

For example, the following function accepts an ANYDATA and returns a text version of the value stored inside the ANYDATA. This function isn't very useful because even creating a trivial example of ANYDATA requires a lot of weird code:

```
--Function that uses ANYDATA to process "anything".
create or replace function process_anything(p_anything anydata)
    return varchar2
is
    v_typecode pls_integer;
    v_anytype anytype;
```

```
   v_result pls_integer;
   v_number number;
   v_varchar2 varchar2(4000);
begin
   --Get ANYTYPE.
   v_typecode := p_anything.getType(v_anytype);
   --Inspect type and process accordingly.
   if v_typecode = dbms_types.typecode_number then
      v_result := p_anything.GetNumber(v_number);
      return('Number: '||v_number);
   elsif v_typecode = dbms_types.typecode_varchar2 then
      v_result := p_anything.GetVarchar2(v_varchar2);
      return('Varchar2: '||v_varchar2);
   else
      return('Unexpected type: '||v_typecode);
   end if;
end;
/
```

The following query shows that we can choose the data types at run time:

```
--Call PROCESS_ANYTHING from SQL.
select
   process_anything(anydata.ConvertNumber(1)) result1,
   process_anything(anydata.ConvertVarchar2('A')) result2,
   process_anything(anydata.ConvertClob('B')) result3
from dual;

RESULT1     RESULT2       RESULT3
---------   -----------   --------------------
Number: 1   Varchar2: A   Unexpected type: 112
```

In practice, most highly generic programming in SQL or PL/SQL is a mistake. To do anything interesting with data, we have to have an idea of what that data looks like. The ANY types are neat, but they have some strange bugs and performance problems. Before we invest too much effort in a solution using an ANY type, we should ensure that the program can scale. Almost all of our database processing should be done in boring strings, numbers, and dates. Instead of one smart function that accepts anything, it is usually better to dynamically generate a dumb function for each type.

APEX

Application Express (APEX) is a free web-based development environment for creating websites. APEX integrates seamlessly with an Oracle database and makes creating front ends for our data almost trivial.

To recreate the examples in this section, we need to install APEX on our database or create a free account at `https://apex.oracle.com`. After we install or create an account, we need to create a workspace, which is a collection of applications. Then we need to create an application, which is a collection of pages.

When inside the application, there are two main utilities – SQL Workshop and App Builder. In SQL Workshop we can quickly create, edit, and run SQL queries and SQL*Plus scripts.

If you installed APEX on your local database, then APEX already has access to the space data set. If you are using Oracle's website, then you need to load some sample data; see this chapter's worksheet in the GitHub repository for a tiny amount of sample data. On Oracle's website, you will need to create a script, copy and paste the commands from the repository, and then run the script.

After the data is loaded, we get to the most important part of APEX – the App Builder. After creating an application, which is done with a few simple clicks, it's time to create a page. To show how simple creating a page is, here are the entire steps: click "Create Page," click "Interactive Report," enter "Launch" for the Page Name, click "Next" twice, choose the LAUNCH table from the drop-down list, and click "Create." To see the page, click the Run Page button and enter a username and password, and then we should see something like Figure 19-2.

Launch Id	Launch Tag	Launch Date	Launch Category	Launch Status
1	1942-A01	13-JUN-42	military missile	failure
10	1943-A03	17-FEB-43	military missile	success
100	1944-M02	13-SEP-44	military missile	success
1000	1951-A11	12-APR-51	atmospheric rocket	success
10000	1963-S479	05-OCT-63	military missile	success

Figure 19-2. APEX launch report

This simple example only scratches the surface of APEX's features. We can use APEX to build complex interactive forms, reports, charts, REST services, custom authentication, or anything else we might find on a modern website. Simple pages can be built with a few clicks. Intermediate-level pages can be built using our SQL skills to define the data. Advanced pages can use custom SQL, PL/SQL, CSS, and JavaScript.

APEX is a great choice if we want to quickly create a front end for an Oracle database. Even if we don't want to build a website, installing APEX gives us access to several useful PL/SQL packages. For example, the powerful APEX_DATA_PARSER is great for declaratively reading several common file types.

Oracle Text

Oracle Text lets us build powerful search engine functionality in an Oracle database. Standard and custom PL/SQL functions are good enough for most text searching. Oracle Text is useful if we need a tool that *understands* language. Oracle Text features include fuzzy matching (matching different spellings of the same words), stopwords (minor words not worth indexing), case, thesauruses, different languages, and more.

Oracle Text works by creating special indexes on our data. There are three different index types, and each has a different purpose and syntax and different properties. CONTEXT is for indexing large documents and uses the CONTAINS operator. CTXCAT is for indexing text fragments combined with other columns and uses the CATSEARCH operator. CTXRULE is used for document classification and uses the MATCHRULE operator.

For example, let's search for GPS launches in the LAUNCH table. The MISSION column contains unstructured text, and dozens of the launches contain the string GPS. The following code is typical approach to look for GPS:

```
--GPS launches using LIKE operator.
select count(*) total
from launch
where lower(mission) like '%gps%';

TOTAL
-----
   72
```

The preceding query will always use a full table scan. Even a function-based index on the expression LOWER(MISSION) will not help. B-tree indexes sort data by the leading characters in the value. A B-tree index can help us find 'gps%', but a B-tree index cannot help us find '%gps '.

Text indexes work with words and can imitate a leading wildcard search. The following code creates a CONTEXT index on LAUNCH.MISSION:

```
--Create CONTEXT index on MISSION.
--(Text indexes need CREATE TABLE privileges on schema owner.)
grant create table to space;

create index launch_mission_text
    on launch(mission) indextype is ctxsys.context;
```

Using Oracle Text indexes requires changing the predicates. Instead of using LIKE we need to use CONTAINS. CONTAINS returns a score for ranking relevancy. If we're just looking for the existence of a word, we can filter with > 0.

The following query uses the CONTAINS operator and returns the same number of rows as the LIKE operator. The execution plan shows the CONTEXT index being used by a DOMAIN NAME operation:

```
--GPS launches using CONTAINS operator.
explain plan for
select count(*) total
from launch
where contains(mission, 'gps', 1) > 0;

select * from table(dbms_xplan.display(format => 'basic'));

Plan hash value: 4034124262

-------------------------------------------------
| Id | Operation         | Name                  |
-------------------------------------------------
|  0 | SELECT STATEMENT  |                       |
|  1 |  SORT AGGREGATE   |                       |
|  2 |   DOMAIN INDEX    | LAUNCH_MISSION_TEXT   |
-------------------------------------------------
```

One of the downsides to CONTEXT indexes is that they are not automatically updated after each transaction. We must manually synchronize the index like this:

```
--Synchronize index after DML on the LAUNCH table.
begin
    ctx_ddl.sync_index(idx_name =>
        sys_context('userenv', 'current_schema')||
        '.launch_mission_text');
end;
/
```

The preceding example only shows one simplistic use of Oracle Text. There are many hidden gems described in the 293-page *Text Application Developer's Guide*. For example, Oracle Text has offered machine learning algorithms for classification long before the feature became a buzzword.

Multilingual Engine

Although SQL and PL/SQL are powerful enough to solve any problem, there are clearly times when other programming languages are helpful. Oracle 21c introduced the multilingual engine (MLE), which integrates JavaScript with SQL and PL/SQL.

Java in the database was supposed to bring polyglot programming to Oracle, but it failed for several technical and sociological reasons explained in Chapter 15. Hopefully MLE can avoid some of those traps, and so far, the technology looks promising. But MLE currently only works on 21c, an innovation release, and only supports JavaScript, so it's too soon to tell what impact it will have.

The simplest way to call JavaScript is to use `console.log` and view the results in the DBMS output:

```
--Simple multilingual engine example.
begin
   dbms_mle.eval
   (
      context_handle => dbms_mle.create_context(),
      language_id    => 'JAVASCRIPT',
      source         => 'console.log("Hello World!");'
   );
end;
/

Hello World!
```

The preceding trivial example only shows one way to integrate PL/SQL and JavaScript. The DBMS_MLE package also lets us pass variables back and forth between PL/SQL and JavaScript. And an MLE SQL driver allows the server-side JavaScript to run and process SQL queries. It might seem foolish to use PL/SQL to run JavaScript to run SQL, when it's easier to cut out the middleman and just use PL/SQL to run the SQL. But server-side JavaScript allows web developers using APEX to avoid PL/SQL and stick to the language they know best.

As an example of how MLE could help a database developer, there have been a few times in the past when I've needed to use numbers with an arbitrary precision. Oracle's NUMBER data type has more than enough precision for the physical values we typically store in a database, like the number of employees or the results of practical equations.

But there's no easy way in PL/SQL to perform the kind of arbitrary precision math necessary for cryptography; NUMBER doesn't have enough precision, and there is no open source PL/SQL library as far as I know.

The following code shows how Oracle numbers eventually lose their precision. After about 41 digits, the numbers start to round, and we see zeroes instead of the expected values:

```
--Example of where Oracle's precision starts to fail.
select
    to_char(123456789012345678901234567890123456789 0123, 'TM') value
from dual;

VALUE
-------------------------------------------
12345678901234567890123456789012345678900 00
```

While JavaScript is not commonly touted for its math skills, there are several ways we can use MLE to quickly enable higher precision. There are several open source arbitrary precision math libraries available for JavaScript, but as of version 21c, the process of loading JavaScript libraries is complicated.[1] Alternatively, we can use the JavaScript BigInt type by placing the letter n at the end of the number, and then all of the digits are preserved:

```
--Use BigInt for better precision.
begin
    dbms_mle.eval
    (
        context_handle => dbms_mle.create_context(),
        language_id    => 'JAVASCRIPT',
        source         => 'console.log(
            12345678901234567890123456789012345678901 23n
            .toString());'
    );
```

---

[1] See this link for an example of creating a table to hold JavaScript libraries, loading the table, and then using the libraries: https://medium.com/graalvm/javascript-as-a-server-side-language-in-oracle-apex-20-2-457e073ca4ca

```
end;
/
```

```
123456789012345678901234567890123456789012345
```

We will inevitably run into integration issues because SQL and PL/SQL have to store the result as a string. But the alternative is to build our own math library, which is no easy task. SQL and PL/SQL will always be our main languages for Oracle data processing, but it's great to have JavaScript as another option for some extreme cases. And MLE will likely improve in future versions. Based on the previous betas, the next version of MLE is likely to support Python as another language, and it is likely to include improved mechanisms for loading and managing libraries.

Spatial

With Oracle Spatial, we can build geographic information systems in Oracle. Spatial can store, index, and query geometric information. Operations like joining take on a completely different meaning with geometric shapes. Historically, the Spatial option was an expensive add-on that very few organizations purchased. Now that the option is free, it's worth considering using Oracle Spatial for simple operations like finding the distance between geographic coordinates.

The spatial functions are generic and powerful, so they are commonly hidden behind a simpler interface that spares us from the many hard-coded values. There are many coordinate systems, but in practice most organizations only need a simple function to return the miles between two points, like the following function provides:

```
--Create function to get miles between two geographic coordinates.
create or replace function get_miles_between
(
    p_latitude1  number,
    p_longitude1 number,
    p_latitude2  number,
    p_longitude2 number
) return number is
begin
```

```
    return sdo_geom.sdo_distance
    (
        sdo_geometry(2001,4326,null,sdo_elem_info_array(1, 1, 1),
            sdo_ordinate_array(p_latitude1,p_longitude1)),
        sdo_geometry(2001,4326,null,sdo_elem_info_array(1, 1, 1),
            sdo_ordinate_array(p_latitude2,p_longitude2))
        ,1
        ,'unit=mile'
    );
end get_miles_between;
/
```

With that function, we can now easily calculate the distance between launch sites, like the popular Wallops Flight Facility and the White Sands Missile Range:

```
--Miles between Wallops and White Sands.
select round(get_miles_between(
    wallops.latitude,      wallops.longitude,
    white_sands.latitude, white_sands.longitude)) miles
from (select * from site where site_id = 1821) wallops
cross join (select * from site where site_id = 1895) white_sands;

MILES
-----
 2152
```

That simple, hard-coded example only scratches the surface of what Oracle Spatial can do. A more realistic example could involve creating geofences around launch sites and then detecting when a ship or airplane gets too close. A naïve, $O(N^2)$ solution would be to calculate the distance between all points and all vehicles. With Oracle Spatial, we could build a multidimensional R-tree index to more quickly find any vehicle that gets too close.

Other Features

This section briefly discusses some of the less popular options and features that can significantly extend the capabilities of our database. Although these options are uncommon, they are not small. Most of these features are the subject of one or more books in the Oracle documentation library. Some developers may spend a large part of their career working with one of these options.

Machine Learning

Oracle has had machine learning features for a long time. Past versions were called data mining or advanced analytics, and they required an expensive license that very few organizations paid for. Luckily, the option is now free, and there are many tools, algorithms, and APIs available for machine learning.

Machine learning has many APIs available in SQL, PL/SQL, R, and Python. Those interfaces let us create and train models on relational or non-relational tables. There's even a SQL Developer plug-in to help us quickly create data mining solutions.

There are certainly more popular choices for machine learning frameworks. Oracle's advantage is the time to production. If the data is already in a database, it's faster to move the algorithms to the data than it is to move the data to the algorithms.

OLAP

Online analytical processing is a different way of querying data. OLAP uses a multidimensional model and used to be a popular choice for data warehouses and business intelligence applications. There are many stand-alone OLAP products, but Oracle's OLAP is a licensable option embedded in the database. The option allows creating dimensions, cubes, and other OLAP structures. The product also comes with a separate Analytic Workspace Manager GUI.

OLAP is not as common as it used to be, and the core Oracle database is gradually adding OLAP-like features. For example, recent versions have added `ANALYTIC VIEW`, `ATTRIBUTE DIMENSION`, `DIMENSION`, and `HIERARCHY` to the database, without the need for an OLAP license.

Property Graph

Property graph is a tool for analyzing graphs – data that consists of vertexes and the edges between them. With property graph we can query existing Oracle tables using the property graph query language (PGQL). PGQL is a SQL-like language, but unfortunately PGQL is not embedded in Oracle SQL. Even evaluating property graph would require multiple external tools. Hopefully a future version of Oracle will better integrate PGQL with the database.

Virtual Private Database

Virtual private database augments normal database security with fine-grained access controls. Through VPD we can transparently insert predicates into relevant SQL statements to enforce access rules.

Setting up VPD requires several objects to work together. A logon trigger initializes a context, and that context will identify the users and their access. A package contains a function, and that function uses the context to return the right predicate. A policy must be set up to tie the functions to specific tables.

For example, VPD could restrict each user to only see rows in the LAUNCH table that are related to their assigned site. Any query against the LAUNCH table will automatically include that predicate. For example, a user might run the query SELECT * FROM LAUNCH, but Oracle would secretly run SELECT * FROM LAUNCH WHERE SITE_ID = 1.

VPD is a neat feature that solves unique security problems. But we should be careful before using VPD. Changing security through triggers and secret predicates can be confusing. Even administrators are affected, and they may not see the results they expect. And the execution plan will not show the added predicates. If we build a VPD system, we must thoroughly document the system and share that documentation with all users and administrators.

Database In-Memory

Database in-memory can significantly improve query performance by storing data in a columnar format. The columnar format allows superior compression, SIMD processing, in-memory storage indexes, join groups, optimized vector aggregation, etc. The in-memory column store can be useful if we have to process a large amount of data based on a small number of columns.

A columnar format is not always better, and Oracle will still store data in rows, blocks, disks, and the traditional memory structures. The in-memory licensable option requires allocating additional memory for columnar storage. Since 19c, we can use up to 16 GB for in-memory without a license.

Advanced Compression

The advanced compression licensable option enables better compression features. Basic table compression works per block and only works for direct-path writes. Advanced table compression can compress data better and can work with regular DML statements. Advanced compression also enables CLOB compression and deduplication, improved index compression, and export data pump compression. Compression features aren't just about saving space; saving space can also improve performance because Oracle has less data to read from disk.

Converged Database and Connections

Oracle's converged database model brings virtually every IT concept either inside the database or closely connected to the database. Every workload, programming paradigm, and data model can be built inside Oracle. But even when our data is stored in another system, Oracle provides tools to access it.

Connectivity is one of Oracle's greatest strengths compared with other databases. The power and simplicity of database links can be extended to many non-Oracle database systems through ODBC or the heterogeneous services option. Accessing external files can be easily done through PL/SQL APIs, BFILEs, or external tables. Newer versions even make it easy for Oracle to connect to object stores through data pump and external tables. Big data connectors allow Oracle to access NoSQL sources, like the Hadoop Distributed File System, and also allow those sources to process Oracle data.

Summary

Whenever someone asks, "Can I do this in an Oracle database?", the answer is always "yes." We don't always *want* to solve everything in Oracle, but the option always exists. Oracle is much more than a simple bit bucket. If our organization has already invested a lot of time and money into Oracle, we shouldn't ignore the arcane features discussed in this chapter.

CHAPTER 20

Use SQL More Often with Advanced Dynamic SQL

SQL is Oracle's greatest strength. Dynamic SQL is important because it gives us more opportunities to use SQL. Chapter 14 introduced the basic features: using dynamic SQL for DDL, unknown objects, and simplifying privileges; EXECUTE IMMEDIATE and bind variable syntax; simplifying dynamic code with multiline strings, alternative quoting syntax, and templating; and the benefit of generating code instead of creating generic code.

Now it's time to discuss advanced dynamic SQL. These features let us push Oracle to its limits and let us walk the fine line between overly generic madness and epic solutions. Programming is hard enough; programming program generators is incredibly difficult.

The topics discussed here should only be used after careful consideration. There's usually a simpler, more boring way to solve our problems. But it's worth remembering these solutions because some of the toughest programming problems cannot be solved without advanced dynamic SQL.

Parsing

Parsing SQL is ridiculously hard and is even listed as an anti-pattern in Chapter 15. Oracle's SQL syntax is huge and cannot be accurately parsed with a mere string function or regular expression. When possible, we should look for ways to constrain our code; if we can force code to look a certain way, then a simple string function may be sufficient.

As our input code becomes more generic, we must become more creative in our solutions. Parsing is one of those problems where we do not want to jump straight to

543

© Jon Heller 2023
J. Heller, *Pro Oracle SQL Development*, https://doi.org/10.1007/978-1-4842-8867-2_20

the most powerful programs, because the most powerful programs have huge learning curves. If we're lucky, our problem has already been solved and is stored somewhere in the data dictionary. A fair number of code inspection problems can be solved with VSQL, VSQL_PLAN, DBA_DEPENDENCIES, DBMS_XPLAN.DISPLAY, and other data dictionary views and tools. For more complex problems, we should look at tools like PL/Scope, PLSQL_LEXER, and ANTLR.

PL/Scope

PL/Scope is a tool for inspecting the identifiers and SQL statements used in PL/SQL programs. The information PL/Scope provides can help with simple code analysis and dependencies. PL/Scope doesn't provide a huge amount of information, but the program is easily accessible and accurate.

For example, we can analyze a small program by setting a session variable and recompiling:

```
--Generate identifier information.
alter session set plscope_settings='identifiers:all';

create or replace procedure temp_procedure is
    v_count number;
begin
    select count(*)
    into v_count
    from launch;
end;
/
```

The PL/Scope data is stored in the data dictionary and can be read with a query like this:

```
--Identifiers in the procedure.
select
    lpad(' ', (level-1)*3, ' ') || name name,
    type, usage, line, col
from
(
```

```
    select *
    from user_identifiers
    where object_name = 'TEMP_PROCEDURE'
) identifiers
start with usage_context_id = 0
connect by prior usage_id = usage_context_id
order siblings by line, col;
```

NAME	TYPE	USAGE	LINE	COL
TEMP_PROCEDURE	PROCEDURE	DECLARATION	1	11
TEMP_PROCEDURE	PROCEDURE	DEFINITION	1	11
V_COUNT	VARIABLE	DECLARATION	2	4
NUMBER	NUMBER DATATYPE	REFERENCE	2	12

We can also get information about the SQL statements called by the program. This information can simplify tuning because it's otherwise difficult to find the SQL_ID of all statements called by a program:

```
--Statements in the procedure.
select text, type, line, col, sql_id
from user_statements;
```

TEXT	TYPE	LINE	COL	SQL_ID
SELECT COUNT(*) FROM LAUNCH	SELECT	4	4	046cuu31c149u

PL/Scope provides high-level information, but it cannot truly parse our programs. In practice, I've rarely found a use for PL/Scope. Even for a task like identifying dependencies, PL/Scope is often insufficient because the program only finds *static* dependencies.

PLSQL_LEXER

Language problems require breaking a program into small pieces. The smallest pieces would be bytes and characters, but those are too low level to be useful. The atomic units of parsing are tokens. A token is a sequence of characters categorized in a way to be useful to a compiler. Lexical analysis is the process of breaking a program into tokens.

Even a lexical analysis of SQL or PL/SQL is too difficult for small string functions or regular expressions. Features like comments and the alternative quoting mechanism make it difficult to pull a token out of the middle of a program. I built the open source package PLSQL_LEXER[1] to break SQL and PL/SQL into tokens. Once we have the tokens, we can begin to understand the code, change the tokens, and reassemble the tokens into a new version of the program. The following is a simple example of creating tokens from a SQL statement:

```
--Tokenize a simple SQL statement.
select type, to_char(value) value, line_number, column_number
from plsql_lexer.lex('select*from dual');
```

TYPE	VALUE	LINE_NUMBER	COLUMN_NUMBER
word	select	1	1
*	*	1	7
word	from	1	8
whitespace		1	12
word	dual	1	13
EOF		1	17

The preceding output is very low level, which is exactly what we need in order to dynamically analyze and modify programs. With tokens we can do things like classify a statement (because dynamic SQL must treat a SELECT different than a CREATE), remove statement terminators (because dynamic SQL cannot have a semicolon at the end), or perform some simple linting (check for common errors like putting a hint comment in the wrong location). Working with tokens is painful but necessary to solve challenging language problems.

ANTLR

ANTLR is an open source parser generator that can understand and modify almost any programming language. ANTLR comes with a pre-built PL/SQL lexer and parser that can be used to break SQL and PL/SQL into parse trees. These parse trees are similar to the railroad diagrams in the language references.

---

[1] The example assumes you have installed https://github.com/method5/plsql_lexer

After a lot of downloading, configuring, and compiling, we can generate parse trees with a command like this:

```
C:\ >grun PlSql sql_script -gui
BEGIN
    NULL;
END;
/
^Z
```

The preceding code will open a GUI with the parse tree shown in Figure 20-1.

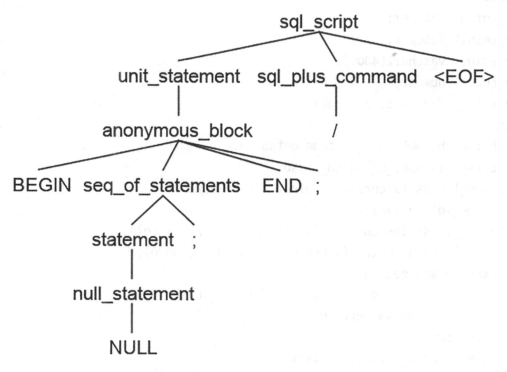

Figure 20-1. *ANTLR parse tree for a simple PL/SQL program*

ANTLR is the most powerful parsing tool for Oracle SQL and PL/SQL. But there are many issues with the program; the code is in Java, which may not work in our database, the PL/SQL grammar is not complete, and generating the parse tree is only the beginning of the real work.

DBMS_SQL

DBMS_SQL is the original way to run dynamic SQL. DBMS_SQL is much less convenient than EXECUTE IMMEDIATE and not as fast, but it has several advantages. Only DBMS_SQL can execute SQL over a database link, parse[2] the SQL and retrieve column metadata, and return or bind an unknown number of items.

For example, the following code parses a SQL statement, finds the column type and name, runs the statement, and retrieves the results:

```
--Example of dynamically retrieving data and metadata.
declare
    v_cursor integer;
    v_result integer;
    v_value  varchar2(4000);
    v_count  number;
    v_cols   dbms_sql.desc_tab4;
begin
    --Parse the SQL and get some metadata.
    v_cursor := dbms_sql.open_cursor;
    dbms_sql.parse(v_cursor, 'select * from dual',
        dbms_sql.native);
    dbms_sql.describe_columns3(v_cursor, v_count, v_cols);
    dbms_sql.define_column(v_cursor, 1, v_value, 4000);
    --Execute and get data.
    v_result := dbms_sql.execute_and_fetch(v_cursor);
    dbms_sql.column_value(v_cursor, 1, v_value);
    --Close cursor.
    dbms_sql.close_cursor(v_cursor);
    --Display metadata and data.
    dbms_output.put_line('Type: '||
        case v_cols(1).col_type
            when dbms_types.typecode_varchar then 'VARCHAR'
            --Add more types here (this is painful)...
```

---

[2] Although DBMS_SQL can parse SQL, it does not make the entire parse tree available the way ANTLR does. DBMS_SQL can only solve a small number of our parsing problems.

```
      end
   );
   dbms_output.put_line('Name: '||v_cols(1).col_name);
   dbms_output.put_line('Value: '||v_value);
end;
/

Type: VARCHAR
Name: DUMMY
Value: X
```

The preceding syntax is tricky, and we'll probably need to look at the manual whenever we write code for DBMS_SQL. The package also has some unexpected behavior. The PARSE function automatically runs DDL commands, so we need to be careful even describing statements. Despite these problems, DBMS_SQL is still a great tool to programmatically inspect, build, and run SQL statements.

DBMS_XMLGEN

DBMS_XMLGEN.GETXML is a useful function that converts the results of a query into an XML type. The following is a simple example of the function:

```
--Convert query to XML.
select dbms_xmlgen.getxml('select * from dual') result
from dual;

<?xml version="1.0"?>
<ROWSET>
 <ROW>
  <DUMMY>X</DUMMY>
 </ROW>
</ROWSET>
```

GETXML was probably only intended to convert relational data into XML for storage or processing in another system. But notice how the query is passed as a string, which means the query is not checked at compile time. That minor design choice lets us do some surprisingly interesting things with this function.

With GETXML, we can dynamically generate and run the query based on another query. With careful code generation and XML parsing, we can query tables that may not exist, return values from an unknown set of tables, etc. Most importantly, we can run dynamic SQL entirely in SQL. There is no need to create any PL/SQL objects.

For example, the following query counts all tables in the SPACE schema that have a name like LAUNCH*:

```
--Number of rows in all LAUNCH* tables in SPACE schema.
--
--Convert XML to columns.
select
   table_name,
   to_number(extractvalue(xml, '/ROWSET/ROW/COUNT')) count
from
(
   --Get results as XML.
   select table_name,
      xmltype(dbms_xmlgen.getxml(
         'select count(*) count from '||table_name
      )) xml
   from all_tables
   where owner = sys_context('userenv', 'current_schema')
      and table_name like 'LAUNCH%'
)
order by table_name;

TABLE_NAME          COUNT
------------------  -----
LAUNCH              70535
LAUNCH_AGENCY       71884
LAUNCH_PAYLOAD_ORG  21214
...
```

Using XML is tricky because we have to parse the results, and we still need to know something about the output columns ahead of time. Unfortunately, the query string can be constructed but cannot use a bind variable. And Oracle's XML processing also isn't as robust as its relational engine. SQL queries can easily handle millions of rows, but when processing XML we need to be more careful, or we will run into performance problems with medium-sized data sets.

PL/SQL Common Table Expressions

We can also run dynamic SQL inside SQL using PL/SQL common table expressions. We can define a function in a SQL statement and call EXECUTE IMMEDIATE in that function. We need to use PL/SQL, but we don't have to create and manage any permanent PL/SQL objects.

For example, the following query returns the same results as the last query:

```
--Number of rows in all LAUNCH* tables in the current schema.
with function get_rows(p_table varchar2) return varchar2 is
   v_number number;
begin
   execute immediate 'select count(*) from '||
      dbms_assert.sql_object_name(p_table)   into v_number;
   return v_number;
end;
select table_name, get_rows(table_name) count
from all_tables
where owner = sys_context('userenv', 'current_schema')
   and table_name like 'LAUNCH%'
order by table_name;
/
```

The preceding query is more robust than the DBMS_XMLGEN.GETXML technique, but PL/SQL common table expressions do not work in every context. And both techniques still require knowledge about the shape of the result set.

Method4 Dynamic SQL

Dynamic SQL statements can be ranked by how generic they are. Per Oracle's nomenclature, method 1 is for non-query statements, method 2 is for non-query statements with bind variables, method 3 is for queries that return a known number of items, and method 4 is for queries that return an unknown number of items. So far in this book, even when dynamic SQL is used, the programs still know what output to expect. SQL becomes much more difficult when we don't even know what the statements will return.

Applications frequently use method 4 technologies. For example, our IDE can run any query and determine the columns at run time. And many applications can consume a dynamically generated ref cursor, which does not necessarily have a known set of columns. It's rare for a SQL or PL/SQL program to need a solution as generic as method 4.

Before we create those generic solutions, a word of caution is in order. While it's fun to build generic programs, it's quite unusual in a database to have no idea what the results will be. In order to do anything useful with data, we generally at least need to know the shape of the data. In practice, the vast majority of SQL programs with a method 4 solution are better served by hard-coding the columns.

Oracle data cartridge provides interfaces that let us extend the database and build method 4 solutions in SQL. Data cartridges can be used to build custom indexes (such as Oracle Text), custom analytic functions, custom statistics, and functions with dynamic return types.

Building a data cartridge is challenging and requires using the ANY types to fully describe all inputs and outputs. Luckily, there are pre-built open source solutions, such as my unoriginally named Method4 program.[3] For example, with that program we can recreate the count-all-the-LAUNCH-tables query with the following SQL statement:

```
--Method4 dynamic SQL in SQL.
select * from table(method4.dynamic_query(
q'[
   select replace(
      q'!
         select '#TABLE_NAME#' table_name, count(*) count
         from #TABLE_NAME#
      !', '#TABLE_NAME#', table_name) sql_statement
   from all_tables
   where owner = sys_context('userenv', 'current_schema')
      and table_name like 'LAUNCH%'
```

---

[3] The example assumes you have installed https://github.com/method5/method4

```
]'
))
order by table_name;
```

The preceding example returns the same results as the previous two queries. But this new version has an important difference – the first line of the query uses * instead of a hard-coded list of columns. Method4 dynamically generates columns each time the query runs. This allows us to solve some rare but difficult problems, such as dynamic pivoting or generating and running queries based on configuration data stored in tables.

Writing a query inside a query, inside a query, leads to weird-looking strings. The data cartridge code is complex, slow, and buggier than average PL/SQL code. Those penalties are the price we pay to reach the pinnacle of query flexibility.

Polymorphic Table Functions

Polymorphic table functions are a new feature in 18c, and they also have a dynamically generated return type. Polymorphic table functions are sort of like a high-level data cartridge solution; they are much easier to implement, but the shape of the query results is typically constrained by table and column names.

The following example creates a polymorphic table function that doesn't do anything particularly useful. The function merely returns everything from the input table. Creating a fully functional sample would take too much space. Even generating this mostly worthless function is complicated enough:

```
--Create polymorphic table function package.
create or replace package ptf as
    function describe(p_table in out dbms_tf.table_t)
    return dbms_tf.describe_t;
    function do_nothing(tab in table)
    return table pipelined
    row polymorphic using ptf;
end;
/

create or replace package body ptf as
    function describe(p_table in out dbms_tf.table_t)
```

```
    return dbms_tf.describe_t as
    begin
        return null;
    end;
end;
/
```

With the preceding package in place, we can call the DO_NOTHING function against any table, and the function will return the entire output of that table:

```
--Call polymorphic table function.
select * from ptf.do_nothing(dual);
```

```
DUMMY
-----
X
```

While the preceding output may look unimpressive, returning a generic relational result with only a few lines of code is amazing compared with the hundreds of lines of code it takes to accomplish the same thing with Oracle data cartridge. But we still need to do something useful with the data, and it's hard to demonstrate that without a few hundred lines of code, so we'll need to use our imagination here.

A simple but more realistic use of polymorphic table functions is to return every column from a table *except* for certain columns. For quick data analysis on many tables with many columns, where most of the columns are auditing columns we want to ignore, it can help to quickly run queries like this: SELECT * FROM EVERYTHING_BUT(EMPLOYEE, COLUMNS(CREATE_DATE, CREATE_USER, ...)); That function would look similar to the preceding function, except we would have to loop through the columns and set the property PASS_THROUGH to FALSE for the relevant columns.[4]

We can create generic conversion functions to turn any table, or any SQL statement, into JSON, CSV, XML, or any other format. Or we could do the opposite and create generic conversion functions that turn those file formats into relational data. (However, in practice, it is probably wiser to use pre-built packages like APEX_DATA_PARSER to handle file conversions. That package may return hundreds of extra columns, but dealing with extra columns is easier than trying to reimplement conversion routines.)

---

[4] See this page for the source code of a full polymorphic table function example: https://oracle-base.com/articles/18c/polymorphic-table-functions-18c#remove-columns

We can almost create our own SQL syntax. We could dynamically change columns and column names, create our own definition of how * works, dynamically pivot, and lots of weird things I can't even imagine.

SQL Macros

Normal PL/SQL functions execute every time a SQL statement calls them. For example, if we have a specific date formatting requirement and we don't want to repeat that logic multiple times, we can encapsulate that logic inside a function named TO_ISO8601. If our application consistently uses that format, our database may be littered with calls to that function, like SELECT TO_ISO8601(START_DATE), TO_ISO8601(STOP_DATE) FROM SITE. There are tricks we can use to reduce the overhead of calling the function, but we may still end up spending more time context switching between SQL and PL/SQL than doing real work. We have to make a trade-off; repeating the TO_CHAR logic as SQL expressions improves performance, but using the function reduces the chance of a developer creating a bug.

SQL macros give us the best of both worlds and eliminate the need for that trade-off. Macros are PL/SQL functions that are replaced at compile time with a SQL expression or SQL query. Macros don't return *values*; they return *strings* that will form part of our final SQL statement.

The following **scalar macro** can help optimize our queries, but there are a few odd features in this function. Notice how the function parameter P_DATE is not used directly in the function; it is neither concatenated to the return string nor passed into the string as a bind variable. But when Oracle evaluates the macro at compile time, P_DATE is replaced with the relevant column name or expression, and a valid SQL statement is created:

```
--Convert a date into a specific kind of ISO8601 formatted string.
create or replace function to_iso8601(p_date date)
    return varchar2 sql_macro(scalar) is
begin
    return
    q'!
        to_char(p_date, 'YYYY-MM-DD"T"HH24:MI:SS"Z"')
    !';
end;
/
```

SQL macros are a PL/SQL trick that helps us avoid using too much PL/SQL. But we should be cautious not to overuse this feature. SQL macros were introduced in 21c and back ported to 19c, but there is some ambiguity over exactly which features are available in which version of 19c. We should usually stick with static code instead of dynamic code, although it's debatable if a macro counts as "dynamic." Macros don't suffer from the same problems as regular dynamic SQL, such as the concern for SQL injection. On the other hand, since macros only return strings, we can't tell if there is an error until the function is used. And there may be some confusion over how to tune these statements; the final SQL text shows up in a 10053 trace file but not in GV$SQL.SQL_FULLTEXT. We should only use scalar macros when we have a confirmed performance problem.

A **table macro** returns a string that will be evaluated as a table function that returns rows of data. With table macros, we can finally create parameterized views.

Like with scalar macros, we should be cautious of overusing table macros. Although developers have been asking for parameterized views for a long time, there's still not always a clear advantage of parameterized views over regular views. The following example creates a simple view and a simple table macro:

```
--Compare a regular view with a table macro parameterized view.
create or replace view launch_view as select * from launch;

create or replace function launch_macro(p_launch_category varchar2) return
varchar2 sql_macro is
begin
   return
   q'[
      select *
      from launch
      where launch_category = p_launch_category
   ]';
end;
/

select * from launch_view where launch_category = 'orbital';

select * from launch_macro(p_launch_category => 'orbital');
```

Selecting from the table macro isn't any easier than selecting from the view. There might be an advantage to a table macro if the condition is complex and the macro hides that complexity from the user. But we can accomplish the same thing in a regular view by projecting a complex expression and then using it in a simple condition. Also, there's no performance advantage of table macros over regular views. Oracle already treats regular views like a macro in some ways; the optimizer transforms SQL as if the outer query and the view text are hard-coded together into one large statement.

The real advantage of table macros is when we create polymorphic views by passing in table or column names as arguments. The following code is yet another way to dynamically count the number of rows for a table. But once again, the macro code is not quite as dynamic as we're used to. The table name parameter, P_TABLE, is simply used as is in the returned string, and we don't have to worry about concatenation, bind variables, or SQL injection. And when we call the function, we're not passing in a string that represents the table name; we're passing in the table name directly as an identifier:

```
--SQL Macro for counting the number of rows in a table.
create or replace function get_row_count
(
    p_table dbms_tf.table_t
) return varchar2 sql_macro(table) is
begin
    return
    q'!
        select count(*) row_count
        from p_table
    !';
end;
/

select * from get_row_count(launch);

ROW_COUNT
---------
    70535
```

The preceding solution is only slightly more dynamic than simply hard-coding the query SELECT COUNT(*) FROM LAUNCH. But that's not a bad thing – it's good to have a range of solutions from hard-coded to fully dynamic. And these small examples don't fully explore the power of SQL macros. Just like polymorphic table functions, table macros can use the package DBMS_TF to loop through columns and build ridiculously dynamic queries. SQL macros provide yet another way to solve complex challenges like comparing generic row sets, dynamic pivoting, or any time we need to process "anything" in the database.

Summary

With the right advanced packages and features, we can solve any problem in Oracle. Dynamic SQL not only creates new opportunities for database programs, but a little advanced code in the right place can vastly simplify our programs by letting us focus on Oracle's best feature – SQL. Most of the features in this chapter rely on PL/SQL, and it's time to stop using PL/SQL only indirectly. The next chapter directly focuses on PL/SQL and shows how to take our database code to the highest level.

CHAPTER 21

Level Up Your Skills with PL/SQL

If you use Oracle SQL long enough, you will eventually want to learn PL/SQL. SQL is the primary language for Oracle development, but we need PL/SQL to package our work and to call APIs that control and extend database functionality. If we decide to learn PL/SQL, the first step is to create a safe playground. There's not enough room here for a full PL/SQL tutorial, but we can at least discuss the features most likely to help us enhance our SQL. To become a true Oracle master, you'll need PL/SQL to help you teach others and create programs.

Is PL/SQL Worth Mastering?

Before you spend even more time learning about Oracle, it's worth briefly considering if PL/SQL is worth investing in. SQL is often good enough, there are technology trends moving away from products like Oracle SQL and PL/SQL, and there are arguments against specialization.

No matter where you go from here with Oracle database development, the focus remains on SQL. PL/SQL is a great language precisely because it integrates so well with SQL. PL/SQL is considered more advanced than SQL, but advanced does not always mean better. PL/SQL code is rarely faster or simpler than SQL code, so we must resist the urge to use obscure PL/SQL features instead of ordinary SQL features. For example, parallel pipelined functions are a neat way to parallelize PL/SQL code. That feature is better than single-threaded PL/SQL, but the best option is usually a single parallel SQL statement.

Learning the proprietary PL/SQL language means we are betting a part of our career on the fortunes of Oracle Corporation and the market for relational databases. Oracle Corporation is one of the largest software companies, SQL is one of the most popular

© Jon Heller 2023
J. Heller, *Pro Oracle SQL Development*, https://doi.org/10.1007/978-1-4842-8867-2_21

programming languages, Oracle has the largest market share of any relational database, and PL/SQL is the best procedural language extension for SQL. On the other hand, Oracle Corporation's revenue is stagnant, their cloud business is struggling, technologies like NoSQL are growing at the expense of relational databases, and open source technologies and languages are growing at the expense of proprietary code.

We also need to consider the argument about being a technology generalist instead of a specialist. We don't want to be a jack of all trades, master of none. On the other hand, developers with a broad background and a resume that looks like alphabet soup are what recruiters look for.

There are great reasons to learn more about PL/SQL, but at some point, our time might be better spent learning a completely different language.

Create a PL/SQL Playground

We need a safe playground to learn new skills, but building a sandbox can be challenging in conservative Oracle development environments. Many developers don't have private databases, private schemas, or even the privileges to create objects. But even in the worst-case environment, we can still learn PL/SQL.

Obviously, we could always create a private database on our home PC or in the cloud, or we could use websites like `https://dbfiddle.uk/` and `https://livesql.oracle.com/`. But the easiest way to learn a skill is to use it at work or at least with work data, and we can't put our company's data in our private database. Luckily, there are tricks that let us write PL/SQL on any database with no additional privileges.

Anonymous blocks are the best way to get started with PL/SQL in a highly limited environment. We can run anonymous blocks that don't change anything without anyone ever knowing. This book has used many simple anonymous blocks, but anonymous blocks don't have to be simple. We can use anonymous blocks to imitate large packages, stored procedures, and functions. The following example shows an anonymous block with an embedded function, and the function has an embedded procedure:

```
--PL/SQL block with nested procedure and function.
declare
    v_declare_variables_first number;
    function some_function return number is
        procedure some_procedure is
```

```
      begin
         null;
      end some_procedure;
   begin
      some_procedure;
      return 1;
   end some_function;
begin
   v_declare_variables_first := some_function;
   dbms_output.put_line('Output: '||v_declare_variables_first);
end;
/
```

Output: 1

We can embed functions and procedures as deep as necessary to imitate large packages. To practice using PL/SQL objects in SQL code, we can use PL/SQL common table expressions. As long as we have access to an Oracle database, there's always a way to experiment with PL/SQL.

PL/SQL Integration Features

This chapter is not a full PL/SQL tutorial. Much of the basic syntax, like variable assignment, IF statements, and looping, can be learned through osmosis. And much of the syntax works the same in both SQL and PL/SQL; most operators, expressions, conditions, and functions work the same way in both languages.

PL/SQL has many of the same benefits as SQL. PL/SQL is a high-level language meant for processing data and is highly portable. A PL/SQL program written for HP-UX on Itanium works just fine on Windows on Intel x86-64.

To fully understand the PL/SQL language, I recommend reading the *PL/SQL Language Reference*. The manual is the most accurate source even if it isn't always the easiest to read. This chapter only focuses on the PL/SQL features that promote integration between SQL and PL/SQL.

Tips for Packaging Code

The first and most obvious tip for packaging our code is to use PACKAGEs to encapsulate related code. We don't want to pollute a schema with all our procedures and functions. A simple rule to help with organizing code is to think of packages as nouns and their procedures and functions as verbs.

By default, procedures, functions, and variables should only be defined in the package body, which makes them private. Procedures, functions, and variables defined in the package specification are public. We always want to minimize the number of entry points and public interfaces to our programs. Every part of our program that we expose to the world is another thing we have to support and maintain.

When we build programs for other developers, we must think carefully about the program's dependencies. Other developers may not have Enterprise Edition, the latest version, elevated privileges, the ability to dedicate an entire schema to a project, optional components like Java, licensed options like partitioning, etc.

Session Data

There are several ways to store and share data within a session using PL/SQL. But before we turn to PL/SQL solutions, we should first evaluate if a heap table, global temporary table, or private temporary table can be used instead. If tables don't work, we can use the **session state** to persist information for the duration of a session. Session state is built with global variables defined in package specifications and bodies. The values of those global package variables are retained in between calls to the package.

Global variables defined in a package specification are public. Global public variables are easier to access, but they are considered a bad programming practice because we can't control how they are used. If we need to maintain global variables in our packages, we should almost always define them in the package body to make them private and then create getters and setters for them. SQL cannot directly access package global variables; we'll have to create setters and getters anyway, so we might as well use private variables as much as possible. The following code shows these rules in action:

```
--Create a package with global public and private variables.
create or replace package test_package is
   g_public_global number;
   procedure set_private(a number);
```

```
   function get_private return number;
end;
/

--Create a package body that sets and gets private variables.
create or replace package body test_package is
   g_private_global number;
   procedure set_private(a number) is
   begin
      g_private_global := a;
   end;
   function get_private return number is
   begin
      return g_private_global;
   end;
end;
/

--Public variables can be get or set directly in PL/SQL.
begin
   test_package.g_public_global := 1;
end;
/

--Private variables cannot be set directly. This code raises
--"PLS-00302: component 'G_PRIVATE_GLOBAL' must be declared"
begin
   test_package.g_private_global := 1;
end;
/

--Public variables still cannot be read directly in SQL.
--This code raises "ORA-06553: PLS-221: 'G_PUBLIC_GLOBAL' is
-- not a procedure or is undefined"
select test_package.g_public_global from dual;
```

```
--Setters and getters with private variables are preferred.
begin
    test_package.set_private(1);
end;
/

--This function can be used in SQL.
select test_package.get_private from dual;

GET_PRIVATE
-----------
          1
```

Global variables create a package state that persists until the session ends. The error "ORA-04068: existing state of packages has been discarded" may be frustrating, but the error is usually our own fault. If we create global variables, and the package is recompiled, Oracle can't possibly know what to do with the existing package state. The best way around that error is to avoid using global variables unless we truly need them.

Sometimes it's helpful to store data in a **context** and read it with the SYS_CONTEXT function. Context data has been used several times throughout this book, such as SYS_CONTEXT('USERENV', 'CURRENT_SCHEMA'). Many of our session settings are available through the default USERENV context, but we can also create our own contexts. Custom contexts can be useful for passing data to parallel statements since parallel sessions do not inherit package state.

As we create session data, we must remember that our resources are not infinite. Session data will consume PGA memory, so we should avoid loading large tables into PL/SQL variables. Sessions also consume PGA for sorting and hashing, as well as temporary tablespace for sorting and hashing, and may require lots of undo data for large and long-running statements. If we use connection pooling and the sessions accumulate large amounts of private data, the application may need to call the procedures DBMS_SESSION.RESET_PACKAGE, DBMS_SESSION.FREE_UNUSED_USER_MEMORY, and DBMS_SESSION.CLEAR_ALL_CONTEXT('CONTEXT_NAME'). A basic understanding of Oracle architecture is helpful for managing session resources.

Transactions I: COMMIT, ROLLBACK, and SAVEPOINT

Atomicity is one of the greatest strengths of a relational database – changes are either completely committed or not committed at all. Oracle provides the mechanisms to enable atomicity, but it is our responsibility to use transaction control statements to precisely define logical transactions. Our PL/SQL code may include many DML statements, and we need to use COMMIT, ROLLBACK, and SAVEPOINT to ensure that our changes make sense.

Oracle automatically begins a transaction for the first DML statement in a session, but Oracle does not automatically commit or roll back that transaction. However, there are notable exceptions to that rule; your client or IDE may be set to auto-commit, and DDL commands like TRUNCATE and CREATE are automatically committed.

Most of our commits should be manually requested, and we should only issue a COMMIT when a logical unit of work is done. That advice may sound obvious to some, but it may sound dubious to those who are familiar with other database architectures where locks and transactions are expensive things to be avoided. In Oracle, we do not want to blindly commit after every change. Over-committing causes performance problems and may cause a weird half-changed state if there is an application error.

There is a subtle difference between a ROLLBACK command and a rollback caused by an error. The ROLLBACK command will undo all uncommitted changes in the *transaction*. An implicit rollback, caused by an exception, will only undo the *statement*. Implicit rollbacks act like a rollback to a SAVEPOINT created at the beginning of the PL/SQL block.

To demonstrate transaction control, we need to start by creating a simple table for our examples:

```
--Create a simple table for transaction tests.
create table transaction_test(a number);
```

Exceptions do not automatically roll back the entire transaction. If we run the following commands, the initial INSERT works, the UPDATE fails, but the table still contains the row created by the initial INSERT:

```
--Insert one row:
insert into transaction_test values(1);

--Fails with: ORA-01722: invalid number
update transaction_test set a = 'B';
```

```
--The table still contains the original inserted value:
select * from transaction_test;
```

```
A
-
1
```

The preceding example behaves differently if it's wrapped in PL/SQL, because a PL/SQL block is considered a single statement. The INSERT still succeeds, and the UPDATE still fails, but that failure causes the rollback of everything, and we are left with no data in the table:

```
--Reset the scratch table.
truncate table transaction_test;
```

```
--Combine good INSERT and bad UPDATE in a PL/SQL block.
--Raises: "ORA-01722: invalid number"
begin
    insert into transaction_test values(1);
    update transaction_test set a = 'B';
end;
/
```

```
--The table is empty:
select * from transaction_test;
```

```
A
-
```

This rollback behavior means that we usually do not need to create extra EXCEPTION blocks only to include a ROLLBACK command. A PL/SQL exception is already going to roll back the whole block. If we include an explicit ROLLBACK command, it will roll back the entire transaction, including things that happened before the PL/SQL block.

If we already have an EXCEPTION block for some other purpose, we still probably don't need to include a ROLLBACK as long as we also include a RAISE. As long as the exception is propagated, the statement will roll back.

If we remember how implicit statement rollback works, we can avoid unnecessary exception handling, like in the following example:

```
--Unnecessary exception handling.
begin
    insert into transaction_test values(1);
    update transaction_test set a = 'B';
exception when others then
    rollback;
    raise;
end;
/
```

The preceding, unnecessary exception handling does too much, but we can also get in trouble if our exception handling does too little. For example, imagine if the preceding exception code was EXCEPTION WHEN OTHERS THEN NULL. The INSERT still works, and the UPDATE still fails, but the block ignores the exception; the statement appears to complete successfully even though half of it failed, and we may end up with half-committed changes. Transaction control is another example of where doing no exception handling is often the best choice.

While it's safe to rely on implicit rollbacks of PL/SQL blocks, we cannot always rely on implicit rollbacks for our SQL client. SQL*Plus, like most SQL clients, defaults to COMMIT on a successful exit and ROLLBACK if the session was abnormally terminated. But that default behavior is configurable in SQL*Plus and other clients. It's always safest to include a COMMIT or ROLLBACK at the end of our work.

Transactions II: Implicit Cursor Attributes

Implicit cursor attributes are often useful for managing transactions. After a DML statement executes, we may want to know how many rows were changed. The number of rows can be useful for logging or for determining if the statement was successful. We can use SQL%ROWCOUNT to find the number of rows affected, but we must reference implicit cursor attributes before a COMMIT or ROLLBACK. The following example shows how to correctly and incorrectly use SQL%ROWCOUNT:

```
--Correct: SQL%ROWCOUNT is before ROLLBACK.
begin
    insert into transaction_test values(1);
    dbms_output.put_line('Rows inserted: '||sql%rowcount);
```

```
   rollback;
end;
/
```

Rows inserted: 1

```
--Incorrect: SQL%ROWCOUNT is after ROLLBACK.
begin
   insert into transaction_test values(1);
   rollback;
   dbms_output.put_line('Rows inserted: '||sql%rowcount);
end;
/
```

Rows inserted: 0

Transactions III: Row-Level Locking

Running SQL statements in PL/SQL becomes more complicated in a multiuser environment. Luckily, Oracle's robust implementation of a multiversion consistency model avoids the locking problems seen in many other databases. Due to the way Oracle implements locking, we don't have to worry about lock escalation or readers and writers blocking each other. But every consistency and locking system has subtle details we need to watch out for.

A good way to demonstrate Oracle's row-level locking mechanism is with a weird, unrealistic example. The following code demonstrates that sessions *initially* wait because of a row lock, but the sessions *continue* to wait until the blocking transaction completes. With SAVEPOINT and ROLLBACK, a transaction can release a lock without completing, thus creating an opportunity for another session to "steal" a lock:

```
--Session #1: These commands all run normally.
insert into transaction_test values(0);
commit;
savepoint savepoint1;
update transaction_test set a = 1;
```

```
--Session #2: This command hangs, waiting for the locked row.
update transaction_test set a = 2;

--Session #1: Rollback to the previous savepoint.
--Notice that session #2 is still waiting.
rollback to savepoint1;

--Session #3: This command steals the lock and completes.
--Notice that session #2 is still waiting, on a row that is
-- no longer locked.
update transaction_test set a = 3;
commit;
```

This odd lock-stealing behavior is a consequence of the way Oracle stores lock data. Oracle does not have a separate table that stores all the row locks. If such a table existed, we could use it to prevent the lock-stealing scenario, and we could use it to answer questions like "What rows are locked right now?" But in practice, lock-stealing is not a problem, and we rarely need to know precisely what rows are locked if they are not blocking anything. Those two minor disadvantages are a good price to pay for not having a lock table that would require a tremendous amount of extra overhead.

Instead of using a separate table, locks are stored inside the data block that contains the locked rows, in the Interested Transaction List. The ITL is a tiny data structure that lists which transaction is locking which row. In the preceding example, when session #2 tried to lock a row, it saw that session #1 already had the lock. By rolling back to the save point, session #1 gave up that lock, but session #2 is not notified. Session #2 can't be expected to check the individual rows – that would require constantly rereading the tables. Instead, session #2 waits for session #1 to finish, which never happens. Rolling back to a save point gives up a lock but doesn't end the transaction. This creates an opportunity for session #3 to cut in line and steal the lock.

We could argue that Oracle doesn't really implement row-level locking if we are able to "steal" a lock like this. In practice this situation is very unlikely to ever occur. This example is not a warning; it's only meant to teach how row-level locking works by demonstrating one of its quirks.

Transactions IV: Isolation and Consistency

Oracle provides mechanisms to allow our PL/SQL applications to act like they are the only database user. This *isolation* is necessary to avoid transaction integrity problems such as dirty reads (reading uncommitted data from another transaction) and non-repeatable or phantom reads (running the same query twice in a transaction and getting different results). Oracle provides two different isolation levels to prevent those problems.

The default isolation level is called **read committed**. Read committed mode prevents dirty reads and ensures that every *statement* is consistent. Statement-level consistency means that a single SQL statement will always read and process data as of a specific point in time. Even if another session deletes all the rows of a table while we are querying that table, our session won't notice.

For example, the following SQL statement reads from the LAUNCH table twice. The following query will always return the same results for each COUNT(*), regardless of what read or write operations other sessions are executing. This statement-level consistency is provided by the undo data that is generated by every change:

```
--These subqueries will always return the same number.
select
    (select count(*) from transaction_test) count1,
    (select count(*) from transaction_test) count2
from dual;
```

Consistency gets more difficult when we use multiple queries in PL/SQL. If consistency only applies *within* a SQL statement, the following PL/SQL block may return different numbers for the same query run at two different times:

```
--These queries may return different numbers.
declare
    v_count1 number;
    v_count2 number;
begin
    select count(*) into v_count1 from transaction_test;
    dbms_output.put_line(v_count1);
    dbms_lock.sleep(5);
```

```
    select count(*) into v_count2 from transaction_test;
    dbms_output.put_line(v_count2);
end;
/
```

If we use a **serializable** transaction, then everything in our session happens as if it was run at the beginning of the transaction. If we change the session's isolation level, the previous example will always return the same numbers within the same transaction. The only difference between these PL/SQL blocks is the SET TRANSACTION command, but that command makes a big difference:

```
--These queries will always return the same number.
declare
    v_count1 number;
    v_count2 number;
begin
    set transaction isolation level serializable;
    select count(*) into v_count1 from transaction_test;
    dbms_output.put_line(v_count1);
    dbms_lock.sleep(5);
    select count(*) into v_count2 from transaction_test;
    dbms_output.put_line(v_count2);
end;
/
```

Enabling a serializable transaction doesn't magically solve all our problems. It ensures transaction-level read consistency, but it can't fix problems with writing data. If another session changes data in the middle of a serializable transaction, and the serializable transaction tries to change the same rows, it will raise the exception "ORA-08177: can't serialize access for this transaction." We may need to preemptively lock the rows we're processing with a SELECT ... FOR UPDATE command.

Simple Variables

Moving data between SQL and PL/SQL is easy because their type systems are so compatible. We rarely need to worry about issues like formatting, precision, character sets, and size limitations when we move numbers, dates, and strings between SQL and PL/SQL. Unfortunately, the type systems do not perfectly match, so we need to be aware of how to work around some issues.

The **%TYPE** attribute can help us safely transfer data between SQL and PL/SQL. Instead of hard-coding a data type, we can set a variable to always match a column's data type. The following code uses %TYPE and avoids the need to specify exactly how large the data from LAUNCH_CATEGORY can be. If a future version of the space data set increases the column size, the PL/SQL variable size will also increase. Synchronizing the data types can avoid errors like "ORA-06502: PL/SQL: numeric or value error: character string buffer too small":

```
--Demonstrate %TYPE.
declare
    v_launch_category launch.launch_category%type;
begin
    select launch_category
    into v_launch_category
    from launch
    where rownum = 1;
end;
/
```

Booleans are fully supported in PL/SQL. The syntax and the keywords TRUE and FALSE let us effortlessly store, compare, and modify Boolean variables. Unfortunately, SQL does not support Boolean data types, so we need to use workarounds to pass or store Boolean data.

SQL statements cannot call PL/SQL functions that receive or return Booleans. Instead of code that looks like WHERE IS_THIS_TRUE, we must design our functions and queries to look like WHERE IS_THIS_TRUE = 'Yes'. For storing Boolean data, there is no universally agreed-upon standard, so we have to decide if we want to use "Yes/No," "YES/NO," "Y/N," "1/0," "True/False," "sí/no," etc. We must enforce our choice with a check constraint because inevitably someone will try to insert an unexpected value:

```
--A table designed for Boolean data.
create table boolean_test
(
   is_true varchar2(3) not null,
   constraint boolean_test_ck
      check(is_true in ('Yes', 'No'))
);
```

Booleans are easy to compare in PL/SQL. As the following conversion code demonstrates, we don't need to check for = TRUE or = FALSE. Instead, we can directly use the variable in the condition CASE WHEN V_BOOLEAN. But we have to change the Boolean into a string before we can insert the value into a table:

```
--Convert PL/SQL Boolean to SQL Boolean.
declare
   v_boolean boolean := true;
   v_string varchar2(3);
begin
   v_string := case when v_boolean then 'Yes' else 'No' end;
   insert into boolean_test values(v_string);
   rollback;
end;
/
```

VARCHAR2 types have a different maximum size in SQL and PL/SQL. The default maximum size in SQL is 4000 bytes, and the maximum size in PL/SQL is 32,767 bytes. Oracle 12.2 can be modified to allow 32,767 bytes in SQL, but only if the parameter MAX_STRING_SIZE is changed. Modifying that parameter is a surprisingly difficult process with significant performance implications, since large strings are internally stored as CLOBs instead of VARCHAR2. I doubt many organizations have changed MAX_STRING_SIZE, so to be safe we should assume the SQL limit is still 4,000 bytes.

PL/SQL has extra data types such as PLS_INTEGER and BINARY_INTEGER. A lot of built-in functions return PLS_INTEGER, and that data type has some performance benefits compared with NUMBER. But we shouldn't go out of our way to convert NUMBER to PLS_INTEGER, unless we're coding small loops or doing scientific programming.

Cursors

Cursors are pointers to SQL statements. There are many ways to create and use cursors, and the technology has changed significantly over the years. We need to be aware of all the options so that we can use the right option in the right context. And we want to avoid using the old, inefficient options when possible.

A **ref cursor** is a common way to pass data to an application. Ref cursors are pointers that are opened in PL/SQL code, but the query does not run and return results until the application begins fetching rows. Ref cursors are great for passing data to applications, but they are not convenient for processing data inside a database. The following code shows how easy it is to create a function that returns a ref cursor, and it demonstrates both a static and a dynamic ref cursor. But there is no example here of consuming ref cursors because that code is different for every application and IDE:

```
--Simple example of a ref cursor.
create or replace function ref_cursor_test
return sys_refcursor is
   v_cursor sys_refcursor;
begin
   --Static ref cursor based on a query.
   open v_cursor for select * from launch;
   --Dynamic ref cursor based on a string.
   --(A more realistic example would include bind variables.)
   open v_cursor for 'select * from launch';
   return v_cursor;
end;
/
```

An **explicit cursor** is one of the oldest techniques for looping through rows in PL/SQL. But as described in Chapter 15, we should avoid the CURSOR/OPEN/FETCH/CLOSE syntax whenever possible. That syntax is almost always uglier, more error prone, and slower than cursor FOR loops or a single SQL statement. Explicit cursor processing can be sped up with features like FORALL and LIMIT, but we're still usually better off using different cursor techniques. One of the few times we're forced to use explicit cursors is when we're using a dynamic query that returns multiple rows (although 21c has a new syntax that lets cursor FOR loops work with dynamic SQL).

The vast majority of cursor processing in a database should be done with one of the remaining three options: SELECT INTO, cursor FOR loops, and SELECT BULK COLLECT INTO. Table 21-1 describes when we want to use these three techniques.

Table 21-1. *When to Use Different Cursor Types*

	One Row	**Many Rows**
Static SQL	SELECT INTO	Cursor FOR loop
Dynamic SQL	SELECT INTO	SELECT BULK COLLECT INTO

SELECT INTO is best for static or dynamic queries that return one row. This syntax has already been used a few times in this book because it's the fastest and easiest way to get simple values. The following is a simple example of the static and dynamic SQL syntax:

```
--Static and dynamic SELECT INTO for one row.
declare
    v_count number;
begin
    select count(*) into v_count from launch;
    execute immediate 'select count(*) from launch' into v_count;
end;
/
```

Problems happen when a SELECT INTO returns zero rows or more than one row. Queries that return zero rows will raise the exception "ORA-01403: no data found." Queries that return more than one row will raise the exception "ORA-01422: exact fetch returns more than requested number of rows." But those exceptions are easy to handle. The tricky part of SELECT INTO is when something goes wrong but an exception is not raised.

In PL/SQL, every SELECT must have an INTO. It makes no sense to run a query and do nothing with the results. In the preceding example, if we remove the INTO V_COUNT from the *static* query, the PL/SQL block understandably raises the exception "PLS-00428: an INTO clause is expected in this SELECT statement." But if we remove the INTO V_COUNT from the *dynamic* query, the query is partially run, and the PL/SQL block does not raise an exception.

The most confusing example of missing exceptions is when the no-data-found exception is raised in a SQL context. For example, look at the following function. This function combines a SELECT INTO with WHERE 1=0, which is a recipe for no-data-found exceptions. Yet when the function is run in a SQL statement, the function returns NULL instead of raising an exception:

```
--This function fails yet does not raise an exception in SQL.
create or replace function test_function return number is
    v_dummy varchar2(1);
begin
    select dummy into v_dummy from dual where 1=0;
    return 999;
end;
/

select test_function from dual;


TEST_FUNCTION
-------------
<NULL>
```

SQL is built to work with things that return nothing. In this context, "nothing" doesn't mean NULL; it means no results at all. For example, an inline view with a condition like WHERE 1=0 won't return any data, but the statement still runs. We expect SQL to work when no data is found, but we expect PL/SQL to fail when no data is found. It's easy to forget that when we combine PL/SQL and SQL, the no-data-found exceptions are ignored.

If we want to see those no-data-found exceptions in SQL, we must catch and reraise them as a different exception. Normally, catching and reraising is a bad idea because it's easy to lose details of the call stack. In this case, we have no choice. The following function shows how to catch a no-data-found exception and raise a different kind of exception that won't be ignored by SQL:

```
--This function re-raises NO_DATA_FOUND exceptions.
create or replace function test_function2 return number is
    v_dummy varchar2(1);
```

```
begin
    select dummy into v_dummy from dual where 1=0;
    return 999;
exception when no_data_found then
    raise_application_error(-20000, 'No data found detected.');
end;
/

--Raises: "ORA-20000: No data found detected.".
select test_function2 from dual;
```

We don't need to include exception handling with every SELECT INTO. We only need to reraise exceptions for SELECT INTOs that will be called from SQL and have a chance of raising no-data-found exceptions.

Cursor FOR loops are best for static queries that return multiple rows. With cursor FOR loops, we don't need to explicitly open and close the cursor or define variables or worry about batching or limiting the results. Oracle takes care of all the details for us.

We've already seen code similar to the following example. This code is worth repeating because too many developers waste too many lines of code dealing with explicit cursors. All we need to do is loop through the results:

```
--Simple cursor FOR loop example.
begin
    for launches in
    (
        --Put huge query here:
        select * from launch where rownum <= 5
    ) loop
        --Do something with result set here:
        dbms_output.put_line(launches.launch_tag);
    end loop;
end;
/
```

BULK COLLECT INTO is best for dynamic queries that return multiple rows. To use this feature, we first need to understand the basics of records and collections, which are discussed in the next sections.

Records

So far, our PL/SQL variables have been simple, scalar types. But as we do more processing in PL/SQL, the complexity of our PL/SQL data structures must grow. SQL data grows in complexity from a single column value to a row and to a table of rows. PL/SQL data grows in complexity from a single scalar variable to a record and to a collection. Figure 21-1 shows the relationship between the terminology for the relational model, SQL, and PL/SQL.[1]

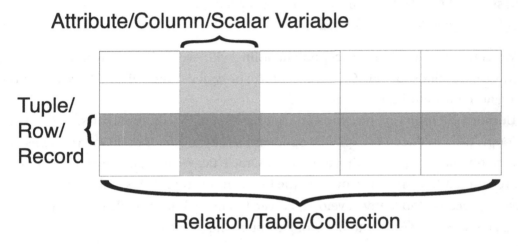

Figure 21-1. *Relational, SQL, and PL/SQL terminology for similar concepts. Based on an image created by Chris Martin and is in the public domain*

Records can be created in three different ways, and each technique has different advantages. Using %ROWTYPE is the simplest and most accurate way to copy a table's data structure. Defining a RECORD type gives us complete control over the type definition. User-defined types are defined in SQL instead of PL/SQL; they aren't technically records, but they act in a similar way.

The following code shows the three different ways to define and populate records. Populating records is often repetitive, so the example uses the simplest table in the space data set, PROPELLANT. Notice how records use the dot notation to access the individual fields:

---

[1] This diagram is not strictly true for PL/SQL. A PL/SQL collection is not always made up of PL/SQL records. We can bypass records and build PL/SQL collections as sets of scalar variables.

```
--Build user defined type, which is similar to PL/SQL record.
create or replace type propellant_type is object
(
   propellant_id    number,
   propellant_name varchar2(4000)
);

--Example of %ROWTYPE, IS RECORD, and user defined type.
declare
   --Define variables and types.
   v_propellant1 propellant%rowtype;

   type propellant_rec is record
   (
      propellant_id   number,
      propellant_name varchar2(4000)
   );
   v_propellant2 propellant_rec;

   v_propellant3 propellant_type := propellant_type(null, null);
begin
   --Populating data can work the same for all three options:
   v_propellant1.propellant_id := 1;
   v_propellant1.propellant_name := 'test1';
   v_propellant2.propellant_id := 2;
   v_propellant2.propellant_name := 'test2';
   v_propellant3.propellant_id := 3;
   v_propellant3.propellant_name := 'test3';

   --Since 18c, records can use qualified expressions:
   v_propellant2 := propellant_rec(2, 'test2');
   --User-defined types can also use constructors:
   v_propellant3 := propellant_type(3, 'test3');
end;
/
```

Records help keep related data together, and it's easier to pass a single record as a parameter instead of passing multiple scalar parameters. The biggest benefit of records is when they are used to build collections, which are the PL/SQL equivalent of "tables" of data.

Collections

Collections are sets of records or scalar variables. Collections can create multidimensional data, but don't let the word "multidimensional" scare you. In practice, collections are mostly used to create two-dimensional data that looks like a table, although we can nest data structures and create more complex shapes if we want. There are three types of collections: nested tables, associative arrays, and varrays.

Nested tables are the most useful collection type for integrating SQL and PL/SQL. A nested table is an unordered heap of records, similar to the way a table is an unordered heap of rows.

Nested tables can be easily populated with static and dynamic SQL, using the BULK COLLECT INTO syntax. The following code uses %ROWTYPE to define a nested table type and then creates a variable of that type. The nested table variable, like all collections, has a COUNT property that can be used to loop through the results. Each record can be accessed with a numeric index, using parentheses. And the relevant field can be accessed using the dot notation:

```
--Define, populate, and iterate nested tables using %ROWTYPE.
declare
    type launch_nt is table of launch%rowtype;
    v_launches launch_nt;
begin
    --Static example:
    select *
    bulk collect into v_launches
    from launch;
    --Dynamic example:
    execute immediate 'select * from launch'
    bulk collect into v_launches;
    --Iterating the nested table:
```

```
for i in 1 .. v_launches.count loop
    dbms_output.put_line(v_launches(i).launch_id);
    --Only print one value.
    exit;
end loop;
end;
/
```

Whenever we use BULK COLLECT INTO, we should think about the maximum possible size of the collection. Collections use PGA memory, and each session can only be allocated a certain amount. If necessary, we could use a loop and a LIMIT clause to only retrieve N rows at a time. In practice, the LIMIT clause is overused. The preceding example puts the entire LAUNCH table into memory, which sounds bad until we realize that the table only uses 4 megabytes of space. We might get into trouble if we have hundreds of sessions running the code at the same time, but otherwise we don't need to worry about loading a few megabytes into memory.

If we have simple data, like a list of numbers or strings, we may not even have to create our own collection data types. Oracle already has many pre-built user-defined types that are useful for collection processing. Two popular examples are SYS.ODCIVARCHAR2LIST and SYS.ODCINUMBERLIST. Those types are VARRAY(32767) OF VARCHAR2(4000)/NUMBER. Those aren't the easiest names to remember, and the maximum number of elements isn't always large enough. On the plus side, those types are publicly available to all schemas and are safe to use because they are listed in the manual and won't suddenly disappear in the next version.

Associative arrays are key–value pairs, known as hash maps or dictionaries in other languages. This collection type is useful in PL/SQL but is not as convenient as nested tables for working with SQL data.

Associative arrays can be indexed by either PLS_INTEGER or VARCHAR2, but an associative array indexed by a number isn't very different than a nested table. Associative arrays are usually indexed by a string, which is convenient because it lets us use almost anything as the key. Unfortunately, Oracle can only directly load SQL into associative arrays indexed by numbers, not strings, and those numbers cannot be larger than 2147483647.

To build an associative array indexed by a string, we must loop through the rows and build the collection ourselves. One advantage of associative arrays is that we can create elements simply by referencing them, and there's no need for an EXTEND function.

Another advantage is that results are automatically sorted as they are loaded into the collection. A disadvantage of associative arrays is that it's a bit awkward to loop through the keys, as shown in the following code:

```
--Define, populate, and iterate an associative array.
declare
    type string_aat is table of number index by varchar2(4000);
    v_category_counts string_aat;
    v_category varchar2(4000);
begin
    --Load categories.
    for categories in
    (
        select launch_category, count(*) the_count
        from launch
        group by launch_category
    ) loop
        v_category_counts(categories.launch_category) :=
            categories.the_count;
    end loop;
    --Loop through and print categories and values.
    v_category := v_category_counts.first;
    while v_category is not null loop
        dbms_output.put_line(v_category||': '||
            v_category_counts(v_category));
        v_category := v_category_counts.next(v_category);
    end loop;
end;
/

atmospheric rocket: 2600
ballistic missile test: 78
deep space: 184

...
```

Varrays, variable-size arrays, are similar to nested tables. The differences between varrays and nested tables only matter if we're storing collections in the database or if we're deleting items from the collections. To avoid breaking the relational model, we shouldn't store collections in a table anyway. And we should also avoid deleting items from collections; it's best to avoid loading unwanted elements in the first place, by using better filtering in our SQL statements that load data.

There's much more to the collection syntax than described in this section. There are many PL/SQL functions for reading, inserting (EXTEND), deleting (DELETE), updating (assignment), combining (MULTISET UNION/INTERSECT/EXCEPT), and loading collections into SQL (FORALL and TABLE). If we stick with a SQL-first approach and simple nested tables, we can usually avoid those features. If you need to do a lot of collection processing, you might want to read the "PL/SQL Collections and Records" chapter of the *PL/SQL Language Reference*.

Functions

We can extend the functionality of our database with user-defined functions. A PL/SQL function can accept arguments, execute procedural code, and return a value that can be easily used in SQL. We can use functions to organize our code and avoid repeating ourselves.

Procedures are similar to functions, except a procedure does not return a value. Procedures can use OUT parameters to allow returning multiple values, but those procedures cannot be directly called by SQL. (Functions can also have OUT parameters, but there's rarely a reason to return data in multiple ways.) There's not a huge difference between functions and procedures, so only functions are discussed here. (Be careful if you look online for a list of differences between functions and procedures. There are a lot of myths surrounding the differences, probably because there's a more significant difference in other databases.)

As an example of a function, let's say we want to calculate the orbital period of the satellites – the time it takes for each satellite to orbit Earth. The SATELLITE table already has an ORBIT_PERIOD column, so let's see if we can duplicate it using the apogee (furthest distance from Earth) and perigee (closest distance to Earth). The math behind Kepler's third law of planetary motion isn't super-complicated, but we wouldn't want to have to repeat it in our SQL statements multiple times:

```
--Calculate orbital period in minutes, based on apogee
--and perigee in kilometers.  (Only works for Earth orbits.)
create or replace function get_orbit_period
(
    p_apogee number,
    p_perigee number
) return number is
    c_earth_radius constant number := 6378;
    v_radius_apogee number := p_apogee + c_earth_radius;
    v_radius_perigee number := p_perigee + c_earth_radius;
    v_semi_major_axis number :=
        (v_radius_apogee+v_radius_perigee)/2;
    v_standard_grav_param constant number := 398600.4;
    v_orbital_period number := 2*3.14159*sqrt(
        power(v_semi_major_axis,3)/v_standard_grav_param)/60;
    --pragma udf;
begin
    return v_orbital_period;
end;
/
```

Calling a custom function is as simple as calling a built-in function. The following code compares the pre-calculated value with our custom function:

```
--Orbital periods for satellites.
Select
    norad_id,
    orbit_period,
    round(get_orbit_period(apogee,perigee),2) my_orbit_period
from satellite
where orbit_period is not null
order by norad_id;
```

```
NORAD_ID   ORBIT_PERIOD   MY_ORBIT_PERIOD
--------   ------------   ---------------
000001            96.18             96.19
000002            96.18             96.19
000003           103.73            103.73
...
```

Most of the values are a close match. There will be differences because of rounding, satellites orbiting another planet, and probably many other complexities I'm overlooking. The point of the GET_ORBIT_PERIOD function is that it encapsulates a lot of logic that we wouldn't want to see repeated in SQL statements.

The biggest problem with user-defined functions is the performance penalty. Oracle SQL and PL/SQL are separate languages, and there's a small price to pay for context switching between them. Also, if we use the function as a condition, the optimizer will have to take a wild guess at how selective the condition is. And the function itself may also be expensive.

If we have many user-defined functions, we should carefully track the number of times our functions are called, using tools like V$SQL, execution plans, and the hierarchical profiler. Luckily, there are several things we can do to potentially improve function performance.

Simply adding PRAGMA UDF cuts the run time in half. That pragma tells the compiler to optimize the function for running in a SQL context. We may also want to define the function with PARALLEL_ENABLE (to allow the SQL statement to run in parallel), DETERMINISTIC (a promise to the compiler that the function always returns the same results for the same inputs, thereby enabling some additional optimizations and features), and RESULT_CACHE (to enable caching the function results, which is useful if the function is frequently called with the same parameters). There are also different compiler optimization settings that might be helpful. Or, as described in Chapter 20, we could rebuild the function as a SQL macro.

In addition to performance problems, functions may also introduce consistency issues. A SQL statement is consistent, but a recursive SQL statement inside a user-defined function will read new data every time it's executed.

Table Functions

Table functions return collections that can be used as a row source in SQL statements. A common example of table functions is when we view explain plans with SELECT * FROM TABLE(DBMS_XPLAN.DISPLAY). With custom table functions, we can use both declarative and procedural code to build table data. There are three kinds of table functions: regular table functions, pipelined table functions, and parallel pipelined table functions.

Regular table functions return an entire collection all at once. Before we move to more advanced pipelined functions or Oracle data cartridge, we should first consider using a simple table function. The process of passing in a collection, processing the collection, and returning a new collection is powerful enough for many tasks.

For example, let's say we want to create a custom distinct function in PL/SQL. The following code first creates a nested table to hold a collection of numbers. Then the code creates a function that accepts a collection of numbers, runs the SET function to get distinct values from the collection, and returns the new collection:

```
--Simple nested table and table function that uses it.
create or replace type number_nt is table of number;

create or replace function get_distinct(p_numbers number_nt)
return number_nt is
begin
    return set(p_numbers);
end;
/
```

We can use the preceding function to find all distinct launch apogees (the furthest distance an object travels from Earth). The first step is to bundle the values into a specific kind of collection, which is done with the CAST and COLLECT functions. Then the collection is passed to the new function, which processes the data and returns another collection. Finally, the TABLE operator turns that new collection back into relational results:

```
--Distinct launch apogees from a custom PL/SQL function.
select *
from table(get_distinct
((
```

```
   select cast(collect(apogee) as number_nt)
   from launch
)))
order by 1;

COLUMN_VALUE
------------
          0
          1
          2
...
```

The preceding function is a poor version of SELECT DISTINCT APOGEE FROM LAUNCH. The point of the code is to lay the groundwork for more useful functions that need to take advantage of procedural code.

Pipelined Functions

Pipelined functions are a special kind of table function. Pipelined functions return collections, but they return collections one row a time. Row-by-row processing is usually a bad thing, but in this case there are advantages. By returning rows immediately we can chain the functions and have multiple steps of a process working concurrently.

The following is a simple pipelined function that returns three numbers. Notice how the function definition includes the keyword PIPELINED. These functions do not RETURN values; instead, the function must call PIPE ROW for each row returned. Although the function returns a collection, we only pipe one element at a time:

```
--Simple pipelined function.
create or replace function simple_pipe
return sys.odcinumberlist pipelined is
begin
   for i in 1 .. 3 loop
      pipe row(i);
   end loop;
end;
/

select * from table(simple_pipe);
```

```
COLUMN_VALUE
------------
           1
           2
           3
```

Parallel Pipelined Functions

Making pipelined functions run in parallel requires a few changes. Parallel pipelined functions must be passed a cursor, must have a PARALLEL_ENABLE clause that partitions the cursor, and must be called with a parallel hint. Setting up parallel pipelined functions can be a challenge but can significantly improve the performance of procedural code.

The following code accepts any input cursor, but for the code to work properly, the input cursor must select all the columns from the LAUNCH table. As the cursor is iterated, each row is stored in a record and then piped out. This function isn't doing anything particularly useful – it's just demonstrating the concepts:

```
--Parallel pipelined function.
create or replace function parallel_pipe(p_cursor sys_refcursor)
return sys.odcinumberlist pipelined
parallel_enable(partition p_cursor by any) is
    v_launch launch%rowtype;
begin
    loop
        fetch p_cursor into v_launch;
        exit when p_cursor%notfound;
        pipe row(v_launch.launch_id);
    end loop;
end;
/
```

The following code shows how to call the new function. The query passes a SQL statement to the function with the CURSOR keyword. To enable parallelism, we need to use a parallel hint. This example is not exactly a subquery, since Oracle is passing a pointer to a SQL statement instead of passing sets of data:

```
--Call parallel pipelined function.
select *
from table(parallel_pipe(cursor(
   select /*+ parallel(2) */ * from launch
)));

COLUMN_VALUE
------------
      49643
      49644
      49646
...
```

Pipelined functions are powerful tools, but in practice they are overused. An advanced SQL statement is usually better than an advanced pipelined function, and a parallel SQL statement will usually outperform a parallel pipelined function.

Autonomous Transactions for DML and DDL

SELECT statements are meant for reading data and should not change the state of the database. But in practice, there are important exceptions to that rule. There are times when we desperately need to run DML or DDL from a function called by a SELECT statement.

If a function includes a change and we call that function from SQL, we will get an error like "ORA-14552: cannot perform a DDL, commit or rollback inside a query or DML." The way around that limitation is with a pragma – an instruction for the PL/SQL compiler.

The following code demonstrates how to use PRAGMA AUTONOMOUS_TRANSACTION to create and call a function that includes a DDL statement:

```
--Function that changes the database.
create or replace function test_function
return number authid current_user is
   pragma autonomous_transaction;
```

```
begin
    execute immediate 'create table new_table(a number)';
    return 1;
end;
/

--Call the function to create the table.
select /*+ no_result_cache */ test_function from dual;

TEST_FUNCTION
-------------
            1
```

The preceding function is usually a bad idea, since SQL does not guarantee the order of execution or even the number of times each piece will be executed. In theory, the function could be executed zero, one, or many times. (For example, depending on how result cache is configured, Oracle may call the function twice the first time the SQL statement is parsed. That's why the hint /*+ NO_RESULT_CACHE */ is used.) In practice, if we test the code carefully and do not change the way the function is called, these functions can be made mostly reliable.

Autonomous Transactions for Logging

A more common use of autonomous transactions is for maintaining logs. Most of our programs should be instrumented to store metadata that can be useful for debugging and performance tuning. This metadata is gathered while our programs are doing their normal work, but it must be gathered in a slightly different way. Our applications typically roll back when there is an exception, but we do not want to roll back the log entries. Autonomous transactions operate independently from their parent transaction, which lets us keep the log changes while we roll back the other changes.

For example, let's create a simple logging table and a simple program to create log entries. Notice how the procedure is created with PRAGMA AUTONOMOUS_TRANSACTION:

```
--Create simple table to hold application messages.
create table application_log
(
   message  varchar2(4000),
   the_date date
);

--Autonomous logging procedure.
create or replace procedure log_it
(
   p_message varchar2,
   p_the_date date
) is
   pragma autonomous_transaction;
begin
   insert into application_log
   values(p_message, p_the_date);
   commit;
end;
/
```

Next, in a PL/SQL block, we'll write to the table, create a log entry, and roll back the transaction:

```
--Reset the scratch table.
truncate table transaction_test;

--Autonomous transaction works despite rollback.
begin
   insert into transaction_test values(1);
   log_it('Inserting...', sysdate);
   rollback;
end;
/
```

The LOG_IT procedure has a COMMIT, but that COMMIT does not affect the parent transaction. If we look at the two tables, we can see that the original INSERT to the test table was rolled back, but the INSERT to the logging table remains:

```
--The main transaction was rolled back.
select count(*) from transaction_test;

COUNT(*)
--------
       0

--But the logging table has the original log message.
select count(*) from application_log;

COUNT(*)
--------
       1
```

Autonomous transactions let us keep our log entries even if the main program crashes or rolls back. This is important because we're most likely to need our logs when there is an error or a rollback.

Definer's Rights vs. Invoker's Rights

When we build PL/SQL objects, we have to make an important choice about privileges: do the objects run with the privileges of the schema owner or the privileges of the current user? These options are called definer's rights and invoker's rights. In the object definition, we can specify either AUTHID DEFINER or AUTHID CURRENT_USER. The AUTHID property is an annoying detail, but it's something we always have to consider. The choice impacts the security and the simplicity of our PL/SQL code.

The default option is definer's rights. Sometimes the schema owner, the definer, has more privileges, and we want to lend those privileges to another user. Sometimes the current user, the invoker, has more privileges, or we may want to run the SQL against the invoker's schema.

You may have noticed that the last version of TEST_FUNCTION, the version that creates a new table, was built using AUTHID CURRENT_USER. But I can't be 100% certain that the setting is correct for you. The right setting depends on exactly how your user is authorized to create tables. Privileges granted through roles are *not* used in definer's rights procedures.

If your account has access to the CREATE TABLE privilege through a role like DBA, then AUTHID CURRENT_USER is necessary to enable the role. If your account was directly granted the CREATE TABLE privilege, then either setting will work. Most accounts are granted access through roles, which is why I chose AUTHID CURRENT_USER in the function.

Regardless of which option is used, PL/SQL objects are *compiled* without using any roles. For a procedure to compile successfully, all schema objects used in the procedure must either be owned by the same schema, directly granted to the schema owner, or used in dynamic SQL. (However, anonymous blocks are run with the invoker's roles, which is why code often works as an anonymous block but not as a stored procedure.)

The AUTHID option is extremely confusing, but we cannot ignore it. Oracle privileges are complex, and it will take a while before this option makes sense.

Triggers

Triggers contain PL/SQL code that is executed when specific things happen and specific conditions are met. Common uses of triggers are logging and auditing, enforcing multi-table constraints, enabling DML on views, and changing session settings during logon.

Triggers are powerful, but they should not be our first choice for solving problems. We should not use triggers when a simpler declarative constraint or column default can solve the problem instead. Also, triggers are side effects of other changes and can easily surprise developers and administrators who aren't expecting those side effects. Triggers that work row by row can decrease performance, especially when they can prevent direct-path writes. Some organizations have a no-triggers policy; I wouldn't go that far, but I would recommend we be careful when we create triggers.

The trigger syntax is complicated, and there's not enough space to cover everything here. The main parts of triggers are the event clauses (that specify what types of statements fire the triggers), timing points (that specify precisely when triggers fire), WHEN conditions (that optionally constrain when triggers fire), and PL/SQL body, which can often reference the OLD and the NEW values. There are four types of triggers: simple, instead-of, compound, and system.

Event clauses can be a combination of the DML events DELETE, INSERT, and UPDATE. For system triggers the events can be almost any DDL event, such as CREATE or TRUNCATE. System triggers can also include database or schema events, like AFTER STARTUP or AFTER LOGON.

Timing points define precisely when the trigger fires. The self-explanatory options are BEFORE STATEMENT, BEFORE EACH ROW, AFTER STATEMENT, AFTER EACH ROW, and INSTEAD OF EACH ROW. Whether a trigger is BEFORE or AFTER, and whether it's for a STATEMENT or for EACH ROW, determines what information the trigger body can read or change. For example, an AFTER STATEMENT trigger can view the final version of the table, which is helpful for enforcing business rules. But an AFTER STATEMENT trigger is not fired for each row and cannot access individual OLD and NEW values.

The **WHEN (condition)** allows triggers to easily include or exclude rows from processing. Any valid SQL condition can be used to filter the results, and the condition can reference the OLD and NEW values.

Simple DML triggers can respond to changes made through INSERT, UPDATE, DELETE, or MERGE statements. For example, a trigger could set columns such as CHANGED_BY or CHANGED_DATE or could save a copy of the old values before deletion.

In many regulated environments, data can never be fully deleted. In theory we could use backups and tools like LogMiner to get the table history, but in practice it is much more convenient to have audit tables. Oracle's built-in auditing is only for security and does not help us audit data changes. We will not find old copies of our data in DBA_AUDIT_TRAIL. If we want to keep historical records, we must build the tables and triggers ourselves. There are several ways to create audit tables.

One popular choice for creating audit tables is to have a single audit table, with one row for each changed column. This solution is similar to an EAV table; the table is easy to build and easy to write into, but is slow, wastes space for dense changes, and is hard to query. If our data is small and we don't plan on querying the audit trail much, a single table might work fine.

If we have a large amount of data or if we plan to regularly query old data, we should build an audit table for every regular table. This solution is faster and easier to use, but it's more complex because we need to create and maintain an extra set of tables. And storing each row twice is inefficient, especially for sparse changes where we may store an entire new row when only one column changed. But in a highly regulated environment where we need to quickly prove exactly what happened, when it happened, and who did it, those tables are a lifesaver.

The following code creates a row-level AFTER trigger that captures every DML change made to the table TRANSATION_TEST. Notice how the CASE statement in the trigger body can determine exactly what kind of DML is happening with the conditional predicates INSERTING, UPDATING, and DELETING. We need that information to know whether to use the OLD or the NEW value or both. A real trigger would store the changes in an audit table, but this sample trigger is only printing the statement so we can see how triggers work:

```
--Create a trigger to track every row change.
create or replace trigger transaction_test_trg
after insert or update of a or delete on transaction_test
for each row
begin
   case
      when inserting then
         dbms_output.put_line('inserting '||:new.a);
      when updating('a') then
         dbms_output.put_line('updating from '||
            :old.a||' to '||:new.a);
      when deleting then
         dbms_output.put_line('deleting '||:old.a);
   end case;
end;
/
```

The following PL/SQL block shows what happens when we INSERT, UPDATE, and DELETE. (The results assume the table is empty at the beginning of the example.)

```
--Test the trigger.
begin
   insert into transaction_test values(1);
   update transaction_test set a = 2;
   delete from transaction_test;
end;
/

inserting 1
updating from 1 to 2
deleting 2
```

If we need to audit a large number of tables, it may be worth creating a package to automate the building of audit triggers. As discussed in previous chapters about dynamic SQL, we can use the data dictionary and helpful programming styles to easily generate trigger code.

Another use of simple DML triggers is to verify multi-table constraints. The problem with validating multi-table constraints through triggers is the performance; even if we only change one row, we may need to query the entire table. We should at least use an AFTER STATEMENT trigger, so we don't have to verify the conditions for every row. This approach can accomplish the same thing as the materialized view multi-table constraints discussed in Chapter 9.

Instead-of DML triggers can be used to change the way we interact with views. If our views are simple, they may be inherently updatable, and we can natively run DML against them. But non-trivial views are not updatable, and it may not be clear to Oracle how a change to a view should be reflected as a change to a table. With an instead-of DML trigger, we can define the rules for how to handle changes to views. Some applications use tables only as low-level physical storage and only allow users to interact with views that create a high-level abstraction of the system.

Compound DML triggers can combine different timing points into a single trigger. Combining timing points lets us initialize variables in the BEFORE STATEMENT section, gather data in a FOR EACH ROW section, and then process the results in bulk in the AFTER STATEMENT section. Combining the trigger operations can significantly improve performance and can be helpful if we're auditing tables that often undergo large changes.

Compound triggers can also help us avoid the dreaded mutating table error, ORA-04091. Mutating table errors happen when our trigger tries to modify the rows of the same table that fired the trigger. Row-level triggers firing triggers would lead to nondeterministic behavior that would depend on the order the rows were processed. One way to avoid that problem is to gather the relevant data in a FOR EACH ROW section and make the changes in an AFTER STATEMENT section, since the AFTER STATEMENT section does not cause mutating table errors.

System triggers can fire for DDL statements per schema or per system, or they can fire for database events. For example, we can create a system trigger to prevent specific commands from running against specific objects. We must be extremely careful when we create system triggers, or we can prevent Oracle from working. If possible, we should use schema triggers instead of database triggers, since schema triggers affect the smallest possible number of users.

A popular use of system triggers is to create a logon trigger that sets session values, for formatting or optimization. But remember that our server code should never depend on the client format settings. If a procedure only runs with a specific NLS_DATE_FORMAT, that procedure is broken and needs to be fixed.

Many developers use logon triggers to set the NLS_DATE_FORMAT to avoid implicit conversion bugs. I prefer the exact opposite: I like to set an intentionally silly NLS_DATE_FORMAT. Setting a weird value, and then running the unit tests, will ensure the program does not use any implicit date conversions. Notice that the following trigger is only set for my schema, not the whole system. And I've also hard-coded my schema name to ensure this trigger is not accidentally applied in the wrong environment:

```
--Create logon trigger that sets a custom NLS_DATE_FORMAT.
create or replace trigger jheller.custom_nls_date_format_trg
after logon on jheller.schema
begin
    execute immediate
        q'[alter session set nls_date_format = 'J']';
end;
/

--Logout and logon again and run this to see the new format.
select to_char(sysdate) julian_day from dual;

JULIAN_DAY
----------
    2458530
```

Oracle does not have **on-commit triggers,** but we can imitate them with PL/SQL packages like DBMS_ALERT and DBMS_JOB. The package DBMS_SCHEDULER is almost always the best way to create jobs, but DBMS_JOB has one advantage: DBMS_JOB only submits the job when the transaction is committed. The following PL/SQL block shows how to make something happen after the transaction is committed:

```
--Imitation on-commit trigger.
declare
    v_job number;
begin
    --Create a job, but it won't take effect yet.
```

```
dbms_job.submit
(
   job  => v_job,
   what => 'insert into transaction_test values(1);'
);
--A rollback would ignore the job.
--rollback;
--Only a commit will truly create the job.
commit;
end;
/
```

Jobs run asynchronously and may not execute immediately. We may need to wait a while before we see the results of the preceding PL/SQL block.

Conditional Compilation

Conditional compilation lets us choose the source code of our PL/SQL programs depending on the environment. Conditional compilation is more dynamic than regular code but not as dynamic as dynamic SQL; we can choose among several static blocks of code, but we cannot arbitrarily modify source code at run time. When PL/SQL programs are compiled, conditional compilation can read session settings and constants to determine which source code to use. This feature is helpful when we want to use the latest and greatest SQL and PL/SQL features but only when those features are available.

The following example shows how we can use different source code for different versions of the database. The preprocessor control tokens (the keywords that start with dollar signs) use the constants in the package DBMS_DB_VERSION to determine what code is compiled. The source code can be complete gibberish as long as that code is not chosen:

```
--Conditional compilation example.
begin
   $if dbms_db_version.ver_le_9 $then
      This line is invalid but the block still works.
   $elsif dbms_db_version.ver_le_12 $then
      dbms_output.put_line('Version 12 or lower');
```

```
  $elsif dbms_db_version.ver_le_18 $then
     dbms_output.put_line('Version 18');
  $elsif dbms_db_version.ver_le_19 $then
     dbms_output.put_line('Version 19');
  $elsif dbms_db_version.ver_le_21 $then
     dbms_output.put_line('Version 21');
  $else
     dbms_output.put_line('Future version');
  $end
end;
/
```

The preceding code is even trickier than it looks. The version checking must be done in a precise order, or the code will not work. For example, the constant DBMS_DB_VERSION.VER_LE_18 does not exist in Oracle 12.2. The code would fail on 12.2 if the IF condition was written in a different order.

Other PL/SQL Features

We need to know what packages already exist, so we don't reinvent the wheel. Chapter 8 already mentioned several important PL/SQL packages, and it's worth quickly listing them again: DBMS_METADATA, DBMS_METADATA_DIFF, DBMS_OUTPUT, DBMS_RANDOM, DBMS_SCHEDULER, DBMS_SQL, DBMS_SQLTUNE, DBMS_STATS, and DBMS_UTILITY.

Other useful pre-built packages are UTL_MAIL (for sending email), DBMS_DATAPUMP (for exporting and importing data), DBMS_LOB (for large object processing), DBMS_LOCK (has a useful SLEEP function), and UTL_FILE (for reading and writing to the operating system). There's a large list of packages in the voluminous *PL/SQL Packages and Types Reference*. Nobody has the time to read the entire manual, but just skimming through the table of contents is helpful.

There's so much more to PL/SQL than what this chapter covers. Unlike other database systems, Oracle's procedural language extension is a full-blown programming language. There is enough power in PL/SQL to do anything. But SQL should still be the star of our database programs. We should save most of our clever tricks for SQL and use PL/SQL to glue the SQL together.

Start Teaching and Creating

You now have everything you need to become an Oracle SQL guru. A good development process lets you quickly build solutions and experiment with new ideas. Advanced and arcane features give you the technical ability to solve any problem. Elegant programming styles let you build beautiful and manageable code. Understanding Oracle performance lets you build solutions that are lightning fast.

It's time to start sharing your skills with others if you're not already. To truly master Oracle SQL, we need to teach others and create open source projects.

Teach Others

The best way to master a skill is to teach it to someone else. We don't have to be an expert before we start teaching. There are always people less skilled than us whom we can help. And there are always people more skilled than us whom we can learn from. We want to participate in environments where people of any skill level can contribute.

Teaching can start at your job. Teaching might just mean speaking up more at meetings, volunteering to give small presentations, or training other developers. If you feel nervous that you're not good enough or suffer from imposter syndrome, that might just be a good sign that you're getting out of your comfort zone and learning. Don't let that nervousness stop you.

Eventually we'll need to move beyond our job and start sharing our knowledge with the public. To continue our professional growth, we need to join a community where developers can collaborate, provide quick and meaningful feedback, and build a reputation. These communities can be forums, Q&A sites like Stack Overflow, user groups, or one of the many social networks for developers.

Mastering a skill requires *intentional* practice. Just doing the bare minimum at work isn't enough to make us experts. We need the confidence to put ourselves out there, but we also need the humility to learn from our mistakes.

Create Open Source Projects

One of the greatest achievements for a software developer is to create a successful, publicly available program. Most Oracle SQL developers only work on internal applications used by a single customer, but our careers don't have to be so limited. There are many opportunities for us to create public programs using Oracle SQL and PL/SQL.

Building good software is tough because we tend to think about generic software. The simple ideas are taken; the world doesn't need another flashlight app for our phone. The good ideas are too tough; we don't have the time or skills to build a better social network. But don't give up!

We need to be in a lucky situation where we have the opportunity to build something unique but feasible. Those lucky situations won't happen unless we are an expert in something, and if you've read this far, you are on the path to becoming an expert in Oracle SQL. Our first attempts will fail, but we'll learn a lot from those failures. Don't get discouraged – nobody builds successful programs on the first try.

The best way to build public programs is to make them open source. There are many existing communities and tools that support open source development. Many of the technical details of project management are easily handled by open source hosting sites, such as GitHub, GitLab, Bitbucket, SourceForge, and many more. Open sourcing our code invites others to participate and helps us build better software.

When you begin building public programs, watch out for the curse of knowledge. There are countless repositories with great programs that are completely inaccessible because there is no metadata. Every project must at least have a Readme file; a quick description, a simple example, simple installation instructions, and license information are absolutely necessary if we want people to use our projects. If we're going to invest a huge amount of time building something, we should at least spend a few hours making the project presentable and easy to install.

When most people talk about open source, what they really mean is "cheap." Real open source isn't about saving money; it's about freedom, collaboration, and positive sum interactions where everybody wins. Our side projects can be open source, and we may be able to convince our organizations to open some of our internal programs. At the very least, when we post snippets of code online, we should ensure the code is properly licensed for others to use.

Oracle SQL doesn't yet have a huge open source ecosystem. With the right development environment, advanced features, beautiful styles, and performance tuning skills, there are many tools we can create and many knowledge gaps we can fill. And advanced programming skills will certainly help advance our careers.

There are endless opportunities for advanced Oracle developers. Put down this book and go write a program.

PART VI

Appendixes

APPENDIX A

SQL Style Guide Cheat Sheet

Follow these style tips to write clear, powerful SQL statements. This simple list summarizes the programming style recommendations made throughout this book. There are exceptions to every rule, but we should still know what the rules are and why the rules exist:

1. *Use inline views*: Build large SQL statements out of small, independent pieces with simple relational interfaces.

2. *Use ANSI join syntax*: Build SQL statements in an orderly fashion by adding and joining one table at a time.

3. *Adhere to the relational model*: Use dumb columns and dumb tables to create smart schemas. Never store lists of values in a column and never use the wrong data type.

4. *Choose good names*: Avoid unnecessary abbreviations and aliases. Complexity is measured in words, not characters.

5. *Use comments and whitespace*: Important constructs like inline views deserve extra comments, lines, and indenting.

6. *Use left alignment, tabs, and lowercase*: Learn to quickly write code that emphasizes the boundaries between important elements like inline views, not the trivial boundaries between keywords.

7. *Create large SQL statements*: One large query is often better than two small queries.

© Jon Heller 2023
J. Heller, *Pro Oracle SQL Development*, https://doi.org/10.1007/978-1-4842-8867-2_22

8. *Use dynamic SQL*: Use SQL more often and keep the code readable by combining dynamic SQL with multiline strings, alternative quoting syntax, templating, and bind variables.

9. *Maintain a single source of truth*: The golden copy of our code should exist in a version-controlled text file, not a database.

10. *Build MCVE test cases*: Build minimal, complete, verifiable examples to test ourselves and share our knowledge.

11. *Use SQL worksheets*: Create an organized collection of worksheets that contain powerful SQL statements. Use a format that leverages IDE features.

12. *Learn and use advanced features*: SQL is much more than SELECT * FROM EMPLOYEES. Learn advanced SELECT, DML, and DDL features to make our SQL statements more powerful, simpler, and faster.

APPENDIX B

Computer Science Topics

You don't need a computer science degree to apply the practical advice in this book and become a better SQL developer. For database developers it can be useful to branch out in different directions and learn about other languages, system architecture, project management, etc. But a deeper understanding of database processing can also help your career and create interesting opportunities. Use the following list to explore the theoretical foundations of many of the topics in this book:

1. *Relational model and relational algebra*: Normalization and denormalization (OLTP and data warehouse), set theory (thinking about SQL), and ACID (Oracle architecture)

2. *Programming language paradigms*: Declarative (SQL, XQuery), imperative (PL/SQL, MODEL), functional (SQL), object-oriented (object-relational PL/SQL), visual (query builders), literate, aspect-oriented (triggers), and metaprogramming (dynamic SQL, data dictionary, conditional compilation)

3. *Algorithms*: Searching (index traversal vs. full table scan), sorting (join, grouping, and order by clause), hashing (join, grouping, cluster, and partitioning), number of distinct values approximation (quickly calculate and aggregate NDV statistics), and joining (hash, sort-merge, nested loops)

4. *Run-time analysis*: Algorithm analysis worst cases – $1/N$ (batching), 1 (ideal hash partitions/clusters/joins), $LOG(N)$ (B-tree index access), $1/((1-P)+P/N)$ (Amdahl's law), N (full table scan, bad hashing), $N*LOG(N)$ (sorting, joining, iterating index access, gathering statistics), N^2 (cross join, nested loops), N! (join order), and ∞ (satisficing the halting problem for the optimizer)

© Jon Heller 2023
J. Heller, *Pro Oracle SQL Development*, https://doi.org/10.1007/978-1-4842-8867-2_23

5. *Data structures*: B-tree (index), bitmap (index), hash table (joining, grouping, distinct, cluster), bloom filter (hash join), array (nested table, varray), record (PL/SQL record, type objects, collections), object (type objects), key value and graph (NoSQL databases), immutable and blockchain (tables)

6. *Automata theory*: Formal languages (is SQL a programming language, elementary cellular automata, regular expression limitations), lexing and parsing (advanced dynamic SQL language problems), Backus–Naur form (syntax diagrams), and compiler construction (optimizer transformations, hints, pragmas)

7. *Discrete math*: Boolean logic (conditions), De Morgan's law (compound conditions), combinatorics (join order), and Venn diagrams (joins)

8. *Information theory*: Randomness (SAMPLE, DBMS_RANDOM), compression (table and index compression), and cryptography (Oracle's weak password hashes)

9. *Data science*: Machine learning, data mining, unstructured data

10. *Operating system theory*: Processes (parallelism), resource allocation (deadlocks, MVCC row-level locking), and I/O (memory and caching)

Index

A

Abjads, 342

Accidental cross joins, 107, 110–111, 417

Active Session History (ASH), 462, 471, 475, 477–478

Adaptive query plans, 437, 455–459

ADD FUNCTION command, 224

Advanced compression, 231, 541

Advanced grouping
  aggregate functions, 150, 151
  CUBE, 148
  GROUP*, 148
  HAVING clause, 146
  LISTAGG, 149
  orbital and deep space launches, 146
  ORDER BY clauses, 147
  ROLLUP, 147

Advanced SELECT features
  advanced grouping, 146–151
  analytic functions, 151–155
  CASE and DECODE, 131
  common table expressions, 171–175
  joins, 133–140
  JSON, 183–188
  NLS (*see* National Language Support (NLS))
  operators/functions/expressions/ conditions
    precedence rules, 129, 130
    semantics, 128
    simplify, 130, 131
    SQL Language Reference, 128, 129
  pivoting and unpivoting, 163–169
  recursive queries, 175–178
  regular expressions, 155–160
  row limiting, 160–163
  set operators, 142–146
  sorting, 140–142
  table references, 169–171
  XML, 179–183

Advanced aggregate functions, 148, 150, 151

Advanced SQL development, 90, 219

Aggregation, 148

Agile development, 364

Aliases, 137, 179, 260, 337, 338

Allman style, 344

ALL PRIVILEGES option, 268

ALTER commands, 223, 224

Alternative database models, 17–18

Alternative quoting mechanism, 357–361

ALTER PACKAGE command, 224

ALTER SESSION command, 46, 195, 215, 216, 222, 223, 293, 368, 492, 496

ALTER SYSTEM command, 48, 213, 214, 222, 223

ALTER SYSTEM FLUSH BUFFER_CACHE command, 214

ALTER SYSTEM FLUSH SHARED_POOL command, 66, 214, 291

ALTER TABLE command, 43, 224, 234, 238, 250, 253

Amdahl's law, 241, 394, 404–406, 505, 607

Printed in the United States
by Baker & Taylor Publisher Services

Printed in the United States
by Baker & Taylor Publisher Services